Christian Doctrine

Christian Doctrine

A Reader

edited by

**Lindsey Hall, Murray Rae
and Stephen Holmes**

scm press

Published in 2010 by SCM Press
Editorial office
13–17 Long Lane,
London, EC1A 9PN, UK

SCM Press is an imprint of Hymns Ancient and Modern Ltd
(a registered charity)
13a Hellesdon Park Road, Norwich, Norfolk, NR6 5DR

www.scm-canterburypress.co.uk

British Library Cataloguing in Publication data

A catalogue record for this book is available
from the British Library

978-0-334-04345-4

Typeset by Regent Typesetting, London
Printed and bound by
CPI Antony Rowe, Chippenham, SN14 6LH

Contents

5 The Work of Christ

6 The Holy Spirit

Acknowledgements

Full bibliographic details may be found at the foot of each extract, but here we wish to record our gratitude to all those who have permitted us to use copyright material:

To Augsberg Fortress Press for the material in extracts 3.15, 4.22, 5.14 7.24, 8.14, 9.16 and 9.19

To Austin Seminary for the material in extract 9.15

To Baker Academic for the material in extract 6.17: Amos Yong *The Spirit Poured Out on all Flesh*, Baker Academic, a Division of Baker Publishing Group, 2005. Used by Permission.

To Blackwell Press for extract 7.26

To Cambridge University Press for extracts 7.22 and 9.20

To Continuum for extracts 2.6, 2.7, 3.13, 5.11, 6.14, 6.20, 7.14, 8.16, 8.18, 9.12, 9.13, 9.14, 9.18,

To Darton, Longman and Todd for extract 7.16

To Eerdmans for extracts 2.10, 2.12, 7.17, 7.20, 9.11, 9.14, 9.17 and 9.21

To Faber and Faber for extract 4.20

To Handsel for extract 8.20

To Harper Collins for the material in extracts 2.9, 2.11 copyright © 1991 by Catherine Mowry, 5.15 English translation copyright © 1974 by SCM Press, Ltd. Reprinted by permission of HarperCollins Publishers , 6.15, 6.19 and 8.21 English translation copyright © 1977 by SCM Press, Ltd. Reprinted by permission of HarperCollins Publishers

To Henry Holt for extract 4.18

To Hodder & Stoughton for the material in extract 6.16

To James Clarke and Co for the material in extracts 2.8, 6.13 and 7.15

To the Estate of Lesslie Newbigin for the material in extract 8.15

To One in Christ for the material in extract 8.24

To Orbis for the material in extracts 5.16, 5.17, 7.18, 8.23 and 8.26

To Paternoster for the material in extracts 7.23 and 8.19

To SCM/ Canterbury Press for the material in extracts 2.9, 2.12, 3.15, 4.21, 5.14, 5.16, 5.18 8.21, 8.22, 8.23 9.14, 9.16, 9.22

To SPCK for the material in extracts 4.23 and 5.13

To St Vladimir's Press for the material in extract 7.19

To The University of Chicago Press for the material in extract 7.25

To Westminster John Knox Press for the material in extract 8.25 reproduced from *The Church in the Round.* ©1993 Letty Russell. Used by permission of Westminster John Knox Press. www.wjkbooks.com

General Introduction

I

Nine years ago, two of us (MAR and SRH) published a Reader in theological method entitled *The Practice of Theology*, together with our then-colleague at King's College London, the late Professor Colin Gunton. We have been pleased with the reception of that book, and considered more than once the possibility of producing a companion volume, focusing on the subject matter of theology. When Colin Gunton died unexpectedly in 2003, Lindsey Hall joined us for a year at King's to help cover the teaching load. Dr Hall proved herself to be an excellent theological educator, and seemed an obvious collaborator to take Colin's place in working on the second Reader. This book is the fruit of that collaboration.

We began the earlier volume with a determined refusal to apologize for what we had produced, borrowed from Oliver Goldsmith: 'There are a hundred faults in this thing, and a hundred things might be said to prove them beauties.' In the same spirit, we do not want to apologize for the work you have before you, but it is perhaps worth explaining the concept of the task of teaching theology that guided our decisions and selections.

This book contains nine chapters covering between them the standard loci of Christian doctrine in an equally standard order: the doctrine of God (two chapters); creation; Christology (two chapters); pneumatology; anthropology; ecclesiology; and eschatology. There is no treatment of prolegomena, or of the doctrine of revelation, simply because those topics were extensively treated in our earlier book; otherwise, the choice and arrangement of topics should be immediately familiar to anyone who is aware of standard introductory works, and indeed classic major statements (Aquinas's *Summa Theologiae*; Calvin's *Institutes*; Barth's *Church Dogmatics*) in the field.

II

That the arrangement is familiar and traditional is not yet enough reason for adopting it, of course. It is not difficult to point to other classic texts – some as significant as those named above (Schleiermacher's *Christian Faith*); others deserving attention because of their recent influence (Tillich's *Systematic Theology*) – which deliberately depart from the classic pattern for, what their authors and admirers regard as, pressing and compelling reasons. The arrangement here is self-consciously traditional, and deliberately follows, and so privileges, a pattern of dogmatic teaching that is

Western and Catholic (as distinct from Eastern Orthodox) in general, and Reformed in particular.

When we turn to the particular texts that have been selected for inclusion, another issue arises. The question of the 'canon' is live in every discipline within the humanities: half a century ago, we thought we knew which were the great texts, which had to be studied, but today these identifications have been repeatedly challenged. The status of revered texts is questioned routinely as part of a suspicion that intellectual or aesthetic judgements of the quality of a text have too often been covers for oppressive political practices. The old canons were routinely exclusively the work of dead white European males drawn from a particular social class; is it really the case that there were no insightful or talented authors outside this privileged group?

Theology has faced the question of the canon for much longer than most other disciplines, and with a sharpness that is also unusual. The first because there have been competing traditions of theology for centuries, each with their own canon. The classic works of the Anglican tradition and the classic works of the Presbyterian tradition overlapped to some extent, but the canons were different, and were known to be so. Historically, two ways of dealing with this canonical question were employed, often simultaneously. On the one hand, a rhetoric of polemic was much in evidence: my way of doing theology, or at least the way of my group, is correct, and all other ways are just wrong. On the other hand, theologians borrowed, sometimes quietly, the insights and arguments of those from other traditions, and gratefully redeployed them, albeit without reference or acknowledgement. Thus Calvin can fulminate against the arid logic-chopping of the 'scholastics' while at the same time making use of some of their carefully worked-out distinctions to solve problems in his own thought. Perhaps the most honest example of this dual usage is the seventeenth- and eighteenth-century fashion for 'elenctic' theology – theology done using a method of establishing positive doctrine by consideration of the errors and questions of those who are wrong.

The acuteness of theology's recent crisis of authority has to do with the inescapably ethical nature of the discipline: if it is true that the selection of theological texts that students should study has been, however unwittingly, racist, sexist, or oppressive in some other way, then a discipline which sees redemption and the establishment of justice as at the heart of its internal logic must feel the challenge of this with a peculiar intensity. There is not just a general ethical pressure to correct the injustices of earlier ages; instead there is a fundamental internal disciplinary incoherence if injustice is perpetuated in the way we do theology.

All of this is to say that the choosing of texts for a Reader in the present state of the academy is a delicate business, and all the more so within the theological academy. How to negotiate the competing classical canons? Is there a pressing moral duty to revise the traditional lists, and if so in which directions? A glance at our table of contents will demonstrate our answers: we have broadly followed a Reformed, rather than Lutheran, Roman Catholic or Eastern Orthodox tradition; and we have generally chosen not to revise the classical canons.

The reason for the first of these decisions is entirely contextual: while there are many exceptions, and while most are now confessedly and cheerfully ecumenical, the broad tradition of most English-speaking centres of higher theological education is more nearly Reformed than anything else. Greek-language theology is generally ignored not just from the Great Schism of 1054, but from the close of the Council of Chalcedon in 451; it is not just Gregory Palamas and the Hesychasts who are not read, but little or no attention is given to the later christological debates, or to Maximus the Confessor and the iconoclastic controversy. Calvin (and Luther) are read; Trent is probably not, still less the leading Roman theologians of the day. The criticism of classical theology is told with reference to Schleiermacher, not to the Roman Catholic modernists. Mediating theology is found in English Anglicans and Scottish and American Presbyterians, not in the German Lutheran tradition, and the reassertion of historical orthodoxy is a tale of Barth, Brunner and the Niebuhrs, not the members of the French *nouvelle théologie* movement. We do not claim that any of this is necessarily right (a glance at our own teaching syllabi would indicate that each of us demurs from these general decisions at times), but while it is the case, a textbook that is aimed at resourcing these institutions needs to reflect this context if it is to find any users.

The second decision is perhaps more contestable. Our reasoning for accepting the 'grand tradition' without feeling the pressure to correct it on political or ethical grounds turns on a belief that it is good academic practice to understand something before attempting to criticize it, and on an assessment that none of the current criticisms have yet been so successful as to carry the day. The first point might be read as an attempt to determine illegitimately the shape of the debate – the tradition is set; everything else is an attempt at revision. This is a real danger, but also reflects something of the present state of the debate: there is not yet a settled feminist or liberationist or post-colonial canon that we might have followed instead. Rather, we have a series of criticisms, of claims that the tradition has enshrined patriarchy or has aligned itself with oppressive political power, or has assumed the normativity of European (and North American) experience. Any or all of these may be true, but as claims they are only testable by someone who has at least some broad knowledge of the tradition that is being criticized.

Further, we judge that attempts to address the recent criticisms by minor adjustment to the received canon, while well intentioned and sometimes genuinely helpful (in the recovery of this or that writer who deserved to be remembered, even on the old canon's own terms), fundamentally under-estimate the seriousness of the problem. If a systematic patriarchal or colonial prejudice has been operative in the determining of the theological canon, then the inclusion of a few token female or majority-world writers is not adequate response; rather, our narrative of the tradition needs to be rewritten completely, starting with a blank sheet, with just and appropriate selection criteria operative. We no doubt display the (somewhat differing) levels of sympathy we have towards the various contemporary criticisms of the canon in our individual introductions to the different chapters; in the chapters, however, we have included (a version of) the old canon in all its offensiveness, in the belief that this should be known and recognized by students before they attempt to criticize or revise it.

III

If there is a (conscious) bias beyond those named above on display here, it is a focus on the historical development of the various doctrines discussed. It would have been possible to focus far more on contemporary statements, but we see the history of theology as an important part of the discipline. The contemporary trinitarian proposals of Catherine Mowry LaCugna, to take an example, make little sense unless the reader knows Karl Rahner's earlier discussion, which in turn is offered as a revision to a tradition of Roman Catholic dogmatics that reaches back to Thomas Aquinas in the thirteenth century. Further, both Rahner and LaCugna attempt to defend their positions by appeal to the patristic traditions of the first millennium (in LaCugna's case, the first three centuries) of the Christian tradition. One may read LaCugna and appreciate her emphases with no knowledge of what lies behind them, of course; but to appreciate her originality, and to assess what is distinctive about her position, this background is simply necessary.

The historical focus also potentially addresses some, at least, of the recent criticisms noted above. Trivially, of course, most of the significant voices of patristic theology came from Africa (Origen, Athanasius, Augustine) or Asia (the Cappadocian Fathers, the Antiochene tradition) – although almost every significant patristic voice was male (women appear as spiritual teachers (St Macrina, or the Desert Mothers), as significant spiritual influences (St Monica), or as patrons and protectors (Empress Pulcheria), but not as significant theologians in their own right). Much more importantly, a historical awareness prevents the culturally dominant assumptions and prejudices of the modern day being accorded canonical status too easily. If the core demand is that a voice other than that of the majority position of modern Western culture be heard, then the divergent voices of past ages might answer the need. (They might not, of course: Christianity allied itself with the dominant political power in the fourth century, and the maleness of the ancient tradition has already been alluded to; therefore it might be that, for all its diversity, the tradition remains homogenously oppressive and patriarchal.)

Regardless of this, comprehending the sheer strangeness of voices from other ages is a necessary experience for neophyte theologians. Christian theology is a discipline rooted in the attempt to understand a particular historical narrative that begins with Abram and Sarai's departure from Ur and culminates in the resurrection of Jesus Christ from the dead, and the promise that one further, and decisive, moment of this narrative is still to come. As such, historical particularity is central to the practice of theology. This discipline does not, or should not, deal with ideas abstracted from historical context, but with arguments located in the messy and particular lives of those who struggled to formulate or defend them.

There are a variety of ways in which these past voices will challenge the contemporary theologian. For most of its history, the connection of theology to the life of the churches has been assumed; the piety of the theologian was routinely seen as decisive to his/her ability to contribute to the discipline; and the ability of a citation from Scripture to settle an argument was accepted, at least in principle, on every side. That none of these points would now be routinely accepted is only a reason for the aspiring theologian to struggle to imagine what it might feel like to think in these strange and aberrant ways. Equally, for the young theologian hailing from a family background where piety was inculcated and the authority of the Bible assumed, serious progress in the discipline depends on a willingness to face up to the arguments against these traditional assumptions in all their forcefulness – not because they must be believed, but because they must be thoroughly understood if any contribution is to be made to the theological task today.

IV

All Readers, of course, suffer from the inherent limitations of the form, and from the purely practical problems that intervene inevitably between the conception of a volume and its final form in production. On the first, each text included must be understood as only a glimpse of a whole that lies behind it. The Reader as a form could perhaps be compared to the sequence of trailers for upcoming films that precede the main feature in a cinema: if skilfully done, the trailer may convey an impression of the character and attractions of the film it advertises, but it can never be considered an adequate substitute. Just so, the student who has recourse to this book should regard it as a series of invitations to engage seriously with primary texts, a guide to the flavour of what lies out there, if time and effort will be given to exploring. But all we can offer of any particular text is a glimpse, a taste, an impression. There is much more to be experienced beyond what we give here.

Practically, any Reader is limited by length and selection. We come with a desire to present the argument of this author in all its clarity and profundity – but within the length of extract that is possible, what we can offer is only a sorry caricature of the original. In another case an important text might be lost completely because of issues of copyright and our inability to gain permission to reproduce material. In this connection we wish to record our thanks to SCM Press, and particularly to our editor Natalie Watson, for their willingness to allow us the space, and particularly the time, to produce something as close as possible to the work we had envisaged.

V

We have found the study of theology to be endlessly exciting, and profoundly relevant to the most pressing questions of modern life. We offer this book in the hope that others may have the same experience. If it opens the eyes of some to the wonder and the relevance of this strange and ancient discipline, our work will have been more than worthwhile.

1 The Doctrine of God in Patristic Development

Introductory essay

To have two chapters on the doctrine of God in a theological textbook is not unusual; typically, however, they would be divided into a chapter on the Trinity and a chapter on the divine attributes or perfections. We have chosen not to do that. As the excerpts below indicate, the development of the doctrine of the divine perfections and the development of the doctrine of the Trinity go hand-in-hand in theological history, and neither may be understood without the other. This chapter, then, will consider both aspects of the doctrine of God from the beginnings of the Church to the Middle Ages; the next chapter will continue the story from the Reformation to the present day.

Divine 'perfections' or 'attributes' are simply words or concepts that may be predicated of God. Any word that successfully completes the sentence 'God is ...' is a divine perfection. They are thus the common stuff of Christian worship and confession: God is good, loving, merciful, just, omnipotent, eternal, etc. Terming them 'perfections' indicates that God is each of these things to the utmost extent. God is not just 'good'; God is as good as it is possible to be, the ultimate definition of goodness.

The doctrine of the Trinity is the claim that God exists in three persons, Father, Son, and Holy Spirit, each fully divine, and sharing all properties save their particular properties of origin: the Father is unbegotten, the Son begotten of the Father, and the Spirit proceeds from the Father (and the Son). (The question as to whether the Spirit proceeds from the Father alone, or from the Father and the Son together has divided the Eastern Orthodox Church from the Roman Catholic Church, and the later Protestant churches, since 1054; some texts dealing with the controversy can be found in Chapter 6, on the Holy Spirit.)

The perfections of God are visible in different ways throughout the Bible. When God is revealed to Moses in Exodus 34.6, God is described according to various perfections: 'gracious', 'compassionate', 'slow to anger', 'abounding in steadfast love and faithfulness'. When Abraham intercedes with God over the destruction of the cities of the plain, he pleads God's perfections: 'Shall not the Judge of all the earth do what is just?' (Ex. 18.25). Isaiah hears angels praising the perfections of God: 'Holy, holy, holy is the Lord of hosts; the whole earth is full of his glory' (Isa. 6.3). In the New

Testament we read such claims as 'God is spirit' (John 4.24), 'God is one' (Rom. 3.30), 'God is rich in mercy' (Eph. 2.4), and, of course, 'God is love' (1 John 4.8).

From its earliest days, Christianity had to come to terms with a culture shaped by the tradition of Greek philosophy (even the Holy Land had been under Greek, then Roman, rule for most of the three centuries prior to the life of Jesus). Although the focus of Greek philosophical traditions was practical advice on how to live life well, there was an established and sophisticated account of the nature of the divine. It was held to be one, eternal, unchanging, spiritual, and separated from this mutable, material world. These ideas sat uneasily with popular Greek and Roman religion, focusing as it did on gods and goddesses who seemed in the myths to be like human beings writ large.

Into this world, Christianity came, looking rather different. Like any new and apparently subversive religious movement, it was regarded with some suspicion by the authorities when they first noticed it. As a result, the early writers on the doctrine of God we have included are mostly attempting to defend Christianity against different charges. In constructing their defences, they add precision to the inherited expressions of what Christians believe. Strangely enough, the first charge the Christians were confronted with was atheism: they were first noticed in public because they refused to burn incense or sacrifice in the local temples, or to worship the Emperor as a god. Justin Martyr and Athenagoras both protest the Christian belief in one God as not being atheistic, and being far superior to traditional Graeco-Roman polytheism. They call on the philosophical tradition concerning the one unchanging divine essence, Athenagoras even quoting several philosophers, to give cultural credibility to their Christian beliefs.

There is no doubt that their intent was apologetic: they were trying to make their faith comprehensible and believable to the culture around. As we shall see in the next chapter, however, some recent theologians have questioned whether they gave up too much, and in fact produced an almost syncretistic account of God's perfections, which in places owed more to Greek intuitions about what God should be than to the biblical narrative. Much of what Theophilus of Antioch claims in our first extract could have been taught by a Greek philosopher; this does not necessarily make it bad theology, but it does raise a question: does theological rationality differ from philosophical rationality? If so, how, and why?

Stressing belief in one God, as Justin and Athenagoras did, raises immediately the question of the Trinity. Tertullian writes against Praxeas, who seemingly had suggested that Father, Son and Spirit were just different masks the one God wore, not distinct persons. Tertullian tries to explain the precise relations of Father, Son and Spirit in the Godhead, inventing the word 'Trinity' in the process. Tertullian is at pains to distinguish his account of the 'prolation' ('going-forth') of the Son from the Father from similar accounts offered by Gnostic thinkers, the main opponents of the early Christian theologians. He singles out Valentinus, who had conceived the spiritual realm in terms of a series of emanations from perfection, getting less and less perfect, until this material realm is reached (see Chapter 3 for more on such Gnostic ideas of creation); Tertullian claims that the Son is neither separated from the Father, nor any less perfect than the Father, and so what he is talking about is a completely different concept. Tertullian is thus trying to steer a middle course: Praxeas collapses Father, Son and Spirit into one undifferentiated being; Valentinus so stresses the differences that multiple beings, simply unlike each other, are suggested. Tertullian believes in one God, whose life is differentiated into the Father, the Son and the Spirit.

The great period of debate and development concerning trinitarian theology was the fourth century. At the beginning of the century, Arius raised questions about the equality of the Son with the Father (see Chapter 4 for some extracts from Arius, and for some direct responses); this raised the question of how, adequately, to describe the relationship of Father, Son and Spirit. This became a question about how best to speak of the divine nature – the perfections of God. Eunomius claimed that the key divine perfection was to be 'ingenerate': always causing, never caused. If this was the case, then Son and Spirit did not share in the divine perfection. It was, however, impossible to deny that the divine was uncaused. The question of how the divine perfections related to the essence of God suddenly became the decisive question for the doctrine of the Trinity. We have included Hilary of Poitiers, the key defender of Nicene orthodoxy in the West, and Gregory of Nyssa, one of the 'Cappadocian Fathers' (Gregory, his brother Basil of Caesarea, and Gregory of Nazianzus), both showing how disciplined reflection on how to speak of the perfections of God is necessary to understanding the Trinity. Gregory states the position that was finally reached: the essence of God is unknown and unnamed by human theology; all our language of God's perceptions is no more than a series of partial approximations to the reality of what God is.

The excerpt from Gregory of Nazianzus, meanwhile, addresses another of the key issues of the controversy: the Bible nowhere unambiguously speaks of the Holy Spirit as God, so the deity of the Spirit needed to be defended. The argument ran in two stages: first, an ontological claim that there is no gradation in levels of being, such as Tertullian had charged Valentinus with believing. The Spirit cannot be 'nearly' divine, because there is no space to be 'nearly' divine; whatever exists is either God the Creator, eternal and necessary, or a creature, timebound, temporary and contingent. The second stage of the argument is seen in the extract here: the Spirit performs the works of God and is honoured with the titles of God; therefore the Spirit is God.

The doctrine of the Trinity advanced by the Cappadocian Fathers was accepted as orthodox at the Council of Constantinople in 381, and debate in the Greek-speaking Eastern Church turned to Christology. The decisive statement of this orthodox trinitarian theology for the Latin-speaking West was still to be written, however. Augustine's great treatise on the Trinity appeared about 419, although it had been twenty years in the writing. In it, Augustine first expounds the doctrine of the Trinity through discussions of Scripture and philosophy, and then (taking his cue from the biblical claim that human beings are made 'in the image of God') looking for trinitarian analogies in human life. The whole is an intricate and massive masterpiece; the excerpt we give here is Augustine's own summary, giving a flavour of some of the themes.

With the Cappadocian Fathers and Augustine, the Christian doctrine of God reached a settled state that was not seriously questioned for over a thousand years (God's existence might be doubted, but, within Christian Europe, that this was a proper account of the God who did or did not exist went essentially unquestioned). The influence of Greek philosophy on the doctrine of God perhaps reached its highest point in the writings of the pseudo-Dionysius (a writer of the sixth century, probably from Syria, whose works became ascribed to the Dionysius who was converted by Paul in Athens (Acts 17.34), and so were invested with near-apostolic authority). Pseudo-Dionysius presents a grand vision of the universe, and an extremely apophatic doctrine of God (that is, a doctrine of God that focuses strongly on the unknowability of God). In the extract we present he argues that our language is utterly incapable of speaking of the divine, and that we speak more truly when we say what God is not than when we attempt to say what God is. This is in recognizable continuity with the arguments of Gregory of Nyssa also included here, but is far more radical than anything found in any of the Cappadocian Fathers.

The chapter closes with three representatives from the medieval West: Anselm of Canterbury, Richard of St Victor, and Thomas Aquinas. Each in different ways illustrates the desire to demonstrate that the Christian doctrine of God is rational. Anselm's *Monologium* is an extended attempt to prove orthodox trinitarianism from first principles; Richard of St Victor attempts to show that God must exist in a plurality of persons if God is held to be perfect; and Thomas Aquinas's famous 'five ways' are a set of arguments from the nature of the world, that each terminate in the existence of 'that which all call God'.

There seems little doubt that these writers believed they were offering logical arguments for Christian doctrine; with the eyes of a more sceptical age, however, we might notice how many distinctively Christian ideas they simply assume. Richard of St Victor, for instance, assumes that perfection must include love; an idea that it seems at least possible to doubt for those of us who are aware of Indian religious traditions which see detachment as the highest perfection. Anselm's arguments almost read like a direct inversion of some of Augustine's psychological analogies for the Trinity; in a culture that had learnt its account of human nature in part from Augustine's attempts to map it on to the doctrine of God, it is not surprising that an analysis of this account resolves into that same doctrine of God. Christian Europe had achieved a stable theological synthesis; God was in heaven and that made sense of the world.

SRH

1.1 Theophilus of Antioch, from *To Autolycus*

Theophilus discusses the different titles given to God and what they teach about God's nature and activity.

You will say, then, to me, 'Do you, who see God, explain to me the appearance of God.' Hear, O man. The appearance of God is ineffable and indescribable, and cannot be seen by eyes of flesh. For in glory He is incomprehensible, in greatness unfathomable, in height inconceivable, in power incomparable, in wisdom unrivalled, in goodness inimitable, in kindness unutterable. For if I say He is Light, I name but His own work; if I call Him Word, I name but His sovereignty; if I call Him Mind, I speak but of His wisdom; if I say He is Spirit, I speak of His breath; if I call Him Wisdom, I speak of His offspring; if I call Him Strength, I speak of His sway; if I call Him Power, I am mentioning His activity; if Providence, I but mention His goodness; if I call Him Kingdom, I but mention His glory; if I call Him Lord, I mention His being judge; if I call Him Judge, I speak of Him as being just; if I call Him Father, I speak of all things as being from Him; if I call Him Fire, I but mention His anger. You will say, then, to me, 'Is God angry?' Yes; He is angry with those who act wickedly, but He is good, and kind, and merciful, to those who love and fear Him; for He is a chastener of the godly, and father of the righteous; but he is a judge and punisher of the impious.

And He is without beginning, because He is unbegotten; and He is unchangeable, because He is immortal. And he is called God [*Theos* in Greek] on account of His having placed all things on security afforded by Himself; and on account of [*Theein*], for [*Theein*] means running, and moving, and being active, and nourishing, and foreseeing, and governing, and making all things alive. But he is Lord, because He rules over the universe; Father, because he is before all things; Fashioner and Maker, because He is creator and maker of the universe; the Highest, because of His being above all; and Almighty, because He Himself rules and embraces all. For the heights of heaven, and the depths of the abysses, and the ends of the earth, are in His hand, and there is no place of His rest. For the heavens are His work, the earth is His creation, the sea is His handiwork; man is His formation and His image; sun, moon, and stars are His elements, made for signs, and seasons, and days, and years, that they may serve and be slaves to man; and all things God has made out of things that were not into things that are, in order that through His works His greatness may be known and understood.

Source: *Theophilus of Antioch*, To Autolycus *I.3–4, trans. Marcus Dods, in Alexander Roberts, James Donaldson and A. Cleveland Coxe (eds)*, Ante-Nicene Fathers, *vol. 2, Buffalo, NY: Christian Literature Publishing Co., 1885.*

1.2 Justin Martyr, from *First Apology*

Justin explains why Christians do not worship like other people: it is not because they are atheists, but because they do not believe in idols, or use sacrifices.

Hence are we called atheists. And we confess that we are atheists, so far as gods of this sort are concerned, but not with respect to the most true God, the Father of righteousness and temperance and the other virtues, who is free from all impurity. But both Him, and the Son (who came forth from Him and taught us these things, and the host of the other good angels who follow and are made like to Him), and the prophetic Spirit, we worship and adore, knowing them in reason and truth, and declaring without grudging to every one who wishes to learn, as we have been taught.

...

And neither do we honour with many sacrifices and garlands of flowers such deities as men have formed and set in shrines and called gods; since we see that these are soulless and dead, and have not the form of God (for we do not consider that God has such a form as some say that they imitate to His honour), but have the names and forms of those wicked demons which have appeared. For why need we tell you who already know, into what forms the craftsmen, carving and cutting, casting and hammering, fashion the materials? And often out of vessels of dishonour, by merely changing the form, and making an image of the requisite shape, they make what they call a god; which we consider not only senseless, but to be even insulting to God, who, having ineffable glory and form, thus gets His name attached to things that are corruptible, and require constant service. And that the artificers of these are both intemperate, and, not to enter into particulars, are practised in every vice, you very well know; even their own girls who work along with them they corrupt. What infatuation! that dissolute men should be said to fashion and make gods for your worship, and that you should appoint such men the guardians of the temples where they are enshrined; not recognising that it is unlawful even to think or say that men are the guardians of gods.

...

What sober-minded man, then, will not acknowledge that we are not atheists, worshipping as we do the Maker of this universe, and declaring, as we have been taught, that He has no need of streams of blood and libations and incense; whom we praise to the utmost of our power by the exercise of prayer and thanksgiving for all things wherewith we are supplied, as we have been taught that the only honour that is worthy of Him is not to consume by fire what He has brought into being for our sustenance, but to use it for ourselves and those who need, and with gratitude to Him to offer thanks by invocations and hymns for our creation, and for all the means of health, and for the various qualities of the different kinds of things, and for the changes of the seasons; and to present before Him petitions for our existing again in incorruption

13

through faith in Him. Our teacher of these things is Jesus Christ, who also was born for this purpose, and was crucified under Pontius Pilate, procurator of Judaea, in the times of Tiberius Caesar; and that we reasonably worship Him, having learned that He is the Son of the true God Himself, and holding Him in the second place, and the prophetic Spirit in the third, we will prove. For they proclaim our madness to consist in this, that we give to a crucified man a place second to the unchangeable and eternal God, the Creator of all; for they do not discern the mystery that is herein, to which, as we make it plain to you, we pray you to give heed.

Source: Justin Martyr, First Apology *6–13, trans. Marcus Dods and George Reith in* Alexander Roberts, James Donaldson and A. Cleveland Coxe (eds), Ante-Nicene Fathers, *vol. 2, Buffalo, NY: Christian Literature Publishing Co., 1885.*

1.3 Athenagoras, from *A Plea for the Christians*

Athenagoras here argues that even the best of the pagan thinkers knew that there is only one God, and then describes an early trinitarian account.

Philolaus, too, when he says that all things are included in God as in a stronghold, teaches that He is one, and that He is superior to matter. Lysis and Opsimus thus define God: the one says that He is an ineffable number, the other that He is the excess of the greatest number beyond that which comes nearest to it ... Plato, then, says, 'To find out the Maker and Father of this universe is difficult; and, when found, it is impossible to declare Him to all,' conceiving of one uncreated and eternal God. And if he recognises others as well, such as the sun, moon, and stars, yet he recognises them as created: 'gods, offspring of gods, of whom I am the Maker, and the Father of works which are indissoluble apart from my will; but whatever is compounded can be dissolved.' If, therefore, Plato is not an atheist for conceiving of one uncreated God, the Framer of the universe, neither are we atheists who acknowledge and firmly hold that He is God who has framed all things by the Logos, and holds them in being by His Spirit. Aristotle, again, and his followers, recognising the existence of one whom they regard as a sort of compound living creature, speak of God as consisting of soul and body, thinking His body to be the etherial space and the planetary stars and the sphere of the fixed stars, moving in circles; but His soul, the reason which presides over the motion of the body, itself not subject to motion, but becoming the cause of motion to the other. The Stoics also, although by the appellations they employ to suit the changes of matter, which they say is permeated by the Spirit of God, they multiply the Deity in name, yet in reality they consider God to be one ...

Since, therefore, the unity of the Deity is confessed by almost all, even against their will, when they come to treat of the first principles of the universe, and we in our turn likewise assert that He who arranged this universe is God – why is it that they can say and write with impunity what they please concerning the Deity, but that against us a law lies in force, though we are able to demonstrate what we apprehend and justly believe, namely that there is one God, with proofs and reason accordant with truth? For poets and philosophers, as to other subjects so also to this, have applied themselves in the way of conjecture, moved, by reason of their affinity with the afflatus from God, each one by his own soul, to try whether he could find out and apprehend the truth; but they have not been found competent fully to apprehend it, because they thought fit to learn, not from God concerning God, but each one from himself; hence they came each to his own conclusion respecting God, and matter, and forms, and the world. But we have for witnesses of the things we apprehend and believe, prophets, men who have pronounced concerning God and the things of God, guided by the Spirit of God. And you too will admit, excelling all others as you do in intelligence and in piety towards the true God, that it would be irrational for us to cease to believe in the Spirit from God, who moved the mouths of the prophets like musical instruments, and to give heed to mere human opinions.

As regards, then, the doctrine that there was from the beginning one God, the Maker of this universe, consider it in this wise, that you may be acquainted with the argumentative grounds also of our faith. If there were from the beginning two or more gods, they were either in one and the same place, or each of them separately in his own. In one and the same place they could not be. For, if they are gods, they are not alike; but because they are uncreated they are unlike: for created things are like their patterns; but the uncreated are unlike, being neither produced from any one, nor formed after the pattern of any one. Hand and eye and foot are parts of one body, making up together one man: is God in this sense one? Others read affirmatively, 'God is one.' And indeed Socrates was compounded and divided into parts, just because he was created and perishable; but God is uncreated, and, impassible, and indivisible – does not, therefore, consist of parts. But if, on the contrary, each of them exists separately, since He that made the world is above the things created, and about the things He has made and set in order, where can the other or the rest be? For if the world, being made spherical, is confined within the circles of heaven, and the Creator of the world is above the things created, managing that by His providential care of these, what place is there for the second god, or for the other gods? ...

That we are not atheists, therefore, seeing that we acknowledge one God, uncreated, eternal, invisible, impassible, incomprehensible, illimitable, who is apprehended by the understanding only and the reason, who is encompassed by light, and beauty, and spirit, and power ineffable, by whom the universe has been created through His Logos, and set in order, and is kept in being – I have sufficiently demonstrated. I say 'His Logos', for we acknowledge also a Son of God. Nor let any one think it ridiculous that God should have a Son. For though the poets, in their fictions, represent the gods as no better than men, our mode of thinking is not the same as theirs, concerning either God the Father or the Son. But the Son of God is the Logos of the Father, in idea and in operation; for after the pattern of Him and by Him were all things made, the Father and the Son being one. And, the Son being in the Father and the Father in the Son, in oneness and power of spirit, the understanding and reason of the Father is the Son of God. But if, in your surpassing intelligence, it occurs to you to inquire what is meant by the Son, I will state briefly that He is the first product of the Father, not as having been brought into existence (for from the beginning, God, who is the eternal mind had the Logos in Himself, being from eternity instinct with Logos); but inasmuch as He came forth to be the idea and energizing power of all material things, which lay like a nature without attributes, and an inactive earth, the grosser particles being mixed up with the lighter. The prophetic Spirit also agrees with our statements. 'The Lord,' it says, 'made me, the beginning of His ways to His works.' The Holy Spirit Himself also, which operates in the prophets, we assert to be an effluence of God, flowing from Him, and returning back again like a beam of the sun. Who, then, would not be astonished to hear men who speak of God the Father, and of God the Son, and of the Holy Spirit, and who declare both their power in union and their distinction in order, called atheists? Nor is our teaching in what relates to the divine nature confined to these points; but we recognise also a multitude of angels and ministers, whom God the Maker and Framer of the world distributed and appointed to their several posts by His Logos, to occupy themselves about the elements, and the heavens, and the world, and the things in it, and the goodly ordering of them all.

Source: Athenagoras, A Plea for the Christians 6—10, trans. Marcus Dods and George Reith, in Alexander Roberts, James Donaldson and A. Cleveland Coxe (eds), Ante-Nicene Fathers, vol. 2, Buffalo, NY: Christian Literature Publishing Co., 1885.

1.4 Tertullian, from *Against Praxeas*

Tertullian here defends the unity of the Father, Son and Spirit in the God-head, against the claim that any doctrine of the Trinity must amount to worshipping three gods.

For before all things God was alone – being in Himself and for Himself universe, and space, and all things. Moreover, He was alone, because there was nothing external to Him but Himself. Yet even not then was He alone; for He had with Him that which He possessed in Himself, that is to say, His own Reason. For God is rational, and Reason was first in Him; and so all things were from Himself. This Reason is His own Thought (or Consciousness), which the Greeks call 'Logos,' by which term we also designate 'Word' or 'Discourse,' and therefore it is now usual with our people, owing to the mere simple interpretation of the term, to say that the Word was in the beginning with God; although it would be more suitable to regard Reason as the more ancient; because God had not Word from the beginning, but He had Reason even before the beginning; because also Word itself consists of Reason, which it thus proves to have been the prior existence as being its own substance. Not that this distinction is of any practical moment. For although God had not yet sent out His Word, He still had Him within Himself, both in company with and included within His very Reason, as He silently planned and arranged within Himself everything which He was afterwards about to utter through His Word. Now, whilst He was thus planning and arranging with His own Reason, He was actually causing that to become Word which He was dealing with in the way of Word or Discourse. And that you may the more readily understand this, consider first of all, from your own self, who are made 'in the image and likeness of God,' for what purpose it is that you also possess reason in yourself, who are a rational creature, as being not only made by a rational Artificer, but actually animated out of His substance. Observe, then, that when you are silently conversing with yourself, this very process is carried on within you by your reason, which meets you with a word at every movement of your thought, at every impulse of your conception. Whatever you think, there is a word; whatever you conceive, there is reason. You must needs speak it in your mind; and while you are speaking, you admit speech as an interlocutor with you, involved in which there is this very reason, whereby, while in thought you are holding converse with your word, you are (by reciprocal action) producing thought by means of that converse with your word. Thus, in a certain sense, the word is a second person within you, through which in thinking you utter speech, and through which also (by reciprocity of process) in uttering speech you generate thought. The word is itself a different thing from yourself. Now how much more fully is all this transacted in God, whose image and likeness even you are regarded as being, inasmuch as He has reason within Himself even while He is silent, and involved in that Reason His Word! I may therefore without rashness first lay this down (as a fixed principle) that even then before the creation of the universe God was not alone, since He had within

Himself both Reason, and, inherent in Reason, His Word, which He made second to Himself by agitating it within Himself.

This power and disposition of the Divine Intelligence is set forth also in the Scriptures under the name of Wisdom; for what can be better entitled to the name of Wisdom than the Reason or the Word of God? Listen therefore to Wisdom herself, constituted in the character of a Second Person: 'At the first the Lord created me as the beginning of His ways, with a view to His own works, before He made the earth, before the mountains were settled; moreover, before all the hills did He beget me.' ...

Then, therefore, does the Word also Himself assume His own form and glorious garb, His own sound and vocal utterance, when God says, 'Let there be light.' This is the perfect nativity of the Word, when He proceeds forth from God – formed by Him first to devise and think out all things under the name of Wisdom – 'The Lord created or formed me as the beginning of His ways;' then afterward begotten, to carry all into effect – 'When He prepared the heaven, I was present with Him' (Prov. 8). Thus does He make Him equal to Him: for by proceeding from Himself He became His first-begotten Son, because begotten before all things; and His only-begotten also, because alone begotten of God, in a way peculiar to Himself, from the womb of His own heart – even as the Father Himself testifies: 'My heart,' says He, 'hath emitted my most excellent Word' (Ps. 140:1). The Father took pleasure evermore in Him, who equally rejoiced with a reciprocal gladness in the Father's presence: 'Thou art my Son, today have I begotten Thee' (Ps. 2:7); even before the morning star did I beget Thee. The Son likewise acknowledges the Father, speaking in His own person, under the name of Wisdom: 'The Lord formed Me as the beginning of His ways, with a view to His own works; before all the hills did He beget Me' (Prov. 8:22–25). For if indeed Wisdom in this passage seems to say that She was created by the Lord with a view to His works, and to accomplish His ways, yet proof is given in another Scripture that 'all things were made by the Word, and without Him was there nothing made' (Jn 1:3); as, again, in another place (it is said), 'By His word were the heavens established, and all the powers thereof by His Spirit' (Ps. 33:6) – that is to say, by the Spirit (or Divine Nature) which was in the Word: thus is it evident that it is one and the same power which is in one place described under the name of Wisdom, and in another passage under the appellation of the Word, which was initiated for the works of God. Nor need we dwell any longer on this point, as if it were not the very Word Himself, who is spoken of under the name both of Wisdom and of Reason, and of the entire Divine Soul and Spirit. He became also the Son of God, and was begotten when He proceeded forth from Him. Do you then (you ask), grant that the Word is a certain substance, constructed by the Spirit and the communication of Wisdom? Certainly I do. But you will not allow Him to be really a substantive being, by having a substance of His own; in such a way that He may be regarded as an objective thing and a person, and so be able (as being constituted second to God the Father,) to make two, the Father and the Son, God and the Word. For you will say, what is a word, but a voice and sound of the mouth, and (as the grammarians teach) air when struck against, intelligible to the ear, but for the rest a sort of void, empty, and incorporeal thing.

19

I, on the contrary, contend that nothing empty and void could have come forth from God, seeing that it is not put forth from that which is empty and void; nor could that possibly be devoid of substance which has proceeded from so great a substance, and has produced such mighty substances: for all things which were made through Him, He Himself (personally) made. How could it be, that He Himself is nothing, without whom nothing was made? How could He who is empty have made things which are solid, and He who is void have made things which are full, and He who is incorporeal have made things which have body? For although a thing may sometimes be made different from him by whom it is made, yet nothing can be made by that which is a void and empty thing. Is that Word of God, then, a void and empty thing, which is called the Son, who Himself is designated God? 'The Word was with God, and the Word was God' (Jn 1:1) ...

If any man from this shall think that I am introducing some 'prolation' [i.e., going forth] of one thing out of another, as Valentinus does when he sets forth Aeon from Aeon, one after another – then this is my first reply to you: Truth must not therefore refrain from the use of such a term, and its reality and meaning, because heresy also employs it. The fact is, heresy has rather taken it from Truth, in order to mould it into its own counterfeit. Was the Word of God put forth or not? Here take your stand with me, and flinch not. If He was put forth, then acknowledge that the true doctrine has a prolation; and never mind heresy, when in any point it mimics the truth. The question now is, in what sense each side uses a given thing and the word which expresses it. Valentinus divides and separates his prolations from their Author, and places them at so great a distance from Him, that the Aeon does not know the Father: he longs, indeed, to know Him, but cannot; nay, he is almost swallowed up and dissolved into the rest of matter. With us, however, the Son alone knows the Father, and has Himself unfolded 'the Father's bosom' (Jn 1:18). He has also heard and seen all things with the Father; and what He has been commanded by the Father, that also does He speak. And it is not His own will, but the Father's, which He has accomplished, which He had known most intimately, even from the beginning. 'For what man knoweth the things which be in God, but the Spirit which is in Him?' (1 Cor. 2:11). But the Word was formed by the Spirit, and (if I may so express myself) the Spirit is the body of the Word. The Word, therefore, is both always in the Father, as He says, 'I am in the Father;' (Jn 14:11) and is always with God, according to what is written, 'And the Word was with God' (Jn 1:1); and never separate from the Father, or other than the Father, since 'I and the Father are one' (Jn 10:30). This will be the prolation, taught by the truth, the guardian of the Unity, wherein we declare that the Son is a prolation from the Father, without being separated from Him. For God sent forth the Word, as the Paraclete also declares, just as the root puts forth the tree, and the fountain the river, and the sun the ray. For these are prolations, or emanations, of the substances from which they proceed. I should not hesitate, indeed, to call the tree the son or offspring of the root, and the river of the fountain, and the ray of the sun; because every original source is a parent, and everything which issues from the origin is an offspring. Much more is (this true of) the Word of God, who has actually received as His own peculiar designation the name of Son. But still the tree is not severed from the root, nor the river from the fountain, nor the ray from the sun; nor, indeed, is the Word separated from God. Following, therefore, the form of these analogies, I confess that I call God and His Word – the Father and His Son – two. For the root and the tree are distinctly two things, but correlatively joined; the fountain and the river are also two forms, but indivisible; so likewise the sun and the ray are two forms, but coherent ones. Everything which proceeds from something else must needs be second to that from which it proceeds, without being on that account separated. Where, however, there is a second, there must be two; and where there is a third, there must be three. Now the Spirit indeed is third from God and the Son; just as the fruit of the tree is third from the root, or as the stream out of the river is third from the fountain, or as the apex of the ray is third from the sun. Nothing, however, is alien from that original source whence it derives its own properties. In like manner the Trinity, flowing down from the Father through intertwined and connected steps, does not at all disturb the Monarchy, whilst it at the same time guards the state of the Economy.

Bear always in mind that this is the rule of faith which I profess; by it I testify that the Father, and the Son, and the Spirit are inseparable from each other, and so will you know in what sense this is said. Now, observe, my assertion is that the Father is one, and the Son one, and the Spirit one, and that They are distinct from Each Other. This statement is taken in a wrong sense by every uneducated as well as every perversely disposed person, as if it predicated a diversity, in such a sense as to imply a separation among the Father, and the Son, and the Spirit. I am, moreover, obliged to say this, when (extolling the Monarchy at the expense of the Economy) they contend for the identity of the Father and Son and Spirit, that it is not by way of diversity that the Son differs from the Father, but by distribution: it is not by division that He is different, but by distinction; because the Father is not the same as the Son, since they differ one from the other in the mode of their being. For the Father is the entire substance, but the Son is a derivation and portion of the whole, as He Himself acknowledges: 'My Father is greater than I' (Jn 14:28). In the Psalm His inferiority is described as being 'a little lower than the angels' (Ps. 8:5). Thus the Father is distinct from the Son, being greater than the Son, inasmuch as He who begets is one, and He who is begotten is another; He, too, who sends is one, and He who is sent is another; and He, again, who makes is one, and He through whom the thing is made is another. Happily the Lord Himself employs this expression of the person of the Paraclete, so as to signify not a division or severance, but a disposition (of mutual relations in the Godhead); for He says, 'I will pray the Father, and He shall send you another Comforter … even the Spirit of truth' (Jn 14:16), thus making the Paraclete distinct from Himself, even as we say that the Son is also distinct from the Father; so that He showed a third degree in the Paraclete, as we believe the second degree is in the Son, by reason of the order observed in the Economy. Besides, does not the very fact that they have the distinct names of Father and Son amount to a declaration that they are distinct in personality? For, of course, all things will be what their names represent them to be; and what they are and ever will be, that will they be called; and the distinction indicated by the names does not at all admit of any confusion, because there is none in the things which they designate. 'Yes is yes, and no is no; for what is more than these, cometh of evil' (Mt. 5:37).

Source: Tertullian, Against Praxeas *5—9, trans. Peter Holmes, in Alexander Roberts, James Donaldson and A. Cleveland Coxe (eds),* Ante-Nicene Fathers, *vol. 3, Buffalo, NY: Christian Literature Publishing Co., 1885.*

1.5 Hilary of Poitiers, from *On the Trinity*

Hilary here reflects on the necessary perfection of God and how the biblical revelation demonstrates it.

Again, some worshipped in the elements of earth and air the actual bodily and visible forms of created things; and, finally, some made their gods dwell within images of men or of beasts, tame or wild, of birds or of snakes, and confined the Lord of the universe and Father of infinity within these narrow prisons of metal or stone or wood. These, I was sure, could be no exponents of truth, for though they were at one in the absurdity, the foulness, the impiety of their observances, they were at variance concerning the essential articles of their senseless belief. My soul was distracted amid all these claims, yet still it pressed along that profitable road which leads inevitably to the true knowledge of God. It could not hold that neglect of a world created by Himself was worthily to be attributed to God, or that deities endowed with sex, and lines of begetters and begotten, were compatible with the pure and mighty nature of the Godhead. Nay, rather, it was sure that that which is Divine and eternal must be one without distinction of sex, for that which is self-existent cannot have left outside itself anything superior to itself. Hence omnipotence and eternity are the possession of One only, for omnipotence is incapable of degrees of strength or weakness, and eternity of priority or succession. In God we must worship absolute eternity and absolute power.

While my mind was dwelling on these and on many like thoughts, I chanced upon the books which, according to the tradition of the Hebrew faith, were written by Moses and the prophets, and found in these words spoken by God the Creator testifying of Himself 'I Am that I Am, and again, He that is hath sent me unto you' [Ex. 3.14]. I confess that I was amazed to find in them an indication concerning God so exact that it expressed in the terms best adapted to human understanding an unattainable insight into the mystery of the Divine nature. For no property of God which the mind can grasp is more characteristic of Him than existence, since existence, in the absolute sense, cannot be predicated of that which shall come to an end, or of that which has had a beginning, and He who now joins continuity of being with the possession of perfect felicity could not in the past, nor can in the future, be non-existent; for whatsoever is Divine can neither be originated nor destroyed. Wherefore, since God's eternity is inseparable from Himself, it was worthy of Him to reveal this one thing, that He is, as the assurance of His absolute eternity.

For such an indication of God's infinity the words 'I Am that I Am' were clearly adequate; but, in addition, we needed to apprehend the operation of His majesty and power. For while absolute existence is peculiar to Him Who, abiding eternally, had no beginning in a past however remote, we hear again an utterance worthy of Himself issuing from the eternal and Holy God, Who says, Who holdeth the heaven in His palm and the earth in His hand, and again, The heaven is My throne and the earth is the footstool of My feet. What house will ye build Me or what shall be the place of My rest? The whole heaven is held in the palm of God, the whole earth grasped in His hand. Now the word of God, profitable as it is to the cursory thought of a pious mind, reveals a deeper meaning to the patient student than to the momentary hearer. For this heaven which is held in the palm of God is also His throne, and the earth which is grasped in His hand is also the footstool beneath His feet. This was not written that from throne and footstool, metaphors drawn from the posture of one sitting, we should conclude that He has extension in space, as of a body, for that which is His throne and footstool is also held in hand and palm by that infinite Omnipotence. It was written that in all born and created things God might be known within them and without, overshadowing and indwelling, surrounding all and interfused through all, since palm and hand, which hold, reveal the might of His external control, while throne and footstool, by their support of a sitter, display the subservience of outward things to One within Who, Himself outside them, encloses all in His grasp, yet dwells within the external world which is His own. In this wise does God, from within and from without, control and correspond to the universe; being infinite He is present in all things, in Him Who is infinite all are included. In devout thoughts such as these my soul, engrossed in the pursuit of truth, took its delight.

Source: Hilary of Poitiers, On the Trinity *I.4–6, trans. E. W. Watson and L. Pullan, in Philip Schaff and Henry Wace (eds),* Nicene and Post-Nicene Fathers, *second series, vol. 9, Buffalo, NY: Christian Literature Publishing Co., 1899.*

1.6 Gregory of Nyssa, from *To Ablabius: 'On Not Three Gods'*

Gregory claims that the divine nature is indivisible and unnameable.

We say, then, to begin with, that the practice of calling those who are not divided in nature by the very name of their common nature in the plural, and saying they are 'many men,' is a customary abuse of language, and that it would be much the same thing to say they are 'many human natures.' And the truth of this we may see from the following instance. When we address any one, we do not call him by the name of his nature, in order that no confusion may result from the community of the name, as would happen if every one of those who hear it were to think that he himself was the person addressed, because the call is made not by the proper appellation but by the common name of their nature: but we separate him from the multitude by using that name which belongs to him as his own – that, I mean, which signifies the particular subject. Thus there are many who have shared in the nature – many disciples, say, or apostles, or martyrs – but the man in them all is one; since, as has been said, the term 'man' does not belong to the nature of the individual as such, but to that which is common. For Luke is a man, or Stephen is a man; but it does not follow that if any one is a man he is therefore Luke or Stephen: but the idea of the persons admits of that separation which is made by the peculiar attributes considered in each severally, and when they are combined is presented to us by means of number; yet their nature is one, at union in itself, and an absolutely indivisible unit, not capable of increase by addition or of diminution by subtraction, but in its essence being and continually remaining one, inseparable even though it appear in plurality, continuous, complete, and not divided with the individuals who participate in it. And as we speak of a people, or a mob, or an army, or an assembly in the singular in every case, while each of these is conceived as being in plurality, so according to the more accurate expression, 'man' would be said to be one, even though those who are exhibited to us in the same nature make up a plurality. Thus it would be much better to correct our erroneous habit, so as no longer to extend to a plurality the name of the nature, than by our bondage to habit to transfer to our statements concerning God the error which exists in the above case. But since the correction of the habit is impracticable (for how could you persuade any one not to speak of those who are exhibited in the same nature as 'many men'? – indeed, in every case habit is a thing hard to change), we are not so far wrong in not going contrary to the prevailing habit in the case of the lower nature, since no harm results from the mistaken use of the name: but in the case of the statement concerning the Divine nature the various use of terms is no longer so free from danger: for that which is of small account is in these subjects no longer a small matter. Therefore we must confess one God, according to the testimony of Scripture, 'Hear, O Israel, the Lord thy God is one Lord,' even though the name of Godhead extends through the Holy Trinity. This I say according to the account we have given in the case of human nature, in which we have learnt that it is improper to extend the name of the nature by the mark of plurality. We must, however, more carefully examine the name of 'Godhead,' in order to obtain, by means of the significance involved in the word, some help towards clearing up the question before us.

Most men think that the word 'Godhead' is used in a peculiar degree in respect of nature: and just as the heaven, or the sun, or any other of the constituent parts of the universe are denoted by proper names which are significant of the subjects, so they say that in the case of the Supreme and Divine nature, the word 'Godhead' is fitly adapted to that which it represents to us, as a kind of special name. We, on the other hand, following the suggestions of Scripture, have learnt that that nature is unnameable and unspeakable, and we say that every term either invented by the custom of men, or handed down to us by the Scriptures, is indeed explanatory of our conceptions of the Divine Nature, but does not include the signification of that nature itself. And it may be shown without much difficulty that this is the case. For all other terms which are used of the creation may be found, even without analysis of their origin, to be applied to the subjects accidentally, because we are content to denote the things in any way by the word applied to them so as to avoid confusion in our knowledge of the things signified. But all the terms that are employed to lead us to the knowledge of God have comprehended in them each its own meaning, and you cannot find any word among the terms especially applied to God which is without a distinct sense. Hence it is clear that by any of the terms we use the Divine nature itself is not signified, but some one of its surroundings is made known. For we say, it may be, that the Deity is incorruptible, or powerful, or whatever else we are accustomed to say of Him. But in each of these terms we find a peculiar sense, fit to be understood or asserted of the Divine nature, yet not expressing that which that nature is in its essence. For the subject, whatever it may be, is incorruptible: but our conception of incorruptibility is this, that that which is, is not resolved into decay: so, when we say that He is incorruptible, we declare what His nature does not suffer, but we do not express what that is which does not suffer corruption. Thus, again, if we say that He is the Giver of life, though we show by that appellation what He gives, we do not by that word declare what that is which gives it. And by the same reasoning we find that all else which results from the significance involved in the names expressing the Divine attributes either forbids us to conceive what we ought not to conceive of the Divine nature, or teaches us that which we ought to conceive of it, but does not include an explanation of the nature itself.

Source: Gregory of Nyssa, To Ablabius: 'On Not Three Gods', *trans. H. A. Wilson, in Philip Schaff and Henry Wace (eds),* Nicene and Post-Nicene Fathers, *second series, vol. 5, Buffalo, NY: Christian Literature Publishing Co., 1893.*

1.7 Gregory of Nazianzus, from *Oration XXXI* ('The fifth theological oration')

Gregory argues for the full deity of the Holy Spirit.

This, then, is my position with regard to these things, and I hope it may be always my position, and that of whosoever is dear to me; to worship God the Father, God the Son, and God the Holy Ghost, Three Persons, One Godhead, undivided in honour and glory and substance and kingdom, as one of our own inspired philosophers not long departed shewed. Let him not see the rising of the Morning Star, as Scripture saith, nor the glory of its brightness, who is otherwise minded, or who follows the temper of the times, at one time being of one mind and of another at another time, and thinking unsoundly in the highest matters. For if He is not to be worshipped, how can He deify me by Baptism? but if He is to be worshipped, surely He is an Object of adoration, and if an Object of adoration He must be God; the one is linked to the other, a truly golden and saving chain. And indeed from the Spirit comes our New Birth, and from the New Birth our new creation, and from the new creation our deeper knowledge of the dignity of Him from Whom it is derived.

This, then, is what may be said by one who admits the silence of Scripture. But now the swarm of testimonies shall burst upon you from which the Deity of the Holy Ghost shall be shewn to all who are not excessively stupid, or else altogether enemies to the Spirit, to be most clearly recognized in Scripture. Look at these facts: Christ is born; the Spirit is His Forerunner. He is baptized; the Spirit bears witness. He is tempted; the Spirit leads Him up. He works miracles; the Spirit accompanies them. He ascends; the Spirit takes His place. What great things are there in the idea of God which are not in His power? What titles which belong to God are not applied to Him, except only Unbegotten and Begotten? For it was needful that the distinctive properties of the Father and the Son should remain peculiar to Them, lest there should be confusion in the Godhead Which brings all things, even disorder itself, into due arrangement and good order. Indeed I tremble when I think of the abundance of the titles, and how many Names they outrage who fall foul of the Spirit. He is called the Spirit of God, the Spirit of Christ, the Mind of Christ, the Spirit of The Lord, and Himself The Lord, the Spirit of Adoption, of Truth, of Liberty; the Spirit of Wisdom, of Understanding, of Counsel, of Might, of Knowledge, of Godliness, of the Fear of God. For He is the Maker of all these, filling all with His Essence, containing all things, filling the world in His Essence, yet incapable of being comprehended in His power by the world; good, upright, princely, by nature not by adoption; sanctifying, not sanctified; measuring, not measured; shared, not sharing; filling, not filled; containing, not contained; inherited, glorified, reckoned with the Father and the Son; held out as a threat; the Finger of God; fire like God (to manifest, as I take it, His consubstantiality); the Creator-Spirit, Who by Baptism and by Resurrection creates anew; the Spirit That knoweth all things, That teacheth, That bloweth where and to what extent He listeth; That guideth, talketh, sendeth forth, separateth, is angry or tempted; That revealeth, illumineth, quickeneth, or rather is the very Light and Life; That maketh Temples; That deifieth; That perfecteth so as even to anticipate Baptism, yet after Baptism to be sought as a separate gift; That doeth all things that God doeth; divided into fiery tongues; dividing gifts; making Apostles, Prophets, Evangelists, Pastors, and Teachers; understanding manifold, clear, piercing, undefiled, unhindered, which is the same thing as Most wise and varied in His actions; and making all things clear and plain; and of independent power, unchangeable, Almighty, all-seeing, penetrating all spirits that are intelligent, pure, most subtle (the Angel Hosts I think); and also all prophetic spirits and apostolic in the same manner and not in the same places; for they lived in different places; thus showing that He is uncircumscript.

Source: Gregory of Nazianzus, Oration XXXI *('The fifth theological oration') 28–9, trans. Charles Gordon Browne and James Edward Swallow, in Philip Schaff and Henry Wace (eds),* Nicene and Post-Nicene Fathers, *second series, vol. 7, Buffalo, NY: Christian Literature Publishing Co., 1894.*

1.8 Augustine of Hippo, from *On the Holy Trinity*

Augustine here offers a summary of his great work on the Trinity, describing the contents of each book.

But since the necessities of our discussion and argument have compelled us to say a great many things in the course of fourteen books, which we cannot view at once in one glance, so as to be able to refer them quickly in thought to that which we desire to grasp, I will attempt, by the help of God, to the best of my power, to put briefly together, without arguing, whatever I have established in the several books by argument as known, and to place, as it were, under one mental view, not the way in which we have been convinced of each point, but the points themselves of which we have been convinced; in order that what follows may not be so far separated from that which precedes, as that the perusal of the former shall produce forgetfulness of the latter; or at any rate, if it have produced such forgetfulness, that what has escaped the memory may be speedily recalled by re-perusal.

In the first book, the unity and equality of that highest Trinity is shown from Holy Scripture. In the second, and third, and fourth, the same: but a careful handling of the question respecting the sending of the Son and of the Holy Spirit has resulted in three books; and we have demonstrated, that He who is sent is not therefore less than He who sends because the one sent, the other was sent; since the Trinity, which is in all things equal, being also equally in its own nature unchangeable, and invisible, and everywhere present, works indivisibly. In the fifth – with a view to those who think that the substance of the Father and of the Son is therefore not the same, because they suppose everything that is predicated of God to be predicated according to substance, and therefore contend that to beget and to be begotten, or to be begotten and unbegotten, as being diverse, are diverse substances – it is demonstrated that not everything that is predicated of God is predicated according to substance, as He is called good and great according to substance, or anything else that is predicated of Him in respect to Himself, but that some things also are predicated relatively, i.e. not in respect to Himself, but in respect to something which is not Himself; as He is called the Father in respect to the Son, or the Lord in respect to the creature that serves Him; and that here, if anything thus relatively predicated, i.e. predicated in respect to something that is not Himself, is predicated also as in time, as, e.g., 'Lord, Thou hast become our refuge' [Ps. 90.1], then nothing happens to Him so as to work a change in Him, but He Himself continues altogether unchangeable in His own nature or essence. In the sixth, the question how Christ is called by the mouth of the apostle 'the power of God and the wisdom of God' [1 Cor. 1.24], is so far argued that the more careful handling of that question is deferred, viz. whether He from whom Christ is begotten is not wisdom Himself, but only the father of His own wisdom, or whether wisdom begat wisdom. But be it which it may, the equality of the Trinity became apparent in this book also, and that God was not triple, but a Trinity; and that the Father and the Son are not, as it were, a double as opposed to the single Holy Spirit: for therein three are not anything more than one. We considered, too, how to understand the words of Bishop Hilary [i.e., Hilary of Poitiers], 'Eternity in the Father, form in the Image, use in the Gift.' In the seventh, the question is explained which had been deferred: in what way that God who begat the Son is not only Father of His own power and wisdom, but is Himself also power and wisdom; so, too, the Holy Spirit; and yet that they are not three powers or three wisdoms, but one power and one wisdom, as one God and one essence. It was next inquired, in what way they are called one essence, three persons, or by some Greeks one essence, three substances; and we found that the words were so used through the needs of speech, that there might be one term by which to answer, when it is asked what the three are, whom we truly confess to be three, viz. Father, and Son, and Holy Spirit. In the eighth, it is made plain by reason also to those who understand, that not only the Father is not greater than the Son in the substance of truth, but that both together are not anything greater than the Holy Spirit alone, nor that any two at all in the same Trinity are anything greater than one, nor all three together anything greater than each severally. Next, I have pointed out, that by means of the truth, which is beheld by the understanding, and by means of the highest good, from which is all good, and by means of the righteousness for which a righteous mind is loved even by a mind not yet righteous, we might understand, so far as it is possible to understand, that not only incorporeal but also unchangeable nature which is God; and by means, too, of love, which in the Holy Scriptures is called God, by which, first of all, those who have understanding begin also, however feebly, to discern the Trinity, to wit, one that loves, and that which is loved, and love. In the ninth, the argument advances as far as to the image of God, viz. man in respect to his mind; and in this we found a kind of trinity, i.e. the mind, and the knowledge whereby the mind knows itself, and the love whereby it loves both itself and its knowledge of itself; and these three are shown to be mutually equal, and of one essence. In the tenth, the same subject is more carefully and subtly handled, and is brought to this point, that we found in the mind a still more manifest trinity of the mind, viz. in memory, and understanding, and will. But since it turned out also, that the mind could never be in such a case as not to remember, understand, and love itself, although it did not always think of itself; but that when it did think of itself, it did not in the same act of thought distinguish itself from things corporeal; the argument respecting the Trinity, of which this is an image, was deferred, in order to find a trinity also in the things themselves that are seen with the body, and to exercise the reader's attention more distinctly in that. Accordingly, in the eleventh, we chose the sense of sight, wherein that which should have been there found to hold good might be recognized also in the other four bodily senses, although not expressly mentioned; and so a trinity of the outer man first showed itself in those things which are discerned from without, to wit, from the bodily object which is seen, and from the form which is thence impressed upon the eye of the beholder, and from the purpose of the will combining the two. But these three things, as was patent, were not mutually equal and of one substance. Next, we found yet another trinity in the mind itself, introduced into it, as it were, by the things perceived from without; wherein the same three things, as it appeared, were of one substance: the image of the bodily object which is in the memory, and the form thence impressed when the mind's eye of the thinker is turned to it, and the purpose of the will combining the two. But we found this trinity to pertain to the outer man, on this account, that it was introduced into the mind from bodily objects which are perceived from without. In the twelfth, we thought good to distinguish wisdom from knowledge, and to seek first, as being the lower of the two, a kind of appropriate and special trinity in that which is specially called knowledge; but that although we have got now in this to something pertaining to the inner man, yet it is not yet to be either called or thought an image of God. And this is discussed in the thirteenth book by the commendation of Christian faith. In the fourteenth we discuss the true wisdom of man, viz. that which is granted him by God's gift in the partaking of that very God Himself, which is distinct from knowledge; and the discussion reached this point, that a trinity is discovered in the image of God, which is man in respect to his mind, which mind is 'renewed in the knowledge' of God, 'after the image of Him that created' man; 'after His own image;' and so obtains wisdom, wherein is the contemplation of things eternal.

Source: Augustine of Hippo, On the Holy Trinity, *Book 15, trans. Arthur West Haddan, in* Philip Schaff (ed.), Nicene and Post-Nicene Fathers, *first series, vol. 3, Buffalo, NY: Christian Literature Publishing Co., 1887.*

1.9 Pseudo-Dionysius, from *Mystical Theology*

Dionysius teaches that no words are adequate to name God.

[E]ven now, when entering into the gloom which is above mind, we shall find, not a little speaking, but a complete absence of speech, and absence of conception. In the other case, the discourse, in descending from the above to the lowest, is widened according to the descent, to a proportionate extent; but now, in ascending from below to that which is above, in proportion to the ascent, it is contracted, and after a complete ascent, it will become wholly voiceless, and will be wholly united to the unutterable. But, for what reason in short, you say, having attributed the Divine attributes from the foremost, do we begin the Divine abstraction from things lowest? Because it is necessary that they who place attributes on that which is above every attribute, should place the attributive affirmation from that which is more cognate to it; but that they who abstract, with regard to that which is above every abstraction, should make the abstraction from things which are further removed from it. Are not life and goodness more (cognate) than air and stone? and He is not given to debauch and to wrath, more (removed) than He is not expressed nor conceived.

We say then – that the Cause of all, which is above all, is neither without being, nor without life – nor without reason, nor without mind, nor is a body – nor has shape – nor form – nor quality, or quantity, or bulk – nor is in a place – nor is seen – nor has sensible contact – nor perceives, nor is perceived, by the senses – nor has disorder and confusion, as being vexed by earthly passions – nor is powerless, as being subject to casualties of sense – nor is in need of light – neither is It, nor has It, change, or decay, or division, or deprivation, or flux – or any other of the objects of sense.

On the other hand, ascending, we say, that It is neither soul, nor mind, nor has imagination, or opinion, or reason, or conception; neither is expressed, nor conceived; neither is number, nor order, nor greatness, nor littleness; nor equality, nor inequality; nor similarity, nor dissimilarity; neither is standing, nor moving; nor at rest; neither has power, nor is power, nor light; neither lives, nor is life; neither is essence nor eternity, nor time; neither is Its touch intelligible, neither is It science, nor truth; nor kingdom, nor wisdom; neither one, nor oneness; neither Deity, nor Goodness; nor is It Spirit according to our understanding; nor Sonship, nor Paternity; nor any other thing of those known to us, or to any other existing being; neither is It any of non-existing nor of existing things, nor do things existing know It, as It is; nor does It know existing things, qua existing; neither is there expression of It, nor name, nor knowledge; neither is It darkness, nor light; nor error, nor truth; neither is there any definition at all of It, nor any abstraction. But when making the predications and abstractions of things after It, we neither predicate, nor abstract from It; since the all-perfect and uniform Cause of all is both above every definition and the pre-eminence of Him, Who is absolutely freed from all, and beyond the whole, is also above every abstraction.

Source: Pseudo-Dionysius, Mystical Theology 3—5, *in* The Works of Dionysius the Areopagite, *trans. John Parker, London: James Parker, 1897.*

1.10 Anselm of Canterbury, from the *Monologion*

Anselm attempts to prove that it is logically necessary to believe in the Trinity.

Hence, it may be clearly apprehended in the supreme Wisdom, which always thinks of itself, just as it remembers itself, that, of the eternal remembrance of it, its coeternal Word is born. Therefore, as the Word is properly conceived of as the child, the memory most appropriately takes the name of parent. If, then, the child which is born of the supreme Spirit alone is the child of his memory, there can be no more logical conclusion than that his memory is himself. For not in respect of the fact that he remembers himself does he exist in his own memory, like ideas that exist in the human memory, without being the memory itself; but he so remembers himself that he is his own memory.

It therefore follows that, just as the Son is the intelligence or wisdom of the Father, so he is that of the memory of the Father. But, regarding whatever the Son has, wisdom or understanding, this he likewise remembers. The Son is, therefore, the memory of the Father, and the memory of memory, that is, the memory that remembers the Father, who is memory, just as he is the wisdom of the Father, and the wisdom of wisdom, that is, the wisdom wise regarding the wisdom of the Father; and the Son is indeed memory, born of memory, as he is wisdom, born of wisdom, while the Father is memory and wisdom born of none.

But, while I am here considering with interest the individual properties and the common attributes of Father and Son, I find none in them more pleasurable to contemplate than the feeling of mutual love. For how absurd it would be to deny that the supreme Spirit loves himself, just as he remembers himself, and conceives of himself! since even the rational human mind is convinced that it can love both itself and him, because it can remember itself and him, and can conceive of itself and of him; for idle and almost useless is the memory and conception of any object, unless, so far as reason requires, the object itself is loved or condemned. The supreme Spirit, then, loves himself, just as he remembers himself and conceives of himself.

It is, at any rate, clear to the rational man that he does not remember himself or conceive of himself because he loves himself, but he loves himself because he remembers himself and conceives of himself; and that he could not love himself if he did not remember and conceive of himself. For no object is loved without remembrance or conception of it; while many things are retained in memory and conceived of that are not loved.

It is evident, then, that the love of the supreme Spirit proceeds from the fact that he remembers himself and conceives of himself. But if, by the memory of the supreme Spirit, we understand the Father, and by his intelligence by which he conceives of anything, the Son, it is manifest that the love of the supreme Spirit proceeds equally from Father and Son.

But if the supreme Spirit loves himself, no doubt the Father loves himself, the Son loves himself, and the one the other; since the Father separately is the supreme Spirit, and the Son separately is the supreme Spirit, and both at once one Spirit. And, since each equally remembers himself and the other, and conceives equally of himself and the other; and since what is loved, or loves in the Father, or in the Son, is altogether the same, necessarily each loves himself and the other with an equal love.

How great, then, is this love of the supreme Spirit, common as it is to Father and Son! But, if he loves himself as much as he remembers and conceives of himself; and, moreover, remembers and conceives of himself in as great a degree as that in which his essence exists, since otherwise it cannot exist; undoubtedly his love is as great as he himself is.

But, what can be equal to the supreme Spirit, except the supreme Spirit? That love is, then, the supreme Spirit. Hence, if no creature, that is, if nothing other than the supreme Spirit, the Father and the Son, ever existed; nevertheless, Father and Son would love themselves and one another.

It therefore follows that this love is nothing else than what the Father and the Son are, which is the supreme Being. But, since there cannot be more than one supreme Being, what inference can be more necessary than that Father and Son and the love of both are one supreme Being? Therefore, this love is supreme Wisdom, supreme Truth, the supreme Good, and whatsoever can be attributed to the substance the supreme Spirit.

It should be carefully considered whether there are two loves, one proceeding from the Father, the other from the Son; or one, not proceeding as a whole from one, but in part from the Father, in part from the Son; or neither more than one, nor one proceeding in part from each separately, but one proceeding as a whole from each separately, and likewise as a whole from the two at once.

But the solution of such a question can, without doubt, be apprehended from the fact that this love proceeds not from that in which Father and Son are more than one, but from that in which they are one. For, not from their relations, which are more than one, but from their essence itself, which does not admit of plurality, do Father and Son equally produce so great a good.

Therefore, as the Father separately is the supreme Spirit, and the Son separately is the supreme Spirit, and Father and Son at once are not two, but one Spirit; so from the Father separately the love of the supreme Spirit emanates as a whole, and from the Son as a whole, and at once from Father and Son, not as two, but as one and the same whole.

Source: Anselm of Canterbury, Monologion *48—54, in* Proslogion; Monologion, an Appendix on Behalf of the Fool by Gaunilon; and Cur Deus Homo, *trans. Sidney Norton Deane, Chicago: Open Court Co., 1903.*

1.11 Richard of St Victor, from *Of the Trinity*

Richard here argues that, if God is perfect in love (he uses the word 'charity') and in happiness, then God must exist as a plurality of persons.

We have learned above that in that supreme and altogether perfect good there is fullness and perfection of all goodness. However, where there is fullness of all goodness, true and supreme charity cannot be lacking. For nothing is better than charity; nothing is more perfect than charity. However, no one is properly said to have charity on the basis of his own private love of himself. And so it is necessary for love to be directed toward another for it to be charity. Therefore, where a plurality of persons is lacking, charity cannot exist.

But you might say, 'Even if there were only one person in that true Divinity, nevertheless He could still have charity toward His creation – indeed He would have it.' But certainly He could not have *supreme* charity toward a created person. For charity would be disordered if He loved supremely someone who should not be supremely loved. But in that supremely wise goodness it is impossible for charity to be disordered. Therefore a divine person could not have supreme charity toward a person who was not worthy of supreme love. However, in order that charity be supreme and supremely perfect, it is necessary that it be so great that nothing greater can exist and that it be of such a kind that nothing better can exist. However, as long as anyone loves no one else as much as he loves himself, that private love which he has for himself shows clearly that he has not yet reached the supreme level of charity. But a divine person certainly would not have anyone to love as worthily as Himself if He did not have a person of equal worth. However, a person who is not God would not be equal in worth to a divine person. Therefore, so that fullness of charity might have a place in that true Divinity, it is necessary that a divine person not lack a relationship with an equally worthy person, who is, for this reason, divine.

Therefore see how easily reason clearly shows that in true Divinity plurality of persons cannot be lacking. Certainly God alone is supremely good. Therefore God alone ought to be loved supremely. A divine person could not show supreme love to a person who lacked divinity. However, fullness of Divinity could not exist without fullness of goodness. But fullness of goodness could not exist without fullness of charity, nor could fullness of charity exist without a plurality of divine persons.

What the fullness of goodness clearly shows and proves concerning the plurality of persons, the fullness of happiness demonstrates by a similar reason. What one says, the other confirms. In one and the same confirmation of truth, the one speaks out and the other applauds.

Let each person examine his consciousness; without doubt and without contradiction he will discover that just as nothing is better than charity, so nothing is more pleasing than charity. Nature herself teaches us this; many experiences do the very same. Therefore, just as that than which nothing is better cannot be lacking in the fullness of true goodness, so also that than which nothing is more pleasing cannot be lacking in the fullness of supreme happiness. Therefore, in supreme happiness it is necessary that charity not be lacking. However, so that charity may be in the supreme good, it is impossible that there be lacking either one who can show charity or one to whom charity can be shown. However, it is a characteristic of love, and one without which it cannot possibly exist, to wish to be loved much by the one whom you love much. Therefore, love cannot be pleasing if it is not also mutual. Therefore, in that true and supreme happiness, just as pleasing love cannot be lacking, so mutual love cannot be lacking. However, in mutual love it is absolutely necessary that there be both one who gives love and one who returns love. Therefore one will be the offerer of love and the other the returner of love. Now, where the one and the other are clearly shown to exist, true plurality is discovered. In that fullness of true happiness, a plurality of persons cannot be lacking. However, it is agreed that supreme happiness is nothing other than Divinity itself. Therefore, the showing of love freely given and the repayment of love that is due prove without any doubt that in true Divinity a plurality of persons cannot be lacking.

Source: Richard of St Victor, Of the Trinity *III.2–3, trans. Grover A. Zinn, in* Richard of St Victor, *Classics of Western Spirituality, New York: Paulist Press, 1979.*

1.12 Thomas Aquinas, from the *Summa Theologica*

Thomas argues that God's existence may be demonstrated in five ways.

The existence of God can be proved in five ways.

The first and more manifest way is the argument from motion. It is certain, and evident to our senses, that in the world some things are in motion. Now whatever is in motion is put in motion by another, for nothing can be in motion except it is in potentiality to that towards which it is in motion; whereas a thing moves inasmuch as it is in act. For motion is nothing else than the reduction of something from potentiality to actuality. But nothing can be reduced from potentiality to actuality, except by something in a state of actuality. Thus that which is actually hot, as fire, makes wood, which is potentially hot, to be actually hot, and thereby moves and changes it. Now it is not possible that the same thing should be at once in actuality and potentiality in the same respect, but only in different respects. For what is actually hot cannot simultaneously be potentially hot; but it is simultaneously potentially cold. It is therefore impossible that in the same respect and in the same way a thing should be both mover and moved, i.e. that it should move itself. Therefore, whatever is in motion must be put in motion by another. If that by which it is put in motion be itself put in motion, then this also must needs be put in motion by another, and that by another again. But this cannot go on to infinity, because then there would be no first mover, and, consequently, no other mover; seeing that subsequent movers move only inasmuch as they are put in motion by the first mover; as the staff moves only because it is put in motion by the hand. Therefore it is necessary to arrive at a first mover, put in motion by no other; and this everyone understands to be God.

The second way is from the nature of the efficient cause. In the world of sense we find there is an order of efficient causes. There is no case known (neither is it, indeed, possible) in which a thing is found to be the efficient cause of itself; for so it would be prior to itself, which is impossible. Now in efficient causes it is not possible to go on to infinity, because in all efficient causes following in order, the first is the cause of the intermediate cause, and the intermediate is the cause of the ultimate cause, whether the intermediate cause be several, or only one. Now to take away the cause is to take away the effect. Therefore, if there be no first cause among efficient causes, there will be no ultimate, nor any intermediate cause. But if in efficient causes it is possible to go on to infinity, there will be no first efficient cause, neither will there be an ultimate effect, nor any intermediate efficient causes; all of which is plainly false. Therefore it is necessary to admit a first efficient cause, to which everyone gives the name of God.

The third way is taken from possibility and necessity, and runs thus. We find in nature things that are possible to be and not to be, since they are found to be generated, and to corrupt, and consequently, they are possible to be and not to be. But it is impossible for these always to exist, for that which is possible not to be at some time is not. Therefore, if everything is possible not to be, then at one time there could have been nothing in existence. Now if this were true, even now there would be nothing in existence, because that which does not exist only begins to exist by something already existing. Therefore, if at one time nothing was in existence, it would have been impossible for anything to have begun to exist; and thus even now nothing would be in existence – which is absurd. Therefore, not all beings are merely possible, but there must exist something the existence of which is necessary. But every necessary thing either has its necessity caused by another, or not. Now it is impossible to go on to infinity in necessary things which have their necessity caused by another, as has been already proved in regard to efficient causes. Therefore we cannot but postulate the existence of some being having of itself its own necessity, and not receiving it from another, but rather causing in others their necessity. This all men speak of as God.

The fourth way is taken from the gradation to be found in things. Among beings there are some more and some less good, true, noble and the like. But 'more' and 'less' are predicated of different things, according as they resemble in their different ways something which is the maximum, as a thing is said to be hotter according as it more nearly resembles that which is hottest; so that there is something which is truest, something best, something noblest and, consequently, something which is uttermost being; for those things that are greatest in truth are greatest in being, as it is written in *Metaph*. ii. Now the maximum in any genus is the cause of all in that genus; as fire, which is the maximum heat, is the cause of all hot things. Therefore there must also be something which is to all beings the cause of their being, goodness, and every other perfection; and this we call God.

The fifth way is taken from the governance of the world. We see that things which lack intelligence, such as natural bodies, act for an end, and this is evident from their acting always, or nearly always, in the same way, so as to obtain the best result. Hence it is plain that not fortuitously, but designedly, do they achieve their end. Now whatever lacks intelligence cannot move towards an end, unless it be directed by some being endowed with knowledge and intelligence; as the arrow is shot to its mark by the archer. Therefore some intelligent being exists by whom all natural things are directed to their end; and this being we call God.

Source: Thomas Aquinas, Summa Theologica, *I.2.3, trans. Fathers of the English Dominican Province, London: Burns, Oates & Washbourne, 1924–34.*

2 The Doctrine of God from the Reformation to the Present Day

Introductory essay

The great disruption to the stability of Christian Europe that was the Reformation began with Martin Luther questioning a relatively minor pastoral practice, the sale of indulgences. In the ferment that followed, however, the received doctrine of God was essentially unquestioned, by the main players at least. (There were isolated individuals who questioned trinitarian doctrine – most famously, perhaps, Michael Servetus and Laelius and Faustus Socini – but in the major debates, the question was simply not raised.) If there is a distinctively Reformation doctrine of God, it is in a sense that the doctrine is useful – not just something to be believed, but something that practically affects the way we choose to live our lives. Luther's exposition of the First Commandment stresses that idolatry is not primarily a matter of believing wrongly, but is a matter of where we seek security, and the ends to which we order our lives. To believe rightly in God is to have the basis and goal of life right; nothing else. He points to certain devotional practices of the Church of his day to suggest that, despite its orthodox doctrine of God, it was in fact serially guilty of idolatry – it said the right things, but lived wrongly.

In our second extract, John Calvin offers his brief exposition of the doctrine of the Trinity. He shows a certain impatience with debates over the aptness of particular terms – for Calvin, too, theology is to be useful, not merely argumentative – but in essence he is doing no more than repeating the received doctrine, affirming that this, at least, had come down to the Church unsullied. The third extract, from Jonathan Edwards two centuries later, is rather different. Not that Edwards denies the inherited doctrine of the Trinity, but his account is bolder and more speculative. It stands in a recognizable tradition of Christian Platonism, which Edwards inherited from Ralph Cudworth and Henry Moore; the Son is the Father's perfect idea of himself; the Spirit the Father's perfect delight in himself. Edwards stands in the Reformed tradition, however, and immediately this speculative account is put to practical use: if all this is true, then we may make claims about the relationship with God that Christians enjoy.

Atheism and Unitarianism were becoming much more common in Europe in Edwards's day, and the collapse of the calm and stable synthesis was immanent. Friedrich Schleiermacher is the first great mind to attempt a reconstruction of theology after its classical forms had seemed to fail. He sees the basis of theology as reflection on human religious experience; each doctrine is to be recast in this form. When he comes to the divine perfections, then, he argues that they are not particularly about God, so much as about our feeling of absolute dependence (the basic religious experience which Schleiermacher holds to be common to all human beings).

Charles Hodge lived a generation after Schleiermacher, but was less convinced of the bankruptcy of classical theology than his predecessor. It is clear that Hodge knew what Schleiermacher was doing, but he generally chose not to address it directly, but to attempt to demonstrate that the older way of doing theology could still have life and power in the middle of the nineteenth century. We include from him a calm and clear reassertion of the older tradition concerning the divine perfections. Hodge is perhaps less conscious of the difficulties of applying human language to God than some of the older theologians, but his deliberate alignment with the seventeenth-century Westminster Confession, and his straightforward and unpolemical rehearsal of standard points, are both perhaps as impressive as they are reactionary.

In the next extract we have another reaction to Schleiermacher, coming from a rather different direction. The great Swiss-German theologian Karl Barth found much of worth in the older Reformed dogmatics that Hodge was seeking to reaffirm, but Barth saw profound problems too. His massive attempt to restate the whole of Christian doctrine, the unfinished *Church Dogmatics*, certainly stands closer to the tradition than Schleiermacher did, but it is still a work of reconstruction. This is already evident in the discussion of the doctrine of revelation in the first part-volume, from which the extract here is taken. God's self-revelation, asserts Barth, is triune in character, and so from the very fact of revelation we can already derive the doctrine of the Trinity.

This idea of giving priority in the arrangement of doctrines to the Trinity is, Barth recognizes, almost unique in the tradition that he received, and yet it has become almost normal since Barth's day. His own arguments are one reason for that; another is found in our next extract, from the Roman Catholic theologian Karl Rahner. Rahner addresses specifically the relationship between the treatment of two doctrines in Catholic dogmatics. Typically, the doctrine of God began, he claims, with a treatment of the oneness of God, including the divine perfections, and then moved on to a treatment of the Trinity. Rahner protests against this division, suggesting that it has had many damaging effects on theology. With a sense of tradition that could only come from a Roman Catholic theologian, he claims it is rather novel, beginning in the thirteenth century only. Our own decision to arrange our two chapters on the doctrine of God the way we have is indicative of the success his argument has had.

Rahner goes on in the extract to make another point, equally influential in theology since. Trinitarian doctrine, he claims, is not abstract and speculative; it is about human salvation. Who God is in the economy of salvation must be the same as who God is in all eternity; or, to state it in Rahner's formulation, so successful that it has become known as 'Rahner's rule', 'the economic Trinity is the immanent Trinity and the immanent Trinity is the economic Trinity'.

Paul Tillich may seem an odd figure to insert into the story at this point. His analysis of the origins of the idea of the Trinity recalls Schleiermacher's attempt to find a general account of 'religiousness' in its attempt to categorize world religions in a meaningful order, with Christianity at the apex. However, Tillich sees with clarity the success of the doctrine of the Trinity in offering an account of mediation between humanity and God; he seems to assume that the doctrine developed because it was successful in this way; those theologians who followed Barth and Rahner in creating a 'trinitarian revival' in the second half of the twentieth century will have more to say about categories such as revelation, but will borrow Tillich's idea that Trinitarianism is uniquely successful in accounting for mediation with some gratitude.

The extract from Jürgen Moltmann's classic *The Crucified God* is an example of the application of 'Rahner's rule' in a radical way, a way that has recently become popular. The immanent Trinity is the economic Trinity – and so the crucifixion of Christ becomes an event in God's own life. What of such divine perfections as impassibility and immutability? These are pagan Greek ideas, from which the Christian doctrine of God urgently needs to be set free. God suffers, dies, is crucified. This is central, definitive of what it means for God to be God in a properly Christian understanding. Wolfhart Pannenberg takes the same thesis forward in a more general way in our next extract, the crucifixion, yes, but the history of the world more generally is decisive for God's life. God has 'made himself dependent upon the course of history'.

For another theologian working in these areas, we offer Catherine Mowry LaCugna. She suggests that Rahner's rule needs yet further collapsing. Pre-Nicene theology (that is, theology from before the Council of Nicaea in AD 325) knew no distinction between economy and eternity, she claims; God's life simply was his story with Israel and the Church. If we can return to that purity, the doctrine of the Trinity becomes an account of how God is present and active in the world and with the Church now, and thus a profoundly practical doctrine.

The final extract comes from a theologian who was very involved with this trinitarian revival, although by no means uncritical of some of the emphases in Moltmann, Pannenberg and LaCugna. In the extract included here, however, Colin Gunton is treating the divine perfections. The Trinity becomes a key principle for rewriting the doctrine; the pagan Greek infection of theology is assumed, and the task we face is to cure it. There is a sense of excitement about the possibilities and the usefulness of a theology like this. The doctrine of God has moved from being a stable set of propositions to be affirmed, to being a vibrant motor for ethical and practical reflection.

SRH

2.1 Martin Luther, from the *Large Catechism*

In an exposition of the First Commandment, Luther outlines what it means to believe in God.

The First Commandment: Thou shalt have no other gods before Me.

That is: Thou shalt have [and worship] Me alone as thy God. What is the force of this, and how is it to be understood? What does it mean to have a god? or, what is God?

Answer: A god means that from which we are to expect all good and to which we are to take refuge in all distress, so that to have a God is nothing else than to trust and believe Him from the [whole] heart; as I have often said that the confidence and faith of the heart alone make both God and an idol. If your faith and trust be right, then is your god also true; and, on the other hand, if your trust be false and wrong, then you have not the true God; for these two belong together, faith and God. That now, I say, upon which you set your heart and put your trust is properly your god.

Therefore it is the intent of this commandment to require true faith and trust of the heart which settles upon the only true God and clings to Him alone. That is as much as to say: 'See to it that you let Me alone be your God, and never seek another,' i.e.: Whatever you lack of good things, expect it of Me, and look to Me for it, and whenever you suffer misfortune and distress, creep and cling to Me. I, yes, I, will give you enough and help you out of every need; only let not your heart cleave to or rest in any other.

This I must unfold somewhat more plainly, that it may be understood and perceived by ordinary examples of the contrary. Many a one thinks that he has God and everything in abundance when he has money and possessions; he trusts in them and boasts of them with such firmness and assurance as to care for no one. Lo, such a man also has a god, Mammon by name, i.e., money and possessions, on which he sets all his heart, and which is also the most common idol on earth. He who has money and possessions feels secure, and is joyful and undismayed as though he were sitting in the midst of Paradise. On the other hand, he who has none doubts and is despondent, as though he knew of no God. For very few are to be found who are of good cheer, and who neither mourn nor complain if they have not Mammon. This sticks and clings to our nature, even to the grave.

So, too, whoever trusts and boasts that he possesses great skill, prudence, power, favor, friendship, and honor has also a god, but not this true and only God. This appears again when you notice how presumptuous, secure, and proud people are because of such possessions, and how despondent when they no longer exist or are withdrawn. Therefore I repeat that the chief explanation of this point is that to have a god is to have something in which the heart entirely trusts.

Besides, consider what in our blindness, we have hitherto been practising and doing under the Papacy. If any one had toothache, he fasted and honored St. Apollonia; if he was afraid of fire, he chose St. Lawrence as his helper in need; if he dreaded pestilence, he made a vow to St. Sebastian or Rochio, and a countless number of such abominations, where every one selected his own saint, worshiped him, and called for help to him in distress. Here belong those also, as, e.g., sorcerers and magicians, whose idolatry is most gross, and who make a covenant with the devil, in order that he may give them plenty of money or help them in love-affairs, preserve their cattle, restore to them lost possessions, etc. For all these place their heart and trust elsewhere than in the true God, look for nothing good to Him nor seek it from Him.

Thus you can easily understand what and how much this commandment requires, namely, that man's entire heart and all his confidence be placed in God alone, and in no one else. For to have God, you can easily perceive, is not to lay hold of Him with our hands or to put Him in a bag, or to lock Him in a chest. But to apprehend Him means when the heart lays hold of Him and clings to Him. But to cling to Him with the heart is nothing else than to trust in Him entirely. For this reason He wishes to turn us away from everything else that exists outside of Him, and to draw us to Himself, namely, because He is the only eternal good. As though He would say: Whatever you have heretofore sought of the saints, or for whatever [things] you have trusted in Mammon or anything else, expect it all of Me, and regard Me as the one who will help you and pour out upon you richly all good things.

Lo, here you have the meaning of the true honor and worship of God, which pleases God, and which He commands under penalty of eternal wrath, namely, that the heart know no other comfort or confidence than in Him, and do not suffer itself to be torn from Him, but, for Him, risk and disregard everything upon earth. On the other hand, you can easily see and judge how the world practises only false worship and idolatry. For no people has ever been so reprobate as not to institute and observe some divine worship; every one has set up as his special god whatever he looked to for blessings, help, and comfort.

Thus, for example, the heathen who put their trust in power and dominion elevated Jupiter as the supreme god; the others, who were bent upon riches, happiness, or pleasure, and a life of ease, Hercules, Mercury, Venus or others; women with child, Diana or Lucina, and so on; thus every one made that his god to which his heart was inclined, so that even in the mind of the heathen to have a god means to trust and believe. But their error is this that their trust is false and wrong for it is not placed in the only God, besides whom there is truly no God in heaven or upon earth. Therefore the heathen really make their self-invented notions and dreams of God an idol, and put their trust in that which is altogether nothing. Thus it is with all idolatry; for it consists not merely in erecting an image and worshiping it, but rather in the heart, which stands gaping at something else, and seeks help and consolation from creatures, saints, or devils, and neither cares for God, nor looks to Him for so much good as to believe that He is willing to help, neither believes that whatever good it experiences comes from God.

Besides, there is also a false worship and extreme idolatry, which we have hitherto practised, and is still prevalent in the world, upon which also all ecclesiastical orders are founded, and which concerns the conscience alone that seeks in its own works help, consolation, and salvation, presumes to wrest heaven from God, and reckons how many bequests it has made, how often it has fasted, celebrated Mass, etc. Upon such things it depends, and of them boasts, as though unwilling to receive anything from God as a gift, but desires itself to earn or merit it superabundantly, just as though He must serve us and were our debtor, and we His liege lords. What is this but reducing God to an idol, yea, an apple-god, and elevating and regarding ourselves as God? But this is slightly too subtle, and is not for young pupils.

But let this be said to the simple, that they may well note and remember the meaning of this commandment, namely, that we are to trust in God alone, and look to Him and expect from Him naught but good, as from one who gives us body, life, food, drink, nourishment, health, protection, peace, and all necessaries of both temporal and eternal things. He also preserves us from misfortune, and if any evil befall us, delivers and rescues us, so that it is God alone (as has been sufficiently said) from whom we receive all good, and by whom we are delivered from all evil. Hence also, I think, we Germans from ancient times call God (more elegantly and appropriately than any other language) by that name from the word good as being an eternal fountain which gushes forth abundantly nothing but what is good, and from which flows forth all that is and is called good.

For even though otherwise we experience much good from men, still whatever we receive by His command or arrangement is all received from God. For our parents, and all rulers, and every one besides with respect to his neighbor, have received from God the command that they should do us all manner of good, so that we receive these blessings not from them, but, through them, from God. For creatures are only the hands, channels, and means whereby God gives all things, as He gives to the mother breasts and milk to offer to her child, and corn and all manner of produce from the earth for nourishment, none of which blessings could be produced by any creature of itself.

Therefore no man should presume to take or give anything except as God has commanded, in order that it may be acknowledged as God's gift, and thanks may be rendered Him for it, as this commandment requires. On this account also these means of receiving good gifts through creatures are not to be rejected, neither should we in presumption seek other ways and means than God has commanded. For that would not be receiving from God, but seeking of ourselves.

Let every one, then, see to it that he esteem this commandment great and high above all things, and do not regard it as a joke. Ask and examine your heart diligently, and you will find whether it cleaves to God alone or not. If you have a heart that can expect of Him nothing but what is good, especially in want and distress, and that, moreover renounces and forsakes everything that is not God, then you have the only true God. If on the contrary, it cleaves to anything else, of which it expects more good and help than of God, and does not take refuge in Him, but in adversity flees from Him, then you have an idol, another god.

Source: Luther's Large Catechism *1.1, trans. F. Bente and W. H. T. Dau, Triglot Concordia: The Symbolical Books of the Evangelical Lutheran Church, St Louis: Concordia Publishing House, 1921, pp. 565–773.*

2.2 John Calvin, from the *Institutes of Christian Religion*

Calvin here explains what is to be believed concerning the Trinity.

The doctrine of Scripture concerning the immensity and the spirituality of the essence of God, should have the effect not only of dissipating the wild dreams of the vulgar, but also of refuting the subtleties of a profane philosophy. One of the ancients thought he spake shrewdly when he said that everything we see and everything we do not see is God. In this way he fancied that the Divinity was transfused into every separate portion of the world. But although God, in order to keep us within the bounds of soberness, treats sparingly of his essence, still, by the two attributes which I have mentioned, he at once suppresses all gross imaginations, and checks the audacity of the human mind. His immensity surely ought to deter us from measuring him by our sense, while his spiritual nature forbids us to indulge in carnal or earthly speculation concerning him. With the same view he frequently represents heaven as his dwelling-place. It is true, indeed, that as he is incomprehensible, he fills the earth also, but knowing that our minds are heavy and grovel on the earth, he raises us above the worlds that he may shake off our sluggishness and inactivity. And here we have a refutation of the error of the Manichees, who, by adopting two first principles, made the devil almost the equal of God. This, assuredly, was both to destroy his unity and restrict his immensity. Their attempt to pervert certain passages of Scripture proved their shameful ignorance, as the very nature of the error did their monstrous infatuation. The Anthropomorphites also, who dreamed of a corporeal God, because mouth, ears, eyes, hands, and feet, are often ascribed to him in Scripture, are easily refuted. For who is so devoid of intellect as not to understand that God, in so speaking, lisps with us as nurses are wont to do with little children? Such modes of expression, therefore, do not so much express what kind of a being God is, as accommodate the knowledge of him to our feebleness. In doing so, he must, of course, stoop far below his proper height.

But there is another special mark by which he designates himself, for the purpose of giving a more intimate knowledge of his nature. While he proclaims his unity, he distinctly sets it before us as existing in three persons. These we must hold, unless the bare and empty name of Deity merely is to flutter in our brain without any genuine knowledge. Moreover, lest any one should dream of a threefold God, or think that the simple essence is divided by the three Persons, we must here seek a brief and easy definition which may effectually guard us from error. But as some strongly inveigh against the term 'Person' as being merely of human inventions let us first consider how far they have any ground for doing so.

When the Apostle calls the Son of God 'the express image of his person' (Heb. 1:3), he undoubtedly does assign to the Father some subsistence in which he differs from the Son. For to hold with some interpreters that the term is equivalent to essence (as if Christ represented the substance of the Father like the impression of a seal upon wax), were not only harsh but absurd. For the essence of God being simple and undivided, and contained in himself entire, in full perfection, without partition or diminution, it is improper, nay, ridiculous, to call it his express image. But because the Father, though distinguished by his own peculiar properties, has expressed himself wholly in the Son, he is said with perfect reason to have rendered his person (hypostasis) manifest in him. And this aptly accords with what is immediately added – viz. that he is 'the brightness of his glory.' The fair inference from the Apostle's words is, that there is a proper subsistence (hypostasis) of the Father, which shines refulgent in the Son. From this, again it is easy to infer that there is a subsistence (hypostasis) of the Son which distinguishes him from the Father. The same holds in the case of the Holy Spirit; for we will immediately prove both that he is God, and that he has a separate subsistence from the Father. This, moreover, is not a distinction of essence, which it were impious to multiply. If credit, then, is given to the Apostle's testimony, it follows that there are three persons (hypostases) in God. The Latins having used the word 'Persona' to express the same thing as the Greek 'hypostasis', it betrays excessive fastidiousness and even perverseness to quarrel with the term. The most literal translation would be subsistence. Many have used substance in the same sense. Nor, indeed, was the use of the term Person confined to the Latin Church. For the Greek Church in like manner, perhaps, for the purpose of testifying their consent, have taught that there are three 'prosopa' (aspects) in God. All these, however, whether Greeks or Latins, though differing as to the word, are perfectly agreed in substance.

Now, then, though heretics may snarl and the excessively fastidious carp at the word 'Person' as inadmissible, in consequence of its human origin, since they cannot displace us from our position that three are named, each of whom is perfect God, and yet that there is no plurality of gods, it is most uncandid to attack the terms which do nothing more than explain what the Scriptures declare and sanction. 'It were better,' they say, 'to confine not only our meanings but our words within the bounds of Scripture, and not scatter about foreign terms to become the future seed-beds of brawls and dissensions. In this way, men grow tired of quarrels about words; the truth is lost in altercation, and charity melts away amid hateful strife.' If they call it a foreign term, because it cannot be pointed out in Scripture in so many syllables, they certainly impose an unjust law – a law which would condemn every interpretation of Scripture that is not composed of other words of Scripture. But if by foreign they mean that which, after being idly devised, is superstitiously defended – which tends more to strife than edification – which is used either out of place, or with no benefit which offends pious ears by its harshness, and leads them away from the simplicity of God's Word, I embrace their soberness with all my heart. For I think we are bound to speak of God as reverently as we are bound to think of him. As our own thoughts respecting him are foolish, so our own language respecting him is absurd. Still, however, some medium must be observed. The unerring standard both of thinking and speaking must be derived from the Scriptures: by it all the thoughts of ours minds, and the words of our mouths, should be tested. But in regard to those parts of Scripture which, to our capacities, are dark and intricate, what forbids us to explain them in clearer terms – terms, however, kept in reverent and faithful subordination to Scripture truth, used sparingly and modestly, and not without occasion? Of this we are not without many examples. When it has been proved that the Church was impelled, by the strongest necessity, to use the words 'Trinity' and 'Person', will not he who still inveighs against novelty of terms be deservedly suspected of taking offence at the light of truth, and of having no other ground for his invective, than that the truth is made plain and transparent?

...

Where names have not been invented rashly, we must beware lest we become chargeable with arrogance and rashness in rejecting them. I wish, indeed, that such names were buried, provided all would concur in the belief that the Father, Son, and Spirit, are one God, and yet that the Son is not the Father, nor the Spirit the Son, but that each has his peculiar subsistence. I am not so minutely precise as to fight furiously for mere words. For I observe, that the writers of the ancient Church, while they uniformly spoke with great reverence on these matters, neither agreed with each other, nor were always consistent with themselves ...

But to say nothing more of words, let us now attend to the thing signified. By person, then, I mean a subsistence in the Divine essence – a subsistence which, while related to the other two, is distinguished from them by incommunicable properties. By subsistence we wish something else to be understood than essence. For if the Word were God simply and had not some property peculiar to himself, John could not have said correctly that he had always been with God. When he adds immediately after, that the Word was God, he calls us back to the one essence. But because he could not be with God without dwelling in the Father, hence arises that subsistence, which, though connected with the essence by an indissoluble tie, being incapable of separation, yet has a special mark by which it is distinguished from it. Now, I say that each of the three subsistences while related to the others is distinguished by its own properties. Here relation is distinctly expressed, because, when God is mentioned simply and indefinitely the name belongs not less to the Son and Spirit than to the Father. But whenever the Father is compared with the Son, the peculiar property of each distinguishes the one from the other. Again, whatever is proper to each I affirm to be incommunicable, because nothing can apply or be transferred to the Son which is attributed to the Father as a mark of distinction. I have no objections to adopt the definition of Tertullian, provided it is properly understood, 'that there is in God a certain arrangement or economy, which makes no change on the unity of essence.'

Source: John Calvin, Institutes of the Christian Religion *I.13.1–6, trans. Henry Beveridge (1559), Grand Rapids: Eerdmans, 1989.*

2.3 Jonathan Edwards, from 'An Unpublished Essay on the Trinity'

Edwards here attempts to argue that the doctrine of the Trinity can be proved rationally.

It is common when speaking of the Divine happiness to say that God is infinitely happy in the enjoyment of Himself, in perfectly beholding and infinitely loving, and rejoicing in, His own essence and perfection, and accordingly it must be supposed that God perpetually and eternally has a most perfect idea of Himself, as it were an exact image and representation of Himself ever before Him and in actual view, and from hence arises a most pure and perfect act or energy in the Godhead, which is the Divine love, complacence and joy. The knowledge or view which God has of Himself must necessarily be conceived to be something distinct from His mere direct existence. There must be something that answers to our reflection. The reflection as we reflect on our own minds carries something of imperfection in it. However, if God beholds Himself so as thence to have delight and joy in Himself He must become his own object. There must be a duplicity. There is God and the idea of God, if it be proper to call a conception of that that is purely spiritual an idea.

If a man could have an absolutely perfect idea of all that passed in his mind, all the series of ideas and exercises in every respect perfect as to order, degree, circumstance and for any particular space of time past, suppose the last hour, he would really to all intents and purpose be over again what he was that last hour. And if it were possible for a man by reflection perfectly to contemplate all that is in his own mind in an hour, as it is and at the same time that it is there in its first and direct existence; if a man, that is, had a perfect reflex or contemplative idea of every thought at the same moment or moments that that thought was and of every exercise at and during the same time that that exercise was, and so through a whole hour, a man would really be two during that time, he would be indeed double, he would be twice at once. The idea he has of himself would be himself again.

...

Therefore as God with perfect clearness, fullness and strength, understands Himself, views His own essence (in which there is no distinction of substance and act but which is wholly substance and wholly act), that idea which God hath of Himself is absolutely Himself. This representation of the Divine nature and essence is the Divine nature and essence again: so that by God's thinking of the Deity [it] must certainly be generated. Hereby there is another person begotten, there is another Infinite Eternal Almighty and most holy and the same God, the very same Divine nature.

And this Person is the second person in the Trinity, the Only Begotten and dearly Beloved Son of God; He is the eternal, necessary, perfect, substantial and personal idea which God hath of Himself; and that it is so seems to me to be abundantly confirmed by the Word of God.

Nothing can more agree with the account the Scripture gives us of the Son of God, His being in the form of God and His express and perfect image and representation: (II Cor. 4:4) 'Lest the light of the glorious Gospel of Christ Who is the image of God should shine unto them.' (Phil. 2:6) 'Who being in the form of God.' (Col. 1:15) 'Who is the image of the invisible God.' (Heb. 1:3) 'Who being the brightness of His glory and the express image of His person.'

Christ is called the face of God (Exod. 33:14): the word in the original signifies face, looks, form or appearance. Now what can be so properly and fitly called so with respect to God as God's own perfect idea of Himself whereby He has every moment a view of His own essence: this idea is that 'face of God' which God sees as a man sees his own face in a looking glass. 'Tis of such form or appearance whereby God eternally appears to Himself. The root that the original word comes from signifies to look upon or behold: now what is that which God looks upon or beholds in so eminent a manner as He doth on His own idea or that perfect image of Himself which He has in view. This is what is eminently in God's presence and is therefore called the angel of God's presence or face (Isa. 63:9). But that the Son of God is God's own eternal and perfect idea is a thing we have yet much more expressly revealed in God's Word. First, in that Christ is called 'the wisdom of God.' If we are taught in the Scripture that Christ is the same with God's wisdom or knowledge, then it teaches us that He is the same with God's perfect and eternal idea. They are the same as we have already observed and I suppose none will deny. But Christ is said to be the wisdom of God (I Cor. 1:24, Luke 11:49, compare with Matt. 23:34); and how much doth Christ speak in Proverbs under the name of Wisdom especially in the 8th chapter.

The Godhead being thus begotten by God's loving an idea of Himself and shewing forth in a distinct subsistence or person in that idea, there proceeds a most pure act, and an infinitely holy and sacred energy arises between the Father and Son in mutually loving and delighting in each other, for their love and joy is mutual (Prov. 8:30), 'I was daily His delight rejoicing always before Him.' This is the eternal and most perfect and essential act of the Divine nature, wherein the Godhead acts to an infinite degree and in the most perfect manner possible. The Deity becomes all act, the Divine essence itself flows out and is as it were breathed forth in love and joy. So that the Godhead therein stands forth in yet another manner of subsistence, and there proceeds the third Person in the Trinity, the Holy Spirit, viz., the Deity in act, for there is no other act but the act of the will.

We may learn by the Word of God that the Godhead or the Divine nature and essence does subsist in love. (I John 4:8) 'He that loveth not knoweth not God; for God is love.' In the context of which place I think it is plainly intimated to us that the Holy Spirit is that Love, as in the 12th and 13th verses. 'If we love one another, God dwelleth in us, and His love is perfected in us; hereby know we that we dwell in Him … because He hath given us of His Spirit.' 'Tis the same argument in both verses. In the 12th verse the apostle argues that if we have love dwelling in us we have God dwelling in us, and in the 13th verse He clears the force of the argument by this that love is God's Spirit. Seeing we have God's Spirit dwelling in us, we have God dwelling in [us], supposing it as a thing granted and allowed that God's Spirit is God. 'Tis evident also by this that God's dwelling in us and His love or the love that he hath exerciseth, being in us, are the same thing. The same is intimated in the same manner in the last verse of the foregoing chapter. The apostle was, in the foregoing verses, speaking of love as a sure sign of sincerity and our acceptance with God, beginning with the 18th verse, and he sums up the argument thus in the last verse, 'and hereby do we know that He abideth in us by the Spirit that He hath given us.'

...

I can think of no other good account that can be given of the apostle Paul's wishing grace and peace from God the Father and the Lord Jesus Christ in the beginning of his Epistles, without ever mentioning the Holy Ghost – as we find it thirteen times in his salutations in the beginnings of his Epistles – but that the Holy Ghost is Himself love and grace of God the Father and the Lord Jesus Christ; and in his blessing at the end of his second Epistle to the Corinthians where all three Persons are mentioned he wishes grace and love from the Son and the Father [except that] in the communion or the partaking of the Holy Ghost, the blessing is from the Father and the Son in the Holy Ghost. But the blessing from the Holy Ghost is Himself, the communication of Himself. Christ promises that He and the Father will love believers (John 14:21,23), but no mention is made of the Holy Ghost, and the love of Christ and the love of the Father are often distinctly mentioned, but never any mention of the Holy Ghost's love.

(This I suppose to be the reason why we have never any account of the Holy Ghost's loving either the Father or the Son, or of the Son's or the Father's loving the Holy Ghost, or of the Holy Ghost's loving the saints, tho these things are so often predicated of both the other Persons.)

And this I suppose to be that blessed Trinity that we read of in the Holy Scriptures. The Father is the Deity subsisting in the prime, un-originated and most absolute manner, or the Deity in its direct existence. The Son is the Deity generated by God's understanding, or having an idea of Himself and subsisting in that idea. The Holy Ghost is the Deity subsisting in act, or the Divine essence flowing out and breathed forth in God's Infinite love to and delight in Himself. And I believe the whole Divine essence does truly and distinctly subsist both in the Divine idea and Divine love, and that each of them are properly distinct Persons.

Source: Jonathan Edwards, 'An Unpublished Essay on the Trinity', from http://153.106.5.3/ ccel/edwards/trinity/files/trinity.html.

2.4 Friedrich Schleiermacher, from *The Christian Faith*

Schleiermacher here argues that God's attributes are merely aspects of our experience of God.

All attributes which we ascribe to God are to be taken as denoting not something special in God, but only something special in the manner in which the feeling of absolute dependence is to be related to Him.

... [H]istory teaches us concerning speculation that, ever since it took the divine essence as an object of thought, it has always entered the same protest against all detailed description, and confined itself to representing God as the Original Being and the Absolute Good. And, indeed, it has frequently been recognized that even in these concepts there remains a certain inadequacy, in so far as they still contain an element of opposition or other analogy to finite being. This method of treatment, therefore, owes its origin first of all to religious poetry, particularly to hymns and other lyrics, and also to the more uncultured experience of common life which harmonizes with poetry and tries to vivify and establish the simple idea of the Supreme Being by the employment of expressions which we use about finite beings. Both methods proceed from religious interests, and have far more the aim of representing the immediate impression in its different forms than of establishing scientific knowledge. Therefore, just because both have been taken over from Judaism, it has been from the beginning the business of Christian Dogmatics to regulate these representations, so that the anthropomorphic element, to be found more or less in all of them, and the sensuous which is mixed in with many, may be rendered as harmless as possible, and that no retrogression towards polytheism should result. And in this direction the age of Scholasticism contributed much that was profound and excellent ...

... [O]ur proposition denies in general the speculative character of the content of all the divine attributes to be affirmed in Christian doctrine, just for that reason and in so far as they are manifold. For if as such they present a knowledge of the Divine Being, each one of them must express something in God not expressed by the others; and if the knowledge is appropriate to the object, then, as the knowledge is composite, the object too must be composite. Indeed, even if these attributes only asserted relations of the Divine to the world, God Himself, like the finite life, could only be understood in a multiplicity of functions; and as these are distinct one from another, and relatively opposed one to another, and at least partly exclusive one of another, God likewise would be places in the sphere of contradiction. This does not fulfil the requirements of the speculative reason, and definitions of this kind could not pass for speculative propositions; and just as little could the interests of religion be satisfied if dogmatic definitions were interpreted in this way. For if differentiations were assumed in God, even the feeling of absolute dependence could not be treated as such and as always and everywhere the same. For in that case there must be differences having their source in something beyond the difference of the life-moments through which the feeling (of dependence) makes its appearance in the mind ...

But as concerns method, in the treatment of Dogmatics up to the present a double procedure is found to predominate. First, rules are put forward as to how one can arrive at right ideas of the divine attributes, and then further, certain rubrics are given under which the various conceptions of divine attributes are to be divided. Now since both aim at systematizing these ideas, the same general assumption has to be made. If the list of these attributes be regarded as a complete summary of definitions to be related to God Himself, then a complete knowledge of God must be derivable from conceptions, and an explanation in due theoretic form would take the place of the ineffability of the Divine Being which the Scriptures – so far as they mention divine attributes – recognize so clearly on every page that we need not quote passages. We have therefore to strive against that completeness alone which guards against letting any of the different moments of the religious self-consciousness pass without asking what are the divine attributes corresponding to them. And with this procedure the classification emerges of its own accord, because in each division only the attributes belonging there can be subjects of exposition ...

Now we may remark concerning these methods that there are three accepted ways of arriving at the divine attributes – the way of removal of limits (*via eminentiae*), the way of negation or denial (*via negationis*), and the way of causality (*via causalitatis*). Now it is self-evident that these are by no means homogenous or coordinate. For in the first two something apart from God must be posited as an attribute; and this, after it has been freed from all limitations, is ascribed to Him, or else its negation is ascribed to Him; while on the other hand causality stands in the closest connexion with the feeling of absolute dependence itself. And if the first two be viewed in their relation to each other, it is clear that negation by itself is no way to posit any attribute, unless something positive remains behind the negation. In that case the negation will consist simply in the fact that the limits of the positive are denied. But in the same manner the way of the removal of limits is a negation, for something is posited of God, but the limits which elsewhere would be co-posited are not posited of God. The identity of these two methods becomes quite obvious in the idea of Infinity, which is at the same time the general form of the absence of limits, for what is posited as infinite is also freed from limitation; but at the same time it shows quite generally (by the fact that it is a negation in which nothing is immediately posited but in which everything may be posited which can be thought of as either limited or unlimited), that by negation we can only posit an attribute in so far as something positive remains behind the negation. Both these methods then can only be applied either haphazard with reference to the question whether something, which as such could only be absolutely denied of God, can be conceived as unlimited and posited as a divine attribute; or, if this is to be avoided, the application of these methods must be preceded by a definition as to what kind of attribute-conceptions are rightly to be ascribed to God in an unlimited fashion, and what kind simply must be denied of Him. The third method, on the contrary, is certainly an independent one. And even if we do not wish to maintain that all divine attributes corresponding to any modification of our feeling of dependence can equally be derived immediately from the idea of causality, but rather here at the start must premise for one thing that to this conception the other methods must first be applied, *i.e.* that the finitude of causality must be denied and its productivity posited as unlimited; and again, that in so far as a plurality of attributes is developed out of the idea of the divine causality, this differentiation can correspond to nothing real in God; indeed, that neither in isolation nor taken together do the attributes express the Being of God itself (for the essence of that which has been active can never be known simply from its activity alone) – yet this at least is certain, that all the divine attributes to be dealt with in Christian Dogmatics must somehow go back to the divine causality, since they are only meant to explain the feeling of absolute dependence.

Source: Friedrich Daniel Ernst Schleiermacher, The Christian Faith, *§50, trans. H. R. Mackintosh and J. S. Stewart, Edinburgh: T. & T. Clark, 1928, pp. 194–200.*

2.5 Charles Hodge, from *Systematic Theology*

Hodge here asks whether 'God' can be defined, and if so, what the best definition is.

The question whether God can be defined, depends for its answer on what is meant by definition ... No creature, much less man, can know all that is proper to God; and, therefore, no creature can give an exhaustive statement of all that God is.

To define, however, is simply to bound, to separate, or distinguish; so that the thing defined may be discriminated from all other things. This may be done (1.) By stating its characteristics. (2.) By stating its genus and its specific difference. (3.) By analyzing the idea as it lies in our minds. (4.) By an explanation of the term or name by which it is denoted. All these methods amount to much the same thing. When we say we can define God, all that is meant is, that we can analyze the idea of God as it lies in our mind; or, that we can state the class of beings to which He belongs, and the attributes by which He is distinguished from all other beings. Thus, in the simple definition, God is *ens perfectissimum* ['most perfect being'], the word *ens* designates Him as a being, not an idea, but as that which has real, objective existence; and absolute perfection distinguishes Him from all other beings. The objection to this and most other definitions of God is, that they do not bring out with sufficient fulness the contents of the idea ... Probably the best definition of God ever penned by man, is that given in the 'Westminster Catechism': 'God is a Spirit, infinite, eternal, and unchangeable, in his being, wisdom, power, holiness, justice, goodness, and truth.' This is a true definition; for it states the class of beings to which God is to be referred. He is a Spirit; and He is distinguished from all other spirits in that He is infinite, eternal, and unchangeable in his being and perfections. It is also a complete definition, in so far as it is an exhaustive statement of the contents of our idea of God.

In what sense, however, are these terms used? What is meant by the words 'being,' and 'perfections,' or 'attributes' of God? In what relation do his attributes stand to his essence and to each other? These are questions on which theologians, especially during the scholastic period, expended much time and labor.

By being is here meant that which has a real, substantive existence. It is equivalent to substance, or essence. It is opposed to what is merely thought, and to a mere force or power. We get this idea, in the first place, from consciousness. We are conscious of self as the subject of the thoughts, feelings, and volitions, which are its varying states and acts. This consciousness of substance is involved in that of personal identity. In the second place, a law of our reason constrains us to believe that there is something which underlies the phenomena of matter and mind, of which those phenomena are the manifestation. It is impossible for us to think of thought and feeling, unless there be something that thinks and feels. It is no less impossible to think of action, unless there be something that acts; or of motion, unless there be something that moves. To assume, therefore, that mind is only a series of acts and states,

55

and that matter is nothing but force, is to assume that nothing (nonentity) can produce effects.

God, therefore, is in his nature a substance, or essence, which is infinite, eternal, and unchangeable; the common subject of all divine perfections, and the common agent of all divine acts. This is as far as we can go, or need to go. We have no definite idea of substance, whether of matter or mind, as distinct from its attributes. The two are inseparable. In knowing the one we know the other. We cannot know hardness except as we know something hard. We have, therefore, the same knowledge of the essence of God, as we have of the substance of the soul. All we have to do in reference to the divine essence, as a Spirit, is to deny of it, as we do of our own spiritual essence, what belongs to material substances; and to affirm of it, that in itself and its attributes it is infinite, eternal, and unchangeable. When, therefore, we say there is a God, we do not assert merely that there is in our minds the idea of an infinite Spirit; but that, entirely independent of our idea of Him, such a Being really exists ...

...

To the divine essence, which in itself is infinite, eternal, and unchangeable, belong certain perfections revealed to us in the constitution of our nature and in the word of God. These divine perfections are called attributes as essential to the nature of a divine Being, and necessarily involved in our idea of God. The older theologians distinguished the attributes of God, (1.) From predicates which refer to God in the concrete, and indicate his relation to his creatures, as creator, preserver, ruler, etc. (2.) From properties, which are technically the distinguishing characteristics of the several persons of the Trinity. There are certain acts or relations peculiar or proper to the Father, others to the Son, and others to the Spirit. And (3.) From accidents or qualities which may or may not belong to a substance, which may be acquired or lost. Thus holiness was not an attribute of the nature of Adam, but an accident, something which he might lose and still remain a man; whereas intelligence was an attribute, because the loss of intelligence involves the loss of humanity. The perfections of God, therefore, are attributes, without which He would cease to be God.

...

Some ... preclude all necessity of a classification of the attributes, by reducing them all to unity, or regarding them as different phases under which we contemplate the Supreme Being as the ground of all things. With them the whole discussion of the divine attributes is an analysis of the idea of the Infinite and Absolute.

Others arrange the attributes according to the mode in which we arrive at the knowledge of them. We form our idea of God, it is said, (1.) By the way of causation; that is, by referring to Him as the great first cause of every virtue manifested by the effects which He produces. (2.) By the way of negation; that is, by denying to Him the limitations and imperfections which belong to his creatures. (3.) By the way of eminence, in exalting to an infinite degree or without limit the perfections which belong to an infinite Being. If this is so, the attributes conceived of by one of these methods belong to one class, and those conceived of, or of which we attain the knowledge by another method, belong to another class. This principle of classification is perhaps the one most generally adopted. It gives rise, however, really but to two classes, namely, the positive and negative, i.e., those in which something is affirmed, and those in which something is denied concerning God. To the negative class are commonly referred simplicity, infinity, eternity, immutability; to the positive class, power, knowledge, holiness, justice, goodness, and truth. Instead of calling the one class negative and the other positive, they are often distinguished as absolute and relative. By an absolute attribute is meant one which belongs to God, considered in Himself, and which implies no relation to other beings; by a relative attribute is meant one which implies relation to an object. They are also distinguished as immanent and transient, as communicable and incommunicable. These terms are used interchangeably. They do not express different modes of classification, but are different modes of designating the same classification. Negative, absolute, immanent, and incommunicable, are designations of one class; and positive, relative, transitive, and communicable, are designations of the other class.

...

Others again seek the principle of classification in the nature of the attributes themselves. Some include the idea of moral excellence, and others do not. Hence they are distinguished as natural and moral. The word natural, however, is ambiguous. Taking it in the sense of what constitutes or pertains to the nature, the holiness and justice of God are as much natural as his power or knowledge. And on the other hand, God is infinite and eternal in his moral perfections, although infinity and eternity are not distinctively moral perfections. In the common and familiar sense of the word natural, the terms natural and moral express a real distinction.

Source: Charles Hodge, Systematic Theology, *vol. 1, London: James Clarke, 1960, pp. 366–376.*

2.6 Karl Barth, from *Church Dogmatics* I.1

Barth argues that the structure of revelation, the very basis of theological knowledge, is already necessarily triune.

... The question of the self-revealing God which thus forces itself upon us as the first question cannot, if we follow the witness of Scripture, be separated in any way from the second question: How does it come about, how is it actual, that this God reveals Himself? Nor can it be separated from the third question: What is the result? What does this event do to the man to whom it happens? Conversely the second and third questions cannot possibly be separated from the first. So impossible is any separation here that the answer to any one of the questions, for all the autonomy and distinctiveness it has and must continue to have as the answer to a particular question, is essentially identical with the answer to the other two. *God* reveals Himself. He reveals Himself *through Himself*. He reveals *Himself*. If we really want to understand revelation in terms of its subject, i.e., God, then the first thing we have to realise is that this subject, God, the Revealer, is identical with His act in revelation and also identical with its effect. It is from this fact, which in the first instance we are merely indicating, that we learn we must begin the doctrine of revelation with the doctrine of the triune God.

...

Thus the man who asks about the God who reveals Himself according to the witness of the Bible must also pay heed to the self-revealing as such and to the men to whom this self-revealing applies.

The fact that in putting the first question we are led on at once to a second and a third is what first brings us close to the problem of the doctrine of the Trinity. Close, for we could not say that these considerations summon us to develop the doctrine of the Trinity. The one thing we now know is that the God who reveals Himself in the Bible must also be known in His revealing and in His being revealed if He is to be known ...

The question: Who is the self-revealing God? always receives a full and unrestricted answer also in what we learn about God's self-revealing as such and about His being revealed among men. God Himself is not just Himself. He is also His self-revealing.

...

Again, He Himself is not just Himself but also what He creates and achieves in men.

...

Thus it is God Himself, it is the same God in unimpaired unity, who according to the Biblical understanding of revelation is the revealing God and the event of revelation and its effect on man.

It does not seem possible, nor is any attempt made in the Bible, to dissolve the unity of the self-revealing God, His revelation and His being revealed into a union in which the barriers that separate the above three forms of His divine being in revelation are removed and they are reduced to a synthetic fourth and true reality.

...

Thus to the same God who in unimpaired unity is the Revealer, the revelation and the revealedness, there is also ascribed in unimpaired differentiation within Himself this threefold mode of being.

It is only – but very truly – by observing the unity and the differentiation of God in His biblically attested revelation that we are set before the problem of the doctrine of the Trinity.

...

In putting the doctrine of the Trinity at the head of all dogmatics we are adopting a very isolated position from the standpoint of dogmatic history.

Yet not wholly isolated, for in the Middle Ages Peter Lombard in his *Sentences* and Bonaventura in his *Breviloquium* took the same position.

Otherwise it neither has been nor is the custom to give this place to the doctrine of the Trinity. The reason for this strange circumstance can be sought only in the fact that with overwhelming unanimity it has obviously been thought that a certain formally very natural and illuminating scheme of questioning should be followed in which one can and should speak first of Holy Scripture (or in Roman Catholic dogmatics the authority of the teaching office, or in Modernist dogmatics the reality and truth of religion) as the *principium cognoscendi* [i.e., basis on which we can know things] (apart from the actual content of faith), and then that even in the doctrine of God itself one can and should deal first with God's existence, nature and attributes (again, apart from the concrete givenness of what Christians call 'God').

Source: Karl Barth, Church Dogmatics *I.1, ed. and trans. Geoffrey Bromiley and T. F. Torrance, Edinburgh: T. & T. Clark, 1936, pp. 295–300.*

2.7 Karl Rahner, from *The Trinity*

Rahner here discusses how the dogmatic discussion of the divine essence
– the treatise 'On the One God' – and the dogmatic discussion of the Trinity
– the treatise 'On the Triune God' – should be related.

The above remarks shed light on other facts as well, especially on the separation immemorially taken for granted between the two treatises On the One God and On the Triune God, and on the sequence in which they are taught. Not a few authors have explicitly defended both as being quite essential … Yet it is impossible to use tradition as a cogent argument on behalf of the usual separation and sequence of the two treatises. For they became customary only after the Sentences of Peter Lombard were superseded by the Summa of St Thomas. If, with Scripture and the Greeks, we mean by ὁ Θεος in the first place the Father, then the trinitarian structure of the Apostles' Creed, in line with the Greek theology of the Trinity, would lead us to treat first of the Father and to consider also, in this first chapter of the doctrine of God, the 'essence' of God, the Father's godhead. Thus the Master of the Sentences subsumed the general doctrine of God under a doctrine of the Trinity. Likewise in the Summa Alexandri there is yet no clear separation between the two treatises. As we said above, this separation took place for the first time in St Thomas, for reasons which have not yet been fully explained. Here the first topic under study is not God the Father as the unoriginate origin of divinity and reality, but as the essence common to all three persons. Such is the method which has prevailed ever since. Thus the treatise of the Trinity locks itself in even more splendid isolation, with the ensuing danger that the religious mind finds it devoid of interest. It looks as if everything which matters for us in God has already been said in the treatise On the One God. This separation of the two treatises and the sequence in which they are explained probably derives from the Augustinian-Western concept of the Trinity, as contrasted with the Greek conception, even though the Augustinian conception had not, in the High Middle Ages, developed the kind of monopoly it would later enjoy. It begins with the one God, the divine essence as a whole, and only afterwards does it see God as three in persons. Of course, great care is then taken, and must be taken, not to set up this divine 'essence' itself as a 'fourth' reality pre-existing in the three persons. The Bible and the Greeks would have us start from the one unoriginate God, who is already Father even when nothing is known yet about generation and spiration. He is known as the one unoriginate hypostasis which is not positively conceived as 'absolute' even before it is explicitly known as relative.

But the medieval-Latin starting point happens to be different. And thus one may believe that Christian theology too may and should put a treatise on the one God before the treatise on the triune God. But since this approach is justified by the unicity of the divine essence, the only treatise which one writes, or can write, is 'on the one divinity'. As a result the treatise becomes quite philosophical and abstract and refers hardly at all to salvation history. It speaks of the necessary metaphysical properties of God, and not very explicitly of God as experienced in salvation history in his free relations to his creatures.

For should one make use of salvation history, it would soon become apparent that one speaks always of him whom Scripture and Jesus himself calls the Father, Jesus' Father, who sends the Son and who gives himself to us in the Spirit, in his Spirit. On the other hand, if one starts from the basic Augustinian-Western conception, an a-trinitarian treatise 'on the one God' comes as a matter of course before the treatise on the Trinity. In this event, however, the theology of the Trinity must produce the impression that it can make only purely formal statements about the three persons, with the help of concepts about the two processions and about the relations. Even these statements, however, refer only to a Trinity which is absolutely locked within itself – one which is not, in its reality, open to anything distinct from it; one, further, from which we are excluded, of which we happen to know something only through a strange paradox ...

The isolation of the treatise of the Trinity has to be wrong. There must be a connection between Trinity and man. The Trinity is a mystery of salvation, otherwise it would never have been revealed. We should show why it is such a mystery. We must point out in every dogmatic treatise that what it says about salvation does not make sense without referring to this primordial mystery of Christianity. Wherever this permanent perichoresis between the treatises is overlooked, we have a clear indication that either the treatise on the Trinity or the other treatises have not clearly explained connections to show how the mystery of the Trinity is for us a mystery of salvation, and why we meet it wherever our salvation is considered, even in the other dogmatic treatises.

The basic thesis which establishes this connection between the treatises and presents the Trinity as a mystery of salvation (in its reality and not merely as a doctrine) might be formulated as follows: The 'economic' Trinity is the 'immanent' Trinity and the 'immanent' Trinity is the 'economic' Trinity.

...

The 'economic' Trinity is the immanent Trinity, according to the statement which interests us. In one way this statement is a defined doctrine of the faith. Jesus is not simply God in general, but the Son. The second divine person, God's Logos, is man, and only he is man. Hence there is at least one 'mission', one presence in the world, one reality of salvation history which is not merely appropriated to some divine person, but which is proper to him. Here we are not merely speaking 'about' this person in the world. Here something occurs 'outside' the intra-divine life in the world itself, something which is not a mere effect of the efficient causality of the triune God acting as one in the world, but something which belongs to the Logos alone, which is the history of one divine person, in contrast to the other divine persons. This remains true even if we admit that this hypostatic union which belongs exclusively to the Logos is causally effected by the whole Trinity. At any rate, this one case shows up as false the statement that there is nothing in salvation history, in the economy of salvation, which cannot equally be said of the triune God as a whole and of each person in particular. On the other hand, the following statement too is false: that a doctrine of the Trinity treating of the divine persons in general and of each person in particular can speak only of that which occurs within the divinity itself. And we are sure that the following statement is true: that no adequate distinction can be made between the doctrine of the Trinity and the doctrine of the economy of salvation.

Source: Karl Rahner, The Trinity, *trans. Joseph Donceel, Tunbridge Wells: Burns & Oates, 1970, pp. 15–24.*

2.8 Paul Tillich, from *Systematic Theology*

*Tillich argues that trinitarian ideas naturally arise as a solution to the prob-
lems of transcendence that any monotheistic religion faces.*

The general outline of the typological analysis of the history of religion follows from the tension of the elements in the idea of God. The concreteness of
man's ultimate concern drives him toward polytheistic structures; the reaction
of the absolute element against these drives him toward monotheistic structures; and the need for a balance between the concrete and the absolute drives
him towards trinitarian structures.

...

Polytheism could not exist unless it included monotheistic elements. But in
all types of polytheism the concrete element in the idea of God prevails over
the element of ultimacy. In monotheism the opposite is the case. The divine
powers of polytheism are subjected to a highest divine power. However, just
as there is no absolute polytheism, so there is no absolute monotheism. The
concrete element in the idea of God cannot be destroyed.

Monarchic monotheism lies on the boundary between polytheism and
monotheism. The god-monarch rules over the hierarchy of inferior gods and
godlike beings ... there are elements of monarchic monotheism not only in
many non-Christian religions but also in Christianity itself. The 'Lord of Hosts'
of whom the Old Testament and Christian liturgy often speak is a monarch
who rules over heavenly beings, angels, and spirits ...

The second type of monotheism is the mystical. Mystical monotheism
transcends all realms of being and value, and their divine representatives, in
favour of the divine ground and abyss from which they come and in which
they disappear. All conflicts between the gods, between the divine and the
demonic, between gods and things, are overcome in the ultimate which transcends all of them ...

Yet even this most radical negation of the concrete element in the idea of
God is not able to suppress the quest for concreteness. Mystical monotheism
does not exclude divine powers in which the ultimate embodies itself temporally. And, once admitted, the gods can regain their lost significance, especially
for people who are unable to grasp the ultimate in its purity and abstraction
from everything concrete ...

Monotheism is able to resist polytheism radically only in the form of
exclusive monotheism, which is created by the elevation of a concrete god to
ultimacy and universality without the loss of his concreteness and without the
assertion of a demonic claim. Such a possibility contradicts every expectation
which can be derived from the history of religion. It is the result of an astound-
ing constellation of objective and subjective factors in Israel, especially in the
prophetic line of its religion. Theologically speaking, exclusive monotheism
belongs to final revelation, for it is a direct preparation for it.

The God of Israel is the concrete God who has led his people out of Egypt,
'the God of Abraham, Isaac, and Jacob.' At the same time he claims to be the

God who judges the gods of the nations, before whom the nations of the world are 'as a drop in a bucket' ...

Like the God of mystical monotheism, the God of exclusive monotheism is in danger of losing the concrete element in the idea of God. His ultimacy and universality tend to swallow his character as a living god. The personal traits in his picture are removed as anthropomorphisms which contradict his ultimacy, and the historical traits in his character are forgotten as accidental factors which contradict his universality ... Nevertheless, exclusive monotheism needs an expression of the concrete element in man's ultimate concern. This posits the trinitarian problem.

...

In exclusive monotheism an abstract transcendence of the divine develops ... But since the concrete element demands its rights, mediating powers of a threefold character appear and posit the trinitarian problem. The first group of these mediators is made up of hypostasised divine qualities, like Wisdom, Word, Glory. The second group is the angels, the divine messengers who represent special divine functions. The third is the divine-human figure through whom God works the fulfilment of history, the Messiah. In all these the God who had become absolutely transcendent and unapproachable now becomes present and concrete in time and space ... When early Christianity calls Jesus of Nazareth the Messiah and identifies him with the divine Logos, the trinitarian problem becomes the central problem of religious existence. The basic motive and the different forms of trinitarian monotheism become effective in the trinitarian dogma of the Chrisitan church. But the Christian solution is founded on the paradox that the Messiah, the mediator between God and man, is identical with a personal human life, the name of which is Jesus of Nazareth.

Source: Paul Tillich, Systematic Theology, *vol. 1, London: Nisbet & Co., 1953, pp. 245– 54.*

2.9 Jürgen Moltmann, from *The Crucified God*

Moltmann here asserts that the event of the crucifixion, as an event in God's own life, drives a wedge between Christian ideas of God and philosophical ideas of God.

Is the theistic concept of God applicable to Christian belief in the crucified God?

For metaphysics, the nature of the divine being is determined by its unity and indivisibility, its lack of beginning and end, its immovability and immutability. As the nature of divine being is conceived of for the sake of finite being, it must embrace all the determinations of finite being and exclude those determinations which are directed against finite being. Otherwise finite being could not find a support and stay against the threatening nothingness of death, suffering and chaos in the divine being. Death, suffering and mortality must therefore be excluded from the divine being. Christian theology has adopted this concept of God from philosophical theology down to the present day, because in practice down to the present day Christian faith has taken into itself the religious need of finite, threatened and mortal man for security in a higher omnipotence and authority. Even Schleiermacher conceived of God as pure causality for the feeling of absolute dependence, and therefore had to exclude God, as pure activity, from all suffering which would make God the object of human activity. In the metaphysical concept of God from ancient cosmology and the modern psychological concept of God, the being of the Godhead, of the origin of all things or the unconditioned mover, as the zone of the impossibility of death, stands in juxtaposition to human being as the zone of the necessity of death. If this concept of God is applied to Christ's death on the cross, the cross *must*, be 'evacuated' of deity, for by definition God cannot suffer and die. He is pure causality. But Christian theology must think of God's being in suffering and dying and finally in the death of Jesus, if it is not to surrender itself and lose its identity. Suffering, dying and similar negations simply cannot be predicated of that which is conceived of as pure causality and the unconditioned mover. The God who was the subject of suffering could not be truly God.

At this point, the controversy between Christian theology and the philosophical concept of God must now be taken further. After the very long period during which the theologian has been confronted in the picture of Christ with the 'unmoving, unemotional countenance of the God of Plato, bedecked with some features of Stoic ethics' (Elert) the time has finally come for differentiating the Father of Jesus Christ from the God of the pagans and the philosophers in the interest of Christian faith. On the theoretical level this corresponds to the critical disestablishment of Christianity from the bourgeois religions of the particular societies in which that theism has predominated. The theology of the early church advanced furthest in this direction in developing the trinitarian doctrine of God, for the doctrine of the Trinity speaks of God in respect of the incarnation and death of Jesus and in so doing breaks the spell of the old philosophical concept of God, at the same time destroying the idols of national political religions.

The modern surrender of the doctrine of the Trinity or its reduction to an empty, orthodox formula is a sign of the assimilation of Christianity to the religions felt to be needed in modern society.

With the Christian message of the cross of Christ, something new and strange has entered the metaphysical world. For this faith must understand the deity of God from the event of the suffering and death of the Son of God and thus bring about a fundamental change in the orders of being of metaphysical thought and the value tables of religious feeling. It must think of the suffering of Christ as the power of God and the death of Christ as God's potentiality. Conversely, it must think of freedom from suffering and death as a possibility for man. So Christian theology cannot seek to understand the death of Jesus on the presupposition of that metaphysical or moral concept of God. If this presupposition holds, the death of Jesus cannot be understood at all in theological terms. Rather, faith must take an opposite course and 'understand God's Godness from the event of this death' (Jüngel) ...

Source: Jürgen Moltmann, The Crucified God, *trans. John Bowden, London: SCM Press and Philadelphia: Fortress Press, 1974, pp. 214–15.*

2.10 Wolfhart Pannenberg, from *Systematic Theology*

Pannenberg here takes forward the theses of Barth and Rahner to claim that 'the world is the history of God'.

Karl Barth demanded that we base the doctrine of the Trinity on the revelation of God in Jesus Christ. He did not succeed in meeting his own demand, but Karl Rahner has taken it up and sharpened it with his thesis of an identity between the immanent and the economic Trinity. This thesis means that the doctrine of the Trinity does not merely begin with the revelation of God in Jesus Christ and then work back to a trinity in the eternal essence of God, but that it must constantly link the trinity in the eternal essence of God to his historical revelation, since revelation cannot be viewed as extraneous to his deity.

...

The starting point for Rahner's thesis is the assertion that Jesus Christ is in person the Son of God, so that the incarnation is not just ascribed to the Son, as distinct from the other persons of the Trinity, by external appropriation. The man Jesus is a real symbol of the divine Logos. His history is the existence of the Logos with us as our salvation, revealing the Logos. In the context of the work of the trinitarian God in salvation history, the incarnation is a specific instance of the intervention of a divine person in worldly reality. It is true that the instance of the hypostatic union of the divine Logos with the man Jesus is unique. Nevertheless, it belongs to the context of a work of the trinitarian God in the world which embraces the whole economy of salvation. Extending the thought of Rahner, one might thus say that creation is brought into the relations of the trinitarian persons and participates in them. Nevertheless, only the persons of the Son and Spirit act directly in creation. The Father acts in the world only through the Son and Spirit. He himself remains transcendent. This fact comes to expression in the 'sendings' of the Son and Spirit into the world.

Through the Son and Spirit, however, the Father, too, stands in relation to the history of the economy of salvation. Even in his deity, by the creation of the world and the sending of his Son and Spirit to work in it, he has made himself dependent upon the course of history. This results from the dependence of the trinitarian persons upon one another as the kingdom is handed over and handed back in connection with the economy of salvation and the intervention of the Son and Spirit in the world and its history. The dependence of the deity of the Father upon the course of events in the world of creation was first worked out by Jüngel and then by Moltmann, who illustrated it by the crucifixion of Jesus. The deity of the Father was itself called into question by the death of Jesus on the cross if it was the death of the Son ...

Source: Wolfhart Pannenberg, Systematic Theology, *vol. 1, trans. Geoffrey W. Bromiley, Grand Rapids: Eerdmans, 1991, pp. 327–9.*

2.11 Catherine Mowry LaCugna, from *God for Us*

LaCugna argues that the traditional distinction between the economic and immanent trinities is in need of profound revision.

The great merit of Rahner's theology is the principle that no adequate distinction can be made between the doctrine of the Trinity and the doctrine of the economy of salvation. This affirms the essential unity of *oikonomia* [i.e., the economy, God's activity in the world] and *theologia* [i.e., God as God is in God's own eternal life]. As for the nature of this unity, there cannot be a strict identity, either epistemological or ontological, between God and God for us. Transposed into the language of Orthodox theology, there is an essential unity though not strict identity between the divine essence and divine energies. We can incorporate the essential concerns of both the economic–immanent and the essence–energies distinctions, with the biblical, creedal, ante-Nicene vision of the economy, in the following principle: *theologia* is fully revealed and bestowed in *oikonomia*, and *oikonomia* truly expresses the ineffable mystery of *theologia*. Up to this point Rahner's principle is valid and useful. However, Rahner evidences that he is caught in the stranglehold of the post-Nicene problematic when he uses the undeniable distinctions of persons in the economy to posit an intradivine self-communication, *intra*divine relations, God in Godself. As Roger Haight points out, Rahner simply asserts but does not explain what difference it makes that there be real differentiations in God. This is a return to Thomas Aquinas' understanding of theology as the science of God in Himself, and is at odds with the Bible, creeds, and Greek theology that Rahner explicitly seeks to follow …

By contrast, the biblical and pre-Nicene sense of the economy is the one dynamic movement of God (Father) outward, a personal self-sharing by which God is forever bending towards God's 'other' (cf. Eph. 1:3–14). The economy is not a mirror dimly reflecting a hidden realm of intradivine relations; the economy is God's concrete existence in Christ and as Spirit. The economy is the 'distribution' of God's life lived with and for the creature. Economy and theology are two aspects of *one* reality: the mystery of divine–human communion …

This chiastic model of emanation and return, *exitus* and *reditus*, expresses the one ecstatic movement of God outward by which all things originate from God through Christ in the power of the Holy Spirit, and all things are brought into union with God and returned to God. There is neither an economic nor an immanent Trinity; there is only the *oikonomia* that is the concrete realization of the mystery of *theologia* in time, space, history, and personality. In this framework, the doctrine of the Trinity encompasses much more than the immanent Trinity, envisioned in static ahistorical and transeconomic terms; the subject matter of the Christian theology of God is the one dynamic movement of God, *a Patre ad Patrem* ['from the Father to the Father']. There is no reason to stop at any one point along the curve, no reason to single out one point as if it could be fixed or frozen in time. Christology is no more and no less prominent than pneumatology. Any analysis of the immanent structure of this economy could not separate itself from the economy of salvation. In contrast, in the scheme generally accepted, the divine persons belong to a transeconomic realm, even if they act also within the economy. The existence of such an intradivine realm is precisely what cannot be established on the basis of the economy, despite the fact that it has functioned within speculative theology ever since the late fourth century.

This revision of the basic trinitarian framework obviates the need to adhere to the language of economic and immanent Trinity. These terms are bound inextricably to the framework that operates with a gap between *oikonomia* and *theologia*. The revision – more accurately, the return to the biblical and pre-Nicene pattern of thought – suggests not only that we abandon the misleading terms, economic and immanent Trinity, but that we also clarify the meaning of *oikonomia* and *theologia*. *Oikonomia* is not the Trinity *ad extra* but the comprehensive plan of God reaching from creation to consummation, in which God and all creatures are destined to exist together in the mystery of love and communion. Similarly, *theologia* is not the Trinity *in se*, but, much more modestly and simply, the mystery of God. As we know from the experience of being redeemed by God through Jesus Christ, the mystery of God is the mystery of God with us. With this understanding in mind, we are well on our way to an understanding of trinitarian theology that justifies our initial thesis that the doctrine of the Trinity is ultimately a practical doctrine with radical consequences for Christian life.

Source: Catherine Mowry LaCugna, God for Us: The Trinity and Christian Life, *New York: HarperCollins, 1991, pp. 221–4.*

2.12 Colin Gunton, from *Act and Being*

Gunton attempts to define what we can know of God's attributes through a trinitarian rereading of the tradition.

The church's theologians and philosophers have not necessarily been wrong in the lists of attributes they have, over the centuries, assembled. What have often been wrong are, first, the way in which they have understood them and, second, the way they have, often by the order of the treatment, weighted them wrongly, emphasizing in particular the negative over against the positive, the cosmological and timeless against the historical and temporal. It may be that there is a place for most or all of the traditional attributes, though it may be necessary to consider carefully the form of some of them, perhaps especially simplicity and impassibility ...

God is interesting in and for himself. That is a slogan much loved by Eberhard Jüngel – repeated in a recent book – and it provides the principle for our discussion. The worship and knowledge of God is not based on self-interest, or any other end, though other ends may be attained by it, but is simply because God is who and what he is, to be worshipped and glorified for ever. The celebration of God's being is just that. So Barth begins his treatment of the divine attributes: 'God is. This is the simple statement which we have to develop and explain ...' As we have seen, the Bible, and especially the New Testament, is for Christological reasons insistent that God is knowable because he is known. In Jesus, and in those anticipations of the incarnation we meet in the Old Testament, God communicates something of himself: he gives himself in his Son. This in its turn generates two subsidiary principles. The first is Christological: 'God gives himself, but he does not give himself away' (Barth). God does not empty himself into the world, but relates to it while retaining his integrity as God and his distinction from the world. The second subsidiary principle is pneumatological. God is known by us when and in so far as he himself wills. This applies to all forms of the knowledge of God, even – especially – to that which is claimed to be possible through what is called natural revelation. In the light of human sin and blindness, the Spirit has to dispel our ignorance, so that we may see what is there.

The principle that God is trinitarianly knowable is one which is most neglected in the tradition, and, indeed, may raise the question of whether we need one traditional attribute, that of the unknowability of God, at all. It undoubtedly calls into question the way the matter has often been put in both East and West. In the East, the official doctrine, associated especially with Gregory Palamas, is that we do not know the being or essence of God, but know him through his energies. In the West, certainly until the late medievals – beginning, as we have seen, with Scotus – and the Reformers began their critique, the doctrine was the Neoplatonically formed teaching that we do not know God in himself, but from his effects. It seems to me that both of these ways of putting it are at best misleading, and that in the light of the gospel we must be free to confess that we are granted to know the very being of God.

Therefore what may seem, in the light of much of the Christian tradition, to be an outrageous claim must be made: that it is a part of the Christian claim to truth that human beings are given to know the being of God. To be sure, there are two senses in which knowledge of the divine essence is excluded. (1) One cannot have a full rational account of or define finally in conceptual terms what it is for God to be God. Indeed, it is a part of the burden of the first three chapters to claim that a deep-seated weakness of much of the tradition is its claim confidently to know too much, particularly of the negative attributes, and that this is not as paradoxical as it may appear. In this regard at least – in this regard only – a version of the doctrine of God's unknowability is essential. Although God is objectively knowable, he sets the conditions of and limits to human knowledge of himself. (2) Nor can one have, so to speak, an inside view of the being of God, to know God by direct vision; that, according to part of the Christian tradition, is reserved for the kingdom of heaven, when the blessed will be granted the beatific vision. God is incomprehensible in not being graspable; but not incomprehensible in the sense of being entirely beyond our understanding. He can and does give himself to be conceived by us ...

In order to move to an account of what we can know, let me begin by revising the two slogans. 'We can know God only by his effects': yes, if by 'effect' is meant not a cosmologically abstracted first cause, but the *actions* of God – creation, redemption, etc. – towards and in the created world; God not abstracted from matter, but involved in it. We know the divine energies: yes, but only if energies refer not to something midway between the world and the divine persons but also to the action of the Holy Spirit. Thus Colossians 2.12 speaks of: 'the *energeias* of him who raised Jesus Christ from the dead', while Ephesians 1.19f., literally translated, reads, 'through the *energeian* of the strength of his might which he exercised (*energeken*) in Christ, raising him from the dead ...'. Unless they are glossed in this way, the traditional slogans effectively deny the mediatorial work of the Son and the Spirit in making the Father known. But if we *know* the hypostases – by the mediation of scripture and the church's life and proclamation – then we know the *substance*, being, essence, *Wesen*, etc., of God, for there is nothing else to be known. The three persons *are* the being of God, and if we know the Father through the Son and in the Spirit we know the being of God.

To repeat, this does not imply that we have an 'inside' sight, or an exhaustive knowledge; indeed, it is not a matter of sight or of that kind of knowledge at all. Rather, knowledge is a form of personal relation, a version of the notion of knowledge by acquaintance. Nor is there a claim that our words as they stand begin to be adequate to the task, but the Spirit makes them adequate, as and in so far as God pleases, and if the Fourth Gospel, to mention but one, is right, God has so pleased and continues to do so. In sum God's being is known in and through his action, his triune act. God's action is triune in the sense that it is the action of Father, Son and Spirit, whose *opera ad extra* are inseparable from one another, though they are distributed, so to speak, between the three persons: the Father being the originating source of action, which he performs through the Son's involvement in the created world and the Spirit's perfecting of created things in anticipation of and on the Last Day.

Source: Colin Gunton, Act and Being, *London: SCM Press, 2002, pp. 109–13.*

3 Creation and Providence

Introductory essay

The doctrine of creation has often been offered as a 'point of contact' between different religious traditions. Whatever else may change, it is held, the claim that the universe owes its origin to the divine is a belief shared by all. To say this, however, is to ignore the distinctiveness of differing accounts of creation, and how they relate to other areas of doctrine and practice within particular faith traditions. In the history of Christian doctrine, the articulation of the doctrine of creation is one of the crucial developments in distinguishing Christianity from the philosophical traditions which surrounded it in its early centuries. Far from being a shared belief, it is one of the major early distinctives.

There was a lively debate within Greek philosophy concerning the origin of matter. The Greeks generally identified the material with changeableness and imperfection, and so, often, they assumed that matter was evil, or at least the source of all imperfection in the world. The material world was something to be escaped from, into a spiritual realm; the divine must be separate from the material, and relate to it, if at all, only through a series of intermediaries to prevent contamination. Because of this, the question of the origin of matter became an important one for later Greek philosophy; the origin of matter was the source of all evil and suffering, after all.

This, of course, raised problems for the early Christian theologians. In one of the earliest, and greatest, treatments of the doctrine of creation, Irenaeus of Lyons rejects such ideas on two grounds: first, the doctrine of the incarnation necessarily denies that God is in any way opposed to matter; second, the eucharistic feast demands that we acknowledge the goodness of the material realm. Creation is good; God deals with it directly, not through endless intermediaries, and takes flesh as his own. He saves us not from the material world, but through the material world – through the body and blood of Christ. We include here two extracts from Irenaeus; in the first, he argues that God relates to the world directly, not through intermediaries. In a memorable image, Irenaeus pictures the Father using his 'two hands', the Son and the Spirit, to interact with the world he has created. The second addresses the question of creation, and the origin of matter. Irenaeus meets head on speculations offered by various religious groups he calls Gnostics, either that the material world was created by an evil and inferior God, or that material things are somehow the products of different bits of a divine being. Instead, Irenaeus claims, God created everything out of nothing. Irenaeus is not quite the first writer to claim this, but creation out of nothing (*ex nihilo*) has become the central doctrine concerning creation in Christian theology. In origin, we see, it serves to protect the truth that the material world is good not evil, and that it is wholly within God's control.

Suspicion of the material world did not go away, however: it was too ingrained in the culture for that. A little after Irenaeus, Origen of Alexandria (whose intellect and industry marked him out as perhaps the most powerful theologian of the first three centuries of the Church) advanced his own idiosyncratic theory of a two-stage creation. In the extract included here he suggests that the driving motivation is justice: people are clearly born with advantages or disadvantages, and there must, thinks Origen, be some reason for this. However, a traditional suspicion of the goodness of the material world is clearly at play in his thinking. He suggests that the material world is not God's original intention, which was a purely spiritual creation, but when that went wrong, because some of the spirits created turned away from God and towards evil, there was a need for a place of expiation and education, and the material world was to be it. The advantages or disadvantages some people are born with are the just result of their previous actions in the spirit world, and reflect the journey they need to make to return to the presence of God from which we have all fallen.

Athanasius was also born in Alexandria, two generations after Origen, and in many ways was heir to the intellectual achievements of his predecessor. His own account of creation, however, shows no hesitation over the goodness of the material world. For Athanasius, the essential point is very simple: God is good, and so God's creation must be good. Athanasius is chiefly remembered for defending (and developing) the doctrine of the incarnation in opposition to Arius; the goodness of matter is a necessary component, or perhaps consequence, of this doctrine.

Augustine, living a century after Athanasius, was the towering intellect of the Latin-speaking Western Church. He regularly repeats Athanasius' insistence on the goodness of creation; in the extract here, however, he is exploring the nature of creation, specifically time. Time is a part of what God created – God is not bound by time. God endures, whereas creatures are constantly passing away; the essence of time, then, is separation and lostness. It is a profound imperfection, which marks creatures out as limited and reliant on God's perfection for their existence.

Jumping forward eight centuries or so, Thomas Aquinas addresses this theme of God's preservation of the creatures in our next extract, quoting Augustine on the point. Thomas believes that it can be demonstrated by logical argument that all things rely on God not just for their first existence (creation), but for their continuing existence moment by moment. It is not that God sets the universe going and then steps back to watch, but God is constantly upholding and preserving the universe, and all its parts, in being. That said, God's relationship to creation needs to be carefully described, according to Thomas. He addresses this in our second extract from his writings, arguing that, while creation depends entirely on God for its being, God's own being is in no way dependent on, or even affected by, creation. The God–world relationship is constitutive of the world, but does not change God at all.

Thomas Aquinas is an example of the careful logical exploration of subtle ideas that was one of the chief glories of the medieval period; in studying theology it is rather too easy to forget that this intellectual achievement went hand in hand with a profound piety, and an aesthetic achievement which gave us the great cathedrals of Europe, among other treasures. For this reason we include Francis of Assisi's 'Song of all the Creatures' – an uncomplicated and beautiful celebration of the goodness of the created order. Throughout, Francis recognizes that humanity is a part of God's creation, and so calls the other creatures 'brother' and 'sister' to stress his solidarity with the world. The most interesting part of the poem, however, is perhaps the penultimate stanza, praising God for sister death. In context, this cannot be read as a denial of the goodness of the body; rather, it is a sober recognition that the fullness of human flourishing lies on the far side of death and resurrection, and that for one living in confident faith in the gospel promises, death can be welcomed as a release from the troubles and cares of this life.

Those troubles and cares were often at the forefront of the mind of Martin Luther, as he found himself battling with the Church. The doctrine of providence, God's continual upholding of all created things, becomes a profound source of comfort for Luther. We include here a part of his exposition of the book of Genesis, where he draws this lesson from the story of Jacob, and applies it at length to the particular troubles of his own day. He is especially concerned about the advance of 'the Turks' – the Ottoman Empire under Suleiman the Magnificent was expanding northward in Luther's day (indeed, its troops reached the gates of Vienna) – but draws a lesson concerning God's providential care in this.

John Calvin reflects on a similar theme in our next extract, but, whereas Luther offers urgent and specific reflection on current events, Calvin's discussion is more abstract and more philosophical. How does the providential care of God relate to 'inferior causes' – that is, to the normal run of events? The story of Joseph famously ends with the claim 'Even though you intended to do harm to me, God intended it for good' (Gen. 50.20, NRSV) – how are we to relate the jealousy of Joseph's half-brothers, the deceit of Potiphar's wife, the memory and gratitude of Pharoah's cupbearer, the weather patterns that caused the Egyptian drought, and so on, to the purposes of God? Calvin (following, it happens, Thomas Aquinas) suggests that God's providential purposes are generally worked out precisely through such 'mundane' events and causes, and that recognizing both the creaturely cause, and the divine intention behind it, is the right attitude for the Christian.

This is arguably an unstable position to hold, without any account of how divine and creaturely causes hold together. In the eighteenth century, it became common to collapse it in one direction or the other. The better-known direction, at least today, was the suggestion that if an event could be adequately explained by natural causes, then there was no need to invoke any account of the divine. The debates over the causes of the horrific Lisbon earthquake of 1755 offer the classic illustration: it was to be seen as a natural disaster, not a supernatural warning or punishment. The opposite position was also explored at length in the eighteenth century, however, and our extract from Jonathan Edwards illustrates that. Edwards will not live with Calvin's account of dual causation, but instead of affirming natural causes and denying divine involvement in the world, he denies the reality of creaturely causation. Even the continued existence of a thing is not caused by its previous existence, but by the direct creative action of God. What we perceive as natural causes are only the consequences of God's constancy – because God is not capricious, the same events happen in the same way time after time.

Edwards – and others who held similar ideas, such as the philosophers Geulincx and Berkeley – lost the argument, and by the end of the eighteenth century the idea of direct divine involvement in the course of history was seen as backward and eccentric by Europe's intellectual elites, at least. At the same time, the early efforts of higher biblical criticism had begun (in the works of Reimarus and others), and so appeals to the text of Scripture as authoritative were not found convincing. What future was there for theology? Friedrich Schleiermacher suggested that all human beings share a fundamentally religious experience, and that theology should start from reflecting on this experience and what it implied. Older doctrines could be reinterpreted through this lens. We see this happening in the extract from his *Christian Faith*: creation and providence, here, are treated as attempts to articulate our religious awareness that we owe our life to something beyond ourselves, that we are fundamentally dependent. For Schleiermacher, creation is precisely a shared religious intuition, a point of contact between different religious traditions.

A century later, Karl Barth famously and angrily rejected Schleiermacher's legacy. Here we include an extract in which Barth insists that the Christian doctrine of creation must be a specifically Christian idea, derived from Scripture, confessed in the Creed. It is not a shared concept that can be generated from reason or experience; rather it is something distinctive. The Scottish theologian T. F. Torrance was one of Barth's students. He simply agreed with his teacher on this point; however, he had a lifelong interest in natural science, and the question of how a specifically Christian account of creation should relate to natural science was an important one for him.

He addressed it in various ways; we include a discussion of the theological basis of the sciences – the method of experimentation to discover knowledge in fact assumes many things about the nature of the world, things that (Torrance claims) can only be demonstrated by Christian theology.

Mention of science raises some of the most pressing ethical issues of the present time. Our final extract has Sallie McFague reflecting on theological resources for ecology. She suggests that our dominant metaphor for the God–world relationship has been that of a king and his realm – like all metaphors, it both communicates and distorts the truth. Perhaps, McFague wonders, we should try a different metaphor – the world as 'God's body'; what would theology look like under this rubric? Would it help us contribute to some of the vital questions of the day?

SRH

3.1 Irenaeus of Lyons, from *Against Heresies* (1)

Irenaeus argues that God created the world through the Son and the Spirit, not through any other intermediaries.

As regards His greatness, therefore, it is not possible to know God, for it is impossible that the Father can be measured; but as regards His love (for this it is which leads us to God by His Word), when we obey Him, we do always learn that there is so great a God, and that it is He who by Himself has established, and selected, and adorned, and contains all things; and among the all things, both ourselves and this our world. We also then were made, along with those things which are contained by Him. And this is He of whom the Scripture says, 'And God formed man, taking clay of the earth, and breathed into his face the breath of life' (Gen. 2:7). It was not angels, therefore, who made us, nor who formed us, neither had angels power to make an image of God, nor any one else, except the Word of the Lord, nor any Power remotely distant from the Father of all things. For God did not stand in need of these beings, in order to accomplish what He had Himself determined with Himself beforehand should be done, as if He did not possess His own hands. For with Him were always present the Word and Wisdom, the Son and the Spirit, by whom and in whom, freely and spontaneously, He made all things, to whom also He speaks, saying, 'Let Us make man after Our image and likeness' (Gen. 1:26); He taking from Himself the substance of the creatures formed, and the pattern of things made, and the type of all the adornments in the world.

...

I have also largely demonstrated, that the Word, namely the Son, was always with the Father; and that Wisdom also, which is the Spirit, was present with Him, anterior to all creation, He declares by Solomon: 'God by Wisdom founded the earth, and by understanding hath He established the heaven. By His knowledge the depths burst forth, and the clouds dropped down the dew' (Prov. 3:19–20). And again: 'The Lord created me [as] the beginning of His ways in His work: He set me up from everlasting, in the beginning, before He made the earth, before He established the depths, and before the fountains of waters gushed forth; before the mountains were made strong, and before all the hills, He brought me forth' (Prov. 8:22–25). And again: 'When He prepared the heaven, I was with Him, and when He established the fountains of the deep; when He made the foundations of the earth strong, I was with Him preparing [them]. I was He in whom He rejoiced, and throughout all time I was daily glad before His face, when He rejoiced at the completion of the world, and was delighted in the sons of men' (Prov. 8:27–31).

There is therefore one God, who by the Word and Wisdom created and arranged all things; but this is the Creator who has granted this world to the human race, and who, as regards His greatness, is indeed unknown to all who have been made by Him (for no man has searched out His height, either among the ancients who have gone to their rest, or any of those who are now alive); but as regards His love, He is always known through Him by whose means He ordained all things. Now this is His Word, our Lord Jesus Christ, who in the last times was made a man among men, that He might join the end to the beginning, that is, man to God. Wherefore the prophets, receiving the prophetic gift from the same Word, announced His advent according to the flesh, by which the blending and communion of God and man took place according to the good pleasure of the Father, the Word of God foretelling from the beginning that God should be seen by men, and hold converse with them upon earth, should confer with them, and should be present with His own creation, saving it, and becoming capable of being perceived by it, and freeing us from the hands of all that hate us, that is, from every spirit of wickedness; and causing us to serve Him in holiness and righteousness all our days, in order that man, having embraced the Spirit of God, might pass into the glory of the Father.

Source: Irenaeus of Lyons, Against Heresies *IV.20, trans. Alexander Roberts and William Rambaut, in Alexander Roberts, James Donaldson and A. Cleveland Coxe (eds),* Ante-Nicene Fathers, *vol. 1, Buffalo, NY: Christian Literature Publishing Co., 1885.*

3.2 Irenaeus of Lyons, from *Against Heresies* (2)

Irenaeus refutes the speculations of the Gnostics concerning the origin of matter, insisting instead that God made everything out of nothing.

But these heretics, while striving to explain passages of Scripture and parables, bring forward another more important, and indeed impious question, to this effect, 'Whether there be really another god above that God who was the Creator of the world?' They are not in the way of solving the questions which they propose; for how could they find means of doing so? But they append an important question to one of less consequence, and thus insert in their speculations a difficulty incapable of solution. For in order that they may know 'knowledge' itself (yet not learning this fact, that the Lord, when thirty years old, came to the baptism of truth), they do impiously despise that God who was the Creator, and who sent Him for the salvation of men. And that they may be deemed capable of informing us whence is the substance of matter, while they believe not that God, according to His pleasure, in the exercise of His own will and power, formed all things (so that those things which now are should have an existence) out of what did not previously exist, they have collected a multitude of vain discourses. They thus truly reveal their infidelity; they do not believe in that which really exists, and they have fallen away into the belief of that which has, in fact, no existence.

For, when they tell us that all moist substance proceeded from the tears of Achamoth, all lucid substance from her smile, all solid substance from her sadness, all mobile substance from her terror, and that thus they have sublime knowledge on account of which they are superior to others – how can these things fail to be regarded as worthy of contempt, and truly ridiculous? They do not believe that God (being powerful, and rich in all resources) created matter itself, inasmuch as they know not how much a spiritual and divine essence can accomplish. But they do believe that their Mother, whom they style a female from a female, produced from her passions aforesaid the so vast material substance of creation. They inquire, too, whence the substance of creation was supplied to the Creator; but they do not inquire whence were supplied to their Mother (whom they call the Enthymesis and impulse of the Aeon that went astray) so great an amount of tears, or perspiration, or sadness, or that which produced the remainder of matter.

For, to attribute the substance of created things to the power and will of Him who is God of all is worthy both of credit and acceptance. It is also agreeable to reason, and there may be well said regarding such a belief, that 'the things which are impossible with men are possible with God' (Lk 18:27). While men, indeed, cannot make anything out of nothing, but only out of matter already existing, yet God is in this point pre-eminently superior to men, that He Himself called into being the substance of His creation, when previously it had no existence. But the assertion that matter was produced from the Enthymesis of an Aeon going astray, and that the Aeon [referred to] was far separated from her Enthymesis, and that, again, her passion and feeling, apart from herself, became matter, is incredible, infatuated, impossible, and untenable.

Source: Irenaeus of Lyons, Against Heresies *II.10, trans. Alexander Roberts and William Rambaut, in Alexander Roberts, James Donaldson and A. Cleveland Coxe (eds),* Ante-Nicene Fathers, *vol. 1, Buffalo, NY: Christian Literature Publishing Co., 1885.*

3.3 Origen, from *On First Principles*

Origen asks about the justice of creation, given the variety of conditions we are born into. He suggests that there was an earlier creation of souls, or 'understandings', which all fell away from God by different degrees. Our stations in this life, then, reflect divine justice and our needs.

But let us now return to the order of our proposed discussion, and behold the commencement of creation, so far as the understanding can behold the beginning of the creation of God. In that commencement, then, we are to suppose that God created so great a number of rational or intellectual creatures (or by whatever name they are to be called), which we have formerly termed 'understandings', as He foresaw would be sufficient. It is certain that He made them according to some definite number, predetermined by Himself: for it is not to be imagined, as some would have it, that creatures have not a limit, because where there is no limit there can neither be any comprehension nor any limitation. Now if this were the case, then certainly created things could neither be restrained nor administered by God. For, naturally, whatever is infinite will also be incomprehensible. Moreover, as Scripture says, 'God has arranged all things in number and measure' (Wis. 11:20); and therefore number will be correctly applied to rational creatures or understandings, that they may be so numerous as to admit of being arranged, governed, and controlled by God. But measure will be appropriately applied to a material body; and this measure, we are to believe, was created by God such as He knew would be sufficient for the adorning of the world. These, then, are the things which we are to believe were created by God in the beginning, i.e., before all things. And this, we think, is indicated even in that beginning which Moses has introduced in terms somewhat ambiguous, when he says, 'In the beginning God made the heaven and the earth' (Gen. 1:1). For it is certain that the firmament is not spoken of, nor the dry land, but that heaven and earth from which this present heaven and earth which we now see afterwards borrowed their names.

But since those rational natures, which we have said above were made in the beginning, were created when they did not previously exist, in consequence of this very fact of their nonexistence and commencement of being, are they necessarily changeable and mutable; since whatever power was in their substance was not in it by nature, but was the result of the goodness of their Maker. What they are, therefore, is neither their own nor endures for ever, but is bestowed by God. For it did not always exist; and everything which is a gift may also be taken away, and disappear. And a reason for removal will consist in the movements of souls not being conducted according to right and propriety. For the Creator gave, as an indulgence to the understandings created by Him, the power of free and voluntary action, by which the good that was in them might become their own, being preserved by the exertion of their own will; but slothfulness, and a dislike of labour in preserving what is good, and an aversion to and a neglect of better things, furnished the beginning of a departure from goodness. But to depart from good is nothing else than to be made bad. For it is certain that to want goodness is to be wicked. Whence it happens that, in proportion as one falls away from goodness, in the same proportion does he become involved in wickedness. In which condition, according to its actions, each understanding, neglecting goodness either to a greater or more limited extent, was dragged into the opposite of good, which undoubtedly is evil. From which it appears that the Creator of all things admitted certain seeds and causes of variety and diversity, that He might create variety and diversity in proportion to the diversity of understandings, i.e., of rational creatures, which diversity they must be supposed to have conceived from that cause which we have mentioned above. And what we mean by variety and diversity is what we now wish to explain.

Now we term world everything which is above the heavens, or in the heavens, or upon the earth, or in those places which are called the lower regions, or all places whatever that anywhere exist, together with their inhabitants. This whole, then, is called world. In which world certain beings are said to be super-celestial, i.e., placed in happier abodes, and clothed with heavenly and resplendent bodies; and among these many distinctions are shown to exist, the apostle, e.g., saying, 'That one is the glory of the sun, another the glory of the moon, another the glory of the stars; for one star differeth from another star in glory' (1 Cor. 15:41). Certain beings are called earthly, and among them, i.e., among men, there is no small difference; for some of them are Barbarians, others Greeks; and of the Barbarians some are savage and fierce, and others of a milder disposition. And certain of them live under laws that have been thoroughly approved; others, again, under laws of a more common or severe kind; while some, again, possess customs of an inhuman and savage character, rather than laws. And certain of them, from the hour of their birth, are reduced to humiliation and subjection, and brought up as slaves, being placed under the dominion either of masters, or princes, or tyrants. Others, again, are brought up in a manner more consonant with freedom and reason: some with sound bodies, some with bodies diseased from their early years; some defective in vision, others in hearing and speech; some born in that condition, others deprived of the use of their senses immediately after birth, or at least undergoing such misfortune on reaching manhood. And why should I repeat and enumerate all the horrors of human misery, from which some have been free, and in which others have been involved, when each one can weigh and consider them for himself? ...

Seeing, then, that all things which have been created are said to have been made through Christ, and in Christ, as the Apostle Paul most clearly indicates, when he says, 'For in Him and by Him were all things created, whether things in heaven or things on earth, visible and invisible, whether they be thrones, or powers, or principalities, or dominions; all things were created by Him, and in Him' (Col. 1:16); and as in his Gospel John indicates the same thing, saying, 'In the beginning was the Word, and the Word was with God, and the Word was God: the same was in the beginning with God: all things were made by Him; and without Him was not anything made' (Jn 1:1–2); and as in the Psalm also it is written, 'In wisdom hast Thou made them all' (Ps. 104:24) – seeing, then, Christ is, as it were, the Word and Wisdom, and so also the Righteousness, it will undoubtedly follow that those things which were created in the Word and Wisdom are said to be created also in that righteousness which is

Christ; that in created things there may appear to be nothing unrighteous or accidental, but that all things may be shown to be in conformity with the law of equity and righteousness. How, then, so great a variety of things, and so great a diversity, can be understood to be altogether just and righteous, I am sure no human power or language can explain, unless as prostrate suppliants we pray to the Word, and Wisdom, and Righteousness Himself, who is the only-begotten Son of God, and who, pouring Himself by His graces into our senses, may deign to illuminate what is dark, to lay open what is concealed, and to reveal what is secret; if, indeed, we should be found either to seek, or ask, or knock so worthily as to deserve to receive when we ask, or to find when we seek, or to have it opened to us when we knock. Not relying, then, on our own powers, but on the help of that Wisdom which made all things, and of that Righteousness which we believe to be in all His creatures, although we are in the meantime unable to declare it, yet, trusting in His mercy, we shall endeavour to examine and inquire how that great variety and diversity in the world may appear to be consistent with all righteousness and reason. I mean, of course, merely reason in general; for it would be a mark of ignorance either to seek, or of folly to give, a special reason for each individual case.

Now, when we say that this world was established in the variety in which we have above explained that it was created by God, and when we say that this God is good, and righteous, and most just, there are numerous individuals, especially those who, coming from the school of Marcion, and Valentinus, and Basilides, have heard that there are souls of different natures ... In the next place, they object to us, with regard to terrestrial beings, that a happier lot by birth is the case with some rather than with others; as one man, e.g., is begotten of Abraham, and born of the promise; another, too, of Isaac and Rebekah, and who, while still in the womb, supplants his brother, and is said to be loved by God before he is born ... Their argument accordingly is this: If there be this great diversity of circumstances, and this diverse and varying condition by birth, in which the faculty of free-will has no scope (for no one chooses for himself either where, or with whom, or in what condition he is born); if, then, this is not caused by the difference in the nature of souls, i.e., that a soul of an evil nature is destined for a wicked nation, and a good soul for a righteous nation, what other conclusion remains than that these things must be supposed to be regulated by accident and chance? And if that be admitted, then it will be no longer believed that the world was made by God, or administered by His providence; and as a consequence, a judgment of God upon the deeds of each individual will appear a thing not to be looked for. In which matter, indeed, what is clearly the truth of things is the privilege of Him alone to know who searches all things, even the deep things of God.

We, however, although but men, not to nourish the insolence of the heretics by our silence, will return to their objections such answers as occur to us, so far as our abilities enable us. We have frequently shown, by those declarations which we were able to produce from the holy Scriptures, that God, the Creator of all things, is good, and just, and all-powerful. When He in the beginning created those beings which He desired to create, i.e., rational natures, He had no other reason for creating them than on account of Himself, i.e., His own goodness. As He Himself, then, was the cause of the existence of those things which were to be created, in whom there was neither any variation nor change, nor want of power, He created all whom He made equal and alike, because there was in Himself no reason for producing variety and diversity. But since those rational creatures themselves, as we have frequently shown, and will yet show in the proper place, were endowed with the power of free-will, this freedom of will incited each one either to progress by imitation of God, or reduced him to failure through negligence. And this, as we have already stated, is the cause of the diversity among rational creatures, deriving its origin not from the will or judgment of the Creator, but from the freedom of the individual will. Now God, who deemed it just to arrange His creatures according to their merit, brought down these different understandings into the harmony of one world, that He might adorn, as it were, one dwelling, in which there ought to be not only vessels of gold and silver, but also of wood and clay (and some indeed to honour, and others to dishonour), with those different vessels, or souls, or understandings. And these are the causes, in my opinion, why that world presents the aspect of diversity, while Divine Providence continues to regulate each individual according to the variety of his movements, or of his feelings and purpose. On which account the Creator will neither appear to be unjust in distributing (for the causes already mentioned) to every one according to his merits; nor will the happiness or unhappiness of each one's birth, or whatever be the condition that falls to his lot, be deemed accidental; nor will different creators, or souls of different natures, be believed to exist.

Source: Origen, On First Principles 2.9, trans. Frederick Crombie, in Alexander Roberts, James Donaldson and A. Cleveland Coxe (eds), Ante-Nicene Fathers, vol. 4, Buffalo, NY: Christian Literature Publishing Co., 1885.

3.4 Athanasius, from *On the Incarnation*

Athanasius indicates that we must believe in the goodness of the created world, because it is the creation of a good God.

In our former book we dealt fully enough with a few of the chief points about the heathen worship of idols, and how those false fears originally arose. We also, by God's grace, briefly indicated that the Word of the Father is Himself divine, that all things that are owe their being to His will and power, and that it is through Him that the Father gives order to creation, by Him that all things are moved, and through Him that they receive their being. Now, Macarius, true lover of Christ, we must take a step further in the faith of our holy religion, and consider also the Word's becoming Man and His divine Appearing in our midst. That mystery the Jews traduce, the Greeks deride, but we adore; and your own love and devotion to the Word also will be the greater, because in His Manhood He seems so little worth. For it is a fact that the more unbelievers pour scorn on Him, so much the more does He make His Godhead evident. The things which they, as men, rule out as impossible, He plainly shows to be possible; that which they deride as unfitting, His goodness makes most fit; and things which these wiseacres laugh at as 'human' He by His inherent might declares divine. Thus by what seems His utter poverty and weakness on the cross He overturns the pomp and parade of idols, and quietly and hiddenly wins over the mockers and unbelievers to recognize Him as God.

Now in dealing with these matters it is necessary first to recall what has already been said. You must understand why it is that the Word of the Father, so great and so high, has been made manifest in bodily form. He has not assumed a body as proper to His own nature, far from it, for as the Word He is without body. He has been manifested in a human body for this reason only, out of the love and goodness of His Father, for the salvation of us men. We will begin, then, with the creation of the world and with God its Maker, for the first fact that you must grasp is this: the renewal of creation has been wrought by the Self-same Word Who made it in the beginning. There is thus no inconsistency between creation and salvation for the One Father has employed the same Agent for both works, effecting the salvation of the world through the same Word Who made it in the beginning.

In regard to the making of the universe and the creation of all things there have been various opinions, and each person has propounded the theory that suited his own taste. For instance, some say that all things are self-originated and, so to speak, haphazard. The Epicureans are among these; they deny that there is any Mind behind the universe at all. This view is contrary to all the facts of experience, their own existence included. For if all things had come into being in this automatic fashion, instead of being the outcome of Mind, though they existed, they would all be uniform and without distinction. In the universe everything would be sun or moon or whatever it was, and in the human body the whole would be hand or eye or foot. But in point of fact the sun and the moon and the earth are all different things, and even within the human body there are different members, such as foot and hand and head. This distinctness of things argues not a spontaneous generation but a prevenient Cause; and from that Cause we can apprehend God, the Designer and Maker of all.

Others take the view expressed by Plato, that giant among the Greeks. He said that God had made all things out of pre-existent and uncreated matter, just as the carpenter makes things only out of wood that already exists. But those who hold this view do not realize that to deny that God is Himself the Cause of matter is to impute limitation to Him, just as it is undoubtedly a limitation on the part of the carpenter that he can make nothing unless he has the wood. How could God be called Maker and Artificer if His ability to make depended on some other cause, namely on matter itself? If He only worked up existing matter and did not Himself bring matter into being, He would be not the Creator but only a craftsman.

Then, again, there is the theory of the Gnostics, who have invented for themselves an Artificer of all things other than the Father of our Lord Jesus Christ. These simply shut their eyes to the obvious meaning of Scripture. For instance, the Lord, having reminded the Jews of the statement in Genesis, 'He Who created them in the beginning made them male and female ...' and having shown that for that reason a man should leave his parents and cleave to his wife, goes on to say with reference to the Creator, 'What therefore God has joined together, let no man put asunder' (Mt 19:4–6). How can they get a creation independent of the Father out of that? And, again, St. John, speaking all inclusively, says, 'All things became by Him and without Him came nothing into being' (Jn 1:3). How then could the Artificer be someone different, other than the Father of Christ?

Such are the notions which men put forward. But the impiety of their foolish talk is plainly declared by the divine teaching of the Christian faith. From it we know that, because there is Mind behind the universe, it did not originate itself; because God is infinite, not finite, it was not made from pre-existent matter, but out of nothing and out of non-existence, absolute and utter God brought it into being through the Word. He says as much in Genesis: 'In the beginning God created the heavens and the earth' (Gen. 1:1); and again through that most helpful book *The Shepherd*, 'Believe thou first and foremost that there is One God Who created and arranged all things and brought them out of non-existence into being' (*Shepherd of Hermas* 2:1). Paul also indicates the same thing when he says, 'By faith we understand that the worlds were framed by the Word of God, so that the things which we see now did not come into being out of things which had previously appeared' (Heb. 11:3). For God is good – or rather, of all goodness He is Fountainhead, and it is impossible for one who is good to be mean or grudging about anything. Grudging existence to none therefore, He made all things out of nothing through His own Word, our Lord Jesus Christ and of all these His earthly creatures He reserved especial mercy for the race of men. Upon them, therefore, upon men who, as animals, were essentially impermanent, He bestowed a grace which other creatures lacked – namely the impress of His own Image, a share in the reasonable being of the very Word Himself, so that, reflecting Him and themselves becoming reasonable and expressing the Mind of God even as He does, though in limited degree they might continue for ever in the blessed and only true life of the saints in paradise.

Source: St Athanasius, On the Incarnation, *trans. Sister Penelope Lawson, London: Mowbray and Crestwood, NY: St Vladimir's Orthodox Theological Seminary, 1953.*

3.5 Augustine of Hippo, from *Confessions*

Augustine meditates on the nature of time, and on God's eternity.

But if the roving thought of any one should wander through the images of bygone time, and wonder that Thou, the God Almighty, and All-creating, and All-sustaining, the Architect of heaven and earth, didst for innumerable ages refrain from so great a work before Thou wouldst make it, let him awake and consider that he wonders at false things. For whence could innumerable ages pass by which Thou didst not make, since Thou art the Author and Creator of all ages? Or what times should those be which were not made by Thee? Or how should they pass by if they had not been? Since, therefore, Thou art the Creator of all times, if any time was before Thou madest heaven and earth, why is it said that Thou didst refrain from working? For that very time Thou madest, nor could times pass by before Thou madest times. But if before heaven and earth there was no time, why is it asked, What didst Thou then? For there was no 'then' when time was not.

Nor dost Thou by time precede time; else wouldest not Thou precede all times. But in the excellency of an ever-present eternity, Thou precedest all times past, and survivest all future times, because they are future, and when they have come they will be past; but 'Thou art the same, and Thy years shall have no end' (Ps. 102:27). Thy years neither go nor come; but ours both go and come, that all may come. All Thy years stand at once since they do stand; nor were they when departing excluded by coming years, because they pass not away; but all these of ours shall be when all shall cease to be. Thy years are one day, and Thy day is not daily, but today; because Thy today yields not with tomorrow, for neither doth it follow yesterday. Thy today is eternity; therefore didst Thou beget the Co-eternal, to whom Thou saidst, 'This day have I begotten Thee' (Ps. 2:7). Thou hast made all time; and before all times Thou art, nor in any time was there not time.

At no time, therefore, hadst Thou not made anything, because Thou hadst made time itself. And no times are co-eternal with Thee, because Thou remainest for ever; but should these continue, they would not be times. For what is time? Who can easily and briefly explain it? Who even in thought can comprehend it, even to the pronouncing of a word concerning it? But what in speaking do we refer to more familiarly and knowingly than time? And certainly we understand when we speak of it; we understand also when we hear it spoken of by another. What, then, is time? If no one ask of me, I know; if I wish to explain to him who asks, I know not. Yet I say with confidence, that I know that if nothing passed away, there would not be past time; and if nothing were coming, there would not be future time; and if nothing were, there would not be present time. Those two times, therefore, past and future, how are they, when even the past now is not; and the future is not as yet? But should the present be always present, and should it not pass into time past, time truly it could not be, but eternity. If, then, time present – if it be time – only comes into existence because it passes into time past, how do we say that even this is, whose cause of being is that it shall not be – namely, so that we cannot truly say that time is, unless because it tends not to be?

Source: Augustine of Hippo, Confessions *XI.13, trans. J. G. Pilkington, in Philip Schaff (ed.),* Nicene and Post-Nicene Fathers, *first series, vol. 1, Buffalo, NY: Christian Literature Publishing Co., 1887.*

3.6 Thomas Aquinas, from *Summa contra Gentiles* (1)

Aquinas argues that God preserves all things in being moment by moment.

Now, from the fact that God rules things by His providence it follows that He preserves them in being.

Indeed, everything whereby things attain their end pertains to the governance of these things. For things are said to be ruled or governed by virtue of their being ordered to their end. Now, things are ordered to the ultimate end which God intends, that is, divine goodness, not only by the fact that they perform their operations, but also by the fact that they exist, since, to the extent that they exist, they bear the likeness of divine goodness which is the end for things, as we showed above. Therefore, it pertains to divine providence that things are preserved in being.

Again, the same principle must be the cause of a thing and of its preservation, for the preservation of a thing is nothing but the continuation of its being. Now, we showed above that God, through His understanding, and will, is the cause of being for all things. Therefore, He preserves all things in being through His intellect and will.

Besides, no particular univocal agent can be the unqualified cause of its species; for instance, this individual man cannot be the cause of the human species, for he would then be the cause of every man, and, consequently, of himself – which is impossible. But this individual man is the cause, properly speaking, of that individual man. Now, this man exists because human nature is present in this matter, which is the principle of individuation. So, this man is not the cause of a man, except in the sense that he is the cause of a human form coming to be in this matter. This is to be the principle of the generation of an individual man. So, it is apparent that neither this man, nor any other univocal agent in nature, is the cause of anything except the generation of this or that individual thing. Now, there must be some proper agent cause of the human species itself; its composition shows this, and also the ordering of its parts, which is uniform in all cases unless it be accidentally impeded. And the same reasoning applies to all the other species of natural things.

Now, this cause is God, either mediately or immediately. For we have shown that He is the first cause of all things. So, He must stand in regard to the species of things as the individual generating agent in nature does to generation, of which he is the direct cause. But generation ceases as soon as the operation of the generative agent ceases. Therefore, all the species of things would also cease as soon as the divine operation ceased. So, He preserves things in being through His operation.

Moreover, though motion may occur for any existing thing, motion is apart from the being of the thing. Now, nothing corporeal, unless it be moved, is the cause of anything, for no body acts unless by motion, as Aristotle proves. Therefore, no body is the cause of the being of anything, in so far as it is being, but it is the cause of its being moved toward being, that is, of the thing's becoming. Now, the being of any thing is participated being, since no thing is its own act of being, except God, as we proved above. And thus, God Himself,

Who is His own act of being, must be primarily and essentially the cause of every being. So, divine operation is related to the being of things as the motion of a corporeal mover is to the becoming and passive movement of the things that are made or moved. Now, it is impossible for the becoming and passive movement of a thing to continue if the motion of the mover cease. Therefore, it is impossible for the being of a thing to continue except through divine operation.

Furthermore, just as art work presupposes a work of nature, so does a work of nature presuppose the work of God the creator. In fact, the material for art products comes from nature, while that of natural products comes through creation by God. Moreover, art objects are preserved in being by the power of natural things; a home, for instance, by the solidity of its stories. Therefore, all natural things are preserved in being by nothing other than the power of God.

Again, the impression of an agent does not continue in the product, if the agent's action ceases, unless the impression be converted into the nature of the product. Indeed, the forms of things generated, and their properties, remain in them after generation until the end, since they become natural to them. And likewise, habits are difficult to change because they are turned into a nature. But dispositions and passions, whether of the body or soul, endure for a little while after the action of the agent, but not forever, since they are present in a state transitional to nature. Now, whatever belongs to the nature of a higher type of being does not last at all after the action of the agent; light, for instance, does not continue in a diaphanous body when the source of light has gone away. Now, to be is not the nature or essence of any created thing, but only of God, as we showed in Book One. Therefore, no thing can remain in being if divine operation cease.

Furthermore, there are two positions regarding the origin of things: one, from faith, holding that things have been brought into being by God, at the beginning; and the position of certain philosophers, that things have emanated from God eternally. Now, in either position one has to say that things are preserved in being by God. For, if things are brought into being by God, after they were not existing, then the being of things, and similarly their non-being, must result from the divine will; for He has permitted things not to be, when He so willed; and He made things to be, when He so willed. Hence, they exist just as long as He wills them to be. Therefore, His will is the preserver of things.

But, if things have eternally emanated from God, we cannot give a time or instant at which they first flowed forth from God. So, either they never were produced by God, or their being is always flowing forth from God as long as they exist. Therefore, He preserves things in being by His operation.

Hence it is said: 'Upholding all things by the word of His Power' (Heb. 1:3). And Augustine says: 'The power of the Creator, and the strength of the Omnipotent and All-sustaining is the cause of the subsistence of every creature. And, if this power were ever to cease its ruling of the things which have been created, their species would at once come to an end, and all nature would collapse. For the situation is not like that of a man who has built a house and has then gone away, and, while he is not working and is absent, his work stands. For, if God were to withdraw His rule from it, the world could not stand, even for the flick of an eye.'

Source: Thomas Aquinas, Summa contra Gentiles *III.65, trans. Vernon J. Bourke, South Bend: University of Notre Dame Press, 1991.*

3.7 Thomas Aquinas, from *Summa contra Gentiles* (SCG) (2)

Thomas argues that God is genuinely related to creation, but not in such a way that the act of creation changes God at all.

These relations [i.e. God's various relations with creatures] however which refer to His effects cannot possibly be in God.

For they cannot be in Him as accidents in a subject, since no accident is in Him, as we proved in the First Book [*SCG* 23]. Neither can they be God's very substance: because, since relative terms 'are those which essentially refer somehow to something else,' as the Philosopher [i.e., Aristotle] says, it would follow that God's substance is essentially referred to something else. Now that which is essentially referred to another, depends in some way thereon, since it can neither exist nor be understood without it. Hence it would follow that God's substance is dependent on something else outside it: and thus it would not be of itself necessary being, as we have proved in the First Book [*SCG* 13]. Therefore suchlike relations are not really in God.

Again: It was proved in the First Book [*SCG* 13] that God is the first measure of all beings. Therefore God is compared to other beings as knowable things to our knowledge: since 'opinion or speech is true or false according as a thing is or is not,' according to the Philosopher. Now though a thing is said to be knowable in relation to knowledge, the relation is not really in the knowable, but only in the knowledge: wherefore according to the Philosopher the knowable is so called relatively, 'not because it is itself related, but because something else is related to it'. Therefore the said relations are not really in God.

Further: The aforesaid relations are said of God not only with respect to those things that are actual, but also with respect to those that are in potentiality: because He both has knowledge of them, and in reference to them is called the first being and the sovereign good. But that which is actual has no real relation to that which is not actual but potential: else it would follow that there are actually an infinite number of relations in the same subject, since potentially infinite numbers are greater than the number two which is prior to them all. Now God is not related to actual things otherwise than to potential things, for He is not changed by the fact that He produces certain things. Therefore He is not related to other things by a relation really existing in Him.

Moreover: Whatever receives something anew, must needs be changed, either essentially or accidentally. Now certain relations are said of God anew: for instance that He is Lord or governor of a thing which begins anew to exist. Wherefore if a relation were predicated of God as really existing in Him, it would follow that something accrues to God anew, and consequently that He is changed either essentially or accidentally: the contrary of which was proved in the First Book [*SCG* 13].

Nevertheless, it cannot be said that the aforesaid relations exist extraneously as something outside God.

For since God is the first being and sovereign good, it would be necessary to consider yet other relations of God to those relations that are realities. And if these also are realities, we shall again have to find third relations: and so on indefinitely. Therefore the relations by which God is referred to other things are not really existing outside God.

Again: A thing is predicated denominatively in two ways. For a thing may be denominated from that which is outside it; for instance from place a person is said to be *somewhere*, and from time *somewhen*: and a thing may be denominated from that which is in it, as a person is denominated *white* from whiteness. On the other hand a thing is not found to be denominated from a relation that is extraneous, but as inherent: for a man is not denominated a father except from fatherhood which is in him. Therefore it is impossible for the relations whereby God is referred to creatures to be realities outside Him.

Since then it has been proved that they are not really in Him, and yet are predicated of Him, it remains that they are ascribed to Him according only to our way of understanding, from the fact that other things are referred to Him. For our intellect, in understanding one thing to be referred to another, understands at the same time that the latter is related to the former; although sometimes it is not really related at all.

Wherefore it is also evident that the aforesaid relations are not said of God in the same way as other things predicated of God. For all other things, as wisdom, will, predicate His essence, whereas the aforesaid relations do not by any means, but solely according to our way of understanding. And yet our understanding is not false. Because from the very fact that our intellect understands that the relations of the divine effects terminate in God Himself, it predicates certain things of Him relatively: even so we understand and express the knowable relatively from the fact that our knowledge is referred to it.

Source: Thomas Aquinas, Summa contra Gentiles *II.12–13, trans. Fathers of the English Dominican Province, London: Burns, Oates & Washbourne, 1924.*

3.8 Francis of Assisi, from 'The Song of All the Creatures'

Francis praises God for all of creation.

O most high, almighty, good Lord God, to thee belong praise, glory, honour, and all blessing!

[To thee alone, Most High, do they belong, and no mortal lips are worthy to pronounce thy Name.]

Praised be my Lord God with all his creatures, and specially our brother the sun, who brings us the day and who brings us the light; fair is he and shines with a very great splendour: O Lord, he signifies to us thee!

Praised be my Lord for our sister the moon, and for the stars, the which he has set clear and lovely in heaven.

Praised be my Lord for our brother the wind, and for air and cloud, calms and all weather by the which thou upholdest life in all creatures.

Praised be my Lord for our sister water, who is very serviceable unto us and humble and precious and clean.

Praised be my Lord for our brother fire, through whom thou givest us light in the darkness; and he is bright and pleasant and very mighty and strong.

Praised be my Lord for our mother the earth, the which doth sustain us and keep us, and bringeth forth divers fruits and flowers of many colours, and grass.

Praised be my Lord for all those who pardon one another for his love's sake, and who endure weakness and tribulation; blessed are they who peaceably shall endure, for thou, O most Highest, shalt give them a crown.

Praised be my Lord for our sister, the death of the body, from which no man escapeth. Woe to him who dieth in mortal sin! Blessed are they who are found walking by thy most holy will, for the second death shall have no power to do them harm.

Praise ye and bless the Lord, and give thanks unto him and serve him with great humility.

Source: Paul Sabatier, The Life of Francis of Assisi, *trans. Louise Seymour Houghton, New York: Scribner's Sons, 1914, pp. 305–6.*

3.9 Martin Luther, from *Lectures on Genesis*

Luther, commenting on the narrative of Jacob, explains how belief in creation and active providence should change our understanding of history and experience of the events of our own lives.

The Holy Spirit reminds us by this example that we should learn the doctrine of creation correctly, namely, that all things are in God's hand and that we should accustom and encourage ourselves to confident trust in our Creator, which, to be sure, is still very small and weak in us. For if we firmly concluded that God is our Creator, we would certainly believe that He has heaven and earth in His hands and all things which are contained by these. To be sure, if we saw the world shattered and falling into ruin with all the elements and hanging over our necks, we would nevertheless say: 'Even in falling you will not fall unless God wills it.' Even if it were hanging over our head, we would say: 'You will do no harm and not overwhelm me. And even if it seems good to God that I should be overwhelmed by your huge mass, let what is good in the Lord's eyes be done. My times are in His hands. But if it seems otherwise, I shall scoff at you, O heaven and earth, together with the Turks and papists and all other ragings of the whole world.'

In this way sure and final devastation was hanging over the house of Jacob. Nor were the Canaanites lacking in strength and will, plans, arms, and manpower. But what hindered them? The Lord said: 'No! Here shall your proud waves be stayed,' as He says in Job (38:11) and as Ps. 65:7 says: 'Who dost still the roaring of the seas, the roaring of their waves, the tumult of the peoples. The nations are in turmoil, and those who dwell at earth's farthest bounds are afraid of Thy signs.' ...

The same can be seen in all the threats of the world in raising a tumult against the church. The Turk is like an ocean swelling and turgid with billows, and if he had to be repressed by our strength it would have long since been all over with us. For we Germans are snoring, buried in sleep and wine, and we are destitute of leaders who could measure up in wisdom, strategy, and strength of heart to manage such great undertakings. If the Turk had moved forward, he would long ago have occupied all of Germany. For there is no one who could protect us, neither the emperor, nor kings, nor princes: God alone fights for us. Nor will an assault be launched on Germany unless it is in accordance with God's distinct decision and will. Otherwise the Turk would have overwhelmed us in our laziness long ago without any trouble. For both the princes and nobles have been completely ruined by luxury and pleasures. But that we are saved comes to pass by the power and goodness of God, and the prayer and faith of the church also obtains this defense. Accordingly, the emperor will make no progress in Belgium and will vent his rage no further than God has previously appointed. These matters, then, are handed down to us for our consolation and to arouse our faith so that we may make invocation and believe with more fervour.

...

This is the true knowledge and faith regarding creation, and this lesson should be carefully meditated and practised so that we stir up ourselves to pray and to believe. For it is ungodly and useless to place confidence in fortifications, ramparts, and guns ... But when we bend our knees and cry out to our Creator, He will be able to surround us with walls of fire, as is testified in Ps. 125:2: 'As the mountains are round about Jerusalem, so the Lord is round about His people, from this time forth and forevermore.' Likewise we read in Ps. 34:7: 'The angel of the Lord encamps around those who fear Him.' I hate that mass of ramparts and fortifications, for it is nothing else but a waste of money and a display of extreme folly. We should rather aim to make it our firm determination that we are in the hand of the Creator, and not only we but also our enemies and the devils with all the gates of hell. For if the devil had free power to fall upon us, none of us would remain alive for one moment.

...

Therefore let those who have God's promise remember that they should have the confidence that God wants to be our Keeper, Defender, Shepherd, and Father on account of the Son, as Christ testifies: 'The Father Himself loves you, because you have loved Me.' 'In the world you have tribulation; but be of good cheer, I have overcome the world.' 'If the world hates you, know that it has hated Me before it hated you.' 'And yet,' He means to say, 'your life in this sinful body is in My hand.' Why, then, are we alarmed and terrified at the threats and power of the enemy? To be sure, we rather rejoice in the Lord, who has called us with His holy calling and taught us to trust and to conquer in Himself.

Source: Martin Luther, Lectures on Genesis, *in Jaroslav Pelikan (ed.),* Luther's Works, *vol. 6, Saint Louis: Concordia, 1970, pp. 242–5.*

3.10 John Calvin, from the *Institutes of the Christian Religion*

Calvin explores the evidences of providence in the biblical history, and encourages a proper piety in believers.

These calumnies, or rather frenzied dreams, will easily be dispelled by a pure and holy meditation on Divine Providence, meditation such as piety enjoins, that we may thence derive the best and sweetest fruit. The Christian, then, being most fully persuaded, that all things come to pass by the dispensation of God, and that nothing happens fortuitously, will always direct his eye to him as the principal cause of events, at the same time paying due regard to inferior causes in their own place. Next, he will have no doubt that a special providence is awake for his preservation, and will not suffer anything to happen that will not turn to his good and safety. But as its business is first with men and then with the other creatures, he will feel assured that the providence of God reigns over both. In regard to men, good as well as bad, he will acknowledge that their counsels, wishes, aims and faculties are so under his hand, that he has full power to turn them in whatever direction, and constrain them as often as he pleases. The fact that a special providence watches over the safety of believers, is attested by a vast number of the clearest promises ... Nay, the chief aim of the historical books of Scripture is to show that the ways of his saints are so carefully guarded by the Lord, as to prevent them even from dashing their foot against a stone. Therefore, as we a little ago justly exploded the opinion of those who feign a universal providence, which does not condescend to take special care of every creature, so it is of the highest moment that we should specially recognise this care towards ourselves. Hence, our Saviour, after declaring that even a sparrow falls not to the ground without the will of his Father, immediately makes the application, that being more valuable than many sparrows, we ought to consider that God provides more carefully for us. He even extends this so far, as to assure us that the hairs of our head are all numbered. What more can we wish, if not even a hair of our head can fall, save in accordance with his will? I speak not merely of the human race in general. God having chosen the Church for his abode, there cannot be a doubt, that in governing it, he gives singular manifestations of his paternal care.

The servant of God being confirmed by these promises and examples, will add the passages which teach that all men are under his power, whether to conciliate their minds, or to curb their wickedness, and prevent it from doing harm. For it is the Lord who gives us favour, not only with those who wish us well, but also in the eyes of the Egyptians (Exod. 3:21), in various ways defeating the malice of our enemies. Sometimes he deprives them of all presence of mind, so that they cannot undertake anything soundly or soberly. In this ways he sends Satan to be a lie in the mouths of all the prophets in order to deceive Ahab (1 Kings 22:22), by the counsel of the young men he so infatuates Rehoboam, that his folly deprives him of his kingdom (1 Kings 12:10, 15).

Sometimes when he leaves them in possession of intellect, he so fills them with terror and dismay that they can neither will nor plan the execution of what they had designed. Sometimes, too, after permitting them to attempt what lust and rage suggested, he opportunely interrupts them in their career, and allows them not to conclude what they had begun. Thus the counsel of Ahithophel, which would have been fatal to David, was defeated before its time (2 Sam. 17:7, 14). Thus, for the good and safety of his people, he over-rules all the creatures, even the devil himself who, we see, durst not attempt any thing against Job without his permission and command. This knowledge is necessarily followed by gratitude in prosperity, patience in adversity, and incredible security for the time to come. Every thing, therefore, which turns out prosperous and according to his wish, the Christian will ascribe entirely to God, whether he has experienced his beneficence through the instrumentality of men, or been aided by inanimate creatures. For he will thus consider with himself: Certainly it was the Lord that disposed the minds of these people in my favour, attaching them to me so as to make them the instruments of his kindness. In an abundant harvest he will think that it is the Lord who listens to the heaven, that the heaven may listen to the earth, and the earth herself to her own offspring; in other cases, he will have no doubt that he owes all his prosperity to the divine blessing, and, admonished by so many circumstances, will feel it impossible to be ungrateful.

...

At the same time, the Christian will not overlook inferior causes. For, while he regards those by whom he is benefited as ministers of the divine goodness, he will not, therefore, pass them by, as if their kindness deserved no gratitude, but feeling sincerely obliged to them, will willingly confess the obligation, and endeavour, according to his ability, to return it. In fine, in the blessings which he receives, he will revere and extol God as the principal author, but will also honour men as his ministers, and perceive, as is the truth, that by the will of God he is under obligation to those, by whose hand God has been pleased to show him kindness. If he sustains any loss through negligence or imprudence, he will, indeed, believe that it was the Lord's will it should so be, but, at the same time, he will impute it to himself. If one for whom it was his duty to care, but whom he has treated with neglect, is carried off by disease, although aware that the person had reached a limit beyond which it was impossible to pass, he will not, therefore, extenuate his fault, but, as he had neglected to do his duty faithfully towards him, will feel as if he had perished by his guilty negligence. Far less where, in the case of theft or murder, fraud and preconceived malice have existed, will he palliate it under the pretext of Divine Providence, but in the same crime will distinctly recognise the justice of God, and the iniquity of man, as each is separately manifested. But in future events, especially, will he take account of such inferior causes. If he is not left destitute of human aid, which he can employ for his safety, he will set it down as a divine blessing; but he will not, therefore, be remiss in taking measures, or slow in employing the help of those whom he sees possessed of the means of assisting him. Regarding all the aids which the creatures can lend him, as hands offered him by the Lord, he will avail himself of them as the legitimate instruments of Divine

Providence. And as he is uncertain what the result of any business in which he engages is to be (save that he knows, that in all things the Lord will provide for his good), he will zealously aim at what he deems for the best, so far as his abilities enable him. In adopting his measures, he will not be carried away by his own impressions, but will commit and resign himself to the wisdom of God, that under his guidance he may be led into the right path. However, his confidence in external aid will not be such that the presence of it will make him feel secure, the absence of it fill him with dismay, as if he were destitute. His mind will always be fixed on the Providence of God alone, and no consideration of present circumstances will be allowed to withdraw him from the steady contemplation of it. Thus Joab, while he acknowledges that the issue of the battle is entirely in the hand of God, does not therefore become inactive, but strenuously proceeds with what belongs to his proper calling, 'Be of good courage,' says he, 'and let us play the men for our people, and for the cities of our God; and the Lord do that which seemeth him good' (2 Sam. 10:12). The same conviction keeping us free from rashness and false confidence, will stimulate us to constant prayer, while at the same time filling our minds with good hope, it will enable us to feel secure, and bid defiance to all the dangers by which we are surrounded.

Source: John Calvin, Institutes of the Christian Religion, *I.17.6–9, trans. Henry Beveridge (1559), Grand Rapids: Eerdmans, 1989.*

3.11 Jonathan Edwards, from 'The Great Christian Doctrine of *ORIGINAL SIN* Defended; Evidences of its Truth produced, And Arguments to the Contrary answered'

Edwards argues that the continued existence of creatures is equivalent to a repeated new creation out of nothing every moment.

And with respect to the identity of created substance itself, in the different moments of its duration, I think we shall greatly mistake, if we imagine it to be like that absolute, independent identity of the first being, whereby he is the same yesterday, today, and for ever. Nay, on the contrary, it may be demonstrated, that even this oneness of created substance, existing at different times, is a merely dependent identity; dependent on the pleasure and sovereign constitution of him who worketh all in all. This will follow from what is generally allowed, and is certainly true, that God not only created all things, and gave them being at first, but continually preserves them, and upholds them in being. This being a matter of considerable importance, it may be worthy here to be considered with a little attention. Let us inquire therefore, in the first place, whether it be not evident, that God does continually, by his immediate power, uphold every created substance in being; and then let us see the consequence.

That God does, by his immediate power, uphold every created substance in being, will be manifest, if we consider that their present existence is a dependent existence, and therefore is an effect and must have some cause; and the cause must be one of these two; either the antecedent existence of the same substance, or else the power of the Creator. But it cannot be the antecedent existence of the same substance. For instance, the existence of the body of the moon, at this present moment, cannot be the effect of its existence at the last foregoing moment. For not only was what existed the last moment, no active cause, but wholly a passive thing; but this also is to be considered, that no cause can produce effects in a time and place in which itself is not. It is plain, nothing can exert itself, or operate, when and where it is not existing. But the moon's past existence was neither where nor when its present existence is. In point of time, what is past entirely ceases, when present existence begins; otherwise it would not be past. The past moment has ceased, and is gone, when the present moment takes place; and no more coexists with it, than any other moment that had ceased, twenty years ago. Nor could the past existence of the particles of this moving body produce effects in any other place, than where it then was. But its existence at the present moment, in every point of it, is in a different place, from where its existence was at the last preceding moment. From these things, I suppose, it will certainly follow, that the present existence, either of this, or any other created substance, cannot be an effect of its past existence. The existences (so to speak) of an effect, or thing dependent, in different parts of space or duration, though ever so near one to another, do not at all co-exist one with the other; and therefore are as truly different effects, as if those parts of space and duration were ever so far asunder. And the prior existence can no more be the proper cause of the new existence, in the next moment, or next part of space, than if it had been in an age before, or at a thousand miles' distance, without any existence to fill up the intermediate time or space. Therefore the existence of created substances, in each successive moment, must be the effect of the immediate agency, will, and power of God.

If any shall insist upon it, that their present existence is the effect or consequence of past existence, according to the nature of things; that the established course of nature is sufficient to continue existence once given; I allow it. But then it should be remembered, what nature is in created things; and what the established course of nature is; that, as has been observed already, it is nothing, separate from the agency of God; and that, as Dr. T. says, God, the original of all being, is the only cause of all natural effects. A father, according to the course of nature, begets a child; an oak, according to the course of nature, produces an acorn, or a bud; so according to the course of nature, the former existence of the trunk of the tree is followed by its new or present existence. In one case, and the other, the new effect is consequent on the former, only by the established laws and settled course of nature; which is allowed to be nothing but the continued immediate efficiency of God, according to a constitution that he has been pleased to establish. Therefore, according to what our author urges, as the child and the acorn which come into existence according to the course of nature, in consequence of the prior existence and state of the parent and the oak, are truly immediately created by God; so must the existence of each created person and thing, at each moment, be from the immediate continued creation of God. It will certainly follow from these things, that God's preserving of created things in being, is perfectly equivalent to a continued creation, or to his creating those things out of nothing at each moment of their existence. If the continued existence of created things be wholly dependent on God's preservation, then those things would drop into nothing upon the ceasing of the present moment, without a new exertion of the divine power to cause them to exist in the following moment. If there be any who own, that God preserves things in being, and yet hold that they would continue in being without any further help from him, after they once have existence; I think, it is hard to know what they mean. To what purpose can it be, to talk of God preserving things in being, when there is no need of his preserving them? Or to talk of their being dependent on God for continued existence, when they would of themselves continue to exist, without his help; nay, though he should wholly withdraw his sustaining power and influence?

It will follow from what has been observed, that God's upholding of created substance, or causing of its existence in each successive moment, is altogether equivalent to an immediate production out of nothing, at each moment. Because its existence at this moment is not merely in part from God, but wholly from him; and not in any part, or degree, from its antecedent existence. For, to suppose that its antecedent existence concurs with God in efficiency, to produce some part of the effect, is attended with all the very same absurdities, which have been shown to attend the supposition of its producing it wholly. Therefore the antecedent existence is nothing, as to any proper influence or assistance in the affair: and consequently God produces the effect as much from nothing, as if there had been nothing before. So that this effect differs not at all from the first creation, but only circumstantially; as, in the first creation there had been no such act and effect of God's power before: whereas, his giving existence afterwards, follows preceding acts and effects of the same kind, in an established order.

Source: Jonathan Edwards, 'The Great Christian Doctrine of ORIGINAL SIN *Defended; Evidences of its Truth produced, And Arguments to the Contrary answered' IV.III, from http://www.mountainretreatorg.net/classics/jonathanedwards/original_sin.shtml.*

3.12 Friedrich Daniel Ernst Schleiermacher, from *The Christian Faith*

Schleiermacher here argues that both the traditional doctrines of creation and providence are best understood as representations of our immediate experience of the world's dependence on God.

The original expression of this relation, i.e. *that the world exists only in absolute dependence upon God, is divided in Church doctrine into the two propositions – that the world was created by God, and that God sustains the world.*

The proposition that the totality of finite being exists only in dependence upon the Infinite is the complete description of that basis of every religious feeling which is here to be set forth. We find ourselves always and only in a continuous existence; our life is always moving along a course; consequently just so far as we regard ourselves as finite being, apart from all other things, our self-consciousness can represent this being only in its continuity. And this in so complete a sense that (the feeling of absolute dependence being so universal an element in our self-consciousness) we may say that in whatever part of the whole or at whatever point of time we may be placed in every full act of reflection we should recognize ourselves as thus involved in continuity, and should extend the same thought to the whole of finite being. The proposition that God sustains the world, considered in itself, is precisely similar. At least it only seems to have acquired another and lesser content because we have grown accustomed to think of preservation and creation together, and thus a beginning is excluded from the range of the idea of preservation. On the other hand, the proposition, 'God has created,' considered in itself, lays down absolute dependence, but only for the beginning, with the exclusion of development; and whether the creation is conceived as taking place once for all or in the manner of one part after another, it lays down something which is not immediately given in our self-consciousness. Thus this proposition appears to belong to Dogmatics only so far as creation is complementary to the idea of preservation, with a view of reaching again the idea of unconditional all-inclusive dependence.

Thus there is no sufficient reason for retaining this division instead of the original expression which is so natural. And there can have been no reason for bringing this distinction into Dogmatics originally except that it was already to be found in traditional religious teaching, and that both the suitability of such expressions and the right measure of their use could be better guarded and established if the distinction were also adopted into the system of doctrine. Thus it did not originally arise on purely dogmatic grounds; and not only so, but it is not the outcome of any purely religious interest (which would find complete satisfaction in the simple expression); and thus, left to itself, the distinction between creation and preservation would fall into oblivion.

But for a human imagination only partially awakened, the beginning of all spatial and temporal existence is a subject which it cannot leave alone; consequently the treatment of the question is older than the abstract scientific phase of speculation, and belongs to the period of mythology. The question is linked up for us with the Mosaic account of creation [i.e., Gen. 1—3], but that by itself does not give it a religious or Christian character any more than other things in the Pentateuch which have been brought over in the same way from primitive and prehistoric times. Yet for a long time this representation had to submit to being used for purposes of speculation and of science as well, and, indeed, for the purpose of supporting opposing theories or even as their source.

Source: Friedrich Daniel Ernst Schleiermacher, The Christian Faith, *§36, trans. H. R. Mackintosh and J. S. Stewart, Edinburgh: T. & T. Clark, 1928, pp. 142–4.*

3.13 Karl Barth, from *Church Dogmatics* III.1

Barth here resists attempts to ground belief in creation in reason or experience, insisting it must be understood as an article of faith.

The first article of the 'Apostles'' creed says: I believe in God the Father Almighty, Maker of heaven and earth. These last words – not by themselves, but together with what goes before, and with all that follows in the second and third articles – are the simplest and most comprehensive form of the teaching of the Church on creation. Though they speak of God, they do not speak only of God, but also of a reality which is distinct from God, i.e., of heaven and earth as the two great distinctive but related spheres, intersecting in man, of the whole being of the 'world' as it exists apart from God. They say that He who alone is God the Father Almighty is not alone. And in order not to be alone and to have this other quite different reality before, with and near Him, He deliberately gave it an existence and definite form. They say that God is its Creator, that is, that heaven and earth and man between them owe to Him the fact as well as the content and manner of their being. Before these words, however, as before the whole creed, there stands the word *credo*, 'I believe'.

Our first emphasis is on this final point that the doctrine of the creation no less than the whole remaining content of Christian confession is an article of faith, i.e., the rendering of a knowledge which no man has procured for himself or ever will; which is neither native to him nor accessible by way of observation and logical thinking; for which he has no organ and no ability; which he can in fact achieve only in faith; but which is actually consummated in faith, i.e., in the reception of and response to the divine witness, so that he is made to be strong in his weakness, to see in his blindness and to hear in his deafness by the One who, according to the Easter story, goes through closed doors. It is a faith and doctrine of this kind which is expressed when in and with the whole of Christendom we confess that God is the Creator of heaven and earth.

...

We must first try to realise why it is that the doctrine of creation is a doctrine of faith and its content a secret; why it is, therefore, that it belongs to the creed and to Church dogmatics. There are three reasons why it cannot be other than an *articulus fidei* ['statement of faith'], and there is then a positive and decisive reason why it is actually and necessarily an *articulus fidei*.

...

To sum up, the statement concerning creation cannot be anything but an *articulus fidei* because (1) its assertion of the reality of the world maintained in it and (2) its grounding of this reality in God are possible only as a statement of faith, and because (3) it is determined in all its elements (subject, predicate and object) by the linguistic usage of Holy Scripture and the content of the terms employed – which means again that it can be understood only as a statement of faith.

We now turn to the positive exposition of our first thesis that the doctrine of creation is a doctrine of faith, that it is knowledge and confession in the reception of the divine self-witness and response to it. The positive meaning of this thesis has necessarily emerged already in the ... proof which we have advanced, and especially in the analysis of the biblical witness regarding the individual elements of the creation dogma. But we will now set it in the forefront.

How do we know that God created heaven and earth and man, that they are therefore reality, and that they owe it to God that this is so? The question is not: How do we come to be justified in supposing this? ... Nor is it, of course: What good does it do us that it is so? ... No, the question is: How do we arrive at the position where we can simply say that we *know* that it is so? How is it that the Christian Church – whether or not it is illuminating and pleasing to itself and the world, and in spite of every objection and contrary opinion – can publicly confess this work of God the Father, the creation of heaven and earth, as truth and indeed as absolute and exclusive truth?

...

If a thorough and precise answer is to be given to the strict question concerning the basis of this statement, it is not enough to say that it occurs at the very beginning of the Bible, that it is developed in the form of a twofold creation narrative, and that it is plainly recalled and explained in many subsequent passages and texts in the Old and New Testaments. This is, of course, perfectly true, and has to be said. The impregnable basis of this statement is indeed the *fact* that it is in the Bible. And the *form* in which it is there will occupy us intensively in what follows. But the fact that the Bible gives us a reliable basis for our knowledge and confession, that it tells the truth on which we can rely, on which the Church can base its proclamation, and on which each individual Christian can confidently build his own conclusions, is itself true in and by reason of the fact that the Bible gives us God's own witness to Himself, that it gives us the witness to Jesus Christ. Its word in all words is this Word. And it is this Word, its witness to Jesus Christ, which makes all its words the infallible Word of God. As the organ of the Spirit it helps us to this knowledge of the Father through the Son. In what it says about creation it also helps us to the knowledge of the Creator through the One in whom the Creator has reconciled the creature to Himself, in whom He has ordered the relationship of the creature to Himself, in whom He has given to the creature His eternal future, in accordance with the fact that in Him He loved and willed it from all eternity. The whole Bible speaks figuratively and prophetically of Him, of Jesus Christ, when it speaks of creation, the Creator and the creature. If, therefore, we are rightly to understand and estimate what it says about creation, we must first see that – like everything else it says – this refers and testifies first and last to Him. At this point, too, He is the primary and ultimate object of its witness ...

Source: Karl Barth, Church Dogmatics III.1, *trans and ed. Geoffrey Bromiley and T. F. Torrance, Edinburgh: T. & T. Clark, 1958, pp. 3–24.*

3.14 T. F. Torrance, from *Divine and Contingent Order*

Torrance here argues that the practice of natural science in fact relies on assumptions that can only be demonstrated theologically.

The basic problem that faces us in the relations between theological science and natural science has to do with a deep paradox in the heart of natural science itself. The understanding of the contingent nature of the cosmos upon which all empirico-theoretical enquiry rests, derives not from natural science but from Judaeo-Christian theology, i.e. from the doctrine of God as Creator of the orderly universe, who brought it into existence out of nothing and who continuously preserves it from lapsing back into chaos and nothingness. Nevertheless scientific investigation of this created order, rigorously in accordance with its distinctive nature, must be pursued without reference to God or any recourse to theological reasoning. The paradox may be succinctly formulated in terms of two classical statements of Reformed theology: nothing can be established about contingence except through divine revelation (*nihil constat de contingentia nisi ex revelatione*), and, divine creation requires us to investigate the contingent world out of its own natural processes alone, without including God in the given (*acsi deus non daretur*).

Natural science tacitly assumes the contingence, as well as the orderliness, of the universe. If there were no order immanent in the universe, if there were chaos and not a cosmos, the universe would not be accessible to scientific knowledge; if the universe were not characterised by contingence, the laws of nature would be derived from it immediately and necessarily through logico-deductive processes without experimental questioning of nature to induce it to reveal its secrets – which would make empirical science quite pointless. It is through relying on the indissoluble bond between contingence and order in the universe that natural science has come to operate with the distinctive interconnection between experiment and theory which has characterized our greatest advances in knowledge of the physical world. Yet we cannot prove that there is order in the universe, for we have to assume it in order ever to attempt proof of it; while genuine contingence is something that natural science on its own cannot come up with, but is rather something that natural science, through its ways of determining regularities in nature and formulating universal laws, is always on the point of resolving away. Quite evidently science must assume conceptions and principles that are themselves not logically derivable, explainable, or provable, but without which it could not function. Contingence and order are assumptions of that kind, yet we do not derive them from natural science but from a fundamental outlook upon the nature of the universe that is the correlative of a distinctive doctrine of God as the Creator of the universe.

Source: T. F. Torrance, Divine and Contingent Order, *Edinburgh: T. & T. Clark, 1998, pp. 26–7.*

3.15 Sallie McFague, from *Models of God*

McFague explores the implications of re-visioning the God–world relationship through a new metaphor, the world as God's body.

We are letting the metaphor of the world as God's body try its chance. We are experimenting with a bit of nonsense to see if it can make a claim to truth. What if, we are asking, the 'resurrection of the body' were not seen as the resurrection of particular bodies that ascend, beginning with Jesus of Nazareth, into another world, but as God's promise to be with us always in God's body, our world? What if God's promise of permanent presence to all space and time were imagined as a worldly reality, a palpable, bodily presence? What if, then, we did not have to go somewhere special (church) or somewhere else (another world) to be in the presence of God but could feel ourselves in that presence at all times and in all places? What if we imagined God's presence as in us and in all others, including the last and the least?

... The metaphor of the world as God's body has the opposite problem to the metaphor of the world as the king's realm: if the latter puts too great a distance between God and the world, the former verges on too great a proximity. Since both metaphors are inadequate, we have to ask which one is better in our time, and to qualify it with other metaphors and models. Is it better to accept an imaginative picture of God as the distant ruler controlling his realm through external and benevolent power or one of God so intimately related to the world that the world can be imagined as God's body? There are, of course, different understandings of 'better'. Is it better in terms of our and the world's preservation and fulfilment? Is it better in terms of coherence, comprehensibility, and illumination? Is it better in terms of expressing the Christian understanding of the relationship between God and the world?

...

Christians should, given their tradition, be inclined to find sense in 'body' language, not only because of the resurrection of the body but also because of the bread and wine of the Eucharist as the body and blood of Christ, and the church as the body with Christ as its head. Christians have a surprisingly 'bodily' tradition; nonetheless, there is a difference between the traditional uses of 'body' and seeing the world as God's body: when the world is viewed as God's body, that body includes more than just Christians and more than just human beings. It is possible to speculate that if Christianity had begun in a culture less dualistic and antiphysical than that of the first-century Mediterranean world, it might have been willing, given the more holistic anthropology and theology of its Hebraic roots, to extend its body metaphor to God. At any rate, in view of the contemporary holistic understanding of personhood, in which embodiment is the sine qua non, the thought of an embodied personal deity is not more incredible than that of a disembodied one; in fact, it is less so. In a dualistic culture where mind and body, spirit and flesh, are separable, a disembodied, personal God is more credible, but not in ours. This is only to suggest that the idea of God's embodiment – the idea as such, quite apart from particulars – should not be seen as nonsense; it is less nonsense than the idea of a disembodied personal God.

A more central issue is whether the metaphor of the world as God's body is pantheistic or, to put it another way, reduces God to the world. The metaphor does come far closer to pantheism than the king-realm model, which verges on deism, but it does not totally identify God with the world any more than we totally identify ourselves with our bodies. Other animals may be said to be bodies that have spirits; we may be said to be spirits that possess bodies. This is not to introduce a new dualism but only to recognize that although our bodies are expressions of us both unconsciously and consciously, we can reflect about them and distance ourselves from them. The very fact that we can speak about our bodies is evidence that we are not totally one with them. On this model, God is not reduced to the world if the world is God's body. Without the use of personal agential metaphors, however, including among others God as mother, lover, and friend, the metaphor of the world as God's body would be pantheistic, for the body would be all there were. Nonetheless, the model is monist and perhaps most precisely panentheistic ...

Nevertheless, though God is not reduced to the world, the metaphor of the world as God's body puts God 'at risk.' If we follow out the implications of the metaphor, we see that God becomes dependent through becoming bodily, in a way that a totally invisible, distant God would never be. Just as we care about our bodies, are made vulnerable by them, and must attend to their well-being, God will be liable to bodily contingencies. The world as God's body may be poorly cared for, ravaged, and as we are becoming well aware, essentially destroyed, in spite of God's own loving attention to it, because of one creature, ourselves, who can choose or not choose to join with God in conscious care of the world. Presumably, were this body blown up, another could be formed; hence, God need not be seen to be as dependent on us or on any particular body as we are on our own bodies. But in the metaphor of the universe as the self-expression of God – God's incarnation – the notions of vulnerability, shared responsibility, and risk are inevitable. This is a markedly different basic understanding of the God–world relationship than in the monarch-realm metaphor, for it emphasises God's willingness to suffer for and with the world, even to the point of personal risk. The world as God's body, then, may be seen as a way to remythologize the inclusive, suffering love of the cross of Jesus of Nazareth. In both instances, God is at risk in human hands: just as once upon a time in a bygone mythology, human beings killed their God in the body of a man, so now we once again have that power, but, in a mythology more appropriate to our time, we would kill our God in the body of the world. Could we actually do this? To believe in the resurrection means we could not. God is not in our power to destroy, but the incarnate God is the God at risk: we have been given central responsibility to care for God's body, our world.

Source: Sallie McFague, Models of God: Theology for an Ecological, Nuclear Age, *Philadelphia: Fortress Press and London: SCM Press, 1987, pp. 69–73.*

4 The Person of Christ

Introductory essay

From its very beginnings Christian faith has advanced the claim that Jesus Christ is not merely some prophet or teacher, more or less like many others before him and since, but that he is in some manner the presence of God with us. Nor is he simply a moral or spiritual exemplar to the faithful. He is proclaimed, rather, to be the Saviour of the world. These are, of course, enormous claims. It is the task of Christology to investigate what they mean and to consider both their coherence and their truth.

The primary witness to Jesus Christ comes, of course, through the writings of the New Testament. In forming their proclamation of Jesus, the New Testament writers drew not only upon their own experience of Jesus and the collective memory of him in the early Church, but also upon the Scriptures of the Hebrew Bible. The faith and story of Israel provided the Church with theological resources that profoundly shaped the expression of its faith that in Jesus of Nazareth the God made known to Israel had now come among them in person.

The use of Jewish conceptuality to speak of Jesus' significance is a process begun, arguably, by Jesus himself. In Mark's Gospel, for instance, Jesus himself appeals to the Davidic tradition to justify the conduct of his disciples (Mark 2.23–28), he accepts the title 'Son of David' (Mark 10.46–52) and appears to accept the Messianic overtones of that designation (Mark 12.35–37). Elsewhere in the Gospels Jesus clearly prefers the title 'Son of Man' among the many titles used of him. This title too is drawn from the Old Testament and is associated with the coming judge. So too with many of the other titles applied to Jesus: the Messiah, the High Priest, the second Adam, and so on.

Beyond the use of such titles, the New Testament writers constantly draw upon Old Testament passages to interpret the person and work of Jesus. Again, this is a process that begins with Jesus himself. In Luke 4, for instance, we have the account of Jesus going to the synagogue and drawing from the book of Isaiah in order to outline the nature of his own ministry (Luke 4.16–21). Beyond the sayings of Jesus himself, the New Testament writers drew upon Old Testament traditions in order to proclaim the significance of Jesus. Matthew, for instance, in recounting the story of Jesus' birth draws heavily upon the Exodus tradition of Israel. Jesus is represented as a new Mosaic figure leading his people from bondage to freedom. Similarly, the three Old Testament offices of prophet, priest and king figure prominently in the New Testament interpretations of Jesus, and the Isaianic anticipation of the suffering servant is frequently drawn upon in order to make clear who Jesus is.

It is a commonplace to observe that the various New Testament writings are characterized by considerable diversity of expression, emphasis, historical detail, and indeed, of theology, in their witness to Jesus Christ. There are many scholars today who take this diversity to be subversive of orthodox Christian faith. Such an attitude, however, requires a glib dismissal of the very considerable unity of purpose among the New Testament writers who unanimously testify that Jesus of Nazareth is to be understood as the saviour through whom God works out his redemptive purposes for the world. That unifying theme of the New Testament surely deserves to be taken seriously, without precluding there being a great variety of ways in which that truth is brought to expression.

It would be surprising, in fact, if there were not considerable diversity in the New Testament witness. The New Testament writers were seeking for ways, against varying backgrounds and in response to particular contextual challenges, to find images and titles and modes of speaking which would communicate the news that Jesus was the saviour of the world. In some contexts and for some audiences, an emphasis upon Jesus' continuity with the history of Israel and an expression of the ways in which he was the fulfilment of Israel's hopes, would be required. In other contexts, it would be necessary to tell the story of Jesus in ways that recognized the Greek language and conceptuality of the intended audience. Similarly, as Christology has developed through the centuries, differing contextual challenges have given rise to diverse expressions of the Christian conviction that Jesus is Lord.

This chapter takes up the story of that development beginning with a brief extract from Irenaeus (c. AD 115–90) in which we see emerging the trinitarian conception of God by which the Church brought conceptual clarity to its confession that in the figure of Jesus Christ and through his Spirit the one God of Israel is at work.

Because the proclamation of Jesus' divinity required of those who heard it a radical transformation of their previous theology, that proclamation inevitably encountered resistance, even among some who counted themselves as belonging to the Church. Of particular importance in the development of orthodox Christology was the resistance to it provided by the fourth-century Alexandrian presbyter Arius (c. 250–336) and his followers. 'The Confession of the Arians' outlines the nature of their resistance. The controversy surrounding Arius prompted the Emperor Constantine to call a Council at Nicaea in 325, from which emerged 'The Faith of Nicaea', a slightly adapted and extended form of which was endorsed by the Council of Constantinople in 381 and is now known as the Nicene Creed. Chief among the opponents of Arius was Athanasius (c. 296–377) who issued a volley of arguments against the Arian conception of Christ as a saviour who was less than fully divine. The extract provided here, opposing the Arian claim that 'there was [a time] when the Son was not', focuses on the eternal existence of the Son.

Although Athanasius eventually won the day, debate about various aspects of Christ's person continued. In particular, questions emerged about how the relation between the divinity and the humanity of Christ should be conceived. In many cases the views of those eventually judged by the Church to have been mistaken helped the Church to develop its own view. Apollinarius, Nestorius, Theodore of Mopsuestia and Eutyches are important cases in point. Gregory of Nazianzus, Gregory of Nyssa, Cyril of Alexandria and Pope Leo I made important contributions to the debate in opposition to the aforementioned, and helped to shape the orthodox position affirmed at the Council of Chalcedon in 451. Leo's Tome sent to the Council was adopted as one of the confessional documents setting out the orthodox position. In the sixth century, Pope Vigilius was a strong supporter of the Chalcedonian position. This orthodoxy was reconfirmed at the Council of Constantinople in 553. The selection of extracts included in this chapter present the key points of the debate.

Further debates about the two natures of Christ were pursued through the Middle Ages and into the Reformation period. Such debates are represented by extracts from Bonaventure (1221–74), who considers the maleness of Christ, and by Martin Luther (1483–1546), who explores the question of the *communicatio idiomatum*. This question, to which a range of responses was developed during the Reformation, concerns the extent to which attributes of the divine nature of Christ may be communicated to the human nature, and vice versa.

Further discussion of how the humanity and the divinity of Christ are to be conceived is provided in the extract from Friedrich Schleiermacher (1768–1834). Schleiermacher is a giant of the theological tradition, representing nineteenth-century liberal theology at its best, but it remains open to question whether his account of the identity of Christ does justice to the Nicene confession that Christ is of one being with the Father. Divinity, on Schleiermacher's account, appears to be equated with the highest attainments of human nature.

In the nineteenth century the identity of Jesus became again a matter of controversy and debate. Following upon the work of Samuel Reimarus (1694–1768) and G. E. Lessing (1729–81), new questions were being raised about the historical reality of Jesus and the theological accounts of that reality given in the New Testament. It was increasingly supposed that the true identity of Jesus could be discovered only by stripping away the overlay of theological interpretation that had been 'imposed' upon him by the Church. The 'Quest of the historical Jesus' thus developed as an effort to lay bare the life of Jesus 'as it really was'. D. F. Strauss was one of the leading proponents of this Quest and an early advocate of the view that much of the New Testament writing about Jesus should be regarded as myth. The question then for Strauss was, what did this myth serve to express? Following Hegel, Strauss claimed that the New Testament myth expresses the idea of the unity of the divine and the human, a unity applying not uniquely to Jesus but to the whole of the human race.

Martin Kähler (1835–1912) rejected the 'Life of Jesus Movement' and claimed instead that the real Christ is revealed through the witness of the New Testament. Contemporary with Kähler, Albert Schweitzer rejected the Quest for rather different reasons. Schweitzer argued that we do not have the resources to write a 'life of Jesus'. We must engage instead with Jesus' teaching in which he urged our participation in his religion of love and in the coming kingdom of God.

Schweitzer's declaration of the futility of the Quest, along with Kähler's emphasis on the authority of New Testament preaching about Christ, set the scene for the next fifty years. The most important theological voices of the early twentieth century were those of the dialectical theologians. Most prominent among them was Karl Barth (1886–1968).

Other leading theologians of the same generation were Rudolf Bultmann (1884–1976) and Dietrich Bonhoeffer (1906–45). Bonhoeffer's call for a Christology that begins in silence before the Word has much in common with Barth's position. Not through historical inquiry but through faithful attentiveness to Scripture will the truth of Christ be learned.

Dialectical theology offered, undoubtedly, a necessary corrective, but its neglect of historical inquiry has subsequently been challenged. There emerged in the latter half of the twentieth century a renewed interest in the importance for Christology of historical inquiry. Among theologians, Wolfhart Pannenberg (1928–) has been a leading advocate of this view (see extract 4.21), while numerous New Testament scholars are engaged in modified forms of the Quest of the historical Jesus. A key theme of contemporary inquiry is the focus upon the Jewishness of Jesus as is evident in the extract from N. T. Wright.

Two further twentieth-century emphases complete this section; the first is represented in Donald Baillie's revisiting of the question of Christ's two natures. The second theme is represented only briefly here but will be encountered more fully in the next section. It is the growing recognition that Jesus has been studied, in the main, by white Western males, and that this fact has obscured aspects of the reality of Christ more readily recognized by women and by non-Western readers of the Bible. The reading from Patricia Wilson-Kastner indicates the direction Christology might take when conducted according to this broader scope.

MAR

4.1 Irenaeus of Lyon, from *The Demonstration of the Apostolic Preaching*

Irenaeus argues that the Son and the Father are one God.

So then the Father is Lord and the Son is Lord, and the Father is God and the Son is God; for that which is begotten of God is God. And so in the substance and power of His being there is shown forth one God; but there is also according to the economy of our redemption both Son and Father. Because to created things the Father of all is invisible and unapproachable, therefore those who are to draw near to God must have their access to the Father through the Son. And yet more plainly and evidently does David speak concerning the Father and the Son as follows: *Thy throne, O God, is for ever and ever: thou hast loved righteousness and hated unrighteousness: therefore God hath anointed thee with the oil of gladness above thy fellows* [Psalm 45.6]. For the Son, as being God, receives from the Father, that is, from God, the throne of the everlasting kingdom, and the oil of anointing above His fellows. The oil of anointing is the Spirit, wherewith He has been anointed; and His fellows are prophets and righteous men and apostles, and all who receive the fellowship of His kingdom, that is to say, His disciples.

Source: Irenaeus of Lyon, The Demonstration of the Apostolic Preaching *47, trans. from the Armenian with introduction and notes by J. Armitage Robinson, London: SPCK and New York: Macmillan, 1920.*

4.2 Arius, from *Letter to Eusebius*

In this letter to Eusebius, Arius explains that he is declared a heretic because of his belief that the Son was created.

To my very dear lord, the faithful and orthodox man of God Eusebius, Arius, unjustly persecuted by Pope Alexander for the sake of the all-conquering truth of which you also are a defender, sends greeting in the Lord.

Since my father Ammonius was coming to Nicomedia, it seemed to me fitting and proper to send you greetings by him, and also to bring to your attention, in the natural love and affection which you have for the brethren, for the sake of God and his Christ, that the bishop greatly injures and persecutes us and does all he can against us trying to drive us out of the city as godless men, since we do not agree with him when he says publicly, 'Always Father, always Son' 'Father and Son together,' 'The Son exists unbegottenly with God,' 'The eternal begotten,' 'Unbegotten-only-one,' 'Neither in thought nor by a single instant is God before the Son,' 'Always God, always Son,' 'The Son is God himself.'

And since your brother Eusebius in Caesarea and Theodotus and Paulinus and Athanasius and Gregorius and all the bishops of the East say that God exists without beginning before the Son, they are anathematised, except Philogonius, Hellanicus, and Macarius, [and such] heretical and uninstructed men, some of who speak of the Son as an emission, others as a projection, others as co-unbegotten. But we cannot bear even to listen to such impieities, though the heretics should threaten us with a thousand deaths. What is it that we say, and think, and have taught, and teach? That the Son is not unbegotten, nor a part of the unbegotten in any way, nor [formed out] of any substratum, but that he was constituted by [God's] will and counsel, before times and before ages, full (of grace and truth), divine, unique, unchangeable. And before he was begotten or created or ordained or founded, he was not. For he was not unbegotten. We are persecuted because we say, 'The Son has a beginning, but God is without beginning.' For this we are persecuted, and because we say, 'He is [made] out of things that were not.' But this is what we say, since he is neither a part of God nor [formed] out of any substratum. For this we are persecuted and you know the rest. So I pray that you may prosper in the Lord, remembering our afflictions, fellow Lucianist, truly Eusebius.

Source: Arius, Letter to Eusebius, *in Edward Rochie Hardy in collaboration with Cyril Charles Richardson,* Christology of the Later Fathers, *Philadelphia: Westminster Press, 1977, pp. 329–31.*

4.3 Confession of the Arians

The Confession of the Arians is an account of why they do not believe that the Son is also God, because God is indivisible.

To our blessed pope and bishop Alexander the presbyters and deacons send greeting in the Lord.

Our faith which we received from our forefathers and have also learned from you is this. We know there is one God, the only unbegotten, only eternal, only without beginning, only true, who only has immortality, only wise, only good, the only potentate, judge of all, governor, dispenser, unalterable and unchangeable, righteous and good, God of the Law and the Prophets and the New Covenant. Before everlasting ages he begot his unique Son, through whom he made the ages and all things. He begot him not in appearance, but in truth, constituting him by his own will, unalterable and unchangeable, a perfect creature of God, but not as one of the creatures – an offspring, but not as one of things begotten. Neither [was] the offspring of the Father a projection, as Valentinius taught, nor, as Manicheus introduced, was the offspring a consubstantial part of the Father, nor [was he], as Sabellius said, dividing the Monad, a Son-Father, nor as Hieracas [taught], a lamp [kindled] from a lamp, or like a torch [divided] into two; nor did he first exist, later being begotten or re-created into a Son – as you also, blessed pope, in the midst of the Church and in council often refuted those who introduced these [ideas]. But as we said, by the will of God [he was] created before times and before ages and received life and being and glories from the Father, the Father so constituting him. Nor did the Father in giving him the inheritance of all things deprive himself of what he possesses unbegottenly in himself, for he is the fount of all things. Thus there are three *hypostases*. God being the cause of all things is without beginning and most unique, while the Son, begotten timelessly by the Father and created before ages and established, was not before he was begotten – but, begotten timelessly before all things, he alone was constituted by the Father. He is neither eternal nor co-eternal nor co-unbegotten with the Father, nor does he have his being together with the Father, as some say 'others with one,' introducing [the idea of] two unbegotten sources. But as Monad and cause of all, God is thus before all. Therefore he is also prior to the Son, as we learned from what you preached in the midst of the Church.

So therefore, as he has being and glories from God, and life and all things were given him, accordingly God is his source. For he precedes him as his God and as being before him. But if the [phrases] 'of him' and 'out of the womb' and 'I came forth from the Father and am come' are understood by some as [meaning] a part of the consubstantial himself and a projection, then according to them the Father is compound and divisible and alterable and a body, and according to them presumably, the bodiless God [is thought of as] suffering what belongs to a body.

We pray that you may fare well in the Lord, blessed pope. Arius, Aeithales, Achilleus, Carpones, Sarmatas, Arius, presbyters. Deacons, Euzoius, Lucius,

Julius, Menas, Helladius, Gaius. Bishops, Secundis of Penapolis, Theonas of Libya, Pistus (whom the Arians installed at Alexandria).

Source: Confession of the Arians, *in Edward Rochie Hardy in collaboration with Cyril Charles Richardson,* Christology of the Later Fathers, *Philadelphia: Westminster Press, 1977, pp. 332–4.*

4.4 Athanasius, from *First Discourse against the Arians*

In his First Discourse against the Arians Athanasius defends the eternal existence of the Son by adducing a range of biblical texts. He then goes on to explain why Jesus is properly understood as 'Son'.

14. When these points are thus proved, [the Arians'] profaneness goes further. 'If there never was, when the Son was not,' say they, 'but He is eternal, and coexists with the Father, you call Him no more the Father's Son, but brother.' O insensate and contentious! For if we said only that He was eternally with the Father, and not His Son, their pretended scruple would have some plausibility; but if, while we say that He is eternal, we also confess Him to be Son from the Father, how can He that is begotten be considered brother of Him who begets? And if our faith is in Father and Son, what brotherhood is there between them? And how can the Word be called brother of Him whose Word He is? This is not an objection of men really ignorant, for they comprehend how the truth lies; but it is a Jewish pretence, and that from those who, in Solomon's words, 'through desire separate themselves' [Prov. 18.1] from the truth. For the Father and the Son were not generated from some pre-existing origin, that we may account Them brothers, but the Father is the Origin of the Son and begat Him; and the Father is Father, and not born the Son of any; and the Son is Son, and not brother. Further, if He is called the eternal offspring of the Father, He is rightly so called. For never was the essence of the Father imperfect, that what is proper to it should be added afterwards; nor, as man from man, has the Son been begotten, so as to be later than His Father's existence, but He is God's offspring, and as being proper Son of God, who is ever, He exists eternally. For, whereas it is proper to men to beget in time, from the imperfection of their nature, God's offspring is eternal, for His nature is ever perfect. If then He is not a Son, but a work made out of nothing, they have but to prove it; and then they are at liberty, as if imagining about a creature, to cry out, 'There was once when He was not;' for things which are originated were not, and have come to be. But if He is Son, as the Father says, and the Scriptures proclaim, and 'Son' is nothing else than what is generated from the Father; and what is generated from the Father is His Word, and Wisdom, and Radiance; what is to be said but that, in maintaining 'Once the Son was not,' they rob God of His Word, like plunderers, and openly predicate of Him that He was once without His proper Word and Wisdom, and that the Light was once without radiance, and the Fountain was once barren and dry? For though they pretend alarm at the name of time, because of those who reproach them with it, and say, that He was before times, yet whereas they assign certain intervals, in which they imagine He was not, they are most irreligious still, as equally suggesting times, and imputing to God an absence of Reason.

15. But if on the other hand, while they acknowledge with us the name of 'Son,' from an unwillingness to be publicly and generally condemned, they deny that the Son is the proper offspring of the Father's essence, on the ground that this must imply parts and divisions; what is this but to deny that He is very Son, and only in name to call Him Son at all? And is it not a grievous

error, to have material thoughts about what is immaterial, and because of the weakness of their proper nature to deny what is natural and proper to the Father? It does but remain, that they should deny Him also, because they understand not how God is, and what the Father is, now that, foolish men, they measure by themselves the Offspring of the Father. And persons in such a state of mind as to consider that there cannot be a Son of God, demand our pity; but they must be interrogated and exposed for the chance of bringing them to their senses. If then, as you say, 'the Son is from nothing,' and 'was not before His generation,' He, of course, as well as others, must be called Son and God and Wisdom only by participation; for thus all other creatures consist, and by sanctification are glorified. You have to tell us then, of what He is partaker. All other things partake of the Spirit, but He, according to you, of what is He partaker? Of the Spirit? Nay, rather the Spirit Himself takes from the Son, as He Himself says; and it is not reasonable to say that the latter is sanctified by the former. Therefore it is the Father that He partakes; for this only remains to say. But this, which is participated, what is it or whence? If it be something external provided by the Father, He will not now be partaker of the Father, but of what is external to Him; and no longer will He be even second after the Father, since He has before Him this other; nor can He be called Son of the Father, but of that, as partaking which He has been called Son and God. And if this be unseemly and irreligious, when the Father says, 'This is My Beloved Son' [Matt. 3.17], and when the Son says that God is His own Father, it follows that what is partaken is not external, but from the essence of the Father. And as to this again, if it be other than the essence of the Son, an equal extravagance will meet us; there being in that case something between this that is from the Father and the essence of the Son, whatever that be.

16. Such thoughts then being evidently unseemly and untrue, we are driven to say that what is from the essence of the Father, and proper to Him, is entirely the Son; for it is all one to say that God is wholly participated, and that He begets; and what does begetting signify but a Son? And thus of the Son Himself, all things partake according to the grace of the Spirit coming from Him; and this shows that the Son Himself partakes of nothing, but what is partaken from the Father, is the Son; for, as partaking of the Son Himself, we are said to partake of God; and this is what Peter said 'that ye may be partakers in a divine nature' [2 Peter 1.4]; as says too the Apostle, 'Know ye not, that ye are a temple of God?' and, 'We are the temple of a living God' [1 Cor. 3.16; 2 Cor. 6.16]. And beholding the Son, we see the Father; for the thought and comprehension of the Son, is knowledge concerning the Father, because He is His proper offspring from His essence. And since to be partaken no one of us would ever call affection or division of God's essence (for it has been shown and acknowledged that God is participated, and to be participated is the same thing as to beget); therefore that which is begotten is neither affection nor division of that blessed essence. Hence it is not incredible that God should have a Son, the Offspring of His own essence; nor do we imply affection or division of God's essence, when we speak of 'Son' and 'Offspring;' but rather, as acknowledging the genuine, and true, and Only-begotten of God, so we believe. If then, as we have stated and are showing, what is the Offspring of the Father's essence be the Son, we cannot hesitate, rather we must be certain,

that the same is the Wisdom and Word of the Father, in and through whom He creates and makes all things; and His Brightness too, in whom He enlightens all things, and is revealed to whom He will; and His Expression and Image also, in whom He is contemplated and known, wherefore 'He and His Father are one' [John 10.30], and whoso looketh on Him looketh on the Father; and the Christ, in whom all things are redeemed, and the new creation wrought afresh. And on the other hand, the Son being such Offspring, it is not fitting, rather it is full of peril, to say, that He is a work out of nothing, or that He was not before His generation. For he who thus speaks of that which is proper to the Father's essence, already blasphemes the Father Himself; since he really thinks of Him what he falsely imagines of His offspring.

Source: Athanasius, First Discourse Against the Arians, *trans. John Henry Newman and Archibald Robertson, in Philip Schaff and Henry Wace (eds),* Nicene and Post-Nicene Fathers, *second series, vol. 4, Buffalo, NY: Christian Literature Publishing Co., 1892.*

4.5 Apollinarius, from *The Teaching of Apollinarius*

In The Teaching of Apollinarius, *the Bishop of Laodicea accounts for the mystery of the incarnation by denying that Jesus was both fully man and fully God, and claiming that in Jesus God commingled with human flesh.*

If God had been conjoined with man, i.e. perfect God with perfect man, there would be two, one Son of God by nature, the other by adoption.

The supreme point in our salvation is the incarnation of the Word. We believe therefore that with no change in his Godhead, the incarnation of the Word took place for the renewal of man. For neither change nor shifting nor circumspection took place in spirit with respect to the power of God, but the power remained the same and accomplished the work of incarnation for the salvation of the world, and the Word of God having had this citizenship on earth in the human sphere maintained likewise his divine presence over all things, having filled all things and commingled with the flesh in a way peculiar to himself, and in the occurrence of the sufferings of the flesh, the (divine) power preserved its own impassibility.

...

And since certain have troubled us, seeking to upset our faith toward our Lord Jesus the Christ, not confessing him God incarnate, but a man conjoined with God, we therefore make confession about the aforesaid faith and drive away their faithless disputation. For God incarnate in human flesh preserves his own activity unimpaired, being Mind that cannot be overcome by passions of the soul and of flesh, but maintaining the flesh and the affection of the flesh in a Godlike way and without sin, not only being unconquerable by death, but abolishing death. And he is true God, that is without flesh, revealed in flesh, perfect in his true and divine perfection, not two persons or two natures.

...

We confess that the Word of God has not descended upon a holy man, a thing which happened in the case of the prophets, but that the Word himself has become flesh without having assumed a human mind, i.e. a mind changeable and enslaved to filthy thoughts, but existing as a divine mind immutable and heavenly.

Source: Apollinarius, The Teaching of Apollinarius, *in J. Stevenson (ed.),* Creeds, Councils and Controversies, *London: SPCK, 1987, pp. 95–6.*

4.6 Gregory of Nazianzus, from *Criticisms of Apollinarius*

In his Criticisms of Apollinarius, *Gregory of Nazianzus argues that in order to redeem the human race Christ must have been fully human. The discussion here begins with whether Mary can properly be called Mother of God – Theotokos – and continues with an explanation of why the one Son must be understood as both divine and human.*

Do not let the men deceive themselves and others with the assertion that the 'Man of the Lord', as they call him, who is rather our Lord and God, is without human mind. For we do not serve the Man from the Godhead, but we lay down as a dogma the unity and identity of Person, who of old was not man but God, and the only Son before all ages, unmingled with body or anything corporeal; but who, in all these last days, has assumed manhood also for our salvation; passible in his flesh, impassible in his Godhead; circumscribed in the body, uncircumscribed in the Spirit; at once earthly and heavenly, tangible and intangible, comprehensible and incomprehensible; that by one and the same Person, complete man and also God, the complete man, fallen through sin, might be created anew.

If anyone does not believe that holy Mary is *Theotokos*, he is severed from the Godhead. If any one should assert that he passed through the Virgin as through a channel, and was not at once divinely and humanly formed in her (divinely, because without the intervention of a man; humanly, because in accordance with the laws of gestation), he is in like manner godless. If any assert that the manhood was formed, and that afterwards God insinuated himself into the manhood, he is to be condemned. For this is not a generation of God, but a shirking of generation. If any introduce the notion of two sons, one of God the Father, the other of the mother, and discredits the unity and identity, may he lose his part in the adoption promised to those who believe aright. For God and man are two natures, as also soul and body are; but there are not two Sons or two Gods. For neither in this life are there two manhoods; though Paul speaks in some such language of the inner and the outer man. And (if I am to speak concisely) the Saviour is made of elements which are distinct from one another (for the invisible is not the same as the visible, nor the timeless as that which is subject to time), yet he is not two. God forbid! For both are one by the combination, the Deity being made man and the manhood deified, or however one should express it. And I say different elements, because it is the reverse of what is the case in the Trinity; for there we acknowledge different Persons so as not to confound the *Hypostases*; but not different elements, for the Three are one and the same in Godhead.

...

If anyone has not put his trust in him as a man without a human mind, he is really bereft of mind and quite unworthy of salvation. For that which he has not assumed, he has not healed; but that which is united to his Godhead, is also saved. If only half Adam fell then that which Christ assumes and saves may be half also; but if the whole of Adam fell, he must be united to the whole nature of him that was begotten, and so be saved as a whole. Let them not then begrudge us our complete salvation, or clothe the Saviour only with bones and nerves and the portraiture of man. For if his manhood is without soul, even the Arians admit this, that they may attribute his passion to the Godhead, as that which gives motion to the body is also that which suffers. But if he has a soul, and yet is without a mind, how is he man? For man is not a mindless animal. And this would necessarily involve that while his form and tabernacle was human, his soul should be that of a horse or an ox, or some other of the brute creation. This, then would also be what it saved; and I have been deceived by the Truth, and led to boast of an honour which had been bestowed upon another. But if his manhood is intellectual, and not without mind, let them cease to be thus really mindless.

But says such an one, the Godhead took the place of the human intellect. How does this touch me? For Godhead joined to flesh alone is not man, nor to soul alone, nor to both apart from intellect, which is the most essential part of man. Keep then the whole man, and mingle Godhead therewith, that you may benefit me in my completeness.

But he asserts, he could not contain two complete natures. Not if you only look at him in a bodily fashion. For a bushel measure will not hold two bushels, nor will the space of one body hold two or more bodies. But if you will look at what is mental and incorporeal, remember that I in my one personality can contain soul and reason and mind and the Holy Spirit; and before me, this world, by which I mean the system of things visible and invisible, contained Father, Son and Holy Ghost. For such is the nature of intellectual existences that they can mingle with one another and with bodies, incoporeally and invisibly. For many sounds are comprehended by one ear; and the eyes of many are occupied by the same visible objects, and the smell by odours; nor are the senses narrowed by each other, nor crowded out, nor the objects of sense diminished by the multitude of the perceptions.

Source: Gregory of Nazianzus, Criticisms of Apollinarius, *in J. Stevenson (ed.),* Creeds, Councils and Controversies, *London: SPCK, 1987, pp. 97–100.*

4.7 Gregory of Nyssa, from *Address on Religious Instruction*

In his Address on Religious Instruction, *Gregory of Nyssa discusses some objections to the claim that Jesus is God and man.*

One who has followed the course of our argument up to this point will probably agree with it, since we do not appear to have said anything unbefitting a right conception of God. He will not, however, take a similar view of what follows, although it substantiates the revelation of the truth in a special way. I refer to the human birth, the advance from infancy to manhood, the eating and drinking, the weariness, the sleep, the grief, the tears, the false accusations, the trial, the cross, the death, and the putting in the tomb. For these facts included as they are in the revelation, in some way blunt the faith of little minds, so that they do not accept the sequel of our argument because of what precedes. Owing to the unworthiness connected with the death, they do not admit that the resurrection from the dead was worthy of God.

For myself, however, I think we must for a moment divert our thoughts from the coarseness of the flesh, and consider what real goodness and its contrary are, and by what distinctive marks each is known. For I imagine that no one who has seriously thought about it will gainsay that one thing alone in the universe is by nature shameful, viz., the malady of evil, while no shame at all attaches to what is alien to evil. What is unmixed with shame is certainly understood to be comprised in the good, and what is genuinely good is unmixed with its opposite.

Now everything we see included in the good is fitting to God. In consequence, either our opponents must show that the birth, the upbringing, the growth, the natural advance to maturity, the experience of death and the return from it are evil. Or else, if they concede that these things fall outside the category of evil, they must of necessity acknowledge there is nothing shameful in what is alien to evil. Since we have shown that what is good is altogether free from all shame and evil, must we not pity the stupidity of those who claim that the good is unbefitting to God?

10. But, they object, is not human nature paltry and circumscribed, while Deity is infinite? How, then, could the infinite be contained in an atom? But who claims that the infinity of the Godhead was contained within the limits of the flesh as in a jar? For in our own case the intellectual nature is not enclosed in the limits of the flesh. The body's bulk, to be sure, is circumscribed by its particular parts, but the soul is free to embrace the whole creation by the movement of thought. It ascends to the heavens, sets foot in the depths, traverses the dimensions of the world, and in its constant activity makes its way to the underworld. Often it is involved in contemplating the marvels of the heavens, and it is not loaded down by being attached to the body.

If, then, the soul of man, although united to the body by natural necessity, is free to roam everywhere, why do we have to say that the Godhead is confined in a fleshly nature? Why should we not rather rely on examples we can understand, in order to form some sort of proper conception of God's plan of salvation? To illustrate: We see the flame of a lamp laying hold of the material which feeds it. Now reason distinguishes between the flame on the material, and the material which kindles the flame, though we cannot actually divorce the one from the other and point out the flame as something separate from the material. The two together form a single whole. So it is with the incarnation. (My illustration must not be pressed beyond the point where it is appropriate. What is incongruous must be omitted, and the perishable character of fire must not be taken as part of the example.) Just, then, as we see the flame hugging the material and yet not encased in it, what prevents us from conceiving of a similar union and connection of the divine nature with the human? Can we not preserve a right idea of God even when we hold to this connection, by believing that the divine is free from all circumscription despite the fact he is in man?

11. If you inquire how the Deity is united with human nature, it is appropriate for you first to ask in what way the soul is united to the body. If the manner in which your soul is joined to your body is a mystery, you must certainly not imagine this former question is within your grasp. In the one case, while we believe the soul to be something different from the body because on leaving the flesh it renders it dead and inactive, we are ignorant of the manner of the union. Similarly in the other case we realize that the divine nature by its greater majesty differs from that which is mortal and perishable; but we are unable to detect how the divine is mingled with the human. Yet we have no doubt, from the recorded miracles, that God underwent birth in human nature. But *how* this happened we decline to investigate as a matter beyond the scope of reason. While we believe that the corporeal and intelligent creation owes its being to the incorporeal and uncreated nature, our faith in this regard does not involve an examination of the source and manner of this. The fact of creation we accept; but we renounce a curious investigation of the way the universe was framed as a matter altogether ineffable and inexplicable.

Source: Gregory of Nyssa, Address on Religious Instruction, *in Edward Rochie Hardy in collaboration with Cyril Charles Richardson*, Christology of the Later Fathers, *Philadelphia: Westminster Press, 1977, pp. 286–8.*

4.8 Cyril of Alexandria, from *Second Letter to Nestorius*

The Second Letter of Cyril to Nestorius *was declared by the Council of Ephesus to be in agreement with Nicaea. Cyril explains what is meant by the phrase 'the Word became flesh'.*

The holy and great synod, therefore, stated that the 'only begotten Son, begotten of God the Father according to nature, true God from true God, the light from the light, the one through whom the Father made all things, came down, became incarnate, became man, suffered, rose on the third day and ascended to heaven.' We too ought to follow these words and these teachings and consider what is meant by saying that the Word from God took flesh and became man.

For we do not say that the *nature* of the Word was changed and became flesh, nor that he was turned into a whole man made of body and soul. Rather do we claim that the Word in an unspeakable, inconceivable manner united to himself hypostatically flesh enlivened by a rational soul, and so became man and was called son of man, not by God's will alone or good pleasure, nor by the assumption of a person alone. Rather did two different natures come together to form a unity, and from both arose one Christ, one Son. It was not as though the distinctness of the natures was destroyed by the union, but divinity and humanity together made perfect for us one Lord and one Christ, together marvellously and mysteriously combining to form a unity. So he who existed and was begotten of the Father before all ages is also said to have been begotten according to the flesh of a woman, without the divine nature either beginning to exist in the holy virgin, or needing of itself a second begetting after that from his Father. (For it is absurd and stupid to speak of the one who existed before every age and is coeternal with the Father, needing a second beginning so as to exist.) The Word is said to have been begotten according to the flesh, because for us and for our salvation he united what was human to himself hypostatically and came forth from a woman. For he was not first begotten of the holy virgin, a man like us, and then the Word descended upon him; but from the very womb of his mother he was so united and then underwent begetting according to the flesh, making his own the begetting of his own flesh.

In a similar way we say that he suffered and rose again, not that the Word of God suffered blows or piercing with nails or any other wounds in his own nature (for the divine, being without a body, is incapable of suffering), but because the body which became his own suffered these things, he is said to have suffered them for us. For he was without suffering, while his body suffered. Something similar is true of his dying. For by nature the Word of God is of itself immortal and incorruptible and life and life-giving, but since on the other hand his own body by God's grace, as the apostle says, tasted death for all, the Word is said to have suffered death for us, not as if he himself had experienced death as far as his own nature was concerned (it would be sheer lunacy to say or to think that), but because, as I have just said, his flesh tasted death. So too, when his flesh was raised to life, we refer to this again as his resurrection, not as though he had fallen into corruption – God forbid – but because his body had been raised again.

So we shall confess one Christ and one Lord. We do not adore the man along with the Word, so as to avoid any appearance of division by using the word 'with'. But we adore him as one and the same, because the body is not other than the Word, and takes its seat with him beside the Father, again not as though there were two sons seated together but only one, united with his own flesh. If, however, we reject the hypostatic union as being either impossible or too unlovely for the Word, we fall into the fallacy of speaking of two sons. We shall have to distinguish and speak both of the man as honoured with the title of son, and of the Word of God as by nature possessing the name and reality of sonship, each in his own way. We ought not, therefore, to split into two sons the one Lord Jesus Christ. Such a way of presenting a correct account of the faith will be quite unhelpful, even though some do speak of a union of persons. For scripture does not say that the Word united the person of a man to himself, but that he became flesh. The Word's becoming flesh means nothing else than that he partook of flesh and blood like us; he made our body his own, and came forth a man from woman without casting aside his deity, or his generation from God the Father, but rather in his assumption of flesh remaining what he was.

This is the account of the true faith everywhere professed. So shall we find that the holy fathers believed. So have they dared to call the holy virgin, *Theotokos*, not as though the nature of the Word or his godhead received the origin of their being from the holy virgin, but because there was born from her his holy body rationally ensouled, with which the Word was hypostatically united and is said to have been begotten in the flesh.

Source: Second Letter of Cyril to Nestorius, *from http://www.dailycatholic.org/history/ 3ecumen1.htm#Second%20letter%20of%20Cyril%20to%20Nestorius.*

4.9 Nestorius, from *Second Letter to Cyril*

In his Second Letter to Cyril, *which was condemned by the Council of Ephesus in* AD *431, Nestorius argues for a distinction between the human Jesus and the second person of the Godhead.*

'The holy and great synod states that the only begotten Son, begotten of God the Father according to nature, true God from true God, the light from the light, the one through whom the Father made all things, came down, became incarnate, became man, suffered, rose.'

These are the words of your reverence and you may recognise them. Now listen to what we say, which takes the form of a brotherly exhortation to piety of the type of which the great apostle Paul gave an example in addressing his beloved Timothy: 'Attend to the public reading of scripture, to preaching, to teaching. For by so doing you will save both yourself and your hearers' [1 Tim. 4.16]. Tell me, what does 'attend' mean? By reading in a superficial way the tradition of those holy men (you were guilty of a pardonable ignorance), you concluded that they said that the Word who is coeternal with the Father was passible. Please look more closely at their language and you will find out that that divine choir of fathers never said that the consubstantial godhead was capable of suffering, or that the whole being that was coeternal with the Father was recently born, or that it rose again, seeing that it had itself been the cause of resurrection of the destroyed temple. If you apply my words as fraternal medicine, I shall set the words of the holy fathers before you and shall free them from the slander against them and through them against the holy scriptures.

'I believe', they say, 'also in our Lord Jesus Christ, his only begotten Son'. See how they first lay as foundations 'Lord' and 'Jesus' and 'Christ' and 'only begotten' and 'Son', the names which belong jointly to the divinity and humanity. Then they build on that foundation the tradition of the incarnation and resurrection and passion. In this way, by prefixing the names which are common to each nature, they intend to avoid separating expressions applicable to sonship and lordship and at the same time escape the danger of destroying the distinctive character of the natures by absorbing them into the one title of 'Son'. In this Paul was their teacher who, when he remembers the divine becoming man and then wishes to introduce the suffering, first mentions 'Christ', which, as I have just said, is the common name of both natures and then adds an expression which is appropriate to both of the natures. For what does he say? 'Have this mind among yourselves, which is yours in Christ Jesus who though he was in the form of God, did not count equality with God a thing to be grasped' [Phil. 2.5–6], and so on until, 'he became obedient unto death, even death on a cross'. For when he was about to mention the death, to prevent anyone supposing that God the Word suffered, he says 'Christ', which is a title that expresses in one person both the impassible and the passible natures, in order that Christ might be called without impropriety both impassible and passible, impassible in godhead, passible in the nature of his body.

...

I applaud your division of natures into manhood and godhead and their conjunction in one person. I also applaud your statement that God the Word needed no second generation from a woman, and your confession that the godhead is incapable of suffering. Such statements are truly orthodox and equally opposed to the evil opinions of all heretics about the Lord's natures. If the remainder was an attempt to introduce some hidden and incomprehensible wisdom to the ears of the readers, it is for your sharpness to decide. In my view these subsequent views seemed to subvert what came first. They suggested that he who had at the beginning been proclaimed as impassible and incapable of a second generation had somehow become capable of suffering and freshly created, as though what belonged to God the Word by nature had been destroyed by his conjunction with his temple or as though people considered it not enough that the sinless temple, which is inseparable from the divine nature, should have endured birth and death for sinners, or finally as though the Lord's voice was not deserving of credence when it cried out to the Jews: 'Destroy this temple and in three days I will raise it up' [John 2.19]. He did not say, 'Destroy my godhead and in three days it will be raised up.'

Again I should like to expand on this but am restrained by the memory of my promise. I must speak therefore but with brevity. Holy scripture, wherever it recalls the Lord's economy, speaks of the birth and suffering not of the godhead but of the humanity of Christ, so that the holy virgin is more accurately termed mother of Christ than mother of God. Hear these words that the gospels proclaim: 'The book of the generation of Jesus Christ, son of David, son of Abraham' [Matt. 1.1]. It is clear that God the Word was not the son of David. Listen to another witness if you will: 'Jacob begat Joseph, the husband of Mary, of whom was born Jesus, who is called the Christ' [Matt. 1.16]. Consider a further piece of evidence: 'Now the birth of Jesus Christ took place in this way. When his mother Mary had been betrothed to Joseph, she was found to be with child of the holy Spirit' [Matt. 1.18]. But who would ever consider that the godhead of the only begotten was a creature of the Spirit? Why do we need to mention: 'the mother of Jesus was there'? And again what of: 'with Mary the mother of Jesus'; or 'that which is conceived in her is of the holy Spirit'; and 'Take the child and his mother and flee to Egypt'; and 'concerning his Son, who was born of the seed of David according to the flesh'? Again, scripture says when speaking of his passion: 'God sending his own Son in the likeness of sinful flesh and for sin, he condemned sin in the flesh'; and again 'Christ died for our sins' and 'Christ having suffered in the flesh'; and 'This is', not 'my godhead', but 'my body, broken for you'.

Ten thousand other expressions witness to the human race that they should not think that it was the godhead of the Son that was recently killed but the flesh which was joined to the nature of the godhead. (Hence also Christ calls himself the lord and son of David: '"What do you think of the Christ? Whose son is he?" They said to him, "The son of David." Jesus answered and said to them, "How is it then that David inspired by the Spirit, calls him Lord, saying, 'The Lord said to my Lord, sit at my right hand [Matt. 22.42]'?"' He said this as being indeed son of David according to the flesh, but his Lord according to his godhead.) The body therefore is the temple of the deity of the Son, a temple which is united to it in a high and divine conjunction, so that the divine nature accepts what belongs to the body as its own. Such a confession is noble and worthy of the gospel traditions. But to use the expression 'accept as its own' as a way of diminishing the properties of the conjoined flesh, birth, suffering and entombment, is a mark of those whose minds are led astray, my brother, by Greek thinking or are sick with the lunacy of Apollinarius and Arius or the other heresies or rather something more serious than these.

For it is necessary for such as are attracted by the name 'propriety' to make God the Word share, because of this same propriety, in being fed on milk, in gradual growth, in terror at the time of his passion and in need of angelical assistance. I make no mention of circumcision and sacrifice and sweat and hunger, which all belong to the flesh and are adorable as having taken place for our sake. But it would be false to apply such ideas to the deity and would involve us in just accusation because of our calumny.

Source: Second Letter of Nestorius to Cyril, *from http://www.dailycatholic.org/history/ 3ecumen1.htm#Second%20letter%20of%20Nestorius%20to%20Cyril.*

4.10 The Chalcedonian Definition of Faith (451)

The Chalcedonian Definition of Faith affirms and expands upon the statements agreed upon at Nicaea and Constantinople and further confirms that there is only one Son, the Lord Jesus Christ.

For [the Council of Constantinople] opposes those who try to divide the mystery of the dispensation into a dyad of Sons; and those who dare to say that the Godhead of the only-begotten is passible it expels away from the company of the priests; and it resists those who think of a mixture or confusion of the two natures of Christ; and it drives away those who fancy that the form of a servant which he took of us was of a heavenly or some other substance; and those who imagine two natures of the Lord before the union but invent one after the union it anathematizes.

Following therefore the holy Fathers, we confess one and the same our Lord Jesus Christ, and we all teach harmoniously [that he is] the same perfect in Godhead, the same perfect in manhood, truly God and truly man, the same of a reasonable soul and body; consubstantial with the Father in Godhead, and the same consubstantial with us in manhood like us in all things except sin; begotten before ages of the Father in Godhead, the same in the last days for us; and for our salvation [born] of Mary the virgin *theotokos* in manhood, one and the same Christ, Son, Lord, unique, acknowledged in two natures without confusion, without change, without division, without separation – the difference of the natures being by no means taken away because of the union, but rather the distinctive character of each nature being preserved, and [each] combining in one Person and *hypostasis* – not divided or separated into two Persons, but one and the same Son and only-begotten God, Word, Lord Jesus Christ; as the prophets of old and the Lord Jesus Christ himself taught us about him, and the symbol of the Fathers has handed down to us.

Source: The Chalcedonian Decree, *in Edward Rochie Hardy in collaboration with Cyril Charles Richardson,* Christology of the Later Fathers, *Philadelphia: Westminster Press, 1977, pp. 372–4.*

4.11 Pope Vigilius, from *Letter to Eutychius of Constantinople*

In Pope Vigilius' Letter to Eutychius of Constantinople *he condemns those who argue that Christ is two persons.*

As a result of this investigation it became evident that in the sayings of Theodore of Mopsuestia (which are spoken against on all hands) there are contained very many things contrary to the right faith and to the teachings of the holy Fathers; and for this very reason these same holy Fathers have left for the instruction of the Church treatises which they had written against him.

For among other blasphemies of his we find that he openly said that God the Word was one [Person] and Christ another [Person], vexed with the passions of the soul and with the desires of the flesh, and that he little by little advanced from a lower to a higher stage of excellence by the improvement of his works, and became irreprehensible in his manner of life. And further he taught that it was a mere man who was baptized in the Name of the Father and of the Son and of the Holy Ghost, and that he received through his baptism the grace of the Holy Spirit, and merited his adoption; and therefore that Christ could be venerated in the same way that the image of the Emperor is venerated as being the persona of God the Word. And he also taught that [only] after his resurrection he became immutable in his thoughts and altogether impeccable.

Moreover he said that the union of the Word of God was made with Christ as the Apostle says the union is made between a man and his wife: They twain shall be one flesh; and that after his resurrection, when the Lord breathed upon his disciples and said, Receive the Holy Ghost, he did not give to them the Holy Spirit. In like strain of profanity he dared to say that the confession which Thomas made, when he touched the hands and side of the Lord after his resurrection, saying, My Lord and my God, did not apply to Christ (for Theodore did not acknowledge Christ to be God); but that Thomas gave glory to God being filled with wonder at the miracle of the resurrection, and so said these words.

But what is still worse is this, that in interpreting the Acts of the Apostles, Theodore makes Christ like to Plato, and Manichaeus, and Epicurus, and Marcian, saying: Just as each of these were the authors of their own peculiar teachings, and called their disciples after their own names, Platonists, and Manichaeans, and Epicureans, and Marcionites, just so Christ invented dogmas and called his followers Christians after himself.

Let therefore the whole Catholic Church know that justly and irreproachably we have arrived at the conclusions contained in this our constitution. Wherefore we condemn and anathematize Theodore, formerly bishop of Mopsuestia, and his impious writings, together with all other heretics, who (as is manifest) have been condemned and anathematized by the four holy Synods aforesaid, and by the Catholic Church: also the writings of Theodoret which are opposed to the right faith, and are against the Twelve Chapters of

St. Cyril, and against the first Council of Ephesus, which were written by him in defence of Theodore and Nestorius.

Source: Pope Vigilius, Letter to Eutychius of Constantinople, *trans. Henry Percival, in* Philip Schaff and Henry Wace (eds), Nicene and Post-Nicene Fathers, *second series, vol. 14, Buffalo, NY: Christian Literature Publishing Co., 1900.*

4.12 The Anathemas of the Second Council of Constantinople

The Second Council at Constantinople took place in 553. The extracts from the Council's statements included here affirm the Chalcedonian understanding of Christ, and define even further what is the Christian understanding of the person of Christ.

I. If anyone does not confess that the Father and the Son and the Holy Spirit are one nature or essence, one power or authority, worshipped as a trinity of the same essence, one deity in three hypostases or persons, let him be anathema. For there is one God and Father, of whom are all things, and one Lord Jesus Christ, through whom are all things, and one Holy Spirit, in whom are all things.

II. If anyone does not confess that God the Word was twice begotten, the first before all time from the Father, non-temporal and bodiless, the other in the last days when he came down from the heavens and was incarnate by the holy, glorious, God-bearer, ever-virgin Mary, and born of her, let him be anathema.

III. If anyone says that God the Word who performed miracles is one and Christ who suffered is another, or says that God the Word was together with Christ who came from woman, or that the Word was in him as one person is in another, but is not one and the same, our Lord Jesus Christ, the Word of God, incarnate and become human, and that the wonders and the suffering which he voluntarily endured in flesh were not of the same person, let him be anathema.

IV. If anyone says that the union of the Word of God with man was only according to grace or function or dignity or equality of honour or authority or relation or effect or power or according to his good pleasure, as though God the Word was pleased with man, or approved of him, as the raving Theodosius says; or that the union exists according to similarity of name, by which the Nestorians call God the Word Jesus and Christ, designating the man separately as Christ and as Son, speaking thus clearly of two persons, but when it comes to his honour, dignity, and worship, pretend to say that there is one person, one Son and one Christ, by a single designation; and if he does not acknowledge, as the holy Fathers have taught, that the union of God is made with the flesh animated by a reasonable and intelligent soul, and that such union is according to synthesis or hypostasis, and that therefore there is only one person, the Lord Jesus Christ one of the holy Trinity – let him be anathema. As the word 'union' has many meanings, the followers of the impiety of Apollinaris and Eutyches, assuming the disappearance of the natures, affirm a union by confusion. On the other hand the followers of Theodore and of Nestorius rejoicing in the division of the natures, introduce only a union of relation. But the holy Church of God, rejecting equally the impiety of both heresies, recognizes the union of God the Word with the flesh according to synthesis, that is according to hypostasis. For in the mystery of Christ the

135

union according to synthesis preserves the two natures which have combined without confusion and without separation.

...

VII. If anyone using the expression, 'in two natures,' does not confess that our one Lord Jesus Christ is made known in the deity and in the manhood, in order to indicate by that expression a difference of the natures of which the ineffable union took place without confusion, a union in which neither the nature of the Word has changed into that of the flesh, nor that of the flesh into that of the Word (for each remained what it was by nature, even when the union by hypostasis had taken place); but shall take the expression with regard to the mystery of Christ in a sense so as to divide the parties, let him be anathema. Or if anyone recognizing the number of natures in the same our one Lord Jesus Christ, God the Word incarnate, does not take in contemplation only the difference of the natures which compose him, which difference is not destroyed by the union between them – for one is composed of the two and the two are in one – but shall make use of the number two to divide the natures or to make of them persons properly so called, let him be anathema.

VIII. If anyone confesses that the union took place out of two natures or speaks of the one incarnate nature of God the Word and does not understand those expressions as the holy Fathers have taught, that out of the divine and human natures, when union by hypostasis took place, one Christ was formed; but from these expressions tries to introduce one nature or essence of the Godhead and manhood of Christ; let him be anathema. For in saying that the only-begotten Word was united by hypostasis personally we do not mean that there was a mutual confusion of natures, but rather we understand that the Word was united to the flesh, each nature remaining what it was. Therefore there is one Christ, God and man, of the same essence with the Father as touching his Godhead, and of the same essence with us as touching his manhood. Therefore the Church of God equally rejects and anathematizes those who divide or cut apart or who introduce confusion into the mystery of the divine dispensation of Christ.

IX. If anyone says that Christ ought to be worshipped in his two natures, in the sense that he introduces two adorations, the one peculiar to God the Word and the other peculiar to the man; or if anyone by destroying the flesh, or by confusing the Godhead and the humanity, or by contriving one nature or essence of those which were united and so worships Christ, and does not with one adoration worship God the Word incarnate with his own flesh, as the Church of God has received from the beginning; let him be anathema.

X. If anyone does not confess that our Lord Jesus Christ who was crucified in the flesh is true God and the Lord of Glory and one of the Holy Trinity; let him be anathema.

Source: http://www.reformed.org/documents/index.html?mainframe=http://www.reformed. org/documents/2_council_of_constan.html.

4.13 Bonaventure, from his *Commentary on Peter Lombard's Sentences*

In this extract, Bonaventure in his commentary on Peter Lombard's Sentences outlines some of the arguments given for why Christ should have assumed female rather than male flesh. He refutes these arguments by appeal to the Scriptures and to Aristotle.

Concerning the condition of the nature [assumed] according to gender.

QUESTION I

Whether it would have been fitting that God assume the womanly gender.
About the first it is thus proceeded and asked, whether it would have been fitting that God assume the womanly gender to repair the human race. And that [this is] so, it seems [from the following]:

1. Since the order of reparation should respond to that of the fall by opposites; but our ruin was through a woman: therefore [also should be its] relief. But the relief must be accomplished by the nature assumed ...

2. Likewise, for this reason did God assume a fragile nature, so that, while with His own fragility He might conquer the strong one, the power of God might shine forth wonderful in this: if therefore the gender of a woman is more fragile, it seems, that His power would have been more manifested, if in the womanly gender He had conquered the devil: therefore it was more suitable, that a woman rather than a man be assumed by the Word of God.

3. Likewise, the rational spirit is so indifferently unitable to the womanly gender, as to the manly one: therefore by equal reckoning also is the uncreated spirit: therefore the sexes of both are considered indifferently to union, in as much as it is on the part of the nature [assumed]. If therefore the gender of a woman had been more depressed in misery than that of a man; since the Son of God had become incarnate to relieve our misery, it seems, that it would have been more fitting that He assume the femine gender than the manly one.

4. Likewise, an offspring should be likened to its principle: but Christ was born from a Virgin mother alone: therefore if He drew [His] flesh from the woman, He should be likened to His mother more than to others: therefore if He did not become unlike His parent, He should rather draw from her [even] the gender, which the Virgin had, rather than another.

ON THE CONTRARY:

1. The Philosopher [Aristotle] says in his book On Animals, that 'a woman is a premature man,' that is an imperfect [man]: therefore if the human assumed should be the most perfect, it should not be a woman, but rather a masculine one.

2. Likewise, what is greater, the Apostle in the eleventh [chapter] of [his] First [Letter] to the Corinthians says, that the head of a woman is the man,

and not conversely; but the human assumed is the Head of the entire Church: therefore it should not be of the femine gender, lest otherwise there be a perversion of order; that indeed God should not do in His incarnation, so that He should rather repair the order [that has been] destroyed.

3. Likewise, the principle of all generation is the manly gender, for *from one* man *all* [were brought forth], but the human assumed should be the principle of all spiritual generation: not therefore of the womanly gender, but of the manly.

4. Likewise, if He had assumed the womanly gender, therefore when the *communicatio idiomatum* is undertaken, there should be said *goddess* and there should be said *daughter*: if therefore it is not fitting that there be but God and Son in that highest Trinity, not goddess nor daughter; in no manner was it fitting that God assume the woman.

CONCLUSION

Without doubt it would not have been so fitting that God assume the femine gender, as the manly one, into the unity of His Person.

I RESPOND: It must be said, that without doubt it would not have been as fitting that God assume the feminine gender, as the masculine, into the unity of His Person. And the reason for this is, since the womanly gender is not of such dignity, as is the manly. For the manly gender excels the womanly both according to *dignity of beginning*, and according to *virtue in acting*, and according to *authority in presiding*. According to *dignity in beginning*, since all, as much as men as women, were from one man, in whom is the express representation of the going-forth of things by that one First and Highest Principle.

According to *virtue in acting* it similarly overrules, since it belongs to a man *to act*, and it belongs to the woman *to endure*. Whence the manly gender has more of active virtue, on account of which it is even more robust both in reality [*res*] and in name [*nominatio*]. According to *authority in presiding* it even excels beforehand [*praeexcellit*]. For according to right order it is not the woman over the man, but the man who is appointed over the woman as head of the body, as the Apostle says.

Therefore since in the Word assuming a human nature there is a distinguished [*praecipua*] *dignity in beginning* and *a virtue in acting* and *a dominion in presiding*; hence it is, that it is more fitting, that the manly gender rather than the womanly be assumed by the uncreated Word, since those [perfections] of the assumed nature should have shared these three [perfections] in an excellent manner. And on that account the reasons in favour of this side must be conceded.

1. To that therefore which is at first objected to the contrary, that the ruin was through a woman; it must be said, that the strength in the womanly gender was our inchoate ruin, however in the manly gender it was consummated. And since our reparation had to be consummated in the assumed nature, hence it is, that according to a right correspondence it is more befitting, that a man be assumed than a woman.

2. To that which is objected concerning fragility, it must be said, that thus it

was suitable, that Christ conquer through fragility in suffering, so that soon He would conquer through virtue in resurrecting; and on that account He should have assumed such a gender, which would also be fragile in respect to time, on account of [its] quality of passibility, and nevertheless [also] ordainable [i.e. useful] in respect to virtue, according to the quality of [its] nature; and such was the manly gender rather than the womanly.

3. To that which is objected concerning the union of a rational spirit to either gender, it must be said, that it is not the same thing: *first*, since the spirit is united to the body, so that from these one thing be made, and there is no *communicatio idiomatum*; not so however concerning the eternal Word, who maintained His own property [of being], communicating to the assumed man His own properties [of being], to communicate which things the manly gender was more competent than the womanly. *Besides*, it is not the same thing, since the uncreated spirit is the most noble, and union, by which it unites Itself to our nature in its Person, is the most noble; and on that account It should assume the more noble gender. Not so, however, is it concerning the rational spirit.

4. To that which is objected, that the offspring should be assimilated to its principle; it must be said, that that is true, when it produces an offspring entirely according to its own virtue of its nature; not so, however, is it in the proposition. For the Virgin conceived, moved and aided by the Holy Spirit; and on that account the offspring had rather the gender, which the Holy Spirit chose, than the gender, which is found in the mother. Nor in such a generation is there a *becoming-unlike-one's-kind* (*degeneratio*), but rather an ennoblement; since it is not against the nature of a woman to conceive the manly gender, on the contrary the woman rather desires naturally to have a masculine son than a femine [daughter].

Source: Commentary on the Book of Sentences of Peter Lombard, from http://www. franciscan-archive.org/bonaventura/opera/bon03270.html.

4.14 Martin Luther, from his Disputation with Schwenkfeld

Martin Luther explains to Schwenkfeld that because of the communication of attributes what can be said of one nature of Christ can also be said of the other.

I

Argument: A human person is one thing, a divine person another. But in Christ there are both divinity and humanity. Therefore there are two persons in Christ.

Response: This is the fallacy of composition and division. In the major premise you divide the human nature and the divine; in the minor premise you join them. This is a philosophical solution; but we are speaking theologically. I deny the consequence, for this reason, that in Christ the humanity and the divinity constitute one person. But these two natures are distinct in theology, with respect, that is, to the natures, but not with respect to [*secundum*] the person. For then they are undivided [*indistinctae*], but two distinct natures, yet belonging to an undivided person [*indistinctae personae*]. There are not two distinct persons, but what is distinct is undivided [*sed sunt distinctae indistinctae*], that is, there are distinct natures, but an undivided person.

II

Argument: Christ was not a man before the creation of the world. Therefore it is not rightly said that the man Christ created the world. Or thus: When the world was created, Christ did not create it as a man [*tamquam homo*]. Therefore it is not rightly said that a man created the world.

Response: There is the communication of attributes; and moreover [this is] a philosophical argument. This stands: The natures are distinct, but after that communication, there is a union, that is, there is one person, not two persons. But that person is God and man, one and the same person, who was before the creation of the world; even though he was not man born of the Virgin Mary before the world, nonetheless he was the Son of God, who is now man. Thus, for example, when I see a king in purple and crowned on his throne, I say, 'This king was born of a woman, naked and without a crown.' How can this be, and yet he sits on a great throne crowned and clothed in purple? But these things he put on after he was made king, and yet nonetheless he is one and the same person; and so too here in Christ God and man are joined in one person and must not be distinguished. But it is true that Christ created the world before he was made man, and yet such a strict unity exists that it is impossible to say different things [of the divinity and the humanity]. Therefore whatever I say of Christ as man, I also say rightly of God, that he suffered, was crucified.

Objection: But God cannot be crucified or suffer.

Response: This is true, when he was not yet man. From eternity he has not suffered; but when he was made man, he was passible. From eternity he was not man; but now being conceived by the Holy Ghost, that is, born of the Virgin, God and man are made one person, and the same things are truly said of God and man [*sunt eadem praedicata Dei et hominis*]. Here the personal union is accomplished. Here the humanity and divinity are joined [*Da gehet's inein-ander humanitas et divinitas*]. The union holds everything together [*Die unitas, die helt's*]. I confess that there are two natures, but they cannot be separated. This is accomplished by the union [*unitas*], which is a greater and stronger union [*coniunctio*] than that of soul and body, because soul and body are separated, but never the immortal and divine nature and the mortal human nature [in Christ], but they are united in one person. That is to say, Christ, the impassible Son of God, God and man, was crucified under Pontius Pilate.

Source: Martin Luther, Disputation on the Divinity and Humanity of Christ, *from http:// www.intratext.com/IXT/ENG0192/_P4.HTM.*

4.15 Friedrich Daniel Ernst Schleiermacher, from *The Christian Faith*

Schleiermacher offers an account of the distinct identity of Jesus Christ.

§ 94. The Redeemer, then, is like all men in virtue of the identity of human nature, but distinguished from them all by the constant potency of His God-consciousness, which was a veritable existence of God in Him.

1. That the Redeemer should be entirely free from all sinfulness is no objection at all to the complete identity of human nature in Him and others, for we have already laid down that sin is so little an essential part of the being of man that we can never regard it as anything else than a disturbance of nature. It follows that the possibility of a sinless development is in itself not incongruous with the idea of human nature; indeed, this possibility is involved, and recognized, in the consciousness of sin as guilt, as that is universally understood. This likeness, however, is to be understood in such a general sense that even the first man before the first sin stood no nearer the Redeemer, and was like Him in no higher sense, than all other men. For if even in the life of the first man we must assume a time when sin had not yet appeared, yet every first appearance of sin leads back to a sinful preparation. But the Redeemer too shared in the same vicissitudes of life, without which we can hardly imagine the entrance of sin at a definite moment even in Adam, for they are essential to human nature. Furthermore, the first man was originally free from all the contagious influences of a sinful society, while the Redeemer had to enter into the corporate life when it had already advanced far in deterioration, so that it would hardly be possible to attribute His sinlessness to external protection – which we certainly must somehow admit in the case of the first man, if we would not involve ourselves in contradictions. Of the Redeemer, on the contrary, we must hold that the ground of His sinlessness was not external to Himself, but that it was a sinlessness essentially grounded in Himself, if He was to take away, through what He was in Himself, the sinfulness of the corporate life. Therefore, so far as sin is concerned, Christ differs no less from the first man than from all others.

The identity of human nature further involves this, that the manner in which Christ differs from all others also has its place in this identity. This would not be the case if it were not involved in human nature that individuals, so far as the measure of the different functions is concerned, are originally different from each other, so that to every separate corporate life (regarded in space as well as in time) there belong those who are more and less gifted; and we only arrive at the truth of life when we thus correlate those who differ from each other. In the same way, therefore, all those who in any respect give character to an age or a district are bound up with those over whom (as being defective in that particular respect) they extend an educative influence, even as Christ is bound up with those whom His preponderatingly powerful God-consciousness links to the corporate life thus indicated. The greater the difference, and the more specific the activity, the more must these also have established themselves against the hindering influences of a worthless environment, and they can be understood only by reference to this self-differentiating quality of human nature, not by reference to the group in which they stand; although by divine right they belong to it, as the Redeemer does to the whole race.

2. But in admitting that what is peculiar in the Redeemer's kind of activity belongs to a general aspect of human nature, we by no means wish to reduce this activity, and the personal dignity by which it is conditioned, to the same measure as that of others. The simple fact that faith in Christ postulates a relation on His part to the whole race, while everything analogous is valid only for definite individual times and places, is sufficient to prove this. For no one has yet succeeded, in any sphere of science or art, and no one will ever succeed, in establishing himself as head, universally animating and sufficient for the whole human race.

For this peculiar dignity of Christ, however, in the sense in which we have already referred back the ideality of His person to this spiritual function of the God-consciousness implanted in the self-consciousness, the terms of our proposition alone are adequate; for to ascribe to Christ an absolutely powerful God-consciousness, and to attribute to Him an existence of God in Him, are exactly the same thing. The expression, 'the existence of God in anyone,' can only express the relation of the omnipresence of God to this one. Now since God's existence can only be apprehended as pure activity, while every individualized existence is merely an inter-mingling of activity and passivity – the activity being always found apportioned to this passivity in every other individualized existence – there is, so far, no existence of God in any individual thing, but only an existence of God in the world. And only if the passive conditions are not purely passive, but mediated through vital receptivity, and this receptivity confronts the totality of finite existence (so far, *i.e.*, as we can say of the individual as a living creature that, in virtue of the universal reciprocity, it in itself represents the world), could we suppose an existence of God in it. Hence this clearly does not hold of what is individualized as an unconscious thing; for since an unconscious thing brings no living receptivity to meet all the forces of consciousness it cannot represent these forces in itself. But just as little and for the same reason can what is conscious but not intelligent represent them, so that it is only in the rational individual that an existence of God can be admitted. How far this is also true similarly and without distinction if we regard reason as functioning in objective consciousness lies outside our investigation. But so far as the rational self-consciousness is concerned, it is certain that the God-consciousness which (along with the self-consciousness) belongs to human nature originally, before the Redeemer and apart from all connexion with Him, cannot fittingly be called an existence of God in us, not only because it was not a pure God-consciousness (either in polytheism or even in Jewish monotheism, which was everywhere tinctured with materialistic conceptions, whether cruder or finer), but also because, such as it was, it did not assert itself as activity, but in these religions was always dominated by the sensuous self-consciousness. If, then, it was able neither to portray God purely and with real adequacy in thought, nor yet to exhibit itself as pure activity, it cannot be represented as an existence of God in us. But just as the unconscious forces of nature and non-rational life become a revelation of God

143

to us only so far as we bring that conception with us, so also that darkened and imperfect God-consciousness by itself is not an existence of God in human nature, but only in so far as we bring Christ with us in thought and relate it to Him. So that originally it is found nowhere but in Him, and He is the only 'other' in which there is an existence of God in the proper sense, so far, that is, as we posit the God-consciousness in His self-consciousness as continually and exclusively determining every moment, and consequently also this perfect indwelling of the Supreme Being as His peculiar being and His inmost self. Indeed, working backwards we must now say, if it is only through Him that the human God-consciousness becomes an existence of God in human nature, and only through the rational nature that the totality of finite powers can become an existence of God in the world, that in truth He alone mediates all existence of God in the world and all revelation of God through the world, in so far as He bears within Himself the whole new creation which contains and develops the potency of the God-consciousness.

Source: *Friedrich Daniel Ernst Schleiermacher,* The Christian Faith, *§ 94, trans. H. R. Mackintosh and J. S. Stewart, Edinburgh: T. & T. Clark, 1963, pp. 385–9.*

4.16 D. F. Strauss, from *The Life of Jesus Critically Examined*

In this extract Strauss argues in Hegelian fashion that it was not only in Christ that divinity and humanity were united, but that this is true for all humans.

§ 150 The Speculative Christology

Kant had already said that the good principle did not descend from heaven merely at a particular time, but had descended on mankind invisibly from the commencement of the human race; and Schelling laid down the proposition: the incarnation of God is an incarnation from eternity. But while the former understood under that expression only the oral instinct, which, with its ideal of good, and its sense of duty, has been from the beginning implanted in man; the latter understood under the incarnate Son of God the finite itself, in the form of the human consciousness, which in its contradistinction to the infinite, wherewith it is nevertheless one, appears as a suffering God, subjected to the conditions of time.

In the most recent philosophy this idea has been further developed in the following manner. When it is said of God that he is a Spirit, and of man that he also is a Spirit, it follows that the two are not essentially distinct. To speak more particularly, it is the essential property of a spirit, in the distribution of itself into distinct personalities, to remain identical with itself, to possess itself in another than itself. Hence the recognition of God as a spirit implies, that God does not remain as a fixed and immutable Infinite encompassing the Finite, but enters into it, produces the Finite, Nature, and the human mind, merely as a limited manifestation of himself, from which he eternally returns into unity. As man, considered as a finite spirit, limited to his finite nature, has not truth; so God, considered exclusively as an infinite spirit, shut up in his infinitude, has not reality. The infinite spirit is real only when it discloses itself in finite spirits; as the finite spirit is true only when it merges itself in the infinite. The true and real existence of spirit, therefore, is neither in God by himself, nor in man by himself, but in the God-man; neither in the infinite alone, nor in the finite alone, but in the interchange of impartation and withdrawal between the two, which on the part of God is revelation, on the part of man religion.

If God and man are in themselves *one*, and if religion is the human side of this unity: then must this unity be made evident to man in religion, and become in him consciousness and reality. Certainly, so long as man knows not that he is a spirit, he cannot know that God is man: while he is under the guidance of nature only, he will deify nature; when he has learned to submit himself to law, and thus to regulate his natural tendencies by external means, he will set God before him as a lawgiver. But when, in the vicissitudes of the world's history, the natural state discloses its corruptions, the legal its misery;

the former will experience the need of a God who elevates it above itself, the latter, of a God who descends to its level. Man being once mature enough to receive as his religion the truth that God is man, and man of a divine race; it necessarily follows; since religion is the form in which the truth presents itself to the popular mind, that this truth must appear, in a guise intelligible to all, as a fact obvious to the senses: in other words, there must appear a human individual who is recognised as the visible God. This God-man uniting in a single being the divine essence and the human personality, it may be said of him that he had the Divine Spirit for a father and a woman for his mother. His personality reflecting itself not in himself, but in the absolute substance, having the will to exist only for God, and not at all for itself, he is sinless and perfect ...

Does not the fact that the human nature is subject to death preclude the idea that that nature is one with the divine? No: the God-man dies, and thus proves that the incarnation of God is real, that the infinite spirit does not scorn to descend into the lowest depths of the finite, because he knows how to find a way of return into himself, because in the most entire alienation of himself, he can retain his identity. Further, the God-man, in so far as he is a spirit reflected in his infinity, stands contrasted with men, in so far as they are limited to their finiteness: hence opposition and contest result, and the death of the God-Man becomes a violent one, inflicted by the hands of sinners; so that to physical degradation is added the moral degradation of ignominy and accusation of crime. If God then finds a passage from heaven to the grave, so must a way be discoverable for man from the grave to heaven: the death of the prince of life is the life of mortals. By his entrance into the world as God-man, God showed himself reconciled to man; by his dying, in which act he cast off the limitations of mortality, he showed moreover the way in which he perpetually effects that reconciliation: namely, by remaining, throughout his manifestation of himself under the limitations of a natural existence, and, his suppression of that existence, identical with himself. Inasmuch as the death of the God-man is merely the cessation of his state of alienation from the infinite, it is in fact an exaltation and return to God, and thus the death is necessarily followed by the resurrection and ascension.

The God-man, who during his life stood before his contemporaries as an individual distinct from themselves, and perceptible by the senses, is by death taken out of their sight; he enters into their imagination and memory: the unity of the divine and human in him, becomes a part of the general consciousness; and the church must repeat spiritually, in the souls of its members, those events of his life which he experienced externally. The believer, finding himself environed with the conditions of nature, must, like Christ, die to nature – but only inwardly, as Christ did outwardly – must spiritually crucify himself and be buried with Christ, that by the virtual suppression of his own sensible existence, he may become, in so far as he is a spirit, identical with himself: and participate in the bliss and glory of Christ.

§ 151 The Last Dilemma

...

If reality is ascribed to the idea of the unity of the divine and human natures, is this equivalent to the admission that this unity must actually have been once manifested, as it never had been, and never more will be, in one individual? This is indeed not the mode in which Idea realizes itself; it is not wont to lavish all its fulness on one exemplar, and be niggardly towards all others – to express itself perfectly in that one individual, and imperfectly in all the rest: it rather loves to distribute its riches among a multiplicity of exemplars which reciprocally complete each other – in the alternate appearance and suppression of a series of individuals. And is this no true realization of the idea? Is not the idea of the unity of the divine and human natures a real one in a far higher sense, when I regard the whole race of mankind as its realization, than when I single out one man as such a realization? Is not an incarnation of God from eternity, a truer one than an incarnation limited to a particular point of time?

This is the key to the whole of Christology, that, as subject of the predicate which the church assigns to Christ, we place, instead of an individual, an idea; but an idea which has an existence in reality, not in the mind only, like that of Kant. In an individual, a God-man, the properties and functions which the church ascribes to Christ contradict themselves; in the idea of the race, they perfectly agree. Humanity is the union of the two natures – God become man, the infinite manifesting itself in the finite, and the finite spirit remembering its infinitude; it is the child of the visible Mother and the invisible Father, Nature and Spirit; it is the worker of miracles, in so far as in the course of human history the spirit more and more completely subjugates nature, both within and around man, until it lies before him as the inert matter on which he exercises his active power; it is the sinless existence, for the course of its development is a blameless one, pollution cleaves to the individual only, and does not touch the race or its history. It is Humanity that dies, rises, and ascends to heaven, for from the negation of its phenomenal life there ever proceeds a higher spiritual life; from the suppression of its mortality as a personal, national, and terrestrial spirit, arises its union with the infinite spirit of the heavens. By faith in this Christ, especially in his death and resurrection, man is justified before God; that is, by the kindling within him of the idea of Humanity, the individual man participates in the divinely human life of the species. Now the main element of that idea is, that the negation of the merely natural and sensual life, which is itself the negation of the spirit (the negation of negation, therefore), is the sole way to true spiritual life.

This alone is the absolute sense of Christology: that it is annexed to the person and history of one individual, is a necessary result of the historical form which Christology has taken ... But mind having once taken occasion by this external fact, to bring under its consciousness the idea of humanity as one with God, sees in the history only the presentation of that idea; the object of faith is completely changed; instead of a sensible, empirical fact, it has become a spiritual and divine idea, which has its confirmation no longer in history but in philosophy. When the mind has thus gone beyond the sensible history, and entered into the domain of the absolute, the former ceases to be essential; it takes a subordinate place, above which the spiritual truths suggested by the history stand self-supported; it becomes as the faint image of a dream which belongs only to the past, and does not, like the idea, share the permanence of the spirit which is absolutely present to itself.

Source: D. F. Strauss, The Life of Jesus Critically Examined, *§§150–1, New York: Calvin Blanchard, 1860, pp. 892–7.*

4.17   Martin Kähler, from *The So-Called Historical Jesus and the Historic, Biblical Christ*

In this passage, Kähler rejects both the search to find details of the life of the 'real' Jesus, and the emphasis on historical research. Rather, he suggests that what is important about the detail of Jesus' life is that it is through him that we can know God.

The Life-of-Jesus movement is completely in the right insofar as it sets the Bible against an abstract dogmatism. It becomes illegitimate as soon as it begins to rend and dissect the Bible without having acquired a clear understanding of the special nature of the problem and the peculiar significance of Scripture for such understanding. In other cases the problem is simply historical; here that is not so. The justification for the movement can be expressed in Luther's statement that we can never draw God's Son deep enough into our flesh, into our humanity. Every truly evangelical movement shares this point of view in reflecting upon our Savior – ever since John 1 and I John 1:1ff were written. But Luther's statement makes sense only if Christ is more than a mere man. It has no meaning at all for those who wish to maintain and demonstrate that he is of no more importance to us than any other significant figure of the past. This was not Luther's view, nor can it be ours, so long as we agree with the apostle that 'if you confess with your lips that Jesus is Lord, you will be saved' (Rom. 10:9). If we believe with Christian dogmatics in the Christ who is more than a mere man in his essence, his mission, and his present function – i.e., if we believe in the supra-historical Savior – then the historical Jesus acquires for us that incomparable worth that moves us to confess before the biblical picture of Jesus,

> My soul it shall refresh, my ear
> Can apprehend no tale more dear.

Every detail that we can learn about him becomes precious and meaningful for us. The tradition about him cannot be studied diligently and faithfully enough. Hence a person may immerse himself in Jesus' actions, trying to understand them and to trace them to their presuppositions. So he plumbs the depths of Jesus' consciousness and development before his public ministry; he accompanies the boy Jesus through ravines and fields. From his mother's bosom to his father's workshop and into the synagogue and then he is most certainly heading up a blind alley!

...

To substantiate such a negative verdict some scientific assertions must now be made which at first sight may seem startling: we do not possess any sources for a 'Life of Jesus' which a historian can accept as reliable and adequate. I repeat: we have no sources for a biography of Jesus of Nazareth which measure up to the standards of contemporary historical science. A trustworthy picture of the Savior for believers is a very different thing, and of this more will be said later. Our sources, that is, the Gospels, exist in such isolation that without them we would know nothing at all about Jesus, although the time and setting of his life are otherwise entirely clear to historians. He could be taken for a product of the church's fantasy around the year AD 100. Furthermore, these sources cannot be traced with certainty to eyewitnesses. In addition to this, they tell us only about the shortest and last period of his life. And finally, these sources appear in two basic forms whose variations must – in view of the proximity of the alleged or probable time of origin of these forms – awaken serious doubts about the faithfulness of the recollections. Consequently the 'unbiased' critic finds himself confronted by a vast field strewn with the fragments of various traditions. From these fragments he is called upon to conjure up a new shape if his task is to compose, according to modern requirements, a biography of this figure who looms up out of the mist. Even the task of establishing the external course of his life is fraught with serious difficulties – leaving us often with mere probabilities.

…

Obviously we would not deny that historical research can help to explain and clarify particular features of Jesus' actions and attitudes as well as many aspects of his teaching. Nor will I exaggerate the issue by casting doubt on the historian's capacity to trace the broad outlines of the historical institutions and forces which influenced the human development of our Lord. But it is common knowledge that all this is wholly insufficient for a biographical work in the modern sense. Such a work is never content with a modest retrospective analysis, for in reconstructing an obscure event in the past it also wishes to convince us that its *a posteriori* conclusions are accurate. The biographical method likes to treat that period in Jesus' life for which we have no sources and in particular seeks to explain the course of his spiritual development during his public ministry. To accomplish that something other than cautious analysis is required. Some outside force must rework the fragments of the tradition. This force is nothing other than the theologian's imagination – an imagination that has been shaped and nourished by the analogy of his own life and of human life in general. If, in other areas, the historian's muse often paints pictures which lack every breath of the past and its distinctive characteristics, what will it make of this unique material? The Gospels confront each of us with an Either/Or. The question is whether the historian will humble himself before the unique sinless Person – the only proper attitude in the presence of the norm of all morality.

…

This brings us to the crux of the matter: *Why* do we seek to know the figure of Jesus? I rather think it is because we believe him when he says, 'He who has seen me has seen the Father' (John 14:9), because we see in him the revelation of the invisible God. Now if the Word became flesh in Jesus, which is the revelation, the flesh or the Word? Which is the more important for us, that wherein Jesus is like us, or that wherein he was and is totally different from us? Is it not the latter, namely, that which he offers us, not from our own hearts, but from the heart of the living God? I do not want to be misunderstood. That he was like us is, of course, incomparably significant for us and is treasured by us; Scripture always emphasizes it, too, but hardly ever without adding expressions like 'without sin', 'by grace', 'in humility and perfect obedience', etc. (Hebrews 4:15; 7:26, 27; II Corinthians 8:9; Phil. 2:6ff.). How he was like us is self-evident. It is also fairly obvious why the evidence of his likeness to us is to be found on every page of the Gospels. And yet how we have to search to muster such a biblical proof from statements which deliberately emphasize that likeness. Does this not explain why we recognize the emphasis on Jesus' moral achievement as a distinguishing peculiarity of the Epistle to the Hebrews? (Cf. 2:17, 18; 4:15; 5:7ff., perhaps also 12:2, 3.) If a person really asks himself what he is looking for when he reads the Gospels, he will admit to himself, 'I am not seeking someone like myself, but rather my opposite, my fulfilment, my Savior.' When a person reflects on what he finds when reading the Gospels, he will say, 'No man has ever spoken or acted thus; never has such a man existed.' He will not say that no one has ever said the same things Jesus said. For Jesus repeated many things which religious thinkers had written and said prior to him – things which become different, however, when he says them. Nor will a reader of the Gospels maintain that everything Jesus did was unique, for he stands surrounded by a cloud of witnesses. And yet, there is something unique in the *way* he did things, for there has never been a man like him.

Why, in the final analysis, do we commune with the Jesus of our Gospels? What does he offer us? 'In him we have redemption through his blood, the forgiveness of our trespasses' (Eph. 1:7). Do I really need to know more of him than what Paul 'delivered to [the Corinthians] as of first importance, what [he] also received, that Christ died for our sins in accordance with the Scriptures, that he was buried, that he was raised on the third day in accordance with the Scriptures, and that he appeared' (I Corinthians 15:3f.)? This is the good news brought in the name of God (I Corinthians 15:12f.; Romans 1:1f.; II Corinthians 5:18f.; Galatians 1:6f.). This is the witness and confession of faith which has overcome the world (I John 5:4). If I have all this I do not need additional information on the precise details of Jesus' life and death.

Then why the Gospels? Why do we need that kind of preaching the content of which is, so often, what Jesus did and taught? We have redemption through *him*. 'Who is to condemn? Is it Christ Jesus, who died, yes, who was raised from the dead, who is at the right hand of God, who indeed intercedes for us?' (Rom. 8:34). 'We have an advocate with the Father, Jesus Christ the righteous' (I John 2:1). 'For we have not a high priest who is unable to sympathize with our weaknesses, but one who in every respect has been tempted as we are, yet without sinning' (Heb. 4:15). We need, we have, and we believe in the living Christ. We believe in him because we know him; we have him as we know him; we know him because he dwelt among us, full of grace and truth, and chose for himself witnesses through whose word we are to believe in him (John 1:13, 14; cf. John 1:1f.; John 15:27; 17:20).

Therefore, the reason we commune with the Jesus of our Gospels is because it is through them that we learn to know that same Jesus whom, with the eyes of faith and in our prayers, we meet at the right hand of God, because we know, with Luther, that God cannot be found except in his beloved Son, because he is God's revelation to us, or, more accurately and specifically, because he who once walked on earth and now is exalted is the incarnate Word of God, the image of the invisible God – because he is for us God revealed.

Source: Martin Kähler, The So-Called Historical Jesus and the Historic, Biblical Christ, *trans., ed. and with an introduction by Carl E. Braaten, Philadelphia: Fortress Press, 1964, pp. 46ff.*

4.18 Albert Schweitzer, from *Out of My Life and Thought*

Schweitzer also rejected the quest for the historical Jesus. However, he believed that the most important thing about Jesus is his teaching.

The ideal would be that Jesus should have preached religious truth in a form independent of any connexion with any particular period and such that it could be taken over simply and easily by each succeeding generation of men. That, however, He did not do, and there is no doubt a reason for it.

And so we must reconcile ourselves to the fact that Jesus' religion of love made its appearance as part of a system of thought that anticipated a speedy end of the world. We cannot make it our own through the concepts in which he proclaimed it but must rather translate it into those of our modern view of the world.

Hitherto we have been doing this ingenuously and covertly. In defiance of what the words of the text said we managed to interpret the teaching of Jesus as if it were in agreement with our own view of the world. Now, however, it must be clear to us that we can only harmonize these two things by an act, for which we claim the right of necessity.

We are obliged, that is, to admit the evident fact that religious truth varies from age to age.

How is this to be understood? So far as its essential spiritual and ethical nature is concerned, Christianity's religious truth remains the same through the centuries. The variations belong only to the outward form which it assumes in the ideas belonging to different world-views. Thus Jesus' religion of love which made its first appearance within the framework of late Jewish eschatological expectation, finds a place later on within the late-Greek, the medieval, and the modern views of the world. Nevertheless, it remains through the centuries what it is essentially. Whether it is worked out in terms of one system of thought or another is only a matter of relative importance. What is decisive is the amount of influence over mankind won by the spiritual and ethical truth which it has held from the very first.

We of to-day do not, like those who were able to hear the preaching of Jesus, expect to see a Kingdom of God realizing itself in supernatural events. Our conviction is that it can only come into existence by the power of the spirit of Jesus working in our hearts and in the world. The one important thing is that we shall be as thoroughly dominated by the idea of the Kingdom, as Jesus required His followers to be.

The mighty thought underlying the Beatitudes of the Sermon on the Mount, that we come to know God and belong to Him through love, Jesus introduces into the late-Jewish, Messianic expectation, without being in any way concerned to spiritualize those realistic ideas of the Kingdom of God and of blessedness. But the spirituality which lies in this religion of love must gradually, like a refiner's fire, seize upon all ideas which come into communication with it. Thus it is the destiny of Christianity to develop through a constant process of spiritualization.

Jesus never undertakes to expound the late-Jewish dogmas of the Messiah and the Kingdom. His concern is, not how believers ought to picture things but that love, without which no one can belong to God, and attain to membership of the Kingdom, shall be powerful within it. The subject of all His preaching is love, and, more generally, the preparation of the heart for the Kingdom. The Messianic dogma remains in the background. If He did not happen to mention it now and then, one could forget that it is presupposed all through. That explains why it was possible to overlook for so long the fact that His religion of love was conditioned by Time.

...

There is a deep significance in the fact that whenever we hear the sayings of Jesus we have to enter a realm of thought which is not ours. Our own affirmative attitude to the world and toward life threatens constantly to externalize Christianity. The Gospel of Jesus which speaks to us out of an expectation of the end of the world leads us off the highway of busy service for the Kingdom of God on to the footpath of inwardness, and urges us, in spiritual freedom from the world to seek true strength for working in the spirit of the Kingdom of God. The essence of Christianity is an affirmation of the world that has passed through a rejection of the world. Within a system of thought that rejects the world and anticipates its end Jesus sets up the ethic of active love!

Even if the historical Jesus has something strange about Him, yet His personality, as it really is, influences us much more strongly and immediately than when He approached us in dogma and in the results attained up to the present by research. In dogma His personality became less alive; recent research has been modernizing and belittling Him.

Anyone who ventures to look the historical Jesus straight in the face and to listen for what He may have to teach him in His powerful sayings, soon ceases to ask what this strange-seeming Jesus can still be to him. He learns to know Him as One who claims authority over him.

The true understanding of Jesus is the understanding of will acting on will. The true relation to Him is to be taken possession of by Him. Christian piety of any and every sort is valuable only so far as it means the surrender of our will to His.

Jesus does not require of men to-day that they be able to grasp either in speech or in thought Who He is. He did not think it necessary to give those who actually heard His sayings any insight into the secret of His personality, or to disclose to them the fact that He was that descendant of David who was one day to be revealed as the Messiah. The one thing He did require of them was that they should actively and passively prove themselves men who had been compelled by Him to rise from being as the world to being other than the world, and thereby partakers of His peace.

Because, while I was investigating and thinking about Jesus, all this became a certainty to me, I let my *Quest of the Historical Jesus* end with the words: 'As one unknown and nameless He comes to us, just as on the shore of the lake He approached those men who knew not who He was. His words are the same: "Follow thou Me!" and He puts us to the tasks which He has to carry out in our age. He commands. And to those who obey, be they wise or simple, He will reveal Himself through all that they are privileged to experience in His fellowship of peace and activity, of struggle and suffering, till they come to know, as an inexpressible secret, Who He is ...'

Source: Albert Schweitzer, Out of My Life and Thought: An Autobiography, *trans. C. T. Campion, New York, Henry Holt and Company, 1933, pp. 53–7.*

4.19 Dietrich Bonhoeffer, from *Christology*

In this extract Bonhoeffer argues that Christology can only be done in a context of worshipful silence, and not through historical research or philosophical speculation.

Teaching about Christ begins in silence. 'Be silent, for that is the absolute' (Kierkegaard). This has nothing to do with mystical silence which, in its absence of words, is, nevertheless, the soul secretly chattering away to itself. The church's silence is silence before the Word. In proclaiming the Word, the church must fall silent before the inexpressible: Let what cannot be spoken be worshipped in silence (Cyril of Alexandria). The spoken Word is the inexpressible: that which cannot be spoken is the Word. It must be spoken, it is the great battle cry of the church (Luther). The church utters it in the world, yet it still remains the inexpressible. To speak of Christ means to keep silent; to be silent about Christ means to speak. The proclamation of Christ is the church speaking from a proper silence.

We are concerned here with the meaning of this proclamation. Its content is revealed only in the proclamation itself. To speak of Christ, then, will be to speak within the context of the silence of the church. We must study Christology in the humble silence of the worshipping community. Prayer is to be silent and to cry out at the same time, before God in the presence of his Word. We have come together as a community to study Christ, God's Word. We have not met in church, but in the lecture room. We have academic work to do.

Christology is a peculiar discipline, because its subject is Christ himself, the Word, the Logos. Christology is the science of the Word of God. Christology is *logology*. Christology is *the* science, because it is concerned with the Logos. Were this Logos our Own Logos, then Christology would be a matter of the Logos reflecting upon itself. But this Logos is the Logos of God, whose transcendence makes Christology the crown of learning and whose coming from outside makes it the centre of scholarship. The subject remains transcendent and yet the Logos with whom we are concerned here is a person. This man is transcendent.

That means two things :

1. The Logos is not only an idea. Where the idea is thought of as the final reality of the Logos there can ultimately be no understanding of the central character of Christology or of its pre-eminent place.

2. Because of its claim to be *the* discipline *par excellence* and the centre of its sphere, Christology stands alone. There is no proof by which it can demonstrate the transcendence of its subject. Its statement that this transcendence, namely the Logos, is a person, a man, is a presupposition and not subject to proof. A transcendence which is allowed to be subject to proof instead of being the presupposition of thought is simply reason coming to an understanding of itself. Only a discipline which knows itself to be within the sphere of the church will be able to agree here that Christology is the centre of the academic world. For the rest, it remains the unknown and hidden centre of the *universitas litterarum*. Man's ultimate presupposition lies in his human Logos, which

engages in this process of classification. What happens if doubt is cast on this presupposition of his scientific activity? What if somewhere the claim is raised that this human Logos is superseded, judged, dead? What happens if an Anti-Logos appears which refuses to be classified? A Logos which annihilates the first? What if the proclamation goes out that the old order has been dissolved, that it is out of date, and that the counterpart of a new world has already begun? What answer does man's Logos give when it is addressed like this?

First of all, the human Logos repeats its old question. How is such a claim possible? How can such a claim be understood within its own order? It thus keeps on with its question, 'How?' But under this threat to its dominion from outside it now surpasses itself. It forestalls the claim by negating itself and at the same time asserting that this negation is a necessary development of its own being. This is the ultimate deceit and the ultimate power of this Logos. This is what Hegel did in his philosophy. This reaction of the Logos under the attack of the Anti-Logos is no narrow-minded repudiation of the other Logos, as in the Enlightenment, but the great insight into its power of self-negation. Self-negation, however, means self-affirmation. By limiting itself, the Logos reinstates itself in power. Nevertheless, the Logos recognizes the claim of the Anti-Logos. Thus the attempt to attack its ultimate presupposition seems to have failed. The Logos has assimilated the Anti-Logos into itself.

But what if the Anti-Logos raises his claim in a completely new form? If he is no longer an idea, but a Word, which challenges the supremacy of the Logos? If he appears at some time and in some place in history as a person? If he declares himself to be a judgment on the human Logos and points to him-self: I am the Way, the Truth and the Life; I am the death of the human Logos, I am the life of God's Logos; man with his Logos must die, he falls into my hands; I am the first and the last?

If the Anti-Logos no longer appears in history as an idea, but as the Word incarnate, there is no longer any possibility of incorporating him into the order of man's own Logos. There is in fact only one question left: 'Who are you? Speak!' The question 'Who are you?' is the question of deposed, distraught reason. But it is equally the question of faith: Who are you? Are you God him-self? This is the question with which Christology is concerned. Christ is the Anti-Logos. There is no longer any possibility of classification because the existence of this Logos means the end of the human Logos. The question 'Who are you?' is the only appropriate question. To this question the phenomenon discloses itself. Christ gives an answer to the question 'Who?'

The question 'Who?' is the question of transcendence. The question 'How?' is the question of immanence. Because the one who is questioned here is the Son, the immanent question cannot grasp him. Not, 'How are you possible?' – that is the godless question, the serpent's question – but 'Who are you?' The question 'Who?' expresses the strangeness and otherness of the encounter and at the same time reveals itself as the question of the very existence of the enquirer himself. He enquires about the being which is alien to his own being, about the boundaries of his own existence. Transcendence puts his own being in question. With the answer that his Logos has found its limit man comes up against the boundaries of his existence. So the question of transcendence is the question of existence and the question of existence is the question of transcendence. In theological terms: man only knows who he is in the light of God.

Source: Dietrich Bonhoeffer, Christology, *trans. John Bowden, London: Collins, 1966, pp. 27–33.*

4.20 D. M. Baillie, from *God Was in Christ*

In this extract, Donald Baillie describes and then rejects the account of Christology known as Kenotic Christology, from the Greek kenosis *which means 'emptying out'.*

The Kenotic Theory of the Incarnation belongs distinctively to modern times. It takes its title indeed from St. Paul's language in the second chapter of the Epistle to the Philippians, where he says that Christ 'emptied himself' [v. 7], and the idea of the divine self-emptying has been widely used in Christian theology. But the Kenotic Theory is something more specific and can hardly claim the direct support of that lyrical Pauline passage or mistake its poetry for theological theory! It is doubtful whether anything corresponding to the theory can be found in ancient Christian thought. The beginnings of it in the modern world are sometimes traced to Zinzendorf, but it was only in the nineteenth century that the idea was taken up and elaborated theologically as a theory of the Incarnation, mainly on the European continent. During the last half century it has played a considerable part in British theology, and has been adopted by a good many prominent divines in this country as a basis for Christology. I do not propose to examine the details of these various essays in Christological thinking which can be regarded as forms of the modern Kenotic Theory, but only to scrutinize the central idea and to ask whether it really meets the problem of the Incarnation.

According to the central idea of the Kenotic Theory, what happened in the Incarnation was that the Son of God, the Second Person of the Trinity, the Divine Logos, laid aside His distinctively divine attributes (omnipotence, omniscience, omnipresence) and lived for a period on earth within the limitations of humanity.

It is easy to see why this theory belongs peculiarly to the modern world, and why in the modern world it looks at first sight very promising. It is because it apparently enables us to combine a full faith in the deity of Jesus Christ with a completely frank treatment of His life on earth as a human phenomenon, the life of a man. Thus it tackles the Christological problem in the peculiarly sharp form which it has assumed in modern times. It gets away entirely from the docetism which has so often infected Christology and which explained away the humanity of Jesus by applying to the story of His life a kind of supra-human psychology. It is able to go the whole way in using human categories about Jesus: He lived a man's life, His mind worked as a man's mind, His knowledge was limited to human knowledge, His equipment to human equipment. But then in what sense was He God? How could God be so limited? The Kenotic Theory has a ready answer. Jesus was indeed identical with the eternal Son of God, one in essence with the Father and equal in power and glory. But in becoming incarnate He 'emptied Himself' of those attributes which essentially differentiate God from man; so that the life He lived on earth was a truly human life, without omnipotence or omnipresence or omniscience, a life subject to the conditions and limitations of humanity, as are the lives of all men. Thus we seem to get a real God–Man, and an intelligible meaning for the

Incarnation, thoroughly congruous both with the New Testament idea of the divine condescension and self-emptying and with the modern treatment of the Gospel story and the rediscovery of the 'Jesus of history'.

Yet I cannot think that this use of the idea of divine self-emptying will bear examination. To say this is not to deny that the *kenosis* of which St. Paul speaks is a reality to which a place must be given in Christian thought. But I cannot think that its right place is that which has been given to it by the holders of the Kenotic Theory in the specific sense indicated above, as a solution to the problem of Christology, a theological account of what happened in the Incarnation. To this there seem to be insuperable objections, which I will proceed to indicate.

1. I am not aware that a good reply has yet been made to the simple question asked by the late Archbishop of Canterbury [William Temple, *Christus Veritas*, p. 142] in objection to the Kenotic Theory. 'What was happening', he asked, 'to the rest of the universe during the period of our Lord's earthly life?' To say that the Infant Jesus was from His cradle exercising providential care over it all is certainly monstrous; but to deny this, and yet to say that the Creative Word was so self-emptied as 'to have no being except in the Infant Jesus, is to assert that for a certain period the history of the world was let loose from the control of the Creative Word.' It is vain to reply that the question presupposes a crude and false separation of the Persons of the Trinity from each other, or to quote the sound principle: *opera Trinitatis ad extra sunt indivisa*. For the Kenotic Christology itself presupposes precisely such a separation, and could not even be stated without it. Thus any crudity or naïveté which may seem to characterize the Archbishop's question derives directly from the theory which it is intended to criticize, since his method is that of *reductio ad absurdum*. Is there any answer?

2. Instead of giving us a doctrine of Incarnation in which Jesus Christ is both God and man, the Kenotic Theory appears to me to give us a story of a temporary theophany, in which He who formerly was God changed Himself temporarily into man, or exchanged His divinity for humanity. This is true even if the Kenoticist maintains the *anhypostasia* in the sense of impersonal humanity. For though the Son of God thus keeps His personal identity in becoming the subject of the human attributes which He assumes, He has divested Himself of the *distinctively divine* attributes; which would imply, if language means anything, that in becoming human He ceased to be divine. If, however, the Kenoticist gives up the idea of the *anhypostasia*, impersonal humanity, and regards Jesus as in every sense *a* man, a human person (as do some holders of the Kenotic Theory) then the situation becomes still stranger. The Kenoticist would then be involved in saying that He who before the Incarnation had been a divine Being now turned into a man, with human instead of divine attributes, for the time. He *had been* God, but now He was a man. If taken in all its implications, that seems more like a pagan story of metamorphosis than like the Christian doctrine of Incarnation, which has always found in the life of Jesus on earth God and man in simultaneous union – the Godhead 'veiled in flesh' but not *changed into* humanity. Surely the relation between the divine and the human in the Incarnation is a deeper mystery than this.

3. The difficulties of the Kenotic Theory become still greater when we go on to ask: Was the *kenosis* merely temporary, confined to the period of the Incarnation of the Son of God, the days of His flesh on earth? The holders of the theory would *logically* have to answer: Yes. The presupposition of the theory is that the distinctive divine attributes (of omniscience, etc.) and the distinctive human attributes (of finitude) cannot be united simultaneously in one life: that is why the Incarnation is explained as a *kenosis*. Therefore when the days of His flesh come to an end, Christ resumes His divine attributes, and His *kenosis*, his humanity, comes to an end. His human life is left behind when He ascends to the right hand of the Father. Thus, on the Kenotic theory in that specific sense (which is what we are concerned with) He is God and Man, not simultaneously in a hypostatic union, but *successively* – first divine, then human, then God again. But if that is really what the theory amounts to – and I do not see how it can be otherwise interpreted – it seems to leave no room at all for the traditional catholic doctrine of the *permanence* of the manhood of Christ, 'who, being the eternal Son of God, became man, and so was, *and continueth to be*, God and man in two distinct natures, and one person, *for ever*'. Now it may indeed be exceedingly difficult to interpret this doctrine and to answer all the questions which it raises. But if we state the problem in such terms at all, surely we cannot deny the doctrine altogether and maintain that the human nature of Christ ended when the days of His flesh on earth ended. That would make nonsense of the Incarnation, and indeed would indicate that the theorist did not regard Jesus Christ as a real man at all.

Source: D. M. Baillie, God Was in Christ, *London: Faber and Faber, 1956, pp. 94–8.*

4.21 Wolfhart Pannenberg, from *Jesus, God and Man*

Pannenberg here discusses the significance of Jesus' resurrection. He considers the Jewish understanding of resurrection and argues that this event confirms that in Jesus God has been revealed.

The following points summarize the most important elements that characterize the immediate inherent significance of Jesus' resurrection.

(a) If Jesus has been raised, then the end of the world has begun.
The universal resurrection of the dead and the judgment are imminent. This comes to expression in Paul's expectation that the resurrection of other men, especially of believers, will immediately follow that of Jesus. Jesus is 'the first-born among many brethren' (Rom. 8:29). Christ is raised as the first-fruits of those who have fallen asleep (I Cor. 15:20). Correspondingly, in Col. 1:18 Jesus is called the firstborn of the dead. The same expression is found in Rev. 1:5, indicating that this is a traditional, widely circulated formulation. The designation of Jesus as 'Author of life,' preserved by Luke in Acts 3:15, is to be understood as materially similar.

To the nearness of the end which began with Jesus' resurrection belongs, as well, the early Christian conviction that the same Spirit of God by which Jesus has been raised now already dwells in the Christians. In early Christianity the Spirit had eschatological significance. The word designated nothing else than the presence of the resurrection life in the Christians.

(b) If Jesus has been raised, this for a Jew can only mean that God himself has confirmed the pre-Easter activity of Jesus.
Jesus' claim to authority, through which he put himself in God's place, was, as we saw in the discussion of the antitheses in the Sermon on the Mount, blasphemous for Jewish ears. Because of this, Jesus was then also slandered by the Jews before the Roman governor as a rebel. Jesus really has been raised, this claim has been visibly and unambiguously confirmed by the God of Israel, who was allegedly blasphemed by Jesus. This was done by Israel's God. A Jew – and for the moment we are speaking only of Jews – could certainly not take an event of this kind as one that came to be apart from the will of his God. That the primitive Christian proclamation in fact understood Jesus' resurrection from the dead as the confirmation of his pre-Easter claim emerges above all in the speeches in Acts, and perhaps also in the old expression that Jesus was shown to be justified in the Spirit.

(c) Through his resurrection from the dead, Jesus moved so close to the Son of Man that the insight became obvious: the Son of Man is none other than the man Jesus who will come again.
In his previously mentioned book, H. E. Tödt has shown that the earliest community, to the extent that its theological thought comes to expression in Q, had already identified Jesus with the Son of Man, although in other respects it

appears only to have continued the proclamation of Jesus himself. This asser-tion of the post-Easter community was not simply an arbitrary act.

It lets the question about the basis of such an identification of Jesus with the Son of Man be put in a meaningful way from the perspective of the event itself as it was experienced by the first Christians. To what extent was the pres-entation of Jesus' relation to the Son of Man different to his disciples after his resurrection from what it had been in his pre-Easter message?

The pre-Easter Jesus had already proclaimed a correspondence in function between his own attitude toward men and the future attitude of the Son of Man: the attitude of men toward Jesus and the community which he grants to others are valid before the forum of the Son of Man. The distinction between these two figures consists only in the fact that the pre-Easter Jesus walked visibly on the earth, whereas the Son of Man was to come only in the future on the clouds of heaven and was expected as a heavenly being. This differ-ence disappeared, however, with Jesus' resurrection. As the one who has been taken away to God, Jesus is a heavenly being. His coming from heaven, which was expected in the immediate future and was probably already initiated by the Easter appearances, will bring on the universal resurrection of the dead and judgment, just as the apocalyptic tradition had predicted of the appear-ance of the Son of Man on the clouds of heaven. Thus it is understandable that Jesus was no longer distinguished from the Son of Man, but was himself seen as the Son of Man whose coming was expected in the future, and the tradition about Jesus down to the details was connected with the expectation of the Son of Man. After Jesus' resurrection it must have become meaningless to expect a second figure in addition to him with the same function and the same mode of coming. By virtue of the resurrection, Jesus had moved into the role of the Son of Man.

(d) If Jesus, having been raised from the dead, is ascended to God and if thereby the end of the world has begun, then God is ultimately revealed in Jesus.
Only at the end of all events can God be revealed in his divinity, that is, as the one who works all things, who has power over everything. Only because in Jesus' resurrection the end of all things, which for us has not yet happened, has already occurred can it be said of Jesus that the ultimate already is present in him, and so also that God himself, his glory, has made its appearance in Jesus in a way that cannot be surpassed. Only because the end of the world is already present in Jesus' resurrection is God himself revealed in him.

If these apocalyptic ideas are translated into Hellenistic terminology and conceptuality, their meaning is: in Jesus, God himself has appeared on earth. God himself – or God's revelatory figure, the Logos, the Son – has been among us as a man in the figure of Jesus. In this sense, in the transition of the Palestinian tradition into the Syrian sphere eschatology was translated throughout into epiphany. This Hellenistic concept of revelation prepared the basic pattern for the subsequent doctrine of incarnation.

The translation of the apocalyptic understanding of Jesus as the one in whom the glory of God is ultimately revealed, because in him the end event has already occurred in advance, into the Hellenistic concept of revelation as epiphany may also have been the path that led to the thesis of the true divinity of Jesus. Jesus' divinity is already implied in some way in the conception of God's appearance in him, even though not with the later orthodox precision.

Source: Wolfhart Pannenberg, Jesus: God and Man, *trans. Lewis L. Wilkins and Duane A. Priebe, London: SCM Press 1968, pp. 66–9.*

4.22 Patricia Wilson-Kastner, from *Faith, Feminism and the Christ*

Wilson-Kastner confronts the question posed by some feminist theologians about whether Christology is irredeemably patriarchal and sexist. She argues that this is not the case and that the significance of Jesus transcends the particularities – maleness, Jewishness – of his human life.

The Christologies available in the mainline Christian tradition all appear to be riddled, tainted with strains of sexism, dualism, patriarchy, and a spirit which splits reality into separate components which have little real relationship to each other. Inevitably, the result is that women are identified with that which is inferior, and males are presented as the superior reality. Must all Christologies and Jesus Christ himself, therefore, be dismissed as hopelessly corrupted with an intrinsic sexism that is necessary to their very being? At this juncture a fundamental division of opinion occurs. It is not between those who are Christian and those who are not, but between those who believe that Jesus' male personhood is of the essence of his meaning as the Christ and those who do not. Some trivializations of Jesus that result from the former view have been well explored in the literature focusing on the questions of the ordination of women. The most fundamental theological objection to such an approach is this: to identify Jesus with maleness (or Jewishness, or living in the first century, and so forth) is to miss the point of Jesus' significance and mission. Jesus became flesh so as to show forth the love of God among us, a love which is not merely an expression of good will, but the power of an energy which is the heart, core, and cohesive force of the universe. The Incarnation – the Word becoming flesh – shows us … God manifest in a human life with all of the possibilities and limitations of human life.

Within this context, Jesus' maleness, like the limited scope of his knowledge, his confinement to the first century in Palestine, and various other specifics of this life, are all examples of God's humility and self-emptying in living among us. Jesus the Christ is the expression of God in *a* human life, not *the* human life. To exalt the concrete details of Jesus' life in an exclusive way is to miss the whole point of the Incarnation, to misapprehend the nature of divine revelation, and in the most proper sense, to espouse heresy. It is the equivalent of mistaking the black type for the white page, or the spoken words for the gospel itself.

Consequently, what a reconstruction of Christology must do is look at the significance and meaning of Jesus Christ as a revelation of the divine love, in the process of learning more about Christ, humanity, and the divine love itself. The whole living tradition of the church throughout the ages must be reconsidered – the Scriptures, the writings of various theologians, liturgies, and popular beliefs and devotion. Some traditions, of course, are far more corrupted by sexism than others, but eventually all must be reexamined. Here we can only begin to make an overture for ways of integrating new insights and questions into the wealth of the Christian tradition. My conviction is that such a process is faithful to the fundamental insights of feminism as well as it is renewing and purifying for Christian theology.

The Christ whom we are considering is, after all, the living Christ, not simply a Palestinian rabbi of the first century. This Christ is the Incarnation of the eternal Word of God, in whom all things came to be, the center of the cosmos, who became human at a particular time and place to manifest God's love among us (John 1:1–18, Ephesians 2:5–10, Colossians 1:15–23). His presence continues among us, not only in the cosmos, but also very tangibly in the church which is called to be the meeting place for divine revelation and the self-awareness of humanity to God.

The search for the Jesus of history, as distinguished from the Christ of faith, which culminated in Albert Schweitzer's *Quest of the Historical Jesus* (1906), is consequently not one of ultimate importance for my theological position. Historical biblical studies are very helpful in understanding Jesus' life, teachings, and context. But finally, one must conclude that all of the biblical material offers different, and developing, perspectives on one Christ, incarnate in Jesus of Nazareth, who still lives in the cosmos and in the church. If one does not take this step, Christ is not one to be venerated, worshiped, or related to, but merely one whose impact can be studied in various guises or who may, under one or another interpretation, be inspiring as a model for behavior.

In the exploration of the nature of Christ, some way must be found to express Christ as a revealer of God to humanity. Christ is the human expression of God to us, and thus we must try to understand what God meant in Christ. Christ is also the inclusive revelation of God's intention for humanity. In Christ we see something of how a divinely renewed humanity acts in the world. Christ is not simply the new male person, but one who shows all persons how to live. As a human he shows us what human self-possession and self-giving are. Thereby Christ shows us the link between divine and human, the cosmos and its conscious inhabitants. Only within such a context, with such concerns, can a feminist Christology emerge. Such a Christology will be feminist not in the sense of making Christ into a female, or merely attributing feminine characteristics to him, but in understanding the significance of Christ as embodying values and ideals which also are sought for and valued by feminists.

Source: Patricia Wilson-Kastner, Faith, Feminism, and the Christ, *Philadelphia: Fortress Press, 1983, pp. 90–2.*

4.23 N. T. Wright, from *Who was Jesus?*

Wright discusses the significance of Jesus in the context of Israel's history and highlights his revolutionary message about the kingdom of God.

The strange thing about Jesus' announcement of the Kingdom of God was that he managed *both* to claim that he was fulfilling the old prophecies, the old hopes, of Israel *and* to do so in a way which radically subverted them. The Kingdom of God is here, he seemed to be saying, *but it's not like you thought it was going to be.*

How so? When Israel's God acts, the Gentiles will benefit as well! When Israel's God brings in his new world, some of Israel's cherished traditions (like the food laws) will be swept away, no longer needed in the new world-wide family! Abraham, Isaac and Jacob will sit down in the Kingdom and welcome people from all over the world, while some of the sons of the Kingdom will be cast out. It's no wonder Jesus needed to use parables to say all this. If too many people realized the doubly revolutionary implications, he wouldn't have lasted five minutes.

Doubly revolutionary: first, anyone saying that Israel's God was becoming King was raising a standard for revolution, and, as Jesus himself wryly noted, all and sundry, particularly those bent on violence, would try to get in on the act. Second, to claim to be announcing the Kingdom while at the same time subverting Israel's national institutions, and/or the fiercely held agendas of certain pressure groups, was asking for trouble. It would be like announcing in a Moslem country that one was fulfilling the will of Allah while apparently vilifying Muhammad and burning a copy of the Koran.

The Great celebration

In particular, Jesus' characteristic behaviour spoke as many volumes as his characteristic teaching. Wherever he went, there was a party. After all, if God is becoming King at last, who wouldn't want to celebrate? But he celebrated *with all the wrong people.* He went into low dives and back alleys. He knocked back the wine with the shady and disrespectable. He allowed women of the street to come and fawn over him. And all the time he seemed to be indicating that, as far as he was concerned, they were in the process being welcomed into the new day that was dawning, the day of God's becoming King. That was the significance of his remarkable healings (which, incidentally, most serious scholars today are prepared to admit as historical).

What had happened to all the old taboos, to Israel's standards of holiness? They seemed to have gone by the board. Jesus was saying – in his actions as much as in his words – that you didn't have to observe every last bit of the Torah before you would count as a real member of Israel. He was saying that you didn't have to make the journey to Jerusalem, offer sacrifice, and go through purity rituals, in order to be regarded as clean, forgiven, restored as a member of Israel. You could be healed, restored, and forgiven right here, where Jesus was, at this party, just by being there with him and welcoming his way of bringing in the Kingdom. No wonder his family said he was out of his mind.

Not only his family. The pressure groups that were urging Israel to become more holy, more faithful to Torah, would be furious. This man was undermining everything they were trying to do. The revolutionaries would be puzzled, then angry. This man was using their language but meaning the wrong thing by it; every serious, radical politician knew that you had to organize, sharpen up the weapons, and be ready to fight. And even Jesus' closest followers, who at a certain point came to the conclusion that Jesus was indeed the Messiah, not just a great prophet, seem to have remained puzzled by what he was actually trying to achieve.

Well, what was he trying to achieve? At this point we are back with Albert Schweitzer's set of questions. What did Jesus expect to happen? Was he disappointed?

The aims of Jesus

We can safely say that Jesus didn't expect the world to come to an end. That bizarre idea, which has been touted around the learned halls of New Testament scholarship all this century, should now be given a pauper's funeral. Schweitzer was 100% right to say that Jesus should be understood in terms of Jewish apocalyptic. He was 100% wrong in saying what that language meant.

The coming crisis

As we have seen, this 'apocalyptic' language meant that Israel was on the verge of the great turn-around of the ages. The long night of exile was coming to an end; the great day of liberation was dawning. Israel was like a bride on the eve of her wedding day, or a prisoner on the verge of release after a mammoth sentence. Everything, everything is going to be different from now on. The world will be a different place. The birds will sound as though they're singing a different song. That's how apocalyptic language works. It invests ordinary events with their total significance. The monsters will be destroyed; the man will be exalted. 'The Son of Man will come on the clouds with power and great glory,' Israel will be vindicated, and her oppressors will trouble her no more.

Jesus picked up this massive expectation – and *applied it to himself*. He had welcomed sinners and outcasts into the Kingdom, calmly and quietly implying that this Kingdom was being redefined around himself. (Is it necessary to say at this point that this *doesn't* mean that he was an egotist, or that he imagined himself to be playing at being 'God' in some high-and-mighty sense?) As many prophets and other leaders had said in olden times (we may think of Elijah, or Isaiah, or John the Baptist), Israel's God was redefining his people, and was now doing so in and through the work of this one man. But what Jesus grasped, which so many of his contemporaries, like so many modern readers, failed to pick up was that Israel's destiny was now moving swiftly towards its vital, crucial moment. Israel, the historical people of the one creator God, was swimming in the stream of history just above a roaring waterfall. If she didn't watch out, she would be swept right over, and fall to her doom.

It didn't take much insight for Jesus to make that last point. Anyone with open eyes and ears could see that the Romans would only take so much provocation, and would then come and smash Jerusalem, and the nation, into little bits. Where Jesus' prophetic insight came into play was in the awesome realization that *when this happened, it would be the judgment of Israel's God on his wayward people*. Israel was called to be the light of the world, but the light was turned inwards on to itself. Israel was called to be the peacemaker, but she was bent on violent revolution. Israel was called to be the healer, but she was determined to dash the pagans to pieces like a potter's vessel. Jesus saw the judgment coming, and realized that it was not just from Rome, but from God. His first aim, therefore, was to summon Israel to 'repent' – not so much of petty individual sins, but of the great national rebellion, against the creator, the covenant God. Failure to repent would lead her inexorably towards disaster.

Jesus and Israel

His second aim, though, was the one that still sends shivers down the spine two thousand years later. As Schweitzer saw in one of his greatest insights, Jesus believed himself called to go out ahead of Israel, to meet the judgment in her place, alone. He drew on the old Jewish beliefs of the coming great tribulation, the time of bitter and harsh suffering and testing for the people of God. This 'tribulation' would surely come; but if he went out to meet it, to take it upon himself, then he might bear it on behalf of his people, so that they would not need to bear it. He would make a way through the tribulation, through the darkest night of Israel's exile and distress, and out the other side into the glorious light of the new day that would then dawn.

Source: N. T. Wright, Who Was Jesus?, *London: SPCK, 1992 and Grand Rapids: Eerdmans, 1993, pp. 97–101.*

5 The Work of Christ

Introductory essay

This Reader follows the convention of treating the subject matter of Christ-ology in two parts, the first dealing with the person of Christ and the second with his work. This convenient distinction, however, should not be allowed to obscure the fact that the work of Christ is not separable from who he is. Jesus is able to be the Saviour of the world because he is the one through whom all things were created and hold together (Col. 1.16–17). He is able to bring to birth the new creation because he is one with the creating Father and the perfecting Spirit. He is able to be *our* Saviour because he is one with us, because he is our brother who represents humanity before God, offers on our behalf the perfect sacrifice of obedience and praise, and intercedes for us at the Father's side.

These are brief and by no means exhaustive summations of the faith diversely expressed in Christian tradition that the communion with God for which humanity was created, but which has been shattered through human sin, is restored and perfected through the person and work of Jesus Christ. In and through him, the world is reconciled to God and set again upon its trajectory to fullness of life in communion with the triune God. That work comes to a particular focus in the crucifixion of Jesus so that the work of Christ is often summed up in the phrase, 'Jesus died for our sins.' A great deal more needs to be said, however, about what that confession means and about how the truth it points to takes its place in the extensive drama of God's creative and redemptive purposes for the world. The eter-nal begetting of the Son and his perichoretic communion with the Father and the Spirit, his incarnation, his growth to human maturity, his baptism and his ministry, his death and resurrection, his ascension and his ses-sion at the right hand of the Father all have a part in the account Christian theology must give of how it is that the world is reconciled to God and will be perfected at the last. It takes more than a collection of extracts such as appears in the following pages to do that task well, but the extracts serve to identify the range and complexity of the matters to be considered in speaking about the work of Christ.

Already in these few lines of introduction a number of terms have been used that variously describe the work of Christ – salvation, reconciliation, redemption, sacrifice, intercession, and so on. The list may be consider-ably extended for no single concept can do all the work necessary to a proper description of Jesus' significance for humanity and for the world. It is to be noted also that the work of Jesus is cosmic in scope. Conceptions of his work concentrated exclusively on the human race, or even more narrowly upon human souls, do not do justice to the biblical vision of the *world* reconciled to God and of the *creation* made new. Nevertheless, just as human beings were appointed to a special role in creation, so their failure in that role occasions the special attention of God as he works through his Son and Spirit to overcome the damage done by human sin.

Adam's failure – the name here encompasses the whole of the human race – is met by God's mercy and forgiving love, and, in the person of the Son, a new Adam takes up the human role of obedient service and praise of God and sees it through to perfection on our behalf. This is a central theme in the theology of Irenaeus seen in the first extract below. Following Paul's lead in Romans 5, Irenaeus draws a sharp contrast between the work of the vanquished first Adam, and that of Christ, the second Adam, who takes humanity's part in the drama of God's creative purposes for the world and recovers on behalf of humanity the true image and likeness of God. It has been a matter of debate in the tradition whether or not the image of God is lost or corrupted through sin. Athanasius follows the Irenaean view in contending that the Son's assumption of true humanity is the means by which human flesh is saved from corruption and death, and by which humanity is renewed in the image of God. The divinity of the Son is not in doubt in either of the texts from Irenaeus or Athanasius. At stake, at this point, was the true nature of his humanity.

A range of metaphors appear in the New Testament concerning the atonement won for humanity on the cross. One of these is the metaphor of ransom, although explicit support for such a metaphor comes only from Mark 10.45. Gregory of Nazianzus in our third extract rejects the idea, developed in later tradition, that ransom should be understood as a price for sin paid either to the devil or to God. Gregory contends that the work of the cross should rather be understood as the defeat of death by our great high priest and sacrifice. Anselm was another who was troubled by the use to which Mark 10.45 had been put. Countering the idea that a ransom was paid to the devil, Anselm developed an understanding of atonement in terms of the satisfaction of a debt owed to God. Justice, according to Anselm, requires that sin be dealt with in some way. It cannot be ignored unless the universe be reduced to moral chaos. It is misleading to suggest, as is often done however, that by Anselm's account God was punishing Christ for human sin. Rather, Christ makes satisfaction for sin, meets humanity's debt to God, and thus sets right the just and moral order of the universe.

Abelard later proposes a theory of the atonement in which the focus rests upon the example of love set by Christ in his passion. Our atonement consists in the love inspired in us by Christ's example. By what means satisfaction was made for human sin is a question considered again in the medieval period by Thomas Aquinas, who considers several aspects of the case, especially, in the extracts presented here, the atoning efficacy of his passion, and the sufficiency of his sacrifice in giving due honour to God. Beyond the selected passage, Aquinas also considers whether salvation was brought about by virtue of Christ's merit or by way of redemption, whether it is proper to regard Christ as the redeemer, and whether the passion was an efficient means of bringing about salvation. In the *Summa Theologica*, from which the extract is taken, Aquinas proceeds first by posing a question for consideration, and second, by offering some standard objections to the proposition entailed by the question. He then responds with a series of replies, first to the question itself, and then to the specific objections raised.

Although there were many factors contributing to the Protestant Reformation, a central theological concern of the Reformers was the question of how the work of Christ is to be understood and appropriated. The Reformers, in debate with the church authorities, sought to clarify what exactly is accomplished through the life, death and resurrection of Jesus, and how it becomes effectual in the life of the believer. That debate impacted upon many areas of Christian doctrine, the evidence for which is presented throughout this volume, but concerned especially the doctrine of justification. Stemming from Luther's conviction that the justice of God is not to be understood in punitive terms, but is revealed through the gospel of Jesus Christ as the means by which the merciful God justifies the sinner, the Reformers argued that justification takes place for us in Christ, without any consideration of merit or works on our part. The Roman Catholic Church, in its initial pontifical response, upheld the principle of justification through grace, but insisted that through grace we acquire merit making us worthy of justification. Later, at the Council of Trent (1545–53), the Church offered a more extensive account of how it understood the relation between justification through divine grace and the continuing merit of works. The debate is represented in what follows by extracts from the Lutheran *Book of Concord*, and from the Council of Trent.

Calvin followed the Lutheran insistence that justification, and, more broadly, salvation, was achieved for us despite our complete lack of merit. Our salvation is accomplished solely through the merit of Christ who is understood, in explicit continuity with the Old Testament, as prophet, king and priest. Exercising these offices, Christ is also the mediator who procures the favour of God for us and brings us into full communion with God; he is pastor to all who believe, and he is judge. One of the questions arising from the Protestant insistence that salvation is accomplished through grace and without consideration of human merit, is whether salvation extends to all people. If Christ takes the cause of sinful humanity upon himself, on what grounds would God limit his grace to only a portion of the human race? That question was taken up by John Owen, among many others, who argues that the saving grace of God is restricted to those whom he 'fore-knew' and with whom he has established a covenant. This argument on its own, however, does not absolve God from the suspicion that his saving will is arbitrary. Accordingly, the Puritan tradition, of which Owen was a part, indulged in numerous attempts to defend the prerogative of God to save whoever he chooses, without thereby giving cause for complaint by human beings, none of whom deserve to be saved in any case.

The nineteenth century saw a return to Abelardian conceptions of Christ's saving work and a particular emphasis on Christ's exemplary role. The 'practical reason' of Immanuel Kant was influential in this regard as were the attention given in biblical scholarship to Jesus' proclamation of the coming kingdom of God, and the widespread nineteenth-century optimism about humanity's capacity to build that kingdom on earth. While critical of Kant in some respects, Albrecht Ritschl sought nevertheless to adapt the Kantian philosophy to a Christian purpose. The work of Christ consists in his representation of humanity before God and his securing for all the status of children of God.

With the dawn of the twentieth century, theologians began to lose confidence in the nineteenth century's optimistic estimations of humanity's capacity to build the kingdom of God on earth. P. T. Forsyth, who studied under Ritschl in Göttingen, rejected such high estimations of humanity's moral capacity for that confidence did not take sufficient account of humanity's propensity for evil. Forsyth was convinced that, far from having the capacity to build the kingdom on earth, humanity stands in need, rather, of forgiveness and atonement. He saw in Jesus Christ the one who makes atonement and confesses on our behalf the true holiness of God. There was a certain amount of prescience in Forsyth's theology for, as the twentieth century unfolded, the questions most urgently confronting Christian faith concerned its response to the atrocities of war and to the growing awareness of injustice, poverty and oppression. Theologians writing on the work of Christ were commonly concerned with the question, 'How does Christ help in the midst of suffering and evil?'

Gustaf Aulén, writing in 1930, sought to recover what he claimed was the dominant idea of atonement in the New Testament, that of Christ's victory over the forces of evil. While that claim has been contested, Aulén's work prompted widespread attention to the several different metaphors used in the New Testament to describe the atoning work of Christ.

Although concerned also with the themes of suffering and evil, the extract from Dorothee Sölle takes up a prominent concern of the 1960s, that of personal identity. Influenced by the existentialist emphasis, she gives an account of how, through the representative action of Christ, the identity of each one of us is secure before God even as we make our way through the sinfulness and incompleteness of human life.

The theme of how God can help in the midst of suffering comes to the fore again in Jürgen Moltmann's widely influential text, *The Crucified God*. Moltmann seeks to understand what the crucifixion of Christ, the second person of the Trinity, means for God himself and concludes that in Christ all human suffering is taken into the very being of God. In that way God takes humanity's cause into the heart of his own life. Moltmann goes on to explain, beyond the extract provided here, that it is only through the resurrection of the crucified one that hope can be found for those who suffer in this world. Liberation theologians of the third world echoed that theme in their conviction that in Christ God takes sides with the poor and the oppressed. Gustavo Gutiérrez, for instance, draws from God's preferential treatment of the poor the political imperative to work towards the relief of suffering, the overcoming of oppression, and the uplifting of the poor. Similar themes are evident in much of the theology that has emerged from Asia. C. S. Song, in the extract provided here, focuses especially upon the plight of oppressed women in Asia and conceives how the work of Christ is directed especially to them. Feminist theologians have also given much attention to this theme. Not all have remained within Christian faith but some, like Rosemary Radford Ruether, are determined to show how the work of Christ challenges the patriarchal practices of society and establishes a new humanity.

The diversity of approaches evident in these readings to the understanding of Christ's saving work reflects something of the diverse testimony to God's saving work in the Bible itself. Concomitant with the variety of the biblical witness, the Christian mystery of salvation has never been articulated definitively through the Councils of the Church. The saving work of Christ has revealed its power in different ways, however, through changing historical circumstances.

MAR

5.1 Irenaeus of Lyons, from *Against Heresies*

In these extracts Irenaeus emphasizes the soteriological importance of the true humanity assumed by the Son of God.

3.18.1   As it has been clearly demonstrated that the Word, who existed in the beginning with God, by whom all things were made, who was also always present with mankind, was in these last days, according to the time appointed by the Father, united to His own workmanship, inasmuch as He became a man liable to suffering, [it follows] that every objection is set aside of those who say, 'If our Lord was born at that time, Christ had therefore no previous existence.' For I have shown that the Son of God did not then begin to exist, being with the Father from the beginning; but when He became incarnate, and was made man, He commenced afresh the long line of human beings, and furnished us, in a brief, comprehensive manner, with salvation; so that what we had lost in Adam – namely, to be according to the image and likeness of God – that we might recover in Christ Jesus.

5.21.1   He has therefore, in His work of recapitulation, summed up all things, both waging war against our enemy, and crushing him who had at the beginning led us away captives in Adam, and trampled upon his head, as thou canst perceive in Genesis that God said to the serpent, 'And I will put enmity between thee and the woman, and between thy seed and her seed; He shall be on the watch for thy head, and thou on the watch for His heel.' For from that time, He who should be born of a woman, [namely] from the Virgin, after the likeness of Adam, was preached as keeping watch for the head of the serpent. This is the seed of which the apostle says in the Epistle to the Galatians, 'that the law of works was established until the seed should come to whom the promise was made.' This fact is exhibited in a still clearer light in the same Epistle, where he thus speaks: 'But when the fulness of time was come, God sent forth His Son, made of a woman.' For indeed the enemy would not have been fairly vanquished, unless it had been a man [born] of a woman who conquered him. For it was by means of a woman that he got the advantage over man at first, setting himself up as man's opponent. And therefore does the Lord profess Himself to be the Son of man, comprising in Himself that original man out of whom the woman was fashioned, in order that, as our species went down to death through a vanquished man, so we may ascend to life again through a victorious one; and as through a man death received the palm [of victory] against us, so again by a man we may receive the palm against death.

Source: Irenaeus of Lyons, Against Heresies *III.18.1 and V.21.1, trans. Alexander Roberts and William Rambaut, in Alexander Roberts, James Donaldson and A. Cleveland Coxe (eds),* Ante-Nicene Fathers, *vol. 1, Buffalo, NY: Christian Literature Publishing Co., 1885.*

5.2 Athanasius, from *On the Incarnation*

In this extract Athanasius places special emphasis on Christ's assumption of human flesh, believing this to be essential to his saving that flesh from corruption and death.

2.8   For this purpose, then, the incorporeal and incorruptible and immaterial Word of God entered our world. In one sense, indeed, He was not far from it before, for no part of creation had ever been without Him Who, while ever abiding in union with the Father, yet fills all things that are. But now He entered the world in a new way, stooping to our level in His love and Self-revealing to us. He saw the reasonable race, the race of men that, like Himself, expressed the Father's Mind, wasting out of existence, and death reigning over all in corruption. He saw that corruption held us all the closer, because it was the penalty for the Transgression; He saw, too, how unthinkable it would be for the law to be repealed before it was fulfilled. He saw how unseemly it was that the very things of which He Himself was the Artificer should be disappearing. He saw how the surpassing wickedness of men was mounting up against them; He saw also their universal liability to death. All this He saw and, pitying our race, moved with compassion for our limitation, unable to endure that death should have the mastery, rather than that His creatures should perish and the work of His Father for us men come to nought, He took to Himself a body, a human body even as our own. Nor did He will merely to become embodied or merely to appear; had that been so, He could have revealed His divine majesty in some other and better way. No, He took *our* body, and not only so, but He took it directly from a spotless, stainless virgin, without the agency of human father – a pure body, untainted by intercourse with man. He, the Mighty One, the Artificer of all, Himself prepared this body in the virgin as a temple for Himself, and took it for His very own, as the instrument through which He was known and in which He dwelt. Thus, taking a body like our own, because all our bodies were liable to the corruption of death, He surrendered His body to death instead of all, and offered it to the Father. This He did out of sheer love for us, so that in His death all might die, and the law of death thereby be abolished because, having fulfilled in His body that for which it was appointed, it was thereafter voided of its power for men. This He did that He might turn again to incorruption men who had turned back to corruption, and make them alive through death by the appropriation of His body and by the grace of His resurrection. Thus He would make death to disappear from them as utterly as straw from fire.

3.13   What was God to do in face of this dehumanising of mankind, this universal hiding of the knowledge of Himself by the wiles of evil spirits? Was He to keep silence before so great a wrong and let men go on being thus deceived and kept in ignorance of Himself? If so, what was the use of having made them in His own Image originally? It would surely have been better for them always to have been brutes, rather than to revert to that condition when once they had shared the nature of the Word. Again, things being as they were, what was the use of their ever having had the knowledge of God? Surely it would have been better for God never to have bestowed it, than that men should subsequently be found unworthy to receive it. Similarly, what possible profit could it be to God Himself, Who made men, if when made they did not worship Him, but regarded others as their makers? This would be tantamount to His having made them for others and not for Himself. Even an earthly king, though he is only a man, does not allow lands that he has colonized to pass into other hands or to desert to other rulers, but sends letters and friends and even visits them himself to recall them to their allegiance, rather than allow His work to be undone. How much more, then, will God be patient and pains-taking with His creatures, that they be not led astray from Him to the service of those that are not, and that all the more because such error means for them sheer ruin, and because it is not right that those who had once shared His Image should be destroyed. What, then, was God to do? What else could He possibly do, being God, but renew His Image in mankind, so that through it men might once more come to know Him? And how could this be done save by the coming of the very Image Himself, our Savior Jesus Christ? Men could not have done it, for they are only made after the Image; nor could angels have done it, for they are not the images of God. The Word of God came in His own Person, because it was He alone, the Image of the Father Who could recreate man made after the Image. In order to effect this re-creation, however, He had first to do away with death and corruption. Therefore He assumed a human body, in order that in it death might once for all be destroyed, and that men might be renewed according to the Image. The Image of the Father only was sufficient for this need.

Source: St Athanasius, On the Incarnation, Chapter 2, §8, and Chapter 3, §13, trans. Sister Penelope Lawson, London: Mowbray and Crestwood, NY: St Vladimir's Orthodox Theological Seminary, 1953.

5.3 Gregory of Nazianzus, from *Oration XLV* ('The Second Oration on Easter')

Gregory here rejects the idea of a ransom paid either to God or to the devil in favour of an account of atonement in which the powers of death are defeated through Christ's death and resurrection.

Now we are to examine another fact and dogma, neglected by most people, but in my judgment well worth enquiring into. To Whom was that Blood offered that was shed for us, and why was It shed? I mean the precious and famous Blood of our God and High Priest and Sacrifice. We were detained in bondage by the Evil One, sold under sin, and receiving pleasure in exchange for wickedness. Now, since a ransom belongs only to him who holds in bondage, I ask to whom was this offered, and for what cause? If to the Evil One, fie upon the outrage! If the robber receives ransom, not only from God, but a ransom which consists of God Himself, and has such an illustrious payment for his tyranny, a payment for whose sake it would have been right for him to have left us alone altogether. [sic] But if to the Father, I ask first, how? For it was not by Him that we were being oppressed; and next, On what principle did the Blood of His Only begotten Son delight the Father, Who would not receive even Isaac, when he was being offered by his Father, but changed the sacrifice, putting a ram in the place of the human victim?

Is it not evident that the Father accepts Him, but neither asked for him nor demanded Him; but on account of the Incarnation, and because Humanity must be sanctified by the Humanity of God, that He might deliver us Himself, and overcome the tyrant, and draw us to Himself by the mediation of His Son, Who also arranged this to the honour of the Father, Whom it is manifest that He obeys in all things? So much we have said of Christ; the greater part of what we might say shall be reverenced with silence. But that brazen serpent was hung up as a remedy for the biting serpents, not as a type of Him that suffered for us, but as a contrast; and it saved those that looked upon it, not because they believed it to live, but because it was killed, and killed with it the powers that were subject to it, being destroyed as it deserved. And what is the fitting epitaph for it from us? 'O death, where is thy sting? O grave, where is thy victory?' Thou art overthrown by the Cross; thou art slain by Him who is the Giver of life; thou art without breath, dead, without motion, even though thou keepest the form of a serpent lifted up on high on a pole.

Source: Gregory of Nazianzus, Oration XLV *('The Second Oration on Easter') 22, trans. Charles Gordon Browne and James Edward Swallow, in Philip Schaff and Henry Wace (eds),* Nicene and Post-Nicene Fathers, *second series, vol. 7, Buffalo, NY: Christian Literature Publishing Co., 1894.*

5.4 Anselm of Canterbury, from *Cur Deus Homo?*

**Cur Deus Homo *takes the form of a dialogue between Anselm and Boso.
Here the question is raised whether God could overcome sin without satisfaction of the debt humanity owes to God.***

Book 1, Chapter XII: *Whether it were proper for God to put away sins by compassion
alone, without any payment of debt.*

Anselm. Let us return and consider whether it were proper for God to put
away sins by compassion alone, without any payment of the honor taken from
him.

Boso. I do not see why it is not proper.

Anselm. To remit sin in this manner is nothing else than not to punish; and
since it is not right to cancel sin without compensation or punishment; if it be
not punished, then is it passed by undischarged.

Boso. What you say is reasonable.

Anselm. It is not fitting for God to pass over anything in his kingdom undischarged.

Boso. If I wish to oppose this, I fear to sin.

Anselm. It is, therefore, not proper for God thus to pass over sin unpunished.

Boso. Thus it follows.

Anselm. There is also another thing which follows if sin be passed by unpunished, viz., that with God there will be no difference between the guilty and
the not guilty; and this is unbecoming to God.

Boso. I cannot deny it.

Anselm. Observe this also. Every one knows that justice to man is regulated
by law, so that, according to the requirements of law, the measure of award is
bestowed by God.

Boso. This is our belief.

Anselm. But if sin is neither paid for nor punished, it is subject to no law.

Boso. I cannot conceive it to be otherwise.

Anselm. Injustice, therefore, if it is cancelled by compassion alone, is more free
than justice, which seems very inconsistent. And to these is also added a further incongruity, viz., that it makes injustice like God. For as God is subject to
no law, so neither is injustice.

Boso. I cannot withstand your reasoning. But when God commands us in every
case to forgive those who trespass against us, it seems inconsistent to enjoin a
thing upon us which it is not proper for him to do himself.

Anselm. There is no inconsistency in God's commanding us not to take upon
ourselves what belongs to Him alone. For to execute vengeance belongs to
none but Him who is Lord of all; for when the powers of the world rightly
accomplish this end, God himself does it who appointed them for the purpose
…

Book 1, Chapter XIII: *How nothing less was to be endured, in the order of things, than that the creature should take away the honor due the Creator and not restore what he takes away.*

Anselm. In the order of things, there is nothing less to be endured than that the creature should take away the honor due the Creator, and not restore what he has taken away.

Boso. Nothing is more plain than this.

Anselm. But there is no greater injustice suffered than that by which so great an evil must be endured.

Boso. This, also, is plain.

Anselm. I think, therefore, that you will not say that God ought to endure a thing than which no greater injustice is suffered, viz., that the creature should not restore to God what he has taken away.

Boso. No; I think it should be wholly denied.

Anselm. Again, if there is nothing greater or better than God, there is nothing more just than supreme justice, which maintains God's honor in the arrangement of things, and which is nothing else but God himself.

Boso. There is nothing clearer than this.

Anselm. Therefore God maintains nothing with more justice than the honor of his own dignity.

Boso. I must agree with you.

Anselm. Does it seem to you that he wholly preserves it, if he allows himself to be so defrauded of it as that he should neither receive satisfaction nor punish the one defrauding him.

Boso. I dare not say so.

Anselm. Therefore the honor taken away must be repaid, or punishment must follow; otherwise, either God will not be just to himself, or he will be weak in respect to both parties; and this it is impious even to think of.

Boso. I think that nothing more reasonable can be said.

Book 1, Chapter XIV: *How the honor of God exists in the punishment of the wicked.*

Boso. But I wish to hear from you whether the punishment of the sinner is an honor to God, or how it is an honor. For if the punishment of the sinner is not for God's honor when the sinner does not pay what he took away, but is punished, God loses his honor so that he cannot recover it. And this seems in contradiction to the things which have been said.

Anselm. It is impossible for God to lose his honor; for either the sinner pays his debt of his own accord, or, if he refuse, God takes it from him. For either man renders due submission to God of his own will, by avoiding sin or making payment, or else God subjects him to himself by torments, even against man's will, and thus shows that he is the Lord of man, though man refuses to acknowledge it of his own accord. And here we must observe that as man in sinning takes away what belongs to God, so God in punishing gets in return what pertains to man. For not only does that belong to a man which he has in present possession, but also that which it is in his power to have. Therefore, since man was so made as to be able to attain happiness by avoiding sin; if, on account of his sin, he is deprived of happiness and every good, he repays from his own inheritance what he has stolen, though he repay it against his will. For although God does not apply what he takes away to any object of his own, as man transfers the money which he has taken from another to his own use; yet what he takes away serves the purpose of his own honor, for this very reason, that it is taken away. For by this act he shows that the sinner and all that pertains to him are under his subjection.

Book 2, Chapter VI: *How no being, except the God-man, can make the atonement by which man is saved.*

Anselm. But this cannot be effected, except the price paid to God for the sin of man be something greater than all the universe besides God.

Boso. So it appears.

Anselm. Moreover, it is necessary that he who can give God anything of his own which is more valuable than all things in the possession of God, must be greater than all else but God himself.

Boso. I cannot deny it.

Anselm. Therefore none but God can make this satisfaction.

Boso. So it appears.

Anselm. But none but a man ought to do this, other wise man does not make the satisfaction.

Boso. Nothing seems more just.

Anselm. If it be necessary, therefore, as it appears, that the heavenly kingdom be made up of men, and this cannot be effected unless the aforesaid satisfaction be made, which none but God can make and none but man ought to make, it is necessary for the God-man to make it.

Boso. Now blessed be God! we have made a great discovery with regard to our question. Go on, therefore, as you have begun. For I hope that God will assist you.

Anselm. Now must we inquire how God can become man.

Source: Anselm of Canterbury, Cur Deus Homo I.5, 12–14, II in Proslogion; Monologion, an Appendix on Behalf of the Fool by Gaunilon; and Cur Deus Homo, *trans. Sidney Norton Deane, Chicago: The Open Court Publishing Company, 1903, reprinted 1926, accessed from http://www.sacred-texts.com/chr/ans/ans117.htm.*

5.5 Abelard, from *Exposition of the Epistle to the Romans*

Abelard here indicates his conception of the atonement as concerned especially with the example of love set by Christ.

Now it seems to us that we have been justified by the blood of Christ and reconciled to God in this way: through this unique act of grace manifested to us – in that his Son has taken upon himself our nature and persevered therein in teaching us by word and example even unto death – he has more fully bound us to himself by love; with the result that our hearts should be enkindled by such a gift of divine grace, and true charity should not now shrink from enduring anything for him.

And we do not doubt that the ancient fathers, waiting in faith for this same gift, were aroused to very great love of God in the same way as men of this dispensation of grace, since it is written: 'And they that went before and they that followed cried, saying: "Hosanna to the Son of David"', etc. Yet everyone becomes more righteous – by which we mean a greater lover of the Lord – after the Passion of Christ than before, since a realised gift inspires greater love than one which is only hoped for. Wherefore, our redemption through Christ's suffering is that deeper affection in us which not only frees us from slavery to sin, but also wins for us the true liberty of sons of God, so that we do all things out of love rather than fear – love to him who has shown us such grace that no greater can be found, as he himself asserts, saying, 'Greater love than this no man hath, that a man lay down his life for his friends.' Of this love the Lord says elsewhere, 'I am come to cast fire on the earth, and what will I, but that it blaze forth?' So does he bear witness that he came for the express purpose of spreading this true liberty of love among men.

Source: Abelard, Exposition of the Epistle to the Romans II, *on Romans 3.19–26, from* A Scholastic Miscellany: Anselm to Ockham, *trans. Eugene R. Fairweather, Library of Christian Classics, London: SCM Press, 1956, pp. 283–4.*

5.6 Thomas Aquinas, from *Summa Theologica*

In this series of deliberations Aquinas considers and affirms several aspects of the saving work of Christ accomplished through the passion.

Question 48: Article 2. *Whether Christ's Passion brought about our salvation by way of atonement?*

Objection 1. It would seem that Christ's Passion did not bring about our salvation by way of atonement. For it seems that to make the atonement devolves on him who commits the sin; as is clear in the other parts of penance, because he who has done the wrong must grieve over it and confess it. But Christ never sinned, according to 1 Peter 2:22: 'Who did no sin.' Therefore He made no atonement by His personal suffering.

Objection 2. Further, no atonement is made to another by committing a graver offense. But in Christ's Passion the gravest of all offenses was perpetrated, because those who slew Him sinned most grievously, as stated above (Question 47, Article 6). Consequently it seems that atonement could not be made to God by Christ's Passion.

Objection 3. Further, atonement implies equality with the trespass, since it is an act of justice. But Christ's Passion does not appear equal to all the sins of the human race, because Christ did not suffer in His Godhead, but in His flesh, according to 1 Peter 4:1: 'Christ therefore having suffered in the flesh.' Now the soul, which is the subject of sin, is of greater account than the flesh. Therefore Christ did not atone for our sins by His Passion.

On the contrary, It is written (Psalm 68:5) in Christ's person: 'Then did I pay that which I took not away.' But he has not paid who has not fully atoned. Therefore it appears that Christ by His suffering has fully atoned for our sins.

I answer that, He properly atones for an offense who offers something which the offended one loves equally, or even more than he detested the offense. But by suffering out of love and obedience, Christ gave more to God than was required to compensate for the offense of the whole human race. First of all, because of the exceeding charity from which He suffered; secondly, on account of the dignity of His life which He laid down in atonement, for it was the life of one who was God and man; thirdly, on account of the extent of the Passion, and the greatness of the grief endured, as stated above (Question 46, Article 6). And therefore Christ's Passion was not only a sufficient but a superabundant atonement for the sins of the human race; according to 1 John 2:2: 'He is the propitiation for our sins: and not for ours only, but also for those of the whole world.'

Reply to Objection 1. The head and members are as one mystic person; and therefore Christ's satisfaction belongs to all the faithful as being His members. Also, in so far as any two men are one in charity, the one can atone for the other as shall be shown later. But the same reason does not hold good of confession and contrition, because atonement consists in an outward action, for which helps may be used, among which friends are to be computed.

Reply to Objection 2. Christ's love was greater than His slayers' malice: and therefore the value of His Passion in atoning surpassed the murderous guilt of those who crucified Him: so much so that Christ's suffering was sufficient and superabundant atonement for His murderer's crime.

Reply to Objection 3. The dignity of Christ's flesh is not to be estimated solely from the nature of flesh, but also from the Person assuming it – namely, inasmuch as it was God's flesh, the result of which was that it was of infinite worth.

Article 3. *Whether Christ's Passion operated by way of sacrifice?*

Objection 1. It would seem that Christ's Passion did not operate by way of sacrifice. For the truth should correspond with the figure. But human flesh was never offered up in the sacrifices of the Old Law, which were figures of Christ: nay, such sacrifices were reputed as impious, according to Psalm 105:38: 'And they shed innocent blood: the blood of their sons and of their daughters, which they sacrificed to the idols of Canaan.' It seems therefore that Christ's Passion cannot be called a sacrifice.

Objection 2. Further, Augustine says (*De Civ. Dei* x) that 'a visible sacrifice is a sacrament – that is, a sacred sign – of an invisible sacrifice.' Now Christ's Passion is not a sign, but rather the thing signified by other signs. Therefore it seems that Christ's Passion is not a sacrifice.

Objection 3. Further, whoever offers sacrifice performs some sacred rite, as the very word 'sacrifice' shows. But those men who slew Christ did not perform any sacred act, but rather wrought a great wrong. Therefore Christ's Passion was rather a malefice than a sacrifice.

On the contrary, The Apostle says (Ephesians 5:2): 'He delivered Himself up for us, an oblation and a sacrifice to God for an odor of sweetness.'

I answer that, A sacrifice properly so called is something done for that honor which is properly due to God, in order to appease Him: and hence it is that Augustine says (*De Civ. Dei* x): 'A true sacrifice is every good work done in order that we may cling to God in holy fellowship, yet referred to that consummation of happiness wherein we can be truly blessed.' But, as is added in the same place, 'Christ offered Himself up for us in the Passion': and this voluntary enduring of the Passion was most acceptable to God, as coming from charity. Therefore it is manifest that Christ's Passion was a true sacrifice. Moreover, as Augustine says farther on in the same book, 'the primitive sacrifices of the holy Fathers were many and various signs of this true sacrifice, one being prefigured by many, in the same way as a single concept of thought is expressed in many words, in order to commend it without tediousness': and, as Augustine observes (*De Trin.* iv), 'since there are four things to be noted in every sacrifice – to wit, to whom it is offered, by whom it is offered, what is offered, and for whom it is offered – that the same one true Mediator reconciling us with God through the peace-sacrifice might continue to be one with Him to whom He offered it, might be one with them for whom He offered it, and might Himself be the offerer and what He offered.'

Reply to Objection 1. Although the truth answers to the figure in some respects, yet it does not in all, since the truth must go beyond the figure. Therefore the figure of this sacrifice, in which Christ's flesh is offered, was flesh right fittingly, not the flesh of men, but of animals, as denoting Christ's. And this is a most perfect sacrifice. First of all, since being flesh of human nature, it is fittingly offered for men, and is partaken of by them under the Sacrament. Secondly, because being passible and mortal, it was fit for immolation. Thirdly, because, being sinless, it had virtue to cleanse from sins. Fourthly, because, being the offerer's own flesh, it was acceptable to God on account of His charity in offering up His own flesh. Hence it is that Augustine says (*De Trin.* iv): 'What else could be so fittingly partaken of by men, or offered up for men, as human flesh? What else could be so appropriate for this immolation as mortal flesh? What else is there so clean for cleansing mortals as the flesh born in the womb without fleshly concupiscence, and coming from a virginal womb? What could be so favorably offered and accepted as the flesh of our sacrifice, which was made the body of our Priest?'

Reply to Objection 2. Augustine is speaking there of visible figurative sacrifices: and even Christ's Passion, although denoted by other figurative sacrifices, is yet a sign of something to be observed by us, according to 1 Peter 4:1: 'Christ therefore, having suffered in the flesh, be you also armed with the same thought: for he that hath suffered in the flesh hath ceased from sins: that now he may live the rest of his time in the flesh, not after the desires of men, but according to the will of God.'

Reply to Objection 3. Christ's Passion was indeed a malefice on His slayers' part; but on His own it was the sacrifice of one suffering out of charity. Hence it is Christ who is said to have offered this sacrifice, and not the executioners.

Source: Thomas Aquinas, Summa Theologica, *Part III, 1a.48.1–3, trans. Fathers of the English Dominican Province, London: Burns, Oates & Washbourne, 1924–34.*

5.7 *The Book of Concord*

The Book of Concord *contains the historic doctrinal standards of the Lutheran Church. The following extracts include Article 4, 'Of Justification', from the Augsburg Confession, the pontifical confutation of Article 4, and Melanchthon's response.*

The Augsburg Confession: Article IV: Of Justification

Also they teach that men cannot be justified before God by their own strength, merits, or works, but are freely justified for Christ's sake, through faith, when they believe that they are received into favor, and that their sins are forgiven for Christ's sake, who, by His death, has made satisfaction for our sins. This faith God imputes for righteousness in His sight. Rom. 3 and 4.

Pontifical Confutation

In the fourth article the condemnation of the Pelagians, who thought that man can merit eternal life by his own powers without the grace of God, is accepted as Catholic and in accordance with the ancient councils, for the Holy Scriptures expressly testify to this. John the Baptist says: 'A man can receive nothing, except it be given him from heaven,' John 3:27. 'Every good gift and every perfect gift is from above, and comes down from the Father of lights,' James 1:17. Therefore 'our sufficiency is of God,' 2 Cor 3:5. And Christ says: 'No man can come to me, Except the Father, which hath sent me, draw him,' John 6:44. And Paul: 'What hast thou that thou didst not receive?' 1 Cor. 4:7. For if any one should intend to disapprove of the merits that men acquire by the assistance of divine grace, he would agree with the Manichaeans rather than with the Catholic Church. For it is entirely contrary to holy Scripture to deny that our works are meritorious. For St. Paul says 'I have fought a good fight, I have finished my course, I have kept the faith; henceforth there is laid up for me a crown of righteousness, which the Lord, the righteous Judge, shall give me at that day,' 2 Tim. 4:7–8. And to the Corinthians he wrote 'We must all appear before the judgment-seat of Christ, that every one may receive the things done in his body, according to that he hath done, whether it be good or bad,' 2 Cor. 5:10. For where there are wages there is merit. The Lord said to Abraham: 'Fear not, Abraham, I am thy shield and thy exceeding great reward,' Gen. 15:1. And Isaiah says: 'Behold, his reward is with him, and his work before him,' Isa. 40:10; and, Isa. 58:7,8: 'Deal thy bread to the hungry, and thy righteousness shall go before thee; the glory of the Lord shall go before thee; the glory of the Lord shall gather thee up.' So too the Lord to Cain: 'If thou doest well shalt thou not be accepted?' Gen. 4:7. So the parable in the Gospel declares that we have been hired for the Lord's vineyard, who agrees with us for a penny a day, and says: 'Call the laborers and give them their hire,' Matt. 20:8. So Paul, knowing the mysteries of God, says: 'Every man shall receive his own reward, according to his own labor,' 1 Cor. 3:8. Nevertheless, all Catholics confess that our works of themselves have no merit, but that

God's grace makes them worthy of eternal life. Thus St. John says: 'They shall walk with me in white; for they are worthy,' Rev. 3:4. And St Paul says to the Colossians 1:12: 'Giving thanks unto the Father, which hath made us meet to be partakers of the inheritance of the saints in light.'

Extracts from Melanchthon's Defense

In the Fourth, Fifth, Sixth, and, below, in the Twentieth Article, they condemn us, for teaching that men obtain remission of sins not because of their own merits, but freely for Christ's sake, through faith in Christ. (They reject quite stubbornly both these statements.) For they condemn us both for denying that men obtain remission of sins because of their own merits, and for affirming that, through faith, men obtain remission of sins, and through faith in Christ are justified. But since in this controversy the chief topic of Christian doctrine is treated, which, understood aright, illumines and amplifies the honor of Christ (which is of especial service for the clear, correct understanding of the entire holy Scriptures, and alone shows the way to the unspeakable treasure and right knowledge of Christ, and alone opens the door to the entire Bible), and brings necessary and most abundant consolation to devout consciences, we ask His Imperial Majesty to hear us with forbearance in regard to matters of such importance. For since the adversaries understand neither what the remission of sins, nor what faith, nor what grace, nor what righteousness is, they sadly corrupt this topic, and obscure the glory and benefits of Christ, and rob devout consciences of the consolations offered in Christ …

All Scripture ought to be distributed into these two principal topics, the Law and the promises. For in some places it presents the Law, and in others the promise concerning Christ, namely, either when (in the Old Testament) it promises that Christ will come, and offers, for His sake, the remission of sins justification, and life eternal, or when, in the Gospel (in the New Testament), Christ Himself, since He has appeared, promises the remission of sins, justification, and life eternal. Moreover, in this discussion, by Law we designate the Ten Commandments, wherever they are read in the Scriptures. Of the ceremonies and judicial laws of Moses we say nothing at present.

Of these two parts the adversaries select the Law, because human reason naturally understands, in some way, the Law (for it has the same judgment divinely written in the mind); (the natural law agrees with the law of Moses, or the Ten Commandments) and by the Law they seek the remission of sins and justification. Now, the Decalog requires not only outward civil works, which reason can in some way produce, but it also requires other things placed far above reason, namely, truly to fear God, truly to love God, truly to call upon God, truly to be convinced that God hears us, and to expect the aid of God in death and in all afflictions; finally, it requires obedience to God, in death and all afflictions, so that we may not flee from these or refuse them when God imposes them.

Here the scholastics, having followed the philosophers, teach only a righteousness of reason, namely, civil works, and fabricate besides that without the Holy Ghost reason can love God above all things. For, as long as the human mind is at ease, and does not feel the wrath or judgment of God, it can imagine that it wishes to love God, that it wishes to do good for God's sake. (But it is sheer hypocrisy.) In this manner they teach that men merit the remission of sins by doing what is in them, i.e., if reason, grieving over sin, elicit an act of love to God, or for God's sake be active in that which is good ...

In this opinion there are many great and pernicious errors, which it would be tedious to enumerate. Let the discreet reader think only of this: If this be Christian righteousness, what difference is there between philosophy and the doctrine of Christ? If we merit the remission of sins by these elicit acts (that spring from our mind], of what benefit is Christ? If we can be justified by reason and the works of reason, wherefore is there need of Christ or regeneration [as Peter declares, 1 Peter 1.18ff.)? And from these opinions the matter has now come to such a pass that many ridicule us because we teach that an other than the philosophic righteousness must be sought after ...

Although the adversaries, not to pass by Christ altogether, require a knowledge of the history concerning Christ, and ascribe to Him that it is His merit that a habit is given us or, as they say, prima gratia, 'first grace,' which they understand as a habit, inclining us the more readily to love God; yet, what they ascribe to this habit is of little importance (is a feeble, paltry, small, poor operation, that would be ascribed to Christ), because they imagine that the acts of the will are of the same kind before and after this habit. They imagine that the will can love God; but nevertheless this habit stimulates it to do the same the more cheerfully. And they bid us first merit this habit by preceding merits; then they bid us merit by the works of the Law an increase of this habit and life eternal. Thus they bury Christ, so that men may not avail themselves of Him as a Mediator, and believe that for His sake they freely receive remission of sins and reconciliation, but may dream that by their own fulfilment of the Law they merit the remission of sins, and that by their own fulfilment of the Law they are accounted righteous before God; while, nevertheless, the Law is never satisfied, since reason does nothing except certain civil works, and, in the mean time, neither (in the heart) fears God, nor truly believes that God cares for it. And although they speak of this habit, yet, without the righteousness of faith, neither the love of God can exist in man, nor can it be understood what the love of God is.

Thus the adversaries teach nothing but the righteousness of reason, or certainly of the Law, upon which they look just as the Jews upon the veiled face of Moses; and, in secure hypocrites who think that they satisfy the Law, they excite presumption and empty confidence in works (they place men on a sand foundation, their own works) and contempt of the grace of Christ. On the contrary, they drive timid consciences to despair, which laboring with doubt, never can experience what faith is, and how efficacious it is; thus, at last they utterly despair ...

For it is false [I thus conclude, and am certain that it is a fiction, and not true] that we merit the remission of sins by our works. False also is this, that men are accounted righteous before God because of the righteousness of reason (works and external piety).

False also is this that reason, by its own strength, is able to love God above all things, and to fulfil God's Law, namely, truly to fear God, to be truly confident that God hears prayer, to be willing to obey God in death and other dispensations of God, not to covet what belongs to others, etc.; although reason can work civil works.

False also and dishonoring Christ is this, that men do not sin who, without grace, do the commandments of God (who keep the commandments of God merely in an external manner, without the Spirit and grace in their hearts).

Because, therefore, men by their own strength cannot fulfil the Law of God, and all are under sin, and subject to eternal wrath and death, on this account we cannot be freed by the Law from sin and be justified, but the promise of the remission of sins and of justification has been given us for Christ's sake, who was given for us in order that He might make satisfaction for the sins of the world, and has been appointed as the (only) Mediator and Propitiator. And this promise has not the condition of our merits (it does not read thus: Through Christ you have grace, salvation etc., if you merit it), but freely offers the remission of sins and justification as Paul says, Rom. 11:6: 'If it be of works, then is it no more grace.' And in another place, Rom. 3:21: 'The righteousness of God without the Law is manifested', i.e., the remission of sins is freely offered. Nor does reconciliation depend upon our merits. Because if the remission of sins were to depend upon our merits, and reconciliation were from the Law, it would be useless. For as we do not fulfil the Law, it would also follow that we would never obtain the promise of reconciliation. Thus Paul reasons, Rom. 4:14: 'For if they which are of the Law be heirs, faith is made void, and the promise made of none effect'. For if the promise would require the condition of our merits and the Law, which we never fulfil, it would follow that the promise would be useless.

But since justification is obtained through the free promise it follows that we cannot justify ourselves. Otherwise wherefore would there be need to promise? (And why should Paul so highly extol and praise grace?) For since the promise cannot be received except by faith, the Gospel which is properly the promise of the remission of sins and of justification for Christ's sake, proclaims the righteousness of faith in Christ, which the Law does not teach. Nor is this the righteousness of the Law. For the Law requires of us our works and our perfection. But the Gospel freely offers, for Christ's sake, to us, who have been vanquished by sin and death, reconciliation which is received not by works, but by faith alone. This faith brings to God not confidence in one's own merits, but only confidence in the promise, or the mercy promised in Christ. This special faith, therefore, by which an individual believes that for Christ's sake his sins are remitted him, and that for Christ's sake God is reconciled and propitious, obtains remission of sins and justifies us. And because in repentance, i.e. in terrors, it comforts and encourages hearts, it regenerates us and brings the Holy Ghost that then we may be able to fulfil God's Law, namely, to love God, truly to fear God, truly to be confident that God hears prayer, and to obey God in all afflictions; it mortifies concupiscence etc. Thus, because faith, which freely receives the remission of sins, sets Christ, the Mediator and Propitiator, against God's wrath, it does not present our merits or our love (which would be tossed aside like a little feather by a hurricane). This faith is the true knowledge of Christ, and avails itself of the benefits of Christ, and regenerates hearts, and precedes the fulfilling of the Law. And of this faith not a syllable exists in the doctrine of our adversaries. Hence we find fault with the adversaries, equally because they teach only the righteousness of the Law, and because they do not teach the righteousness of the Gospel, which proclaims the righteousness of faith in Christ.

Source: The Book of Concord. *Translation:* Triglot Concordia: The Symbolical Books of the Evangelical Lutheran Church: German-Latin-English, *published as a memorial of the quadricentenary jubilee of the Reformation anno Domini 1917 by resolution of the Evangelical Lutheran Synod of Missouri, Ohio, and Other States, St Louis: Concordia Publishing House, 1921.*

5.8 The Council of Trent

The Council of Trent met between 1545 and 1563 and issued a series of decrees in response to 'Protestant heresies'. Here the Council sets out its understanding of the doctrine of justification.

CHAPTER I. *On the Inability of Nature and of the Law to justify man.*

The holy Synod declares first, that, for the correct and sound understanding of the doctrine of Justification, it is necessary that each one recognise and confess, that, whereas all men had lost their innocence in the prevarication of Adam – having become unclean, and, as the apostle says, by nature children of wrath, as (this Synod) has set forth in the decree on original sin – they were so far the servants of sin, and under the power of the devil and of death, that not the Gentiles only by the force of nature, but not even the Jews by the very letter itself of the law of Moses, were able to be liberated, or to arise, therefrom; although free will, attenuated as it was in its powers, and bent down, was by no means extinguished in them.

CHAPTER II. *On the dispensation and mystery of Christ's advent.*

Whence it came to pass, that the heavenly Father, the father of mercies and the God of all comfort, when that blessed fulness of the time was come, sent unto men, Jesus Christ, His own Son – who had been, both before the Law, and during the time of the Law, to many of the holy fathers announced and promised – that He might both redeem the Jews who were under the Law, and that the Gentiles, who followed not after justice, might attain to justice, and that all men might receive the adoption of sons. Him God hath proposed as a propitiator, through faith in his blood, for our sins, and not for our sins only, but also for those of the whole world.

CHAPTER III. *Who are justified through Christ.*

But, though He died for all, yet do not all receive the benefit of His death, but those only unto whom the merit of His passion is communicated. For as in truth men, if they were not born propagated of the seed of Adam, would not be born unjust – seeing that, by that propagation, they contract through him, when they are conceived, injustice as their own – so, if they were not born again in Christ, they never would be justified; seeing that, in that new birth, there is bestowed upon them, through the merit of His passion, the grace whereby they are made just. For this benefit the apostle exhorts us, evermore to give thanks to the Father, who hath made us worthy to be partakers of the lot of the saints in light, and hath delivered us from the power of darkness, and hath translated us into the Kingdom of the Son of his love, in whom we have redemption, and remission of sins.

CHAPTER V. *On the necessity, in adults, of preparation for Justification, and whence it proceeds.*

The Synod furthermore declares, that in adults, the beginning of the said Justification is to be derived from the prevenient grace of God, through Jesus Christ, that is to say, from His vocation, whereby, without any merits existing on their parts, they are called; that so they, who by sins were alienated from God, may be disposed through His quickening and assisting grace, to convert themselves to their own justification, by freely assenting to and co-operating with that said grace: in such sort that, while God touches the heart of man by the illumination of the Holy Ghost, neither is man himself utterly without doing anything while he receives that inspiration, forasmuch as he is also able to reject it; yet is he not able, by his own free will, without the grace of God, to move himself unto justice in His sight. Whence, when it is said in the sacred writings: Turn ye to me, and I will turn to you, we are admonished of our liberty; and when we answer; Convert us, O Lord, to thee, and we shall be converted, we confess that we are prevented by the grace of God.

CHAPTER VI. *The manner of Preparation.*

Now they (adults) are disposed unto the said justice, when, excited and assisted by divine grace, conceiving faith by hearing, they are freely moved towards God, believing those things to be true which God has revealed and promised – and this especially, that God justifies the impious by His grace, through the redemption that is in Christ Jesus; and when, understanding themselves to be sinners, they, by turning themselves, from the fear of divine justice whereby they are profitably agitated, to consider the mercy of God, are raised unto hope, confiding that God will be propitious to them for Christ's sake; and they begin to love Him as the fountain of all justice; and are therefore moved against sins by a certain hatred and detestation, to wit, by that penitence which must be performed before baptism: lastly, when they purpose to receive baptism, to begin a new life, and to keep the commandments of God. Concerning this disposition it is written; He that cometh to God, must believe that he is, and is a rewarder to them that seek him; and, Be of good faith, son, thy sins are forgiven thee; and, The fear of the Lord driveth out sin; and, Do penance, and be baptized every one of you in the name of Jesus Christ, for the remission of your sins, and you shall receive the gift of the Holy Ghost; and, Going, therefore, teach ye all nations, baptizing them in the name of the Father, and of the Son, and of the Holy Ghost; finally, Prepare your hearts unto the Lord.

CHAPTER VII. *What the justification of the impious is, and what are the causes thereof.*

This disposition, or preparation, is followed by Justification itself, which is not remission of sins merely, but also the sanctification and renewal of the inward man, through the voluntary reception of the grace, and of the gifts, whereby man of unjust becomes just, and of an enemy a friend, that so he may be an heir according to hope of life everlasting.

Of this Justification the causes are these: the final cause indeed is the glory of God and of Jesus Christ, and life everlasting; while the efficient cause is a merciful God who washes and sanctifies gratuitously, signing, and anointing with the holy Spirit of promise, who is the pledge of our inheritance; but the meritorious cause is His most beloved only-begotten, our Lord Jesus Christ, who, when we were enemies, for the exceeding charity wherewith he loved us, merited Justification for us by His most holy Passion on the wood of the cross, and made satisfaction for us unto God the Father; the instrumental cause is the sacrament of baptism, which is the sacrament of faith, without which (faith) no man was ever justified; lastly, the alone formal cause is the justice of God, not that whereby He Himself is just, but that whereby He maketh us just, that, to wit, with which we being endowed by Him, are renewed in the spirit of our mind, and we are not only reputed, but are truly called, and are, just, receiving justice within us, each one according to his own measure, which the Holy Ghost distributes to every one as He wills, and according to each one's proper disposition and co-operation. For, although no one can be just, but he to whom the merits of the Passion of our Lord Jesus Christ are communicated, yet is this done in the said justification of the impious, when by the merit of that same most holy Passion, the charity of God is poured forth, by the Holy Spirit, in the hearts of those that are justified, and is inherent therein: whence, man, through Jesus Christ, in whom he is ingrafted, receives, in the said justification, together with the remission of sins, all these (gifts) infused at once, faith, hope, and charity. For faith, unless hope and charity be added thereto, neither unites man perfectly with Christ, nor makes him a living member of His body. For which reason it is most truly said, that Faith without works is dead and profitless; and, In Christ Jesus neither circumcision, availeth anything, nor uncircumcision, but faith which worketh by charity ...

Source: The Council of Trent, *ed. and trans. J. Waterworth, London: Dolman, 1848.*

5.9 John Calvin, from the *Institutes of the Christian Religion*

Calvin sets out the threefold office of Christ as prophet, king and priest. It becomes clear here that the saving work of Christ, undertaken on our behalf, is inseparable from who he is.

Therefore, that faith may find in Christ a solid ground of salvation, and so rest in him, we must set out with this principle, that the office which he received from the Father consists of three parts. For he was appointed both Prophet, King, and Priest; though little were gained by holding the names unaccompanied by a knowledge of the end and use ...

2. Moreover, it is to be observed, that the name *Christ* refers to those three offices: for we know that under the law, prophets as well as priests and kings were anointed with holy oil. Whence, also, the celebrated name of Messiah was given to the promised Mediator. But although I admit (as, indeed, I have elsewhere shown) that he was so called from a view to the nature of the kingly office, still the prophetical and sacerdotal unctions have their proper place, and must not be overlooked. The former is expressly mentioned by Isaiah in these words: 'The Spirit of the Lord God is upon me: because the Lord has anointed me to preach good tidings unto the meek; he has sent me to bind up the broken-hearted, to proclaim liberty to the captive, and the opening of the prison to them that are bound; to proclaim the acceptable year of the Lord' (Is. 60:1, 2). We see that he was anointed by the Spirit to be a herald and witness of his Father's grace, and not in the usual way; for he is distinguished from other teachers who had a similar office. And here, again, it is to be observed, that the unction which he received, in order to perform the office of teacher, was not for himself, but for his whole body, that a corresponding efficacy of the Spirit might always accompany the preaching of the Gospel. This, however, remains certain, that by the perfection of doctrine which he brought, an end was put to all the prophecies, so that those who, not contented with the Gospel, annex somewhat extraneous to it, derogate from its authority. The voice which thundered from heaven, 'This is my beloved Son, hear him' gave him a special privilege above all other teachers. Then from him, as head, this unction is diffused through the members, as Joel has foretold, 'Your sons and your daughters shall prophesy, your old men shall dream dreams, and your young men shall see visions' (Joel 2:28). Paul's expressions, that he was 'made unto us wisdom' (1 Cor. 1:30), and elsewhere, that in him 'are hid all the treasures of wisdom and knowledge' (Col. 2:3), have a somewhat different meaning, namely, that out of him there is nothing worth knowing, and that those who, by faith, apprehend his true character, possess the boundless immensity of heavenly blessings. For which reason, he elsewhere says, 'I determined not to know any thing among you, save Jesus Christ and him crucified' (1 Cor. 2:2). And most justly: for it is unlawful to go beyond the simplicity of the Gospel. The purpose of this prophetical dignity in Christ is to teach us, that in the doctrine which he delivered is substantially included a wisdom which is perfect in all its parts.

3. I come to the Kingly office, of which it were in vain to speak, without previously reminding the reader that its nature is spiritual; because it is from thence we learn its efficacy, the benefits it confers, its whole power and eternity. Eternity, moreover, which in Daniel an angel attributes to the office of Christ (Dan. 2:44), in Luke an angel justly applies to the salvation of his people (Luke 1:33). But this is also twofold, and must be viewed in two ways; the one pertains to the whole body of the Church the other is proper to each member. To the former is to be referred what is said in the Psalms, 'Once have I sworn by my holiness, that I will not lie unto David. His seed shall endure for ever, and his throne as the sun before me. It shall be established for ever, as the moon, and as a faithful witness in heaven' (Ps. 89:35, 37). There can be no doubt that God here promises that he will be, by the hand of his Son, the eternal governor and defender of the Church. In none but Christ will the fulfilment of this prophecy be found; since immediately after Solomon's death the kingdom in great measure lost its dignity, and, with ignominy to the family of David, was transferred to a private individual. Afterwards decaying by degrees, it at length came to a sad and dishonourable end. In the same sense are we to understand the exclamation of Isaiah, 'Who shall declare his generation?' (Isaiah 53:8). For he asserts that Christ will so survive death as to be connected with his members. Therefore, as often as we hear that Christ is armed with eternal power, let us learn that the perpetuity of the Church is thus effectually secured; that amid the turbulent agitations by which it is constantly harassed, and the grievous and fearful commotions which threaten innumerable disasters, it still remains safe. Thus, when David derides the audacity of the enemy who attempt to throw off the yoke of God and his anointed, and says, that kings and nations rage 'in vain' (Ps. 2:2–4), because he who sitteth in the heaven is strong enough to repel their assaults, assuring believers of the perpetual preservation of the Church, he animates them to have good hope whenever it is occasionally oppressed. So, in another place, when speaking in the person of God, he says, 'The Lord said unto my Lord, Sit thou at my right hand, until I make thine enemies thy footstool' (Ps. 110:1), he reminds us, that however numerous and powerful the enemies who conspire to assault the Church, they are not possessed of strength sufficient to prevail against the immortal decree by which he appointed his Son eternal King. Whence it follows that the devil, with the whole power of the world, can never possibly destroy the Church, which is founded on the eternal throne of Christ. Then in regard to the special use to be made by each believer, this same eternity ought to elevate us to the hope of a blessed immortality. For we see that every thing which is earthly, and of the world, is temporary, and soon fades away. Christ, therefore, to raise our hope to the heavens, declares that his kingdom is not of this world (John 18:36). In fine, let each of us, when he hears that the kingdom of Christ is spiritual, be roused by the thought to entertain the hope of a better life, and to expect that as it is now protected by the hand of Christ, so it will be fully realised in a future life.

4. That the strength and utility of the kingdom of Christ cannot, as we have said, be fully perceived without recognising it as spiritual, is sufficiently apparent, even from this, that having during the whole course of our lives to war under the cross, our condition here is bitter and wretched. What then

would it avail us to be ranged under the government of a heavenly King, if its benefits were not realised beyond the present earthly life? We must, therefore, know that the happiness which is promised to us in Christ does not consist in external advantages – such as leading a joyful and tranquil life, abounding in wealth, being secure against all injury, and having an affluence of delights, such as the flesh is wont to long for – but properly belongs to the heavenly life. As in the world the prosperous and desirable condition of a people consists partly in the abundance of temporal good and domestic peace, and partly in the strong protection which gives security against external violence; so Christ also enriches his people with all things necessary to the eternal salvation of their souls and fortifies them with courage to stand unassailable by all the attacks of spiritual foes. Whence we infer, that he reigns more for us than for himself, and that both within us and without us; that being replenished, in so far as God knows to be expedient, with the gifts of the Spirit, of which we are naturally destitute, we may feel from their first fruits, that we are truly united to God for perfect blessedness; and then trusting to the power of the same Spirit, may not doubt that we shall always be victorious against the devil, the world, and every thing that can do us harm. To this effect was our Saviour's reply to the Pharisees, 'The kingdom of God is within you.' 'The kingdom of God cometh not with observation' (Luke 17:21, 22). It is probable that on his declaring himself to be that King under whom the highest blessing of God was to be expected, they had in derision asked him to produce his insignia. But to prevent those who were already more than enough inclined to the earth from dwelling on its pomp, he bids them enter into their consciences, for 'the king-dom of God' is 'righteousness, and peace, and joy in the Holy Ghost' (Rom. 14:17). These words briefly teach what the kingdom of Christ bestows upon us. Not being earthly or carnal, and so subject to corruption, but spiritual, it raises us even to eternal life, so that we can patiently live at present under toil, hunger, cold, contempt, disgrace, and other annoyances; contented with this, that our King will never abandon us, but will supply our necessities until our warfare is ended, and we are called to triumph: such being the nature of his kingdom, that he communicates to us whatever he received of his Father. Since then he arms and equips us by his power, adorns us with splendour and magnificence, enriches us with wealth, we here find most abundant cause of glorying, and also are inspired with boldness, so that we can contend intrep-idly with the devil, sin, and death. In fine, clothed with his righteousness, we can bravely surmount all the insults of the world: and as he replenishes us liberally with his gifts, so we can in our turn bring forth fruit unto his glory.

5. Accordingly, his royal unction is not set before us as composed of oil or aromatic perfumes; but he is called the Christ of God, because 'the Spirit of the Lord' rested upon him; 'the Spirit of wisdom and understanding, the Spirit of counsel and might, the Spirit of knowledge and of the fear of the Lord' (Isaiah 11:2). This is the oil of joy with which the Psalmist declares that he was anointed above his fellows (Ps. 45:7). For, as has been said, he was not enriched privately for himself, but that he might refresh the parched and hun-gry with his abundance. For as the Father is said to have given the Spirit to the Son without measure (John 3:34), so the reason is expressed, that we might all receive of his fulness, and grace for grace (John 1:16). From this fountain

flows the copious supply (of which Paul makes mention, Eph. 4:7) by which grace is variously distributed to believers according to the measure of the gift of Christ. Here we have ample confirmation of what I said, that the kingdom of Christ consists in the Spirit, and not in earthly delights or pomp, and that hence, in order to be partakers with him, we must renounce the world. A visible symbol of this grace was exhibited at the baptism of Christ, when the Spirit rested upon him in the form of a dove. To designate the Spirit and his gifts by the term *'unction'* is not new, and ought not to seem absurd (see 1 John 2:20, 27), because this is the only quarter from which we derive life; but especially in what regards the heavenly life, there is not a drop of vigour in us save what the Holy Spirit instils, who has chosen his seat in Christ, that thence the heavenly riches, of which we are destitute, might flow to us in copious abundance. But because believers stand invincible in the strength of their King, and his spiritual riches abound towards them, they are not improperly called Christians. Moreover, from this eternity of which we have spoken, there is nothing derogatory in the expression of Paul, 'Then cometh the end, when he shall have delivered up the kingdom to God, even the Father' (1 Cor. 15:24); and also, 'Then shall the Son also himself be subject unto him that put all things under him, that God may be all in all' (1 Cor. 15:28); for the meaning merely is, that, in that perfect glory, the administration of the kingdom will not be such as it now is. For the Father has given all power to the Son, that by his hand he may govern, cherish, sustain us, keep us under his guardianship, and give assistance to us. Thus, while we wander far as pilgrims from God, Christ interposes, that he may gradually bring us to full communion with God. And, indeed, his sitting at the right hand of the Father has the same meaning as if he was called the vicegerent of the Father, entrusted with the whole power of government. For God is pleased, mediately (so to speak) in his person to rule and defend the Church. Thus also his being seated at the right hand of the Father is explained by Paul, in the Epistle to the Ephesians, to mean, that 'he is the head over all things to the Church, which is his body' (Eph. 1:20, 22). Nor is this different in purport from what he elsewhere teaches, that God has 'given him a name which is above every name; that at the name of Jesus every knee shall bow, of things in heaven, and things in earth, and things under the earth, and that every tongue should confess that Jesus Christ is Lord, to the glory of God the Father' (Phil. 2:9–11). For in these words, also, he commends an arrangement in the kingdom of Christ, which is necessary for our present infirmity. Thus Paul rightly infers that God will then be the only Head of the Church, because the office of Christ, in defending the Church, shall then have been completed. For the same reason, Scripture throughout calls him *Lord*, the Father having appointed him over us for the express purpose of exercising his government through him. For though many lordships are celebrated in the world, yet Paul says, 'To us there is but one God, the Father, of whom are all things, and we in him; and one Lord Jesus Christ, by whom are all things, and we by him' (1 Cor. 8:6). Whence it is justly inferred that he is the same God, who, by the mouth of Isaiah, declared, 'The Lord is our Judge, the Lord is our Lawgiver, the Lord is our King: he will save us' (Isaiah 33:22). For though he every where describes all the power which he possesses as the benefit and gift of the Father, the meaning simply is, that he reigns by divine authority, because his reason for assuming the office of Mediator was, that descending from the bosom and incomprehensible glory of the Father, he might draw near to us. Wherefore there is the greater reason that we all should with one consent prepare to obey, and with the greatest alacrity yield implicit obedience to his will. For as he unites the offices of King and Pastor towards believers, who voluntarily submit to him, so, on the other hand, we are told that he wields an iron sceptre to break and bruise all the rebellious like a potter's vessel (Ps. 2:9). We are also told that he will be the Judge of the Gentiles, that he will cover the earth with dead bodies, and level down every opposing height (Ps. 110:6). Of this examples are seen at present, but full proof will be given at the final judgment, which may be properly regarded as the last act of his reign.

6. With regard to his Priesthood, we must briefly hold its end and use to be, that as a Mediator, free from all taint, he may by his own holiness procure the favour of God for us. But because a deserved curse obstructs the entrance, and God in his character of Judge is hostile to us, expiation must necessarily intervene, that as a priest employed to appease the wrath of God, he may reinstate us in his favour. Wherefore, in order that Christ might fulfil this office, it behoved him to appear with a sacrifice. For even under the law of the priesthood it was forbidden to enter the sanctuary without blood, to teach the worshipper that however the priest might interpose to deprecate, God could not be propitiated without the expiation of sin. On this subject the Apostle discourses at length in the Epistle to the Hebrews, from the seventh almost to the end of the tenth chapter. The sum comes to this, that the honour of the priesthood was competent to none but Christ, because, by the sacrifice of his death, he wiped away our guilt, and made satisfaction for sin. Of the great importance of this matter, we are reminded by that solemn oath which God uttered, and of which he declared he would not repent, 'Thou art a priest for ever, after the order of Melchizedek' (Ps. 110:4). For, doubtless, his purpose was to ratify that point on which he knew that our salvation chiefly hinged. For, as has been said, there is no access to God for us or for our prayers until the priest, purging away our defilements, sanctify us, and obtain for us that favour of which the impurity of our lives and hearts deprives us. Thus we see, that if the benefit and efficacy of Christ's priesthood is to reach us, the commencement must be with his death. Whence it follows, that he by whose aid we obtain favour, must be a perpetual intercessor. From this again arises not only confidence in prayer, but also the tranquillity of pious minds, while they recline in safety on the paternal indulgence of God, and feel assured, that whatever has been consecrated by the Mediator is pleasing to him. But since God under the Law ordered sacrifices of beasts to be offered to him, there was a different and new arrangement in regard to Christ – viz. that he should be at once victim and priest, because no other fit satisfaction for sin could be found, nor was any one worthy of the honour of offering an only begotten son to God. Christ now bears the office of priest, not only that by the eternal law of reconciliation he may render the Father favourable and propitious to us, but also admit us into this most honourable alliance. For we though in ourselves polluted, in him being priests (Rev. 1:6), offer ourselves and our all to God, and freely enter the heavenly sanctuary, so that the sacrifices of prayer and praise which we present are grateful and of sweet odour before him. To

this effect are the words of Christ, 'For their sakes I sanctify myself,' (John 17:19); for being clothed with his holiness, inasmuch as he has devoted us to the Father with himself (otherwise we were an abomination before him), we please him as if we were pure and clean, nay, even sacred. Hence that unction of the sanctuary of which mention is made in Daniel (Dan. 9:24). For we must attend to the contrast between this unction and the shadowy one which was then in use; as if the angel had said, that when the shadows were dispersed, there would be a clear priesthood in the person of Christ. The more detestable, therefore, is the fiction of those who, not content with the priesthood of Christ, have dared to take it upon themselves to sacrifice him, a thing daily attempted in the Papacy, where the mass is represented as an immolation of Christ.

Source: John Calvin, Institutes of the Christian Religion II.15, *trans. Henry Beveridge (1559), Edinburgh: The Calvin Translation Society, 1845.*

5.10 John Owen, from *Works*

John Owen offers a series of arguments against the universality of redemption. The first, from the nature of the new covenant, is presented here.

Argument I. The first argument may be taken from the nature of the covenant of grace, which was established, ratified, and confirmed in and by the death of Christ; that was the testament whereof he was the testator, which was ratified in his death, and whence his blood is called 'The blood of the new testament,' Matt. xxvi. 28. Neither can any effects thereof be extended beyond the compass of this covenant. But now this covenant was not made universally with all, but particularly only with some, and therefore those alone were intended in the benefits of the death of Christ.

The assumption appears from the nature of the covenant itself, described clearly, Jer. xxxi. 31, 32, 'I will make a new covenant with the house of Israel, and with the house of Judah: not according to the covenant that I made with their fathers in the day that I took them by the hand to bring them out of the land of Egypt; which my covenant they brake, though I was an husband to them, saith the Lord'; and Heb. viii. 9–11, 'Not according to the covenant that I made with their fathers in the day when I took them by the hand to lead them out of the land of Egypt; because they continued not in my covenant, and I regarded them not, saith the Lord. For this is the covenant that I will make with the house of Israel after those days, saith the Lord; I will put my laws in their mind, and write them in their hearts: and I will be to them a God, and they shall be to me a people: and they shall not teach every man his neighbour, and every man his brother, saying, Know the Lord: for all shall know me, from the least to the greatest.' Wherein, first, the condition of the covenant is not said to be required, but it is absolutely promised: 'I will put my fear in their hearts.' And this is the main difference between the old covenant of works and the new one of grace, that in that the Lord did only require the fulfilling of the condition prescribed, but in this he promiseth to effect it in them himself with whom the covenant is made. And without this spiritual efficacy, the truth is, the new covenant would be as weak and unprofitable, for the end of a covenant (the bringing of us and binding of us to God), as the old. For in what consisted the weakness and unprofitableness of the old covenant, for which God in his mercy abolished it? Was it not in this, because, by reason of sin, we were no way able to fulfil the condition thereof, 'Do this, and live'? Otherwise the connection is still true, that 'he that doeth these things shall live.' And are we of ourselves any way more able to fulfil the condition of the new covenant? Is it not as easy for a man by his own strength to fulfil the whole law, as to repent and savingly believe the promise of the gospel? This, then, is one main difference of these two covenants – that the Lord did in the old only require the condition; now, in the new, he will also effect it in all the federates, to whom this covenant is extended. And if the Lord should only exact the obedience required in the covenant of us, and not work and effect it also in us, the new covenant would be a show to increase our misery, and not a serious imparting and communicating of grace and mercy. If, then, this be the nature of the new testament – as appears from the very words of it, and might abundantly be proved – that the condition of the covenant should certainly, by free grace, be wrought and accomplished in all that are taken into covenant, then no more are in this covenant than in whom those conditions of it are effected.

But thus, as is apparent, it is not with all; for 'all men have not faith' – it is 'of the elect of God': therefore, it is not made with all, nor is the compass thereof to be extended beyond the remnant that are according to election. Yea, every blessing of the new covenant being certainly common, and to be communicated to all the covenantees, either faith is none of them, or all must have it, if the covenant itself be general. But some may say that it is true God promiseth to write his law in our hearts, and put his fear in our inward parts; but it is upon condition. Give me that condition, and I will yield the cause. Is it if they do believe? Nothing else can be imagined. That is, if they have the law written in their hearts (as every one that believes hath), then God promiseth to write his law in their hearts! Is this probable, friends? is it likely? I cannot, then, be persuaded that God hath made a covenant of grace with all, especially those who never heard a word of covenant, grace, or condition of it, much less received grace for the fulfilling of the condition; without which the whole would be altogether unprofitable and useless. The covenant is made with Adam, and he is acquainted with it, Gen. iii. 15 – renewed with Noah, and not hidden from him – again established with Abraham, accompanied with a full and rich declaration of the chief promises of it, Gen. xii.; which is most certain not to be effected towards all, as afterwards will appear. Yea, that first distinction, between the seed of the woman and the seed of the serpent is enough to overthrow the pretended universality of the covenant of grace; for who dares affirm that God entered into a covenant of grace with the seed of the serpent?

Most apparent, then, it is that the new covenant of grace, and the promises thereof, are all of them of distinguishing mercy, restrained to the people whom God did foreknow; and so not extended universally to all. Now, the blood of Jesus Christ being the blood of this covenant, and his oblation intended only for the procurement of the good things intended and promised thereby – for he was the surety thereof, Heb. vii. 22, and of that only – it cannot be conceived to have respect unto all, or any but only those that are intended in this covenant.

Source: The Works of John Owen, *vol. 10, Edinburgh: The Banner of Truth Trust, 1967, pp. 236–40.*

5.11 Albrecht Ritschl, from *The Christian Doctrine of Justification and Reconciliation*

In this brief extract Ritschl summarizes his understanding of the relation between the redemptive work of Christ and the moral end to which that redemption is directed.

Since Jesus himself ... saw in the Kingdom of God the moral end of the religious fellowship He had to found ...; since He understood by it not the common exercise of worship, but the organization of humanity through action inspired by love, any conception of Christianity would be imperfect and therefore incorrect which did not include this specifically teleological aspect. We must further remember that Christ did not describe this moral task, to be carried out by the human race, in the form of a philosophical doctrine, and propagate it in a school: He entrusted it to His disciples. At the same time He constituted them a religious community through training of another kind. For when good action towards our fellow-men is subsumed under the conception of the Kingdom of God, this whole province is placed under the rule and standard of religion. And so, were we to determine the unique quality of Christianity merely by its teleological element, namely, its relation to the moral Kingdom of God, we should do injustice to its character as a religion. This aspect of Christianity, clearly, is meant to be provided for in Schleiermacher's phrase – 'in which everything is referred to the redemption wrought by Jesus.' For redemption is a presupposition of the Christian's peculiar dependence on God; but dependence on God is, for Schleiermacher, the general form of religious experience as distinct from a moral relationship. Now it is true that in Christianity everything is 'related' to the moral organisation of humanity through love-prompted action; but at the same time everything is also 'related' to redemption through Jesus, to spiritual redemption, *i.e.* to that freedom from guilt and over the world which is to be won through the realised Fatherhood of God. Freedom in God, the freedom of the children of God, is the private end of each individual Christian, as the Kingdom of God is the final end of all. And this double character of the Christian life – perfectly religious and perfectly ethical – continues, because its realisation in the life of the individual advances through the perpetual interaction of the two elements. For the life and activity of the Founder of Christianity issued at once in the redemption and the setting up of the Kingdom of God. The same fidelity in His Divine vocation enabled Him to preserve and secure both His own fellowship with the Father, and the power to lead sinners back into the same fellowship with God; and the same effect has two aspects – His disciples acknowledge Him as the Head of the Kingdom of God, and God as their Father.

Christianity, then, is the monotheistic, completely spiritual, and ethical religion which is based on the life of its Author as Redeemer and as Founder of the Kingdom of God, consists in the freedom of the children of God, involves the impulse to conduct from the motive of love, aims at the moral organisation of mankind, and grounds blessedness on the relation of sonship to God, as well as on the Kingdom of God.

Source: Albrecht Ritschl, The Christian Doctrine of Justification and Reconciliation, trans. and ed. H. R. Mackintosh and A. B. Macaulay, Edinburgh: T. & T. Clark, 1900, pp. 12–13.

5.12 P. T. Forsyth, from *The Work of Christ*

In this extract Forsyth gives an account of penal substitution and describes the work of Christ in terms of God's offering and humanity's confession.

From what I have said you will be prepared to hear me state that reconciliation is effected by the representative sacrifice of Christ crucified, by Christ crucified as the representative of God on the one hand and of Humanity, or the Church, on the other hand. Also it was by Christ crucified in connection with the divine judgment. Judgment is a far greater idea than sacrifice. For you see great sacrifices made for silly or mischievous causes, sacrifices which show no insight whatever into the moral order or the divine sanctity. Now this sacrifice of Christ, when you connect it with the idea of judgment, must in some form or other be described as a penal sacrifice. Round that word penal there rages a great deal of controversy. And I am using the word with some reserve, because there are forms of interpreting it which do the idea injustice. The sacrifice of Christ was a penal sacrifice. In what sense is that so? We can begin by clearing the ground, by asking, In what sense is it not true that the sacrifice of Christ was penal? Well, it cannot be true in the sense that God punished Christ. That is an absolutely unthinkable thing. How could God punish Him in whom He was always well pleased? The two things are a contradiction in terms. And it cannot be true in the sense that Christ was in our stead in such a way as to exclude and exempt us. The sacrifice of Christ, then, was penal not in the sense of God so punishing Christ that there is left us only religious enjoyment, but in this sense. There is a penalty and curse for sin; and Christ consented to enter that region. Christ entered voluntarily into the pain and horror which is sin's penalty from God. Christ, by the deep intimacy of His sympathy with men, entered deeply into the blight and judgment which was entailed by man's sin, and which must be entailed by man's sin if God is a holy and therefore a judging God. It is impossible for us to say that God was angry with Christ; but still Christ entered the wrath of God ... He entered the penumbra of judgment, and from it He confessed in free action, He praised and justified by act, before the world, and on the scale of all the world, the holiness of God. You can therefore say that although Christ was not punished by God, He bore God's penalty upon sin. That penalty was not lifted even when the Son of God passed through. Is there not a real distinction between the two statements? To say that Christ was punished by God who was always well pleased with Him is an outrageous thing. Calvin himself repudiates the idea. But we may say that Christ did, at the depth of that great act of self-identification with us when He became man, He did enter the sphere of sin's penalty and the horror of sin's curse, in order that, from the very midst and depth of it, His confession and praise of God's holiness might rise like a spring of fresh water at the bottom of the bitter sea, and sweeten all. He justified God in His judgment and wrath. He justified God in this thing.

§

So the act of Christ had this twofold aspect. On the one hand it was God offering, and on the other hand it was man confessing. Now, what was it that Christ chiefly confessed? I hope you have read McLeod Campbell on the Atonement. Every minister ought to know that book, and know it well. But there is one criticism to be made upon the great, fine, holy book. And it is this. It speaks too much, perhaps, about Christ confessing human sin, about Christ becoming the Priest and Confessor before God of human sin and exposing it to God's judgment. The horror of the Cross expresses the repentance of the race before a holy God for its sin. But considerable difficulties arise in that connection, and critics were not slow to point them out. How could Christ in any real sense confess a sin, even a racial sin, with whose guilt He had nothing in common? Now that is rather a serious criticism if the confession of sin were the first charge upon either Christ or us, if the confession of human sin were the chief thing that God wanted or Christ did. I think it is certainly a defect in that great book that it fixes our attention too much upon Christ's vicarious confession *of human sin.* The same criticism applies to another very fine book, that by the late Canon Moberly, of Christ Church, 'Atonement and Personality.' I once had the privilege of meeting Canon Moberly in discussion on this subject, and ventured to point out that defect in his theory, and I was relieved to find that on the occasion the same criticism was also made by Bishop Gore. But we get out of the difficulty, in part at least, if we recognise that the great work of Christ, while certainly it did confess human sin, was yet not to confess that, but to confess something greater, namely, God's holiness in His judgment upon sin. His confession, indeed, was not in so many words, but in a far more mighty way, by act and deed of life and death. The great confession is not by word of mouth – it is by the life, in the sense, not of mere conduct, but in the great personal sense in which life contains conduct and transcends death. Christ confessed not merely human sin – which in a certain sense, indeed, He could not do – but He confessed God's holiness in reacting mortally against human sin, in cursing human sin, in judging it to its very death. He stood in the midst of human sin full of love to man, such love as enabled Him to identify Himself in the most profound, sympathetic way with the evil race; fuller still of love to the God whose name He was hallowing; and, as with one mouth, as if the whole race confessed through Him, as with one soul, as though the whole race at last did justice to God through His soul, He lifted up His face unto God and said, 'Thou art holy in all Thy judgments, even in this judgment which turns not aside even from Me, but strikes the sinful spot if even I stand on it.' The dereliction upon the Cross, the sense of love's desertion by love, was Christ's practical confession of the holy God's repulsion of sin. He accepted the divine situation – the situation of the race before God. By God's will He did so. By His own free consent He did so. Remember the distinction between God's changeless love and God's varying treatment of the soul. God made Him sin, treated Him as if He were sin; He did not view Him as sinful. That is quite another matter. God made Him to be sin – it does not say He made Him sinful. God lovingly treated Him as human sin, and with His consent judged human sin in Him and on Him. Personal guilt Christ could never confess. There is that in guilt which can only be confessed by the guilty. 'I did it.' That kind of confession Christ could never make. That is the part of the confession that we make, and we cannot make it effectually until we are in union with Christ and His great lone work of perfectly and practically confessing the holiness of God. There is a racial confession that can only be made by the holy; and there is a personal confession that can only be made by the guilty. That latter, I say, is a confession Christ could never make. In that respect Christ did not die, and did not suffer, did not confess, in our stead. We alone, the guilty, can make that confession; but we cannot make it with Christian effect without the Cross and the confession there. We say then not only 'I did this,' but 'I am guilty before the holiness confessed in the Cross.' The grand sin is not to sin against the law but against the Cross. The sin of sins is not transgression, but unfaith. So also of holiness, there is a confession of holiness which can only be made by God, the Holy. If God's holiness was to be fully confessed, in act and deed, in life, and death, and love transcending both, it can only be done by Godhead itself.

§

Therefore we press the words to their fullness of meaning: 'God was in Christ reconciling,' not reconciling through Christ, but actually present as Christ reconciling, doing in Christ His own work of reconciliation. It was done by Godhead itself, and not by the Son alone. The old theologians were right when they insisted that the work of redemption was the work of the whole Trinity – Father, Son, and Holy Spirit; as we express it when we baptize into the new life of reconcilement in the threefold name. The holiness of God was confessed in man by Christ, and this holy confession of Christ's is the source of the truest confession of our sin that we can make. Our saving confession is not merely 'I did so and so,' but 'I did it against a holy, saving God.' 'I have sinned against heaven and in thy sight,' sinned before infinite holiness and forgiving grace. God could not forgive until man confessed and confessed not only his own sin but confessed still more – God's holiness in the judgment of sin. The confession also had to be made in life and action, as the sin was done. That is to say, it had to be made religiously and not theologically, by an experience and not an utterance. A verbal confession, however sincere, could not fully own an actual sin. If we sin by deed we must so confess. It is made thus religiously, spiritually, experimentally, practically by Jesus Christ's life, its crown of death, and His life eternal. The more sinful man is, the less can he thus confess either his own sin or God's holiness. Therefore God did it in man by a love which was as great as it was holy, by an infinite love. That is to say, by a love which was as closely and sympathetically identified with man as it was identified with the power of the holy God. So we have arrived at this. The great confession was made not alone in the precise hour of Christ's death, although it was consummated there. It had to be made in life and act, and not in a mere feeling or statement; and for this purpose death must be organically one with the whole life. You cannot sever the death of Christ from the life of Christ. When you think of the self-emptying which brought Christ to earth, His whole life here was a living death. The death of Christ must be organic with His whole personal life and action. And that means not only His earthly life previous to the Cross, but His whole celestial life from the beginning, and to this hour, and to all eternity. The death of Christ is the central point of eternity as well as of human history. His own eternal life revolves on it. And we shall never be so good and holy at any point, even in eternity, that we shall not look into the Cross of Christ as the centre of all our hope in earth or heaven. It is Christ that works out His own redemption and reconciliation, from God's right hand, throughout the course of history. I would gather that up in one phrase. Christ is the perpetual providence of His own salvation. Christ, acting through His Spirit, is the eternal providence of His own salvation. The apostles never separated reconciliation in any age from the Cross and blood of Jesus Christ. If ever we do that (and many are doing it today) we throw the New Testament overboard.

Source: P. T. Forsyth, The Work of Christ, *2nd edn, Blackwood, South Australia: New Creation Publications, 1994, pp. 145–54.*

5.13 Gustaf Aulén, from *Christus Victor*

Aulén here contends that among the several metaphors of the atonement evident in the New Testament, the idea of Christ victorious over the evil powers is the predominant one.

There is a form of the idea of the Atonement which this account of the matter either ignores altogether or treats with very much less than justice, but whose suppression falsifies the whole perspective, and produces a version of the history which is seriously misleading. This type of view may be described provisionally as the 'dramatic.' Its central theme is the idea of the Atonement as a Divine conflict and victory; Christ – Christus Victor – fights against and triumphs over the evil powers of the world, the 'tyrants' under which mankind is in bondage and suffering, and in Him God reconciles the world to Himself. Two points here require to be pressed with special emphasis: first, that this is a doctrine of Atonement in the full and proper sense, and second, that this idea of the Atonement has a clear and distinct character, of its own, quite different from the other two types.

First, then, it must not be taken for granted that this idea may rightly be called only a doctrine of salvation, in contrast with the later development of a doctrine of Atonement properly so called. Certainly it describes a work of salvation, a drama of salvation; but this salvation is at the same time an atonement in the full sense of the word, for it is a work wherein God reconciles the world to Himself, and is at the same time reconciled. The background of the idea is dualistic;[1] God is pictured as in Christ carrying through a victorious conflict against powers of evil which are hostile to His will. This constitutes Atonement, because the drama is a cosmic drama, and the victory over the hostile powers brings to pass a new relation, a relation of reconciliation, between God and the world; and, still more, because in a measure the hostile powers are regarded as in the service of the Will of God the Judge of all, and the executants of His judgment. Seen from this side, the triumph over the opposing powers is regarded as a reconciling of God Himself; He is reconciled by the very act in which He reconciles the world to Himself.

Secondly, it is to be affirmed that this 'dramatic' view of the Atonement is a special type, sharply distinct from both the other types. We shall illustrate its character fully in the course of these lectures; for the present a preliminary sketch must suffice.

The most marked difference between the 'dramatic' type and the so-called 'objective' type lies in the fact that it represents the work of Atonement or reconciliation as from first to last a work of God Himself, a *continuous* Divine work; while according to the other view, the act of Atonement has indeed its origin in God's will, but is, in its carrying-out, an offering made to God by

---

1 [Dualism] is not used in the sense of a metaphysical Dualism between the Infinite and the finite, or between spirit and matter; nor, again, in the sense of the absolute Dualism between Good and Evil ... It is used in the sense in which the idea constantly occurs in Scripture, of the opposition between God and that which in His own created world resists His will; between the Divine Love and the rebellion of created wills against Him ...

Christ as man and on man's behalf, and may therefore be called a *discontinuous* Divine work.

On the other hand, it scarcely needs to be said that this 'dramatic' type stands in sharp contrast with the 'subjective' type of view. It does not set forth only or chiefly a change taking place in men; it describes a complete change in the situation, a change in the relation between God and the world, and a change also in God's own attitude. The idea is, indeed, thoroughly 'objective'; and its objectivity is further emphasised by the fact that the Atonement is not regarded as affecting men primarily as individuals, but is set forth as a drama of a world's salvation.

Since, then, the objective character of the 'dramatic' type is definite and emphatic, it can hardly help to a clear understanding of the history of the idea of Atonement to reserve the term 'objective Atonement' for the type of view which commonly bears that name. The result can only be a confusion of two views of the Atonement which need to be clearly distinguished. I shall therefore refer to the type of view commonly called objective as the 'Latin' type, because it arose and was developed on Western, Latin soil, and to the dualistic-dramatic view as 'the classic idea' of the Atonement.

The classic idea has in reality held a place in the history of Christian doctrine whose importance it would not be easy to exaggerate. Though it is expressed in a variety of forms, not all of which are equally fruitful, there can be no dispute that it is the dominant idea of the Atonement throughout the early church period. It is also in reality, as I shall hope to show, the dominant idea in the New Testament; for it did not suddenly spring into being in the early church, or arrive as an importation from some outside source. It was, in fact, the ruling idea of the Atonement for the first thousand years of Christian history. In the Middle Ages it was gradually ousted from its place in the theological teaching of the church, but it survived still in her devotional language and in her art. It confronts us again, more vigorously and profoundly expressed than ever before, in Martin Luther, and it constitutes an important part of his expression of the Christian faith. It has therefore every right to claim the title of the *classic Christian idea of the Atonement*. But if this be the case, any account of the history of the doctrine which does not give full consideration to this type of view cannot fail to be seriously misleading.

Source: Gustaf Aulén, Christus Victor, *London: SPCK and New York: The Macmillian Co., 1931, pp. 20–3.*

5.14 Dorothee Sölle, from *Christ the Representative*

In this extract, Sölle offers an account of how Christ acts representatively on behalf of all humanity in holding open our place before God.

Who am I? How do I achieve identity? These questions almost seem to have dropped out of view in the course of our theological inquiry into the treatment of representation in the Bible and in tradition. Yet even when speaking of magical exchange or voluntary suffering, of *satisfactio* and *imputatio*, of reconciliation in alienation and of exclusive substitution in our place, it is indirectly we ourselves who are involved, since such concepts describe the way in which the kingdom of identity is established.

The Christian faith answers all these questions by saying that from now on representation is not just a postulate of the reason, nor an everyday occurrence, but the really decisive event of all human history. Anthropology and christology are related as question and answer. In Tillich's terminology, they exist in correlation. To ask about the structures of living representation is necessarily to ask about Christ. In other words, it is to ask how we may define the representation which the concrete person Jesus (historicity) is said to carry out voluntarily for all (universalization).

Certain as it is that my quest for one who can represent me (and my possibilities) reaches out beyond the society in which I live, it is equally important for me as a person that this representative should not replace me. The answer given by the Christian faith to the quest for one who acts and suffers in my place is misunderstood if it is presented in perfectionistic and final terms. This tears identity and the kingdom apart. Identity degenerates into a substitutionary act on the part of Christ, and the kingdom of identity is postponed for ever. But Christ represents us only for a time, conditionally and incompletely. Christ does not substitute himself for us; he represents us for a time. And this must be maintained in opposition to all forms of christocratic perfectionism. We remain irreplaceable precisely because we need him as representative. He who in our place believes, hopes and loves – and who therefore does what we have failed to do – does not obliterate us so that nothing now depends on us. Christ does not replace our life, making us superfluous, not counted on by anyone any longer. Christological perfectionism turns Jesus, who is our brother, into a 'superman' who replaces us if this term 'superman' ever applied to anyone. But at the same time, this perfectionism turns God into an idol for whom man is exchangeable. But can it ever be a matter of indifference to God what becomes of me?

Any doctrine of representation which treats us, our sins, our history, as 'over and done with', not only destroys the irreplaceable individual but also abandons the God for whom men are not interchangeable. God, who despite the satisfaction already made, is still not content with the representative, continues to count on us, continues to look to us, to wait for us. For him, our hope, which is fixed on him, is not detachable and already settled. God is *not* content with our representative. Our representative speaks for us, but we ourselves have to learn to speak. He believes *for* us, but we ourselves have to learn to believe. He hopes when we are without hope, but that is not the end of the story. The Spirit who intercedes for us with 'inarticulate groans' (Rom. 8.26) does not intend to replace our own praying. But certainly he represents those whose only prayer is ignorance of what to pray for. By his representation he holds their place open for them lest they should lose it. Expressing it metaphorically, we need Christ so that God should not 'sack' us. Without Christ, God would dismiss us on the spot. Christ does not press for our dismissal, like some ambitious and more successful colleague. He is a representative, not a replacement. So God does not tear up our contract of employment.

But can this metaphorical statement be transposed into the realities of human history? Our 'place' or 'post' would in that case mean our freedom as God's children who have responsibility for the world. To say that because of Christ, God does not 'sack' us, means that he allows us this freedom so that we should no longer be the prey of mythical preconceptions and prejudices. The New Testament declares this freedom began in Christ: it is celebrated in the hymn to Christ in Philippians which the apostle derived from the tradition of the primitive Church. The cosmic powers – under, above, and on the earth – have paid homage to Christ (Phil. 2.10). It was all up with them as 'powers', as mythical, fateful forces, the moment they acknowledged Christ. They have lost the power to terrorize anyone. If at any time they are invoked, and appeal is made to their power (whether in the guise of blood and soil, party and state, or ministerial office and hierarchy), it can be pointed out that they have been disarmed. They now have to justify themselves as secular powers at the bar of reason, since no higher sanction can any longer be assigned them.

The recognition of Christ resulted in the abdication of the powers. Once lords of the world, they no longer have any say. When man is still imprisoned in mythical thinking, he feels himself hemmed in by the world. He is caught in its toils, so it cannot become for him the medium of his self-realization. At the mercy of irrational powers, he remains a child, under age, immature. But Christ, the man of God, reveals in his life what liberation from these powers, which still boast of their invincibility, could be like. He demythologizes them. In mythical language, we express this by saying that he compels them to abdicate. In this way Christ ensures that we do not lose our 'post' as God's co-workers on earth. Without Christ, the earth would have been less subject to us, and consequently less habitable than it actually is. The freedom which dawned in him exists, of course, even where it does not appeal to him. Yet it can be said that his name is the indelible seal of this freedom. Whenever this freedom is threatened, whenever worldly powers, parading as myths, demand unconditional obedience, there too the secular consciousness is present in Christ's right and name. That, for the sake of Christ, God does not 'sack' us, then, means that he maintains in us this consciousness of freedom over against all such powers. By virtue of his radical freedom from every form of regimentation of the world, the 'place' promised us remains open – the 'place' of lords of the world, the 'place' *he* took in order that we might occupy it.

The engagement undertaken by Christ on our behalf can only be an incomplete and temporary representation, since it is on behalf of those who are and in Christ's view remain irreplaceable. Because Christ at no point sacrifices our identity to some higher goal, he necessarily acts for us 'incompletely'. Because we continue to be irreplaceable to God, Christ cannot sacrifice us to history, or to historical ends realizable only in the future – not even to a mythically interpreted final world judgment at the end of history. Representation is a kind of restoration of the damaged present, which is now once more given its due; something which is only possible, of course, insofar as the future is kept open for it. Christ does not include us all on one great account, for the simple reason that by representing us he shows that he expects more of us than we yet are.

He died for us – namely, in our place – but we too must learn to die. The Christian life is lived out as a learning to die in which physical death is only one, and that not necessarily the most concrete, form of dying. Using traditional language, we may say with Luther that this learning to die means acknowledging God's wrath as the truth concerning ourselves, and submitting ourselves completely to the dependence upon God implied in the concept of imputation. Of course, terms like 'God's wrath', 'dependence on God', require to be interpreted and translated into secular terms. This we try to do in what follows. It was for us, in our place, that Christ entered into life, but we ourselves have to learn to live. This means recognizing the human condition, and its characteristic estrangement, not as something alien to God but rather as a mode of His being with and among us. It also means perceiving identity in the non-identical – that is to say, living on the basis of this identity. The very goal of Christ's work would be destroyed if this work were in any way complete and perfect. Incompleteness constitutes the mode of his being for us.

Source: Dorothee Sölle, Christ the Representative: An Essay in Theology after the Death of God, *Philadelphia: Fortress Press and London: SCM Press, 1967, pp. 102–6.*

5.15 Jürgen Moltmann, from *The Crucified God*

In this extract Moltmann considers what it means for God that Jesus Christ the second person of the Trinity should suffer and die on the cross.

The death of Jesus on the cross is the *centre* of all Christian theology. It is not the only theme of theology, but it is in effect the entry to its problems and answers on earth. All Christian statements about God, about creation, about sin and death have their focal point in the crucified Christ. All Christian statements about history, about the church, about faith and sanctification, about the future and about hope stem from the crucified Christ. The multiplicity of the New Testament comes together in the event of the crucifixion and resurrection of Jesus and flows out again from it. It is one event and one person. The addition of 'cross and resurrection' represents only the inevitable temporality which is a part of language; it is not a sequence of facts. For cross and resurrection are not facts on the same level; the first expression denotes a historical happening to Jesus, the second an eschatological event. Thus the centre is occupied not by 'cross and resurrection', but by *the resurrection of the crucified Christ,* which qualifies his death as something that has happened for us, and the cross of the risen Christ, which reveals and makes accessible to those who are dying his resurrection from the dead.

In coming to terms with this Christ event, the christological tradition closely followed the Christ hymn in Phil. 2. It therefore understood the incarnation of the Son of God as his course towards the humiliation on the cross. The incarnation of the Logos is completed on the cross. Jesus is born to face his passion. His mission is fulfilled once he has been abandoned on the cross. So it is impossible to speak of an incarnation of God without keeping this conclusion in view. There can be no theology of the incarnation which does not become a theology of the cross. 'As soon as you say incarnation, you say cross.' God did not become man according to the measure of our conceptions of being a man. He became the kind of man we do not want to be: an outcast, accursed, crucified. *Ecce homo*! Behold the man! is not a statement which arises from the confirmation of our humanity and is made on the basis of 'like is known by like'; it is a confession of faith which recognizes God's humanity in the dehumanized Christ on the cross. At the same time the confession says *Ecce deus*! Behold God on the cross! Thus God's incarnation 'even unto the death on the cross' is not in the last resort a matter of concealment; this is his utter humiliation, in which he is completely with himself and completely with the other, the man who is dehumanized. Humiliation to the point of death on the cross corresponds to God's nature in the contradiction of abandonment. When the crucified Jesus is called the 'image of the invisible God', the meaning is that *this* is God, and God is like *this*. God is not greater than he is in this humiliation. God is not more glorious than he is in this self-surrender. God is not more powerful than he is in this helplessness. God is not more divine than he is in this humanity. The nucleus of everything that Christian theology says about 'God' is to be found in this Christ event. The Christ event on the cross is a God event. And conversely, the God event takes place on the cross of the risen Christ. Here God has not just acted externally, in his unattainable glory and eternity. Here he has acted in himself and has gone on to suffer in himself. Here he himself is love with all his being. So the new christology which tries to think of the 'death of Jesus as the death of God', must take up the elements of truth which are to be found in *kenoticism* (the doctrine of God's emptying of himself). It cannot seek to maintain only a dialectical relationship between the divine being and human being, leaving each of these unaffected; in its own way the divine being must encompass the human being and vice versa. That means that it must understand the event of the cross in God's being in both trinitarian and personal terms. In contrast to the traditional doctrine of the two natures in the person of Christ, it must begin from the totality of the person of Christ and understand the relationship of the death of the Son to the Father and the Spirit. The doctrine of kenosis, the self-emptying of God, was still conceived within the framework of the distinction of the two natures of God and man. It attempted, however, to understand God's being in process. It has found few followers, because the framework of thought which it has preserved leads to difficult and impossible statements. But Paul Althaus is right in saying:

> Christology must be done in the light of the cross: the full and undiminished deity of God is to be found in the complete helplessness, in the final agony of the crucified Jesus, at the point where no 'divine nature' is to be seen. In faith in Jesus Christ, we recognize as a law of the life of God himself a saying of the Lord which Paul applied to his own life ('My strength is made perfect in weakness', II Cor. 12.9). Of course the old idea of the immutability of God shatters on this recognition. Christology must take seriously the fact that God himself really enters into the suffering of the Son and in so doing is and remains completely God. This divine miracle cannot be rationalized by a theory which makes God present and active in Jesus Christ only so long as the limits of being human as we understand it are not crossed. Yet on the other hand the Godhead may not be located ontologically in the humanity of Jesus. The Godhead is there hidden under the manhood, only open to faith and not to sight. It is therefore beyond any possibility of a theory. That this is the case, that God enters into the hiddenness of his Godhead beneath the human nature, is kenosis.

With this attitude to the old doctrine of kenosis, Althaus comes very near to a personal understanding of the suffering and death of Jesus as that of the Son in relationship to the Father. He has put in question the theory of the immutability of God and with it the axiom of the impassibility of the divine nature. But at that point he has returned to the old dialectic of Godhead and manhood and has therefore barred the way towards a trinitarian understanding of kenosis. The 'mystical theology of the Eastern church', unrestricted by the doctrine of the two natures by which God and man are distinguished, could go further here and say: 'The kenosis ... [and] the work of the incarnate Son [is] the work of the entire most holy Trinity, from which Christ cannot be separated.' But if the kenosis of the Son to the point of death upon the cross is the 'revelation of the entire Trinity', this event too can only be presented as a God-event in trinitarian terms. What happens on the cross manifests the relationships of Jesus, the Son, to the Father, and vice versa. The cross and its liberating effect makes possible the movement of the Spirit from the Father to us. The cross stands at the heart of the trinitarian being of God; it divides and conjoins the persons in their relationships to each other and portrays them in a specific way. For as we said, the theological dimension of the death of Jesus on the cross is what happens between Jesus and his Father in the spirit of abandonment and surrender. In these relationships the person of Jesus comes to the fore in its totality as the Son, and the relationship of the Godhead and the manhood in his person fall into the background. Anyone who really talks of the Trinity talks of the cross of Jesus, and does not speculate in heavenly riddles. Consequently, we must make more of a differentiation than is suggested by the phrase 'the death of God' which appeared at the beginning of this section.

Jesus' death cannot be understood 'as the death of God', but only as death in God. The 'death of God' cannot be designated the origin of Christian theology, even if the phrase has an element of truth in it; the origin of Christian theology is only the death on the cross in God and God in Jesus' death. If one uses the phrase, it is advisable to abandon the concept of God and to speak of the relationships of the Son and the Father and the Spirit at the point at which 'God' might be expected to be mentioned. From the life of these three, which has within it the death of Jesus, there then emerges who God is and what his Godhead means. Most previous statements about the specifically Christian understanding of talk about 'the death of God' have lacked a dimension, the trinitarian dimension. 'On the cross, God stretched out his hands to embrace the ends of the earth,' said Cyril of Jerusalem. This is a symbolic expression. He invites the whole earth to understand his suffering and his hopes in the outstretched arms of the crucified Jesus and therefore in God. 'O blessed tree on which God was outstretched.' This symbol is an invitation to understand the Christ hanging on the cross as the 'outstretched' God of the Trinity.

Source: Jürgen Moltmann, The Crucified God, *London: SCM Press and Philadelphia: Fortress Press, 1974, pp. 204–7.*

5.16 Gustavo Gutiérrez, from *A Theology of Liberation*

Guttiérrez considers the relation between the liberation from sin accom-
plished on the cross and the political liberation of the poor and oppressed
peoples of this world.

The approach we have been considering opens up for us – and this is of utmost importance – unforeseen vistas on the problem of sin. An unjust situation does not happen by chance; it is not something branded by a fatal destiny: there is human responsibility behind it. The prophets said it clearly and energetically and we are rediscovering their words now. This is the reason why the Medellin Conference refers to the state of things in Latin America as a 'sinful situation,' as a 'rejection of the Lord.' This characterization, in all its breadth and depth, not only criticizes the individual abuses on the part of those who enjoy great power in this social order; it challenges all their practices, that is to say, it is a repudiation of the whole existing system – to which the Church itself belongs.

In this approach we are far, therefore, from that naive optimism which denies the role of sin in the historical development of humanity. This was the criticism, one will remember, of the Schema of Ariccia and it is frequently made in connection with Teilhard de Chardin and all those theologies enthusiastic about human progress. But in the liberation approach sin is not considered as an individual, private, or merely interior reality – asserted just enough to necessitate 'spiritual' redemption which does not challenge the order in which we live. Sin is regarded as a social, historical fact, the absence of fellowship and love in relationships among persons, the breach of friendship with God and with other persons, and, therefore, an interior, personal fracture. When it is considered in this way, the collective dimensions of sin are rediscovered. This is the biblical notion that José Maria Gonzalez Ruiz calls the 'hamartiosphere,' the sphere of sin: 'a kind of parameter or structure which objectively conditions the progress of human history itself.' Moreover, sin does not appear as an afterthought, something which one has to mention so as not to stray from tradition or leave oneself open to attack. Nor is this a matter of escape into a fleshless spiritualism. Sin is evident in oppressive structures, in the exploitation of humans by humans, in the domination and slavery of peoples, races, and social classes. Sin appears, therefore, as the fundamental alienation, the root of a situation of injustice and exploitation. It cannot be encountered in itself, but only in concrete instances, in particular alienations. It is impossible to understand the concrete manifestations without understanding the underlying basis and vice versa. Sin demands a radical liberation, which in turn necessarily implies a political liberation. Only by participating in the historical process of liberation will it be possible to show the fundamental alienation present in every partial alienation.

This radical liberation is the gift which Christ offers us. By his death and resurrection he redeems us from sin and all its consequences, as has been well said in a text we quote again: 'It is the same God who, in the fullness of time, sends his Son in the flesh, so that he might come to liberate all men from all slavery to which sin has subjected them: hunger, misery, oppression, and ignorance, in a word, that injustice and hatred which have their origin in human selfishness.' This is why the Christian life is a passover, a transition from sin to grace, from death to life, from injustice to justice, from the subhuman to the human. Christ introduces us by the gift of his Spirit into communion with God and with all human beings. More precisely, it is because he introduces us into this communion, into a continuous search for its fullness, that he conquers sin – which is the negation of love – and all its consequences.

In dealing with the notion of liberation in Chapter 2, we distinguished three levels of meaning: political liberation, human liberation throughout history, liberation from sin and admission to communion with God. In the light of the present chapter, we can now study this question again. These three levels mutually affect each other, but they are not the same. One is not present without the others, but they are distinct: they are all part of a single, all encompassing salvific process, but they are to be found at different levels. Not only is the growth of the Kingdom not reduced to temporal progress; because of the Word accepted in faith, we see that the fundamental obstacle to the Kingdom, which is sin, is also the root of all misery and injustice; we see that the very meaning of the growth of the Kingdom is also the ultimate precondition for a just society and a new humanity. One reaches this root and this ultimate precondition only through the acceptance of the liberating gift of Christ, which surpasses all expectations. But, inversely, all struggle against exploitation and alienation, in a history which is fundamentally one, is an attempt to vanquish selfishness, the negation of love. This is the reason why any effort to build a just society is liberating. And it has an indirect but effective impact on the fundamental alienation. It is a salvific work, although it is not all of salvation. As a human work it is not exempt from ambiguities, any more than what is considered to be strictly 'religious' work. But this does not weaken its basic orientation or its objective results.

Temporal progress – or, to avoid this aseptic term, human liberation – and the growth of the Kingdom both are directed toward complete communion of human beings with God and among themselves. They have the same goal, but they do not follow parallel roads, not even convergent ones. The growth of the Kingdom is a process which occurs historically in liberation, insofar as liberation means a greater human fulfilment. Liberation is a precondition for the new society, but this is not all it is. While liberation is implemented in liberating historical events, it also denounces their limitations and ambiguities, proclaims their fulfilment, and impels them effectively towards total communion. This is not an identification. Without liberating historical events, there would be no growth of the Kingdom. But the process of liberation will not have conquered the very roots of human oppression and exploitation without the coming of the Kingdom, which is above all a gift. Moreover, we can say that the historical, political liberating event is the growth of the Kingdom and is a salvific event; but it is not the coming of the Kingdom, not *all* of salvation. It is the historical realization of the Kingdom and, therefore, it also proclaims its fullness. This is where the difference lies. It is a distinction made from a dynamic viewpoint, which has nothing to do with the one which holds for the existence of two juxtaposed 'orders,' closely connected or convergent, but deep down different from each other.

The very radicalness and totality of the salvific process require this relationship. Nothing escapes this process, nothing is outside the pale of the action of Christ and the gift of the Spirit. This gives human history its profound unity. Those who reduce the work of salvation are indeed those who limit it to the strictly 'religious' sphere and are not aware of the universality of the process. It is those who think that the work of Christ touches the social order in which we live only indirectly or tangentially, and not in its roots and basic structure. It is those who in order to protect salvation (or to protect their interests) lift salvation from the midst of history, where individuals and social classes struggle to liberate themselves from the slavery and oppression to which other individuals and social classes have subjected them, it is those who refuse to see that the salvation of Christ is a radical liberation from all misery, all despoliation, all alienation. It is those who by trying to 'save' the work of Christ will 'lose' it.

In Christ the all-comprehensiveness of the liberating process reaches its fullest sense. His work encompasses the three levels of meaning which we mentioned above. A Latin American text on the missions seems to us to summarize this assertion accurately: 'All the dynamism of the cosmos and of human history, the movement towards the creation of a more just and fraternal world, the overcoming of social inequalities among persons, the efforts, so urgently needed on our continent, to liberate humankind from all that depersonalizes it – physical and moral misery, ignorance and hunger – as well as the awareness of human dignity (*Gaudium et spes*, no. 22) – all these originate, are transformed, and reach their perfection in the saving work of Christ. In him and through him salvation is present at the heart of human history, and there is no human act which, in the last instance, is not defined in terms of it.'

Source: Gustavo Gutiérrez, A Theology of Liberation, Maryknoll, NY: Orbis Books and London: SCM Press, 2001, pp. 173–7.

5.17 Choan-Seng Song, from *Theology from the Womb of Asia*

This extract offers, from an Asian perspective, a further consideration of the relation between the liberation accomplished on the cross and political liberation for the oppressed.

In Asia, not only women are building their vision of tomorrow on the rejection of the wrongs of yesterday; outcasts too – the untouchables in India, the Burakumin in Japan, the aborigines in Australia – have begun to do the same.

The vision of tomorrow extends as well to economic and political reality in Asia. It is the reality of economic progress at the cost of workers forced to sell their labor for a pittance. It is the reality of political oppression by those who hold power – the power that breaks families and destroys lives. The lament of a Korean wife whose beloved husband was beaten, tortured, and finally hanged by the Korean Central Intelligence Agency in 1974 reminds us of the tragic reality of many countries in Asia today:

Where should I go,
where should I go
from now on, to meet you again?

    Turning your head again and again
    you'd leave our home in the morning,
    and always come back in the evening,
    always you came back to me …

Last spring, all of a sudden
you were taken away
without any reason.

    After the spring, summer came
    and autumn passed without
    any sign of your return.

All through the long winter
I waited for spring to come
for, if spring came, I could see you
and I kept dreaming of that joyous day.
Even that dream I'm deprived of now,
I am refused even to feel the pain
that I had gone through
by waiting for you.

    You were all that I lived for,
    the spring where my strength to live came from,
    Beloved one!

I would rather,
I would rather lie next to you
holding your pale tortured hands,
holding them tightly, tightly
and with a smile.
I would rather lie next to you peacefully,
peacefully,
and quietly.

The lament moves one to tears. It is heartrending. It fills one with anger at the brutal political power that thinks nothing of destroying such a beautiful union between husband and wife.

This is a dirge. It is the dirge of a bereaved wife for her departed husband. But it is also a dirge for a government that cruelly took the life of her husband and the lives of many others. It is a dirge for a political power that multiplies widows and orphans.

But it is also a love song. The song is a dedication to that tender love of the husband who would, on his way out to work in the morning, 'turn his head again and again' toward his wife standing at the door to see him off. The song is a confession of the love of the wife who 'would rather lie next to her dead husband, holding his pale tortured hands tightly.' Such love is indestructible. Police brutality cannot break it. Political cruelty cannot destroy it. It still binds the wife to her husband. It puts to shame those whose love is weak and calculating. It will kindle hope in those who have a vision of tomorrow built on the ruins of today.

With such love, tomorrow will become possible – not only possible but real. That love is the power of tomorrow, the energy of the future, and the glory of God's reign in the world. One recalls Jesus on his way to the cross. 'Great numbers of people followed,' Luke tells us, 'many women among them, who mourned and lamented over him' (Luke 23:27). How much these women loved Jesus! They were like mothers and sisters to him, and he was to them like a son and a brother. But he is being taken to be executed on a cross. How could they not mourn? Who could stop them from lamenting? Their mourning and their lament must have filled the air. It must have gone into the heart of spectators. it must have reached the hearts of those religious leaders who conspired to have all this happen; it must have shaken their souls. And it must have also reached Pontius Pilate, the Roman governor who became, against his better judgment, an accomplice in the hideous abuse of law and sent an innocent Jesus to die a shameful and painful death on the cross. It must have given unrest to his heart the rest of his life.

The crying of these women must have deeply touched Jesus. What he saw were tears of love. He 'turned to them and said, "Daughters of Jerusalem, do not weep for me; no, weep for yourselves and your children" ' (23:28). Yes, for the city of God that is going to be deprived of Jesus, the Son of God, they should weep. Over the nation favored by God, the nation that murdered prophets and now is going to murder God's only Son, they should lament. And for themselves who looked for a messiah in him and now have to accompany him on his way to death, they should cry.

But Jesus had something else to say to those weeping women: 'For the days are surely coming when they will say, "Happy are the barren, the wombs that never bore a child, the breasts that never fed one" ' (23:29). These are words of strong warning about God's judgment. This is an apocalyptic warning. This is a striking parallel to that apocalyptic passage in Mark's Gospel where it is said: 'Alas for women with child in those days, and for those who have children at their breast!' (Mark 13:17). A city that is going to crucify the Son of God – is there a warning of future catastrophe strong enough for it? These words could have been put on Jesus' lips by the earliest Christian community. But if they had indeed come from him, Jesus must have said them with deep compassion.

But Jesus had to face up to the cross. He had to walk that road of death to the end. But that road to Golgotha was not the final end. It was the beginning of the road to life. The tomorrow of the resurrection dawned out of the yesterday and today of the cross. Some of those women who wept at the foot of Jesus' cross were the first ones to meet the risen Christ and announce his resurrection. It was Mary of Magdala who went to the disciples and broke the incredible news: 'I have seen the Lord!' (John 20:18).

Source: Choan-Seng Song, Theology from the Womb of Asia, *Maryknoll, NY: Orbis Books, 1986 and London: SCM Press, 1988, pp. 211–14.*

5.18 Rosemary Radford Ruether, from *To Change the World*

Rosemary Radford Ruether provides an example of how feminist theologians have explored the implications of Christ's liberating work for women oppressed by patriarchal culture.

Another perspective on christology is being elaborated by liberation theologies. Liberation theologies go back to nineteenth-century movements of Christian socialism that began to seek alliances between the gospel and the Left. Liberation theologies base their christologies particularly on the Jesus of the synoptic gospels. Here is a Jesus who does not sacralize existing ruling classes. The messianic prophet proclaims his message as an iconoclastic critique of existing élites, particularly religious élites. The gospel drama is one of prolonged conflict between Christ and those religious authorities who gain their social status from systems of ritualized righteousness. Jesus proclaims an iconoclastic reversal of this system of religious status. The leaders of the religious establishment are blind guides and hypocrites, while the outcasts of the society, socially and morally, prostitutes, publicans, Samaritans, are able to hear the message of the prophet. In Matthew's language, 'Truly the tax collectors and the harlots go into the kingdom of God before you', i.e., the scribes and Pharisees (Matt. 21.31). The gospel turns upside down the present order; the first shall be last and the last first.

This reversal of order is not simply a turning upside down of the present hierarchy, but aims at a new order where hierarchy itself is overcome as a principle of rule. This may have been the source of the messianic struggle between Jesus and his own disciples. It certainly has been the root of misunderstanding of Jesus by the church historically. When the sons of Zebedee ask Jesus if they can sit on his left and right hands when he comes into his Kingdom, he confronts them with his different vision of the way into the messianic future.

> You know that the rulers of the Gentiles lord it over them, and their great men exercise authority over them. It shall not be so among you; but whoever would be great among you must be your servant, and whoever would be first among you must be your slave; even as the Son of man came not to be served but to serve and to give his life as a ransom for many. (Matt. 20.25–27)

The meaning of servanthood in this oft-quoted and oft-misused text of Jesus cannot be understood either as a sacralized Christian lordship that calls itself 'servant', but reproduces the same characteristics of domination, or as the romanticizing of servitude. This is why neither existing lords nor existing servants can serve as a model for this servanthood, but only the Christ, the messianic person, who represents a new kind of humanity. The essence of servanthood is that it is possible only for liberated persons, not people in servitude. Also it exercises power and leadership, but in a new way, not to reduce others to dependency, but to empower and liberate others. This means, in the language of liberation theology, that God as liberator acts in history to liberate all through opting for the poor and the oppressed of the present system. The poor, the downcast, those who hunger and thirst, have a certain priority in God's work of redemption. Part of the signs of the kingdom is that the lame walk, the blind see, the captives are freed, the poor have the gospel preached to them. Christ goes particularly to the outcasts, and they, in turn, have a special affinity for the gospel. But the aim of this partiality is to create a new whole, to elevate the valleys and make the high places low, so that all may come into a new place of God's reign, when God's will is done on earth.

How does the question of the subjugation and emancipation of women fit into such a vision of the iconoclastic prophetic Christ? This world view is not concerned with the dualism of male and female, either as total groups or as representatives of some cosmic principles that need to be related to each other. But women are not ignored in this vision. Indeed, if one can say that Christ comes to the oppressed and the oppressed especially hear him, then it is women within these marginal groups who are often seen both as the oppressed of the oppressed and also as those particularly receptive to the gospel. The dialogue at the well takes place not just with a Samaritan, but with a Samaritan woman. Not just a Syro-Phoenician, but a Syro-Phoenician woman is the prophetic seeker who forces Jesus to concede redemption to the non-Jews. Among the poor it is widows who are the exemplars of the most destitute; among the moral outcasts it is the prostitutes who represent the bottom of the list. This is not accidental. It means that, in the iconoclastic messianic vision, it is the women of the despised and outcast peoples who are seen as the bottom of the present hierarchy and hence, in a special way, the last who shall be first in the kingdom.

How does this vision of the redemptive work of Christ, that addresses itself particularly to the women among the outcast, differ from those messianic visions of the new age of the 'feminine' which we described earlier? It seems to me that it has some affinities with them, in the sense that Christ is seen as critic rather than vindicator of the present hierarchical social order. The meaning of Christ is located in a new future order still to come that transcends the power structures of historical societies, including those erected in the Christian era in 'Christ's name'.

But this biblical vision also differs in important ways from the romantic vision of the advent of the new age of the feminine. These gnostic and romantic traditions abstract the human person as male and female into a dualism of opposite principles, masculinity and femininity. They give different valuations to each side and then try to set up a scheme to unite the two in a new whole. This sets up an insoluble problem for human personhood until these qualities labelled masculine and feminine are seen as the product of social power relations rather than 'nature'. 'Woman-as-body-sensuality' and 'woman-as-pure-altruistic-love' are both abstractions of human potential created when one group of people in power is able to define other groups of people over against themselves. To abstract these definitions into eternal essences is to miss the social context in which these definitions arise.

223

The world of the gospels returns us to concrete social conditions in which maleness and femaleness are elements of a complex web in which humans have defined status, superiority and inferiority. The gospel returns us to the world of Pharisees and priests, widows and prostitutes, homeless Jewish prophets and Syro-Phoenician women. Men and women interact with each other within a multiplicity of social definitions: sexual status, but also ethnicity, social class, religious office and law define relations with each other. Jesus as liberator calls for a renunciation and dissolution of this web of status relationships by which societies have defined privilege and unprivilege. He speaks especially to outcast women, not as representatives of the 'feminine', but because they are at the bottom of this network of oppression. His ability to be liberator does not reside in his maleness, but, on the contrary, in the fact that he has renounced this system of domination and seeks to embody in his person the new humanity of service and mutual empowerment.

Together, Jesus and the Syro-Phoenician woman, the widow and the prostitute, not as male and female principles, but as persons responding authentically to each other, point us to that new humanity of the future. This new humanity is described in simple and earthy terms by Jesus as the time when 'all receive their daily bread, when each remits the debts which the others owe to them, when we are not led into temptations (including messianic temptations) but are delivered from evil'.

Source: Rosemary Radford Ruether, To Change the World, *New York: Crossroad, 1981 and London: SCM Press, 1984, pp. 53–6.*

6 The Holy Spirit

Introductory essay

Christian theology has as its principal source and authority the Scriptures of the Old and New Testaments which bear witness to the self-disclosure of God to and through Israel and with particular concentration in the person of Jesus Christ. As the early Christian community reflected on the person and work of Jesus they came to understand that what had been learned of God through Israel's history was brought to a particular focus and fulfilment in Jesus Christ and in such a way as to elicit from those who were his disciples the confession that in encountering Jesus their brother they were also entering into communion with God. This Jesus who had come among them spoke and acted with the authority of God and claimed for himself prerogatives that were thought to have belonged to God alone.

At the same time, however, Jesus spoke to and of his 'Father' and promised to send the Spirit, each of whom were distinct from Jesus himself and yet were apparently intimately related to him. Whether Jesus said it himself or whether it forms part of the interpretative activity of the early Church, it seemed appropriate for Jesus to say, 'the Father and I are one' and 'whoever has seen me has seen the Father'. Further indication of a unique unity between God the Father and Jesus, which embraces the Spirit too, is given through Jesus' promise: 'I will send you from the Father – the Spirit of truth that issues from the Father – he will bear witness to me' (John 15.26).

A new theology thus emerges, a theology that regards the Word and Spirit referred to in the Old Testament not merely as impersonal energies emanating from God, but rather as distinct persons in a threefold differentiation of God's being. Irenaeus in our first reading below thus identified the Son and Spirit made known in the New Testament with the Word and Spirit of the Old Testament who were the instruments of God's self-communication and who were with God in the beginning. His was the first attempt to say that while God is disclosed to us through these three persons, it is nevertheless the one God who acts in and through each of them. In the years that followed, the Church sought to clarify further this threefold understanding of God.

Both Irenaeus and Tertullian sought to distinguish a biblical understanding of the Spirit from that of the Gnostics. While accepting that the Son and Spirit 'emanate' from the Father – thus using language favoured by the Gnostic writer Valentinus – Tertullian, in opposition to Valentinus, insists, as seen below, that there is no separation between the Father, Son and Spirit.

The Spirit is not to be counted among created things. Origen in our next reading is likewise insistent upon preserving the ontological unity of Father, Son and Spirit, and begins to trace the role of the Spirit in teaching us of Christ and in uniting us with the Father and the Son.

In the third century the Arian controversy led to the confession, drafted at Nicaea in 325 and confirmed at Constantinople in 381, that Jesus was 'true God from true God' and 'of one being with the Father'. The divine identity of the Spirit was not in contention at Nicaea but became a matter of controversy with the expulsion of Macedonius from the See of Constantinople in 360. Macedonius was an Arian bishop who apparently denied the divinity of the Spirit. Though long regarded as the founder of a group called the Pneumatomachians (Spirit-fighters), this is doubtful. Macedonius, however, advocated the use of the term *homoiousion* ('of like being' with the Father) as applied to both the Son and to the Spirit. This implied that the Son and Spirit were something other than fully divine. Eustathius of Sebaste, whom J. N. D Kelly describes as 'the leader of the Spirit-fighters',[1] was a more strident advocate of the subordination of the Spirit. Kelly further explains that the position of the Pneumatomachians 'is aptly summarized in the statement attributed to Eustathius that he did "not choose to call the Spirit God nor presume to call him a creature"'.[2]

As seen in the next reading, Cyril of Jerusalem, though prone to the use of questionable terminology sought to uphold the Nicene affirmation of the ontological unity of the Father and Son and advocated the same in respect of the Spirit. His catechetical lectures were an effort to articulate a view of the Spirit faithful to the biblical witness.

Athanasius, who was at the forefront of opposition to the Arians, became involved too in the debate about the Spirit. His treatise on the matter took the form of a series of letters to Serapion (*Ad Serapionem*), 359–60. In these letters Athanasius opposes an Egyptian group he calls the Tropici because of their figurative exegesis of Scripture (Gk *tropos* = figure). This group denied the divinity of the Spirit and argued that the Spirit was a creature brought into existence out of nothing and took the form of an angel. Athanasius, by contrast, and with particular emphasis on scriptural 'proofs', argued that the Spirit is fully divine, consubstantial with the Father and the Son.

In 374 Amphilocius, a first cousin of Gregory of Nazianzus and friend of Basil of Caesarea, visited Basil and urged him to write a treatise on the Spirit. Although he had been circumspect on the matter until then, Basil complied and wrote a treatise from which the next extract is taken and in which he urged that the Spirit be accorded the same glory and honour and worship as the Father and the Son. He nowhere calls the Spirit 'God', but he does insist that we worship the Spirit because the Spirit is 'not alien to

---

1 J. N. D. Kelly, *Early Christian Doctrines*, 5th edn, London: A&C Black, 1977, p. 259.
2 Kelly, *Early Christian Doctrines*, p. 260.

the divine nature'. Three key features of his argument are: (a) The Spirit's greatness and dignity, along with his power, are testified to in Scripture; (b) the Spirit is associated with the Father and the Son in whatever they accomplish, especially in the work of sanctification and *theosis*; (c) the Spirit is *personally* related to the Father and Son. Precisely how the Spirit is related to the Father and Son became a particular concern of Augustine in his treatise *De Trinitate*. It is in that work, extracted below, that Augustine develops the widely influential view that the Spirit is the bond of love between Father and Son. Augustine contends that the biblical phrase 'God is love' may be applied most especially to the Spirit.

By the turn of the ninth century John of Damascus was able to summarize the 'orthodox' faith with a series of affirmations that left no doubt that the Spirit was to be worshipped with the Father and Son as Lord and Creator of all things. The Damascene distinguishes the Spirit, however, as the one who 'proceeded' from the Father *simultaneously* with the generation of the Son, thus distancing himself from those who had begun to confess through an addition to the Nicene-Constantinopolitan Creed that the Spirit proceeds from the Father *and the Son* (*filioque*). The controversy over the addition of that clause was soon to be the cause of the schism between Constantinople and Rome.

The distinct personal identity of the Spirit has sometimes been obscured in the tradition. Whereas the personhood of the Father and Son shines forth clearly in the New Testament, the Spirit sometimes appears as the power or energy of God without distinct personal identity. Whatever the merits of Augustine's identification of the Spirit as the bond of love, that formulation has contributed to the effacement of the personhood of the Spirit. Thomas Aquinas in our next reading is thus concerned to show that the name 'Holy Ghost' applies to a distinct person of the Trinity rather than to a power held in common by the persons of the Godhead. Relying less upon the gifts of rational deliberation and more upon the powerful testimony of visionary experience, Hildegard of Bingen in a short devotional passage testifies to the life-giving power of the Holy Spirit. In just a short extract Hildegard speaks of the Spirit as the fiery force blazing in the beauty of nature, as the breath that brings all things to life, and as the giver of wisdom and reason. Here and throughout her work, the Spirit is represented with powerful imagery, and takes a very prominent role in the divine economy.

At the time of the Reformation the central concern was not the Spirit's personal identity, nor the Spirit's divinity along with the Father and Son, but rather the role of the Spirit in the economy of salvation. This concern is evident in the extract from John Calvin's *Institutes of the Christian Religion*. There is a polemical edge to Calvin's words for the Reformers attributed to the authority of the Spirit, rather than the authority of the Church, the possibility that Christians might read the Scriptures for themselves and learn what is necessary for salvation. Contemporary with Calvin, however,

227

Laelius Socinus denied the divinity of both Christ and the Spirit. The Unitarian faith of Socinius became influential in Europe and so, as seen in the next reading, John Owen in the following century found it necessary to retrace the ground of earlier doctrinal battles and affirm once more both the divinity and the personality of the Spirit. Owen ties the work of the Spirit very closely to that of the Son, and stresses that the benefits of Christ's work are applied to our souls through the love, grace and power of the Spirit.

In Israel's Scripture and in the New Testament the Spirit is portrayed as the giver of life. The *ruach* of God is breathed into humankind, and that same Spirit inspires, empowers and equips human beings for life in communion with God. The intimate connection between the life-giving Spirit of God and the human spirit can lead to a confusion of the two and consequent elevation of those who claim a special gifting of the Spirit. Friedrich Schleiermacher, as seen in our next reading, is determined to avoid that confusion while nevertheless offering an account of how the Spirit works in union with human nature. Drawing upon the New Testament accounts of Jesus promising to send the Spirit after his departure from the disciples, Schleiermacher tries to distinguish the distinctive gift of the Spirit to believers from a more general presence of the Spirit in creation. Edward Irving is likewise concerned to identify specifically what difference to the individual is made through baptism in the Spirit. While Irving acknowledges that the gift of life itself, the capacity to live, love and experience sensation and emotion is possible only on account of the Spirit's work, there is also a special work of the Spirit in giving new life to the fallen and disobedient creature and enabling us to live a holy life in communion with God. Renewed communion with God and with our neighbour is identified by H. Wheeler Robinson as the principal characteristic of life in the Spirit. This new relation between God and humanity and between persons is best expressed, Robinson contends, 'in the Spirit of the Cross of Christ'.

One of the most tragic of many schisms in the Church took place in 1054 and divided the Western (Roman Catholic) from the Eastern (Orthodox) Church. The immediate cause of the schism was a dispute over the Spirit and whether or not it was appropriate to say in the Nicene Creed that the Spirit proceeds from the Father *and from the Son* (*filioque*). This chapter includes accounts of that issue from a Western point of view (Karl Barth) and from an Eastern perspective (Theodore Stylianopoulos). It is fair to say, however, that these two extracts indicate but by no means encompass the full scope of what remains a serious point of difference between the Eastern and Western theological traditions.

The emergence of the Pentecostal and Charismatic Movements in the twentieth century prompted renewed attention to the gifts of the Spirit, and to the Spirit's empowering of the Church. These traditions and their contributions to a renewed concentration upon the work of the Spirit are represented below by extracts from Tom Smail and Amos Yong, but three further readings reveal that more traditional churches, as, for instance, the Roman Catholic Church in the encyclical *Lumen Gentium*, have also taken up the theme. Jürgen Moltmann (Reformed) and Hans Küng (Roman Catholic) offer further consideration of the Spirit's work in the Church. There are, of course, several dimensions of the work of the Spirit in the Church and in the world. Roman Catholic theologian Yves Congar considers especially Jesus' promise recalled in John's Gospel that 'the Spirit will lead you into all truth'.

Moving beyond the role of the Spirit within the community of faith, Wolfhart Pannenberg draws attention to the pervasive activity of the Spirit throughout creation. Without wishing to diminish the personal identity of the third person of the Trinity, Pannenberg employs a metaphor from science, the 'field of force', to describe the all-pervasive, life-giving presence of the Spirit in creation and in human life. The Spirit is the immanence of God throughout all creation, the 'field' within which all life is sustained, and the force that directs creation towards its eschatological completion. Pannenberg here recovers an ancient theme, namely, that the Spirit is the one who is 'the perfecting cause', bringing creation to its intended life-giving communion with God. Pannenberg's focus on the work of the Spirit throughout creation reflects a widespread concern in contemporary theology.

Summarizing, then, the principal themes in the Church's reflection upon the Spirit, they are the divinity and distinct personal identity of the Spirit, the role of the Spirit in revealing the truth of Christ, the relation between the Spirit, the Father and the Son and the particular work of the Spirit in the Church and in creation.

MAR

6.1 Irenaeus of Lyons, from *Against Heresies*

Irenaeus explains that the Spirit was with the Father in the beginning and is co-eternal with the Word.

1. As regards His greatness, therefore, it is not possible to know God, for it is impossible that the Father can be measured; but as regards His love (for this it is which leads us to God by His Word), when we obey Him, we do always learn that there is so great a God, and that it is He who by Himself has established, and selected, and adorned, and contains all things; and among the all things, both ourselves and this our world. We also then were made, along with those things which are contained by Him. And this is He of whom the Scripture says, 'And God formed man, taking clay of the earth, and breathed into his face the breath of life.'

It was not angels, therefore, who made us, nor who formed us, neither had angels power to make an image of God, nor any one else, except the Word of the Lord, nor any Power remotely distant from the Father of all things. For God did not stand in need of these [beings], in order to the accomplishing of what He had Himself determined with Himself beforehand should be done, as if He did not possess His own hands. For with Him were always present the Word and Wisdom, the Son and the Spirit, by whom and in whom, freely and spontaneously, He made all things, to whom also He speaks, saying, 'Let Us make man after Our image and likeness;' He taking from Himself the substance of the creatures [formed], and the pattern of things made, and the type of all the adornments in the world.

3. I have also largely demonstrated, that the Word, namely the Son, was always with the Father; and that Wisdom also, which is the Spirit, was present with Him, anterior to all creation, He declares by Solomon: 'God by Wisdom founded the earth, and by understanding hath He established the heaven. By His knowledge the depths burst forth, and the clouds dropped down the dew.' And again: 'The Lord created me the beginning of His ways in His work: He set me up from everlasting, in the beginning, before He made the earth, before He established the depths, and before the fountains of waters gushed forth; before the mountains were made strong, and before all the hills, He brought me forth.'

And again: 'When He prepared the heaven, I was with Him, and when He established the fountains of the deep; when He made the foundations of the earth strong, I was with Him preparing [them]. I was He in whom He rejoiced, and throughout all time I was daily glad before His face, when He rejoiced at the completion of the world, and was delighted in the sons of men.'

Source: Irenaeus of Lyons, Against Heresies IV.20.1 and 3, trans. Alexander Roberts and William Rambaut, in Alexander Roberts, James Donaldson and A. Cleveland Coxe (eds), Ante-Nicene Fathers, vol. 1, Buffalo, NY: Christian Literature Publishing Co., 1885.

6.2 Tertullian, from *Against Praxeas*

Tertullian explains, against Valentinus, that there is no separation between the Spirit, the Son and the Father.

If any man from this shall think that I am introducing some *probole* – that is to say, some prolation of one thing out of another, as Valentinus does when he sets forth Aeon from Aeon, one after another – then this is my first reply to you: Truth must not therefore refrain from the use of such a term, and its reality and meaning, because heresy also employs it. The fact is, heresy has rather taken it from Truth, in order to mould it into its own counterfeit. Was the Word of God put forth or not? Here take your stand with me, and flinch not. If He was put forth, then acknowledge that the true doctrine has a prolation; and never mind heresy, when in any point it mimics the truth. The question now is, in what sense each side uses a given thing and the word which expresses it. Valentinus divides and separates his prolations from their Author, and places them at so great a distance from Him, that the Aeon does not know the Father: he longs, indeed, to know Him, but cannot; nay, he is almost swallowed up and dissolved into the rest of matter.

With us, however, the Son alone knows the Father, He has also heard and seen all things with the Father; and what He has been commanded by the Father, that also does He speak. And it is not His own will, but the Father's, which He has accomplished, which He had known most intimately, even from the beginning. 'For what man knoweth the things which be in God, but the Spirit which is in Him?' But the Word was formed by the Spirit, and (if I may so express myself) the Spirit is the body of the Word. The Word, therefore, is both always in the Father, as He says, 'I am in the Father;' and is always with God, according to what is written, 'And the Word was with God;' and never separate from the Father, or other than the Father, since 'I and the Father are one.' This will be the prolation, taught by the truth, the guardian of the Unity, wherein we declare that the Son is a prolation from the Father, without being separated from Him. For God sent forth the Word, as the Paraclete also declares, just as the root puts forth the tree, and the fountain the river, and the sun the ray. For these are *probolai, or emanations*, of the substances from which they proceed. I should not hesitate, indeed, to call the tree the son or offspring of the root, and the river of the fountain, and the ray of the sun; because every original source is a parent, and everything which issues from the origin is an offspring. Much more is (this true of) the Word of God, who has actually received as His own peculiar designation the name of *Son*. But still the tree is not severed from the root, nor the river from the fountain, nor the ray from the sun; nor, indeed, is the Word separated from God. Following, therefore, the form of these analogies, I confess that I call God and His Word – the Father and His Son – *two*. For the root and the tree are distinctly two things, but correlatively joined; the fountain and the river are also two forms, but indivisible; so likewise the sun and the ray are two forms, but coherent ones. Everything which proceeds from something else must needs be second to that from which it proceeds, without being on that account separated. Where, however, there is a second, there must be two; and where there is a third, there must be three. Now the Spirit indeed is third from God and the Son; just as the fruit of the tree is third from the root, or as the stream out of the river is third from the fountain, or as the apex of the ray is third from the sun. Nothing, however, is alien from that original source whence it derives its own properties. In like manner the Trinity, flowing down from the Father through intertwined and connected steps, does not at all disturb the *Monarchy*, whilst it at the same time guards the state of the *Economy*.

Source: Tertullian, Against Praxeas *VIII, trans. Peter Holmes, in Alexander Roberts, James Donaldson and A. Cleveland Coxe (eds),* Ante-Nicene Fathers, *vol. 3, Buffalo, NY: Christian Literature Publishing Co., 1885.*

6.3 Origen, from *On First Principles*

Origen seeks to preserve the ontological unity of Father, Son and Spirit, and begins to trace the role of the Spirit in teaching us of Christ and in uniting us with the Father and the Son.

2. Now, what the Holy Spirit is, we are taught in many passages of Scripture, as by David in the fifty first Psalm, when he says, 'And take not thy Holy Spirit from me', and by Daniel where it is said, 'The Holy Spirit which is in thee.' And in the New Testament we have abundant testimonies, as when the Holy Spirit is described as having descended upon Christ, and when the Lord breathed upon His apostles after His resurrection, saying, 'Receive the Holy Spirit;' and the saying of the angel to Mary, 'The Holy Spirit will come upon thee;' the declaration by Paul, that no one can call Jesus Lord, save by the Holy Spirit. In the Acts of the Apostles, the Holy Spirit was given by the imposition of the apostles' hands in baptism.

From all which we learn that the person of the Holy Spirit was of such authority and dignity, that saving baptism was not complete except by the authority of the most excellent Trinity of them all, i.e., by the naming of Father, Son, and Holy Spirit, and by joining to the unbegotten God the Father, and to His only-begotten Son, the name also of the Holy Spirit. Who, then, is not amazed at the exceeding majesty of the Holy Spirit, when he hears that he who speaks a word against the Son of man may hope for forgiveness; but that he who is guilty of blasphemy against the Holy Spirit has not forgiveness, either in the present world or in that which is to come!

3. That all things were created by God, and that there is no creature which exists but has derived from Him its being, is established from many declarations of Scripture; those assertions being refuted and rejected which are falsely alleged by some respecting the existence either of a matter co-eternal with God, or of unbegotten souls, in which they would have it that God implanted not so much the power of existence, as equality and order. For even in that little treatise called *The Pastor or Angel of Repentance*, composed by Hermas, we have the following: 'First of all, believe that there is one God who created and arranged all things; who, when nothing formerly existed, caused all things to be; who Himself contains all things, but Himself is contained by none.'

And in the book of Enoch also we have similar descriptions. But up to the present time we have been able to find no statement in holy Scripture in which the Holy Spirit could be said to be made or created, not even in the way in which we have shown above that the divine wisdom is spoken of by Solomon, or in which those expressions which we have discussed are to be understood of the life, or the word, or the other appellations of the Son of God. The Spirit of God, therefore, which was borne upon the waters, as is written in the beginning of the creation of the world, is, I am of opinion, no other than the Holy Spirit, so far as I can understand; as indeed we have shown in our exposition of the passages themselves, not according to the historical, but according to the spiritual method of interpretation ...

4. ... We must understand ... that as the Son, who alone knows the Father,

reveals Him to whom He will, so the Holy Spirit, who alone searches the deep things of God, reveals God to whom He will: 'For the Spirit bloweth where He listeth.'

We are not, however, to suppose that the Spirit derives His knowledge through revelation from the Son. For if the Holy Spirit knows the Father through the Son's revelation, He passes from a state of ignorance into one of knowledge; but it is alike impious and foolish to confess the Holy Spirit, and yet to ascribe to Him ignorance. For even although something else existed before the Holy Spirit, it was not by progressive advancement that He came to be the Holy Spirit; as if any one should venture to say, that at the time when He was not yet the Holy Spirit He was ignorant of the Father, but that after He had received knowledge He was made the Holy Spirit. For if this were the case, the Holy Spirit would never be reckoned in the Unity of the Trinity, i.e., along with the unchangeable Father and His Son, unless He had always been the Holy Spirit. When we use, indeed, such terms as 'always' or 'was,' or any other designation of time, they are not to be taken absolutely, but with due allowance; for while the significations of these words relate to time, and those subjects of which we speak are spoken of by a stretch of language as existing in time, they nevertheless surpass in their real nature all conception of the finite understanding ...

8. Having made these declarations regarding the Unity of the Father, and of the Son, and of the Holy Spirit, let us return to the order in which we began the discussion. God the Father bestows upon all, existence; and participation in Christ, in respect of His being the word of reason, renders them rational beings. From which it follows that they are deserving either of praise or blame, because capable of virtue and vice. On this account, therefore, is the grace of the Holy Ghost present, that those beings which are not holy in their essence may be rendered holy by participating in it. Seeing, then, that firstly, they derive their existence from God the Father; secondly, their rational nature from the Word; thirdly, their holiness from the Holy Spirit – those who have been previously sanctified by the Holy Spirit are again made capable of receiving Christ, in respect that He is the righteousness of God; and those who have earned advancement to this grade by the sanctification of the Holy Spirit, will nevertheless obtain the gift of wisdom according to the power and working of the Spirit of God. And this I consider is Paul's meaning, when he says that to 'some is given the word of wisdom, to others the word of knowledge, according to the same Spirit.' And while pointing out the individual distinction of gifts, he refers the whole of them to the source of all things, in the words, 'There are diversities of operations, but one God who worketh all in all.'

Source: Origen, On First Principles *I.3, trans. Frederick Crombie, in Alexander Roberts, James Donaldson and A. Cleveland Coxe (eds),* Ante-Nicene Fathers, *vol. 4, Buffalo, NY: Christian Literature Publishing Co., 1885.*

6.4 Cyril of Jerusalem, from *Catecheses*

Cyril here offers a commentary on the creedal article, 'And in one Holy Spirit'.

On the Article, And in One Holy Ghost, the Comforter, Which Spake in the Prophets.

> 1 Corinthians xii. 1, 4: *Now concerning spiritual gifts, brethren, I would not have you ignorant … Now there are diversities of gifts, but the same Spirit, &c.*

1. Spiritual in truth is the grace we need, in order to discourse concerning the Holy Spirit; not that we may speak what is worthy of Him, for this is impossible, but that by speaking the words of the divine Scriptures, we may run our course without danger. For a truly fearful thing is written in the Gospels, where Christ has plainly said, *Whosoever shall speak a word against the Holy Ghost, it shall not be forgiven him, neither in this world, nor in that which is to come.* And there is often fear, lest a man should receive this condemnation, through speaking what he ought not concerning Him, either from ignorance, or from supposed reverence. The Judge of quick and dead, Jesus Christ, declared that he hath no forgiveness; if therefore any man offend, what hope has he?

2. It must therefore belong to Jesus Christ's grace itself to grant both to us to speak without deficiency, and to you to hear with discretion; for discretion is needful not to them only who speak, but also to them that hear, lest they hear one thing, and misconceive another in their mind. Let us then speak concerning the Holy Ghost nothing but what is written; and whatsoever is not written, let us not busy ourselves about it. The Holy Ghost Himself spoke the Scriptures; He has also spoken concerning Himself as much as He pleased, or as much as we could receive. Let us therefore speak those things which He has said; for whatsoever He has not said, we dare not say.

3. There is One Only Holy Ghost, the Comforter; and as there is One God the Father, and no second Father – and as there is One Only-begotten Son and Word of God, who hath no brother – so is there One Only Holy Ghost, and no second spirit equal in honour to Him. Now the Holy Ghost is a Power most mighty, a Being divine and unsearchable; for He is living and intelligent, a sanctifying principle of all things made by God through Christ. He it is who illuminates the souls of the just; He was in the Prophets, He was also in the Apostles in the New Testament. Abhorred be they who dare to separate the operation of the Holy Ghost! There is One God, the Father, Lord of the Old and of the New Testament: and One Lord, Jesus Christ, who was prophesied of in the Old Testament, and came in the New; and One Holy Ghost, who through the Prophets preached of Christ, and when Christ was come, descended, and manifested Him.

4. Let no one therefore separate the Old from the New Testament; let no one say that the Spirit in the former is one, and in the latter another; since thus he offends against the Holy Ghost Himself, who with the Father and the

Son together is honoured, and at the time of Holy Baptism is included with them in the Holy Trinity. For the Only-begotten Son of God said plainly to the Apostles, *Go ye, and make disciples of all the nations, baptizing them into the name of the Father, and of the Son, and of the Holy Ghost.* Our hope is in Father, and Son, and Holy Ghost. We preach not three Gods; let the Marcionites be silenced; but with the Holy Ghost through One Son, we preach One God. The Faith is indivisible; the worship inseparable. We neither separate the Holy Trinity, like some; nor do we as Sabellius work confusion. But we know according to godliness One Father, who sent His Son to be our Saviour; we know One Son, who promised that He would send the Comforter from the Father; we know the Holy Ghost, who spake in the Prophets, and who on the day of Pentecost descended on the Apostles in the form of fiery tongues, here, in Jerusalem, in the Upper Church of the Apostles; for in all things the choicest privileges are with us. Here Christ came down from heaven; here the Holy Ghost came down from heaven. And in truth it were most fitting, that as we discourse concerning Christ and Golgotha here in Golgotha, so also we should speak concerning the Holy Ghost in the Upper Church; yet since He who descended there jointly partakes of the glory of Him who was crucified here, we here speak concerning Him also who descended there: for their worship is indivisible.

Source: Cyril of Jerusalem, Catecheses XVI, 1–4, Catechetical Lectures, *trans. Edwin Hamilton Gifford, in Philip Schaff and Henry Wace (eds),* Nicene and Post-Nicene Fathers, *second series, vol. 7, Buffalo, NY: Christian Literature Publishing Co., 1894.*

6.5 Basil, from *On the Holy Spirit*

In one of the most substantial treatises on the Spirit in Patristic theology, Basil urges that the Spirit be accorded the same glory and honour and worship as the Father and the Son.

Chapter XIX: *Against those who assert that the Spirit ought not to be glorified.*

48. 'Be it so,' it is rejoined, 'but glory is by no means so absolutely due to the Spirit as to require His exaltation by us in doxologies.' Whence then could we get demonstrations of the dignity of the Spirit, 'passing all understanding,' if His communion with the Father and the Son were not reckoned by our opponents as good for testimony of His rank? It is, at all events, possible for us to arrive to a certain extent at intelligent apprehension of the sublimity of His nature and of His unapproachable power, by looking at the meaning of His title, and at the magnitude of His operations, and by His good gifts bestowed on us or rather on all creation. He is called Spirit, as 'God is a Spirit,' and 'the breath of our nostrils, the anointed of the Lord.' He is called holy, as the Father is holy, and the Son is holy, for to the creature holiness was brought in from without, but to the Spirit holiness is the fulfilment of nature, and it is for this reason that He is described not as being sanctified, but as sanctifying. He is called good, as the Father is good, and He who was begotten of the Good is good, and to the Spirit His goodness is essence. He is called upright, as 'the Lord is upright,' in that He is Himself truth, and is Himself Righteousness, having no divergence nor leaning to one side or to the other, on account of the immutability of His substance. He is called Paraclete, like the Only begotten, as He Himself says, 'I will ask the Father, and He will give you another comforter.' Thus names are borne by the Spirit in common with the Father and the Son, and He gets these titles from His natural and close relationship. From what other source could they be derived? Again He is called royal, Spirit of truth, and Spirit of wisdom. 'The Spirit of God,' it is said 'hath made me,' and God filled Bezaleel with 'the divine Spirit of wisdom and understanding and knowledge.' Such names as these are super-eminent and mighty, but they do not transcend His glory.

49. And His operations, what are they? For majesty ineffable, and for numbers innumerable. How shall we form a conception of what extends beyond the ages? What were His operations before that creation whereof we can conceive? How great the grace which He conferred on creation? What the power exercised by Him over the ages to come? He existed; He pre-existed; He co-existed with the Father and the Son before the ages. It follows that, even if you can conceive of anything beyond the ages, you will find the Spirit yet further above and beyond. And if you think of the creation, the powers of the heavens were established by the Spirit, the establishment being understood to refer to disability to fall away from good. For it is from the Spirit that the powers derive their close relationship to God, their inability to change to evil, and their continuance in blessedness. Is it Christ's advent? The Spirit is forerunner. Is there the incarnate presence? The Spirit is inseparable. Working of

miracles, and gifts of healing are through the Holy Spirit. Demons were driven out by the Spirit of God. The devil was brought to naught by the presence of the Spirit. Remission of Sins was by the gift of the Spirit, for 'ye were washed, ye were sanctified … in the name of the Lord Jesus Christ, and in the holy Spirit of our God.' There is close relationship with God through the Spirit, for 'God hath sent forth the Spirit of His Son into your hearts, crying Abba, Father.' The resurrection from the dead is effected by the operation of the Spirit, for 'Thou sendest forth thy spirit, they are created; and Thou renewest the face of the earth.' If here creation may be taken to mean the bringing of the departed to life again, how mighty is not the operation of the Spirit, Who is to us the dispenser of the life that follows on the resurrection, and attunes our souls to the spiritual life beyond? Or if here by creation is meant the change to a better condition of those who in this life have fallen into sin (for it is so understood according to the usage of Scripture, as in the words of Paul 'if any man be in Christ he is a new creature'), the renewal which takes place in this life, and the transmutation from our earthly and sensuous life to the heavenly conversation which takes place in us through the Spirit, then our souls are exalted to the highest pitch of admiration. With these thoughts before us are we to be afraid of going beyond due bounds in the extravagance of the honour we pay? Shall we not rather fear lest, even though we seem to give Him the highest names which the thoughts of man can conceive or man's tongue utter, we let our thoughts about Him fall too low? …

50. But, it is said that 'He maketh intercession for us.' It follows then that, as the suppliant is inferior to the benefactor, so far is the Spirit inferior in dignity to God. But have you never heard concerning the Only-begotten that He 'is at the right hand of God, who also maketh intercession for us'? Do not, then, because the Spirit is in you – if indeed He is at all in you – nor yet because He teaches us who were blinded, and guides us to the choice of what profits us – do not for this reason allow yourself to be deprived of the right and holy opinion concerning Him. For to make the loving kindness of your benefactor a ground of ingratitude were indeed a very extravagance of unfairness. 'Grieve not the Holy Spirit;' hear the words of Stephen, the first fruits of the martyrs, when he reproaches the people for their rebellion and disobedience; 'you do always,' he says, 'resist the Holy Ghost;' and again Isaiah – 'They vexed His Holy Spirit, therefore He was turned to be their enemy;' and in another passage, 'the house of Jacob angered the Spirit of the Lord.' Are not these passages indicative of authoritative power? I leave it to the judgment of my readers to determine what opinions we ought to hold when we hear these passages; whether we are to regard the Spirit as an instrument, a subject, of equal rank with the creature, and a fellow servant of ourselves, or whether, on the contrary, to the ears of the pious the mere whisper of this blasphemy is not most grievous. Do you call the Spirit a servant? But, it is said, 'the servant knoweth not what his Lord doeth,' and yet the Spirit knoweth the things of God, as 'the spirit of man that is in him.'

Source: Basil of Caesarea, On the Holy Spirit, *trans. Blomfield Jackson, in Philip Schaff and Henry Wace (eds),* Nicene and Post-Nicene Fathers, *second series, vol. 8, Buffalo NY: Christian Literature Publishing Co., 1895.*

6.6 Augustine of Hippo, from *On the Holy Trinity*

Augustine here develops the widely influential view that the Spirit is the bond of love between Father and Son.

28. '*God*,' then, '*is love*;' but the question is, whether the Father, or the Son, or the Holy Spirit, or the Trinity itself: because the Trinity is not three Gods, but one God. But I have already argued above in this book, that the Trinity, which is God, is not so to be understood from those three things which have been set forth in the trinity of our mind, as that the Father should be the memory of all three, and the Son the understanding of all three, and the Holy Spirit the love of all three; as though the Father should neither understand nor love for Himself, but the Son should understand for Him, and the Holy Spirit love for Him, but He Himself should remember only both for Himself and for them; nor the Son remember nor love for Himself, but the Father should remember for Him, and the Holy Spirit love for Him, but He Himself understand only both for Himself and them; nor likewise that the Holy Spirit should neither remember nor understand for Himself, but the Father should remember for Him, and the Son understand for Him, while He Himself should love only both for Himself and for them; but rather in this way, that both all and each have all three each in His own nature. Nor that these things should differ in them, as in us memory is one thing, understanding another, love or charity another, but should be some one thing that is equivalent to all, as wisdom itself; and should be so contained in the nature of each, as that He who has it is that which He has, as being an unchangeable and simple substance. If all this, then, has been understood, and so far as is granted to us to see or conjecture in things so great, has been made patently true, I know not why both the Father and the Son and the Holy Spirit should not be called Love, and all together one love, just as both the Father and the Son and the Holy Spirit is called Wisdom, and all together not three, but one wisdom. For so also both the Father is God, and the Son God, and the Holy Ghost God, and all three together one God.

29. And yet it is not to no purpose that in this Trinity the Son and none other is called the Word of God, and the Holy Spirit and none other the Gift of God, and God the Father alone is He from whom the Word is born, and from whom the Holy Spirit principally proceeds. And therefore I have added the word principally, because we find that the Holy Spirit proceeds from the Son also. But the Father gave Him this too, not as to one already existing, and not yet having it; but whatever He gave to the only-begotten Word, He gave by begetting Him. Therefore He so begot Him as that the common Gift should proceed from Him also, and the Holy Spirit should be the Spirit of both. This distinction, then, of the inseparable Trinity is not to be merely accepted in passing, but to be carefully considered; for hence it was that the Word of God was specially called also the Wisdom of God, although both Father and Holy Spirit are wisdom. If, then, any one of the three is to be specially called Love, what more fitting than that it should be the Holy Spirit? – namely, that in that simple and highest nature, substance should not be one thing and love another, but that substance itself should be love, and love itself should be substance, whether

in the Father, or in the Son, or in the Holy Spirit; and yet that the Holy Spirit should be specially called Love.

Source: Augustine, On the Holy Trinity, *Book XV, trans. Arthur West Haddan, in Philip Schaff (ed.),* Nicene and Post-Nicene Fathers, *first series, vol. 3, Buffalo, NY: Christian Literature Publishing Co., 1887.*

6.7 John of Damascus, from *Exposition of the Orthodox Faith*

John distinguishes the Spirit as the one who 'proceeded' from the Father simultaneously with the generation of the Son, thus distancing himself from those who had begun to confess through an addition to the Nicene-Constantinopolitan Creed that the Spirit proceeds from the Father and the Son (filioque).

Likewise we believe also in one Holy Spirit, the Lord and Giver of Life: Who proceedeth from the Father and resteth in the Son: the object of equal adoration and glorification with the Father and Son, since He is co-essential and co-eternal: the Spirit of God, direct, authoritative, the fountain of wisdom, and life, and holiness: God existing and addressed along with Father and Son: uncreate, full, creative, all-ruling, all-effecting, all-powerful, of infinite power, Lord of all creation and not under any lord: deifying, not deified: filling, not filled: shared in, not sharing in: sanctifying, not sanctified: the intercessor, receiving the supplications of all: in all things like to the Father and Son: proceeding from the Father and communicated through the Son, and participated in by all creation, through Himself creating, and investing with essence and sanctifying, and maintaining the universe: having subsistence, existing in its own proper and peculiar subsistence, inseparable and indivisible from Father and Son, and possessing all the qualities that the Father and Son possess, save that of not being begotten or born. For the Father is without cause and unborn: for He is derived from nothing, but derives from Himself His being, nor does He derive a single quality from another. Rather He is Himself the beginning and cause of the existence of all things in a definite and natural manner. But the Son is derived from the Father after the manner of generation, and the Holy Spirit likewise is derived from the Father, yet not after the manner of generation, but after that of procession. And we have learned that there is a difference between generation and procession, but the nature of that difference we in no wise understand. Further, the generation of the Son from the Father and the procession of the Holy Spirit are simultaneous.

Source: John of Damascus, Exposition of the Orthodox Faith, *Book 1, trans. E. W. Watson and L. Pullan, in Philip Schaff and Henry Wace (eds),* Nicene and Post-Nicene Fathers, *second series, vol. 9, Buffalo, NY: Christian Literature Publishing Co., 1899.*

6.8 Thomas Aquinas, from *Summa Theologica*

Aquinas is concerned to show that the name 'Holy Ghost' applies to a distinct person of the Trinity rather than to a power held in common by the persons of the Godhead.

Article 1. Whether this name 'Holy Ghost' is the proper name of one divine person?

Objection 1. It would seem that this name, 'Holy Ghost,' is not the proper name of one divine person. For no name which is common to the three persons is the proper name of any one person. But this name of 'Holy Ghost' is common to the three persons; for Hilary (*De Trinitate*, viii) shows that the 'Spirit of God' sometimes means the Father, as in the words of Isaiah 61:1: 'The Spirit of the Lord is upon me;' and sometimes the Son, as when the Son says: 'In the Spirit of God I cast out devils' (Matthew 12:28), showing that He cast out devils by His own natural power; and that sometimes it means the Holy Ghost, as in the words of Joel 2:28: 'I will pour out of My Spirit over all flesh.' Therefore this name 'Holy Ghost' is not the proper name of a divine person.

Objection 2. Further, the names of the divine persons are relative terms, as Boethius says (*De Trinitate*). But this name 'Holy Ghost' is not a relative term. Therefore this name is not the proper name of a divine Person.

Objection 3. Further, because the Son is the name of a divine Person He cannot be called the Son of this or of that. But the spirit is spoken of as of this or that man, as appears in the words, 'The Lord said to Moses, I will take of thy spirit and will give to them' (Numbers 11:17) and also 'The Spirit of Elias rested upon Eliseus' (2 Kings 2:15). Therefore 'Holy Ghost' does not seem to be the proper name of a divine Person.

On the contrary, It is said (1 John 5:7): 'There are three who bear witness in heaven, the Father, the Word, and the Holy Ghost.' As Augustine says (*De Trinitate*, vii, 4): 'When we ask, Three what? we say, Three persons.' Therefore the Holy Ghost is the name of a divine person.

I answer that, While there are two processions in God, one of these, the procession of love, has no proper name of its own, as stated above (27, 4, and 3). Hence the relations also which follow from this procession are without a name (28, 4): for which reason the Person proceeding in that manner has not a proper name. But as some names are accommodated by the usual mode of speaking to signify the aforesaid relations, as when we use the names of procession and spiration, which in the strict sense more fittingly signify the notional acts than the relations; so to signify the divine Person, Who proceeds by way of love, this name 'Holy Ghost' is by the use of scriptural speech accommodated to Him. The appropriateness of this name may be shown in two ways.

Firstly, from the fact that the person who is called 'Holy Ghost' has something in common with the other Persons. For, as Augustine says (*De Trinitate*, xv, 17; v, 11), 'Because the Holy Ghost is common to both, He Himself is called that properly which both are called in common. For the Father also is a spirit, and the Son is a spirit; and the Father is holy, and the Son is holy.'

Secondly, from the proper signification of the name. For the name spirit in things corporeal seems to signify impulse and motion; for we call the breath and the wind by the term spirit. Now it is a property of love to move and impel the will of the lover towards the object loved. Further, holiness is attributed to whatever is ordered to God. Therefore because the divine person proceeds by way of the love whereby God is loved, that person is most properly named 'The Holy Ghost.'

Reply to Objection 1. The expression Holy Spirit, if taken as two words, is applicable to the whole Trinity: because by 'spirit' the immateriality of the divine substance is signified; for corporeal spirit is invisible, and has but little matter; hence we apply this term to all immaterial and invisible substances. And by adding the word 'holy' we signify the purity of divine goodness. But if Holy Spirit be taken as one word, it is thus that the expression, in the usage of the Church, is accommodated to signify one of the three persons, the one who proceeds by way of love, for the reason above explained.

Reply to Objection 2. Although this name 'Holy Ghost' does not indicate a relation, still it takes the place of a relative term, inasmuch as it is accommodated to signify a Person distinct from the others by relation only. Yet this name may be understood as including a relation, if we understand the Holy Spirit as being breathed [*spiratus*].

Reply to Objection 3. In the name Son we understand that relation only which is of something from a principle, in regard to that principle: but in the name 'Father' we understand the relation of principle; and likewise in the name of Spirit inasmuch as it implies a moving power. But to no creature does it belong to be a principle as regards a divine person; but rather the reverse. Therefore we can say 'our Father,' and 'our Spirit'; but we cannot say 'our Son.'

Source: Thomas Aquinas, Summa Theologica *1 q.36, trans. Fathers of the English Dominican Province, London: Burns, Oates & Washbourne, 1924–34.*

6.9 Hildegard of Bingen, from *Liber Divinorum Operum*

Hildegard testifies to the life-giving power of the Spirit.

I am the supreme and fiery force who has kindled all sparks of life and breathed forth none of death and I judge them as they are. I have rightly established that order, encircling it with my upper wings, that is, embracing them with wisdom. I, the fiery life of the divine substance, blaze in the beauty of the fields, shine in the waters, and burn in the sun, moon and stars. And as the all-sustaining invisible force of the aerial wind, I bring all things to life … I am also Reason, having the wind of the sounding word by which all things were created, and I breathe in them all, so that none may die, because I am Life.

Source: Hildegard of Bingen, Liber Divinorum Operum, *Vision 1, chapter 2, cited and trans. Sabina Flanagan,* Hildegard of Bingen, 1098–1179: A Visionary Life, *London: Routledge, 1989, p. 143.*

6.10 John Calvin, from the *Institutes of the Christian Religion*

Calvin explores the role of the Spirit in the economy of salvation.

1. We must now see in what way we become possessed of the blessings which God has bestowed on his only-begotten Son, not for private use, but to enrich the poor and needy. And the first thing to be attended to is, that so long as we are without Christ and separated from him, nothing which he suffered and did for the salvation of the human race is of the least benefit to us. To communicate to us the blessings which he received from the Father, he must become ours and dwell in us. Accordingly, he is called our Head, and the first-born among many brethren, while, on the other hand, we are said to be ingrafted into him and clothed with him, all which he possesses being, as I have said, nothing to us until we become one with him. And although it is true that we obtain this by faith, yet since we see that all do not indiscriminately embrace the offer of Christ which is made by the gospel, the very nature of the case teaches us to ascend higher, and inquire into the secret efficacy of the Spirit, to which it is owing that we enjoy Christ and all his blessings. I have already treated of the eternal essence and divinity of the Spirit (Book 1 chap. 13 sect. 14, 15); let us at present attend to the special point, that Christ came by water and blood, as the Spirit testifies concerning him, that we might not lose the benefits of the salvation which he has purchased. For as there are said to be three witnesses in heaven, the Father, the Word, and the Spirit, so there are also three on the earth, namely, water, blood, and Spirit. It is not without cause that the testimony of the Spirit is twice mentioned, a testimony which is engraven on our hearts by way of seal, and thus seals the cleansing and sacrifice of Christ. For which reason, also, Peter says, that believers are 'elect' 'through sanctification of the Spirit, unto obedience and sprinkling of the blood of Jesus Christ' (1 Pet. 1: 2). By these words he reminds us, that if the shedding of his sacred blood is not to be in vain, our souls must be washed in it by the secret cleansing of the Holy Spirit. For which reason, also, Paul, speaking of cleansing and purification, says, 'but ye are washed, but ye are sanctified, but ye are justified in the name of the Lord Jesus and by the Spirit of our God' (1 Cor. 6: 11). The whole comes to this that the Holy Spirit is the bond by which Christ effectually binds us to himself. Here we may refer to what was said in the last Book concerning his anointing.

2. But in order to have a clearer view of this most important subject we must remember that Christ came provided with the Holy Spirit after a peculiar manner, namely, that he might separate us from the world, and unite us in the hope of an eternal inheritance. Hence the Spirit is called the Spirit of sanctification, because he quickens and cherishes us, not merely by the general energy which is seen in the human race, as well as other animals, but because he is the seed and root of heavenly life in us. Accordingly, one of the highest commendations which the prophets give to the kingdom of Christ is, that under it the Spirit would be poured out in richer abundance. One of the most

remarkable passages is that of Joel, 'It shall come to pass afterward, that I will pour out my Spirit upon all flesh' (Joel 2: 28). For although the prophet seems to confine the gifts of the Spirit to the office of prophesying, he yet intimates under a figure, that God will, by the illumination of his Spirit, provide himself with disciples who had previously been altogether ignorant of heavenly doctrine. Moreover, as it is for the sake of his Son that God bestows the Holy Spirit upon us, and yet has deposited him in all his fulness with the Son, to be the minister and dispenser of his liberality, he is called at one time the Spirit of the Father, at another the Spirit of the Son: 'Ye are not in the flesh but in the Spirit, if so be that the Spirit of God dwell in you. Now, if any man have not the Spirit of Christ, he is none of his' (Rom. 8: 9); and hence he encourages us to hope for complete renovation: 'If the Spirit of him that raised up Jesus from the dead dwell in you, he that raised up Christ from the dead shall also quicken your mortal bodies by his Spirit that dwelleth in you' (Rom. 8: 11). There is no inconsistency in ascribing the glory of those gifts to the Father, inasmuch as he is the author of them, and, at the same time, ascribing them to Christ, with whom they have been deposited, that he may bestow them on his people. Hence he invites all the thirsty to come unto him and drink (John 7: 37). And Paul teaches, that 'unto every one of us is given grace, according to the measure of the gift of Christ,' (Eph. 4: 7). And we must remember, that the Spirit is called the Spirit of Christ, not only inasmuch as the eternal Word of God is with the Father united with the Spirit, but also in respect of his office of Mediator; because, had he not been endued with the energy of the Spirit, he had come to us in vain. In this sense he is called the 'last Adam,' and said to have been sent from heaven 'a quickening Spirit' (1 Cor. 15: 45), where Paul contrasts the special life which Christ breathes into his people, that they may be one with him with the animal life which is common even to the reprobate. In like manner, when he prays that believers may have 'the grace of our Lord Jesus Christ, and the love of God,' he at the same time adds, 'the communion of the Holy Ghost,' without which no man shall ever taste the paternal favor of God, or the benefits of Christ. Thus, also, in another passage he says, 'The love of God is shed abroad in our hearts by the Holy Ghost, which is given unto us' (Rom. 5: 5).

Source: John Calvin, Institutes of the Christian Religion III.1, trans. Henry Beveridge (1559), Edinburgh: The Calvin Translation Society, 1845.

6.11 John Owen, from *The Holy Spirit, His Gifts and Power*

Owen retraces the ground of earlier doctrinal battles and affirms once more both the divinity and the personality of the Spirit and ties the work of the Spirit very closely to that of the Son.

First, then, we may observe, That the doctrine of the Spirit of God, is the second great article of those gospel truths, in which the glory of God and the good of souls, are most eminently concerned; without true knowledge of which in its truth, and the improvement of it in its power, the first will be altogether useless. For when God designed the great and glorious work of recovering fallen man, and of saving sinners to the praise of the glory of his grace, he appointed in his infinite wisdom two great means thereof: The one was, the giving of his Son for them; and the other was, the giving of his Spirit to them. And hereby a way was opened for the manifestation of the glory of the whole blessed Trinity; which is the utmost end of all the works of God. Hereby, were the love, grace and wisdom of the Father, in the design and projection of the whole; the love, grace and condescension of the Son, in the execution of the plan of Salvation; with the love, grace and power of the Spirit, in the application of all to the souls of men, made gloriously conspicuous. Hence, from the first entrance of sin, there were two general heads of the promises of God concerning salvation. The one respected the sending his Son to take our nature, and to suffer for us therein; the other, related to the giving his Spirit, to make the effects and fruits of the incarnation, obedience, and suffering of his Son effectual to us. The great promise of the Old Testament, the principal object of the faith and hope of believers, was that of the coming of the Son of God in the flesh but when that was accomplished, the principal remaining promise of the New Testament respects the coming of the Holy Spirit. Hence the doctrine of his person, work and grace, is the peculiar subject of the New Testament; and a most eminent object of the Christian's faith. And this must be insisted upon, as we have to do with some, who will scarcely allow him to be of any consideration in these matters.

1. It is of great moment, and sufficient of itself to maintain the cause as proposed, that when our Lord Jesus Christ was about to leave the world, he promised to send his Holy Spirit to his disciples, to supply his absence. Of what use the presence of Christ was to them, we may in some measure conceive; for their hearts were filled with sorrow on the mention of his departure, John xvi. 5, 6. Designing to relieve them in this great distress, he makes them this promise; assuring them thereby of greater advantage than the continuance of his bodily presence among them. Consider what he says to this purpose In his last discourse. 'I will pray the Father, and he shall give you another Comforter, that he may abide with you for ever; even the Spirit of truth, who in the world cannot receive, because it seeth him not, neither knoweth him; but ye know him, for he dwelleth with you, and shall be in you. I will not leave you comfortless, I will come unto you;' that is, by his Spirit. 'These things I have

spoken unto you, being present with you; but the Comforter, who is the Holy Ghost, whom the Father will send in my name, he shall teach you all things. Now I go my way – and sorrow hath filled your hearts. Nevertheless – it is expedient for you that I go away; for if I go not away, the Comforter will not come. When he is come, he will convince the world of sin, and of righteousness, and of judgment. He will guide you into all truth – and show you things to come. He shall glorify me; for he shall receive of mine, and show it unto you,' chap. xiv. 16, &c., xv. 26, xvi. 7, &c. This was the great legacy which Jesus bequeathed to his sorrowful disciples; and because of its importance, he frequently repeats it, enlarging on the benefits they should thereby receive. After his resurrection, they would have been again embracing and rejoicing in his human nature, but as he said to Mary, 'touch me not,' to wean her from any carnal consideration of him; so he instructs them now to look for him only in the promise of the Holy Ghost. They were no longer to 'know him after the flesh,' 2 Cor. v. 16; for though it was a great privilege so to know him, yet it was a much greater to enjoy him in the dispensation of the Spirit. It is in vain pretended, that only the apostles or primitive Christians were concerned in this promise; for though it was made to them in a peculiar manner, yet it belongs to believers, universally, and to the end of time. As far as it respects his gracious operations, what Christ prayed for, and so promised to, his apostles he 'prayed not for them alone, but for them also which should believe on him through their word,' John xvii. 20. And his promise is, to be 'with his, always, even to the end of the world,' Matt. xxviii. 20. And also that 'wherever two or three are gathered together in his name, there he would be in the midst of them,' chap. xviii. 20; which he is no otherwise than by his Spirit. And this one consideration is sufficient to evince the importance of the doctrine. For is it possible that any Christian should be so supinely negligent, so careless about the things on which his present comfort and future happiness depend, as not to inquire, with the utmost diligence, into what Christ has left us to supply his absence, and at length to bring us to himself? He who despises these things, has neither part nor lot in Christ himself; for 'if any man have not the Spirit of Christ, he is none of his,' Rom. viii. 9.

2. The great work of the Holy Ghost, in the dispensation of the gospel, is another evidence to the same purpose. Hence the gospel itself is called, 'the ministration of the Spirit,' in opposition to that of the law, which is called 'the ministration of the letter; of condemnation; and of death,' 2 Cor. iii. 6–8. The 'ministry of the Spirit,' is either that ministry which the Spirit makes effectual, or that ministry whereby the Spirit in his gifts and graces is communicated to men. And this alone gives glory and efficacy to the gospel. Take away the Spirit from the gospel, and you render it 'a dead letter;' of no more use to Christians, than the Old Testament is of to the Jews. It is therefore a mischievous imagination, proceeding from ignorance and unbelief, that there is no more in the gospel, than what is contained under any other doctrine or declaration of truth; that it is nothing but a hook for men to exercise their reason upon, and to improve the things of it by the same faculty. This is to separate the Spirit from it, which is in truth to destroy it: and to reject the covenant of God, which is, that 'his word and spirit shall go together,' Isa. lix. 21. We shall therefore prove, that the whole use and efficacy of the ministry of the gospel,

depend on the promised ministry of the Spirit, with which it is accompanied. If therefore we have any concern in the gospel, we have signal duty before us in the present subject.

3. There is not one spiritual good from first to last communicated to us; or that we by the grace of God partake of; but it is revealed to us, and bestowed on us, by the Holy Ghost. He who never experienced the special work of the Spirit upon him, never received any special mercy from God. How is it possible? For whatever God works in us, is by his Spirit; he therefore who has no work of the Spirit on his heart, never received either mercy or grace from God. To renounce therefore the work of the Spirit, is to renounce all interest in the mercy and grace of God.

4. There is not any thing done by us, that is holy and acceptable to God, but it is an effect of the Spirit's operation. 'Without him we can do nothing;' John xv. 5; for without Christ we cannot; and by him alone, is the grace of Christ communicated. By him we are regenerated; by him we are sanctified; by him we are cleansed; by him we are assisted in every good work. Surely then, we ought to inquire into time cause and spring of all that is good in us.

5. God assures us, that the only remediless sin, is the sin against the Holy Ghost. This alone may convince us how necessary it is, to be well instructed in what concerns him. Thus saith our Lord, 'All sins shall be forgiven to the sons of men, and blasphemies wherewith soever they shall blaspheme; but he that shall blaspheme against the Holy Ghost hath never forgiveness,' Mark iii. 28, 29, and Matt. xii. 32. There remains nothing for him who 'doth despite to the Spirit of grace, but a certain fearful looking for of judgment and fiery indignation,' Heb. x. 27, 29. This is that 'sin unto death,' whose remission is not to be prayed for, 1 John v. 16. For he, having undertaken to make effectual to us, the great remedy in the blood of Christ for the pardon of our sins; if he, in the prosecution of that work, be despitefully used and blasphemed, there can be no relief or pardon for that sin. For, whence should it arise? For as God has not another Son to offer another sacrifice for sin; so that he by whom his sacrifice is despised, can have none remaining for him; neither has he another Spirit to make that sacrifice effectual to us, if the Holy Ghost in his work be despised and rejected. This therefore is a tender place. We cannot be too diligent in our inquiries after what God has revealed concerning his Spirit, and his work; seeing there may be so fatal a miscarriage in an opposition to him, as human nature is incapable of in any other instance.

Source: John Owen, The Holy Spirit: His Gifts and Power, *Grand Rapids, MI: Kregel Publications, 1954, pp. 20–5.*

6.12 Edward Irving, from *The Trinitarian Face of God*

Irving attempts to identify the specific benefits of the Spirit's work in the believer.

Now, the third work, which I have named inhabitation, and which is the proper subject of this discourse being what is called the 'baptism of the Holy Ghost', the 'promise of the Father', and the gift of 'power from on high', is superinduced upon the two other, but neither stints nor supersedes them. They go on beneath; the mighty hand of the Father sustaining the nothingness of the creature's being; the mighty hand of the Son redeeming the sinfulness of it; and now the mighty hand of the Holy Ghost comes in to fill it with Divine attributes of wisdom and knowledge and power. The Father gives the materials, the Son frames them into a living temple, the Holy Ghost fills them with the glory of God. This work of the Comforter is the most wonderful of all. That what came out of and in itself is nothing should be capable of producing the various sensations, emotions, and affections of human life, is wonderful: that what is become mortal, pressed down on all sides with the law of sin and dissolution, should be recovered, against itself, to bring forth the fruits of holy living, is still more wonderful: but that it should be made capable of receiving and sustaining the life of God, of having his mind, and of working his works, is a thing which passeth understanding, being in very deed the mighty power of God. The great account which is made of the resurrection of Christ, in all the Scriptures, as 'the exceeding greatness of God's mighty working' (Eph. i), and of the baptism of the Holy Ghost, which is the first-fruits thereof – called 'the power from on high', as if nothing else were worthy of that name – do prove how much more vast is this than every other manifestation of God-head unto men. To make this erroneous mind of ours capable of discerning truth infallibly, to make this trembling and stammering lip capable of utter-ing words before which death and the grave and the devil stand discovered and dismantled, to make this fearful heart capable of confidence in the face of all ungodly conditions, and this palsied hand to strengthen with all the power of God – these are things which far surpass the speculation, and almost the belief, of man. And had we not seen it accomplished in the feebleness of Jesus Christ, who calleth himself 'a work, and no man', we should not have believed it possible to be done in mortal man: and had we not the assurance of Him who is the Truth, that the like works, and greater were to be done in them who believe, we should have thought it a very wonderful thing, done once, upon an extraordinary occasion, for an extraordinary end, by one who was an extraordinary person, God as well as man, and never to be renewed again: but having his word and the facts of all the Apostolical history for it, we believe, as we have written, that this is the third and highest sphere of God's operation in man, carried on under the hand of the Holy Ghost, whose part it is to bring both the Father and the Son, or the Son indwelt by the Father, the life of glori-fied manhood, into all the members of the body, that is, into all who believe.

Source: Graham W. P. McFarlane (ed.), Edward Irving: The Trinitarian Face of God, *Edin-burgh: Saint Andrew Press, 1996, pp. 78–9.*

6.13 H. Wheeler Robinson, from *The Christian Experience of the Holy Spirit*

Robinson here traces what he conceives to be the practical implications of the doctrine of the Holy Spirit.

The practical value of the doctrine of the Holy Spirit is not to be measured by the intellectual results of our inquiry. To keep the mind steadily and reverently fixed on this subject is to open a way for a new experience of God. The interpretation of His ways with us makes possible a new fact, indeed, the ultimate fact – the fellowship of spirit with Spirit. This is the doctrine of the Lifegiver, the vitalizing doctrine to all other portions of Christian truth. Whilst it draws its content from them, they draw their vitality from it. He who finds that the familiar truths of the Gospel or the traditional ways of the Church fail to arouse him to devotion and loyalty because of their remoteness from his living interests, does well to ask whether the lacuna in his experience does not arise from the lack of any real understanding of the doctrine of the Holy Spirit. This specially concerns those who are professionally concerned with religion. They are always in danger of a familiarity which breeds, not contempt, but the atrophy of spiritual response. They need always to be climbing above their own professional duties, like Father Hilary in D. G. Rossetti's poem ('World's Worth'), to the roof of their church, where the winds of God blow, and they may inhale for themselves

> the breath
> Of God in man that warranteth
> The inmost, utmost things of faith.

This is the doctrine of a dynamic God. His limitless resources roll in on the shores of human life like the waves of the sea, ceaseless and unnumbered, terrible in wrath, majestic in their encompassing might, mysterious by their far horizon. Yet for all the immensity of that 'sea of the Spirit' (a better metaphor than the wind for an island-race), it does not disdain to enter into our little lives, shaping itself to our pattern, rippling its way into the tiny pools, lifting the pink shells and floating the fronds of weed; nothing is too small for the dynamic activities of the Spirit, as nothing is too great. When the Christian truths are baptized into the consciousness of this, they become what the Gospel is meant to be: the *dunamis* of God unto salvation (Rom. 1:16).

This, too, is the doctrine of divine personality, which brings God near in all the intimacies of spiritual companionship. The basal kinship of God and man is lifted to a new level by this growing friendship, this conscious kinship of mind and heart. The inevitable loneliness of life in its inner consciousness here finds its explanation; the truest human friendship cannot replace that of the Father of spirits. As we enter more and more into the experience of what this means, the externality of religion is transfigured into a new relation. Religion is no longer a wearisome burden, a load for weary beasts (Isa. 46:1–4), something to be protected, and if possible saved from the encroachments of other interests. Religion becomes faith in a Burden-bearer, Who carries us and saves us, a God Whom no imagery can ever portray, because He is Spirit.

At an earlier stage, we found the salient marks of the human spirit's activity to be four – it lived by unifying, socializing, transforming, and sacramental-izing life. Practically all that has been said of the work and personality of the Holy Spirit in this book is the expansion of those attributes in relation to the Spirit of God, like unto our spirits, though so far beyond our comprehension. The God of Christian faith is Himself a unity, Who reveals Himself in unify-ing the universe, both in nature and in grace – One God, not three – but God Who is Spirit, and Whose unities are always inclusive and recapitulatory, giv-ing as they receive. We have seen that the essential work of the Holy Spirit is fellowship. Life in the Spirit does not mean simply more of life, it means new life, and the primary content of that new life is in a new relation to other per-sons, a new ethical relation, which is best expressed in the Spirit of the Cross of Christ. The actual world we know is a world half-spoiled in the making – whatever be the ultimate mystery of evil, physical and moral. Yet we see a miracle of transformation wrought in the meaning of things by the attitude of individual spirits, and we dare to believe in an ultimate transformation of the meaning of it all by the Spirit of God – and what of things is left at last in a spiritual universe, save their meaning and practical outcome for spirits? Last of all, we may come back from these studies, that have shewn horizons of speculation whither we cannot pass, to the homely ways of common life with a new conviction that they are sacramental to Spirit:

> – well-spent toilsome days, –
> And natural life, refined by honest love,
> And sweet unselfish liturgies of home,
> Heaven's will, borne onward by obedient souls,
> Careless of what may come.

> Lewis Morris, 'The Wanderer'

'Careless of what may come' – because the care to do God's will can lighten every other care, and because the fruit of the Spirit, given to those who obey God, is love, joy, peace.

Source: H. Wheeler Robinson, The Christian Experience of the Holy Spirit, *London: Nisbet & Co. Ltd, 1928, pp. 286–8.*

6.14 Karl Barth, from *Church Dogmatics*

Karl Barth offers a defence of the Western inclusion of the filioque *clause in the Nicene Creed.*

We have reasons for following the Western tradition as regards the *Filioque*, and since the East–West schism is now a fact and this is one of the issues – whether rightly or wrongly is another question – there is cause to give some account of the matter.

Fundamentally what has brought us to this side is no less than the whole thrust of our attempted understanding of the doctrine of the Holy Spirit and the Trinity generally. Even supporters of the Eastern view do not contest the fact that in the *opus ad extra*, and therefore in revelation (and then retrospectively in creation), the Holy Spirit is to be understood as the Spirit of both the Father and the Son. But we have consistently followed the rule, which we regard as basic, that statements about the divine modes of being antecedently in themselves cannot be different in content from those that are to be made about their reality in revelation. All our statements concerning what is called the immanent Trinity have been reached simply as confirmations or underlinings or, materially, as the indispensable premises of the economic Trinity. They neither could nor would say anything other than that we must abide by the distinction and unity of the modes of being in God as they encounter us according to the witness of Scripture in the reality of God in His revalation. The reality of God in His revelation cannot be bracketed by an 'only,' as though somewhere behind His revelation there stood another reality of God; the reality of God which encounters us in His revelation is His reality in all the depths of eternity. This is why we have to take it so precisely in His revelation. In connexion with the specific doctrine of the Holy Spirit this means that He is the Spirit of both the Father and the Son not just in His work *ad extra* and upon us, but that to all eternity – no limit or reservation is possible here – He is none other than the Spirit of both the Father and the Son. 'And the Son' means that not merely for us, but in God Himself, there is no possibility of an opening and readiness and capacity for God in man – for this is the work of the Holy Ghost in revelation – unless it comes from Him, the Father, who has revealed Himself in His Word, in Jesus Christ, and also, and no less necessarily, from Him who is His Word, from His Son, from Jesus Christ, who reveals the Father. Jesus Christ as the Giver of the Holy Spirit is not without the Father from whom He, Jesus Christ, is. But the Father as the Giver of the Holy Spirit is also not without Jesus Christ to whom He Himself is the Father. The Eastern doctrine does not contest the fact that this is so in revelation. But it does not read off from revelation its statements about the being of God 'antecedently in Himself.' It does not stand by the order of the divine modes of being which by its own admission is valid in the sphere of revelation. It goes beyond revelation to achieve a very different picture of God 'antecedently in Himself.' We must object already at this point quite apart from the results. What gives us the right to take passages like Jn. 15:26, which speak of the procession of the Spirit from the Father, and isolate them from the many others which equally plainly call Him the Spirit of the Son? Is it not much more natural to understand opposing statements like this as mutually complementary, as is freely done in the reality of revelation, and then to acknowledge the reality disclosed thereby as valid to all eternity, as the way it is in the essence of God Himself ? For us the Eastern rejection of the *Filioque* is already suspect from the formal standpoint because it is patently a speculation which interprets individual verses of the Bible in isolation, because it bears no relation to the reality of God in revelation and for faith.

This formal defect, however, takes on at once material significance. The *Filioque* expresses recognition of the communion between the Father and the Son. The Holy Spirit is the love which is the essence of the relation between these two modes of being of God. And recognition of this communion is no other than recognition of the basis and confirmation of the communion between God and man as a divine, eternal truth, created in revelation by the Holy Spirit. The intra-divine two-sided fellowship of the Spirit, which proceeds from the Father and the Son, is the basis of the fact that there is in revelation a fellowship in which not only is God there for man but in very truth – this is the *donum Spiritus sancti* [gift of the Spirit] – man is also there for God. Conversely, in this fellowship in revelation which is created between God and man by the Holy Spirit there may be discerned the fellowship in God Himself, the eternal love of God: discerned as the mystery, surpassing all understanding, of the possibility of this reality of revelation; discerned as the one God in the mode of being of the Holy Spirit.

This whole insight and outlook is lost when the immanent *Filioque* is denied. If the Spirit is also the Spirit of the Son only in revelation and for faith, if He is only the Spirit of the Father in eternity, i.e., in His true and original reality, then the fellowship of the Spirit between God and man is without objective ground or content. Even though revealed and believed, it is a purely temporal truth with no eternal basis, so to speak, in itself. No matter, then, what we may have to say about the communion between God and man, it does not have in this case a guarantee in the communion between God the Father and God the Son as the eternal content of its temporal reality. Does not this mean an emptying of revelation?

It would be even worse if the denial of the *Filioque* were not restricted to the immanent Trinity but were also applied to the interpretation of revelation itself, if, then, the Holy Spirit were to be one-sidedly and exaggeratedly regarded as the Spirit of the Father even in His *opus ad extra*. We must be very careful here, for this is theoretically contested. Yet we cannot avoid asking whether, if that denial, the exclusive *ex Patre* [from the Father], is to obtain as an eternal truth, it is not inevitable that the relation of God to man will be understood decisively from the standpoint of Creator and creature, and that it will thus acquire a more or less developed naturalistic and unethical character, so that the Mediator of revelation, the Son or Word, will be set aside as the basis and origin of the relation, and it will take on the nature of a direct and immediate relation, a mystical union with the *principium et fons Deitatis* [principle and source of Deity].

But be that as it may, in the Eastern view of the relation between the divine modes of being we cannot recognise their reality as we believe we know it from the divine revelation according to the witness of Scripture.

We do not recognise it even in the version in which it does indeed rule out the *ek tou uiou* [from the Son] but is prepared to accept a *dia tou uiou* [through the Son] as a possible interpretation of the *ek tou patros* [from the Father]. For even this *dia tou uiou* does not lead, and according to the intent of Eastern theology it is not meant to lead, to that on which everything seems to us to depend, namely, to the thought of the full consubstantial fellowship between Father and Son as the essence of the Spirit, corresponding as a prototype to the fellowship between God as Father and man as His child the creation of which is the work of the Holy Spirit in revelation.

In accordance with what has been said, the positive meaning of the Western version of the dogma may be summarised as follows.

As God is in Himself Father from all eternity, He begets Himself as the Son from all eternity. As He is the Son from all eternity, He is begotten of Himself as the Father from all eternity. In this eternal begetting of Himself and being begotten of Himself, He posits Himself a third time as the Holy Spirit, i.e., as the love which unites Him in Himself. As He is the Father who begets the Son He brings forth the Spirit of love, for as He begets the Son, God already negates in Himself, from eternity, in His absolute simplicity, all loneliness, self-containment, or self-isolation. Also and precisely in Himself, from eternity, in His absolute simplicity, God is orientated to the Other, does not will to be without the Other, will have Himself only as He has Himself with the Other and indeed in the Other. He is the Father of the Son in such a way that with the Son He brings forth the Spirit, love, and is in Himself the Spirit, love. It is not, of course, to satisfy a law of love, nor because love is a reality even God must obey, that He must be the Father of the Son. The Son is the first in God and the Spirit is the second in God, that is, as God is the Father of the Son, and, as Father, begets the Son, He also brings forth the Spirit and therefore the negation of isolation, the law and the reality of love. Love is God, the supreme law and ultimate reality, because God is love and not vice versa. And God is love, love proceeds from Him as His love, as the Spirit He Himself is, because He posits Himself as the Father and therefore posits Himself as the Son. In the Son of His love, i.e., in the Son in and with whom He brings forth Himself as love, He then brings forth in the *opus ad extra* [work outside of God] too, in creation, the creaturely reality which is distinct from Himself, and in revelation the reconciliation and peace of the creature that has fallen away from Him. The love which meets us in reconciliation, and then retrospectively in creation, is real love, supreme law and ultimate reality, because God is antecedently love in Himself: not just a supreme principle of the relation of separateness and fellowship, but love which even in fellowship wills and affirms and seeks and finds the other or Other in its distinction, and then in separateness wills and affirms and seeks and finds fellowship with it. Because God is antecedently love in Himself, love is and holds good as the reality of God in the work of reconciliation and in the work of creation. But He is love antecedently in Himself as He posits Himself as the Father of the Son. This is the explanation and proof of the *qui procedit ex Patre* [who proceeds from the Father].

But just because we explain and prove it thus, we must now continue that similarly, as God is the Son who comes forth from the Father, He brings forth the Spirit, He brings forth love. In this mode of being, too, He negates loneliness in His absolute simplicity; He is orientated to the Other; He does not will to be without the Other out of whom He is. How else could He be the Son but as the Son of the Father? How could He be less the origin of love in being the Son than in being the Father? Distinct as Father and Son, God is one in the fact that His distinction is that of the Father and the Son, so that it is not the kind of distinction which might also arise in a supreme principle of separateness and fellowship, a loveless distinction, but the distinction which affirms fellowship in separateness and separateness in fellowship. How, then, can the breathing of the Spirit belong less essentially, less properly and originally, to the Son than to the Father? In relation to the *opus ad extra* we must also ask: If it is true that God reveals Himself to us through His only-begotten Son, if it is also true that God's only-begotten Son is no less and no other than God the Father, if it is true again that God's revelation is also the revelation of His love, if revelation would not be revelation without the outpouring and impartation of the Spirit through whom man becomes the child of God, can it be that this Spirit is not directly the Spirit of the Son as well? Is it only indirectly, only derivatively, that the Son is here the Giver of the Spirit, of the revelation of love? But if He is this immediately and directly, how can this be if He is not so in reality, in the reality of God antecedently in Himself? If here, and already in creation when seen from here, love is God's reality in the Son and through the Son, we have no reason and no warrant to think beyond that which is valid here. It is also the love of the Son antecedently in Himself, in eternity. As the Son of the Father He, too, is thus *spirator Spiritus* [breather of the Spirit]. He is this, of course, as the Son of the Father. To that extent the *per Filium* [through the Son] is true. But here *per Filium* cannot mean *per causam instrumentalem* [through instrumental cause]. This Son of this Father is and has all that His Father is and has. He is and has it as the Son. But He is and has it. Thus He, too, is *spirator Spiritus*. He, too, has the possibility of being this. This is how we explain and prove the *qui procedit ex Patre Filioque* [who proceeds from the Father and the Son].

With this explanation and proof, however, we have already said the final thing that has always been said, and must necessarily be said, in explanation of the Western view, namely, that the *ex Patre Filioque* denotes, not a twofold, but rather a common origin of the Spirit from the Father and the Son. The fact that the Father is the Father and the Son the Son, that the former begets and the latter is begotten, is not common to them; in this respect they are different divine modes of being. But the fact that between them and from them, as God's third mode of being, is the Spirit, love – this they have in common. This third mode of being cannot result from the former alone, or the latter alone, or co-operation of the two, but only from their one being as God the Father and God the Son, who are not two 'persons' either in themselves or in co-operation, but two modes of being of the one being God. Thus the one Godness of the Father and Son is, or the Father and the Son in their one Godness are, the origin of the Spirit. What is between them, what unites them, is, then, no mere relation. It is not exhausted in the truth of their being alongside and with one another. As an independent divine mode of being over against them, it is the active mutual orientation and interpenetration of love, because of these two, the Father and the Son, are of one essence, and indeed of divine essence, because God's fatherhood and sonship as such must be related to one another in this active mutual orientation and interpenetration. That the Father and the Son are the one God is the reason why they are not just united but are united in the Spirit in love; it is the reason, then, why God is love and love is God.

Source: Karl Barth, Church Dogmatics *I.1, trans. and ed. by Geoffrey Bromiley and T. F. Torrance, Edinburgh: T. & T. Clark, 1975, pp. 479–87.*

6.15 Theodore Stylianopoulos, from *Conflicts about the Holy Spirit*

This extract offers an account of the Eastern rejection of the filioque *clause.*

For any hopeful breakthrough in the debate over the Filioque, the investigation must move beyond simple comparison of the Filioque and the terminology of the Second Council into consideration of the entire theological approaches behind them and of what in these approaches are crucial divergencies. In this regard three observations are important regarding style, historical context and doctrinal value.

1. Different style

By style is meant the character and spirit of theological exposition. That Augustine's is philosophical whereas Athanasius' and the Cappadocians' is biblical, as sometimes claimed, is not true without qualification. All of these Church fathers use Scripture as their ultimate authority. They all employ an intellectual discursive exposition which includes formal terms and notions such as essence, *hypostasis*, immutability, time, eternity, act according to essence, act according to will and the like. Significantly, Augustine's teaching of the Filioque is derived more from biblical texts, such as John 15:26; 20:22 (*de Trin.* iv, 20) and Gal. 4:6 (xv, 26), as well as from the biblical principle that the Son has whatever the Father has (xv, 26–27), rather than from his philosophical interpretations of the Trinity. After all Augustine himself not infrequently states that his reflections about the Trinity are based on the data of faith and not the reverse. The difference seems to be that, despite his own repeated reservations, Augustine is almost naively bold about what can be conceived of the inner life of the Trinity, gives himself to speculation in terms of several human analogies and ends his book in a prayerful tentative mood by stressing the difficulties in the intellectual task of understanding the Trinity (xv, chaps. 2, 5, 22–24, 28). He gives the impression of presenting his thoughts as a kind of personal theological speculation about the Trinity resting on the security of the Church's dogma about the Trinity.

2. Different historical context

But the case is different with Athanasius and the Cappadocians. While philosophically more sensitive to the incomprehensibility of the essence of God, they firmly argue about the truth of the Church's revealed faith in terms of basic principles which are at stake. They neither give themselves to open speculation, nor do they seek to understand the inner life of the Trinity on the basis of faith, but unhesitatingly they defend the Catholic faith against heretics. If the Son is Saviour, how can he be created? If the Son is uncreated, he cannot be related to the Father in the same way as the world is related to

God because the world is a creation. Is the Spirit created or uncreated? How can both the unity and trinitarian nature of God be defended against heretical teaching that compromised one aspect or the other? Such were their questions. The crucial *historical* factor is this: Athanasius, the Cappadocians and many other fathers who wrote in Greek shared an ongoing debate – an entire historical context of issues, terms, principles, biblical interpretations, Councils and writings of Church fathers and heretics. After a long and hard-won struggle, they hammered out an impressive consensus on the Trinity which involved definite terminology and clear principles. But Augustine was removed from this context. The problem was not geography or time. Augustine simply was not at home with Greek, as he admits. Unable to read in depth the extensive writings of Church fathers and heretics not yet available in Latin translation, Augustine never became integrally rooted in the above trinitarian consensus. While accepting both the Catholic faith and the decrees of the Councils, his gifted mind simply set out on a different path.

3. Different doctrinal value

The matter of doctrinal value is most crucial. If the above remarks are in the main true, then Augustine's teaching of the Filioque has the value of personal theological meditation. It probably cannot even be regarded as a serious alternative interpretation of the Trinity because it does not really take into account the standard interpretation of the Church fathers and Councils hammered out on the anvil of the actual struggle against Sabellianism, Arianism and Eunomianism. Above all Augustine's teaching cannot be viewed as the *normative* teaching of the Church. The only normative teaching about the Trinity is that of the Ecumenical Councils against the background of the trinitarian theology of the Church fathers mentioned above who were the Catholic principals in the trinitarian controversy with the ancient heresies.

Although Augustine unknowingly set a different path, one may still ask what the important divergencies are in trinitarian teaching between him and the Greek fathers. The *heart of the problem* is that Augustine's views, not sharpened by full knowledge of the struggle against the ancient heresies, lack a fundamental theological principle which emerged as a first line of defence against Arianism, namely, that the manner by which the Father 'causes' the existence of the uncreated *Son* and uncreated *Spirit* is *radically different from* that by which the entire Trinity 'causes' the created *world* and manifests Itself in it. The former involves the essence of God and the eternal existence of the Holy Trinity (God in Himself), while the latter involves the will of God and the Trinity's revelation in time and history (God with us). Applied to the former, the Filioque is *unacceptable* for reasons already stated. Applied to the latter the Filioque is *acceptable* according to Maximus the Confessor's interpretation because the entire Trinity shares a common will, action, glory, kingdom and grace, just as the Trinity shares a common essence. Excepting the single case of the incarnation of the Son, which is according to the eternal person of the Son and not only according to the will of the Trinity, all other manifestations of God are absolutely common: the Father always acts through the Son in the Holy Spirit. In this sense, the Spirit who abides in and belongs to the Son

(Gal. 4:6) also proceeds from and is sent to the world (John 15:26) by the Son who is the agent of creation, revelation and redemption. But the Son does not cause the eternal existence of the Spirit. Thus when Jesus imparts the Spirit to the apostles (John 20:20), he does not impart to them the *hypostasis* (person) but the grace of the Holy Spirit which is common to Father, Son and Spirit.

The above differentiation between the Trinity's eternal inner existence and volitional activity toward the world is impossible unless God's essence and will are distinguished, as they are by Athanasius and the Cappadocians against the Arians. This is the crucial distinction of 'essence' and 'energies' in God on which Orthodox theologians insist in order to maintain both the personal immanence of God in his creation as well as his radical difference from it. God is one, yet revealed and hidden; partially revealed by his will or activity, absolutely hidden in his inner being or essence. This distinction, far from negating the simplicity of God who is perfect and present at all times and in all places according to both essence and will, affirms the biblical faith in the living God of Abraham, Isaac and Jacob who acts in creation and history, has personal communion with human beings in prayer, sacrament and righteous living, while he remains ineffably transcendent in himself. At this level of doctrinal interpretation the Filioque becomes a matter about the truth of God as revealed to us and about our relations with him – a matter of salvation …

Source: Theodore Stylianopoulos, 'The Orthodox Position', in Hans Küng and Jürgen Moltmann (eds), Conflicts about the Holy Spirit, *New York: Seabury Press, 1979, pp. 23–30, here pp. 26–9.*

6.16 Tom Smail, from *The Giving Gift*

Smail, a leading theologian of the charismatic movement, explores the Holy Spirit as the 'giving gift'.

1. To describe the Holy Spirit as Gift emphasises that we are here in the realm of grace. Free giving is not by any means the only kind of exchange that can take place between two parties. A cheque can pass from me to you as a contracted payment of wages in return for services rendered. It is then not a gift but a payment, a *quid pro quo* in which one party fulfils agreed conditions and the other party is in duty bound to pay the agreed reward.

Some Christians have tended to understand God's sending of the Holy Spirit in this contractual way. God gives the Spirit when we fulfil the conditions that he has laid down. This view has both a typically Roman Catholic and a typically Protestant form.

In much traditional Catholic spirituality the full indwelling of the Holy Spirit is seen as the reward of a long laborious effort after sanctity, so that the gifts and fruit of the Spirit are the end product of an extended process of disciplined prayer, stern self-denial and costly strivings for holiness, perhaps in a monastic setting. They are thus the prerogatives of the saints and indeed the signs and proofs of their sainthood.

The Catholic charismatic renewal has rebelled against that approach. What was seen as a reward for the few who could attain to the heights of holiness, is now seen as a gift freely offered to all who belong to Christ and indeed implicit in their baptismal initiation into his grace. What was once shut up in the cloister has been set free in a popular movement. Once more the Spirit is seen not as a reward for the few but as a free gift to the many. Far from being a reversal of Catholic tradition, this is a return to its basic insight that God lavishes his Spirit and his gifts on his people not in proportion to their achievements but in the freedom of his mercy and grace.

The Protestant form of the same contractual approach is deeply entrenched in much denominational pentecostalism and often shows itself in the mainline charismatic renewal. It holds that the Spirit and his gifts are given when we have repented enough, prayed enough, claimed enough, 'tarried' enough.

Such an approach almost inevitably leads to a preoccupation with ourselves and how we can receive the Spirit, rather than with God and his willingness to give the Spirit. It can also threaten the very notion that the Spirit is Gift. What sort of a gift is it that can be bestowed only when required conditions have been fulfilled? It is a bit like the 'free gifts' offered by the cornflakes' manufacturers to induce us to buy their product. It is in fact neither gift nor free, because the value of the gift is included in the cost of the product. That may be good trade but it is bad theology. God does not extract a hidden payment for his gifts. His gifts have lifechanging consequences, but no preconditions, except the willingness to receive them. In the New Testament, as we shall see, even that willingness is regarded as itself a gift of God rather than a precondition for receiving a gift.

If that is true of all God's gifts, it is supremely true of his supreme Gift, the

Holy Spirit. In his Pentecost sermon Peter offers that Gift to potential converts as part of the beginning of their Christian life (Acts 2:38). The faith and
repentance with which the Gift is to be received are not things that his Jewish
hearers have to produce out of themselves as their entitlement to the Spirit.
Their willingness to turn round to Christ and hold out empty hands for what
Peter is promising has been produced in them by the word Peter has preached
in the power of the Spirit, by which they 'were cut to the heart' (v. 37). So it
was the Spirit who made them open to the Spirit: their faith and repentance
were themselves his work and gift.

Our sinful hearts are for ever trying to turn the good news of God's grace
into a series of daunting demands for us to fulfil. The result is always guilty
self-absorption rather than rejoicing liberation. To call the Holy Spirit Gift
reminds us that here we are not in the calculating world of benefits conferred
in proportion to conditions fulfilled, but in the kingdom of a gracious Father
who generously imparts his Spirit in free unconditional grace to people who
do not and could not earn such a Gift, and in the same generosity opens and
prepares them to receive it.

2. To describe the Holy Spirit as Gift emphasises that we are in the realm
of dynamic relationships, the movement from a giver to a receiver, the opening up of one person to another. We are concerned with the impartation of
life, truth, love and power from divine persons to human persons, with the
self-giving of God to man that creates and evokes the responsive self-giving
of man to God. The very notion of gift reminds us that the Holy Spirit cannot
be studied in isolation, in and for himself. A gift is meaningless without a
giver and a receiver. So the word Spirit is a word that has meaning only in a
relationship. The Spirit is, in Bishop John V. Taylor's suggestive phrase, 'the
Go-Between God'. He is what he is and does what he does only within a network of divine and divine–human relationships.

It is therefore only from within that set of divine–human relationships that we
call the Church that the Spirit can be identified and recognised, even although
he works unidentified and unrecognised in all men and in all creation. There
can be no theoretical academic knowledge of the Spirit. He can be met only
where God's love is being poured out into people's hearts (Romans 5:5). The
Pentecost of Acts 2 is not solitary ecstasy; it is corporate receptivity. In the
New Testament the Spirit typically comes to groups of people together, not to
individuals alone. Discussions of the so called baptism in the Holy Spirit have
often gone awry. They have not taken account of that corporate dimension
that is so evident in the New Testament from Pentecost on; they have failed to
see that the coming of the Spirit takes place when people are together, and that
it results in new relationships with God and with fellow Christians, not as a
remote consequence but as the heart and centre of what the Spirit is doing.

These relationships are not set and static but dynamic and active. The
three characteristically biblical symbols for the Spirit – wind (John 3:8), water
(John 7:37–39), and fire (Matthew 3:11, Acts 2:3–4) – all point to a mysterious
dynamic energy that destroys one kind of life and gives birth to another. It
is only by involvement in these powerful dynamic relationships that we can
know the Holy Spirit.

3. When we describe the Holy Spirit as Gift we are emphasising that we are

in the personal realm. A gift is a gift in the proper sense only if it embodies the intention of a donor to give it and it is received as a gift only when the recipient acknowledges that intention. A cow does not give milk; she has it taken from her. When I give the cat her food, the fact that I act in goodwill and even affection towards her is a matter of small import as far as she is concerned. But when I give my wife some perfume, the fact that it is redolent of me as well as of Chanel No 5 is what makes it precious to her. It is a gift made and received within a personal relationship and it has its value within that context. In the same way the Holy Spirit conveys and expresses God's love to God's people: that is why he is a Gift.

But in the case of the Holy Spirit, it is not only that a divine person gives and human persons receive, but the Gift is himself a person in a way that we shall have to discuss in detail later. When God in Christ gives us the Spirit, he gives us nothing less than himself. A gift is often an object that is passed from one hand to another. But here the Gift is a subject, living, acting, loving, sovereign and free.

That has not always been clear in the theology of the Christian West, particularly in the Augustinian strand that preferred to speak of the Holy Spirit as Gift. One of Augustine's ways of distinguishing the persons of the Trinity was to say that the Father was the Lover, the Son his Beloved and the Holy Spirit the Love between them. The problem with this analogy is that love is a relationship *between* persons and not itself another person, so that Augustine failed to do justice to the distinct personhood of the Holy Spirit. In the centuries that followed, the failure continued and there was an increasing tendency to understand the gift of God in terms of impersonal grace rather than in terms of a fully personal Spirit.

As a result, the Spirit came to be robbed of that sovereign freedom that is so characteristic of him in the New Testament (cf John 3:8). That is why we have described him in our title not simply as Gift but as Giving Gift. He is not just a passive Gift but himself an active Giver. What God gives us in him is less like a fortune to possess and spend and more like a friend to cultivate and love. His gifts do become our possessions, but as Heribert Mühlen points out, Paul is careful to distinguish between the gifts which we are responsible for using and controlling (I Cor 14:32) and the Spirit who, as the sovereign distributor of these gifts, is not controlled or used by anyone but gives whatever he will to whomsoever he chooses (I Cor 12:11). In all this the Spirit retains his own personal identity. He is in us, but he never becomes part of us. He gives with the greatest generosity, but he himself is never possessed. Our relationship with him is, as we shall soon see, quite different from our relationship with the Son and the Father, but in all his dealings with us he acts as a person whose freedom is always maintained and who eludes all our attempts at manipulation and possession. The value of this Gift is that the one who is given wills to be given, and he comes to us as one who has the divine willingness to give. He is the Giving Gift.

So even at this early stage we have identified, even if in a rather formal and abstract way, some of the defining characteristics of the Holy Spirit. His field of operation is dynamic personal relationships and we are to acknowledge him in the unconditional freedom of his divine grace.

The giver of fellowship

If the central thesis of this book is correct, it is not surprising that Paul should describe the Spirit as the creator of *koinonia*, fellowship, in II Corinthians 13:14. As the Son is characterised by the grace he embodies and as the Father is characterised by the love of which he is the source, so the Spirit is characterised by the *koinonia* in which his own person is rooted and which he produces in us as the primary result of his presence and activity among us.

The word *koinonia*, in the Greek of the New Testament, has a strong meaning which is inadequately represented by the English word, fellowship, which, especially in a religious context, is often weak and vague in meaning. The root meaning of *koinonia* is a having in common, the sharing of a common life. It can be used to describe an intimate spiritual union of persons, but words from the same root can equally well be used to describe the sharing of money and possessions, which was one of the first results of the pouring out of the Spirit at Pentecost. 'All the believers were together and had everything in common (*hapanta koina*)' (Acts 2:44).

According to I John 1:3 the creation of this *koinonia* is the primary purpose and effect of the proclamation of the gospel: 'We proclaim to you what we have seen and heard, so that you also may have *koinonia* with us. And our *koinonia* is with the Father and with his Son Jesus Christ.' These two occurrences of the word clearly indicate the two dimensions of the *koinonia* which the gospel creates. On the hand it is a horizontal sharing of life among believers: on the other it is a *vertical* sharing of life between believers on the one side and the Father and the Son on the other. One could hardly think of a more theologically succinct and practically challenging description of the Church. The Christian Church is, in the purpose and intention of God, that community of people who, as a result of their hearing and believing of the gospel, have been enabled to share through Christ in God's own life, and who, as a result, have begun to share their lives with one another on every level. It is a norm that very few congregations live up to; yet the more they are in Christ and the more the Spirit sets them free, the nearer they come to it.

In the rest of his first letter one of John's central themes is that vertical *koinonia* with God and horizontal *koinonia* with one another are so inseparably connected that you cannot have the one without the other. The only way that one can have *agape*-love for God's people is by being 'born of God', and, on the other hand, to fail to love your brother on the visible level is a sure sign that you do not love God on the invisible level. 'Every one who loves has been born of God and knows God. Whoever does not love does not know God, because God is love' (4:7–8). 'If anyone says, 'I love God', yet hates his brother, he is a liar. For anyone who does not love his brother whom he has seen, cannot love God whom he has not seen' (4:20).

The inseparability of our new relationship with God in Christ and our resultant and very practical sharing of life with one another is demonstrated in Acts 2, precisely in the context of the coming of the Spirit at Pentecost. His coming results, first of all, in the apostles sharing in the authority and power of the risen and exalted Jesus. The preached word of Peter has converting effect on a large scale and the prayer of Peter and John over the lame man at the gate of the temple in the next chapter (Acts 3:6–10) results in his miraculous healing. No sooner is their new sharing through the Spirit in the power of Jesus inaugurated than it results, as we have already indicated, in a new sharing among themselves in spiritual, social and economic ways, 'All the believers were together and had everything in common. Selling their possessions and goods, they gave to anyone as he had need. Every day they continued to meet together in the temple courts. They broke bread in their homes and ate together with glad and sincere hearts' (2:44–46). The key word in that passage is undoubtedly 'together'. The sharing of one Spirit results in their co-ordination into one body in all sorts of visible and practical ways.

One of my very few criticisms of Richard Lovelace's fine book, *Dynamics of Spiritual Life*, concerns the way in which he relegates what he calls the 'community of believers' to the 'secondary elements' of renewal. Such teaching seems to me to owe more to Protestant individualism than to the New Testament. In the gospel, being in Christ and being in the closest fellowship with other Christians are too inseparably connected for one to be thought of as secondary to the other. To be in Christ and to be in the Church, *i.e.* the visible company of believers, are one and the same thing. If you are not in Christ, you are not in the Church: if you are not in the Church, you are not in Christ. To be baptised into Christ is to join a local visible community which is the body of Christ in that place. Any baptism that does not entail the integration of the baptised into the local community of believers in which that baptism is performed is so far a defective baptism. Belonging to the Church is not a secondary consequence of our relationship to Christ but an essential and defining component within it.

The Holy Spirit is the Spirit of relationship: as he opens us up to the Father and the Son, he opens us up to one another as well. Where we stand with the Holy Spirit is much more clearly demonstrated by the state of our relationships with other people than it is by the dramatic gifts that we exercise. The *charismata* are secondary to the *koinonia*. The initial evidence that we share in the Church's baptism in the Spirit is less speaking in tongues and more new relationships of love with God and with others.

Source: Thomas A. Smail, The Giving Gift: The Holy Spirit in Person, *London: Hodder & Stoughton, 1988, pp. 17–22, 182–4.*

6.17 Amos Yong, from *The Spirit Poured Out on All Flesh*

From within the Pentecostal tradition Yong here considers the implications of pneumatology for our understanding of worship.

3.3.3 Meeting Daily in the Spirit: Toward a Pneumatological Theology of the Liturgy.

From this initiatory rite (we were saved) emerges a distinctive pentecostal and pneumatological theology of the liturgy whereby the entire liturgy (or worship service) becomes a 'sacrament of the Spirit' (whereby we are being saved). To put it in thesis form, I suggest that the Holy Spirit breathes life and grace into the believing community by making present and available the resurrection power of Jesus Christ, which inaugurates the eschatological kingdom of God. More concretely, the Holy Spirit transforms the community of faith from moment to moment that it can more fully realize and embody here and now the image and likeness of the eschatological Christ. This happens liturgically (among other means) in the word of worship that is directed to God and enlivened by the Spirit of God, in the word of proclamation of Jesus as the Messiah, and in the word of consumption that is the eucharistic fellowship of the body and blood of Christ. Let me briefly elaborate on each.

A pneumatological theology of the liturgy emphasizes the centrality of the Spirit's presence and activity to enable the true praise and worship of God (John 4:23–24), precisely because no true encounter with God is possible apart from such divine initiative. When the Spirit is present and active, the vertical dimension of relationship between God and the people of God opens up (as experienced by John, who visited the throne of God only in the Spirit; Rev. 4:2). Human beings realize their fallenness, finitude, and unworthiness in the presence of God and their need for the confession of their sins (cf. Isa. 6:5) and are enabled to experience, if only in part, the glory of God because of the mediating and sanctifying work and word of Christ by the Spirit. At this juncture, the life-giving word of Christ is transformed into living words of praise and worship by the people of God, given to God for no other reason than that God is worthy to be magnified. This becomes in turn a transformative experience for the people of God, leading to an ever intensifying realization of the eschatological glory of God amidst the worshiping community.

Yet this relationship opened by the mediating word and work of Christ is not limited to its vertical or eschatological dimension but carries over into the believing community's engagement with reality here and now. Thus a pneumatological theology of the liturgy recognizes the necessity of the Spirit quickening the word of Christ in order to give life to the people of God. When this happens, the letter of the law becomes living and active (John 6:63; 2 Cor. 3:6; Heb. 4:12). This is what pentecostals often call the '*rhema* word,' which speaks God's word anew and afresh to the here-and-now situation of the believer and the believing community. This certainly occurs in the contemporary sermon, the central form of kerygmatic proclamation of the living word of Christ by the power of the Spirit. But because the Spirit of God is no respecter of persons and has been poured out upon all flesh, the rhema word can be spoken at any moment and by any one. Thus the importance of the testimony and confessional praise in pentecostal liturgy as well as ordered moments for the manifestation of the charisms, including the word of wisdom, the word of knowledge, and tongues and their interpretations. The living word of the Spirit is best understood doing things with words and bringing things about with words (illocutionary and perlocutionary speech acts, respectively; see §3.2.2). So the word of Christ spoken by the power of the Spirit accomplishes the transformation of the soul and of the believing community – for example, in the bringing about of a new situation ('Brother Saul … regain your sight and be filled with the Holy Spirit.' Acts 9:17); in the granting of forgiveness ('Your sins are forgiven,' cf. Luke 7:48; John 20:22-23); in the releasing of those captive and oppressed ('There is therefore now no condemnation for those who are in Christ Jesus.' Rom. 8:1); in the reconciling with those estranged ('Go and show yourselves to the priests.' Luke 17:14); and in exorcising the demonic ('Come out of him!' Luke 4:35) – so that the world of the Scriptures becomes alive in the here and now of the liturgical community. In one sense, the Spirit enables us to step into and inhabit the world of the scriptural narrative; in another sense, the Spirit of God calls and empowers the believer and believing community to actualize the word of God in the image and likeness of Jesus.

But the word of God not only returns to God in worship and accomplishes the purposes of God in the world (cf. Isa. 55:11); it is also internalized and, through the Supper, literally embodied by the people of God. So a pneumatological theology of the liturgy highlights the centrality of the working of the Spirit in the fellowship of the meal. In this case, the invocation (*epiklēsis*) of the Spirit becomes essential to the church's memory (*anamnesis*) of Christ, both in the sense of enabling the recollection of the historical Jesus in the present remembering of the body of Christ and in the sense of making present the living Christ in the 'membered' elements of the bread and cup and in the 'members' of the congregation as the living body of Christ. As such, the Lord's Supper becomes a sacramental rite (in the senses defined above) that transforms the worshiping community through word and Spirit. We can see this in at least five dimensions.

First, the Supper is a physical act wherein the word of God is consumed by the body of Christ through the working of the Spirit. The physicality of this experience can be understood in the literal sense of eating and drinking. Indeed, the eating and drinking of the elements used to be literally nourishing (cf. Acts 2:46). Because of abuses, however, Paul instructed the Corinthians to eat and drink to their fill at home before coming to participate around the Lord's Table (1 Cor. 11:17–22). Since Paul's concern was that factions not develop in the body between the haves and the have-nots, there is no reason the Lord's Supper cannot once again become a communal celebration that nourishes physical bodies so long as the congregation is alert to the have-nots in their midst.

But even more than a source of nourishment, the Supper as a physical act, taken with self-discernment, also is an occasion for God's healing grace to be manifest. This is so not only in the sense in which the church fathers understood the Eucharist as a *pharmakon* (or pharmaceutical medicine) but also in the sense in which many pentecostals believe healing to be in the atonement – 'by his wounds you have been healed' (1 Pet. 2:24b) – so that to internalize the body and blood of Christ is to release its healing virtues for broken bodies. And why not, if in fact the material elements of bread and wine or juice some-how mediate the presence of Christ by the power of the Spirit? If pentecostals believe that the healing powers of God and the gift of the Holy Spirit can be and are communicated through material means – for example, handkerchiefs, aprons (Acts 19:12), and the laying on of hands (Acts 8:14–17; 9:17; 13:3; 19:6) – then why not through the eucharistic elements (cf. John 6:51–58)? Believers encounter the living Christ who is present, understood not in the physicalist or consubstantive terms of Aristotelian and neoscholastic substance philosophy but in the interpersonal and intersubjective terms of contemporary pneuma-tological theology.

This means, second, not only that Christ is present to us but that we are present to Christ. This mutual presence is made possible by the Spirit, invited to reign over the Supper. The Spirit enables us to 'respond to Christ's bodily presence and [to] share in the formation of a mutual, personal presence.' In this pneumatological framework, what is important is not the alleged 'tran-substantiation' of the elements into the actual body and blood of Christ, nor the moment of full or mutual presence between Christ and the believing com-munity, but the intersubjective mutuality that is always a matter of degree: the Supper now becomes a mysterious interpersonal encounter wherein Christ and his body are brought into real relationship by the Spirit.

Third, the Supper is thus an ecclesial and social act of solidarity whereby Jesus the resurrected Word is united with the body of Christ through the fellowship of the Spirit. It goes beyond the interpersonal union brought about by consuming the elements, toward the fellowship brought about by the Spirit among those nourished by the body and blood of Jesus. This effects a trans-formation of human relationships within and without the congregation. Not only are those who gather around the Lord's Table required to be sensitive to each other and to be discerning about the body of Christ (cf. 1 Cor. 11:22, 27–34); insofar as the Supper is the consummation of the liturgical activity of the church, the members of the body are not to approach this moment without being reconciled to any and all from whom they are estranged (cf. Matt. 5:23–24). In this way, the Supper becomes a moment of intimate and yet catholic (§3.2.3) fellowship brought about by the Holy Spirit around the body (and blood) of Christ even as it hastens the process of reconciliation between believers and other believers and those not yet followers of the way of Jesus. The eucharistic fellowship can never be only inward-looking but is always already opened to the world, at least in attitude and eschatological anticipa-tion if not in participatory actuality.

Fourth, connected to this is that the Supper is a political and prophetic act whereby the enacted and enacting body of Christ provides and mediates an alternative way of life through the gracious activity of the Spirit. By 'politi-cal,' I am drawing both on themes of exodus and liberation connecting the Supper with the Passover meal and on postliberal perspectives that consider how the Supper in particular and the liturgy in general provide imaginative possibilities for and actually instantiate alternative modes of space-time existence in this world. The church gathered around the Table of the Lord is a spatiotemporal and public body that celebrates its constitution through the transgression of all legal, class, gender, sexual, ethnic, racial, and national boundaries (§3.2.3). Hence, against modernity's privatization of the religious dimension of human experience, the fellowship of the Supper opens up a truly free space for human habitation and provides for a counterdiscourse to the prevailing ideologies of any time, thereby making concrete God's redemptive activity in all spheres and aspects of life. In this way, the Eucharist is also a prophetic act, sanctifying, renewing, and empowering the church for its mission of reconciliation to the world (see *Baptism, Eucharist and Ministry* §§14, 17; §3.2.4 above). It makes real, through the working of the Spirit, a 'participatory politics' that catches up the members of the body into a transformative narrative, thereby freeing individuals-as-communities to enact the kingdom of the future in the present.

This leads, finally, to an understanding of the Supper as an eschatological act whereby the people of God anticipate embodiment of the word of God according to the full image and likeness of Jesus Christ through the resurrection power of the Spirit. After all, the Supper is not only an act of remembering but also an act of anticipation until Jesus returns (1 Cor. 11:26). And this eschatological dimension is the realm of the Spirit, who graces – sometimes violently breaking through – history's times and places with foreshadowings of the coming kingdom. As the Oriental Orthodox put it, it is the Holy Spirit who '"recaptures" the salvific events of the past into the Now and anticipates the "not yet" into the present.'[3] Doing so renders the Supper in particular and the church in general as signs of the eschatological kingdom, which banishes the fallen powers of this world (Luke 11:20) and ushers in justice, righteousness, peace, and the fruits of the Spirit (cf. Isa. 11:1–2; 32:15–17). It also requires that, eschatologically speaking, 'we must regard all human beings, Christians and non-Christians alike, as at least potential members of the body of Christ.'

The Spirit ecclesiology developed here has enabled envisioning a pneumatological theology of the sacraments and of the liturgy. Herein lies the pentecostal response to the postliberal vision of the church as an alternative praxis. Though agreeing with the postliberal ecclesiology in its basic senses, pentecostals would want to emphasize the pragmatic, transformative, and eschatological dimensions of being and becoming the people of God. Put this way, the sacramental liturgy, a gift of God and the Holy Spirit, is now a performance that redeems and transforms all persons, along with their times and places, for the kingdom and glory of God. Here, we are in and not of the world, but also open to the world as the world is opened to the coming kingdom by the presence and activity of the Spirit.

Source: Amos Yong, The Spirit Poured Out on All Flesh, Grand Rapids, MI: Baker Academic, 2005, pp. 160–6.

---

3 Jacob Vellian, 'Role of the Holy Spirit in the Sanctifying Effect of the Sacraments according to the Oriental Perspective', in *Oriental Churches – Theological Dimensions: International Theological Conference of the Catholic Oriental Churches*, ed. Xavier Koodapuzha (Kerala, India: Oriental Institute of Religious Studies, 1988), pp. 101–11; quotation, p. 101.

6.18 The Second Vatican Council, from *Lumen Gentium*

This encyclical, one of the key texts of the Second Vatican Council, explores the role of the Spirit in the Church and in the world.

I. 4. When the work which the Father gave the Son to do on earth (cf. Jn. 17:4) was accomplished, the Holy Spirit was sent on the day of Pentecost in order that He might continually sanctify the Church, and thus, all those who believe would have access through Christ in one Spirit to the Father (cf. Eph. 1:18). He is the Spirit of Life, a fountain of water springing up to life eternal (cf. Jn. 4:14; 7:38–39). To men, dead in sin, the Father gives life through Him, until, in Christ, He brings to life their mortal bodies (cf. Rom. 8:10–11). The Spirit dwells in the Church and in the hearts of the faithful, as in a temple (cf. 1 Cor. 3:16; 6:19). In them He prays on their behalf and bears witness to the fact that they are adopted sons (cf Gal. 4:6; Rom. 8:15–16, 26). The Church, which the Spirit guides in way of all truth (cf. Jn. 16:13) and which He unified in communion and in works of ministry, He both equips and directs with hierarchical and charismatic gifts and adorns with His fruits (cf. Eph. 1:11–12; 1 Cor. 12:4; Gal. 5:22). By the power of the Gospel He makes the Church keep the freshness of youth. Uninterruptedly He renews it and leads it to perfect union with its Spouse. The Spirit and the Bride both say to Jesus, the Lord, 'Come!' (Rev. 22:17).

II. 12. It is not only through the sacraments and the ministries of the Church that the Holy Spirit sanctifies and leads the people of God and enriches it with virtues, but, 'allotting his gifts to everyone according as He wills' (1 Cor. 12:11), He distributes special graces among the faithful of every rank. By these gifts He makes them fit and ready to undertake the various tasks and offices which contribute toward the renewal and building up of the Church, according to the words of the Apostle: 'The manifestation of the Spirit is given to everyone for profit' (cf. 1 Thess. 5:12, 19–21). These charisms, whether they be the more outstanding or the more simple and widely diffused, are to be received with thanksgiving and consolation for they are perfectly suited to and useful for the needs of the Church. Extraordinary gifts are not to be sought after, nor are the fruits of apostolic labor to be presumptuously expected from their use; but judgment as to their genuinity and proper use belongs to those who are appointed leaders in the Church, to whose special competence it belongs, not indeed to extinguish the Spirit, but to test all things and hold fast to that which is good (cf. Jn. 11:52).

Source: Dogmatic Constitution on the Church, Lumen Gentium, 21 November 1964, from http://www.vatican.va/archive/hist_councils/ii_vatican_council/documents/vat-ii_const_19641121_lumen-gentium_en.html.

6.19 Hans Küng and Jürgen Moltmann, from *Conflicts about the Holy Spirit*

Küng and Moltmann explore the role of the Spirit in the Church.

Experience of the Spirit is the basic experience in the charismatic movement. In the Neo-Pentecostalist movement charismatic experience is the most important thing – it is everything. But how is the genuineness of charismatic experience to be determined? Even with what seem outwardly the most reliable experiences there may be weeds mixed with the wheat. Prudence and testing are therefore essential (see 1 John 4:1). The gift of 'discernment of spirits' (1 Cor. 12:10) does not work automatically, but on principles some of which come from the Holy Spirit himself while others are learned by experienced community leaders, ministers and laity. The following criteria for the discernment of spirits is based on holy Scripture, the tradition of the saints and the spiritual experience of the Church.

First, the charismatic experience must start from faith in Jesus Christ and contain a direct or indirect confession of this faith (see 1 John 4:2–3). The Paraclete, the spirit of truth, is sent to believers by Jesus Christ to lead them still further into the fullness of his truth; he glorifies Jesus because what he declares to Christians he takes from Jesus' fullness (John 16:7, 13–14). So no-one who speaks in the Spirit of God can say 'Jesus be cursed!' and no-one can say Jesus is Lord', except in the Holy Spirit (1 Cor. 12:3).

Second, the content of the charismatic experience must agree with the revelations contained in the scriptures and traditions inspired by the Holy Spirit. In all revelations of the Holy Spirit there is unity, continuity and consistency; they contain no contradictions.

Third, spiritual gifts are allotted to believers *in the Church* (see 1 Cor. 12:28). The Church is the mysterious body of the Lord in which everything is made alive and holy by the Holy Spirit. The various gifts of the Holy Spirit are given to equip the saints for the building up of the mystical body of Christ (Eph. 4:12). There may be many defects in the empirical structure of the Church, but it remains nonetheless a divine and human organism in which we can attain sanctification and salvation. Only in the maternal and gracious bosom of the Church can the baptised Christian grow properly and reach the measure of the stature of the fullness of Christ (see Eph. 4:13). Accordingly all Christians, including charismatics, are required to belong to the Church and to be obedient to it (see Matt. 18:17).

Fourth, service to the community, to neighbour, to mankind, is a mark of the spiritual charisms. According to the teaching of the apostles, charisms are gifts for service, given for the benefit of the community, to build it up (1 Cor. 12:4–7; 14:4, 12), for mutual service and not for individual advantage and private enjoyment.

Fifth, genuine striving to preserve the *unity* of the community and of the whole Church and to maintain the fraternal fellowship of its members is a mark of the person who is filled with the Holy Spirit, since the Spirit is a Spirit of unity and fellowship. Dissension and division among Christians mean that they are still of the flesh and behaving in a human way (1 Cor, 1:10; 3:3).

Sixth, the Lord's advice to judge a tree by its fruits (Matt. 7: 16ff.; Luke 6:43–44) gives us an infallible criterion for the discernment of spirits. The 'fruits of the Spirit' listed by the apostle Paul (Gal. 5:22–23) are also irrefutable evidence for the divine origin and nature of spiritual gifts.

Seven, the *agape* which the apostle Paul mentions first among the fruits of the Spirit (Gal. 5:22) is a further infallible criterion for the discernment of spirits. *Agape* is part of the essence of the Christian character and life (John 13:35). Without it no spiritual gift has any value or brings any benefit (1 Cor. 13:1–3).

Eight, humility is an additional mark of the possession of a spiritual gift, because 'God opposes the proud, but gives grace to the humble' (James 4:6).

These criteria could, of course, be expanded, or others added, but I believe that they are sufficient as they stand for a proper discernment of spirits. In attempting discernment it is advisable to beware of hasty judgments, to avoid making a disastrous mistake and saying a word against the Holy Spirit which will not be forgiven either in this world or the world to come (Matt. 12:32). In unclear and complicated cases, when some spiritual gifts are beyond our power of judgment and we are not in a position to reach a wise judgment, it is better to practise tolerance, as the Lord advises (Matt. 13:29–30).

Today all Christian denominations emphasise the role of the Holy Spirit in the world, in history and in the Church. The Holy Spirit is present and at work among Christians and among all men, but he never destroys human freedom or does violence to human will. That is why the apostle Paul appeals to Christians not to extinguish the Spirit (1 Thess. 5:19) but to keep alive the gifts of God which are within them (2 Tim. 1:6). The constant growth of the spiritual gifts given to Christians will produce a lasting renewal.

Source: Hans Küng and Jürgen Moltmann (eds), Conflicts about the Holy Spirit, *New York: Seabury Press, 1979, pp. 111–13.*

6.20 Yves Congar, from *The Word and the Spirit*

A central role of the Spirit, announced in John's Gospel, is to lead us into truth. Congar here explores that theme.

The Paraclete or Holy Spirit is called the 'Spirit of truth' (see Jn 14:17; 15:26; 16:13; 1 Jn 4:6). We are also told that 'the Spirit is the truth' (1 Jn 5:7). Many studies have sought to define the concept of 'truth' assumed in the texts produced in the Johannine circle. Most distinguish between a 'Greek' and a 'biblical' concept of truth and some go so far as to oppose these two ideas. The former is understood in relation to what things are in themselves and consists of a revelation of what they are. The Greek word *aletheia* is formed from the privative *a-* combined with the root *leth*, to be hidden. The knowledge that we have 'is true', as is the formula in which we express that knowledge. This meaning is not unknown in Scripture (see, for example, 1 Kings 10:6: what had been reported to the Queen of Sheba was true. Micaiah is commanded to tell the truth: 1 Kings 22:16 [cf. Jer 9:5[4]; Zech 8:16]) and it would be simplistic to overlook it.

Nevertheless, it is impossible not to recognize the distinctiveness of the biblical concept. The Hebrew word for truth is *'emeth*, derived from the verb *'āman*, which means to be stable, firm, sure, reliable. What is stable, then, 'is true'. Of the 132 times that the word is used in the Old Testament, more than half refer to God. Studies of the biblical concept of 'truth' therefore almost always have, for internal reasons, to end by speaking about God and his attributes. This is of decisive importance for the notion of truth contained in the Bible and for the quality of the truth to which it refers.

On the one hand, God is the first true one because he is the first one who is stable, firm, faithful and reliable: 'Know therefore that the Lord your God is God, the faithful (true) God (*'āman*), who keeps covenant and steadfast love with those who love him … to a thousand generations' (Dt 7:9). In the book of Revelation, the victorious Christ is called 'Faithful and True' (Rev 19:11; cf. 1:5; 3:7, 14). God has this attribute because he *is*. The revelation of his name to Moses (Ex 3:14) has in the past been translated, notably in the Septuagint and the Vulgate, as 'I am (the one) who am', but it is now widely accepted that a better translation is that followed by the *Traduction oecuménique de la Bible*, namely, 'I am who I shall be'. The faithfulness of God, then, his 'truth' and stability, is based on what he is. It is identical with his being and his being is that of the 'living God' who has freely shaped a plan of self-communication and salvation. He is, in other words, the God who is called in the book of Revelation 'the one who is, who was and who is to come' (Rev 1:4, 8; 4:8; cf. 11:17; 16:5).

On the other hand, however, there is another aspect of truth that is very similar to this. The truth which is based on God and which he communicates to his Word as a quality and in the self-revelation of his Word as its content is the truth and faithfulness of his plan of grace. That is why the Second Vatican Council proclaimed in its Dogmatic Constitution *Dei Verbum* on Divine Revelation that 'the books of Scripture must be acknowledged as teaching firmly, faithfully and without error that truth which God wanted put into the sacred writings *for the sake of our salvation'* (11, 2) ...

The truth communicated by the Bible, then, is that of God's plan of grace invested in the facts and the words that have been handed down to us. The book of Genesis is neither a cosmological nor a palaeontological work. It is the first chapter of the history of our salvation. I think Karl Barth was right when he said that everything can be seen from the end onwards, that end being our communion in Christ, aimed at in the decree of election which set everything in motion, and creation itself. It is possible to say that the last two chapters of the book of Revelation render an account of the first two chapters of Genesis. The end, in the sense of finality, determines the form and is what God's plan and the Bible, which reveals that plan, have in view. 'The thought of the Bible is directed towards destinies rather than towards essences' ... The language of the Bible is eschatological and expresses what things and men are called to be according to God's plan.

That is why the Word, which expresses the will of God, is addressed, in man, to the mind and to the 'heart'. What prevents man from hearing that Word is not weakness of intelligence, but hardness of heart and rational pride: 'I thank thee, Father, Lord of heaven and earth, that thou hast hidden these things from the wise and understanding and revealed them to babes' (Mt 11:25). The reply that the martyr Theophilus of Antioch gave to the pagan who asked him 'Show me your God' was: 'Show me your man and I will show you my God. Present, while seeing, the eyes of your soul and, while listening, the ears of your heart' ...

The Spirit is totally relative to Jesus. His coming is linked to the departure and the absence, in a certain sense, of Jesus, to the extent that it is good that Jesus should go away (16:7). His activity is relative to the truth that Jesus was and is. He 'brings to remembrance' what Jesus has said (14:26). He 'bears witness' to Jesus (15:26). He will guide us into (*hodegesai*) the whole truth (6:13), that is, he will make us take the way (*hodos*) of truth and life that Jesus is and that his words are, because they are 'spirit and life' (6:63). The Spirit too is truth, both in his relationship with the incarnate Word and also because he also comes from the Father and Jesus sends him from the Father (15:26).

But how can the Spirit be and do this in history, the time of Jesus' corporeal absence? This is indicated to us in the New Testament in three ways especially:

(1) The Spirit will be *with* the disciples and even *in* them *eis ton aiōna*, for ever. He will be with and in them as the Spirit of truth in order to bear witness with them to Christ and his work (Jn 15:26–27). Even more striking is the text in which John speaks of the witness borne by the Spirit by affirming that 'the Spirit is the truth' and goes on to say: 'There are three witnesses, the Spirit, the water and the blood; and these three agree', in other words, they bear a single witness (1 Jn 5:7–8). One possible way of interpreting this is that the water signifies baptism and the blood the Eucharist, although the context is Christological. The Spirit is mentioned first because he brings about the faith that is a precondition for the other two. Baptism and the Eucharist make the Church. They are relative to Christ and bring him into the heart of the world as the principle of life.

(2) The Acts of the Apostles make us acquainted, in a way that is admittedly reconstructed and schematic, with the life of the apostolic Church. This is putting into practice what Jesus declared: 'When the Counsellor (Paraclete) comes, whom I shall send to you from the Father, even the Spirit of truth, who proceeds from the Father, he will bear witness to me; and you also are witnesses, because you have been with me from the beginning' (Jn 15:26–27). This promise is echoed by Peter and the apostles when they declare to the Sanhedrin: 'We are witnesses to these things (*rhematon*) and so is the Holy Spirit whom God has given to those who obey him' (Acts 5:32). The apostolic Church was in fact a real and active 'concelebration' with the Holy Spirit. Finally, according to Revelation, the book in which the future of that same apostolic Church is unveiled, 'the testimony of Jesus is the spirit of prophecy' (Rev 19:10). This book also closes with an appeal to the eschatological Christ: 'The Spirit and the Bride say, "Come!"' (22:17).

Source: Yves M. J. Congar, The Word and the Spirit, *trans. David Smith, London: Geoffrey Chapman and San Francisco: Harper & Row, 1986, pp. 42–7.*

6.21 Wolfhart Pannenberg, from *An Introduction to Systematic Theology*

Pannenberg considers the role of Spirit in the cosmos as a whole and offers the metaphor of the Spirit as a 'field of force'.

[T]he biblical idea of Spirit, especially as it occurs in the Old Testament, is not primarily related to the concept of mind but is of a more general nature. It evokes the images of wind and breath. Thus 'spirit' is more appropriately conceived as a dynamic force, especially in terms of the creative wind that breathes the breath of life into animals and plants to the effect that, according to Ps. 104:30, they come alive: 'When thou sendest forth thy Spirit, they are created; and thou renewest the face of the ground.' The same idea underlies the account of the creation of Adam in Gen. 2:7: God 'breathed into his nostrils the breath [spirit] of life; and man became a living being.' Literally, it is the human soul that is here reported to be a creation of the spirit, but the modern translations are correct to interpret that phrase as 'living being' and not in terms of a separate soul beside the body. Nor does the creator spirit consist of the power of intelligence that would produce the intelligent soul, which according to Greek philosophical tradition distinguishes the human being from the other animals. In the biblical story the spirit is simply the dynamic principle of life, and the soul is the creature which is alive and yet remains dependent on the spirit as the transcendent origin of its life.

The notions of spirit as well as of soul have been intellectualized in Christian theology under the influence of Platonic philosophy. The decisive figure in this process was Origen, who argued effectively against the Stoic idea of *pneuma*, which he charged to be materialistic. Origen's criticism was successful because of the apparent absurdities such a materialistic conception of spirit would cause in the concept of God who according to John 4:24 is spirit: God would be a body, could be divided and composed of parts, etc. In fact, however, the Stoic conception of *pneuma* as a most subtle element like air was much closer to the biblical language than Origen's identification of *pneuma* with intelligence. The fateful effect of this identification was that the relation of the divine Spirit to the material world and to the process of its creation was obscured. In addition, the divine Spirit was also separated from the created spirit, the human soul. Consequently, the divine Spirit could be reduced almost to a principle of supernatural experience and insight. In the history of Christian thought, on the basis of the reading of the scriptures, there certainly occurred reactions against such a restrictive interpretation of the function of the Spirit. Thus in Orthodox as well as in Calvinist theology the involvement of the Spirit in the act of creation has been emphasized. But in order to recover the broad biblical vision of the Spirit as the creative origin of all life, not just of the new life of faith, it is necessary to overcome the intellectualization of the concept of spirit. In order to achieve this, it may be important to be reminded of the fact that the modern concept of fields of force, so influential in the history of modern physics, is historically rooted in the Stoic doctrine of *pneuma*.

The biblical idea of spirit as dynamic movement of air in the forms of wind, storm, or breath is closer to the modern scientific concept of a field of force than to the notion of intellect. It is only by derivation from the phenomenon of life that the act of intelligence is related to the spirit. The human mind, then, is a phenomenon of heightened life. In this sense, all intellectual life is in need of inspiration, an inspiration that in a certain sense lifts up the creature beyond the limitations of its finite existence.

All spiritual experience has such an ecstatic tinge. But the same is true of life in general. There is no living being that could live without an ecological context. Each plant or animal in a certain way exists outside itself in seeking its food and nourishing itself from its surroundings. When modern bio-chemists describe the phenomenon of life as autocatalytic exploitation of an energy gradient, such a description yields the same idea of life as an ecstatic phenomenon, a phenomenon which is surprisingly close to the Christian idea of faith as described in the theology of the Reformation: an existence outside oneself, realized in the act of trust in God. Could it be that, basically, faith is the uncrippled and untainted enactment of the movement and rhythm of all life as it was intended by the creator? Could it be, conversely, that all life in its self-transcendence is related to God? The psalmist says of the young lions that when they 'roar for their prey' they are 'seeking their food from God' (Ps. 104:21). Can we take this as a clue to the understanding of all life, to the effect that its ecstatic self-transcendence is primarily related to God and that in this way the range of its finite object (including the prey of the lions) is opened up to a living being? Anyway, the ecstatic self-transcendence of life is not something that is in the power of the organism itself, but arises as its response to a power that seizes it and, by lifting it up beyond itself, inspires life into it.

This is, I think, what the biblical tradition intends by talking about the creative function of the Spirit of God. We may add that in arousing the ecstatic response of life, the Spirit cooperates with the Word of creation, because it is the Word that gives each creature its particular form of existence. In doing so, the Word itself is empowered by the Spirit and the Spirit animates the creatures in raising them beyond themselves to participate in some measure in the life of the eternal God, who is Spirit. ...

What has been said so far with special reference to living creatures can now be generalized to comprise all of creation. The Spirit of God can be understood as the supreme field of power that pervades all of creation. Each finite event or being is to be considered as a special manifestation of that field, and their movements are responsive to its forces. The concept of field lends itself to such a theological application, because it does not conceive of force as a function of bodies, but rather of bodies as dependent on forces. In the early modern period, the mechanistic conception of physics tried to reduce all forces to bodies or masses. This contributed to the expulsion of the idea of God from the world of nature, because God cannot be conceived of as a body. If all forces are functions of bodies, then God can no longer be imagined to be operative in the world of nature, because he is not a body. The introduction of the field concept by Michael Faraday turned the issue around in rendering the concept of force independent from body, though in the actuality of natural processes masses may have a decisive role in structuring the dynamics of the field (e.g., as happens in the gravitational field). It is the independence in principle of the field concept of force from the notion of body that makes its theological application possible so as to describe all actions of God in nature and history as field effects. This does not mean to physicalize the theological conception of the creative, sustaining, and redeeming action of God. But it does relate the description of nature in modern physics to a theological perspective. We need only remind ourselves that the field language of science is rooted historically in the *pneuma* theories of classical antiquity This demonstrates the legitimacy of using field concepts in a more general way than in the formalized mathematical fashion of physics. The field theories of science, then, can be considered as approximations to the metaphysical reality of the all-pervading spiritual field of God's creative presence in the universe. It may belong to the limitations of the approximative descriptions of science that the scientific descriptions usually treat field effects as correlative to masses rather than perceiving the occurrence of such a dependency as an inversion of the more profound nature of field effects.

The theological use of the field concept in describing God's creative presence and activity in the world of creation does require, however, a theological interpretation of space and time. There is a particularly intimate dependence of the field concept on space, because it is hardly possible to imagine a field without any form of space. In the perspective of modern thought, space in its turn is dependent on time, since space can be defined as simultaneousness: Everything that coexists simultaneously is somehow organized in spatial relations. The relativity of simultaneity therefore accounts for the relativity of distances in space.

...

There is good reason ... to insist that the intuition of infinite space can be appropriately accounted for only in theological terms, as expressing the immensity and omni-presence of God. The case of time is similar. Plotinus already argued that the transition from one temporal moment to another presupposes the intuition of time as a whole or rather of eternity, since eternity means the whole of time in the form of one undivided presence. Nevertheless, the separateness of temporal moments in the course of their sequence may be considered as connected with the situation of finite beings in the flow of time. Only from the point of view of a finite being is the past lost and the future not yet arrived, while God in his eternity is his own future as well as the world's, and whatever is past is kept in his presence. Thus, God's immensity and eternity can be regarded as constitutive of time and space, and consequently it makes sense to speak of a field of God's spiritual presence in his creation.

If the notion of energy can also be related to this concept of spirit as field, the presence of God's Spirit in his creation can be described as a field of creative presence, a comprehensive field of force that releases event after event into finite existence. Perhaps such a view of energy can be justified in terms of an interpretation of quantum indeterminacy. It would have to regard the indeterminacy of quantum events as not only epistemic but real in the sense that in the microstructure of natural processes individual future events are not derivable from any given situation. They occur contingently from a field of possibility, which is another word for future. Such an interpretation of quantum indeterminacy substantiates a thesis which I tentatively proposed two decades ago in explicating the potential significance of the imminence of the kingdom of God for a Christian doctrine of creation: Every single event as well as the sequence of such events springs contingently from the future of God. This way of looking at the occurrence of events converges, furthermore, with the interrelatedness of time and eternity, because it is through the future that eternity enters into time.

Source: Wolfhart Pannenberg, from An Introduction to Systematic Theology, *Edinburgh: T. & T. Clark, 1991, pp. 43–9.*

7 The Doctrine of Humanity

Introductory essay

The doctrine of humanity explores Christian understandings of personhood. What, in less inclusive times, was called the doctrine of 'man', echoes the Psalmist's question: 'What is man that you should care for him, the son of man that you are mindful of him?' (Ps. 8). In both of the accounts of creation in Genesis, human beings are given a particular place in the created order, and are invited into a relationship with God that is distinct from other species. The most central aspect of this is rooted in the first Genesis account of creation (1.26) that humans are made in the image and likeness of God. Exactly what it means for us to bear the image and likeness of God is much debated over the centuries of Christian history. It is widely accepted that the image is not primarily a physical one; Christian doctrine has not taught that God is embodied in the way that humans are. Rather it is often suggested that humans reflect God in their capacity for rational thought, in their ability to communicate or even as moral agents, able to feely choose their actions and to anticipate the moral consequences of them.

In the first extract, Irenaeus argues that it is the union of flesh and spirit in the human being that is the image and likeness of God. The physical matter of creation is the handiwork of God, and this is perfected by the presence of the Spirit. A being who is not so constituted, according to Irenaeus, is an incomplete human, or not a human being at all as the image and likeness of God is not present. Augustine suggests that the image of God is to be found in the highest point of human being, which for him is the mind. And so Augustine suggests that the faculties of memory, understanding and will are the image of the triune God in the human person. The tendency to associate the *imago Dei* with the rational capacity of human beings has been challenged in more recent times. Reinhold Niebuhr contrasts the Christian view of personhood with a classic, or philosophical view and argues that it is inadequate to describe the image of God as rationality. He suggests that Christian doctrine succeeds, where other philosophies do not, in affirming the necessity of both body and soul to give an account of human being.

Many theologians have argued that although humans were indeed originally made in the image and likeness of God, sin has marred and corrupted this image. Gregory of Nazianzus in the second extract suggests that the image has been damaged as a result of humans exercising their free will. Augustine acknowledges that sin can damage the image of God, but argues that the image cannot be totally destroyed. Thomas Aquinas similarly argues that although sin has greatly diminished the good of human nature, it cannot destroy it entirely. John Calvin, however, regards human beings as totally depraved and argues that humans are so corrupted by sin, not just through acts, but primarily through nature, that without redemption through Christ, humans are characterized by depravity and are unacceptable to God. Although Calvin does believe that, because of the work of Christ, the image of God will be restored in some, in his view humans are capable of so destroying the image of God that the possibility of relationship with God is lost. The human capacity for evil certainly seems to challenge the understanding of the *imago Dei*, but Colin Gunton argues that even those who commit the most heinous of crimes cannot destroy the image of God in them. Humanity, regardless of what a person has done, has a certain status because of the image of God, which demands that every human being be regarded as a person. This of course is also the grounds for Christian ethics. Alistair McFadyen also argues that a proper understanding of personhood provides a basis for Christian ethics.

Exactly what constitutes sin, and whether it is part of human nature, or whether it pertains only to the acts of a person, was debated by Augustine and Pelagius. Augustine argues that sin has pervaded the human race, and that it is no longer possible to exist without sin. He specifically argues against Pelagius, who claims that humans are born, and remain, morally neutral. Sin pertains only to particular acts which can be good or bad, but these do not change the character or nature of the person. Christian tradition has largely sided with Augustine in this debate and has taken the sinful nature of humanity seriously. The recognition that humans live as flawed or imperfect beings has significant consequences. Søren Kierkegaard writes that sin separates us from God and characterizes the human condition. Anselm argues that death is a consequence of sin. He claims that human beings were originally made to be immortal but since humans sinned, they have lost that immortality.

John Wesley rejects the claim that sin is a necessary characteristic of the human condition. He argues that, because of what Christ has already done, it would be possible to live here and now without sin. Wesley's doctrine of Christian perfection takes the idea of sanctification, and suggests that there is no reason why this should not be possible in this life, rather than assuming it can only happen in the next. Gregory Palamas uses the traditional Eastern language of deification to explore the true end of human existence. He argues that although the fulfilment of personhood is found through participation in the divine life, there will remain a distinction between God and humanity. Deification is not the belief that humans will become divine, but is rather concerned with the ultimate union between human and divine existence. Palamas raises two important aspects of a Christian account of personhood, first that there is an insoluble difference between creature and Creator. Humans are created beings. This status brings with it certain limitations, and most significantly the recognition that humans are not the creator. Second, Palamas is clear that Christians anticipate the fulfilment of their human being in the eschaton. This fulfilment will happen in and through Christ. Nicholas Cabasilas argues that it is only possible to know what true humanity is, because it is revealed to us in the person of Christ. He suggests that every human being, including Adam – the first man – was modelled after Jesus. Karl Barth similarly argues that we only know what humanity is through Christ. Kathryn Tanner suggests that humans have already been assumed by Christ, and therefore participate in the mission of God and receive the benefits of God's goodness.

John Zizioulas understands humans as beings in relation. There is no such thing as an individual, autonomous person, but we are person alongside person, in relationship with one another. Zizioulas suggests that the Trinity, the divine relationship of Persons, provides the proper basis for understanding human personhood. Such personhood cannot be realized merely through biological existence, but requires, through baptism, Zizioulas contends, a new 'ecclesial hypostasis', by which we are gathered into one Church, and together participate in the divine community. Leonardo Boff similarly argues that the Trinity reveals authentic personhood, and that we are called to live in relationship. Boff suggests that just as we are invited to participate in the life of the triune God, humans should live in open societies and communities which welcome the outsider and stranger and which are characterized by equality. Karl Rahner proposes what he calls 'transcendental anthropology' in which personhood can only be understood in reference to the other, the God who transcends our experience and knowledge. Indeed, Rahner argues that whenever we say anything about human being, we are also speaking of God.

The meaning of sex and gender and the extent to which they define personhood has been much discussed in the history of Christian thought. The early fathers were interested in this question, and the feminist movements of the last century have brought fresh questions to this particular debate. The primary question concerns whether there is a generic category of humanity, or whether there are just males and females. Gregory of Nyssa argues that celibacy is an important step towards conquering the consequences of sin, namely death. He also suggests that the perfected human being will not exist in gendered form. Sarah Coakley, in the final extract, reflects on Gregory's arguments and contrasts them to those of Augustine, who suggests that the female is an incomplete version of the image of God, but does not think that gender distinctions will cease in the eschaton. Coakley argues that both of these positions are inadequate and do not lead to the full participation of women in the life of the Church. Elaine Storkey understands gender as one of the particularities we are given by God, but argues that it is not the most defining feature of existence. She suggests that the New Testament is primarily concerned with instruction for discipleship, which is the same for males and females. However, Valerie Saiving claims that although we may share a common humanity, the experience of men and the experience of women have been, and remain, very different. She observes that the vast majority of theologians are male and that there has been a tendency through the ages to universalize male experience, and assume it is the experience of all humans. Saiving argues that in terms of theology, this has very particular consequences and that the common definitions of sin as, for example, pride are much more likely to apply to men than to women. The temptations experienced by women are largely different, but tend not to be acknowledged within theological frameworks.

The Christian doctrine of humanity, then, incorporates many different understandings of what it is that makes us human. Humanity is created by God and exists before God. The covenant relationship that God establishes with human beings is central to this. Karl Barth argues that although humans can reject their relationship with God, and can turn away from the covenant, they cannot annul it. Humans are made, not by a disinterested or experimental God, but by a God who makes humans for relationship with Godself, and who remains faithful to that covenant regardless of how often humans turn away. Although the human condition is characterized by sin, this is not the ultimate truth of humanity. In Jesus Christ, full or authentic humanity is revealed. The flawed humanity of this life will finally be perfected in Christ.

LEH

7.1 Irenaeus of Lyons, from *Against Heresies*

Irenaeus explains that it is not only because we are made in the image of God, that humans are perfect, but also because we have been perfected through the Spirit of God. Further, a human can only be rightly understood as a being possessing body, soul and spirit.

1. Now God shall be glorified in His handiwork, fitting it so as to be conformable to, and modelled after, His own Son. For by the hands of the Father, that is, by the Son and the Holy Spirit, man, and not [merely] a *part* of man, was made in the likeness of God. Now the soul and the spirit are certainly a part of *the* man, but certainly not the man; for the perfect man consists in the commingling and the union of the soul receiving the spirit of the Father, and the admixture of that fleshly nature which was moulded after the image of God. For this reason does the apostle declare, 'We speak wisdom among them that are perfect' [1 Cor. 2.6], terming those persons 'perfect' who have received the Spirit of God, and who through the Spirit of God do speak in all languages, as he used Himself also to speak. In like manner we do also hear many brethren in the Church, who possess prophetic gifts, and who through the Spirit speak all kinds of languages, and bring to light for the general benefit the hidden things of men, and declare the mysteries of God, whom also the apostle terms 'spiritual,' they being spiritual because they partake of the Spirit, and not because their flesh has been stripped off and taken away, and because they have become purely spiritual. For if any one take away the substance of flesh, that is, of the handiwork [of God], and understand that which is purely spiritual, such then would not be a spiritual man but would be the spirit of a man, or the Spirit of God. But when the spirit here blended with the soul is united to [God's] handiwork, the man is rendered spiritual and perfect because of the outpouring of the Spirit, and this is he who was made in the image and likeness of God. But if the Spirit be wanting to the soul, he who is such is indeed of an animal nature, and being left carnal, shall be an imperfect being, possessing indeed the image [of God] in his formation (*in plasmate*), but not receiving the similitude through the Spirit; and thus is this being imperfect. Thus also, if any one take away the image and set aside the handiwork, he cannot then understand this as being a man, but as either some part of a man, as I have already said, or as something else than a man. For that flesh which has been moulded is not a perfect man in itself, but the body of a man, and part of a man. Neither is the soul itself, considered apart by itself, the man; but it is the soul of a man, and part of a man. Neither is the spirit a man, for it is called the spirit, and not a man; but the commingling and union of all these constitutes the perfect man. And for this cause does the apostle, explaining himself, make it clear that the saved man is a complete man as well as a spiritual man; saying thus in the first Epistle to the Thessalonians, 'Now the God of peace sanctify you perfect (*perfectos*); and may your spirit, and soul, and body be preserved whole without complaint to the coming of the Lord Jesus Christ' [1 Thess. 5.23]. Now what was his object in praying that these three – that is, soul, body, and spirit – might be preserved to the coming

of the Lord, unless he was aware of the [future] reintegration and union of the three, and [that they should be heirs of] one and the same salvation? For this cause also he declares that those are 'the perfect' who present unto the Lord the three [component parts] without offence. Those, then, are the perfect who have had the Spirit of God remaining in them, and have preserved their souls and bodies blameless, holding fast the faith of God, that is, that faith which is [directed] towards God, and maintaining righteous dealings with respect to their neighbours.

2. Whence also he says, that this handiwork is 'the temple of God,' thus declaring: 'Know ye not that ye are the temple of God, and that the Spirit of God dwelleth in you? If any man, therefore, will defile the temple of God, him will God destroy: for the temple of God is holy, which [temple] ye are' [1 Cor. 3.16]. Here he manifestly declares the body to be the temple in which the Spirit dwells. As also the Lord speaks in reference to Himself, 'Destroy this temple, and in three days I will raise it up. He spake this, however,' it is said, 'of the temple of His body' [John 2.19–21]. And not only does he (the apostle) acknowledge our bodies to be a temple, but even the temple of Christ, saying thus to the Corinthians, 'Know ye not that your bodies are members of Christ? Shall I then take the members of Christ, and make them the members of an harlot?' [1 Cor. 3.17]. He speaks these things, not in reference to some other spiritual man; for a being of such a nature could have nothing to do with an harlot: but he declares 'our body,' that is, the flesh which continues in sanctity and purity, to be 'the members of Christ;' but that when it becomes one with an harlot, it becomes the members of an harlot. And for this reason he said, 'If any man defile the temple of God, him will God destroy.' How then is it not the utmost blasphemy to allege, that the temple of God, in which the Spirit of the Father dwells, and the members of Christ, do not partake of salvation, but are reduced to perdition? Also, that our bodies are raised not from their own substance, but by the power of God, he says to the Corinthians, 'Now the body is not for fornication, but for the Lord, and the Lord for the body. But God hath both raised up the Lord, and shall raise us up by His own power.' [1 Cor. 6.13–14].

Source: Irenaeus of Lyons, Against Heresies *V.6.1, trans. Alexander Roberts and William Rambaut, in Alexander Roberts, James Donaldson and A. Cleveland Coxe (eds),* Ante-Nicene Fathers, *vol. 1, Buffalo, NY: Christian Literature Publishing Co., 1885.*

7.2 Gregory of Nazianzus, from *Oration XLV* ('The Second Oration on Easter')

Gregory expounds on the creation of humans in the image of God, empha-
sizing the original goodness of humanity and the fall from that goodness
because of free will. The only remedy for the wrong choices of humanity is
the Word of God, the one who takes on human flesh for our sake.

VII. Mind then and sense, thus distinguished from each other, had remained
within their own boundaries, and bore in themselves the magnificence of the
Creator-Word, silent praisers and thrilling heralds of His mighty work. Not
yet was there any mingling of both, nor any mixture of these opposites, tokens
of a greater wisdom and generosity in the creation of natures; nor as yet were
the whole riches of goodness made known. Now the Creator-Word, determining to exhibit this, and to produce a single living being out of both (the
invisible and the visible creation, I mean) fashions Man; and taking a body
from already existing matter, and placing in it a Breath taken from Himself
(which the Word knew to be an intelligent soul, and the image of God), as a
sort of second world, great in littleness, He placed him on the earth, a new
Angel, a mingled worshipper, fully initiated into the visible creation, but only
partially into the intellectual; king of all upon earth, but subject to the King
above; earthly and heavenly; temporal and yet immortal; visible and yet intellectual; halfway between greatness and lowliness; in one person combining
spirit and flesh; spirit because of the favour bestowed on him, flesh on account
of the height to which he had been raised; the one that he might continue to
live and glorify his benefactor, the other that he might suffer, and by suffering
be put in remembrance, and be corrected if he became proud in his greatness;
a living creature, trained here and then moved elsewhere; and to complete the
mystery, deified by its inclination to God for to this, I think, tends that light
of Truth which here we possess but in measure; that we should both see and
experience the Splendour of God, which is worthy of Him Who made us, and
will dissolve us, and remake us after a loftier fashion.

VIII. This being He placed in paradise – whatever that paradise may have
been (having honoured him with the gift of free will, in order that good
might belong to him as the result of his choice, no less than to Him Who had
implanted the seeds of it) – to till the immortal plants, by which is perhaps
meant the Divine conceptions, both the simpler and the more perfect; naked
in his simplicity and inartificial life; and without any covering or screen; for
it was fitting that he who was from the beginning should be such. And He
gave Him a Law, as material for his free will to act upon. This Law was a commandment as to what plants he might partake of, and which one he might not
touch. This latter was the Tree of Knowledge; not, however, because it was evil
from the beginning when planted; nor was it forbidden because God grudged
it to men – let not the enemies of God wag their tongues in that direction, or
imitate the serpent. But it would have been good if partaken of at the proper
time; for the Tree was, according to my theory, Contemplation, which it is only

safe for those who have reached maturity of habit to enter upon; but which is not good for those who are still somewhat simple and greedy; just as neither is solid food good for those who are yet tender and have need of milk. But when through the devil's malice and the woman's caprice [Wis. 2.24], to which she succumbed as the more tender, and which she brought to bear upon the man, as she was the more apt to persuade – alas for my weakness, for that of my first father was mine; he forgot the commandment which had been given him, and yielded to the baleful fruit; and for his sin was banished at once from the tree of life, and from paradise, and from God; and put on the coats of skins, that is, perhaps, the coarser flesh, both mortal and contradictory. And this was the first thing which he learnt – his own shame – and he hid himself from God. Yet here too he makes a gain, namely death and the cutting off of sin, in order that evil may not be immortal. Thus, his punishment is changed into a mercy, for it is in mercy, I am persuaded, that God inflicts punishment.

IX. And having first been chastened by many means because his sins were many, whose root of evil sprang up through divers causes and sundry times, by word, by law, by prophets, by benefits, by threats, by plagues, by waters, by fires, by wars, by victories, by defeats, by signs in heaven, and signs in the air, and in the earth, and in the sea; by unexpected changes of men, of cities, of nations (the object of which was the destruction of wickedness) at last he needed a stronger remedy, for his diseases were growing worse; mutual slaughters, adulteries, perjuries, unnatural crimes, and that first and last of all evils, idolatry, and the transfer of worship from the Creator to the creatures. As these required a greater aid, so they also obtained a greater. And that was that the Word of God Himself, Who is before all worlds, the Invisible, the Incomprehensible, the Bodiless, the Beginning of beginning, the Light of Light, the Source of Life and Immortality, the Image of the Archetype, the Immovable Seal, the Unchangeable Image, the Father's Definition and Word, came to His own Image, and took on Him Flesh for the sake of our flesh, and mingled Himself with an intelligent soul for my soul's sake, purifying like by like; and in all points except sin was made Man; conceived by the Virgin, who first in body and soul was purified by the Holy Ghost, for it was needful both that Child-bearing should be honoured and that Virginity should receive a higher honour. He came forth then, as God, with that which He had assumed; one Person in two natures, flesh and Spirit, of which the latter deified the former.

Source: Gregory of Nazianzus, from Oration XLV (*'The Second Oration on Easter'*), 7–9, *trans. Charles Gordon Browne and James Edward Swallow, in Philip Schaff and Henry Wace (eds),* Nicene and Post-Nicene Fathers, *second series, vol. 7, Buffalo, NY: Christian Literature Publishing Co., 1894.*

7.3 Gregory of Nyssa, from *On Virginity*

Gregory of Nyssa explains how humans are responsible for evil. Rather than it being part of God's creation, he suggests that evil is against original human nature and that death is not of God but a consequence of the human choice for evil. Gregory suggests that the celibate life is an important step towards conquering death and living in the Spirit; or living the life that God intended for us.

This reasoning and intelligent creature, man, at once the work and the likeness of the Divine and Imperishable Mind (for so in the Creation it is written of him that 'God made man in His image' [Gen. 1.27]), this creature, I say, did not in the course of his first production have united to the very essence of his nature the liability to passion and to death. Indeed, the truth about the image could never have been maintained if the beauty reflected in that image had been in the slightest degree opposed to the Archetypal Beauty. Passion was introduced afterwards, subsequent to man's first organization; and it was in this way. Being the image and the likeness, as has been said, of the Power which rules all things, man kept also in the matter of a Free-Will this likeness to Him whose Will is over all. He was enslaved to no outward necessity whatever; his feeling towards that which pleased him depended only on his own private judgment; he was free to choose whatever he liked; and so he was a free agent, though circumvented with cunning, when he drew upon himself that disaster which now overwhelms humanity. He became himself the discoverer of evil, but he did not therein discover what God had made; for God did not make death. Man became, in fact, himself the fabricator, to a certain extent, and the craftsman of evil. All who have the faculty of sight may enjoy equally the sunlight; and any one can if he likes put this enjoyment from him by shutting his eyes: in that case it is not that the sun retires and produces that darkness, but the man himself puts a barrier between his eye and the sunshine; the faculty of vision cannot indeed, even in the closing of the eyes, remain inactive, and so this operative sight necessarily becomes an operative darkness rising up in the man from his own free act in ceasing to see … As those who have slipped and fallen heavily into mud, and have all their features so besmeared with it, that their nearest friends do not recognize them, so this creature has fallen into the mire of sin and lost the blessing of being an image of the imperishable Deity; he has clothed himself instead with a perishable and foul resemblance to something else; and this Reason counsels him to put away again by washing it off in the cleansing water of this calling. The earthly envelopment once removed, the soul's beauty will again appear. Now the putting off of a strange accretion is equivalent to the return to that which is familiar and natural; yet such a return cannot be but by again becoming that which in the beginning we were created. In fact this likeness to the divine is not our work at all; it is not the achievement of any faculty of man; it is the great gift of God bestowed upon our nature at the very moment of our birth; human efforts can only go so far as to clear away the filth of sin, and so cause the buried beauty of the soul to shine forth again.

...

But seeing that Paradise is the home of living spirits, and will not admit those who are dead in sin, and that we on the other hand are fleshly, subject to death, and sold under sin, how is it possible that one who is a subject of death's empire should ever dwell in this land where all is life? What method of release from this jurisdiction can be devised? Here too the Gospel teaching is abundantly sufficient. We hear our Lord saying to Nicodemus, 'That which is born of the flesh is flesh; and that which is born of the Spirit is spirit.' [John 3.6]. We know too that the flesh is subject to death because of sin, but the Spirit of God is both incorruptible, and life-giving, and deathless. As at our physical birth there comes into the world with us a potentiality of being again turned to dust, plainly the Spirit also imparts a life-giving potentiality to the children begotten by Himself. What lesson, then, results from these remarks? This: that we should wean ourselves from this life in the flesh, which has an inevitable follower, death; and that we should search for a manner of life which does not bring death in its train. Now the life of Virginity is such a life. We will add a few other things to show how true this is. Every one knows that the propagation of mortal frames is the work which the intercourse of the sexes has to do; whereas for those who are joined to the Spirit, life and immortality instead of children are produced by this latter intercourse; and the words of the Apostle beautifully suit their case, for the joyful mother of such children as these 'shall be saved in child-bearing;' [1 Tim. 2.15]; as the Psalmist in his divine songs thankfully cries, 'He maketh the barren woman to keep house, and to be a joyful mother of children' [Ps. 113.9]. Truly a joyful mother is the virgin mother who by the operation of the Spirit conceives the deathless children, and who is called by the Prophet barren because of her modesty only. This life, then, which is stronger than the power of death, is, to those who think, the preferable one. The physical bringing of children into the world – I speak without wishing to offend – is as much a starting-point of death as of life; because from the moment of birth the process of dying commences. But those who by virginity have desisted from this process have drawn within themselves the boundary line of death, and by their own deed have checked his advance; they have made themselves, in fact, a frontier between life and death, and a barrier too, which thwarts him ... Just as, in the age of Mary the mother of God, he who had reigned from Adam to her time found, when he came to her and dashed his forces against the fruit of her virginity as against a rock, that he was shattered to pieces upon her, so in every soul which passes through this life in the flesh under the protection of virginity, the strength of death is in a manner broken and annulled, for he does not find the places upon which he may fix his sting. If you do not throw into the fire wood, or straw, or grass, or something that it can consume, it has not the force to last by itself; so the power of death cannot go on working, if marriage does not supply it with material and prepare victims for this executioner ... In fact, the Life of Virginity seems to be an actual representation of the blessedness in the world to come, showing as it does in itself so many signs of the presence of those expected blessings which are reserved for us there. That the truth of this statement may be perceived, we will verify it thus. It is so, first, because a man who has thus died once for all to sin lives for the future to God; he brings forth no more fruit unto death; and having so far as in him lies made an end of this life within him according to the flesh, he awaits thenceforth the expected blessing of the manifestation [Titus 2.13] of the great God, refraining from putting any distance between himself and this coming of God by an intervening posterity: secondly, because he enjoys even in this present life a certain exquisite glory of all the blessed results of our resurrection. For our Lord has announced that the life after our resurrection shall be as that of the angels. Now the peculiarity of the angelic nature is that they are strangers to marriage; therefore the blessing of this promise has been already received by him who has not only mingled his own glory with the halo of the Saints, but also by the stainlessness of his life has so imitated the purity of these incorporeal beings. If virginity then can win us favours such as these, what words are fit to express the admiration of so great a grace? What other gift of the soul can be found so great and precious as not to suffer by comparison with this perfection?

Source: Gregory of Nyssa, On Virginity, *trans. William Moore and Henry Austin Wilson, in Philip Schaff and Henry Wace (eds),* Nicene and Post-Nicene Fathers, *second series, vol. 5, Buffalo, NY: Christian Literature Publishing Co., 1893.*

7.4 Augustine of Hippo, from *On Nature and Grace*

Augustine responds to Pelagius' claim that sin is a wrong act and not a substance, a thing, a body or some sort of existence and therefore does not damage the person. Augustine appeals to the Scriptures to argue that sin very clearly causes damage to the person and needs healing. Augustine explains that Christ came to save people from their sins and that he, who created humankind, has more knowledge of the state and needs of humanity than philosophers who argue that we are not defined by sin, but that it is merely a wrong act.

Now, do you not perceive the tendency and direction of this controversy? Even to render of none effect the Scripture where it is said 'Thou shalt call His name Jesus, for He shall save His people from their sins' [Matt. 1.21]. For how is He to save where there is no malady? For the sins, from which this gospel says Christ's people have to be saved, are not substances, and according to this writer are incapable of corrupting. O brother, how good a thing it is to remember that you are a Christian! To believe, might perhaps be enough; but still, since you persist in discussion, there is no harm, nay there is even benefit, if a firm faith precede it; let us not suppose, then, that human nature cannot be corrupted by sin, but rather, believing, from the inspired Scriptures, that it is corrupted by sin, let our inquiry be how this could possibly have come about. Since, then, we have already learnt that sin is not a substance, do we not consider, not to mention any other example, that not to eat is also not a substance? Because such abstinence is withdrawal from a substance, inasmuch as food is a substance. To abstain, then, from food is not a substance; and yet the substance of our body, if it does altogether abstain from food, so languishes, is so impaired by broken health, is so exhausted of strength, so weakened and broken with very weariness, that even if it be in any way able to continue alive, it is hardly capable of being restored to the use of that food, by abstaining from which it became so corrupted and injured. In the same way sin is not a substance; but God is a substance, yea the height of substance and only true sustenance of the reasonable creature. The consequence of departing from Him by disobedience, and of inability, through infirmity, to receive what one ought really to rejoice in, you hear from the Psalmist, when he says: 'My heart is smitten and withered like grass, since I have forgotten to eat my bread' [Ps. 102.4].

But observe how, by specious arguments, he continues to oppose the truth of Holy Scripture. The Lord Jesus, who is called Jesus because He saves His people from their sins [Matt. 1.21], in accordance with this His merciful character, says: 'They that be whole need not a physician, but they that are sick; I am come not to call the righteous, but sinners to repentance' [Matt. 9.12]. Accordingly, His apostle also says: 'This is a faithful saying, and worthy of all acceptation, that Christ Jesus came into the world to save sinners' [1 Tim. 1.15]. This man, however, contrary to the 'faithful saying, and worthy of all acceptation,' declares that 'this sickness ought not to have been contracted by sins, lest the punishment of sin should amount to this, that more sins should be committed.' Now even for infants the help of the Great Physician is sought. This writer asks: 'Why seek Him? They are whole for whom you seek the Physician. Not even was the first man condemned to die for any such reason, for he did not sin afterwards.' As if he had ever heard anything of his subsequent perfection in righteousness, except so far as the Church commends to our faith that even Adam was delivered by the mercy of the Lord Christ. 'As to his posterity also,' says he, 'not only are they not more infirm than he, but they actually fulfilled more commandments than he ever did, since he neglected to fulfil one,' – this posterity which he sees so born (as Adam certainly was not made), not only incapable of commandment, which they do not at all understand, but hardly capable of sucking the breast, when they are hungry! Yet even these would He have to be saved in the bosom of Mother Church by His grace who saves His people from their sins; but these men gainsay such grace, and, as if they had a deeper insight into the creature than ever He possesses who made the creature, they pronounce [these infants] sound with an assertion which is anything but sound itself.

Source: Augustine, On Nature and Grace, Against Pelagius, *trans. Peter Holmes and Robert Ernest Wallis, and revised by Benjamin B. Warfield, in Philip Schaff (ed.),* Nicene and Post-Nicene Fathers, *first series, vol. 5, Buffalo, NY: Christian Literature Publishing Co., 1887.*

7.5 Augustine of Hippo, from *On the Holy Trinity*

Augustine argues that the image of God is found in every person and cannot be totally destroyed. The image of the triune God is present in the mind of each person. The mind is the highest part of the human being, and therefore the aspect of humanity which will most reflect God.

Therefore neither is that trinity an image of God, which is not now, nor is that other an image of God, which then will not be; but we must find in the soul of man, *i.e.*, the rational or intellectual soul, that image of the Creator which is immortally implanted in its immortality. For as the immortality itself of the soul is spoken with a qualification; since the soul too has its proper death, when it lacks a blessed life, which is to be called the true life of the soul; but it is therefore called immortal, because it never ceases to live with some life or other, even when it is most miserable – so, although reason or intellect is at one time torpid in it, at another appears small, and at another great, yet the human soul is never anything save rational or intellectual; and hence, if it is made after the image of God in respect to this, that it is able to use reason and intellect in order to understand and behold God, then from the moment when that nature so marvellous and so great began to be, whether this image be so worn out as to be almost none at all, or whether it be obscure and defaced, or bright and beautiful, certainly it always is. Further, too, pitying the defaced condition of its dignity, divine Scripture tells us, that 'although man walks in an image, yet he disquieteth himself in vain; he heapeth up riches, and cannot tell who shall gather them' [Ps. 39.7]. It would not therefore attribute vanity to the image of God, unless it perceived it to have been defaced. Yet it sufficiently shows that such defacing does not extend to the taking away its being an image, by saying, 'Although man walks in an image.' Wherefore in both ways that sentence can be truly enunciated; in that, as it is said, 'Although man walketh in an image, yet he disquieteth himself in vain,' so it may be said, 'Although man disquieteth himself in vain, yet he walketh in an image.' For although the nature of the soul is great, yet it can be corrupted, because it is not the highest; and although it can be corrupted, because it is not the highest, yet because it is capable and can be partaker of the highest nature, it is a great nature. Let us seek, then, in this image of God a certain trinity of a special kind, with the aid of Him who Himself made us after His own image. For no otherwise can we healthfully investigate this subject, or arrive at any result according to the wisdom which is from Him. But if the reader will either hold in remembrance and recollect what we have said of the human soul or mind in former books, and especially in the tenth, or will carefully re-peruse it in the passages wherein it is contained, he will not require here any more lengthy discourse respecting the inquiry into so great a thing.

...

But we have come now to that argument in which we have undertaken to consider the noblest part of the human mind, by which it knows or can know God, in order that we may find in it the image of God. For although the human mind is not of the same nature with God, yet the image of that nature than which none is better, is to be sought and found in us, in that than which our nature also has nothing better. But the mind must first be considered as it is in itself, before it becomes partaker of God; and His image must be found in it. For, as we have said, although worn out and defaced by losing the participation of God, yet the image of God still remains. For it is His image in this very point, that it is capable of Him, and can be partaker of Him; which so great good is only made possible by its being His image. Well, then, the mind remembers, understands, loves itself; if we discern this, we discern a trinity, not yet indeed God, but now at last an image of God.

Source: Augustine, On the Holy Trinity, *trans. Arthur West Haddan, in Philip Schaff (ed.),* Nicene and Post-Nicene Fathers, *first series, vol. 3, Buffalo, NY: Christian Literature Publishing Co., 1887.*

7.6 Anselm of Canterbury, from *Cur Deus Homo*

Anselm here explains that the purpose of human rational nature is to pursue and enjoy God. In conversation with Boso, Anselm further explains that death is not inherent to the human condition, but is a consequence of sin and that God will restore to their original perfection those who have not persevered in wickedness.

Anselm. It ought not to be disputed that rational nature was made holy by God, in order to be happy in enjoying Him. For to this end is it rational, in order to discern justice and injustice, good and evil, and between the greater and the lesser good. Otherwise it was made rational in vain. But God made it not rational in vain. Wherefore, doubtless, it was made rational for this end. In like manner is it proved that the intelligent creature received the power of discernment for this purpose, that he might hate and shun evil, and love and choose good, and especially the greater good. For else in vain would God have given him that power of discernment, since man's discretion would be useless unless he loved and avoided according to it. But it does not befit God to give such power in vain. It is, therefore, established that rational nature was created for this end, viz., to love and choose the highest good supremely, for its own sake and nothing else; for if the highest good were chosen for any other reason, then something else and not itself would be the thing loved. But intelligent nature cannot fulfil this purpose without being holy. Therefore that it might not in vain be made rational, it was made, in order to fulfil this purpose, both rational and holy. Now, if it was made holy in order to choose and love the highest good, then it was made such in order to follow sometimes what it loved and chose, or else it was not. But if it were not made holy for this end, that it might follow what it loves and chooses, then in vain was it made to love and choose holiness; and there can be no reason why it should be ever bound to follow holiness. Therefore, as long as it will be holy in loving and choosing the supreme good, for which it was made, it will be miserable; because it will be impotent despite of its will, inasmuch as it does not have what it desires. But this is utterly absurd. Wherefore rational nature was made holy, in order to be happy in enjoying the supreme good, which is God. Therefore man, whose nature is rational, was made holy for this end, that he might be happy in enjoying God.

Anselm. Moreover, it is easily proved that man was so made as not to be necessarily subject to death; for, as we have already said, it is inconsistent with God's wisdom and justice to compel man to suffer death without fault, when he made him holy to enjoy eternal blessedness. It therefore follows that had man never sinned he never would have died.

Anselm. From this the future resurrection of the dead is clearly proved. For if man is to be perfectly restored, the restoration should make him such as he would have been had he never sinned.

Boso. It must be so.

Anselm. Therefore, as man, had he not sinned, was to have been transferred with the same body to an immortal state, so when he shall be restored, it must properly be with his own body as he lived in this world.

Boso. But what shall we say to one who tells us that this is right enough with regard to those in whom humanity shall be perfectly restored, but is not necessary as respects the reprobate?

Anselm. We know of nothing more just or proper than this, that as man, had he continued in holiness, would have been perfectly happy for eternity, both in body and in soul; so, if he persevere in wickedness, he shall be likewise completely miserable forever.

Boso. You have promptly satisfied me in these matters.

Anselm. From these things, we can easily see that God will either complete what he has begun with regard to human nature, or else he has made to no end so lofty a nature, capable of so great good. Now if it be understood that God has made nothing more valuable than rational existence capable of enjoying him; it is altogether foreign from his character to suppose that he will suffer that rational existence utterly to perish.

Boso. No reasonable being can think otherwise.

Anselm. Therefore is it necessary for him to perfect in human nature what he has begun. But this, as we have already said, cannot be accomplished save by a complete expiation of sin, which no sinner can effect for himself.

Boso. I now understand it to be necessary for God to complete what he has begun, lest there be an unseemly falling off from his design.

Source: Anselm, Cur Deus Homo, *Book II, Chapters 1–4, in* Proslogion; Monologion, an Appendix on Behalf of the Fool by Gaunilon; and Cur Deus Homo, *trans. Sidney Norton Deane, Chicago: The Open Court Publishing Company, 1903, reprinted 1926.*

7.7 Nicholas Cabasilas, from *The Life in Christ*

Cabasilas explains that Jesus is the archetype of humanity. Although Adam was temporally the first man, even he was made in the image of Christ, the second Adam. Only in Christ do we know what true humanity is.

It was for the new man that human nature was created at the beginning, and for him mind and desire were prepared. Our reason we have received in order that we may know Christ, our desire in order that we might hasten to Him. We have memory in order that we may carry Him in us, since He Himself is the Archetype for those who are created. It was not the old Adam who was the model for the new, but the new Adam for the old, even though it is said that the new Adam was generated according to the likeness of the old (Romans 8:3) because of the corruption which the old Adam initiated. The latter Adam inherited it in order that He might abolish the infirmity of our nature by means of the remedies which He brings and, as Paul says, so 'that which is mortal might be swallowed up by life' (2 Corinthians 5:4).

For those who have known him first, the old Adam is the archetype because of our fallen nature. But for Him who sees all things before they exist the first Adam is the imitation of the second. It was in accordance with His pattern and image that he was formed, but he did not continue thus. Rather, he started to go in His direction but failed to attain to Him. Accordingly, it was the former who received the law but the latter who fulfilled it. Of the old Adam obedience was demanded; the new Adam, as Paul says displayed it 'unto death, even death on a cross' (Philippians 2:8). The one by transgressing the law manifested himself as lacking the things which are required of man, for the law for which the transgressor was liable to punishment did not surpass nature. But the second Adam was perfect in all things and, as He says, 'I have kept my Father's commandments' (John 15:10). The former introduced an imperfect life which needed countless aid, the latter became the Father of immortal life for men. Our nature from the beginning tended to immortality; it achieved it much later in the body of the Saviour who, when He had risen to immortal life from the dead, became the leader of immortality for our race.

To sum it up: the Saviour first and alone showed to us the true man, who is perfect on account of both character and life and in all other respects as well.

Since incorruptible life is truly the end of man, God formed him with a view to this goal. It became possible after his body became pure from corruption and his will free from all sin. The perfection of anything consists in this, that the craftsman makes it all that he thinks it should be, as when the beauty of a statue is achieved by the final touch of the sculptor's hand. But while the former Adam fell greatly short of perfection, the latter was perfect in all respects and imparted perfection to men and adapted the whole human race to Himself. How then would the latter not be the model of the former? We must, then, regard Christ as the Archetype and the former Adam as derived from Him. For it is most absurd to regard the most perfect of all things as striving towards the imperfect, and to posit the inferior as the model of the superior, as though the blind were to lead those who see!

It is not surprising that the imperfect is prior in time when we consider that many things were prepared in advance for the use of men and that man who is the measure of all these came from the earth last of all. But it is fitting to believe that the perfect is the first principle of the imperfect by reason of its perfection.

So then, for all these reasons man strives for Christ by nature, by his will, by his thoughts, not only because of His Godhead which is the goal of all things, but because of His human nature as well. He is the resting place of human desires; He is the food of our thoughts. To love anything besides Him or to meditate on it is a manifest aberration from duty and a turning aside from the first principles of our nature.

Source: Nicholas Cabasilas, The Life in Christ *6:12, trans. Carmino J. De Catanzaro, Crestwood, NY: St Vladimir's Seminary Press, 1974, pp. 190–1.*

7.8 Thomas Aquinas, from the *Summa Theologica*

Aquinas explores whether sin diminishes the good of human nature, and whether it can be destroyed entirely. Aquinas argues that although sin does diminish the goodness of nature, it cannot destroy it completely.

The good of human nature is threefold. First, there are the principles of which nature is constituted, and the properties that flow from them, such as the powers of the soul, and so forth. Secondly, since man has from nature an inclination to virtue ... this inclination to virtue is a good of nature. Thirdly, the gift of original justice, conferred on the whole of human nature in the person of the first man, may be called a good of nature.

Accordingly, the first-mentioned good of nature is neither destroyed nor diminished by sin. The third good of nature was entirely destroyed through the sin of our first parent. But the second good of nature, viz. the natural inclination to virtue, is diminished by sin. Because human acts produce an inclination to like acts, as stated above (Question 50, Article 1). Now from the very fact that thing becomes inclined to one of two contraries, its inclination to the other contrary must needs be diminished. Wherefore as sin is opposed to virtue, from the very fact that a man sins, there results a diminution of that good of nature, which is the inclination to virtue ...

As stated above (Article 1), the good of nature, that is diminished by sin, is the natural inclination to virtue, which is befitting to man from the very fact that he is a rational being; for it is due to this that he performs actions in accord with reason, which is to act virtuously. Now sin cannot entirely take away from man the fact that he is a rational being, for then he would no longer be capable of sin. Wherefore it is not possible for this good of nature to be destroyed entirely.

Since, however, this same good of nature may be continually diminished by sin, some, in order to illustrate this, have made use of the example of a finite thing being diminished indefinitely, without being entirely destroyed. For the Philosopher says (Phys. i, text. 37) that if from a finite magnitude a continual subtraction be made in the same quantity, it will at last be entirely destroyed, for instance if from any finite length I continue to subtract the length of a span. If, however, the subtraction be made each time in the same proportion, and not in the same quantity, it may go on indefinitely, as, for instance, if a quantity be halved, and one half be diminished by half, it will be possible to go on thus indefinitely, provided that what is subtracted in each case be less than what was subtracted before. But this does not apply to the question at issue, since a subsequent sin does not diminish the good of nature less than a previous sin, but perhaps more, if it be a more grievous sin.

We must, therefore, explain the matter otherwise by saying that the aforesaid inclination is to be considered as a middle term between two others: for it is based on the rational nature as on its root, and tends to the good of virtue, as to its term and end. Consequently its diminution may be understood in two ways: first, on the part of its root, secondly, on the part of its term. In the first way, it is not diminished by sin, because sin does not diminish nature, as stated above (Article 1). But it is diminished in the second way, in so far as an obstacle is placed against its attaining its term. Now if it were diminished in the first way, it would needs be entirely destroyed at last by the rational nature being entirely destroyed. Since, however, it is diminished on the part of the obstacle which is placed against its attaining its term, it is evident that it can be diminished indefinitely, because obstacles can be placed indefinitely, inasmuch as man can go on indefinitely adding sin to sin: and yet it cannot be destroyed entirely, because the root of this inclination always remains. An example of this may be seen in a transparent body, which has an inclination to receive light, from the very fact that it is transparent; yet this inclination or aptitude is diminished on the part of supervening clouds, although it always remains rooted in the nature of the body.

Source: Thomas Aquinas, Summa Theologica, *First Part of the Second Part Q85, trans. Fathers of the English Dominican Province, London: Burns, Oates & Washbourne, 1924–34.*

7.9 Gregory Palamas, from *The Triads*

In his work The Triads, *Palamas discusses the idea of deification, and argues that this is not a result of nature, but is only given through God's grace. Thus the deified person is not God, as God is, but participates in the life of God through God's grace.*

You claim that the grace of deification is a natural state, that is, the activity and manifestation of a natural power. Without realising it, you are falling into the error of the Messalians,[1] for the deified man would necessarily be God by nature, if deification depended on our natural powers, and was included among the laws of nature! ... But know that the grace of deification transcends every natural relationship, and there does not exist in nature 'any faculty capable of receiving it.'

For if it were no longer a grace, but a manifestation of the energy which appertains to natural power, there would be nothing absurd in holding that deification occurred according to the measure of the receptive power of nature. Deification would then be a work of nature, not a gift of God, and the deified man would be god by nature and receive the name of 'God' in the proper sense. For the natural power of each thing is simply the continuous activation of nature. But in that case, I cannot understand why deification should cause a man to go out from himself, if it is itself subject to the laws of nature.

The grace of deification thus transcends nature, virtue and knowledge, and (as St. Maximus says) 'all these things are inferior to it'. Every virtue and imitation of God on our part indeed prepares those who practise them for divine union, but the mysterious union itself is effected by grace. It is through grace that 'the entire Divinity comes to dwell in fulness in those deemed worthy', and all the saints in their entire being dwell in God, receiving God in His wholeness, and gaining no other reward for their ascent to Him than God Himself. 'He is conjoined to them as a soul is to its body, to its own limbs'; judging it right to dwell in believers by the authentic adoption, according to the gift and grace of the Holy Spirit. So, when you hear that God dwells in us through the virtues, or that by means of the memory He comes to be established in us, do not imagine that deification is simply the possession of the virtues; but rather that it resides in the radiance and grace of God, which really comes to us through the virtues. As St. Basil the Great says, 'A soul which has curbed its natural impulses by a personal *ascesis* and the help of the Holy Spirit, becomes worthy (according to the just judgment of God) of the splendour granted to the saints.' [*De Spir. Sancto*, 16, 40, PG XXXII, 141AB].

The splendour granted by the grace of God is light, as you may learn from this text: 'The splendour for those who have been purified is light, for the just will shine like the sun [Matt. 13.43]; God will stand in the midst of them, distributing and determining the dignities of blessedness, for they are gods and kings.' No one will deny that this relates to supracelestial and supracosmic

---

1 The Messalian belief that Palamas is referring to is the understanding that sanctification is achieved through human effort, and not through grace.

realities, for 'it is possible to receive the supracelestial light among the promises of good things'. Solomon declares, 'Light shines always for the just' [Prov. 13.9], and the Apostle Paul says, 'We give thanks to God who has counted us worthy to participate in the heritage of the saints in light' [Col. 1.12] …

He who says 'the deifying gift is a state of perfection of the rational nature, which has existed since the first disposition of the world and finds its fulfilment in the most elevated of the rational beings', manifestly opposes himself to Christ's Gospel. If deification does no more than perfect the rational nature, without elevating those made in the form of God beyond that condition; if it is only a state of the rational nature, since it is only activated by a natural power, the deified saints do not transcend nature, they are not 'born of God' [John 1.13], are not 'spirit because born of the Spirit' [John 3.16], and Christ, by coming into the world, has not 'given the power to become children of God' to those alone 'who believe in His name' [John 1.12]. Deification would have belonged to all nations even before He came if it naturally pertains to the rational soul, just as today it would belong to everyone irrespective of faith or piety. For if deification were only the perfection of the rational nature, then the pagan Greeks were not entirely rational, neither are the fallen angels; one cannot charge them with misusing their knowledge, yet they have been deprived of the natural state appropriate to such knowledge. Of what, then, were they really guilty? Even the pagan wise men admit that an essence cannot be more or less essential. How then could an angel or soul be more or less rational?

For imperfection in the case of those not yet mature in years resides not in the nature of the soul, but in that of the body. Is deification then to be identified with the age which brings rational thought? For our part, we consider the fact that some men know more than others belongs not to the nature of the soul, but to the constitution of the body. Is deification then this constitution in its natural state of perfection?

But we know that natural perfection is itself a gift of God, even though knowledge is not only a gift of God, but a state of perfection of the rational nature. However, this state, since it is not supernatural, is not a deifying gift, because the deifying gift is supernatural. Otherwise all men and angels without exception would be more or less gods, and the race of demons would be imperfect gods or demigods … Thus, whatever the state in which the rational nature attains perfection, whether it is a knowledge, a constitution, a natural perfection of body and soul, whether it comes from within them or from outside a man, it can truly make perfect those rational beings who possess it, but it cannot make them gods.

Source: Gregory Palamas, The Triads, *in Saint Gregory Palamas, trans. John Meyendorff and Nicholas Gendle, Classics of Western Spirituality, New York: Paulist Press, 1983, pp. 82–6.*

7.10 Martin Luther, from *Exposition on the Lord's Prayer*

In this exposition of the Lord's Prayer, Luther reflects on the petition, 'Thy will be done on earth, as it is in heaven.' Luther argues that the meaning of the prayer, and indeed the aim of the Christian life, is for the believer to conform to God's will and not their own. Luther argues that this is the only way for the human will to remain free.

A person should learn to know a will which is superior to his and which is opposed to his own. He will never feel uncertain when he finds this one will, knowing that in him these wills are not in conflict with one another, when he accustoms himself to follow the superior will rather than his own. He who has and obeys his own will surely acts contrary to God's will. But as it happens, there is nothing so dear to man and so hard to surrender as his own will. Many people perform fine and good works, but they completely follow their own will and inclinations, assuming all the time that all is well and that they are not doing wrong. They are of the opinion that their will is good and true and that they do not in the least need this petition. They are also without any fear of God.

In the second place, this petition mortifies us through other people who antagonize us, assail us, disquiet us, and oppose our will in every way, who mock not only our worldly actions but also our good spiritual works, such as our prayers, our fasting, our acts of kindness, who, in brief, are never at peace with us. O what a priceless blessing this is! We should really pay such assailants all our goods, for they are the ones who fulfil this petition in us. They are the ones through whom God breaks our will so that his will may be done. This is why Christ says in Matthew 5 [:25], 'Make friends quickly with your accuser.' That is, we must surrender our will and accept our adversary's will as good, for in that way our will is broken. In the breaking of our will God's will is done; for he wants to see our will hindered and broken. Therefore if someone wants to reproach you or make a fool of you, do not oppose him, but say yes to him, deeming it right before God to do so, which as a matter of fact, it is. If he wants to rob you of anything and work you for harm, let him do it as though it were your just desert, for undoubtedly in God's sight it is just. Even if your adversary is doing wrong thereby, you nevertheless are not suffering an injustice, for since everything belongs to God, it is his right to take it from you either through a good or an evil person. Your will must not resist, but must say, 'Thy will be done.' This applies to all things, physical and spiritual. Christ says, 'If anyone takes your coat, let him have your cloak as well' [Matt. 5.40]. But you may say, 'If that is the meaning of doing God's will, who, then can be saved? Who can fulfil this lofty commandment to the extent that he surrenders all things and has no will of his own?' This is my reply: you must learn how important and necessary this petition is, why we must pray it ardently and earnestly, and why it is important that our will be mortified and God's will alone be done. Thus you must confess that you are a sinner who cannot do God's will, who must petition God for help and mercy, to forgive your shortcomings, and to aid you in doing his will. It is imperative that if God's will is to prevail, our will must be submerged, for these two are at war with each other. We can take an example from Christ, our Lord. When he asked his Father in the garden to remove the cup, he also added 'Not my will, but thine, be done' [Luke 22.42]. If Christ had to surrender his will, which after all was good, yes, undoubtedly and always the best, in order that God's will be carried out, why should we poor little worms make such a fuss about our will, which is never free of evil and always deserves to be thwarted?

To understand this we must note the two ways in which our will is evil. In the first place, our will may be openly and patently and undisguisedly evil, as, for example, when we are wilfully inclined to do something that is generally acknowledged by all as being evil; such as a will to be wrathful, to lie, deceive, to harm a neighbour, to be unchaste, and the like. Such a will and leaning show up in everyone, especially when he is incited in their direction. We must ask God's helping opposing it, so that his will may be done, for God wants peace, truth, purity, and gentleness. In the second place, our will may appear cloaked and disguised as something good, as seen for instance in the words in Luke 9 [:54–55], directed by St John and St James against the Samaritans who would not receive Christ, 'Lord, do you want us to bid fire come down from heaven and consume them?' The Lord answered them, 'Do you not know what manner of spirit you are children of; for the Son of man came not to destroy the soul but to save it.'

...

In addition to these two evil wills, there is a just and good will, which also must not be done. David had such a will when he wanted to build a temple to God. The Lord praised him for this, and yet did not permit him to carry it out. Such was the will of Christ in the garden when he was reluctant to drink the cup; his will, though good, did not prevail. Likewise, if you willed to convert the whole world, raise the dead, lead yourself and all others to heaven, and to perform every miracle, you should still not want to do any of this unless you had first consulted God's will and subordinated your will wholly to his, and said, 'My dear God, this or that seems good to me; if you approve, let it be done, but if you disapprove, let it remain undone.'

God very often breaks this good will in his saints to prevent a false, malicious, and evil good will from establishing itself through the semblance of good, and also to help us learn that no matter how good our will may be, it is still immeasurably inferior to God's will. Therefore, our inferior good will must necessarily give way to the infinitely better will of God; it must submit to being destroyed by it.

Third, this good will in us must be hindered for its own improvement. God's only purpose in thwarting our good will is to make of it a better will. And this is done when it subordinates itself to and conforms to the divine will (by which it is hindered), until the point is reached when man is entirely unfettered by his own will, delivered from his own will, and knows nothing except that he waits upon the will of God.

Now that is what is meant by genuine obedience, a thing which, unfortunately, is entirely unknown in our day. Nowadays idle babblers come along and fill all of Christendom with their chatter and mislead the poor people with their doctrines. They fairly shout from the pulpits telling us how to have and how to make a good will, a good opinion, a good resolve. Then they tell the people that if they have done this they can feel secure and that all that they do is good. With this doctrine they merely create self-willed and stubborn people, bold and secure minds, who constantly contend against God's will and do not break or subordinate their own. They feel that their own ideas are good and should therefore prevail, and that whatever obstructs them must be of the devil and not of God. That gives birth to the wolves in sheep's clothing, to those arrogant saints who are the most pernicious people on earth. That is why one bishop fights and feuds and wars with another, one church with another. That is why priests and monks and nuns are at loggerheads with each other. That is why there is dissension everywhere. Yet each faction claims to have a good will, the right opinion, and a godly resolve. And so they carry on their devilish work, thinking it to be the honor and glory of God.

One ought to teach them properly to have a God-fearing will and not to rely in the least on their own will and opinion, yes, to cast from them this accursed belief that they can have or make a good will or intention. Man must despair utterly of ever having or attaining a good will, opinion, or resolve. As I stated before, a good will is found only where there is no will. Where there is no will, God's will, which is the very best, will be present. Therefore these barkers know all about a good or bad will. They come along boldly and encourage us to say with our lips 'Thy will be done,' but with the heart, 'My will be done.' Thus they mock God and us.

You may say, 'Well, did God not endow us with a free will?' I reply: To be sure, he gave you a free will. But why do you want to make it your own will? Why not let it remain free? If you do with it whatever you will, it is not a free will, but your own will. God did not give you or anyone else a will of your own. Your own will comes from the devil and from Adam, who transformed the free will received from God into his own. A free will does not want its own way, but looks only to God's will for direction. By so doing it then also remains free, untrammelled and unshackled.

Source: Luther's Works *XLII*, ed. Jaroslav Pelikan, St Louis: Concordia Publishing House, *1969, pp. 45–8.*

7.11 John Calvin, from the *Institutes of the Christian Religion*

Calvin argues that the human condition is characterized by depravity, not because of the way God made human beings, but because of the corruption of human nature. He further argues that we inherit this corrupt nature and so every human being in this state of sin is 'hateful' to God.

But self-knowledge consists in this, First, When reflecting on what God gave us at our creation, and still continues graciously to give, we perceive how great the excellence of our nature would have been had its integrity remained, and, at the same time, remember that we have nothing of our own, but depend entirely on God, from whom we hold at pleasure whatever he has seen it meet to bestow; secondly When viewing our miserable condition since Adam's fall, all confidence and boasting are overthrown, we blush for shame, and feel truly humble. For as God at first formed us in his own image, that he might elevate our minds to the pursuit of virtue, and the contemplation of eternal life, so to prevent us from heartlessly burying those noble qualities which distinguish us from the lower animals, it is of importance to know that we were endued with reason and intelligence, in order that we might cultivate a holy and honourable life, and regard a blessed immortality as our destined aim.

At the same time, it is impossible to think of our primeval dignity without being immediately reminded of the sad spectacle of our ignominy and corruption, ever since we fell from our original in the person of our first parent. In this way, we feel dissatisfied with ourselves, and become truly humble, while we are inflamed with new desires to seek after God, in whom each may regain those good qualities of which all are found to be utterly destitute.

8. The nature of original sin

But lest the thing itself of which we speak be unknown or doubtful, it will be proper to define original sin. I have no intention, however, to discuss all the definitions which different writers have adopted, but only to adduce the one which seems to me most accordant with truth. Original sin, then, may be defined as hereditary corruption and depravity of our nature, extending to all the parts of the soul, which first makes us obnoxious to the wrath of God, and then produces in us works which in Scripture are termed works of the flesh. This corruption is repeatedly designated by Paul by the term sin (Gal. 5:19), while the works which proceed from it, such as adultery, fornication, theft, hatred, murder, revellings, he terms, in the same way, the fruits of sin, though in various passages of Scripture, and even by Paul himself, they are also termed sins.

The two things, therefore, are to be distinctly observed, viz., that being thus perverted and corrupted in all the parts of our nature, we are, merely on account of such corruption, deservedly condemned by God, to whom nothing is acceptable but righteousness, innocence, and purity. This is not liability for another's fault. For when it is said, that the sin of Adam has made us obnoxious to the justice of God, the meaning is not, that we, who are in ourselves innocent and blameless, are bearing his guilt, but that since by his transgression we are all placed under the curse, he is said to have brought us under obligation. Through him, however, not only has punishment been derived, but pollution instilled, for which punishment is justly due. Hence Augustine, though he often terms it another's sin (that he may more clearly show how it comes to us by descent), at the same time asserts that it is each individual's own sin. And the Apostle most distinctly testifies, that 'death passed upon all men, for that all have sinned' (Rom. 5:12), that is, are involved in original sin, and polluted by its stain. Hence, even infants bringing their condemnation with them from their mother's womb, suffer not for another's, but for their own defect. For although they have not yet produced the fruits of their own unrighteousness, they have the seed implanted in them. Nay, their whole nature is, as it were, a seed-bed of sin, and therefore cannot but be odious and abominable to God. Hence it follows, that it is properly deemed sinful in the sight of God; for there could be no condemnation without guilt.

Next comes the other point, viz., that this perversity in us never ceases, but constantly produces new fruits, in other words, those works of the flesh which we formerly described; just as a lighted furnace sends forth sparks and flames, or a fountain without ceasing pours out water. Hence, those who have defined original sin as the want of the original righteousness which we ought to have had, though they substantially comprehend the whole case, do not significantly enough express its power and energy. For our nature is not only utterly devoid of goodness, but so prolific in all kinds of evil, that it can never be idle. Those who term it concupiscence use a word not very inappropriate, provided it were added (this, however, many will by no means concede) that everything which is in man, from the intellect to the will, from the soul even to the flesh, is defiled and pervaded with this concupiscence; or, to express it more briefly, that the whole man is in himself nothing else than concupiscence.

...

10. *Sin is not our nature, but its derangement*

Let us have done, then, with those who dare to inscribe the name of God on their vices, because we say that men are born vicious. The divine workmanship, which they ought to look for in the nature of Adam, when still entire and uncorrupted, they absurdly expect to find in their depravity. The blame of our ruin rests with our own carnality, not with God, its only cause being our degeneracy from our original condition.

And let no one here glamour that God might have provided better for our safety by preventing Adam's fall. This objection, which, from the daring presumption implied in it, is odious to every pious mind, relates to the mystery of predestination, which will afterwards be considered in its own place. Meanwhile let us remember that our ruin is attributable to our own depravity, that we may not insinuate a charge against God himself, the Author of nature. It is true that nature has received a mortal wound, but there is a great difference between a wound inflicted from without, and one inherent in our first condition. It is plain that this wound was inflicted by sin; and, therefore, we have no ground of complaint except against ourselves. This is carefully taught in Scripture. For the Preacher says, 'Lo, this only have I found, that God made man upright; but they have sought out many inventions' (Eccl. 7:29). Since man, by the kindness of God, was made upright, but by his own infatuation fell away unto vanity, his destruction is obviously attributable only to himself.

11. 'Natural' corruption of the 'nature' created by God

We say then that man is corrupted by a natural viciousness, but not by one which proceeded from nature. In saying that it proceeded not from nature, we mean that it was rather an adventitious event which befell man, than a substantial property assigned to him from the beginning. We, however, call it natural to prevent any one from supposing that each individual contracts it by depraved habit, whereas all receive it by a hereditary law. And we have authority for so calling it. For, on the same grounds the apostle says, that we are 'by nature the children of wrath' (Eph. 2:3). How could God, who takes pleasure in the meanest of his works be offended with the noblest of them all? The offence is not with the work itself, but the corruption of the work. Wherefore, if it is not improper to say, that, in consequence of the corruption of human nature, man is naturally hateful to God, it is not improper to say, that he is naturally vicious and depraved. Hence, in the view of our corrupt nature, Augustine hesitates not to call those sins natural which necessarily reign in the flesh wherever the grace of God is wanting. This disposes of the absurd notion of the Manichees, who, imagining that man was essentially wicked, went the length of assigning him a different Creator, that they might thus avoid the appearance of attributing the cause and origin of evil to a righteous God.

Source: John Calvin, Institutes of the Christian Religion, *II.1, trans. Henry Beveridge (1559), Grand Rapids: Eerdmans, 1989.*

7.12 John Wesley, from *A Plain Account of Christian Perfection*

Wesley argues that the process of sanctification, and the resulting perfection of the person does not only happen in the world to come, but is possible in this life. Here he suggests that it is possible to live without sin, which is not a necessary part of human nature.

In what sense then are they perfect? Observe, we are not now speaking of babes in Christ, but adult Christians. But even babes in Christ are so far perfect as not to commit sin. This St. John affirms expressly; and it cannot be disproved by the examples of the Old Testament. For what, if the holiest of the ancient Jews did sometimes commit sin? We cannot infer from hence, that 'all Christians do and must commit sin as long as they live.'

But does not the Scripture say, 'A just man sinneth seven times a day'? It does not. Indeed it says, 'A just man falleth seven times.' But this is quite another thing; for, First, the words, a day, are not in the text. Secondly, here is no mention of falling into sin at all. What is here mentioned, is, falling into temporal affliction.

But elsewhere Solomon says, 'There is no man that sinneth not.' Doubtless thus it was in the days of Solomon; yea, and from Solomon to Christ there was then no man that sinned not. But whatever was the case of those under the law, we may safely affirm, with St. John, that, since the gospel was given, 'he that is born of God sinneth not.'

The privileges of Christians are in nowise to be measured by what the Old Testament records concerning those who were under the Jewish dispensation; seeing the fullness of time is now come, the Holy Ghost is now given, the great salvation of God is now brought to men by the revelation of Jesus Christ. The kingdom of heaven is now set up on earth, concerning which the Spirit of God declared of old time (so far is David from being the pattern or standard of Christian perfection), 'He that is feeble among them, at that day, shall be as David, and the house of David shall be as the angel of the Lord before them' (Zech. 12:8).

But the Apostles themselves committed sin; Peter by dissembling, Paul by his sharp contention with Barnabas. Suppose they did, will you argue thus: 'If two of the Apostles once committed sin, then all other Christians, in all ages, do and must commit sin as long as they live?' Nay, God forbid we should thus speak. No necessity of sin was laid upon them; the grace of God was surely sufficient for them. And it is sufficient for us at this day.

But St. James says, 'In many things we offend all.' True; but who are the persons here spoken of? Why, those 'many masters' or teachers whom God had not sent; not the Apostle himself, nor any real Christian. That in the word we, used by a figure of speech, common in all other as well as the inspired writings, the Apostle could not possibly include himself, or any other true believer, appears, First, from the ninth verse, 'Therewith bless we God, and therewith curse we men.' Surely not we Apostles! not we believers! Secondly, from the words preceding the text: 'My brethren, be not many masters,' or teachers, 'knowing that we shall receive the greater condemnation. For in many things we offend all.' *We!* Who? Not the Apostles nor true believers, but they who were to 'receive the greater condemnation,' because of those many offences. Nay, Thirdly, the verse itself proves, that 'we offend all,' cannot be spoken either of all men or all Christians. For in it immediately follows the mention of a man who 'offends not,' as the *we* first mentioned did; from whom therefore he is professedly contradistinguished, and pronounced a 'perfect man.'

But St. John himself says, 'If we say that we have no sin, we deceive ourselves;' and, 'If we say we have not sinned, we make him a liar, and his word is not in us.'

I answer, (1.) The tenth verse fixes the sense of the eighth: 'If we say we have no sin,' in the former, being explained by, 'If we say we have not sinned,' in the latter, verse. (2.) The point under consideration is not, whether we have or have not sinned heretofore; and neither of these verses asserts that we do sin, or commit sin now. (3.) The ninth verse explains both the eighth and tenth: 'If we confess our sins, he is faithful and just to forgive us our sins, and to cleanse us from all unrighteousness.' As if he had said, 'I have before affirmed, The blood of Christ cleanseth from all sin.' And no man can say, 'I need it not; I have no sin to be cleansed, from.' If we say, we have no sin, that 'we have not sinned, we deceive ourselves,' and make God a liar: But 'if we confess our sins, he is faithful and just,' not only 'to forgive us our sins,' but also 'to cleanse us from all unrighteousness,' that we may 'go and sin no more.' In conformity, therefore, both to the doctrine of St. John, and the whole tenor of the New Testament, we fix this conclusion: A Christian is so far perfect, as not to commit sin.

This is the glorious privilege of every Christian, yea, though he be but a babe in Christ. But it is only of grown Christians it can be affirmed, they are in such a sense perfect, as, Secondly, to be freed from evil thoughts and evil tempers. First, from evil or sinful thoughts. Indeed, whence should they spring? 'Out of the heart of man,' if at all, 'proceed evil thoughts.' If, therefore, the heart be no longer evil, then evil thoughts no longer proceed out of it: For 'a good tree cannot bring forth evil fruit.'

And as they are freed from evil thoughts, so likewise from evil tempers. Every one of these can say, with St. Paul, 'I am crucified with Christ; nevertheless I live; yet not I, but Christ liveth in me' – words that manifestly describe a deliverance from inward as well as from outward sin. This is expressed both negatively, 'I live not,' my evil nature, the body of sin, is destroyed; and positively, 'Christ liveth in me,' and therefore all that is holy, and just, and good. Indeed, both these, 'Christ liveth in me,' and, 'I live not,' are inseparably connected. For what communion hath light with darkness, or Christ with Belial?

He, therefore, who liveth in these Christians hath 'purified their hearts by faith;' insomuch that every one that has Christ in him, 'the hope of glory, purifieth himself even as he is pure.' He is purified from pride; for Christ was lowly in heart: He is pure from desire and self-will; for Christ desired only to do the will of his Father: And he is pure from anger, in the common sense of the word; for Christ 'was meek and gentle'. I say, *in the common sense of the word;* for he is angry at sin, while he is grieved for the sinner. He feels a displacency at every offence against God, but only tender compassion to the offender.

... It remains, then, that Christians are saved in this world from all sin, from all unrighteousness; that they are now in such a sense perfect, as not to commit sin, and to be freed from evil thoughts and evil tempers.

Source: The Works of John Wesley, *vol. 11, ed. Thomas Jackson, London: John Mason, 1872, pp. 366–446.*

7.13 Søren Kierkegaard, from *The Sickness unto Death*

Here Kierkegaard argues that sin separates humans from each other and from God. Indeed, sin not only separates us from God, but can only be recognized by God, rather than through speculation.

The category of sin is the category of the individual. Speculatively sin cannot be thought at all. The individual man is subsumed under the concept; one cannot think an individual man but only the concept man. Hence it is that Speculation at once reaches the doctrine of the preponderance of the generations over the individual; for it is not to be expected that Speculation should recognize the impotence of the concept in relation to reality. But as one cannot think an individual man, so neither can one think an individual sinner; one can think sin (then it becomes negative), but not an individual sinner. Just for this reason, however, there can be no seriousness about sin when it is merely thought. For seriousness is precisely the fact that thou and I are sinners. Seriousness is not sin in general, but the emphasis of seriousness falls upon the sinner who is an individual. In relation to 'the individual man' Speculation, if it is consistent, must think very scornfully of what it is to be an individual or that it is something which cannot be thought. If it would do anything in this line, it must say to the individual, 'Is that anything to waste time on? Above all try to forget it, to be an individual man is not to be anything – think, and then thou art the whole of humanity, *cogito ergo sum*.' This, however, might perhaps be a lie, and the individual might be the highest. Yet suppose it is so. But to be entirely consistent Speculation must also say, 'The thing of being an individual sinner, that's not to be anything, it is subsumed under the concept, waste no time on it etc.' And then what further? Is one perhaps to think sin instead of being an individual sinner? – just as one was exhorted to think the concept of man instead of being the individual man. And then what further? Does a man become himself 'sin' by thinking sin? *Cogito ergo sum.* A capital proposal! However, one does not even in this case need to be afraid of becoming sin … the pure sin, for sin cannot be thought. This after all Speculation itself might concede, since sin is in fact a falling away from the concept. But not to dispute any longer *e concessis*, the principal difficulty is another. Speculation does not take heed of the fact that in relation to sin the ethical has its place, which employs an emphasis which is the converse of that of Speculation and accomplishes the opposite development; for the ethical does not abstract from reality but goes deeper into reality, operating essentially by the aid of the category of the individual, which is the category overlooked and despised by Speculation. Sin is a characteristic of the individual; it is frivolity and a new sin to act as if it were nothing to be an individual sinner. Here Christianity is in place. It marks a cross before Speculation. It is as impossible for Speculation to get out of this difficulty as for a sailing vessel to sail directly against a contrary wind. The seriousness of sin is its reality in the individual, whether it be thou or I. Speculatively one has to look away from the individual. So it is only frivolously one can talk speculatively about sin. The dialectic of sin is directly contrary to that of Speculation.

Here Christianity begins with the doctrine of sin, and therefore with the individual. The doctrine of the sin of the human race has often been misused because it has not been noticed that sin, common though it is to all, does not gather men together in a common concept, into a society or a partnership ('any more than out in the churchyard the multitude of the dead constitute a society'), but it splits men into individuals and holds every individual fast as a sinner – a splitting which in another sense is both in correspondence with and teleologically in the direction of the perfection of existence. This men have not observed, and so they have let the fallen race become once for all good again in Christ. And so in turn they have saddled God with an abstraction which, as an abstraction, presumes to claim kinship with Him. But this is a false pretext which only makes men insolent. For if the individual is to feel himself akin to God (and this is the doctrine of Christianity), the whole weight of this falls upon him in fear and trembling, and he must discover (if it were not an old discovery) the possibility of offense. But if the individual is to attain this glory through an abstraction, the thing becomes too easy, and essentially it is taken in vain. The individual does not in this case get the prodigious weight of God, which by humiliation presses down as deeply as it uplifts; the individual imagines that he possesses everything as a matter of course by participating in this abstraction. Being a man is not like being an animal, where the specimen is always less than the species. Man is distinguished from other animals not only by the advantages which are commonly enumerated, but qualitatively by the fact that the individual is more than the species. And this characteristic is again dialectical, it means that the individual is a sinner, but then again that it is perfection to be the individual. For it is Christianity to be sure which has taught this about the God-Man, about the likeness between God and man, but Christianity is a great hater of wanton and impertinent forwardness. By the help of the doctrine of sin and of the individual sinner God and Christ have been secured once for all, and far better than any king, against the nation, the people, the crowd, etc., item against every demand for a freer constitution. All these abstractions are before God nonexistent, before God in Christ there live only individual men (sinners) – yet God can well oversee the whole, He can care for the sparrows too. God is wholly a friend of order, and to that end He is Himself present at every point, in every instant, He is omnipresent – which is specified in the text-books as one of the titles by which God is called, which men once in a while think about a little but surely never try to think every instant. His concept is not like that of man under which the individual is subsumed as a thing which cannot be absorbed by the concept, His concept comprises everything, and in another sense He has no concept. God does not help Himself by an abbreviation, He comprehends (*comprehendit*) reality itself, all the individuals; for Him the individual is not subsumed under the concept.

The doctrine of sin, the doctrine that we are sinners, thou and I, which absolutely disperses the 'crowd,' fixes then the qualitative distinction between God and man more deeply than ever it was fixed anywhere – for again this God alone can do, sin is in fact before God etc. In no respect is a man so different from God as in the fact that he is a sinner, as every man is, and is a sinner 'before God,' whereby indeed the opposites are held together in a double sense: they are held together (*continentur*), not allowed to separate from one another; but by being thus held together the differences display themselves all the more strikingly, as when one speaks of holding colors together, *opposita juxta se posita magis illucescunt.* Sin is the only thing universally predicated of man which cannot in any way, either *via negationis* or *via eminentia,* be affirmed of God. It may be affirmed of God that He is not finite as man is, and so, *via negationis,* that He is infinite; but to affirm of God that He is not a sinner is blasphemy. As a sinner man is separated from God by a yawning qualitative abyss. And obviously God is separated from man by the same yawning qualitative abyss when He forgives sins. In case it were possible by a converse kind of accommodation to transfer the divine attributes to a human being, in one respect man will never in all eternity come to resemble God, namely, in forgiving sins.

Source: Søren Kierkegaard, The Sickness Unto Death, *Princeton, NJ: Princeton University Press, 1941, pp. 99ff.*

7.14 Karl Barth, from *Church Dogmatics*

In this passage Barth explains that 'real man', true human being, can only be understood in the light of Christ. He goes on to explain that humans are made to be in covenant relationship with God.

The ontological determination of humanity is grounded in the fact that one man among all others is the man Jesus. So long as we select any other starting point for our study, we shall reach only the phenomena of the human. We are condemned to abstractions so long as our attention is riveted as it were on other men, or rather on man in general, as if we could learn about real man from a study of man in general, and in abstraction from the fact that one man among all others is the man Jesus. In this case we miss the one Archimedean point given us beyond humanity, and therefore the one possibility of discovering the ontological determination of man. Theological anthropology has no choice in this matter. It is not yet or no longer theological anthropology if it tries to pose and answer the question of the true being of man from any other angle.

We remember who and what the man Jesus is. As we have seen, He is the one creaturely being in whose existence we have to do immediately and directly with the being of God also. Again, He is the creaturely being in whose existence God's act of deliverance has taken place for all other men. He is the creaturely being in whom God as the Saviour of all men also reveals and affirms His own glory as the creator. He is the creaturely being who as such embodies the sovereignty of God, or conversely the sovereignty of God which as such actualises this creaturely being. He is the creaturely being whose existence consists in His fulfilment of the will of God. And finally He is the creaturely being who as such not only exists from God and in God but absolutely for God instead of for Himself ...

Real man lives with God as His covenant-partner. For God has created him to participate in the history in which God is at work with him and he with God; to be His partner in this common history of the covenant. He created him as His covenant-partner. Thus real man does not live a godless life – without God. A godless explanation of man, which overlooks the fact that he belongs to God, is from the very outset one which cannot explain real man, man himself. Indeed, it cannot even speak of him. It gropes past him into the void. It grasps only the sin in which he breaks the covenant with God and denies and obscures his true reality. Nor can it really explain or speak of his sin. For to do so it would obviously have to see him first in the light of the fact that he belongs to God, in his determination by the God who created him, and in the grace against which he sins. Real man does not act godlessly, but in the history of the covenant in which he is God's partner by God's election and calling. He thanks God for His grace by knowing Him as God, by obeying Him, by calling on Him as God, by enjoying freedom from Him and to Him. He is responsible before God, i.e., He gives to the Word of God the corresponding answer. That this is the case, that the man determined by God for life with God is real man, is decided by the existence of the man Jesus. Apart from anything else, this is

315

the standard of what his reality is and what it is not. It reveals originally and definitively why God has created man. The man Jesus is man for God. As the Son of God He is this in a unique way. But as He is for God, the reality of each and every other man is decided. God has created man for Himself. And so real man is for God and not the reverse. He is the covenant-partner of God. He is determined by God for life with God. This is the distinctive feature of his being in the cosmos ...

The covenant partner of God can break the covenant. Real man can deny and obscure his reality. This ability for which there is no reason, the mad and incomprehensible possibility of sin, is a sorry fact. And since man is able to sin, and actually does so, he betrays himself into a destructive contradiction in which he is as it were torn apart. On the one hand there is his reality as God's covenant-partner which he has denied and obscured. And on the other, as something quite different and not recognisably connected with this reality, there is his creaturely form, the humanity which runs amok when it is denied and obscured in this way, and plunges like a meteor into the abyss, into empty space ...

The power of sin is great, but not illimitable. It can efface or devastate many things, but not the being of man as such. It cannot reverse the divine operation, and therefore the divine work, that which is effected by God. Sin is not creative. It cannot replace the creature of God by a different reality. It cannot, therefore, annul the covenant. It cannot lead man to more than a fearful and fatal compromising of his reality, his determination. And so his humanity can be betrayed into the extreme danger of inhumanity. It can become a picture which merely mocks him. But man can as little destroy or alter himself as create himself. If there is a basic form of humanity in which it corresponds and is similar to the divine determination of man, in this correspondence and similarity we have something constant and persistent, an inviolable particularity of his creaturely form which cannot be effaced or lost or changed or made unrecognisable even in sinful man ...

The humanity of Jesus is not merely the repetition and reflection of His divinity, or of God's controlling will; it is the repetition and reflection of God Himself, no more and no less. It is the image of God, the *imago Dei*.

The 'image' – we must not forget the limitation implicit in this term. If the humanity of Jesus is the image of God, this means that it is only indirectly and not directly identical with God. It belongs intrinsically to the creaturely world, to the cosmos. Hence it does not belong to the inner sphere of the essence, but to the outer sphere of the work of God. It does not present God in Himself and in His relation to Himself, but in His relation to the reality distinct from himself. In it we have to do with God and man rather than God and God. There is a real difference in this respect. We cannot, therefore, expect more than correspondence and similarity. We cannot maintain identity. Between God and God, the Father and the Son and the Son and the Father, there is unity of essence, the perfect satisfaction of self-grounded reality, and a blessedness eternally self-originated and self-renewed. But there can be no question of this between God and man, and it cannot therefore find expression in the humanity of Jesus, in his fellow-humanity as the image of God. In this case we have a complete disparity between the two aspects. There is total sovereignty and grace on the part of God, but total dependence and need on that of man. Life and blessedness may be had by man wholly in God and only in fellowship with Him, in whom they are to be sought and found. On God's side, therefore, we have a Saviour and Deliverer. And he does not enter into alliance with a second God in His eternal covenant with man as revealed in Jesus Christ. Nor does man become a second God when He takes part in this covenant and is delivered by this Deliverer. The one who enters into this covenant is always the creature, and, who would probably be absolutely threatened without this help and lost if thrown back upon his own resources. It is in the humanity, the saving work of Jesus Christ that the connexion between God and man is brought before us.

Source: Karl Barth, Church Dogmatics III.2, *trans. Harold Knight, ed. Geoffrey Bromiley and T. F. Torrance, Edinburgh: T. & T. Clark, 1960, pp 132–3, 203, 205, 206, 219–20.*

7.15 Reinhold Niebuhr, from *The Nature and Destiny of Man*

Niebuhr contrasts the Christian view of humanity with the classical view, and argues that the Christian understanding of the person includes both body and spirit. Niebuhr also rejects the view that the distinctive thing about humanity is the capacity for rational thought.

The Christian faith in God as Creator of the world transcends the canons and antinomies of rationality, particularly the antinomy between mind and matter, between consciousness and extension. God is not merely mind who forms a previously given formless stuff. God is both vitality and form and the source of all existence. He creates the world. This world is not God; but it is not evil because it is not God. Being God's creation, it is good.

The consequence of this conception of the world upon the view of human nature in Christian thought is to allow an appreciation of the unity of body and soul in human personality which idealists and naturalists have sought in vain. Furthermore, it prevents the idealistic error of regarding the mind as essentially good or essentially eternal and the body as essentially evil. But it also obviated the romantic error of seeking for the good in man-as-nature and for evil in man-as-spirit or as reason. Man is, according to the Biblical view, a created and finite existence in both body and spirit.

The second important characteristic of the Christian view of man is that he is understood primarily from the standpoint of God, rather than from the uniqueness of his rational faculties or his relation to nature. He is made in the 'image of God'. It has been the mistake of many Christian rationalists to assume that this term is no more than a religious-pictorial expression of what philosophy intends when it defines man as a rational animal. We have previously alluded to the fact that the human spirit has the special capacity of standing continually outside itself in terms of indefinite regression. Consciousness is a capacity for surveying the world and determining action from a governing centre. Self-consciousness represents a further degree of transcendence in which the self makes itself its own object in such a way that the ego is finally always subject and not object. The rational capacity of surveying the world, of forming general concepts and analysing the order of the world, is thus but one aspect of what Christianity knows as 'spirit'. The self knows the world, in so far as it knows the world, because it stands outside both itself and the world, which means that it cannot understand from beyond itself and the world.

...

God as will and personality, in concepts of Christian faith, is thus the only possible ground of real individuality, though not the only possible presupposition of self-consciousness. But faith in God as will and personality depends upon faith in His power to reveal Himself. The Christian faith in God's self-disclosure, culminating in the revelation of Christ, is thus the basis of the

Christian concept of personality and individuality. In terms of this faith man can understand himself as a unity of will which finds its end in the will of God. We thus have in the problem of human nature one of the many indications of the relation of general and special revelation which concerns theology so perennially. The conviction that man stands too completely outside of both nature and reason to understand himself in terms of either without misunderstanding himself, belongs to general revelation in the sense that any astute analysis of the human situation must lead to it. But if a man lacks a further revelation of the divine he will also misunderstand himself when he seeks to escape the conditions of nature and reason. He will end by seeking absorption in a divine reality which is at once all and nothing. To understand himself truly means to begin with a faith that he is understood from beyond himself, that he is known and loved of God and must find himself in terms of obedience to the divine will. This relation of the divine to the human will makes it possible for man to relate himself to God without pretending to be God, and to accept his distance from God as a created thing without believing that the evil of his nature is caused by this finiteness. Man's finite existence in the body and in history can be essentially affirmed, as naturalism wants to affirm it. Yet the uniqueness of man's spirit can be appreciated even more than idealism appreciates it, though always preserving a proper distinction between the human and divine. Also the unity of spirit and body can be emphasized in terms of its relation to a Creator and Redeemer who created both mind and body. These are the ultra-rational foundations and presuppositions of Christian wisdom about man.

This conception of man's stature is not, however, the complete Christian picture of man. The high estimate of the human stature implied in the concept of 'image of God' stands in paradoxical juxtaposition to the low estimate of human virtue in Christian thought. Man is a sinner. His sin is defined as rebellion against God. The Christian estimate of human evil is so serious precisely because it places evil at the very centre of human personality – in the will. This evil cannot be regarded complacently as the inevitable consequence of his finiteness or the fruit of his involvement in the contingencies and necessities of nature. Sin is occasioned precisely by the fact that man refuses to admit his 'creatureliness' and to acknowledge himself as merely a member of a total unity of life. He pretends to be more than he is. Nor can he, as in both rationalistic and mystical dualism, dismiss his sins as residing in the part of himself which is involved in physical necessity. In Christianity it is not the eternal man who judges the finite man; but the eternal and holy God who judges sinful man. Nor is redemption in the power of the eternal man who gradually sloughs off finite man. Man is not divided against himself so that the essential man can be extricated from the non-essential. Man contradicts himself within the terms of his true essence. His essence is free self-determination. His sin is the wrong use of his freedom and its consequent destruction.

Man is an individual, but he is not self-sufficing. The law of his nature is love, a harmonious relation of life to life in obedience to the divine centre and source of his life. This law is violated when man seeks to make himself the centre and source of his own life. His sin is therefore spiritual and not carnal, though the infection of rebellion spreads from the spirit to the body and disturbs its harmonies also. Man, in other words, is a sinner not because he is one limited individual within a whole but rather because he is betrayed, by his very ability to survey the whole, to imagine himself the whole ...

[I]t is impossible without the presuppositions of the Christian faith to find the source of sin within man himself. Greek tragedy regards the human evil as the consequence of a conflict between vitality and form, between Dionysian and Olympian divinities. Only in a religion of revelation, whose God reveals Himself to man from beyond himself and from beyond the contrast of vitality and form, can man discover the root of sin to be within himself. The essence of man is his freedom. Sin is committed in that freedom. Sin can therefore not be attributed to a defect in his essence. It can only be understood as a self-contradiction, made possible by the fact of his freedom but not following necessarily from it.

Source: Reinhold Niebuhr, The Nature and Destiny of Man, *vol. 1, London: Nisbett & Co., 1949, pp. 12–18.*

7.16 Karl Rahner, from *Theological Investigations*

Rahner approaches the doctrine of humanity from a specific starting point. That humans have the ability to question, Rahner suggests, allows them to transcend their own reality or experience. Indeed, Rahner argues that we are more than the sum of our experiences but that we can only be understood in reference to God, and God can only be understood in reference to humanity.

As soon as man is understood as the being who is absolutely transcendent in respect of God, 'anthropocentricity' and 'theocentricitry' in theology are not opposites but strictly one and the same thing, seen from two sides. Neither of the two aspects can be comprehended at all without the other. Thus, although anthropocentricity in theology is not the opposite of the strictest theocentricity, it *is* opposed to the idea that in theology man is one particular theme among others, e.g. angels, the material world; or that it is possible to say something about God theologically without thereby automatically saying something about man and vice versa; or that these two kinds of statements are connected with one another in respect of their object, but not in the process of knowing itself.

...

What is revealed and then pondered upon in theology is not an arbitrary matter, but something which is intended for man's salvation. By this statement we do not imply the sort of principle (as in the case of 'fundamentalism') according to which certain objects can be excluded at the outset from the sphere of possible revelation, for what salvation really is is determined materially for the first time in the event of revelation. But the statement must be taken seriously. Only those things can belong to man's salvation which, when lacking, injure his 'being' and wholeness. Otherwise he could eschew salvation without thereby being in danger of losing it. This does not entail a rationalistic and unhistorical reduction of man to the status of an abstract transcendental being in his merely formal structure as such, as if what is historical and not deducible and what is experienced concretely *a posteriori* had no significance for salvation. It means that everything of significance for salvation is to be illuminated by referring it back to this transcendental being (which is not the same as *deducing* the significance *from* the transcendental being). In this sense, 'reduction' does not mean diminution but the process of establishing by reflex investigation. A comparison may clarify what is meant: the concrete beloved person who is the object of my love and in whom it is realized (and without whom it does not exist) cannot be deduced *a priori* from human possibilities, but is rather a historical occurrence, an indissoluble fact which has to be accepted. But in spite of this, such love for this concrete person can only be understood when one comprehends man as the being who must of necessity fulfil himself in love in order to be true to his nature. Even the most unpredictable, concrete love, occurring in history, must therefore be understood transcendentally in this way, in order that it may be what it should be. And this applies above all in the case of salvation. For even if this is a historical event, what it concerns is precisely man's actual nature; it is his nature which is to be consummated in salvation or the loss of it. If revelation and theology are essentially concerned with salvation as such, theology's structure when confronted with any object whatsoever is bound to imply the question as to man's nature, in so far as this nature is susceptible to 'saving' influence from the object involved. In other words, a theological object's significance for salvation (which is a necessary factor in any theological object) can only be investigated by inquiring at the same time as to man's *saving receptivity for* this object. However, this receptivity must not be investigated only 'in the abstract' nor merely presupposed in its most general aspects. It must be reflected upon with reference to the concrete object concerned, which is only *theologically relevant* as a result of and for the purpose of this receptiveness for salvation. Thereby the object also to some extent lays down the conditions for such receptiveness.

Source: Karl Rahner, Theological Investigations, *vol. 9, trans. Graham Harrison, London: Darton, Longman & Todd, 1972, pp. 28, 35–56.*

7.17 Robert Jenson, from *Essays in Theology of Culture*

In this passage Jenson argues that the distinction between humans and other animals is that humans are spoken to by God, and not just spoken about by God. Humans are both subject and object in relation to God.

First. We are not any kind of substance, temporal or eternal, supporting ourselves in being by holding on to certain attributes. We are *creatures*, and that is to say, we are radically contingent. There is nothing we are, do, or can do about maintaining ourselves in being. The most radical and precise formulation of this was by Thomas Aquinas, who – within the Aristotelian framework but in drastic violation of it – distinguished between 'existence' and 'essence'. My 'essence' is the sum total of all the attributes that I indeed do manifest. My 'existence' is the sheer fact that I am. Said Thomas: if we could list everything that is true about me, if we could give a complete description of my essence, on the list we would find no reason that I should be in the first place. None of the characteristics that I manifest are attributes in the genuine Socratic sense; that is to say, none are the support of my contingent reality. Rather I am supported in being and exist at any instant solely because it is willed that I be.

We are intrinsically – now let me use some language that comes out of my own systematics – *objects* of God. He knows us, he wills us, he chooses us. Putting all those together, he *intends* us. His consciousness is aimed at us as mine is now aimed at you. The difference between God and me is that you are there whether I intend you or not, but all there is to our being is being intended by God. God knows and wills us; and in that we are thus his objects, we are.

As Thomas said of the difference between God's knowledge and ours, we know what is already there whereas what God knows is there because he knows it. Switching now to my own system I say: we are in that God talks about us. The converse that between the Father and the Son in the Spirit is the life of God, the eternal, dialogical word that God is, is a word about us. And in that we are thus spoken about in the divine converse, we are and are what we are.

Second. The above is true of all creatures – amoebas, grains of sand, quarks. The specificity of humankind among the creatures, I suggest, is that whereas all creatures are that *about* which God speaks, humans are those creatures *to* whom he speaks. The law and the gospel are the intra-trinitarian converse of God, between the Father and the Son, let out so that we may hear what is said. To be specifically human is to be let in on that converse, to be not merely an object of it but a hearer of it, to be not merely one of those about whom the word of God speaks but also one to whom this same word of God is spoken. To be human, therefore, is to hear the law and the gospel.

Third. If I am not only spoken about but spoken to, I am established not merely as an object, not merely as the target of intention, but as subject also. For to be spoken to is to be called upon to reply. Thus humans are those called upon to reply to God; that is, the behavioural reality of specifically human being is *prayer*. The doing of specifically human being, of being addressed by God, is prayer. An Aristotle-style definition of human being would be: humans are the praying animals.

I really should tell you about penguins. On several occasions I have taught seminars on theological anthropology for the students at Gettysburg. When the discussion thus stretches over a whole semester, we of course spend a lot of time on this matter of what it means to be human as over against being other kinds of being. We run through all the suggestions that are made: humans are the talking animals, or humans are the reasoning animals, or whatever. And then we always get long disquisitions on those chimpanzees that can be taught to use language. Of course, one does not need experimental results; all one has to say is, 'Well, how do you know termites don't talk?' In one seminar, we settled on penguins. For every suggestion that was made, one student always asked, 'But Jenson, how do you know penguins don't …?' (At the end of the semester the class chipped in and bought a wall hanging of penguins, which now hangs on our wall.) The answer is that one does not know. I do not know even that penguins do not pray. But if they pray, then they are human in my sense. In any case, the point that I would want to make is this: the specificity of humankind is not that we talk; the specificity of humankind is to whom we talk.

Fourth. Over against God, that is to say, we are not only objects but also subjects, not only spoken about but also spoken to and drawn to reply. That is to say, we are participants in the conversation that is the divine life. And that is to say, the soteriology of the Eastern church is better than we have thought. Since Harnack, it has been assumed that the Eastern church's language about divinization was a smuggling of Hellenistic mysticism into the pure gospel. This is an error. The Eastern church's talk about divinization is the message that the final fulfilment of human being is to become not merely spectator but participant in the triune life of God; for it is the *triune* God of which they spoke. And that seems to me to be precisely what the Bible says.

Fifth. We are not merely objects of God but also subjects to God; and that duality replicates itself in our existence, for we are only what we are over against God. I am both subject and object, and the marvel is that I am object to myself as subject. This mysterious phenomenon is the first thing anthropological reflection notices whenever such reflection occurs. Somehow I can be outside myself so as to look at myself; somehow I am beyond myself so as to be my own object.

But now, this object that I am to myself as subject, what sort of being is it? It is a subject, just as you are objectively a subject for me. So there are two subjects here. And that means – and here is, I think, the legitimacy of Augustine's doctrine of trinitarian *vestigia* – that like God, I am a conversation within myself, that my lived active being is an interior dialogue. As subject, I know myself as object; but the weird thing is that this object answers back. This is widely observed; depth psychology posits a whole populace of interior voices.

I am an interior conversation; and it is this that Christian theology and, following Christian theology, much philosophy calls 'spirit'. That I am not merely what I am but that I am what I am in a conversation within me about what I am, is what is meant by calling me 'spirit' or, alternatively, 'free'. I am not simply what I am; but I am what I am in a conversation about what I ought to be, what I can be. That is freedom.

Sixth and last in this series. That I am not merely subject but that I am subject and object for myself, and everything that follows from this, is *communally* mediated. That I am subject and then object for myself, and that this is very mysterious, need not remain a mere surd to reflection. Something can be said about how all this comes to pass. You have me as your object. Insofar as we address one another, insofar as we *communicate,* insofar, that is to say, as we establish a common world, within that common world that you and I have together I appear as the object that I am to you. And *so,* I suggest, I am object to myself. Human freedom, human reality as spirit, is communally mediated. I would not have it were I isolated. I am object to myself in that I am object to you and in that you and I share a world in which I am object.

Source: Robert Jenson, Essays in Theology of Culture, *Grand Rapids, MI: Eerdmans, 1995, pp. 111–14.*

7.18 Leonardo Boff, from *Trinity and Society*

Boff argues that personhood is rightly understood as relational. Humans and human communities and societies should reflect the openness of the Godhead, the community of persons who invite us to participate in the divine life.

Consideration of the communion of the three distinct beings of the Trinity produces a critical attitude to personhood, community, society and church. On the personal level, our dominant culture stresses the predominance of isolated personal development, of the rights of individuals divorced from any consideration of their relation to society. The a-trinitarian monotheism of the churches, their ideology of subjectivity, of unity/identity, serve both to reinforce and reflect this distortion. Seeing people as image and likeness of the Trinity implies always setting them in open relationship with others; it is only through being with others, understanding themselves as others see them, being through others, that they can build their own identities. Personal incommunicability exists only so as to allow communion with other people. In the light of the Trinity, being a person in the image and likeness of the divine Persons means acting as a permanently active web of relationships: relating backwards and upwards to one's origin in the unfathomable mystery of the Father, relating outwards to one's fellow human beings by revealing oneself to them and welcoming the revelation of them in the mystery of the Son, relating inwards to the depths of one's own personality in the mystery of the Spirit.

The Trinity forms an open communion going beyond the existence of the three Persons by including creation. So in the same way human beings cannot concentrate on their own interpersonal relations to the exclusion of a sense of their wider, trans-personal and structural relationships, with society and history. Personalization through communion must not lead to a personalism alienated from the conflicts and processes of social change, but must seek to establish new, more participatory and humanizing relationships. The same criticism applies to the community, with its network of close relationships integrating individuals with their work, life and common interest; the community has to place itself within a greater whole, since it cannot exist as a closed and reconciled little world of its own. 'Communitarianism' is close to anarchy.

...

Trinitarian communion is a source of inspiration rather than of criticism in the social sphere. Christians committed to social change based on the needs of majorities, above all, see tri-unity as their permanent utopia. The three 'Differents' uphold their difference one from another; by upholding the other and giving themselves totally to the other, they become 'Differents' in communion. In the Trinity there is no domination by one side, but convergence of the Three in mutual acceptance and giving. They are different but none is greater or lesser, before or after. Therefore a society that takes its inspiration from trinitarian communion cannot tolerate class differences, dominations based on power (economic, sexual or ideological) that subjects those who are different to those who exercise that power and marginalizes the former from the latter.

The sort of society that would emerge from inspiration by the trinitarian model would be one of fellowship, equality of opportunity, generosity in the space available for personal and group expression. Only a society of sisters and brothers whose social fabric is woven out of participation and communion of all in everything can justifiably claim to be an image and likeness (albeit pale) of the Trinity, the foundation and final resting-place of the universe.

Source: Leonardo Boff, Trinity and Society, *trans. Paul Burns, Maryknoll, NY: Orbis Books and Tunbridge Wells: Burns & Oates, 1988, pp. 148–51.*

7.19 John Zizioulas, from *Being as Communion*

Zizioulas rejects biology as the ground of personhood, and argues instead for an ecclesial hypostasis. Humans are recreated through their baptism and exist as free beings, not bound by biological necessity.

The *hypostasis of ecclesial existence* is constituted by the new birth of man, by baptism. Baptism as new birth is precisely an act constitutive of hypostasis. As the conception and birth of a man constitute his biological hypostasis, so baptism leads to a new mode of existence, to a regeneration (1 Peter 1:3,23), and consequently to a new 'hypostasis.' What is the basis of this new hypostasis? How is man hypostasized by baptism and what does he become?

We have seen that the fundamental problem of the biological hypostasis of man lies in the fact that the ecstatic activity which leads to his birth is bound up with the 'passion' of ontological necessity, in the fact that ontologically nature precedes the person and dictates its laws (by 'instinct'), thus destroying freedom at its ontological base. This 'passion' is closely connected with createdness, that is, with the fact that man as a person confronts, as we have already seen, the necessity of existence. Consequently it is impossible for created existence to escape ontological necessity in the constitution of the biological hypostasis: without 'necessary' natural laws, that is, without ontological necessity, the biological hypostasis of man cannot exist.

Consequently, if, in order to avoid the consequences of the tragic aspect of man which we have discussed, the person as absolute ontological freedom needs a hypostatic constitution without ontological necessity, his hypostasis must inevitably be rooted, or constituted, in an ontological reality which does not suffer from createdness. This is the meaning of the phrase in Scripture about being born 'anew' or 'from above' (John 3:3,7). It is precisely this possibility that patristic Christology strives to proclaim, to announce to man as good news ...

Christology consequently is the proclamation to man that his nature can be 'assumed' and hypostasized in a manner free from the ontological necessity of his biological hypostasis, which, as we have seen, leads to the tragedy of individualism and death. Thanks to Christ man can henceforth himself 'subsist,' can affirm his existence as personal not on the basis of the immutable laws of his nature, but on the basis of a relationship with God which is identified with what Christ in freedom and love possesses as Son of God with the Father. This adoption of man by God, the identification of his hypostasis with the hypostasis of the Son of God, is the essence of baptism.

I have called this hypostasis which baptism gives to man 'ecclesial' because, in fact, if one should ask, 'How do we see this new biological hypostasis of man realised in history?' the reply would be, 'In the Church.' In early patristic literature the image of the Church as a mother is often employed. The spirit of this image is precisely that in the Church a birth is brought about; man is born as 'hypostasis,' as person. This new hypostasis of man has all the basic characteristics of what I have called authentic personhood, characteristics which distinguish the ecclesial hypostasis from the first hypostasis, the biological one. In what do these characteristics consist?

The first and most important characteristic of the Church is that she brings man into a kind of relationship with the world which is not determined by the laws of biology. The Christians of the early centuries, when their consciousness of what the Church is was lucid and clear, expressed this transcendence over the relationships created by the biological hypostasis by transferring *to the Church* the terminology which is used of the family. Thus for the new ecclesial hypostasis 'father' was not the physical progenitor but He 'who is in heaven,' and 'brothers' were the members of the Church, not of the family. That this signified not a parallel co-existence of the ecclesial with the biological hypostasis but a transcendence of the latter by the former is apparent from the harshness of sayings like those which demand of Christians the abandonment – even the 'hatred' – of their own relations. These sayings do not signify a simple denial. They conceal an affirmation: the Christian through baptism stands over against the world, he exists as a relationship with the world, as a person, in a manner free from the relationship created by his biological identity. This means that henceforth he can love not because the laws of biology oblige him to do so – something which inevitably colors the love of one's own relations – but *unconstrained* by the natural laws. As an ecclesial hypostasis man thus proves that what is valid for God can also be valid for man: the nature does not determine the person; the person enables the nature to exist; freedom is identified with the being of man.

The result of this freedom of the person from the nature, of the hypostasis from biology, is that in the Church man transcends exclusivism. When man loves as a biological hypostasis, he inevitably excludes others: the family has priority on love over 'strangers,' the husband lays exclusive claim to the love of his wife – facts altogether understandable and 'natural' for the biological hypostasis. For a man to love someone who is not a member of his family *more* than his own relations constitutes a transcendence of the exclusiveness which is present in the biological hypostasis. Thus a characteristic of the ecclesial hypostasis is the capacity of the person to love without exclusiveness, and to do this not out of conformity with a moral commandment ('Love thy Neighbor' etc.), but out of his 'hypostatic constitution,' out of the fact that his new birth from the womb of the Church has made him part of a network of relationships which transcend every exclusiveness. This means that only in the Church has man the power to express himself as a catholic person. Catholicity, as a characteristic of the Church, permits the person to become a hypostasis without falling into individuality, because in the Church two things are realized simultaneously: the world is presented to man not as mutually exclusive portions which he is called upon to unite *a posteriori*, but as a single whole, which is expressed in a catholic manner without division in every concrete being; simultaneously the same man, while relating to the world precisely through this catholic mode of existence that he has, comes to express and realize a catholic presence in the world, a hypostasis which is not an individual but an authentic person. Thus the Church becomes Christ Himself in human existence, but also every member of the Church becomes Christ and Church. The ecclesial hypostasis is the *faith* of man in his capacity to become a person and his *hope* that he will indeed become an authentic person. In other words it is faith and hope in the immortality of man as a person.

Source: John Zizioulas, Being as Communion: Studies in Personhood and the Church, *Crestwood, NY: St Vladimir's Seminary Press and London: Darton, Longman & Todd, 1985, pp. 53–8.*

7.20 Colin Gunton, from *The Triune Creator*

Here Gunton argues that human beings have a unique status in the created order. Humans are made in the image of God, and the image cannot be completely destroyed even by the most evil acts.

The doctrine of the image of God shares with the other topics we have encountered intrinsic difficulties which are complicated by the history of their articulation. The literature on the doctrine of the image of God is immense, and, like other immensities of discussion, comes to no agreed conclusion. If there is something approaching a consensus in recent theology, it is the belief, going at least as far back as Philo of Alexandria, that the image of God consists in human rationality, requires, at the very least, to be radically qualified. Asking what differentiated the human from the non-human creation, many early theologians drew on aspects of philosophical thought to say that it was reason, and then drew the further conclusion that this difference was that in which the image consisted. That might be part of the truth, but none the less derives from asking the wrong question: about the way in which the human is different from the non-human – the secondary question – not the primary one of the distinctive human being-in-relation to God ...

A second problem is that the doctrine of the image appears but rarely in scripture, so that any theological use of the concept must serve as the conceptual means of saying something about human being according to the whole of the teaching of scripture. As with the doctrine of creation as a whole, we are concerned primarily not with the texts which refer to the image explicitly – though we must do justice to them – but with whether or not the concept enables us to articulate something of what it is to be a human creature in relation to God. For historical reasons, we cannot articulate a doctrine of the human creature without putting this concept somewhere near the centre, because it is the vehicle of so much discussion of the topic. Yet, as we have seen, the history is in many ways so problematic that much care is necessary if misunderstanding is not to result.

Third, and complicating the matter systematically, is the fact that in speaking of the image we are not speaking of the order of creation alone. We have seen already that the doctrine of creation cannot be adequately treated without due reference to redemption, both in the present and in eschatological perspective. That is doubly the case here, for not only is man in some way at the heart of the problem of evil, in some way or other involving the created order in the fall, but also in the New Testament the assimilation of image language almost exclusively to Jesus Christ means that the doctrine is now concerned as much with new creation as with creation: with the redemption of the distorted image as much as with its status as creation. We cannot, as has been argued above, begin to understand the creation apart from the meditation of the Son and the Spirit. In relation to the image of God, this becomes, if that is possible, even more crucial a consideration, for while the non-human creation retains a measure of good order, albeit an often disrupted order, the fallen human creature is characterised by an active creativity in evil, as the history of our century only too well testifies. Just as, therefore, we cannot understand the creation apart from Christ, so we fail even more completely to understand human being apart from Christ, and particularly apart from Christ crucified ...

That brings us to the most pressing problem of the doctrine of the image of God. It has to do with the status of our createdness given not only its incompleteness, but its corruption. We may be in the image of God in so far as we are like the human Jesus, but in what sense and how far do those who can be called the ordinarily sinful, let alone the most depraved, remain like him? The situation is similar to, but more difficult than, that of the general problem of the doctrine of creation. In affirming that the creation, because it is the work and gift of God, is good, it is necessary to conclude that evil – in so far as we are sure that we know what that is – is not intrinsic to the creation, but some corruption of, or invasion into, that which is essentially good. In the case of the human creature, we have the case of one not only capable, but also guilty, of offences against others made in the image of God which too often confound the imagination. A doctrine like that of the image of God, which claims universality, must be able to deal with the hardest cases. They are of two kinds.

The first concerns, as we seen, moral corruption: the manifest unfreedom of much of our existence, enslaved as we are, apart from redemption, to sin and 'the powers'. The question is whether those so enslaved to evil as to be virtually deprived of the capacity to love are thus far deprived of personhood, which, as I shall later claim, is the heart of the matter of the image. What are we to make of those who, it appears, can no longer love in freedom: those daemonic persons ... who are so enslaved to the lie that they call evil their good, consigning millions of those made in the image of God to gas chambers or death by war, poisoning or starvation? What are we to make of those who so violate the order of being that their likeness to the human Jesus is discernible only by their physical shape? One cannot locate the image of God in freedom or creativity, if there are those whose creativity is only, or largely, in evil; or even in love when there are those so alienated from their creator that love is overridden by hatred, destructiveness and violence. What God has created, he has created; or, to adapt a saying of Ockham, what God has created stays created unless he chooses to annihilate it, so that we cannot deny even to the perpetrators of monstrous evils the fact that they are made and, in some respects remain, in the image of their creator, uniquely of the whole created order. Similarly, the second and less difficult case theologically, but problem enough in modern culture, there are the physically and mentally handicapped. Again, if we take the worst cases, in what sense are we to regard as in the image of God those so incapacitated as to be incapable of any 'human' response, let alone the rationality or consciousness traditionally ascribed to those in the image: the senile, the victims of brain damage, or, at the other end of the scale of life, the foetus? We must say at least that those whose physical shape is deformed or not yet fully formed retain the intrinsic dignity conferred by virtue of their inextinguishable relation to God the Father through Christ and the Spirit.

More trinitarianly, we should say that even the apparently irremediably lost remain in the likeness of God because he continues, in Christ, to be creator, whether freedom to love is exercised or rejected for slavery. This means that however horrible the deformity, however great the need for redemption in its broadest sense, those created in God's image remain so, and hence Genesis' prohibition on killing one so created. (Here, of course, is the heart of the objection to capital punishment and 'euthanasia'.) At the very least, the human being, simply as created, is of the kind of *being* that a certain radical moral respect is due to every human person, however sunk in villainy and depravity. This entails at the very least the ascription of a certain unique *status*, though what it is can surely not be understood without some form of ontology – because status, certainly status before God, is a mode of being. It would seem to follow, then, that, as created, the image of God is in a sense something given, even though it can finally be perfected only eschatologically, and through redemption. That something given cannot be taken away, except by God, because it is part of what it is to be a created human being.

Source: Colin Gunton, The Triune Creator: A Historical and Systematic Study, *Grand Rapids, MI: Eerdmans and Edinburgh: Edinburgh University Press, 1998, pp. 193–204.*

7.21 Alistair McFadyen, from *The Call to Personhood*

McFadyen explores the meaning of the fall for humanity and argues that human beings remain in the image of God, but have distorted this image by rejecting their relationship with and dependence on God. McFadyen further argues that ethics is not a matter of choosing between right and wrong, but stems from faithful relationship with God.

The choice posed by the Serpent in the story of the fall (Genesis 3) was between the constitution of human being either in obedience and faithfulness on the one hand, or in the making and giving of laws on the other. The choice is between orientating oneself through faithfulness to values transcending oneself (otherness), or to oneself and one's own values alone and without limit. Constitution in fidelity and obedience denotes an ex-centric orientation in the free recognition of values external to but with claims upon the self. In the free (*voluntas*) response there is a recognition of an extrinsic law with an intrinsic claim. Law-giving, in contradistinction, represents a self-constitution which, in a purely individual act of freedom (*arbtrarium*), recognises as binding only that which is self-chosen ... This represents a reversal of creation since it is a rejection of the reality of God and the other as intrinsically related to oneself; their rejection, more precisely, as claim and limit. Instead of accepting the other as other in dialogue, as a transcendent limit and claim who can never be assimilated by oneself, there is here the desire to overcome, deny or possess one's limit. The fall represents the desire to be a self-constituting and isolated being rather than a limited creature.

The fracture of relations with one another and with God is the immediate result of the decision to transgress the limits placed on humanity by God to eat the fruit of the tree of knowledge and become like God. The narrative offers a powerful image of this disruption in terms of shame: Adam and Eve can no longer stand before one another openly, in their nakedness, neither can they stand before God and admit what they have done – first they hide, then Adam blames Eve and Eve the Serpent (3:7–14).

The Christian doctrine of the fall is an attempt to recognise and bring to expression the distortion of human being in the image. The image is a norm for communication which is not presently realised. It exists therefore only as a norm or ideal and has a future aspect. It is both an ontological structure of freedom and a project towards its future reconstitution. The Christian understanding of fall implies that that reconstitution cannot come through human activity alone because, first, the concrete conditions of human communication have become overbearingly distorted and, second, the attempt at reconstitution in isolation from God would only be repetition of the fall and so a further accumulation of its effects. The future orientation of the image is to be understood in terms of the active coinherence of the three Trinitarian Persons who were similarly working together in its creation. In the future enlivening power of the Spirit the image is directed towards God's future communication in creation-redemption, a future in which all three Persons are involved but in which the Spirit and Son/Word have particular significance. Communication cannot be redeemed by our acting alone, but only in partnership with God and one another as we make autonomous responses to God's address as it continues through history. In Christian tradition there is a witness to the mode of this continuance through history as the call of Christ ...

The doctrine of the fall means that the question of the right practice of relations (ethics) has to be relocated. The ethical question cannot be equated with possession of the knowledge of the difference between good and evil, for that is precisely the form of self-possession which led to the fall. Adam and Eve thought they could dispute what God's Word really meant, get behind it to judge both it and God. The assumptions that we have the capacity to know the difference between right and wrong and to act upon it is in itself and on its own already a corruption of the image. It isolates one from God and others because what is right for one and others is assumed to be already known. The assumption that one already knows what is right stops communication because no new information or external agency is necessary.

Source: Alistair McFadyen, The Call to Personhood: A Christian Theory of the Individual in Social Relationships, *Cambridge: Cambridge University Press, 1990, pp. 42–4.*

7.22 Elaine Storkey, from *Created or Constructed*

Storkey discusses the nature of gender and argues that it is part of the cre-
ated order, but that sex or gender are secondary to the shared category of
personhood.

A perspective that would try to be faithful to the historic Christian faith would begin from a different Archimedean point from either biology, culture or experience. It would start from the acceptance that there is a God, and a world of which we are a part. The God who is there is the God whom the Christian Scriptures, in an unfolding revelation, reveal to us: a God who is relational, a God whose name is love, a God who is interpersonal and involved with the creation. This creating God is one who sets boundaries and breathes morality into the creation, and who constantly offers us the opportunity to change our lives for the better. What is more, God is expressed uniquely and personally in Jesus Christ to whom the Scriptures and the Church bear witness. Christ, in union with the whole Godhead, is the one who has given his life for ours, who offers the power of the Spirit to those who ask, who shows a new kind of authority and breaks down barriers between people. Our 'credal' starting point would also have a commitment to the Bible, not simply for its narrative history or theological teachings, but because it discloses who God is and who we are; it unlocks the truth of God for us. But the Bible has to be understood aright, which involves us in also recognizing that we might get it wrong because our experience is not the primary exegetical hermeneutic. Rather, the Bible contains its own hermeneutical tools; it holds the truth to its own meaning and interpretation.

From this perspective, many things follow. To start with, we can accept that our sexuality is indeed 'given', part of the rich created structure of our humanness. The differences in our sexual make-up are part of the rich complementarity which God has breathed into creation. Yet a creational perspective is different from a 'natural' one; sexuality is not simply that which defines our 'nature'. Creation is ordered, not by something people used to call the 'laws of nature' but by complex normative structures which define and delineate our various relationships. For example, we are not to murder, or to commit adultery; we are to love our neighbours as ourselves; we are not to steal or violate one another. God has regulated the structure of reality, breathed an ethical order into it, and that has implications for our sexuality. Far from being driven by the unremitting desire to procreate, we are given responsibility to use our sexuality wisely and to act always in love. How we express our sexuality matters, and we remain accountable to God.

…

The distinction between sex and gender is also important, because it helps to avoid the temptation to reduce everything to sex. Yet I think it would be a mistake to think too rigidly of sex as creational and gender as cultural. This suggests too big a dichotomy, that we accept our sex as a creation of God, but we create our gender for ourselves, according to social variants. In fact, if we believe in a God who has given a normative structure to relationships, we have to believe in a God who is as interested in our gender as in our biology. For the way we shape our gender is also part of our human response before God. And so we do need to address issues of power, discrimination, poor communication, injustice, unfaithfulness, violation, competitiveness and stereotypes, because in all of these areas we can contravene the principles which God has given us for gender relationships. We need to develop loving, just, impartial, faithful and open ways of relating with one another, for then we are responding together to the God who is love, justice, righteousness, faithfulness and truth. God calls us into responsible and right relationships, and gender patterns call from us a response of obedience.

We need, therefore, to resist the crippling stereotypes whether they are racial or gender or whatever else, and we need also to recognize that despite popular exhortations, the Bible does not say a great deal about being masculine for God or feminine for Jesus! So many of the stereotypes which proliferate in 'Christian' literature are far from biblical. In fact, the New Testament does not tell us how to be feminine or masculine at all. It offers us one set of characteristics as a guideline for both sexes, the 'fruits of the Spirit': love, joy, peace, patience, kindness, goodness, faithfulness, gentleness and self-control. The fact that these are often interpreted as 'feminine characteristics' ought to set us thinking ...

Source: Elaine Storkey, Created or Constructed? The Great Gender Debate, *Sydney: University of New South Wales Press and Carlisle: Paternoster Press, 2000, pp. 112–15.*

7.23 Kathryn Tanner, from *Jesus, Humanity and the Trinity*

In this passage, Tanner argues that the primary purpose of human life is not to 'do' anything, but to receive God's gifts. She goes on to argue that human life is perfected only through Christ, and only eschatologically, but that we are already assumed into Christ, regardless of moral merit. This assumption does not deny human freedom but enables it. Christians are called to imitate Christ, but Tanner argues that this should be understood broadly and does not inevitably require suffering and self-sacrifice.

One might begin this discussion of theological ethics by asking what our lives are for, theologically conceived. Why have we been created? For what purpose? What ends are we to serve? My theological anthropology appears, indeed, to be a task – or vocation-oriented one. The Son is sent by the Father in the power of the Spirit to bring us into the gift-giving relations enjoyed among members of the Trinity; living our lives in Christ according to the mode of the Son, should involve, then, our own service to that mission, spreading the gifts of the Father that are ours in Christ, empowered by the Son's own Spirit.

While this is all true, my incarnation-centered Christology, and account of the Trinity as an overflowing superabundant source, undercut in fundamental ways the usual presuppositions of such task-orientated questions. In the final analysis, God does not so much want something *of* us as want to be *with* us. God does not really need us *for* anything. There is nothing yet to achieve beyond what God's own trinitarian perfection already instantiates. In giving rise to the creature and elevating it to God's own level, God is always bringing about something less rather than something more than what the triune God already *is* in itself. Without hopes of any advance on God's own goodness thereby, God's gifts to the creature are a kind of love-filled non-purposive or gratuitous trinitarian overflow – something like the aura or penumbra that a generously fecund sun gives off for nothing into the surrounding darkness of space …

In a similar fashion, an incarnation-centered Christology emphasizes the fact that God does not so much require something of us as want to give something *to* us. Our lives are for nothing in the sense that we are here simply to be the recipients of God's good gifts. Thus, the gift of our assumption into the life of Christ through the power of the Holy Spirit is the presupposition and continual foundation of all our action in the mode of the Son, just as the incarnation was the supporting condition of the sort of life Jesus led. We do not have to achieve anything as a requirement for inclusion in Christ's own life. The acts of ours that initiate and maintain relationship with Christ are brought about by the workings of the Holy Spirit and are acts that point away from our own powers and capacities to Christ and what he has already done for us. Nor are our achievements, particularly in the realm of morals, a requirement for sustaining our assumption by Christ. However good or bad our lives, whether our lives reflect our assumption by Christ adequately or not – most certainly, mostly not – by the power of the Spirit we continue to lead them in Christ.

Within this non-purposive context, however, purposive action, our action for ends, maintains its proper place. The already replete triune God may not need anything from us, but the world does, especially in so far as it is our very sinful actions that hinder the world's reception of God's gifts. We are called to act in a process primarily of self-reformation in service of God's ends for the whole world that the superabundant God wants to be similarly replete with goods ...

That, assumed by Christ, our activity is *free* becomes evident from the nature of our imitation of Christ's life, the nature of our correspondence to it. We are not called to slavishly imitate the events of Jesus' life; there is no need for that. What Jesus does to save us is done by him for us so that we need not repeat it. For example, sin and death are overcome by the Son's assumption of death and sin on the cross; should we suffer at the hands of those resisting the Father's mission of beneficence we need not suffer this for the sake of the same saving purpose. Moreover, we need not slavishly imitate the events of Christ's life because Christ is ours in any case. We do and suffer with Christ all that Christ did and suffered whether or not something like those events recur in our own lives, whether or not, for example, something like a crucifixion occurs in our lives as a consequence of our joining Christ in his mission for others. We are crucified with Christ in any case because we are united with him as the crucified one, because the whole of his life becomes our own in our being assumed by him.

Rather than expect a repetition of Jesus' life in our own, when we are assumed by Christ, it is our lives as the contemporary people we are who are so assumed and transformed thereby according to the form of Christ. We follow Christ where he leads in our own lives, shaped as those lives already are by the forces of contemporary times and cultures. Christ's life is extended in new directions as it incorporates our lives within it. Though the mode of sonship will carry across all differences of space and time, exactly where we will be led in Christ is not easily foreseen from the specifics of Jesus' own life as those reflect an historical distance of two thousand years. Assumed by Christ as Jesus' humanity was assumed by the Son of God, we must do as Jesus did and live out a union with God in ways appropriate to our own circumstances.

What we see here on the topic of human freedom – that imitation of Christ is only properly understood when Jesus' life is not abstracted from incarnation and from the saving point of that – helps clarify the import of imitating Christ on a number of other fronts. For example, we should not make Jesus' holiness in abstraction from the incarnation an object for our imitation through the power of the Spirit. As we saw in the first chapter, Jesus' sinlessness is not a static property for our imitation, but something that takes shape in a process of overcoming temptation as that process is empowered by the fact of Jesus' being the Word incarnate. Jesus does not have his perfection as an achieved state, short of his resurrection, and certainly neither will we, assumed by Christ and battling active sin through the Spirit of Christ that thereby indwells us. We have thus achieved perfection only eschatologically; it is ours now only as we live in Christ's own glorified humanity, and will be our very humanity's own only when its reformation according to the form of Christ is complete – something that never appears to us to be finally the case. If Jesus' humanity is nevertheless perfect from the first – despite his formation in sinlessness in a process over time – this perfection must be nothing like that of a moral hero or moral virtuoso. It seems, on the contrary, to be the perfection of someone wholly devoted to the Father's cause, someone ever recognising his need as a human being, grateful for what he has received and willing in prayer to call upon the Father's help as the source of all good for his own sake and that of others. If Jesus' perfection as an agent cannot be understood apart from the assumption of his humanity by the Son of God or apart from his relation to the Father, then neither should ours. Short of an achieved perfection that is ours only eschatologically, we are sanctified through life in Christ not in virtue of being morally perfect but in virtue of the eccentric, God-ward reference of our efforts, clinging to Christ in the Spirit, and invoking the Father's aid in union with Christ, in our dedication to the Father's own mission of beneficent gift-giving.

When Jesus' life is not abstracted from his humanity's assumption by the Word and its soteriological point, the call to imitate Christ, to correspond in action to Christ's own life, also moves away from any simple valorization of self-denial or self-sacrifice. The sacrifices made in Christ can no longer be primarily identified with Jesus' passive sufferings on the cross. The sacrifice that the Son of God makes by assuming all aspects of human existence in a state of suffering and sin to be his own and the sacrifice that the human being Jesus makes in remaining in solidarity with us suffering sinners despite his unity with the Son, range over the course of Jesus' life, in all that Jesus does or undergoes. These sacrifices should be matched in the whole of our own lives as re-directed by the beneficent mission of the Father. We are to immerse ourselves in the struggle and trouble of the world for the good's sake. The sacrifices of Christ's life, broadly construed now, are not, furthermore, good in and of themselves. They are such only 'economically' as the patristic writers would say, only as a means to overcoming the very sin and suffering to which they are a response. There is nothing good about suffering in a narrow sense, then, apart from efforts to carry out the Son's beneficent mission of the Father, which the Son has shared with us. The suffering undergone by those dedicated to the Father's cause is, moreover, the product of the world's opposition to it, the product of sin's refusal of that beneficence; that suffering is not itself, therefore, a good gift from God. And, finally, such suffering is not self-sacrificial in Christ's life and therefore neither should it be in ours. Jesus' own humanity is exalted and perfected by the sacrifices of Jesus' life; he is not merely acting for others, at the expense of himself.

Source: Kathryn Tanner, Jesus, Humanity and the Trinity: A Brief Systematic Theology, Minneapolis: Fortress Press, 2001, pp. 67–76.

7.24 Valerie Saiving, from 'The Human Situation: A Feminine View'

In this extract Saiving talks about the difference between masculine and feminine experience, and challenges the definitions of sin proposed by many theologians. She argues that for women, temptation and sin are often very different, indeed the opposite of most theological definitions.

I am no longer as certain as I once was that when theologians speak of 'man' they are using the word in its generic sense. It is, after all, a well-known fact that theology has been written almost exclusively by men. This alone should put us on our guard, especially since contemporary theologians constantly remind us that one of man's strongest temptations is to identify his own limited perspective with universal truth ...

It is my contention that there are significant differences between masculine and feminine experience and that feminine experience reveals in a more emphatic fashion certain aspects of the human situation which are present but less obvious in the experience of men. Contemporary theological doctrines of love have, I believe, been constructed primarily upon the basis of masculine experience and thus view the human condition from the male standpoint. Consequently, these doctrines do not provide an adequate interpretation of the situation of women – nor, for that matter, of men, especially in view of certain fundamental changes now taking place in our own society ...

For the temptations of woman *as woman* are not the same as the temptations of man *as man*, and the specifically feminine forms of sin – 'feminine' not because they are confined to women or because women are incapable of sinning in other ways but because they are outgrowths of the basic feminine character structure – have a quality which can never be encompassed by such terms as 'pride' and 'will-to-power.' They are better suggested by such items as triviality, distractibility, and diffuseness; lack of an organizing center or focus; dependence on other's for one's own self-definition; tolerance at the expense of standards of excellence; inability to respect the boundaries of privacy; sentimentality; gossipy sociability, and mistrust of reason – in short, underdevelopment or negation of the self.

This list of specifically feminine sins could be extended. All of them, however, are to be understood as merely one side of the feminine coin. For just as man's distance from nature is the precondition of his creativity, on the one hand, and his self-concern, on the other, so does woman's closeness to nature have dipolar potentialities. Her sureness of her own femininity and thus of her secure place in the scheme of things may, if she accepts the feminine role with joy, enable her to be a source of strength and refreshment to her husband, her children, and the wider community. If she has been brought up to devalue her femininity, on the other hand, this same sense that for her 'anatomy is destiny' may create an attitude of stolid and sterile resignation, a feeling that there is no use in trying. Again, the fact that her whole growth toward womanhood has the character of an inevitable process of bodily maturation rather than that of a challenge and a task may lead her to dissipate herself in activities which are merely trivial. Yet it is the same lack of creative drive which may make it possible for her to perform cheerfully the thousand-and-one routine tasks – the woman's work which is never done – which someone must do if life is to go on. Her capacity for surrendering her individual concerns in order to serve the immediate needs of others – a quality which is so essential to the maternal role – can, on the other hand, induce a kind of diffuseness of purpose, a tendency toward being easily distracted, a failure to discriminate between the more and the less important, and an inability to focus in a sustained manner on the pursuit of any single goal. Her receptivity to the moods and feelings of others and her tendency to merge her selfhood in the joys, sorrows, hopes, and problems of those around her are the positive expressions of an aspect of the feminine character which may also take the negative forms of gossipy sociability, dependence on others (such as husband or children) for the definition of her values, or a refusal to respect another's right to privacy. And her capacity for forgiving love, for cherishing all her children equally without regard to beauty, merit, or intelligence, can also express itself in a kind of indiscriminate tolerance which suspects or rejects all objective criteria of excellence.

All this is not meant to constitute an indictment of the feminine character as such. I have no wish, certainly, to add to the burden of guilt which has been heaped upon women – by themselves as well as by men – for centuries. My purpose, indeed, as far as it concerns women in particular, is quite the opposite. It is to awaken theologians to the fact that the situation of woman, however similar it may appear on the surface of our contemporary world to the situation of man and however much it may be echoed in the life of individual men, is, at bottom, quite different – that the specifically feminine dilemma is, in fact, precisely the opposite of the masculine.

Source: Valerie Saiving, 'The Human Situation: A Feminine View', in Carol Christ and Judith Plaskow (eds), Womanspirit Rising: A Feminist Reader in Religion, *San Francisco: Harper, 1979, pp. 25, 27, 37–9.*

7.25 Sarah Coakley, from *Powers and Submissions*

Coakley reviews Augustine and Gregory of Nyssa's understanding of gen-
der difference and argues that both have led to practices in the Church
that must be rejected by Christian feminists.

According to Gregory [of Nyssa], there is a double creation: in the first instance
a non-sexual and purely spiritual creation (for it is assumed by Gregory that to
be truly 'in the image of God' the creature must be angelic, non-physical); only
in the second instance and 'with a view to the Fall' is bodily nature added,
both male and female. On this view, then, the female creature is not regarded
as intrinsically more physical or bodily than the male; but both the origins and
goal of perfect creatureliness lie in a sort of humanoid state, where sexual differentiation is *irrelevant*. In Augustine, by contrast, the existence of the sexes
is from the start 'intrinsic to creation', and sexual relations – without passion,
however! – are part of God's good intentions. This might appear to be potentially a more promising picture for women, were it not for the sting in the tail:
the disjunction of spirit and corporeality, with woman being fatally identified
with the latter. Augustine sees the male, alone, as the proper and full image
of God. He contains both 'male' spirit and 'female' bodiliness within himself,
whereas the woman is *intrinsically* carnal, subordinate to the male, and in the
image of God only insofar as she conjoins herself with her husband ...

Now if we align this material with the insights already gleaned from attend-
ing to the different emphases of Eastern and Western trinitarianism, we may
arrive at some interesting results. In the East, first, there emerges a fascinating
correlation between the *ideology* of *houmoousian* equality in the 'persons' of
the Godhead on the one hand, and creaturely equality of humanoid souls on
the other. But we cannot help asking whether the *realities* are not in both cases
actually more hierarchical and subordinationist than the ideology allows. For
all its appeal to the natural and fortuitous inclusiveness of its *anthrōpos* language, the Greek Church – we could surely all agree – is not noted for its
granting of equal ministerial roles to women; and it is these *practical* issues
which are the acid test in the long run ...

In the West, however, one may suggest a different point of correlation
between the trinitarian theology of Augustine and his views on male and
female creatureliness, but one that is perhaps also telling. Running through
the various different psychological analogies of the *De Trinitate* is the insistence on the right operation and *harmony* of the faculties of the soul (memory,
understanding and will) which mirror the coinherent relations of the divine
triad. It is not insignificant, I suggest, that what most offends Augustine about
normal sexual activity is the failure of the male will to effect total dispassion-
ate control over the phallus; the harmonious ordering of the soul is disrupted:
the body revolts ... In Augustine, however, it is not the hope of eschatological flight to a non-sexual realm that is held before us, but rather *actual* sexual
relations without loss of control. In this (somewhat joyless) vision of paradise
the woman nonetheless remains intrinsically 'bodily' and subordinate to her
husband's leading spirit. Now when such assumptions are carried over, much

later, into the problematic inner-trinitarian relations of an Anselmian substitutionary atonement theory, a (bodily) female figure may occasionally be brought in visually as the *vinvulum amoris*, effecting a *rapprochement* between Father and Son, whether directly as Holy Spirit or, more usually, as the Virgin replacing the Spirit and warding off the wrath of a visually vengeful Father. Christian feminists may again well ask, however, whether these spontaneous projections of female figures into the Godhead, retrieved and welcomed with enthusiasm by some, are really a viable way forward, recapitulating as they do the Western stereotype of bodily, subordinate dependence for women.

To sum up: if in the East we have detected at least a tendency to announce a spurious (and de-sexed) equality for female creatureliness, in the West a more explicit stereotype of subordinate female bodiliness has been the norm. From a Christian feminist standpoint clearly neither of these solutions is agreeable as a systematic view of female creatureliness.

Source: Sarah Coakley, Powers and Submissions: Spirituality, Philosophy and Gender, *Oxford and New Malden, MA: Blackwell, 2002, pp. 63–5.*

8 The Church

Introductory essay

The Church, or *ecclesia*, the gathering of God's people, is central to the practice of Christianity. However, what exactly the Church is, what its purpose and calling are and how we can identify the true Church have been matters of theological debate over the centuries. From the reports of the structure and activities of the very first Christian churches in the Acts of the Apostles right down to the current 'Fresh Expressions' being explored by mainstream churches in the West, Christians have debated what form the Church should take and how it should fulfil its mission. This raises many questions, about the behaviour of members of the Church, authority within the community, the sacraments and practices of the Church. The questions of ecclesiology, however, are not simply questions of practice – of what we do and how we do it. They are primarily the question of what theological beliefs underpin those practices. In the Nicene Creed, we confess belief in the 'one, holy, catholic and apostolic church'. It may seem odd to affirm 'we believe' in the Church; its existence after all is evidential. But it is also clear that the Church does not appear to be consistently one, holy, catholic or apostolic. The confession of belief is concerned with what the Church should and will be, rather than the experienced reality of the Church.

Understanding the Church and the ways in which it has changed over the centuries is complex, because the story of the Church cannot be separated from stories of politics, social change and economics, among other things. The establishment of Christendom, and the conflation between Church and State in many places, posed a whole new set of challenges for theologians seeking to define the nature and purpose of the Church. For the earliest Christians, participation in the life of the Church was the result of a proactive choice in response to hearing the Gospel proclaimed, or indeed because of the witness of the Christian communities themselves. However, when Christianity became the religion of the Roman Empire, this was no longer necessarily the case. There was often an expectation of church participation and a requirement to conform to the Christian life. Indeed, for some, participation in the Church was a means to power and career opportunities. In such a context, what distinguishes the Church – the people of God – from any other gathering of people? One theological response to this is the distinction between the visible and invisible Church. The people who are gathered and who visibly appear to be part of the Church may not be part of the true, or invisible, Church, whose membership is known only to God. The Reformers held that this distinction was central to an understanding of the Church. Calvin argues that although there are those within the Church who are not part of the elect, or the true Church, who they are is known only to God. He further argues that this does not challenge the unity of the Church, as the true Church is the body of believers who have Christ as their head. Richard Hooker, in his work *On Ecclesiastical Polity*, argues that all who claim to be Christian are part of the visible Church. The invisible part of the Church is those who have gone before, and this mystical body, which is united by Christ, cannot be observed but is known only through the intellect. Pope Pius XII writes that the Church is called to be a visible body that is united through profession of the same faith, following the same practices and under the same authority.

The challenge of unity does not just arise at periods of dramatic change or conflict within the Church. The earliest Christian writers were challenged not only by the fragmentary nature of the Church, but also by those who taught a gospel that was not accepted by the orthodox Church, and who led people away from what they considered to be true, apostolic, teaching. Ignatius in the second extract, writes to the churches in Ephesus, urging them to maintain unity and to accept the authority of the bishop. Irenaeus is concerned to expose those who preach a false gospel, and to respond to those who challenge the true teaching of Christianity. The true gospel, he argues, is that which has been handed down by the apostles. Similarly, Clement of Alexandria is concerned about the false teachings being passed on, but argues that Christians cannot retreat from belief in the gospel because some distort it. Cyprian's concern in his treatise on unity is that the Church can only fulfil its mission and calling by being united through those who have been given authority. In more recent times, the discussion over church unity has inevitably related to the ecumenical movement. Walter Kasper identifies the progress and failings of the ecumenical movement and considers the nature of unity in light of the continuing separation between church communities. Paul Fiddes similarly reflects on the current state of the move towards unity between the churches, and reminds the reader that this is a 'call to unity' which comes from God.

The practice of the sacraments has become one of the defining features of the Church, and also one of the most divisive aspects of church practice. Although there may be differences about the *way* in which the sacraments are practised, the more profound differences lie in the understanding of sacraments in general, and the meaning of each sacrament in particular. During the period of the Reformation, which practices should be considered to be Sacraments, as well as understandings of baptism and Eucharist, were fiercely debated. These discussions were far from being simply theoretical, indeed it was clearly understood by the Reformers that what was at stake were the very souls of believers. Even though the word *sacrament* was probably not used until Tertullian used the Latin *sacramentum* to describe baptism, the concept and practice of what we now refer to as the sacraments was a part of Christian life from the beginning. The first extract, from the *Didache*, offers instruction on the practices of both baptism and Eucharist. By the mid fifteenth century, the Roman Catholic Church had consolidated its understanding of sacraments, and Pope Eugenius in the *Decree for the Armenians* sets out the seven rituals that are understood to be sacraments, and that both contain grace and confer it on those who 'receive them worthily'.

Martin Luther challenged the understanding of sacrament espoused by the Roman Catholic Church, and argued that while many things may be broadly sacramental, only two rituals are in themselves sacraments. Baptism and Eucharist are the only two that attach a material sign to God's promise and are therefore the only two rites that Luther accepts as sacraments. The Council of Trent confirms the position of the Roman Catholic Church that there are seven sacraments and that they are necessary for salvation. However, a person does not need to avail themselves of every sacrament, and indeed one could not have both taken orders and married. Disagreement over the nature of a sacrament was by no means confined to the Roman Catholic Church and the Reformers. The Protestant churches, although largely accepting that there are two sacraments, continue to debate the meaning and practice of Eucharist and baptism. In the Scots Confession written in 1560, the leaders of the Reformation in Scotland assert that they do not hold the sacraments to be mere signs, but that both baptism and Eucharist result in the believer being joined to Christ. Geoffrey Bromiley explores the meaning of baptism and argues that this sacrament is not something that we do for ourselves, but indicates something that God does for us and that lies at the heart of the covenant relationship between God and God's people. Alisdair Heron, in discussing the Eucharist, argues that Christ himself is the sacrament, and that if we reframe our understanding of Eucharist and baptism in these contexts, it is possible to move beyond the views that divide understanding and practice.

Dietrich Bonhoeffer argues that the Church exists because God has called it into being and that it can only be experienced by faith. This Church is the community of saints, the people sanctified by God. The Church is not limited by what we witness or experience of it, but its reality is established by what it will one day be. In this respect, the Church is truly an eschatological community. *Lumen Gentium* anticipates the fulfilment of the Church and suggests that the final perfection of the Church provides us with a model for the character of the Church today. Jürgen Moltmann similarly claims that the Church is characterized by the reality of Christ and the gift of the Spirit and argues that its character should seek to manifest the future character of the fulfilled Church. John Zizioulas describes the Church as an 'eschatological community existing in history' and argues that only through reclaiming a corporate understanding of personhood and a clear trinitarian understanding can we begin to understand the mystery of the Church.

The twentieth century saw a move away from Christendom, as for the first time since the fourth century church attendance in many Western countries became once again a matter of individual, and possibly costly, choice. The characterization of this period as 'post-Christendom' points to the new challenges in understanding the nature and practice of the Church. In this context the teaching and missionary aspects of the Church are given new significance. Leslie Newbiggin argues that the Church has lost its sense of being a missionary community, and that mission is often an 'added extra' to the main activity of the Church. David Bosch, in the final extract, similarly argues that the Church must rediscover its missionary nature as it shares in God's missionary nature. The vast social and political changes of the twentieth century raise very specific challenges for the churches. Latin American liberation theology and feminist theology pose serious challenges to the Church, both in terms of theology and praxis. Jon Sobrino defends the title 'Church of the Poor' as a legitimate description and a reminder of the central place of the poor in the kingdom of God. Leonardo Boff argues that the model of the Church as the Body of Christ has allowed the boundaries of the Church to be narrowly conceived. Letty Russell provides an example of *church in the round* which operates with broad boundaries and challenges inherited models of authority and leadership in the Church.

It would be impossible in this chapter to trace fully the development of the Church over two thousand years of Christianity, but the readings included here provide an indication of the major developments and shifts in thinking about the nature and life of the Church. In many ways, the questions facing theologians about ecclesiology and church practice change little over the centuries, but they are of course shaped and coloured by the contexts in which they are being asked.

LEH

8.1 *Didache*

The Didache *is believed to have been written in the late first or early second century and offers instruction on various matters to do with the living of the Christian life. Parallels between this and the discussion of the Church in the Acts of the Apostles are evident. This section focuses on instruction for baptism, Eucharist and the behaviour expected within the church community.*

7:1 But concerning baptism, thus shall ye baptize.

7:2 Having first recited all these things, baptize [in the name of the Father and of the Son and of the Holy Spirit] in living (running) water.

7:3 But if thou hast not living water, then baptize in other water;

7:4 and if thou art not able in cold, then in warm.

7:5 But if thou hast neither, then pour water on the head thrice in the name of the Father and of the Son and of the Holy Spirit.

7:6 But before the baptism let him that baptizeth and him that is baptized fast, and any others also who are able;

7:7 and thou shalt order him that is baptized to fast a day or two before.

...

9:1 But as touching the eucharistic thanksgiving give ye thanks thus.

9:2 First, as regards the cup:

9:3 We give Thee thanks, O our Father, for the holy vine of Thy son David, which Thou madest known unto us through Thy Son Jesus;

9:4 Thine is the glory for ever and ever.

9:5 Then as regards the broken bread:

9:6 We give Thee thanks, O our Father, for the life and knowledge which Thou didst make known unto us through Thy Son Jesus;

9:7 Thine is the glory for ever and ever.

9:8 As this broken bread was scattered upon the mountains and being gathered together became one, so may Thy Church be gathered together from the ends of the earth into Thy kingdom;

9:9 for Thine is the glory and the power through Jesus Christ for ever and ever.

9:10 But let no one eat or drink of this eucharistic thanksgiving, but they that have been baptized into the name of the Lord;

9:11 for concerning this also the Lord hath said:

9:12 {Give not that which is holy to the dogs.}

...

14:1 And on the Lord's own day gather yourselves together and break bread and give thanks, first confessing your transgressions, that your sacrifice may be pure.

14:2 And let no man, having his dispute with his fellow, join your assembly until they have been reconciled, that your sacrifice may not be defiled;

14:3 for this sacrifice it is that was spoken of by the Lord;

14:4 {In every place and at every time offer Me a pure sacrifice;

14:5 for I am a great king, saith the Lord and My name is wonderful among the nations.}

15:1 Appoint for yourselves therefore bishops and deacons worthy of the Lord, men who are meek and not lovers of money, and true and approved;

15:2 for unto you they also perform the service of the prophets and teachers.

15:3 Therefore despise them not;

15:4 for they are your honourable men along with the prophets and teachers.

15:5 And reprove one another, not in anger but in peace, as ye find in the Gospel;

15:6 and let no one speak to any that has gone wrong towards his neighbour, neither let him hear a word from you, until he repent.

15:7 But your prayers and your almsgivings and all your deeds so do ye as ye find it in the Gospel of our Lord.

Source: The Apostolic Fathers, *trans. and ed. J. B. Lightfoot, London: Macmillan, 1893.*

8.2 Ignatius of Antioch, from *Epistle to the Ephesians*

In this letter from Ignatius to the people in Ephesus, he urges them to main-
tain unity with the bishop and asserts that the Church must be faithful to
its shepherd, the bishop. At the time Ignatius was writing, the Church was
beginning to grow and the questions of structure, authority and obedience
were becoming increasingly important.

For if I in this brief space of time, have enjoyed such fellowship with your
bishop – I mean not of a mere human, but of a spiritual nature – how much
more do I reckon you happy who are so joined to him as the Church is to
Jesus Christ, and as Jesus Christ is to the Father, that so all things may agree
in unity! Let no man deceive himself: if any one be not within the altar, he is
deprived of the bread of God. For if the prayer of one or two possesses [Matt.
18.19] such power, how much more that of the bishop and the whole Church!
He, therefore, that does not assemble with the Church, has even by this manifested his pride, and condemned himself. For it is written, 'God resisteth the
proud' [Prov. 3.34; James 4.6; 1 Peter 5.5]. Let us be careful, then, not to set ourselves in opposition to the bishop, in order that we may be subject to God.

The more, therefore, you see the bishop silent, the more do you reverence
him. For we ought to receive every one whom the Master of the house sends
to be over His household [Matt. 24.25], as we would do Him that sent him. It
is manifest, therefore, that we should look upon the bishop even as we would
look upon the Lord Himself, standing, as he does, before the Lord. For 'it
behoves the man who looks carefully about him, and is active in his business,
to stand before kings, and not to stand before slothful men' [Prov. 22.29]. And
indeed Onesimus himself greatly commends your good order in God, that ye
all live according to the truth, and that no sect has any dwelling-place among
you. Nor indeed do ye hearken to any one rather than to Jesus Christ, the true
Shepherd and Teacher. And ye are, as Paul wrote to you, 'one body and one
spirit, because ye have also been called in one hope of the faith' [Eph. 4.4].
Since also 'there is one Lord, one faith, one baptism, one God and Father of
all, who is over all, and through all, and in all' [Eph. 4.5–6]. Such, then, are ye,
having been taught by such instructors, Paul the Christ-bearer, and Timothy
the most faithful.

But some most worthless persons are in the habit of carrying about the
name [of Jesus Christ] in wicked guile, while yet they practise things unworthy of God, and hold opinions contrary to the doctrine of Christ, to their own
destruction, and that of those who give credit to them, whom you must avoid
as ye would wild beasts. For 'the righteous man who avoids them is saved for
ever; but the destruction of the ungodly is sudden, and a subject of rejoicing'
[Prov. 10.25 and 11.3]. For 'they are dumb dogs, that cannot bark' [Isa. 56.10],
raving mad, and biting secretly, against whom ye must be on your guard,
since they labour under an incurable disease. But our Physician is the only
true God, the unbegotten and unapproachable, the Lord of all, the Father and
Begetter of the only-begotten Son. We have also as a Physician the Lord our
God, Jesus the Christ, the only-begotten Son and Word, before time began, but

who afterwards became also man, of Mary the virgin. For 'the Word was made flesh' [John 1.14]. Being incorporeal, He was in the body; being impassible, He was in a passible body; being immortal, He was in a mortal body; being life, He became subject to corruption, that He might free our souls from death and corruption, and heal them, and might restore them to health, when they were diseased with ungodliness and wicked lusts.

Source: The Epistle of Ignatius to the Ephesians 5—7, *trans. Alexander Roberts and James Donaldson, in Alexander Roberts, James Donaldson and A. Cleveland Coxe (eds),* Ante-Nicene Fathers, *vol. 1, Buffalo, NY: Christian Literature Publishing Co., 1885.*

8.3 Irenaeus of Lyons, from *Against Heresies*

In these extracts from Irenaeus' book Against Heresies *he argues that the Church is united by belief in the gospel as it has been handed on by the apostles. He states that the true churches are those who recognize the authority that has been handed on through a succession of bishops from Peter and Paul.*

Book I, Chapter X: Unity of the Faith of the Church Throughout the Whole World

1. The Church, though dispersed throughout the whole world, even to the ends of the earth, has received from the apostles and their disciples this faith: [She believes] in one God, the Father Almighty, Maker of heaven, and earth, and the sea, and all things that are in them; and in one Christ Jesus, the Son of God, who became incarnate for our salvation; and in the Holy Spirit, who proclaimed through the prophets the dispensations of God, and the advents, and the birth from a virgin, and the passion, and the resurrection from the dead, and the ascension into heaven in the flesh of the beloved Christ Jesus, our Lord, and His [future] manifestation from heaven in the glory of the Father 'to gather all things in one' [Eph. 1.10], and to raise up anew all flesh of the whole human race, in order that to Christ Jesus, our Lord, and God, and Saviour, and King, according to the will of the invisible Father, 'every knee should bow, of things in heaven, and things in earth, and things under the earth, and that every tongue should confess' [Phil. 2.10–11] to Him, and that He should execute just judgment towards all; that He may send 'spiritual wickednesses' [Eph. 4.12], and the angels who transgressed and became apostates, together with the ungodly, and unrighteous, and wicked, and profane among men, into everlasting fire; but may, in the exercise of His grace, confer immortality on the righteous, and holy, and those who have kept His commandments, and have persevered in His love, some from the beginning [of their Christian course], and others from [the date of] their repentance, and may surround them with everlasting glory.

...

Book III, Chapter III: A Refutation of the Heretics, from the Fact That, in the Various Churches, a Perpetual Succession of Bishops Was Kept Up

1. It is within the power of all, therefore, in every Church, who may wish to see the truth, to contemplate clearly the tradition of the apostles manifested throughout the whole world; and we are in a position to reckon up those who were by the apostles instituted bishops in the Churches, and [to demonstrate] the succession of these men to our own times; those who neither taught nor knew of anything like what these [heretics] rave about. For if the apostles had known hidden mysteries, which they were in the habit of imparting to 'the perfect' apart and privily from the rest, they would have delivered them espe-

cially to those to whom they were also committing the Churches themselves. For they were desirous that these men should be very perfect and blameless in all things, whom also they were leaving behind as their successors, delivering up their own place of government to these men; which men, if they discharged their functions honestly, would be a great boon [to the Church], but if they should fall away, the direst calamity.

2. Since, however, it would be very tedious, in such a volume as this, to reckon up the successions of all the Churches, we do put to confusion all those who, in whatever manner, whether by an evil self-pleasing, by vainglory, or by blindness and perverse opinion, assemble in unauthorized meetings; [we do this, I say,] by indicating that tradition derived from the apostles, of the very great, the very ancient, and universally known Church founded and organized at Rome by the two most glorious apostles, Peter and Paul; as also [by pointing out] the faith preached to men, which comes down to our time by means of the successions of the bishops. For it is a matter of necessity that every Church should agree with this Church, on account of its pre-eminent authority, that is, the faithful everywhere, inasmuch as the apostolical tradition has been preserved continuously by those [faithful men] who exist everywhere.

Source: *Irenaeus of Lyons*, Against Heresies *III*, 2.1–2, *trans. Alexander Roberts and James Donaldson, in Alexander Roberts, James Donaldson and A. Cleveland Coxe (eds)*, Ante-Nicene Fathers, *vol. 1, Buffalo, NY: Christian Literature Publishing Co., 1885.*

8.4 Clement of Alexandria, from *Stromata*

Clement acknowledges that the Church is not united and that there are many different versions of the gospel being taught. However, he does not accept that this is a weakness of the gospel itself, or that people should be denied the opportunity of hearing the gospel because some are teaching false versions of it.

Chapter XV.   The Objection to Join the Church on Account of the Diversity of Heresies Answered.

Since it comes next to reply to the objections alleged against us by Greeks and Jews; and since, in some of the questions previously discussed, the sects also who adhere to other teaching give, their help, it will be well first to clear away the obstacles before us, and then, prepared thus for the solution of the difficulties, to advance to the succeeding Miscellany.

First, then, they make this objection to us, saying, that they ought not to believe on account of the discord of the sects. For the truth is warped when some teach one set of dogmas, others another.

To whom we say, that among you who are Jews, and among the most famous of the philosophers among the Greeks, very many sects have sprung up. And yet you do not say that one ought to hesitate to philosophize or Judaize, because of the want of agreement of the sects among you between themselves. And then, that heresies should be sown among the truth, as 'tares among the wheat,' was foretold by the Lord; and what was predicted to take place could not but happen [Matt. 13.28]. And the cause of this is, that everything that is fair is followed by a foul blot. If one, then, violate his engagements, and go aside from the confession which he makes before us, are we not to stick to the truth because he has belied his profession? But as the good man must not prove false or fail to ratify what he has promised, although others violate their engagements; so also are we bound in no way to transgress the canon of the Church. And especially do we keep our profession in the most important points, while they traverse it.

Those, then, are to be believed, who hold firmly to the truth. And we may broadly make use of this reply, and say to them, that physicians holding opposite opinions according to their own schools, yet equally in point of fact treat patients. Does one, then, who is ill in body and needing treatment, not have recourse to a physician, on account of the different schools in medicine? No more, then, may he who in soul is sick and full of idols, make a pretext of the heresies, in reference to the recovery of health and conversion to God.

Further, it is said that it is on account of 'those that are approved that heresies exist' [1 Cor. 11.19]. [The apostle] calls 'approved,' either those who in reaching faith apply to the teaching of the Lord with some discrimination (as those are called skilful money-changers, who distinguish the spurious coin from the genuine by the false stamp), or those who have already become approved both in life and knowledge.

...

On account of the heresies, therefore, the toil of discovery must be undertaken; but we must not at all abandon [the truth]. For, on fruit being set before us, some real and ripe, and some made of wax, as like the real as possible, we are not to abstain from both on account of the resemblance. But by the exercise of the apprehension of contemplation, and by reasoning of the most decisive character, we must distinguish the true from the seeming.

...

But, in my opinion, the nature of plausible arguments is of one character, and that of true arguments of another. And we know that it is necessary that the appellation of the heresies should be expressed in contradistinction to the truth; from which the Sophists, drawing certain things for the destruction of men, and burying them in human arts invented by themselves, glory rather in being at the head of a School than presiding over the Church.

Source: Clement of Alexandria, Stromata, Book 7, trans. William Wilson, in Alexander Roberts, James Donaldson, and A. Cleveland Coxe (eds), Ante-Nicene Fathers, vol. 2, Buffalo, NY: Christian Literature Publishing Co., 1885.

8.5 Cyprian, from *On the Unity of the Church*

In his treatise On the Unity of the Church, *Cyprian argues that the unity of the Church is central to its mission and calling. The unity of the Church stems from Jesus' appointment of Peter as the rock on which the Church is built.*

4. If any one consider and examine these things, there is no need for lengthened discussion and arguments. There is easy proof for faith in a short summary of the truth. The Lord speaks to Peter, saying, 'I say unto thee, that thou art Peter; and upon this rock I will build my Church, and the gates of hell shall not prevail against it. And I will give unto thee the keys of the kingdom of heaven; and whatsoever thou shalt bind on earth shall be bound also in heaven, and whatsoever thou shalt loose on earth shall be loosed in heaven' [Matt. 16.18–19]. And again to the same He says, after His resurrection, 'Feed my sheep' [John 21.15]. And although to all the apostles, after His resurrection, He gives an equal power, and says, 'As the Father hath sent me, even so send I you: Receive ye the Holy Ghost: Whosoever sins ye remit, they shall be remitted unto him; and whosoever sins ye retain, they shall be retained' [John 20.21]; yet, that He might set forth unity, He arranged by His authority the origin of that unity, as beginning from one. Assuredly the rest of the apostles were also the same as was Peter, endowed with a like partnership both of honour and power; but the beginning proceeds from unity. Which one Church, also, the Holy Spirit in the Song of Songs designated in the person of our Lord, and says, 'My dove, my spotless one, is but one. She is the only one of her mother, elect of her that bare her' [Song of Songs 6.9]. Does he who does not hold this unity of the Church think that he holds the faith? Does he who strives against and resists the Church trust that he is in the Church, when moreover the blessed Apostle Paul teaches the same thing, and sets forth the sacrament of unity, saying, 'There is one body and one spirit, one hope of your calling, one Lord, one faith, one baptism, one God?' [Eph. 4.4].

5. And this unity we ought firmly to hold and assert, especially those of us that are bishops who preside in the Church, that we may also prove the episcopate itself to be one and undivided. Let no one deceive the brotherhood by a falsehood: let no one corrupt the truth of the faith by perfidious prevarication. The episcopate is one, each part of which is held by each one for the whole. The Church also is one, which is spread abroad far and wide into a multitude by an increase of fruitfulness. As there are many rays of the sun, but one light; and many branches of a tree, but one strength based in its tenacious root; and since from one spring flow many streams, although the multiplicity seems diffused in the liberality of an overflowing abundance, yet the unity is still preserved in the source. Separate a ray of the sun from its body of light, its unity does not allow a division of light; break a branch from a tree, when broken, it will not be able to bud; cut off the stream from its fountain, and that which is cut off dries up. Thus also the Church, shone over with the light of the Lord, sheds forth her rays over the whole world, yet it is one light which is everywhere diffused, nor is the unity of the body separated. Her fruitful

abundance spreads her branches over the whole world. She broadly expands her rivers, liberally flowing, yet her head is one, her source one; and she is one mother, plentiful in the results of fruitfulness: from her womb we are born, by her milk we are nourished, by her spirit we are animated.

6. The spouse of Christ cannot be adulterous; she is uncorrupted and pure. She knows one home; she guards with chaste modesty the sanctity of one couch. She keeps us for God. She appoints the sons whom she has born for the kingdom. Whoever is separated from the Church and is joined to an adulteress, is separated from the promises of the Church; nor can he who forsakes the Church of Christ attain to the rewards of Christ. He is a stranger; he is profane; he is an enemy. He can no longer have God for his Father, who has not the Church for his mother. If any one could escape who was outside the ark of Noah, then he also may escape who shall be outside of the Church. The Lord warns, saying, 'He who is not with me is against me, and he who gathereth not with me scattereth' [Matt. 12.30]. He who breaks the peace and the concord of Christ, does so in opposition to Christ; he who gathereth elsewhere than in the Church, scatters the Church of Christ. The Lord says, 'I and the Father are one' [John 10.30]; and again it is written of the Father, and of the Son, and of the Holy Spirit, 'And these three are one' [1 John 5.7]. And does any one believe that this unity which thus comes from the divine strength and coheres in celestial sacraments, can be divided in the Church, and can be separated by the parting asunder of opposing wills? He who does not hold this unity does not hold God's law, does not hold the faith of the Father and the Son, does not hold life and salvation.

Source: Cyprian, De Catholicae Ecclesiae Unitate *4—6, trans. Robert Ernest Wallis, in Alexander Roberts, James Donaldson and A. Cleveland Coxe (eds),* Ante-Nicene Fathers, *vol. 5, Buffalo, NY: Christian Literature Publishing Co., 1886.*

8.6 Pope Eugenius, from *Decree for the Armenians*

By the Middle Ages, the arguments over true and false teaching had become centred on which sacraments were deemed to be valid. This Decree for the Armenians was written at the Council of Florence in 1439 and establishes that there are seven sacraments of the Roman Catholic Church.

We have drawn up in the briefest form a statement of the truth concerning the seven sacraments, so that the Armenians, now and in future generations, may more easily be instructed therein.

There are seven sacraments under the new law: that is to say, baptism, confirmation, the mass, penance, extreme unction, ordination, and matrimony. These differ essentially from the sacraments of the old law; for the latter do not confer grace, but only typify that grace which can be given by the passion of Christ alone. But these our sacraments both contain grace and confer it upon all who receive them worthily.

...

To effect these sacraments three things are necessary: the things [or symbols], that is, the 'material'; the words, that is, the 'form'; and the person of the 'ministrant,' who administers the sacrament with the intention of carrying out what the Church effects through him. If any of these things be lacking, the sacrament is not accomplished.

...

BAPTISM

Holy baptism holds the first place among all the sacraments because it is the gate of spiritual life, for by it we are made members of Christ and of the body of the Church. Since through the first man death entered into the world [cf. Rom. 5.12], unless we are born again of water, and of the spirit, we cannot, so saith Truth, enter into the kingdom of heaven [cf. John 3.5]. The material of this sacrament is water, real and natural, it matters nothing whether it be cold or warm. Now the form is: 'I baptize thee in the name of the Father, and of the Son, and of the Holy Ghost.'

...

The ministrant of this sacrament is the priest, for baptism belongs to his office. But in case of necessity not only a priest or deacon may baptize, but a layman or a woman, nay, even a pagan or a heretic, provided he use the form of the Church and intend to do what the Church effects. The efficacy of this sacrament is the remission of all sin, original sin and actual, and of all penalties incurred through this guilt. Therefore no satisfaction for past sin should be imposed on those who are baptized; but if they die before they commit any sin, they shall straightway attain the kingdom of heaven and the sight of God.

CONFIRMATION

The second sacrament is confirmation. The material is the chrism made from oil, which signifies purity of conscience, and from balsam, which signifies the odour of fair fame; and it must be blessed by the bishop. The form is: 'I sign thee with the sign of the cross and confirm thee with the chrism of salvation, in the name of the Father, and of the Son, and of the Holy Ghost.'

The proper ministrant of this sacrament is the bishop. While a simple priest avails to perform the other anointings, this one none can confer save the bishop only, for it is written of the apostles alone that by the laying on of hands they gave the Holy Ghost, and the bishops hold the office of the apostles.

...

THE EUCHARIST

The third sacrament is the Eucharist. The material is wheaten bread and wine of the grape, which before consecration should be mixed very sparingly with water; because, according to the testimony of the holy fathers and doctors of the Church set forth in former times in disputation, it is believed that the Lord himself instituted this sacrament with wine mixed with water, and also because this corresponds with the accounts of our Lord's passion ... Moreover the mixing of water with the wine fitly signifies the efficacy of this sacrament, namely, the union of Christian people with Christ, for water signifies 'people,' according to the passage in the Apocalypse which says, 'many waters, many people' [cf. Rev. 17.15] ...

The form of this sacrament is furnished by the words of the Saviour when he instituted it, and the priest, speaking in the person of Christ, consummates this sacrament. By virtue of these words, the substance of the bread is turned into the body of Christ and the substance of the wine into his blood. This is accomplished in such wise that the whole Christ is altogether present under the semblance of the bread and altogether under the semblance of the wine. Moreover, after the consecrated host and the consecrated wine have been divided, the whole Christ is present in any part of them ...

PENANCE

The fourth sacrament is penance. The material, as we may say, consists in the acts of penitence, which are divided into three parts. The first of these is contrition of the heart, wherein the sinner must grieve for the sins he has committed, with the resolve to commit no further sins. Second comes confession with the mouth, to which it pertains that the sinner should make confession to his priest of all the sins he holds in his memory. The third is satisfaction for sins according to the judgment of the priest, and this is made chiefly by prayer, fasting, and almsgiving. The form of this sacrament consists in the words of absolution which the priest speaks when be says, 'I absolve thee,' etc.; and the minister of this sacrament is the priest, who has authority to absolve either regularly or by the commission of a superior. The benefit of this sacrament is absolution from sins.

EXTREME UNCTION

The fifth sacrament is extreme unction, and the material is oil of the olive, blessed by a bishop. This sacrament shall not be given to any except the sick who are in fear of death. They shall be anointed in the following places: the eyes on account of the sight, the ears on account of the hearing, the nostrils on account of smell, the mouth on account of taste and speech, the hands on account of touch, the feet on account of walking, and the loins as the seat of pleasure. The form of this sacrament is as follows: 'Through this holy unction and his most tender compassion, the Lord grants thee forgiveness for whatever sins thou hast committed by the sight,' and in the same way for the other members.

The minister of this sacrament is a priest. The benefit is even the healing of the mind and, so far as is expedient, of the body also ...

ORDINATION

The sixth sacrament is ordination. The material for the priesthood is the cup with the wine and the paten with the bread; for the deaconate, the books of the Gospel; for the subdeaconate, an empty cup placed upon an empty paten; and in like manner, other offices are conferred by giving to the candidates those things which pertain to their secular ministrations. The form for priests is this: 'Receive the power to offer sacrifice in the Church for the living and the dead, in the name of the Father, and of the Son, and of the Holy Ghost.' And so for each order the proper form shall be used, as fully stated in the Roman pontifical. The regular minister of this sacrament is a bishop; benefit, growth in grace, to the end that whosoever is ordained may be a worthy minister.

MATRIMONY

The seventh sacrament is matrimony, the type of the union of Christ and the Church, according to the apostle who saith, 'This is a great mystery' [Eph. 5.32. In the Vulgate Paul's word *mysterion* is translated *sacramentum*]; 'but I speak concerning Christ and the church.' The efficient cause of marriage is regularly the mutual consent uttered aloud on the spot. These advantages are to be ascribed to marriage: first, the begetting of children and their bringing up in the worship of the Lord; secondly, the fidelity that husband and wife should each maintain toward the other; thirdly the indissoluble character of marriage, for this typifies the indissoluble union of Christ and the Church. Although for the cause of adultery separation is permissible, for no other cause may marriage be infringed, since the bond of marriage once legitimately contracted is perpetual.

Source: Pope Eugenius, Decree for the Armenians, *Council of Florence 1439. Bull Exsultate Domine, in James Harvey Robinson (ed.),* Readings in European History, *vol. I, Boston: Ginn & Co., 1904.*

8.7 Martin Luther, from *On the Babylonian Captivity of the Church*

During the period of Reformation the issue of the number of sacraments and the way in which they should be administered became extremely controversial. Here, Luther argues that many things could be considered sacraments, but that the title is properly used only of the promises of God which have a material sign attached to them. Only baptism and the Eucharist fulfil this criterion, even though Luther himself has previously argued that penance could also be considered a sacrament.

On the Babylonian Captivity of the Church

There are yet a few other things it might seem possible to regard as sacraments; namely, all those to which a divine promise has been given, such as prayer, the Word, and the cross. Christ promised, in many places, that those who pray should be heard; especially in Luke 11, where He invites us in many parables to pray. Of the Word He says: 'Blessed are they that hear the word of God, and keep it' (Luke 11.28). And who will tell how often He promises aid and glory to such as are afflicted, suffer, and are cast down? No, who will recount all the promises of God? The whole Scripture is concerned with provoking us to faith; now driving us with precepts and threats, now drawing us with promises and consolations. Indeed, whatever things are written are either precepts or promises; the precepts humble the proud with their demands, the promises exalt the humble with their forgiveness.

Nevertheless, it has seemed best to restrict the name of sacrament to such promises as have signs attached to them. The remainder, not being bound to signs, are bare promises. Hence there are, strictly speaking, but two sacraments in the Church of God – baptism and bread; for only in these two do we find both the divinely instituted sign and the promise of forgiveness of sins. The sacrament of penance, which I added to these two, lacks the divinely instituted visible sign, and is, as I have said, nothing but a return to baptism. Nor can the scholastics say that their definition fits penance, for they too ascribe to the sacrament a visible sign, which is to impress upon the senses the form of that which it effects invisibly. But penance, or absolution, has no such sign; wherefore they are constrained by their own definition, either to admit that penance is not a sacrament, and thus to reduce the number of sacraments, or else to bring forward another definition.

Baptism, however, which we have applied to the whole of life, will truly be a sufficient substitute for all the sacraments we might need as long as we live. And the bread is truly the sacrament of the dying; for in it we commemorate the passing of Christ out of this world, that we may imitate Him. Thus we may apportion these two sacraments as follows: baptism belongs to the beginning and the entire course of life, the bread belongs to the end and to death. And the Christian should use them both as long as he is in this poor body, until, fully baptised and strengthened, he passes out of this world and is born to the new life of eternity, to eat with Christ in the Kingdom of His Father, as He promised at the Last Supper – 'Amen I say to you, I will not drink from henceforth of this fruit of the vine, until it is fulfilled in the kingdom of God' (Matt. 26.29). Thus He seems clearly to have instituted the sacrament of the bread with a view to our entrance into the life to come. Then, when the meaning of both sacraments is fulfilled, baptism and bread will cease.

Source: Martin Luther, The Babylonian Captivity of the Church *(Op Lat V.16), from http:// www.ctsfw.edu/etext/luther/babylonian/babylonian.htm#9.*

8.8 The Council of Trent, from *Decree on the Seven Sacraments*

The Council of Trent met in the sixteenth century to assert the position of the Roman Catholic Church on certain matters and to speak against emerging Protestant 'heresies'. The Council's Decree on the Sacraments *confirms that there are seven sacraments and that participation in the sacraments is necessary for salvation.*

Decree on the Sacraments

For the completion of the salutary doctrine on Justification, which was promulgated with the unanimous consent of the Fathers in the last preceding Session, it hath seemed suitable to treat of the most holy Sacraments of the Church, through which all true justice either begins, or being begun is increased, or being lost is repaired. With this view, in order to destroy the errors and to extirpate the heresies, which have appeared in these our days on the subject of the said most holy sacraments – as well those which have been revived from the heresies condemned of old by our Fathers, as also those newly invented, and which are exceedingly prejudicial to the purity of the Catholic Church, and to the salvation of souls – the sacred and holy, ecumenical and general Synod of Trent, lawfully assembled in the Holy Ghost, the same legates of the Apostolic See presiding therein, adhering to the doctrine of the holy Scriptures, to the apostolic traditions, and to the consent of other councils and of the Fathers, has thought fit that these present canons be established and decreed; intending, the divine Spirit aiding, to publish later the remaining canons which are wanting for the completion of the work which It has begun.

On the Sacraments in general

CANON I.   If any one saith, that the sacraments of the New Law were not all instituted by Jesus Christ, our Lord; or, that they are more, or less, than seven, to wit, Baptism, Confirmation, the Eucharist, Penance, Extreme Unction, Order, and Matrimony; or even that any one of these seven is not truly and properly a sacrament; let him be anathema.

CANON II.   If any one saith, that these said sacraments of the New Law do not differ from the sacraments of the Old Law, save that the ceremonies are different, and different the outward rites; let him be anathema.

CANON III.   If any one saith, that these seven sacraments are in such wise equal to each other, as that one is not in any way more worthy than another; let him be anathema.

CANON IV.   If any one saith, that the sacraments of the New Law are not necessary unto salvation, but superfluous; and that, without them, or without the desire thereof, men obtain of God, through faith alone, the grace of justification; though all (the sacraments) are not indeed necessary for every individual; let him be anathema.

CANON V.   If any one saith, that these sacraments were instituted for the sake of nourishing faith alone; let him be anathema.

CANON VI.   If any one saith, that the sacraments of the New Law do not contain the grace which they signify; or, that they do not confer that grace on those who do not place an obstacle thereunto; as though they were merely outward signs of grace or justice received through faith, and certain marks of the Christian profession, whereby believers are distinguished amongst men from unbelievers; let him be anathema.

CANON VII.   If any one saith, that grace, as far as God's part is concerned, is not given through the said sacraments, always, and to all men, even though they receive them rightly, but (only) sometimes, and to some persons; let him be anathema.

CANON VIII.   If any one saith, that by the said sacraments of the New Law grace is not conferred through the act performed, but that faith alone in the divine promise suffices for the obtaining of grace; let him be anathema.

CANON IX.   If any one saith, that, in the three sacraments, Baptism, to wit, Confirmation, and Order, there is not imprinted in the soul a character, that is, a certain spiritual and indelible Sign, on account of which they cannot be repeated; let him be anathema.

CANON X.   If any one saith, that all Christians have power to administer the word, and all the sacraments; let him be anathema.

CANON XI.   If any one saith, that, in ministers, when they effect, and confer the sacraments, there is not required the intention at least of doing what the Church does; let him be anathema.

CANON XII.   If any one saith, that a minister, being in mortal sin – if so be that he observe all the essentials which belong to the effecting, or conferring of, the sacrament – neither effects, nor confers the sacrament; let him be anathema.

CANON XIII.   If any one saith, that the received and approved rites of the Catholic Church, wont to be used in the solemn administration of the sacraments, may be contemned, or without sin be omitted at pleasure by the ministers, or be changed, by every pastor of the churches, into other new ones; let him be anathema.

Source: **The Council of Trent, The Seventh Session: The Canons and Decrees of the Sacred and Oecumenical Council of Trent,** *trans. J. Waterworth, London: Dolman, 1848, pp. 53–67.*

8.9 John Calvin, from the *Institutes of the Christian Religion*

In this passage from his Institutes of the Christian Religion, *Calvin argues that we should properly confess that we believe 'the Church' rather than confess belief 'in the Church'. Although it is not the Church itself that is the object of our faith, without being members of the Church we have no hope of salvation.*

2. What is the relationship of church and creed?

When in the Creed we profess to believe the Church, reference is made not only to the visible Church of which we are now treating, but also to all the elect of God, including in the number even those who have departed this life. And, accordingly, the word used is 'believe,' because oftentimes no difference can be observed between the children of God and the profane, between his proper flock and the untamed herd. The particle 'in' is often interpolated, but without any probable ground. I confess, indeed, that it is the more usual form, and is not unsupported by antiquity, since the Nicene Creed, as quoted in Ecclesiastical History, adds the preposition. At the same time, we may perceive from early writers, that the expression received without controversy in ancient times was to believe 'the Church,' and not 'in the Church.' This is not only the expression used by Augustine, and that ancient writer, whoever he may have been, whose treatise, *De Symboli Expositione*, is extant under the name of Cyprian, but they distinctly remark that the addition of the preposition would make the expression improper, and they give good grounds for so thinking. We declare that we believe in God, both because our mind reclines upon him as true, and our confidence is fully satisfied in him. This cannot be said of the Church, just as it cannot be said of the forgiveness of sins, or the resurrection of the body. Wherefore, although I am unwilling to dispute about words, yet I would rather keep to the proper form, as better fitted to express the thing that is meant, than affect terms by which the meaning is ceaselessly obscured.

The object of the expression is to teach us, that though the devil leaves no stone unturned in order to destroy the grace of Christ, and the enemies of God rush with insane violence in the same direction, it cannot be extinguished, – the blood of Christ cannot be rendered barren, and prevented from producing fruit. Hence, regard must be had both to the secret election and to the internal calling of God, because he alone 'knoweth them that are his' (2 Tim. 2:19;) and as Paul expresses it, holds them as it were enclosed under his seal (Eph. 1:13), although, at the same time, they wear his insignia, and are thus distinguished from the reprobate. But as they are a small and despised number, concealed in an immense crowd, like a few grains of wheat buried among a heap of chaff, to God alone must be left the knowledge of his Church, of which his secret election forms the foundation. Nor is it enough to embrace the number of the elect in thought and intention merely. By the unity of the Church we must understand a unity into which we feel persuaded that we are truly ingrafted. For unless we are united with all the other members under Christ our head, no hope of the future inheritance awaits us.

Hence the Church is called Catholic or Universal (August. *Ep.* 48), for two or three cannot be invented without dividing Christ; and this is impossible. All the elect of God are so joined together in Christ, that as they depend on one head, so they are as it were compacted into one body, being knit together like its different members; made truly one by living together under the same Spirit of God in one faith, hope, and charity, called not only to the same inheritance of eternal life, but to participation in one God and Christ. For although the sad devastation which everywhere meets our view may proclaim that no Church remains, let us know that the death of Christ produces fruit, and that God wondrously preserves his Church, while placing it as it were in concealment. Thus it was said to Elijah, 'Yet I have left me seven thousand in Israel' (1 Kings 19:18).

3. 'The communion of saints'

Moreover this article of the Creed relates in some measure to the external Church, that every one of us must maintain brotherly concord with all the children of God, give due authority to the Church, and, in short, conduct ourselves as sheep of the flock. And hence the additional expression, the 'communion of saints;' for this clause, though usually omitted by ancient writers, must not be overlooked, as it admirably expresses the quality of the Church; just as if it had been said, that saints are united in the fellowship of Christ on this condition, that all the blessings which God bestows upon them are mutually communicated to each other. This, however, is not incompatible with a diversity of graces, for we know that the gifts of the Spirit are variously distributed; nor is it incompatible with civil order, by which each is permitted privately to possess his own means, it being necessary for the preservation of peace among men that distinct rights of property should exist among them. Still a community is asserted, such as Luke describes when he says, 'The multitude of them that believed were of one heart and of one soul' (Acts 4:32), and Paul, when he reminds the Ephesians, 'There is one body, and one Spirit, even as ye are called in one hope of your calling' (Eph. 4:4). For if they are truly persuaded that God is the common Father of them all, and Christ their common head, they cannot but be united together in brotherly love, and mutually impart their blessings to each other.

Then it is of the highest importance for us to know what benefit thence redounds to us. For when we believe the Church, it is in order that we may be firmly persuaded that we are its members. In this way our salvation rests on a foundation so firm and sure, that though the whole fabric of the world were to give way, it could not be destroyed. First, it stands with the election of God, and cannot change or fail, any more than his eternal providence. Next, it is in a manner united with the stability of Christ, who will no more allow his faithful followers to be dissevered from him, than he would allow his own members to be torn to pieces. We may add, that so long as we continue in the bosom of the Church, we are sure that the truth will remain with us ...

But in order to embrace the unity of the Church in this manner, it is not necessary, as I have observed, to see it with our eyes, or feel it with our hands. Nay, rather from its being placed in faith, we are reminded that our thoughts are to dwell upon it, as much when it escapes our perception as when it openly appears. Nor is our faith the worse for apprehending what is unknown, since we are not enjoined here to distinguish between the elect and the reprobate (this belongs not to us, but to God only), but to feel firmly assured in our minds, that all those who, by the mercy of God the Father, through the efficacy of the Holy Spirit, have become partakers with Christ, are set apart as the proper and peculiar possession of God, and that as we are of the number, we are also partakers of this great grace.

Source: John Calvin, The Institutes of the Christian Religion *IV.1, trans. Henry Beveridge (1559), Grand Rapids: Eerdmans, 1989.*

8.10 Richard Hooker, from *Of the Lawes of Ecclesiastical Politie*

In his work Of the Lawes of Ecclesiastical Polity *Hooker discusses the nature of the Church as visible and invisible and suggests that there are many who profess to be Christians, but who do not demonstrate the values of the gospel, who are part of the visible Church.*

Book 3 [2.] That Church of Christ, which we properly term his body mystical, can be but one; neither can that one be sensibly discerned by any man, inasmuch as the parts thereof are some in heaven already with Christ, and the rest that are on earth (albeit their natural persons be visible) we do not discern under this property, whereby they are truly and infallibly of that body. Only our minds by intellectual conceit are able to apprehend, that such a real body there is, a body collective, because it containeth an huge multitude; a body mystical, because the mystery of their conjunction is removed altogether from sense. Whatsoever we read in Scripture concerning the endless love and the saving mercy which God sheweth towards his Church, the only proper subject thereof is this Church. Concerning this flock it is that our Lord and Saviour hath promised, 'I give unto them eternal life, and they shall never perish, neither shall any pluck them out of my hands' [John 10.28]. They who are of this society have such marks and notes of distinction from all others, as are not object unto our sense; only unto God who seeth their hearts and understandeth all their secret cogitations, unto him they are clear and manifest. All men knew Nathanael to be an Israelite. But our Saviour piercing deeper giveth further testimony of him than men could have done with such certainty as he did, 'Behold indeed an Israelite in whom is no guile' [John 1.47]. If we profess, as Peter did [John 21.15], that we love the Lord, and profess it in the hearing of men, charity is prone to believe all things, and therefore charitable men are likely to think we do so, as long as they see no proof to the contrary. But that our love is sound and sincere, that it cometh from 'a pure heart and a good conscience and a faith unfeigned' [1 Tim. 1.5], who can pronounce, saving only the Searcher of all men's hearts, who alone intuitively doth know in this kind who are His?

[3.] And as those everlasting promises of love, mercy, and blessedness belong to the mystical Church; even so on the other side when we read of any duty which the Church of God is bound unto, the Church whom this doth concern is a sensibly known company. And this visible Church in like sort is but one, continued from the first beginning of the world to the last end. Which company being divided into two moieties, the one before, the other since the coming of Christ; that part, which since the coming of Christ partly hath embraced and partly shall hereafter embrace the Christian religion, we term as by a more proper name the Church of Christ. And therefore the Apostle affirmeth plainly of all men Christian, that be they Jews or Gentiles, bond or free, they are all incorporated into one company, they all make but *one body*. The unity of which visible body and Church of Christ consisteth in that uniformity which all several persons thereunto belonging have, by reason of that *one Lord* whose servants they all profess themselves, that *one Faith* which they all acknowledge, that *one Baptism* wherewith they are all initiated [Eph. 4.5].

…

[6.] Now although we know the Christian faith and allow of it, yet in this respect we are but entering; entered we are not into the visible Church before our admittance by the door of Baptism. Wherefore immediately upon the acknowledgment of Christian faith, the Eunuch (we see) was baptized by Philip [Acts 8.38], Paul by Ananias [Acts 12.16], by Peter an huge multitude containing three thousand souls [Acts 2.41], which being once baptized were reckoned in the number of souls added to the visible Church.

[7.] As for those virtues that belong unto moral righteousness and honesty of life, we do not mention them, because they are not proper unto Christian men, as they are Christian, but do concern them as they are men. True it is, the want of these virtues excludeth from salvation. So doth much more the absence of inward belief of heart; so doth despair and lack of hope; so emptiness of Christian love and charity. But we speak now of the visible Church, whose children are signed with this mark, 'One Lord, one Faith, one Baptism.' In whomsoever these things are, the Church doth acknowledge them for her children; them only she holdeth for aliens and strangers, in whom these things are not found. For want of these it is that Saracens, Jews, and Infidels are excluded out of the bounds of the Church. Others we may not deny to be of the visible Church, as long as these things are not wanting in them. For apparent it is, that all men are of necessity either Christians or not Christians. If by external profession they be Christians, then are they of the visible Church of Christ; and Christians by external profession they are all, whose mark of recognizance hath in it those things which we have mentioned, yea, although they be impious idolaters, wicked heretics, persons excommunicable, yea, and cast out for notorious improbity. Such withal we deny not to be the imps and limbs of Satan, even as long as they continue such.

Source: Richard Hooker, Of the Lawes of Ecclesiastical Politie, *Oxford: Clarendon Press, 1876.*

8.11 John Knox, from *A Scots Confession*

The Scots Confession *was written as a statement of belief by the leaders of the Reformation in Scotland. They argue that there is one true Church, which unites all who are saved through Christ. The Confession also clarifies that while they believe that there is a distinction between Jesus and the sacramental presence of Jesus, they do not hold the sacraments to be mere symbols.*

Chapter 16 – The Kirk

As we believe in one God, Father, Son, and Holy Ghost, so we firmly believe that from the beginning there has been, now is, and to the end of the world shall be, one Kirk, that is to say, one company and multitude of men chosen by God, who rightly worship and embrace him by true faith in Jesus Christ, who is the only Head of the Kirk, even as it is the body and spouse of Christ Jesus. This Kirk is catholic, that is, universal, because it contains the chosen of all ages, of all realms, nations, and tongues, be they of the Jews or be they of the Gentiles, who have communion and society with God the Father, and with his Son, Christ Jesus, through the sanctification of his Holy Spirit. It is therefore called the communion, not of profane persons, but of saints, who, as citizens of the heavenly Jerusalem, have the fruit of inestimable benefits, one God, one Lord Jesus, one faith, and one baptism. Out of this Kirk there is neither life nor eternal felicity. Therefore we utterly abhor the blasphemy of those who hold that men who live according to equity and justice shall be saved, no matter what religion they profess. For since there is neither life nor salvation without Christ Jesus; so shall none have part therein but those whom the Father has given unto his Son Christ Jesus, and those who in time come to him, avow his doctrine, and believe in him. (We include the children with the believing parents.) This Kirk is invisible, known only to God, who alone knows whom he has chosen, and includes both the chosen who are departed, the Kirk triumphant, those who yet live and fight against sin and Satan, and those who shall live hereafter.

Chapter 21 – The Sacraments

As the fathers under the Law, besides the reality of the sacrifices, had two chief sacraments, that is, circumcision and the Passover, and those who rejected these were not reckoned among God's people; so do we acknowledge and confess that now in the time of the gospel we have two chief sacraments, which alone were instituted by the Lord Jesus and commanded to be used by all who will be counted members of his body, that is, Baptism and the Supper or Table of the Lord Jesus, also called the Communion of His Body and Blood. These sacraments, both of the Old Testament and of the New, were instituted by God not only to make a visible distinction between his people and those who were without the Covenant, but also to exercise the faith of his children and, by participation of these sacraments, to seal in their hearts the assurance of his promise, and of that most blessed conjunction, union, and society, which the chosen have with their Head, Christ Jesus. And so we utterly condemn the vanity of those who affirm the sacraments to be nothing else than naked and bare signs. No, we assuredly believe that by Baptism we are engrafted into Christ Jesus, to be made partakers of his righteousness, by which our sins are covered and remitted, and also that in the Supper rightly used, Christ Jesus is so joined with us that he becomes the very nourishment and food for our souls. Not that we imagine any transubstantiation of bread into Christ's body, and of wine into his natural blood, as the Romanists have perniciously taught and wrongly believed; but this union and conjunction which we have with the body and blood of Christ Jesus in the right use of the sacraments is wrought by means of the Holy Ghost, who by true faith carries us above all things that are visible, carnal, and earthly, and makes us feed upon the body and blood of Christ Jesus, once broken and shed for us but now in heaven, and appearing for us in the presence of his Father. Notwithstanding the distance between his glorified body in heaven and mortal men on earth, yet we must assuredly believe that the bread which we break is the communion of Christ's body and the cup which we bless the communion of his blood. Thus we confess and believe without doubt that the faithful, in the right use of the Lord's Table, do so eat the body and drink the blood of the Lord Jesus that he remains in them and they in him; they are so made flesh of his flesh and bone of his bone that as the eternal Godhood has given to the flesh of Christ Jesus, which by nature was corruptible and mortal, life and immortality, so the eating and drinking of the flesh and blood of Christ Jesus does the like for us. We grant that this is neither given to us merely at the time nor by the power and virtue of the sacrament alone, but we affirm that the faithful, in the right use of the Lord's Table, have such union with Christ Jesus as the natural man cannot apprehend. Further we affirm that although the faithful, hindered by negligence and human weakness, do not profit as much as they ought in the actual moment of the Supper, yet afterwards it shall bring forth fruit, being living seed sown in good ground; for the Holy Spirit, who can never be separated from the right institution of the Lord Jesus, will not deprive the faithful of the fruit of that mystical action. Yet all this, we say again, comes of that true faith which apprehends Christ Jesus, who alone makes the sacrament effective in us. Therefore, if anyone slanders us by saying that we affirm or believe the sacraments to be symbols and nothing more, they are libelous and speak against the plain facts. On the other hand we readily admit that we make a distinction between Christ Jesus in his eternal substance and the elements of the sacramental signs. So we neither worship the elements, in place of that which they signify, nor yet do we despise them or undervalue them, but we use them with great reverence, examining ourselves diligently before we participate, since we are assured by the mouth of the apostle that 'whoever shall eat this bread, and drink this cup of the Lord, unworthily, shall be guilty of the body and blood of the Lord.'

Source: John Knox, The Scots Confession, 1560, from http://www.apuritansmind.com/ Creeds/ScottishConfession.htm#Chapter%2016%20-%20The%20Kirk.

8.12 The Seven Articles of Schleitheim

In 1527 the Swiss Anabaptists set out the principal articles of their faith. These concern the sacraments of baptism and Eucharist, but also outline the role of pastors in the church and set out rules for various aspects of Christian living.

The articles which we discussed and on which we were of one mind are these:
1. Baptism
2. The Ban [excommunication]
3. Breaking of Bread
4. Separation from the Abomination
5. Pastors in the Church
6. The Sword
7. The Oath.

First. Observe concerning baptism: Baptism shall be given to all those who have learned repentance and amendment of life, and who believe truly that their sins are taken away by Christ, and to all those who walk in the resurrection of Jesus Christ, and wish to be buried with Him in death, so that they may be resurrected with Him, and to all those who with this significance request it [baptism] of us and demand it for themselves. This excludes all infant baptism, the highest and chief abomination of the pope. In this you have the foundation and testimony of the apostles. Mt. 28, Mk. 16, Acts 2, 8, 16, 19. This we wish to hold simply, yet firmly and with assurance.

Second. We are agreed as follows on the ban: The ban shall be employed with all those who have given themselves to the Lord, to walk in His commandments, and with all those who are baptized into the one body of Christ and who are called brethren or sisters, and yet who slip sometimes and fall into error and sin, being inadvertently overtaken. The same shall be admonished twice in secret and the third time openly disciplined or banned according to the command of Christ. Mt.18. But this shall be done according to the regulation of the Spirit (Mt. 5) before the breaking of bread, so that we may break and eat one bread, with one mind and in one love, and may drink of one cup.

Third. In the breaking of bread we are of one mind and are agreed [as follows]: All those who wish to break one bread in remembrance of the broken body of Christ, and all who wish to drink of one drink as a remembrance of the shed blood of Christ, shall be united beforehand by baptism in one body of Christ which is the church of God and whose Head is Christ ... Therefore it is and must be [thus]: Whoever has not been called by one God to one faith, to one baptism, to one Spirit, to one body, with all the children of God's church, cannot be made [into] one bread with them, as indeed must be done if one is truly to break bread according to the command of Christ.

Fourth. We are agreed [as follows] on separation: A separation shall be made from the evil and from the wickedness which the devil planted in the world; in this manner, simply that we shall not have fellowship with them [the wicked] and not run with them in the multitude of their abominations. This is the way it is: Since all who do not walk in the obedience of faith, and have not united themselves with God so that they wish to do His will, are a great abomination before God, it is not possible for anything to grow or issue from them except abominable things. For truly all creatures are in but two classes, good and bad, believing and unbelieving, darkness and light, the world and those who [have come] out of the world, God's temple and idols, Christ and Belial; and none can have part with the other.

...

Fifth. We are agreed as follows on pastors in the church of God: The pastor in the church of God shall, as Paul has prescribed, be one who out-and-out has a good report of those who are outside the faith. This office shall be to read, to admonish and teach, to warn, to discipline, to ban in the church, to lead out in prayer for the advancement of all the brethren and sisters, to lift up the bread when it is to be broken, and in all things to see to the care of the body of Christ, in order that it may be built up and developed, and the mouth of the slanderer be stopped.

...

Sixth. We are agreed as follows concerning the sword: The sword is ordained of God outside the perfection of Christ. It punishes and puts to death the wicked, and guards and protects the good. In the Law the sword was ordained for the punishment of the wicked and for their death, and the same [sword] is [now] ordained to be used by the worldly magistrates. In the perfection of Christ, however, only the ban is used for a warning and for the excommunication of the one who has sinned, without putting the flesh to death – simply the warning and the command to sin no more ...

[I]t will be asked concerning the sword, whether a Christian shall pass sentence in worldly disputes and strife such as unbelievers have with one another. This is our united answer: Christ did not wish to decide or pass judgment between brother and brother in the case of the inheritance, but refused to do so. Therefore we should do likewise ...

Seventh. We are agreed as follows concerning the oath: The oath is a confirmation among those who are quarreling or making promises. In the Law it is commanded to be performed in God's Name, but only in truth, not falsely. Christ, who teaches the perfection of the Law, prohibits all swearing to His [followers], whether true or false – neither by heaven, nor by the earth, nor by Jerusalem, nor by our head – and that for the reason which He shortly thereafter gives, For you are not able to make one hair white or black. So you see it is for this reason that all swearing is forbidden: we cannot fulfill that which we promise when we swear, for we cannot change [even] the very least thing on us.

...

Christ also taught us along the same line when He said, Let your communication be Yea, yea; Nay, nay; for whatsoever is more than these cometh of evil. He says, Your speech or word shall be yea and nay. [However] when one does not wish to understand, he remains closed to the meaning. Christ is simply Yea and Nay, and all those who seek Him simply will understand His Word. Amen.

Source: **The Schleitheim Confession of Faith,** *adopted by a Swiss Brethren Conference on 24 February 1527, trans. J. C. Wenger, from http://www.bibleviews.com/Schleitheim.html*

8.13 Pope Pius XII, from *Mystici Corporis Christi*

Pope Pius XII issued this statement on the nature of the Body of Christ in 1943. Here he argues that the Church is identifiable through the profession of the same faith and the practice of the same rites.

68. Our union in and with Christ is first evident from the fact that, since Christ wills His Christian community to be a Body which is a perfect Society, its members must be united because they all work together towards a single end. The nobler the end towards which they strive, and the more divine the motive which actuates this collaboration, the higher, no doubt, will be the union. Now the end in question is supremely exalted; the continual sanctifying of the members of the Body for the glory of God and of the Lamb that was slain. The motive is altogether divine: not only the good pleasure of the Eternal Father, and the most earnest wish of our Savior, but the interior inspiration and impulse of the Holy Spirit in our minds and hearts. For if not even the smallest act conducive to salvation can be performed except in the Holy Spirit, how can countless multitudes of every people and every race work together harmoniously for the supreme glory of the triune God, except in the power of Him, who proceeds from the Father and the Son in one eternal act of love?

69. Now since its Founder willed this social body of Christ to be visible, the cooperation of all its members must also be externally manifest through their profession of the same faith and their sharing the same sacred rites, through participation in the same Sacrifice, and the practical observance of the same laws. Above all, it is absolutely necessary that the Supreme Head, that is, the Vicar of Jesus Christ on earth, be visible to the eyes of all, since it is He who gives effective direction to the work which all do in common in a mutually helpful way towards the attainment of the proposed end. As the Divine Redeemer sent the Paraclete, the Spirit of Truth, who in His name should govern the Church in an invisible way, so, in the same manner, He commissioned Peter and his successors to be His personal representatives on earth and to assume the visible government of the Christian community.

70. These juridical bonds in themselves far surpass those of any other human society, however exalted; and yet another principle of union must be added to them in those three virtues, Christian faith, hope and charity, which link us so closely to each other and to God.

71. 'One Lord, one faith' [Eph. 4.5], writes the Apostle: the faith, that is, by which we hold fast to God, and to Jesus Christ whom He has sent [John 17.3]. The beloved disciple teaches us how closely this faith binds us to God: 'Whosoever shall confess that Jesus is the Son of God, God abideth in him, and he in God' [1 John 4.15]. This Christian faith binds us no less closely to each other and to our divine Head. For all we who believe, 'having the same spirit of faith' [2 Cor. 4.13], are illumined by the same light of Christ, nourished by the same Food of Christ, and live under the teaching authority of Christ. If the same spirit of faith breathes in all, we are all living the same life 'in the faith of the Son of God who loved us and delivered himself for us' [Gal. 2.20]. And once we have received Christ, our Head, through an ardent faith so that

He dwells within our hearts [Eph. 3.17], as He is the author so He will be the finisher of our faith [Heb. 12.2].

...

82. By means of the Eucharistic Sacrifice Christ our Lord willed to give the faithful a striking manifestation of our union among ourselves and with our divine Head, wonderful as it is and beyond all praise. For in this Sacrifice the sacred minister acts as the viceregent not only of our Savior but of the whole Mystical Body and of each one of the faithful. In this act of Sacrifice through the hands of the priest, by whose word alone the Immaculate Lamb is present on the altar, the faithful themselves, united with him in prayer and desire, offer to the Eternal Father a most acceptable victim of praise and propitiation for the needs of the whole Church. And as the Divine Redeemer, when dying on the Cross, offered Himself to the Eternal Father as Head of the whole human race, so 'in this clean oblation' [Mal. 1.11] He offers to the heavenly Father not only Himself as Head of the Church, but in Himself His mystical members also, since He holds them all, even those who are weak and ailing, in His most loving Heart.

83. The Sacrament of the Eucharist is itself a striking and wonderful figure of the unity of the Church, if we consider how in the bread to be consecrated many grains go to form one whole, and that in it the very Author of supernatural grace is given to us, so that through Him we may receive the spirit of charity in which we are bidden to live now no longer our own life but the life of Christ, and to love the Redeemer Himself in all the members of His social Body.

Source: Mystici Corporis Christi, Encyclical of Pope Pius XII on the Mystical Body of Christ to Our Venerable Brethren, Patriarchs, Primates, Archbishops, Bishops and Other Local Ordinaries Enjoying Peace and Communion with the Apostolic See, *29 June 1943,* *from http://www.vatican.va/holy_father/pius_xii/encyclicals/documents/hf_p-xii_enc_* *29061943_mystici-corporis-christi_en.html.*

8.14 Dietrich Bonhoeffer, from *Sanctorum Communio*

Bonhoeffer argues here that the Church does not come into existence when we join it and cannot be 'made' into one thing or another. Rather, Christ calls the Church into being and it is for this reason that the Church exists.

We have been speaking not of the experience of sin and grace but of their theological meaning and their social intentions. It was only thus that we were able to establish the reality of the basic relationships and arrive at a specifically Christian sociology; otherwise it would have been impossible to form a concept of the church as opposed to that of religious community. We cannot deal here with the important problem as to how far faith and experience belong together. The important thing is that so far we have kept to faith not as an experience but in so far as it comprises realities. In so doing I think we have done justice to the special nature of theological method. Essentially the church can be understood only as a divine act, that is, in the utterance of faith; only upon this basis can it be understood as an 'experience'. Only faith comprehends the church as a community established by God. The so-called 'experience of the church' cannot in principle be distinguished from the experience of religious community; and yet there is a genuine experience of the church, just as there is an experience of justification. But far too often nowadays people forget that it is not the experience that makes the church. Supporters of the Youth Movement who speak of the church always fail to see the significance of the church's reality, that is, that it is established by God, and that it exists in principle 'before' any experience ... The church is not 'made' in great experiences of fellowship; it is not only historically but in point of faith too that everyone finds himself already in the church, when he becomes aware of it. We must re-awaken the perception that everyone who is moved by the Spirit stands in the church, and that this is something that is both a gift and a task. The loudly acclaimed 'will for the church' in its most recent forms is to be welcomed only in so far as it expresses not the will to make the church but the will of those concerned to recognise themselves, and be active, as the church moved by the Holy Spirit.

The fact that the 'will for the church' and the 'experience' of the church are for the most part confused with one another is very characteristic. We shall see at once why it is necessary to distinguish between them.

The confusion of community romanticism with the communion of saints is extremely dangerous. The communion of saints must always be recognised as something established by God, and of course as something we ourselves must will; but we ourselves can will it only if it is willed by God through us. It is thus willed by God 'before' all human will for community, and yet at the same time it is effective solely as will for community. This antinomy is overcome only by God's subjection of the human will to his own will. In actual fact this subjection always remains incipient, but God sees what has only begun as already consummated. This means that in speaking only of the present movement of will for community we have not exhausted God's action with us; it is rather that God's merciful judgment considers the new will of the church community, though constantly breaking down, to be something holy now, because he himself purposes to make it holy. God establishes the church in Christ as something which from that time on is in his view perfect at every moment. But to make it actual he uses the wills of men, who are thus both the means and the end. If a community of will is moved by the Spirit it is always *ipso facto* the church. The will for the church is necessary, but genuine only in connection with, or when arising from, faith in the church which is really present, already established by God. 'Experiencing the church' is something else. It is supposed to make it possible for us to experience the 'others' as members of the church of God. There are many weighty dogmatic considerations opposing this. 'We live by faith and not by sight.' None of us knows whether our neighbour has been elected, or has remained impenitent. He is completely non-transparent to us in all that he does. This means not only that nothing is known about a man's *donum perseverantiae*, but also that Christian actions can spring from a hypocritical, misguided heart, governed by false enthusiasm. Only the *opera,* and not the *Persona, quae in manu Dei est* (Calvin), are perceptible; 'the Lord knows those who are his.' How then should it be possible for us really to experience the church, and not just religious community? The church is *impalpabilis, insensibilis*; as Luther says, it must be believed. Even when men reveal their hearts to one another in love no one of them can with certainty state whether the other belongs to the church. It is only through faith that the church can be grasped, and only faith can interpret the experience of communion that necessarily arises as evidence of the presence of the church. Man 'experiences' only the religious community, but knows in faith that this religious community is 'the church'. Even when two or three are gathered together in Christian community, and being one in Christ, profess their faith, they also believe in the church upon the strength of the promise (Isa. 55.11; Matt. 18.20) and their experience is only in faith an experience of the church.

But what does 'believing in the church' mean? We do not believe in an invisible church, nor in the kingdom of God existing in the church as *coetus electorum*; but we believe that God has made the actual empirical church, in which the Word and the sacraments are administered, into his community, that it is the Body of Christ, that is, the presence of Christ in the world, and that according to the promise God's Spirit becomes effective in it. We believe in the church as the church of God and as the communion of saints, of those, that is, who are sanctified by God, but within the historical form of the empirical church. Thus we believe in the means of grace within the empirical church and hence in the holy congregation created by them. We believe in the church as *una*, for it is 'Christ existing as the church', and Christ is the one Lord over those who are all one in him; as *sancta*, since the Holy Spirit is at work in it, and as *catholica*, since as the church of God its call is to the whole world, and it is present wherever God's Word is preached in the world. We believe in the church not as an unattainable ideal, or one which has still to be attained, but as a present reality. What distinguishes Christian thinking from all idealist theories of community is that the Christian community is the church of God in every moment of history and it knows it will never attain perfection within the development of history. It will remain impure so long as history exists, and yet in this its actual form it is God's church.

Source: Dietrich Bonhoeffer, Sanctorum Communio: A Dogmatic Inquiry into the Sociology of the Church, *London: Collins, 1963, pp. 194–8.*

8.15 Lesslie Newbigin, from *The Household of God*

In this passage Newbigin discusses the missionary nature of the Church and argues that mission is fundamental to the being of the Church. He critiques some of the modern approaches to mission, particularly those that view it is an extra activity to the life of the Church, and missionary endeavours that are inseparable from cultural advances.

This truth about the nature of salvation in Christ must obviously be determinative of the doctrine of the Church. The Church has its existence in relation to the salvation which has been wrought at Christ's coming into the world and is to be consummated at His coming again. Since that consummation concerns the whole world, the Church's existence is in the act of being the bearer of that salvation to the whole world. 'The Church exists by mission as fire exists by burning.' It has its being, so to say, in the magnetic field between Christ and the world. Its *koinonia* in Him is a participation in His apostolate to the world. Each Christian congregation is the earnest and foretaste, the *arrabon* of the gathering together of all men of every tribe and tongue around the throne of God and of the Lamb. It is true to its own essential nature only when it takes this fact seriously and therefore treats the world-wide mission of the Church as something which belongs to the very core of its existence as a corporate body. Between the Church militant here on earth, longing for the full possession of that which she has in foretaste, and the consummation for which she longs, the marriage supper of the Lamb, there lies the unfinished missionary task. The first answer to her prayer, 'Come, Lord Jesus,' is His commission, – 'Go ye into all the world – and lo, I am with you.'

If this be true, then it is high time that its implications for the ecumenical discussion of the nature of the Church were realistically faced. The danger about these discussions is that they may concentrate upon the matters upon which the Churches differ, on which they presumably cannot all be right, and may altogether overlook matters upon which the Churches agree but are quite certainly all wrong. In all the discussions between Catholics and Protestants as to the *esse* and *bene esse* of the Church, I do not remember to have heard the fact seriously faced that a Church which has ceased to be a mission has certainly lost the *esse*, and not merely the *bene esse* of a Church. Yet surely this is so. It is impossible to reconcile with the New Testament the view which seems to be more or less accepted among the majority of Churchmen, that while missionary work is an admirable thing to do, within reasonable limits, it is not something without which the Church simply falls to the ground. We must say bluntly that when the Church ceases to be a mission, then she openly denies the titles by which she is adorned in the New Testament. Apart from actual engagement in the task of being Christ's ambassador to the world, the name 'priests and kings into God' is but a usurped title.

I think it is right to spend a few moments looking at some of the evidences, in the life of the Church, of failure to grasp this truth about the Church's essential nature.

1. The most obvious evidence is the fact that, in the thinking of the vast

majority of Christians, the words 'Church' and 'Mission' connote two different kinds of society. The one is conceived to be a society devoted to worship, and the spiritual care and nurture of its members. It is typically represented by a large and ancient building. The other, is conceived to be a society devoted to the propagation of the Gospel, passing on its converts to the safe keeping of 'the Church' ... The two cannot become one until a very deep and widespread change has taken place in the thinking of the Churches about their own nature, until they have come to see, and to express in the ordinary life of the Church, the truth that the Church has all its treasure entrusted to it for the sake of the world, and that therefore mission belongs to the very substance of the Church's life.

2. Less obvious, but equally significant, are the implications of the ordinary conceptions of missionary strategy which operate even in Churches which accept the obligation of world-wide missionary work. It is taken for granted that the missionary obligation is one that has to be met after the needs of the home have been fully met; that existing gains have to be thoroughly consolidated before we go further afield; that the world-wide Church has to be built up with the same sort of prudent calculation of resources and costs as is expected of any business enterprise. Must we not contrast this with the sort of strategy that the New Testament reveals, which seems to be a sort of determination to stake out God's claim to the whole world at once, without expecting that one area should be fully worked out before the next is claimed. Thus our Lord forbids His disciples to stay and argue with those who do not receive them, but tells them to shake off the dust of their feet for a testimony and go on. And Paul's missionary planning leaps to the end of the known world, urging him forward from each field of work to the next, not when the Church has been fully built up, but when the Gospel has been fully preached. He carries in his heart always a deep sorrow concerning the home base. For we must remember that the true home base of the missionary enterprise is the Jews, and that all others can only be called the home base in a secondary sense. Yet he is clear that the right course is not to wait to win the Jews before going on with the Gentile mission, but rather to expect that the conversion of the Gentiles will be the means of life to the Jews. All this is precisely congruous with a conception of the Christian mission which sees it as the sign and instrument of a universal and eschatological salvation, the coming of a kingdom not of this world wherein death shall have been swallowed up in victory. It is the strategy of a kingdom which is God's and not ours.

... St. Paul leaves behind him in Ephesus, after only two years of missionary work, a fully established Church provided with its own ministry, able to stand entirely on its own feet. Two centuries would be regarded as a more reasonable period by a missionary of the modern era, and during most of that period the young Church would be treated as a charge on the personal and financial resources of the home base, precluding further advance into new regions. The contrast is startling and becomes more so the more it is examined in detail. Surely it reveals a fundamental defect in our doctrine of the Church. St. Paul is working with a doctrine of the Church which is dominated by the hope of the coming consummation, a consummation which will be wholly the victory of God, but of which the witness of the Church is the sign and instrument, and of which its life is the foretaste. Our missionary methods seem to suggest that we expect an infinitude of time in which the Church on earth can gradually be extended until it covers the whole globe. But the conception of the Church which we tend to reproduce as the fruit of our missionary work is so much a replica of our own, so much that of a fundamentally settled body existing for the sake of its own members rather than of a body of strangers and pilgrims, the sign and instrument of a supernatural and universal salvation to be revealed, that our missionary advance tends to follow the lines of cultural and political expansion, and to falter when that advance stops. Our present methods show little sign of being able to achieve the enormous new advances which are necessary if the vast unevangelised regions are to be reached.

3. When the eschatological and missionary perspective has been lost from the thinking of the Church, its task comes to be conceived in terms of the rescue of individuals one by one out of this present evil age and their preservation unharmed for the world to come. When this becomes dominant the Church thinks primarily of its duty to care for its own members, and its duty to those outside drops into second place. A conception of pastoral care is developed which seems to assume that the individual believer is primarily a passive recipient of the means of grace which it is the business of the Church to administer. 'The Church', then, comes to mean the paid ministry – and this may and does happen in Churches which claim to repudiate sacerdotalism. There is of course real truth in this picture. The sheep are to be fed by those whom the Lord appoints for the purpose. The faithful steward has to give their due portions to all the household. But when this is taken to be the whole truth, then we must point to other parts of the New Testament which stress the responsibilities of the whole body as a royal priesthood, as the body of Christ in which every member has its proper function. The root of the error lies in the failure to keep in view throughout the *whole* salvation of which the Church is the sign and first-fruit and instrument. If this is done, the Church will be delivered from the tendency to turn in upon itself and will always be turned outwards to the world. It will know itself to be wholly committed in every part to the task of witness to the world in word and in service. It will understand that participation in Christ means participation in His mission to the world, and that therefore true pastoral care, true training in the Christian life, and true use of the means of grace will precisely be in and for the discharge of this missionary task.

Source: Lesslie Newbigin, The Household of God: Lectures on the Nature of the Church, London: SCM Press, 1953, pp. 142–47.

8.16 Walter Kasper, from *That They May All be One*

*In this passage Kasper reflects on the progress of the ecumenical move-
ment, and the nature of the Church* communio. *He refers to* communio *as
participation rather than community and argues that this participation is
not a choice to join together, but the nature of the Church, and is established especially through participation in baptism and Eucharist.*

[Ecumenical dialogue has] shown that incomplete *communio*, which links us
with other churches and ecclesial communities, is not just a theory but a reality which can be experienced. We have found that what unites us is far more
than what, sadly, still divides us. Everybody who has participated in ecumenical dialogue knows what an exhilarating and constantly surprising experience
this is. This discovery represents a twentieth-century *novum* in church history.
The separated churches and ecclesial communities no longer see themselves
as hostile antagonists or at best indifferent neighbours. They see themselves as
brothers and sisters who together have set out on the way to full communion.
The encyclical letter *ut unum sint* speaks about rediscovered brotherliness as
the essential fruit of the ecumenical dialogue (*Ut Unum Sint* [*UUS*] 41.f).

   This new ecclesial reality fills us with gratitude, joy and hope; it is the fruit
of the work of the Holy Spirit (*Unitatis Redintegratio* [*UR*] 1;4). But at the same
time it also causes pain. For the closer we come to each other, the more painful
is the experience that we are not yet in full communion. We are hurt by what
still separates us and hinders us from gathering around the table of the Lord.
We are increasingly dissatisfied with the ecumenical status quo, and ecumenical frustration and sometimes even opposition develops. Paradoxically, it
is the same ecumenical progress which is also the cause of the ecumenical
malaise. This gives increased urgency to the questions: How can we progress?
How can we progress from the already existing incomplete communion to
full *communio*, which is the ultimate goal of the ecumenical movement (*UR* 3;
UUS 14)?

   The answer is not easy because, as so often, there is no one answer. The
present situation is complex and many-layered and there are many reasons
why some people today have the impression that, although a lot is happening
in ecumenical dialogue, no real progress is being made.

...

   The theological understanding of *communio* is often replaced or overlaid by
an anthropological or sociological understanding. The secularized use of the
word *communio* leads to a secular understanding of ecumenism characterized
by non-theological, general social criteria and interpretations.

   In its secularized meaning, *communio* is understood in a 'horizontal' way
as a community of people resulting from the individual's desire for community. *Communio* in this sense is the result of an association of partners who are
in principle free and equal. This understanding is based on the idea of the
social contract which developed during the period of Enlightenment. Such an
understanding of the Church can even become a battle-cry against the hierar-

chical structure of the Church. This conception views the Church 'from below', i.e., the 'base' church as opposed to the 'established' church. This understanding of the *communio* concept of the Church develops the idea of the equality and equal rights of all church members and demands the democratization of the Church, so that decisions are made in open, fearless dialogue, critical discourse, consensus-forming processes or by plebiscite.

Democracy may be considered the best of all bad possibilities. But democracy is far from being salvation. The experiences of the twentieth century, among others, have shown that majorities can be mobilized by populist agitation and often represent the sum of the highest number of private interests capable of forming a majority, at the expense of minorities which cannot mobilize sufficient voices. Democratically evolved majorities, if generally recognized, may have a pacifying influence; but the search for truth cannot be organized by majorities.

...

The sacramental basis of *communio* is the *communio* in the one baptism. For through the one baptism we have all been baptized into the one body of Christ. Baptism is the sacrament of faith. So *communio* through baptism presupposes and implies *communio* in the common faith of the Church, i.e., communion in the Gospel. Both communion in faith and baptism are the foundations of *communio*.

The summit of *communio* is participation in the Eucharist. In the history of theology, the most important text was to become 1 Corinthians 10:16ff ... This text states that the *koinonia* in the one Eucharistic bread is source and sign of the *koinonia* in the one body of the Church; the one Eucharistic body of Christ is source and sign of the one ecclesial body of Christ.

...

We have to fill the interim stage that we have reached (of a real if not complete church *communio*) with real life. The 'ecumenism of love' and the 'ecumenism of truth', which both naturally remain very important, must be complemented by an 'ecumenism of life'. We have to apply all that we have achieved to the way we actually live. The churches did not diverge only through discussion, they diverged through alienation, i.e. the way we lived. Therefore they have to come closer to each other again in their lives; they must get accustomed to each other, pray together, work together and live together, bearing the pain of incomplete *communio* and of not yet being able to share Eucharistic communion around the Lord's table. Thus this ecumenism of life is not to be understood in a static way; it is a process of healing and growing.

Source: Walter Kasper, That They May All Be One: The Call to Unity Today, London: Burns & Oates, 2004, pp. 51–5, 72.

8.17 Second Vatican Council, from *Lumen Gentium*

This document, the title of which means 'light of the nations', was prepared during the Second Vatican Council. In the following section, the fulfilment of the Church is anticipated, and the calling of the Church in the meantime outlined.

Joined with Christ in the Church and signed with the Holy Spirit 'who is the pledge of our inheritance' [Eph. 1.14], truly we are called and we are sons of God [1 John 3.1] but we have not yet appeared with Christ in glory [Col. 3.4], in which we shall be like to God, since we shall see Him as He is [1 John 3.2]. And therefore 'while we are in the body, we are exiled from the Lord [2 Cor. 5.6] and having the first-fruits of the Spirit we groan within ourselves [Rom. 8.23] and we desire to be with Christ' [Phil. 1.23]. By that same charity, however, we are urged to live more for Him, who died for us and rose again [2 Cor. 5.15]. We strive therefore to please God in all things [2 Cor. 5.9] and we put on the armour of God, that we may be able to stand against the wiles of the devil and resist in the evil day [Eph. 6.11–13]. Since however we know not the day nor the hour, on Our Lord's advice we must be constantly vigilant so that, having finished the course of our earthly life [Heb. 9.27], we may merit to enter into the marriage feast with Him and to be numbered among the blessed [Matt. 25.31–46] and that we may not be ordered to go into eternal fire [Matt. 25.41] like the wicked and slothful servant [Matt. 25.26], into the exterior darkness where 'there will be the weeping and the gnashing of teeth' [Matt. 22.13; 25.30]. For before we reign with Christ in glory, all of us will be made manifest 'before the tribunal of Christ, so that each one may receive what he has won through the body, according to his works, whether good or evil' [2 Cor. 5.10] and at the end of the world 'they who have done good shall come forth unto resurrection of life; but those who have done evil unto resurrection of judgment' [John 5.29]. Reckoning therefore that 'the sufferings of the present time are not worthy to be compared with the glory to come that will be revealed in us' [Rom. 8.18], strong in faith we look for the 'blessed hope and the glorious coming of our great God and Saviour, Jesus Christ' [Titus 2.13] 'who will refashion the body of our lowliness, conforming it to the body of His glory' [Phil. 3.21]. and who will come 'to be glorified in His saints and to be marvelled at in all those who have believed' [2 Thess. 1.10].

49. Until the Lord shall come in His majesty, and all the angels with Him [1 Cor. 15.26–27] and death being destroyed, all things are subject to Him, some of His disciples are exiles on earth, some having died are purified, and others are in glory beholding 'clearly God Himself triune and one, as He is'; but all in various ways and degrees are in communion in the same charity of God and neighbour and all sing the same hymn of glory to our God. For all who are in Christ, having His Spirit, form one Church and cleave together in Him. [Eph. 4.16]. Therefore the union of the wayfarers with the brethren who have gone to sleep in the peace of Christ is not in the least weakened or interrupted, but on the contrary, according to the perpetual faith of the Church, is strengthened by communication of spiritual goods. For by reason of the fact that those in

heaven are more closely united with Christ, they establish the whole Church more firmly in holiness, lend nobility to the worship which the Church offers to God here on earth and in many ways contribute to its greater edification [1 Cor. 12.12–27]. For after they have been received into their heavenly home and are present to the Lord [2 Cor. 5.8], through Him and with Him and in Him they do not cease to intercede with the Father for us, showing forth the merits which they won on earth through the one Mediator between God and man [1 Tim. 2.5], serving God in all things and filling up in their flesh those things which are lacking of the sufferings of Christ for His Body which is the Church [Col. 1.24]. Thus by their brotherly interest our weakness is greatly strengthened.

50. Fully conscious of this communion of the whole Mystical Body of Jesus Christ, the pilgrim Church from the very first ages of the Christian religion has cultivated with great piety the memory of the dead, and 'because it is a holy and wholesome thought to pray for the dead that they may be loosed from their sins' [2 Macc. 12.46], also offers suffrages for them. The Church has always believed that the apostles and Christ's martyrs who had given the supreme witness of faith and charity by the shedding of their blood, are closely joined with us in Christ, and she has always venerated them with special devotion, together with the Blessed Virgin Mary and the holy angels. The Church has piously implored the aid of their intercession. To these were soon added also those who had more closely imitated Christ's virginity and poverty, and finally others whom the outstanding practice of the Christian virtues and the divine charisms recommended to the pious devotion and imitation of the faithful.

…

Our union with the Church in heaven is put into effect in its noblest manner especially in the sacred Liturgy, wherein the power of the Holy Spirit acts upon us through sacramental signs. Then, with combined rejoicing we celebrate together the praise of the divine majesty; then all those from every tribe and tongue and people and nation [Rev. 5.9] who have been redeemed by the blood of Christ and gathered together into one Church, with one song of praise magnify the one and triune God. Celebrating the Eucharistic sacrifice therefore, we are most closely united to the Church in heaven in communion with and venerating the memory first of all of the glorious ever-Virgin Mary, of Blessed Joseph and the blessed apostles and martyrs and of all the saints.

Source: **Dogmatic Constitution on the Church, Lumen Gentium,** *21 November 1964, from http://www.vatican.va/archive/hist_councils/ii_vatican_council/documents/vat-ii_const_ 19641121_lumen-gentium_en.html*

8.18 Geoffrey W. Bromiley, from *Children of Promise*

In his book Children of Promise *Bromiley explores the scriptural arguments for the meaning of baptism. He argues that baptism does not depend upon the faith of the recipient, but on the gracious initiative of God.*

When we investigate the matter in scripture we find that the situation is very different. In fact we ought to be warned at the outset by the very character of the baptismal sign. In contrast to the Lord's Supper it is an act in which the recipient has a passive, not an active role. Even an adult convert does not baptize as he takes, eats, or drinks. He is baptized. He does not do something for or to himself. Something is done for, to, and on him. When we turn to the relevant passages in scripture we find that this is not accidental, for baptism is not related primarily to what we do, our faith, or to our decision or confession of faith, but to that which is done for us, to that in which our faith is set. In this again baptism corresponds to circumcision. Paul, as we have seen, undoubtedly links circumcision and faith, yet he does not call circumcision an enactment or expression of faith. He calls it a seal. Moreover, it is not strictly a seal of faith, but a seal of the righteousness of faith. Nor is faith itself the righteousness. According to the whole argument of this first part of Romans righteousness is a gift and work of God reckoned on account of faith. It is here that we begin to see the element of truth which unfortunately undergoes distortion in exaggerated sacramentalist and quasi-magical ideas of baptism.

In relation to baptism, surely the first thing to strike us is the emphasis placed not so much on the person baptized as on the one into whose name he or she is baptized. The words of institution in Matthew 28:19 tell us that baptism is to be in the name of the Father, the Son, and the Holy Spirit. In the Acts accounts we read of baptisms in the name of Jesus Christ, which implies the whole Trinity [e.g. 2.38]. Paul disclaims the importance of the human minister only to enhance the one into whose name we are all baptized [1 Cor. 1.12–15]. All this means that baptism does not primarily summon either ourselves or others to look at us and our faith and confession of faith. It invites both ourselves and others to look first at the one who is the object of our faith and whose gracious work we acknowledge when we confess our faith. To be sure, faith has an indispensable role. Nevertheless, salvation does not lie in our faith. Peter clearly proclaims that salvation lies in the name of Jesus Christ [Acts 4.12] and baptism, as a sign of the gospel like the Supper, was not instituted to witness to our own name as though we were the first thing. It was instituted to witness to the name and act of God into which we are caught up in faith. It is our baptism and confession of Christ only because it is Christ's baptizing and confession of us. Baptism finds its basic and central meaning as a sign and proclamation of the work of God whereby the righteousness of faith is sealed to us. It has only secondary and derivative meaning as the confession of our own faith and conversion …

Now it is evident that neither the forgiveness of sins nor regeneration is or can be a human work or even a human possibility. We can and must do certain things for ourselves within the totality of God's saving work. We are told to repent, call on the name of the Lord, believe, confess our faith, and receive forgiveness and renewal. We have to do these things if salvation is to be ours and we have to do them even if only enabled by virtue of what God does. Forgiveness and regeneration, however, are very plainly the work of God which we cannot and should not try to do. 'Who can forgive sins but God only?' (Mk 2:7) The Pharisees were quite right when they put this accusing question before Jesus. They were wrong in failing to see that in Jesus they were dealing with God. Similarly the new birth is not of blood, nor of the will of man, nor of the will of the flesh, but of God (Jn 1:13). If we are to be born again we must be born from above, born of the Spirit (Jn 3:3–6). This means, however, that if baptism is primarily for remission and regeneration it does not focus on our necessary but secondary and derivative action, faith and the confession of faith. It focuses on the indispensable, primary, and originative action of God, the divine work of reconciliation and renewal. Baptism declares, signifies and seals not what I do but what God has done, does and will do for me.

...

Surely, then, we are forced to the conclusion that baptism is primarily a sign or seal of God's own work. Saying this, however, is simply another way of saying that it is a sign or seal of the covenant and its fulfilment in Jesus Christ. God's reconciling and regenerating work constitutes the fulfilment of the promise which lies at the heart of the covenant and of all God's dealings with his covenant people. From the very beginning the covenant carried with it the creation of a redeemed and renewed people, at first restricted in the main to a single nation but then broadened to embrace all nations. The fulfilment of the covenant in and with the death and resurrection of Jesus Christ means that the word of promise has been succeeded by the word of accomplishment, and the Old Testament signs of anticipation have been succeeded by the New Testament signs of recollection. If this is so, then it is no less perverse to treat baptism as the sign of personal faith than to treat circumcision as the sign of the faith of Abraham. Indeed, if this is possible, it is even more perverse. It is false to the New Testament and destroys the whole balance of the Christian gospel and the Christian life. It substitutes an anthropocentric meaning for the theocentric meaning. It puts the 'I' and its decision in the place of God and his decision. It gives the primacy and honor to man and his work and not as it should to God and his work. It gives this work of man an apparent importance of its own in independence of Jesus Christ and the atonement and the Holy Spirit and regeneration. It finds the critical point in our turning to God rather than his turning to us and his turning us to himself. In other words, it turns the gospel upside down. In so doing it misses the real meaning and purpose of the gospel ordinance or sacrament.

By its very nature baptism is calculated to drive home the personal application of the divine work. The same was true of circumcision. Like circumcision, however, it does so only as it proclaims the divine work which is the work of the covenant fulfilled in Jesus Christ by the Holy Spirit.

Source: Geoffrey Bromiley, Children of Promise: The Case for Baptizing Infants, *Edinburgh: T. & T. Clark, 1979, pp. 27–37.*

8.19 Paul Fiddes, from *Tracks and Traces*

Here Fiddes discusses three trends in the way that churches understand the call to unity. He asserts that moves towards true unity have their origins in God and identifies three aspects of this: unity, fellowship and covenant.

First, the kind of unity that churches are seeking today is one which begins *from the bottom up* rather than top-down ... Whatever fine things have been happening in the airy heights of theological commissions, such as the dialogue between the Baptist World Alliance and the Roman Catholic Church, it is another thing for this to trickle down to the roots. It is better for unity to grow at grass-roots level in the first place, in a sharing of resources for worship, witness and social action at local and regional levels ...

A second general trend I detect is towards the vision of 'full communion' rather than 'one world church'. The picture of visible unity generally on view is that of a continuing variety of churches, each with their own heritage, tradition and emphases, but each in full communion with the other. It is this kind of goal of union which was envisioned by the World Council of Churches (WCC) Assembly at Canberra in 1991: 'when all the churches are able to *recognize* in one another the one, holy, catholic and apostolic church in its fullness.' Such a communion, the statement spells out, will be nurtured in a common sacramental life, will confess a common faith, will have a common life in which members and ministries are mutually recognized and reconciled, and will exercise a common mission in the world.

The stress of communion, or fellowship (*koinonia*), is rooted in a theological vision of God who lives in a fellowship of love as Father, Son and Holy Spirit...The abiding of the communion of the church in the communion of God means that in spite of separation the various churches are *already* in communion. This is a new note that has been struck in recent years, a feeling that churches are not 'out of communion' – they *cannot* be if they exist in God's communion. But they can be said to share 'an existing though imperfect communion' or a 'degree of communion' ...

A third general trend arises from this stress on full communion – that is the acceptance of diversity in the unity. Again appeal is made to the vision of a triune God: just as God lives in unity and true diversity as three persons in one God, so the church in God's image can and should show *legitimate diversity*. The catchword here is 'reconciled diversity' not uniformity. This does raise the question, however, of what are legitimate and illegitimate diversities. The document 'Towards Koinonia' suggests that diversity is not acceptable where it denies the 'common confession of Jesus Christ as God and Saviour', where it justifies discrimination on the basis of race or gender, where it prevents reconciliation, where it hinders the common mission of the church, and where it endangers the life in *koinonia* [WCC, 'Towards Koinonia', para. 57, p. 280].

This is fairly wide-ranging, and while it clearly and properly rules out – for instance – a church based on apartheid, it might also rule out uncomfortable challenges to the status quo which are truly prophetic. Perhaps life in *koinonia* sometimes *needs* to be 'endangered' ...

So, to summarize where we have come so far, the sense of ecumenical call which is widespread at present is a calling to work from the roots, to work towards full communion, and to live with diversity, painful though it is. I have been using the term 'call' because it echoes the statement of Ephesians 4 that we are *called* to be one, and so reminds us that all true movements for unity have their origin in the desire, initiative and the summons of God (cf. the prayer of Jesus in John 17). The opening verses in this chapter in Ephesians have been often quoted in the dialogues of the modern ecumenical movement, in which the readers are urged to be: 'eager to maintain the unity of the spirit in the bond of peace. There is one body and one Spirit, just as you were *called* to the one hope that belongs to your *call*, one Lord, one faith, one baptism, one God and father of us all, who is above all and through all and in all.' This passage either states or hints at three theological ideas that define the call to unity ... First there is the image of the body; second there is an evoking of the fellowship in which God lives, as 'one Spirit ... one Lord (Christ) ... one father'; and thirdly there is the allusion to covenant with the phase 'bond of peace.' One body, one fellowship, one covenant.

Source: Paul Fiddes, Tracks and Traces: Baptist Identity in Church and Theology, *Carlisle: Paternoster Press, 2005, pp. 193–7.*

8.20 Alisdair Heron, from *Table and Tradition*

In this passage Heron reviews some of the inherited views of sacraments and argues that they must be held in complementarity. He then goes on to explain how Jesus himself is the sacrament.

i. Christ the Sacrament

In the last two chapters we have traced two rather different paradigmatic models of 'a sacrament'. One is controlled by the thought *of God acting through the action of the church*, the other by that of *God communicating by his Word to faith*. Yet each model has its strengths and its inherent dangers. The first is based on the sound recognition that a sacrament involves *action* and not merely *words*: 'Do this ... ' is performative and not merely declaratory. The second builds on the equally fundamental awareness that God does not act upon us dumbly or impersonally, but in acting also communicates and evokes an answer. To this extent the two models may be seen as complementary and mutually corrective. Taken on its own, the first can lead to an uncritical identification of God's action and ours, and so to a magical view of sacramental efficacy, and the second to a reduction of 'sacrament' to a 'naked and bare sign', or to an activity of our own in which God is no longer believed to be involved directly. Yet the Word and the action of God cannot be sundered from each other; our own speech and action rest and depend on his; and both the activity of the church and the response of faith have their necessary place in the horizon. Each of the two models has something necessary and valuable to contribute – provided they are held together in proper complementarity rather than torn apart into stark opposition, in which each becomes opaque and absolute, with its more dubious aspects setting the tone.

This recognition, however, can only be a first step towards a profounder re-evaluation. The very concept of 'a sacrament' is not properly to be found in the New Testament at all. Both these conceptions of it rest largely on the theology of the early Latin fathers, and in particular on Augustine's explanations and interpretations of *sacramentum*. Behind that lies a wider tendency in the early church to focus attention on the rite, the sacred action, and to ask what was really happening in it. The danger there is that we can come to concentrate simply on the rite, or on a preferred definition of 'sacrament', and work out from there. Instead we do better to return to the central meaning of the whole matter and to remember that in the New Testament *mysterion* does not refer to ceremonies but to the secret of God's redemptive will, disclosed in Jesus Christ. Jesus Christ is *the* 'sacrament' in whom God and man are united, the Father's purpose for man declared, and man's true identity as the child of God affirmed. It is there that we must begin if we are to get our thought about 'sacraments' into sharper focus.

In this light, the established medieval and Reformation definitions of a sacrament, so far from being dispossessed, take on yet deeper meaning. If it is understood, along scholastic lines, as 'a form and cause of grace', that pattern can be applied, in the strictest propriety, to Jesus Christ himself. He is the actualisation of God's favour present for us in our world, and it is from and through him that that favour is extended to us. In similar style, the Reformed understanding of 'a sign given to confirm God's promise' also leads back into christology; for where is *the* sign and pledge of that promise but in Christ incarnate, crucified, risen and ascended? Obliquely though it may be, both definitions point back to him, and it is in their relation to him that the opposition between them can best be overcome.

In what sense, then, may we understand the claim that he is *the* sacrament? First, he himself, as God's Word made flesh, as true God and true man, is the place of meeting between God and man, the visible and the invisible, the natural and the supernatural. He is himself sign and pledge and reality of God's presence with and for us. Second, from and through him in his person, history and destiny, is given to us the life that is his and in which we share. Here certainly it is better to think less in terms of 'grace' than of the Holy Spirit; for the power and energy of that life is the power and energy of the Spirit that came upon him and was released and sent through his cross and resurrection/ascension. Third, in that Spirit we are gathered together, incorporated with Christ, and in him offered to the Father; and by this the whole creation is recalled to its promised future under the sign of the reign of God. The uniting of God with man, the coming of God to man, and the raising of man to God: these are the three moments which combine in him as the outworking of the *mysterion* which he himself is. It is by reference to this ground and criterion that all 'sacramentality' is established and measured.

...

In view of this it is pertinent to ask whether the categories of 'sacrament' and 'sacramentality' whose roots lie in the early church rather than in the New Testament do not after all have something of value to contribute. Given that the central and fundamental *mysterion* or *sacramentum* is Christ himself, may we not also recognise a strictly secondary and dependent sacramentality in the forms and means of his presence and action? In this sense the church may properly be called a sacramental reality as his body. Its nature and meaning lie deeper than the surface appearance; it is both visible and invisible, both an empirical entity and a divinely grounded mystery. But it is not in and by itself a sacrament apart from Christ, nor is it a sacrament of the same sort as he, for only in him is its own identity grounded, disclosed and promised. It is sacramental as a sacrament of *Christ, the sacrament*, as participant in him, as imaging him, and as witnessing to him.

In this broad sense, every authentic expression of the being and life of the church in the world has sacramental character, for it always rests on and represents the mystery of Christ and his Spirit, of his life for us and our life in him. This applies equally to the life of the believer: there too lies a hidden depth and a secret significance, for there too God in Christ is at work. It is in the divine call and promise in Jesus that our own identity is declared, and it is in response to that call and promise that our true life grows, grasped by the graciousness of the Father and made a testimony in the Spirit to his love in the incarnate Son. Each individual Christian life is essentially sacramental in its core, called and challenged and – however brokenly and fragmentarily

– empowered to be a sign and channel of the everlasting mercy. This is not a recipe for unrealistic perfectionism or for pietistic escapism: rather it has to do with the essential orientation and direction of our human life in the world through which we are travelling. Precisely because it is sacramental, it involves from beginning to end the victory of grace over our failures, of forgiveness over our guilts, of liberation and promise over our enslavements and defeats. And unless the life of the Christian believer is indeed seized by grace, forgiveness, liberation and promise, how shall it be Christian at all?

...

If 'the sacramental' in general, and Baptism and Eucharist in particular, are set in this light, it is possible to move away from the tendency to think of them in the rather juridical terms that marked medieval theology, and also to some degree that of the Reformers. Where attention is focused more on a certain conception of 'validity', or of 'real presence' than on the true presence, or where a legalistic notion of 'what the Lord commanded' obscures the profound connexion of the Eucharist with the very person of the Word made flesh, then eucharistic theology can hardly fail to be diverted on to (doubtless well intentioned) side-tracks. Both can find the needed corrective in a return to the centre of the matter, and in a measured working out from it.

Source: Alisdair Heron, Table and Tradition, *Edinburgh: Handsel Press, 1993 and Louisville: Westminster John Knox Press, 1984, pp. 155–9.*

8.21 Jürgen Moltmann, from *The Church in the Power of the Spirit*

Here Moltmann suggests that the marks of the Church, are in fact marks of Christ and therefore anticipate all that the Church will become. These marks also lead to action as the Church seeks to live the life of the kingdom.

If the church acquires its existence through the activity of Christ, then her characteristics, too, are characteristics of Christ's activity first of all. The acknowledgment of the 'one, holy, catholic and apostolic church' is acknowledgment of the uniting, sanctifying, comprehensive and commissioning lordship of Christ. In so far they are *statements of faith*. 'The *unity* of the church is not primarily the unity of her members, but the unity of Christ who acts upon them all, in all places and at all times.' Christ gathers his church. Consequently the unity of the church lies in his uniting activity. The result of his gathering activity is the unity of believers in Christ (Gal. 3.28) and their unity of mind in the Spirit (Eph. 4.1ff). The *holiness* of the church is not initially the holiness of her members or her cultic assemblies; it is the holiness of the Christ who acts on sinners. Christ sanctifies his church by justifying it. Consequently the holiness of the church lies in his sanctifying activity. The result of his justifying activity is 'the communion of saints'. The *catholicity* of the church is not initially her spatial extent or the fact that she is in principle open to the world; it is the limitless lordship of Christ, to whom 'all authority is given in heaven and on earth'. Where, and so far as, Christ rules, there, consequently, the church is to be found. She acquires her openness to the world in the breadth of his rule. 'She is catholic on the strength of the catholicity of her Lord, which is imputed to her.' Her apostolic *character* is also to be understood in the framework of the mission of Christ and the Spirit. Founded by Christ's apostles in the Spirit, her charge is the apostolate in the world. As the church of Christ the church is bound to be the one, holy, catholic and apostolic church.

If the church acquires her existence from Christ's messianic mission and the eschatological gift of the Spirit, then her characteristics are messianic predicates at the same time. In so far these are *statements of hope*. The *unity* of the church is a 'predicate of the time of salvation', for in the Old Testament the restoration of the unity of God's people and the unity of mankind are prophetic promises. The Messiah of the last days will 'gather' those who have been dispersed, unite the divided and bring about the kingdom of peace. As the Messiah of the time of salvation Christ gathers and unites Jews and Gentiles, Greeks and barbarians, masters and slaves, men and women, making them the new people of the *one* kingdom. According to the prophetic promise, *holiness* is part of the inmost nature of the coming divine glory that is going to fill the earth. 'The Holy One of Israel' will redeem his people. When the church is called 'holy' in the New Testament, this means that it has become the new creation in Christ and therefore partakes of the holiness of the new creation, which the holy God brings about through his Spirit. The church is holy because it is the 'community of the last days'. The apostles and the church's *apostolate* belong to the beginning of the messianic era, like the gospel and evangelization. Finally, the church is catholic to the extent in which it partakes of the *catholicity* of the coming kingdom. In its openness for the kingdom of God it is also open to the world, encompassing it with its mission and intercession. The four characteristics of the church are therefore to be seen as messianic predicates of the church in the perspective of the coming kingdom, for which it exists and which in the church acquires form and testimony. As the church of the kingdom of God, the church is bound to be the one, holy, catholic and apostolic church.

If the characteristics of the church are statements of faith and hope, they also lead to *statements of action*. Because in Christ the church is one, it ought *to be* one. Those who receive its unity in Christ ought to seek its unity. The one people of the one kingdom ought to lay the foundations of unity among men. Because in Christ the church is holy, its members ought to fight sin and sanctify its life through righteousness. Because they are sanctified through the Spirit, they ought in obedience to sanctify all things for the new creation. Because in Christ it is open to the world, it ought to be catholic, testifying everywhere to the all-embracing kingdom. As the church of the Spirit, the one church is the unifying church. The holy church is the church that sanctifies or makes holy. The catholic church is the peace-giving, and so the all-embracing, church. The apostolic church is – through the gospel – the liberating church in the world.

The church's essential nature is given, promised and laid upon it in the characteristics we have named. Faith, hope and action are the genesis of the form of the church visible to the world in unity, holiness, catholicity and apostolicity. That is why theology cannot withdraw to 'the invisible church', 'the church of the future', or 'the church of pure demands'. The church lives in the one, holy, catholic and apostolic rule of Christ through faith, hope and action.

Source: Jürgen Moltmann, The Church in the Power of the Spirit: A Contribution to Messianic Ecclesiology, London: SCM Press, 1977 and New York: Harper & Row, 1992, pp. 338–40.

8.22 Leonardo Boff, from *Church, Charism and Power*

In this extract Boff examines the model of the Church as the body of Christ. He argues that this model must be based on the resurrected body of Christ, which is not bound by physical limitations. A Church modelled on the carnal body of Christ will have narrow boundaries that ignore the cosmic dimensions of the risen Christ.

Expressions such as 'the Church is Christ continued,' 'the Church is one with Christ,' highlight the continuity of a function. Just as Christ achieved salvation for all persons, the Church must prolong that mission throughout the centuries. It has the same mission as Christ. Yet, traditional theology has taken Jesus Christ as the model for understanding the whole Church. Both have parallels, that is, there is a human and divine nature in Christ just as the Church is both human and divine. But there is a preliminary limitation in this understanding of Christ and the Church. Christ has been almost exclusively understood in terms of his incarnation as a man with a body, soul, and divinity. The physical body of Christ has been the comparative model for the Church, the mystical body of Christ. Just as the body has various members and diverse functions, so also does the Church have many members with diverse functions ...

The human body is limited and well defined. The Church, as the body of Christ, is also well defined and limited so that members are clearly defined (one is either a member or non-member) as are the institutions that must maintain the Church's unity and strength in the world. Such a concept of Church is the logical consequence of the model of the physical body of Christ.

However, this Christology and consequent ecclesiology is, basically, too narrow. These theological disciplines, by solely considering the physical body of Christ as the model for the Church, fail to take into account the decisive event of the resurrection. Through the resurrection the body of Jesus Christ was not simply brought back to life. It was completely fulfilled and liberated from every temporal and spatial limitation. He was no longer simply a carnal body, that is, a body subject to an earthly condition, a prisoner to the conditions of space and time, the need to eat and drink, and the limitations of ambiguous communication through word and gesture. His resurrection transformed Jesus' carnal body into a spiritual body ... The body of the risen and pneumatic (spiritual) Christ can no longer be considered as a physically definable entity from which we can deduce the limits of the Church, the body of Christ. Therefore, the expression of the Church as the body of Christ must be carefully defined ...

The Church as institution is not based on the incarnation of the Word but rather in the faith in the power of the apostles, inspired by the Holy Spirit, that caused them to move from eschatology and the end-times to the present situation of the Church, translating the teachings about the Kingdom into a doctrine about the Church. The Church arose from a historical decision by the apostles, enlightened by the Holy Spirit. The Church, born of a decision, will continue to exist only if Christians and all people of faith in the risen Christ and his Spirit continually renew this decision and incarnate the Church in ever new situations. The Church is not a completely defined and established entity; it is always open to new situations and cultural encounters, and within these realities, it must incarnate and proclaim the liberating message of Jesus Christ ...

The pneumatic character of the Church is best seen by analyzing the expression 'The Church is the body of Christ.' As pointed out above, this expression will lead to theological confusion if the term *body* is taken in its carnal sense rather than in its pneumatic meaning. As has already been shown, Christ became spiritual, rather than carnal, through the resurrection (cf. 1 Corinthians 15:45); that is, his nature of body, soul, and divinity is no longer limited to a particular place or time but is, as Spirit, free of all these earthly constraints and acquires a cosmic dimension, open to the totality of all reality. His is a 'spiritual body' (1 Corinthians 15:44). As such, he is present in all things. He is 'all in all things' (Colossians 3:11) and nothing that exists is far from his presence ... the risen Christ tore down all barriers that separate people (Ephesians 2:15–18), abolishing the separation between races, religions, between the sacred and the profane. No longer is there a limit to his ineffable and pneumatic existence.

Where does this reality of Christ appear? For Paul, the local Church constitutes the social manifestation of the risen Christ, especially when the Eucharistic supper is celebrated. It is in eating the body of the risen Lord that the People of God, gathered together, also become the body of Christ, 'in one Spirit all of us were baptized ... and all of us were given to drink of the one Spirit' (1 Corinthians 12:13).

However, if the pneumatic (risen) Christ knows no limitations, neither may his body, the Church, confine itself to the limitations of its own dogma, its rituals, its liturgy, or its canon law. The Church has the same boundaries as the risen Christ; and these dimensions are cosmic in nature. Its functions and mysteries, its structures and services must always be open to the Spirit that blows where it will, as a dynamic force in the world. Therefore, all people of faith, in the Spirit, must be members of the Church and must have their place within its visible structures. No one is outside of the Church because there is no longer an 'outside,' because no one is outside of the reality of God and the risen Christ. Yet, individuals may elect to reject this reality. Even so, they do not cease to be a part of this reality. There is always the possibility of their conversion, accepting the salvation that has already been won for them.

Source: Leonardo Boff, Church: Charism and Power: Liberation Theology and the Institutional Church, *New York: Crossroad Publishing and London: SCM Press, 1985, pp. 144–53.*

8.23 Jon Sobrino, from *The True Church and the Poor*

In this extract Sobrino explains why it is not only legitimate, but the obvious outworking of the resurrection of Christ and the establishment of the Church, to talk about the 'Church of the poor'.

I will analyze first of all the Church that makes its appearance in the New Testament from a theological standpoint in order to see whether and in what way it can be called a 'Church of the poor.' I will also analyze the relationship that must exist between the Church and Christ if the Church is to retain its authentic character. The Church comes into existence after the resurrection of Christ. But this 'after' is not simply a matter of fact, as though after Christ's resurrection the Church could have come into existence or could just as well have not. No, the existence of the Church is an integral part of the resurrection of Christ. The 'after' describes in temporal terms something that is essential to the very resurrection of Christ ...

The resurrection of Christ is therefore essentially impossible without the correlative rise of another reality. The resurrection of Christ is impossible unless it in turn launches history. The resurrection of Christ, the supreme symbol of victory over death and over the wretchedness of history, is impossible – provided we understand it in a Christian way and not just as an extraordinary wonder – unless it in its turn launches a movement aimed at overcoming death and the wretchedness of history. The Church is thus an integral and essential part of the very fact of Christ's resurrection. When Christ makes himself known, a historical movement arises. The Church that comes into existence is not simply the depository of the truth about the resurrection of Christ but is itself the very expression, at the historical level, of the newness that has come in Christ ...

Clearly, then, there is a correlation between the resurrection of Christ and the rise of the Church as far as the fact of the coming into existence of these two new realities is concerned. But the correlation extends to content as well. The deepest reality of the Church is correlative with the content of the Christ who rises from the dead. At this point a basic problem arises that will have serious consequences for the Church's self-understanding and mission.

The Church can organize its entire existence around the plenitude already brought into being in the resurrection of Christ. The Church will then be able to render an account of what it knows, hopes and does (a Kantian phrase for a total response) in terms of the resurrection of Christ. If the Church is asked what it knows about the end of history, it will answer by saying that 'this Jesus God raised up' (Acts 2:32) and that God 'gives life to the dead and calls into existence the things that do not exist' (Rom. 4:17). If the Church is asked what we may hope for, it will answer by saying that 'Christ has been raised from the dead [as] the first fruits of those who have fallen asleep' (1 Cor. 15:20). If the Church is asked what we must do, it will answer by saying that Christ must be 'preached as raised from the dead' (1 Cor. 5:12). If the Church is asked how we are saved, it will answer that 'Christ was raised for our justification' (Rom. 4:25).

...

The risen Christ can present himself to the Church with the wounds of his crucifixion (cf. Jn 10:24–27), as the Christ whom God raised from the dead not by an arbitrary act (as if he might just as well not have raised him) but out of fidelity to the Son who was faithful even to the cross. If the one who appears to the Church is this crucified Jesus, this Christ who has now reached the fulfilment because he was completely faithful within history, then the Church will respond differently to the basic questions about itself and its mission. The difference in responses does not imply a contradiction; it only requires that the previous responses be given a Christian concreteness.

Thus, if the Church is asked what it knows about the last things, it will answer that God gave his Son (cf. Rom. 4:25), that the power and wisdom of God are 'a stumbling block to Jews and folly to Gentiles' (cf. 1 Cor. 1:23–25), and that God is not yet all in all (cf. 1 Cor. 15:20). If it is asked what it may hope for, it will answer that it hopes for liberation, but as one who like Abraham hopes against hope (cf. Rom. 4:18). If it is asked what it must do, it will answer that it must 'have the mind of Christ Jesus by taking the status of a slave, humbling itself, and becoming obedient unto death, death on a cross' (Phil. 2:5–8). If it is asked how we are saved, it will answer by saying that 'Christ died for us' (Rom. 5:8).

These comprehensive theological formulas show that the Church which arises from the resurrection does not forget that the risen Lord is the crucified Jesus. The fullness that belongs to it in the resurrection of Christ and in its own coming into existence comes because it overcomes a scandal, namely, the abandonment of Jesus on the cross by God and his historical abandonment by his disciples.

...

I may state as a theological thesis that according to the New Testament the Church certainly arises because of the resurrection, but also that that which arises is in conformity with a symbol of fulfilment and with a concrete life of solidarity with the poor and of service to them. It is unimportant whether or not this Church calls itself 'Church of the poor'. The important thing from a theological standpoint is that conformity to the risen Christ is not possible solely on the basis of generic kinds of knowing, doing, and hoping but on the basis of the concrete kinds of knowing, doing, and hoping that the risen Lord who has been crucified demands. In our day the formula 'Church of the poor', when properly understood, expresses this formula better than any other formula.

...

When we say that the Church of the poor is the true Church we are not speaking of 'another' Church alongside the Catholic Church or the various Protestant Churches. Nor are we saying that where this Church of the poor exists it exists in a pure form, uncontaminated by sin and error, nor that it is coextensive with the Church of faith. What we are saying is that the Church of the poor is in its structure the true way of being a Church in Jesus; that it provides the structural means of approximating ever more closely to the Church of faith; and that it is more perfectly the historical sacrament of liberation.

If all this is the case and if it is happening in Latin America, it is because Christ has willed to show himself not in any place whatsoever, nor even in the structure, good in principle, which he established, but in the poor. We must describe this new phenomenon of the Church of the poor as representing on the one hand a conversion of the historical Church and on the other its resurrection.

Source: Jon Sobrino, The True Church and the Poor, *Maryknoll, NY: Orbis Books, 1984, pp. 86–90 and 123–4.*

8.24 John Zizioulas, from 'The Mystery of the Church in Orthodox Tradition'

In this extract Zizioulas examines an Orthodox understanding of ecclesiology, and draws from this what he believes the churches hold in common. He focuses on the way in which the Church relates to Christ, and emphasizes the relation of the whole Trinity. He also asserts that the Church is shaped not by past, but by future. The Church is what it is because of its eschatological being.

The ecclesiological question is not simply a matter of dialectic between Christ and Church. It is also a matter of a certain dialectic between Christ and the Father. This affects the entire perspective of ecclesiology. Let me be more explicit by using the following question as an illustration of this somewhat subtle and not easily grasped point.

When the Church prays to God, who prays? In a problematic based on the dialectic Christ–Church, which is normally the problematic we encounter in theological discussions, it is assumed that there is on the one hand a community called 'Church' which is *human,* and a person called 'Christ' who is *divine.* Thus the Chalcedonian dialectic of divine versus human nature is transferred into ecclesiology, and the question arises whether the Church is distinguished enough from Christ or not. But the question of who prays in the Church is far more complex, and takes us away from the dialectic Christ–Church.

When the Church prays to the Father it is Christ who prays to him for us and with us. This is particularly evident in the eucharistic prayers which from the very beginning (including the Lord's prayer, which was eucharistic) were addressed to the Father. As such these prayers are heard by God only because they are brought to him by his only-begotten Son. But this would have been impossible had it not been for the fact that the Son-Christ has identified himself so much with the ecclesial community that any separation, or even distinction in this particular case, would render these prayers meaningless and fruitless. How can one speak in this case of a dialectic between Christ and the Church? Unless the two are identified the eucharistic prayer will lose its meaning as a prayer of the Church addressed *to* the Father by the Son. In this case the three elements Church–Christ–Father will have to be seen as forming a dialectic between Church plus Christ-Father, and not as a 'trialectic', for the prayer will not work.

Of course Christ is not only the one who prays with the community, but also the one who receives the prayers, sitting next to the Father. And yet the fact that the prayer of the community is no other than the prayer of Christ cannot be otherwise understood apart from a total – at that moment – identification of Christ with the Church. Any other conception will turn Christ into a sort of go-between mediator, a third person, who listens first to the Church speaking to him and then like a messenger transmits the prayer to the Father.

Thus, the intra-trinitarian dialectic removes ecclesiology from the dialectic Christ–Church, and leads to an identification of Christ with the Church in *what concerns* that *particular case*. I suggest that a study of the liturgical evidence in some depth shows that the Eucharist was always understood as the act or event in which the identification of the Church with Christ would reach its fullest realisation, and it is for this reason that in the ancient Church *only* the eucharistic prayer would be addressed to the Father, and only the eucharistic communities would be 'churches' in the fullest sense.

...

Does the Eucharist remove all dialectic between Christ and Church by virtue of the fact that another dialectic takes place there, namely that of Father–Christ plus Church? I mentioned earlier on that Christ is not only the praying one but also the recipient of the eucharistic prayers. This suggests that the Eucharist does not remove entirely the dialectic Christ–Church. If we study, and analyse in some depth the prayers of the ancient eucharistic liturgies, we see that they are marked by the following dialectic: when, for example, the bishop enters the church to begin the liturgy, he is greeted by the people as Christ himself coming into the world in his glory – 'Deute, *proskunesomen*', 'Come, let us worship', which signifies a full identification between the bishop and Christ. Immediately, however, the bishop transfers the prayer to Christ, *as if he were not himself Christ*. Thus in the eyes of his people the bishop is Christ; but in his own eyes he is *not*: he prays *to* Christ *for himself*, but to the Father (as if he were Christ) for the *people*. What a complexity of dialectics!

In an approach like this the question whether the Church is human *or* divine looks so naive. In fact she is both at the same time. In this she resembles the Chalcedonian Christ. But this is possible only because there is a personal dialectic between Father and Son, that allows for the Son to be other than the Father and 'side' with man in the eucharistic prayer. The insistence of the Cappadocian Fathers on the full distinction and integrity of the trinitarian Persons is thus an essential presupposition for the proper understanding of the mystery of the Church.

We stressed earlier on that it is important to think of the Spirit as *constitutive of the identity* of Christ, and not simply as an assistant to him. If this is applied to ecclesiology, the implications are quite important. In the first place, it means that Christ's identity is conditioned by the existence of the 'many'. The Spirit is the Spirit of 'communion' and his primary work consists in opening up reality to become *relational*. The Spirit is incompatible with individualism. By being born of the Spirit Christ is inconceivable as an individual: he becomes automatically a relational being. But a relational being draws its identity, its personhood, from its relation with others. One person is no person. The spiritual character of God's own being lies in nothing else but in the relational nature of his existence: there is no Father unless there is a Son and the Spirit. And since the one God is the Father and not the one divine nature or *ousia*, the very identity of God depends on the Father's relationship with persons other than himself. There is no 'one' whose identity is not conditioned by the 'many'. And if this applies to the being of God, it must be made equally to apply also to Christ.

This de-individualisation of Christ is in my view the stumbling-block of all ecclesiological discussions in the ecumenical movement. The insistence of certain people on a clear-cut distinction between Christ and the Church pre-supposes an individualistic understanding of Christ. But this Christ could not be the spiritual being who incorporates all in himself. He cannot be the first-born among many brothers or of creation, of whom Colossians and Ephesians speak. The 'one' without the 'many' is an individual not touched by the Spirit. He cannot be the Christ of our faith.

In order to speak of the identity of Christ one has to make use of the idea of 'corporate personality'. This idea, discovered and proposed by modern bibli-cal scholars such as Wheeler, Robinson, Pedersen, de Frain etc., constitutes a scandal to our western minds, but seems to be the key to an understanding of the Bible. The Semitic mind did not have the difficulty we experience in think-ing of, for example, Abraham as one in whom his 'seed', i.e. all generations after him, is included, forming his own personal identity. Or of Adam as being simultaneously one and many. Or of the Servant of God of Isaiah, the Son of man of Daniel, etc., as being simultaneously one and many. Why do we tend to avoid this way of thinking when we come to Christ, the corporate being par excellence? The mystery of the Church consists above all in the mystery of the 'one' who is 'many' – not of the 'one' who is first one and then, in the *eschata*, becomes 'many', but of the 'one' who is 'one', i.e. unique, and 'other' precisely because he relates with the 'many'.

All this means that Christology without ecclesiology is inconceivable. What is at stake is the very identity of Christ. The existence of the body is a neces-sary condition for the head to be head. A bodiless head is no head at all. If Christ does not draw his identity from his relation with the Church, then he is either an individual of demonic isolationism, or he should be understood only in terms of his relationship with the Father. But in this latter case we risk becoming monophysite in ecciesiology. Christ's 'I' is of course the eternal 'I' that stems from his eternal filial relationship with the Father. But as the incarnate Christ he has introduced into this eternal relationship another ele-ment: us, the many, the Church. If the Church disappears from his identity he is no longer Christ, although he will still be the eternal Son. And yet, the 'mystery hidden before all ages' in the will of the Father is nothing else but the incorporation of this other element, of us, or the many, into the eternal filial relationship between the Father and the Son. This mystery amounts therefore, to nothing but the Church.

Just as Christ, the all-inclusive being, this 'corporate personality', is an eschatological reality existing in a state of conflict with the fallen creation in history, so the Church, by drawing her identity from Christ, is thrown into a world hostile to Christ and to herself, and is forced to live in conflict with it. In leading her historical existence the Church appears to the eyes of the historian as another human community or society. She is no mystery to the sociologist. Quite often she is tempted herself, either for the sake of survival or for the ful-filment of her mission, to adjust so much to the world as to forget that her true citizenship is in heaven and her identity is not drawn from history but from the *eschata*: she is what she will be. In this situation the only way to preserve the eschatological identity is the celebration of the sacraments, particularly the Eucharist, and the encounter of the Word, not as a message coming to her as passed through the channels of historical experience, but as an echo of the future state of things. She is thus obliged to live by faith, not by sight. She is the great *mysterium fidei*, precisely, by being in this world but not *of* this world, by drawing, that is, her identity from what she will be.

Source: John Zizioulas, 'The Mystery of the Church in Orthodox Tradition', One in Christ 24, pp. 296–300.

8.25 Letty Russell, from *Church in the Round*

Russell here approaches ecclesiology from a grass-roots perspective by talking about the theological principles of Church in the round. This form of Church is based on the idea of inclusivity and shared leadership. It is particularly aimed at those on the margins of society and aims to redistribute power among the members.

Discussion of tradition and ecclesiology from a feminist perspective is most definitely a way of talking back to a community whose self-understanding has been shaped in all its aspects of tradition from a patriarchal paradigm of authority as domination. The shift to the metaphor of church in the round is one way of talking back because it reconfigures the paradigm of what evokes assent from the image of the household ruled by a patriarch to one of a household where everyone gathers around the common table to break bread and to share table talk and hospitality. All are welcome to participate in the table talk because in that way they become participants in their own journey of faith and struggle for the mending and liberation of creation.

Round table ecclesiology reflects the self-understanding of the community of faith and struggle about its life in a changing pattern of faith, justice, and hospitality.

...

The word 'church' or *ekklesia* in the Greek Testament was not the only word used to describe the early Christians. An earlier term seems to have been 'people of the Way,' and the word *koinonia*, or community, was often used to refer to the gathering of Christians in each place (Acts 24:14; 2:42). Within a few years it seems that the local churches were described as *ekklesia tou theou* (*ekklesia* of God), gathered in the name of Christ (1 Thess. 2:14). *Ekklesia* had been used in the Septuagint to translate the word *qahal*, meaning assembly, meeting, or gathering. The Greek Testament does not use the word 'synagogue' except to refer to Jewish congregations (except in James 2:2 in the Greek), so it is often assumed that *ekklesia* was to be understood in terms of *qahal* with its overtones of a holy set-apart assembly of Israel (Deut. 23:1–14). Yet is more likely that a new meaning had been attached to the Greek word, which conveyed its particular Christian usage to the Greek-speaking world.

Ekklesia is found only three times in the Gospels: once in the Matthew 16:18 declaration about Peter and twice in Matthew 18:17. It appears that in seeking to convey the openness of the new Christian communities in contrast to the restricted Jewish communities, Paul and others working with the Gentiles used a word to describe the gatherings of Christians that was not so much a reference to *qahal* as a reference to the Greek political assemblies and thus to the theo-political assemblies of the people of God (Acts 19:32, 39–41). In the same way the word 'Christian' was probably coined as a secular word to refer to the Christians as a political group associated with Christ (Acts 11:26).

The usage of the word *ekklesia* reflects its functional character. It is used as a description of the totality of Christians living in any one place – a city or a house (1 Cor. 1:2; 16:19). It is also used to describe the church universal to which all believers belong as part of the eschatological people of God (1 Cor. 12:28). These communities were defined simply by the presence of Christ in their midst and viewed their task as that of proclamation of the Gospel (Matt. 18:20).

...

[I]t is possible to say that ecclesiology is by its very nature not only talking back to tradition but also talking back and forth between tradition and its historical context. Feminist ecclesiology is no different in this respect from any other expression of the church's self-understanding, but it is different in that the self-understanding includes action/reflection on the way faith shapes life in the struggle for justice on behalf of marginalized people. What makes its back talk so startling is that the voices doing the talking have not been those of the church officials and scholars who are the usual interpreters of meaning in the church.

...

In the interpretation of the Apostles' Creed we are called to 'believe the holy catholic church.' This formulation of the creed seems to indicate that we believe the church and not in the church because we believe that no matter what its present failings it is still a community of Christ that offers the possibility of new life and continuing nurture of the faith through the word and sacraments ...

To believe the church is to believe it exists and to risk believing that the particular communities of faith and struggle where we are members partake in some way of the one church of Jesus Christ. Participation in local church is at the same time participation with all who are united to Christ. Churches that are feminist Christian communities or basic Christian communities are also local manifestations of the one church. Those who join them also risk their inadequacy in living up to their calling to be communities of church and struggle. Although the insights of women in struggle for full humanity are key to the interpretation of the gospel among Christian feminists, their insights into ways of being the church of Jesus Christ may contribute to the self-understanding of the whole church. It may well be that the insights of women into the meaning of faithfulness for all Christians will one day make it no longer necessary for women to gather apart to give an account of the hope that is in them.

There is no perfect church, and our imperfect church is the only one we have as we seek to point beyond ourselves to God's new household ...

The same is true for the metaphor of church in the round. There is no perfect expression of this reality of authority shared in community, but at least those of us who take round table talk seriously know that reflection on faith and struggle with those on the margin can at least become a small piece of the round. We move forward with whatever piece we have received in expectation that Christ will be present among us as we crowd together around the table with the one who comes to serve and not to be served (Mark 10:45).

Source: Letty Russell, Church in the Round, *Louisville: Westminster John Knox Press, 1993, pp. 42–5.*

8.26 David Bosch, from *Transforming Mission*

In this passage from Transforming Mission, *Bosch argues that the Church exists only as it is sent out. Its very nature is to share in the mission of God. Thus the Church is a pilgrim Church, constantly moving towards its ultimate goal.*

In the emerging ecclesiology, *the church is seen as essentially missionary*. The biblical model behind this conviction, which finds its classical expression in *Ad Gentes* 9 ('The pilgrim church is missionary by its very nature'), is the one we find in 1 Peter 2:9. Here the church is not the sender but the one sent. Its mission (its 'being sent') is not secondary to its being; the church exists in being sent and in building up itself for the sake of its mission. Ecclesiology therefore does not precede missiology. Mission is not 'a fringe activity of a strongly established Church, a pious cause that [may] be attended to when the home fires [are] first brightly burning ... Missionary activity is not so much the work of the church as simply the Church at work' (John Power *Mission Theology Today* Gill and MacMillan 1970:41,42). It is a duty 'which pertains to the *whole* Church' (*Ad Gentes* 23). Since God is a missionary God (as will be argued in the section on the *missio Dei*), God's people are a missionary people. The question 'Why still mission?' evokes a further question, 'Why still church?' It has become impossible to talk about the church without at the same time talking about mission. One can no longer talk about church *and* mission, only about the mission of the church. One could even say, with Schumacher (Geschichte der Missionstheologie – eine Denkaufgabe, Neue Zeitschrift für Missionswissenschaft, col 26, 1970:183), 'The inverse of the thesis "the church is essentially missionary" is "Mission is essentially ecclesial"' (my translation). Because church and mission belong together from the beginning 'a church without mission or a mission without the church are both contradictions. Such things do exist, but only as pseudostructures' (Carl E Braaten, *The Flamin*, Center Fortress Press, 1977:55). These perspectives have implications for our understanding of the church's catholicity. Without mission, the church cannot be called catholic.

All this does not suggest that the church is always and everywhere overtly involved in missionary projects. Newbigin has introduced the helpful distinction between the church's missionary *dimension* and its missionary *intention*: the church is both 'missionary' and 'missionizing'. The missionary dimension of a local church's life manifests itself, among other ways, when it is truly a worshipping community; it is able to welcome outsiders and make them feel at home; it is a church in which the pastor does not have the monopoly and the members are not merely objects of pastoral care; its members are equipped for their calling in society; it is structurally pliable and innovative; and it does not defend the privileges of a select group. However, the church's missionary dimension evokes *intentional*, that is *direct* involvement in society; it actually moves beyond the walls of the church and engages in missionary 'points of concentration' (Newbigin) such as evangelism and work for justice and peace.

...

The church is viewed as the *people of God* and, by implication then, as a pilgrim church ...

The biblical archetype here is that of the wandering people of God, which is so prominent in the letter to the Hebrews. The church is a pilgrim not simply for the practical reason that in the modern age it no longer calls the tune and is everywhere finding itself in a diaspora situation, rather, to be a pilgrim in the world belongs intrinsically to the church's ex-centric position. It is *ek-klesia*, 'called out' of the world, and sent back into the world. Foreignness is an element of its constitution.

God's pilgrim people need only two things: support for the road, and a destination at the end of it. It has no fixed abode here; it is a *paroikia*, a temporary residence. It is permanently underway, toward the ends of the world and the end of time. Even if there is an unbridgeable difference between the church and its destination – the reign of God – it is called to flesh out, already in the here and now, something of the conditions which are to prevail in God's reign. Proclaiming its own transience the church pilgrimages toward God's future.

Source: David Bosch, Transforming Mission: Paradigm Shifts in Theology of Mission, *Maryknoll, NY: Orbis Books, 1992, pp. 372–4.*

9 Eschatology

Introductory essay

The doctrine of eschatology is concerned with the end times and the fulfilment of God's purposes for creation. It is not a doctrine of speculation about the future, but underpins the reality of Christian life and, most specifically, the Christian hope. The Church's teaching about the life that is to come does not only have future relevance, but provides the framework for this life, in which the kingdom, although not yet fulfilled, has begun. Although, systematically, eschatology is part of every Christian doctrine, the study of eschatology in the narrow sense focuses on the end times, and more particularly on the four Last Things: death, judgement, heaven and hell.

Over the centuries of Christianity, the mystery that inevitably surrounds life beyond death, and indeed death itself, has captured the imagination of many theologians, artists and writers, among others. Versions of Christian debate around the Last Things are picked up in popular culture and sometimes come to dominate understandings of God and Christianity. Much of the popular understanding of life after death distorts the Christian hope and this aspect of doctrine cannot be understood apart from the rest of Christian theology. For example, the image of Christ as Judge was, arguably, the predominant image of Western Christianity in the Middle Ages. Certainly Christianity teaches that Christ will return 'to judge the living and the dead', but this is the same Christ who became incarnate 'for our sake', and who was crucified and resurrected 'for our sake'. Christ as Judge, is only one aspect of who Christ is and the way in which he judges is in accordance with his ministry, death and resurrection. His practice of judgement differs markedly from that of a judge who has a specific role within a legal and political system. Indeed Robert Jenson notes that the Last Judgement is not primarily to mete out punishment, but to set right relationships and to establish the kingdom through the reconciliation of creation. Helmut Thielicke is another among the theologians represented below who discusses the significance of the Final Judgement, and the return of Christ, which he argues is a cosmic event.

The significance of death is sometimes assumed to be only that it opens the door to the next life. However, Karl Rahner explores the meaning of death itself and suggests that it is a moment when the Christian is required to surrender all to God. Kathryn Tanner examines what death can mean in a religious sense, and argues that there is quality of life with God, eternal life, which is not destroyed by death but which continues to be life-giving even beyond death. Christian teaching is that death is a result of sin. Gregory of Nyssa argues that sin and evil cannot last eternally, and that in the next life, humans will be free of sin and the consequences of sin. Gregory suggests that humans will return to the state of perfection that they enjoyed before the fall and the image of God will be fully restored.

Hans Urs von Balthasar considers Jesus' descent to hell on Holy Saturday, and the question of what that means for the scope of salvation. He concludes that although all have heard the Good News of Jesus, it cannot be stated that all are therefore saved. In the first extract, Origen argues that all creatures will finally be restored to their original perfection. He suggests that sin and corruption will be destroyed by a purifying fire, and that all creatures will enter eternal life free from sin. Origen's teaching is sometimes referred to as the *apocatastasis panton*, the reconciliation of all. He is often considered to be the first theologian to have advocated an explicit doctrine of universal salvation. Although the teaching of universalism has continued through the centuries of Christianity, the majority tradition has assumed a separation of fates in the afterlife. Human beings will either end up in heaven or in hell. Purgatory is not taught as an eternal resting place, but rather is preparation for heaven. This doctrine has been controversial, not least because it is difficult to demonstrate any clear biblical warrant for the teaching. This is the question dealt with by Thomas Aquinas who concludes that it has been revealed to the faithful, and therefore can legitimately be taught by the Church.

Aquinas examines the notion of the Beatific Vision and considers how humans could comprehend the infinite God. Jonathan Edwards describes heaven as the place where the glory of God is fully recognized and all things are made perfectly lovely. John Calvin also tries to express the glories of heaven and warns that it is only possible to understand a fraction of it in this life. Calvin contrasts this with hell which is devoid of any joy or goodness at all. William Perkins similarly contrasts the perfection of the saints in heaven and the glory of God with the state of the reprobate in hell. This state is characterized by destruction and misery. The nature of hell is reflected on by Charles Spurgeon in his sermon *Heaven and Hell*. Spurgeon, following his text from Matthew's Gospel, considers what it means to be cast out and argues that the misery of hell results primarily from being separated from God. Although Spurgeon is by no means alone in emphasizing that hell is the place where God is not, he does anticipate many of the more recent discussions of hell, which rather than focusing on physical torment, depict the torture of hell as resulting from isolation and alienation from God.

Although there is a limit to what can be said about the nature of heaven or hell, there are some glimpses of life in the nearer presence of God. Augustine, in the second extract, argues that the Church is already the city of heaven, and will be fully established as such at the consummation of all things. Similarly, John Zizioulas suggests that in the liturgy of the Church, Christians experience a foretaste of the kingdom of God. The calling of the Church to embody the eschaton is also explored by Alan Lewis, who argues that the purpose of mission is the establishment of the new heavens and the new earth.

John Wesley's sermon *The General Deliverance* explores the way in which all creatures are caught up in the consummation of creation. Much theology has focused on the anthropocentric aspect of eschatology, but Wesley takes seriously St Paul's teaching that the whole of creation has been 'groaning together' (Rom. 8.22). Wolfhart Pannenberg also considers the scope of the final transformation to be universal. Rowan Williams, in the last extract, takes the confession from the Nicene Creed and explores what it means to confess belief in 'the resurrection of the body'. He is clear that Christianity is not concerned with a spiritual resurrection, or the salvation of the soul only, but that the eschatological vision is of a transformed and perfected flesh and matter. Very often discussions of the afterlife suggest that a part of the person, namely the soul, will live on after death, while the body and the world which we now occupy are dispensed with. Williams argues that this is not in fact the teaching of Christianity, but rather is the belief of Greek philosophy. That this world will be transformed into the new earth, not only challenges assumptions about eschatology, but also about creation.

St Paul writes to the church at Corinth, 'If there is no resurrection of the dead, then Christ has not been raised; and if Christ has not been raised, then our proclamation has been in vain and your faith has been in vain' (1 Cor. 15.13–14). The resurrection of Christ is the foundation of the Christian hope. Over the centuries of Christianity, much discussion has taken place over the nature of resurrection, and the order of the Last Things. Augustine argues that there will be a two-stage resurrection, the first for the soul and the second for the body. Jürgen Moltmann is also concerned with resurrection, but does not reflect on the mechanisms that may be involved in that process, but rather expresses the joy of the Christian hope and the promise of new life. Karl Barth argues that the glorious fulfilment of creation in the eschaton is God's ultimate 'yes' to humanity, and to God's creation. The Christian hope does not just mean that death is not the end, but is the promise that all will be finally fulfilled through Christ. Thus the Last Things are not last in the sense of final, but are rather the ultimate things.

LEH

9.1 Origen, from *On First Principles*

In this passage, Origen articulates his understanding of the Christian hope. He argues that all things will be reconciled to God their maker so that ultimately nothing will be destroyed, but all will be transformed according to God's good purposes.

5. The last enemy, moreover, who is called death, is said on this account to be destroyed, that there may not be anything left of a mournful kind when death does not exist, nor anything that is adverse when there is no enemy. The destruction of the last enemy, indeed, is to be understood, not as if its substance, which was formed by God, is to perish, but because its mind and hostile will, which came not from God, but from itself, are to be destroyed. Its destruction, therefore, will not be its non-existence, but its ceasing to be an enemy, and (to be) death. For nothing is impossible to the Omnipotent, nor is anything incapable of restoration to its Creator: for He made all things that they might exist, and those things which were made for existence cannot cease to be. For this reason also will they admit of change and variety, so as to be placed, according to their merits, either in a better or worse position; but no destruction of substance can befall those things which were created by God for the purpose of permanent existence. For those things which agreeably to the common opinion are believed to perish, the nature either of our faith or of the truth will not permit us to suppose to be destroyed. Finally, our flesh is supposed by ignorant men and unbelievers to be destroyed after death, in such a degree that it retains no relic at all of its former substance. We, however, who believe in its resurrection, understand that a change only has been produced by death, but that its substance certainly remains; and that by the will of its Creator, and at the time appointed, it will be restored to life; and that a second time a change will take place in it, so that what at first was flesh (formed) out of earthly soil, and was afterwards dissolved by death, and again reduced to dust and ashes ('For dust thou art,' it is said, 'and to dust shalt thou return' [Gen 3.19]) will be again raised from the earth, and shall after this, according to the merits of the indwelling soul, advance to the glory of a spiritual body.

6. Into this condition, then, we are to suppose that all this bodily substance of ours will be brought, when all things shall be re-established in a state of unity, and when God shall be all in all. And this result must be understood as being brought about, not suddenly, but slowly and gradually, seeing that the process of amendment and correction will take place imperceptibly in the individual instances during the lapse of countless and unmeasured ages, some outstripping others, and tending by a swifter course towards perfection, while others again follow close at hand, and some again a long way behind; and thus, through the numerous and uncounted orders of progressive beings who are being reconciled to God from a state of enmity, the last enemy is finally reached, who is called death, so that he also may be destroyed, and no longer be an enemy. When, therefore, all rational souls shall have been restored to a condition of this kind, then the nature of this body of ours will undergo a change into the glory of a spiritual body. For as we see it not to be the case with

413

rational natures, that some of them have lived in a condition of degradation owing to their sins, while others have been called to a state of happiness on account of their merits; but as we see those same souls who had formerly been sinful, assisted, after their conversion and reconciliation to God, to a state of happiness; so also are we to consider, with respect to the nature of the body, that the one which we now make use of in a state of meanness, and corruption, and weakness, is not a different body from that which we shall possess in incorruption, and in power, and in glory; but that the same body, when it has cast away the infirmities in which it is now entangled, shall be transmuted into a condition of glory, being rendered spiritual, so that what was a vessel of dishonour may, when cleansed, become a vessel unto honour, and an abode of blessedness. And in this condition, also, we are to believe, that by the will of the Creator, it will abide for ever without any change, as is confirmed by the declaration of the apostle, when he says, 'We have a house, not made with hands, eternal in the heavens.' ...

8. And now the point for investigation is, whether, when God shall be all in all, the whole of bodily nature will, in the consummation of all things, consist of one species, and the sole quality of body be that which shall shine in the indescribable glory which is to be regarded as the future possession of the spiritual body. For if we rightly understand the matter, this is the statement of Moses in the beginning of his book, when he says, 'In the beginning God created the heavens and the earth' [Gen. 1.1]. For this is the beginning of all creation: to this beginning the end and consummation of all things must be recalled, i.e., in order that that heaven and that earth may be the habitation and resting-place of the pious; so that all the holy ones, and the meek, may first obtain an inheritance in that land, since this is the teaching of the law, and of the prophets, and of the Gospel. In which land I believe there exist the true and living forms of that worship which Moses handed down under the shadow of the law; of which it is said, that 'they serve unto the example and shadow of heavenly things' [Heb. 8.5] – those, viz., who were in subjection in the law. To Moses himself also was the injunction given, 'Look that thou make them after the form and pattern which were showed thee on the mount' [Ex. 25.40]. From which it appears to me, that as on this earth the law was a sort of schoolmaster to those who by it were to be conducted to Christ, in order that, being instructed and trained by it, they might more easily, after the training of the law, receive the more perfect principles of Christ; so also another earth, which receives into it all the saints, may first imbue and mould them by the institutions of the true and everlasting law, that they may more easily gain possession of those perfect institutions of heaven, to which nothing can be added; in which there will be, of a truth, that Gospel which is called everlasting, and that Testament, ever new, which shall never grow old.

Source: Origen, On First Principles *III.6, trans. Frederick Crombie, in Alexander Roberts, James Donaldson and A. Cleveland Coxe (eds)*, Ante-Nicene Fathers, *vol. 4, Buffalo, NY: Christian Literature Publishing Co., 1885.*

9.2 Augustine of Hippo, from *City of God*

In this extract from City of God *Augustine discusses the first resurrection, the resurrection of the soul, and the second resurrection, that of the body. He argues that the second resurrection includes all people, but for some it is the process of judgement.*

After that He [Jesus] adds the words, 'Verily, verily, I say unto you, The hour is coming, and now is, when the dead shall hear the voice of the Son of God; and they that hear shall live. For as the Father hath life in Himself; so hath He given to the Son to have life in Himself' [John 5.25, 26]. As yet He does not speak of the second resurrection, that is, the resurrection of the body, which shall be in the end, but of the first, which now is. It is for the sake of making this distinction that He says, 'The hour is coming, and now is.' Now this resurrection regards not the body, but the soul. For souls, too, have a death of their own in wickedness and sins, whereby they are the dead of whom the same lips say, 'Suffer the dead to bury their dead' [Matt. 8.22] – that is, let those who are dead in soul bury them that are dead in body. It is of these dead, then – the dead in ungodliness and wickedness – that He says, 'The hour is coming, and now is, when the dead shall hear the voice of the Son of God; and they that hear shall live.' 'They that hear,' that is, they who obey, believe, and persevere to the end. Here no difference is made between the good and the bad. For it is good for all men to hear His voice and live, by passing to the life of godliness from the death of ungodliness. Of this death the Apostle Paul says, 'Therefore all are dead, and He died for all, that they which live should not henceforth live unto themselves, but unto Him which died for them and rose again' [2 Cor. 5.14, 15]. Thus all, without one exception, were dead in sins, whether original or voluntary sins, sins of ignorance, or sins committed against knowledge; and for all the dead there died the one only person who lived, that is, who had no sin whatever, in order that they who live by the remission of their sins should live, not to themselves, but to Him who died for all, for our sins, and rose again for our justification, that we, believing in Him who justifies the ungodly, and being justified from ungodliness or quickened from death, may be able to attain to the first resurrection which now is. For in this first resurrection none have a part save those who shall be eternally blessed; but in the second, of which He goes on to speak, all, as we shall learn, have a part, both the blessed and the wretched. The one is the resurrection of mercy, the other of judgment. And therefore it is written in the psalm, 'I will sing of mercy and of judgment: unto Thee, O Lord, will I sing' [Ps. 101.1].

And of this judgment He went on to say, 'And hath given Him authority to execute judgment also, because He is the Son of man.' Here He shows that He will come to judge in that flesh in which He had come to be judged. For it is to show this He says, 'because He is the Son of man'. And then follow the words for our purpose: 'Marvel not at this: for the hour is coming, in the which all that are in the graves shall hear His voice, and shall come forth; they that have done good, unto the resurrection of life; and they that have done evil, unto the resurrection of judgment' [John 5.28, 29]. This judgment He uses

415

here in the same sense as a little before, when He says, 'He that heareth my word, and believeth on Him that sent me, hath everlasting life, and shall not come into *judgment*, but is passed from death to life;' *i.e.*, by having a part in the first resurrection, by which a transition from death to life is made in this present time, he shall not come into damnation, which He mentions by the name of judgment, as also in the place where He says, 'but they that have done evil unto the resurrection of judgment,' *i.e.*, of damnation. He, therefore, who would not be damned in the second resurrection, let him rise in the first. For 'the hour is coming, and now is, when the dead shall hear the voice of the Son of God; and they that hear shall live,' *i.e.*, shall not come into damnation, which is called the second death; into which death, after the second or bodily resurrection, they shall be hurled who do not rise in the first or spiritual resurrection. For 'the hour is coming' (but here He does not say, 'and now is,' because it shall come in the end of the world in the last and greatest judgment of God) 'when all that are in the graves shall hear His voice and shall come forth.' He does not say, as in the first resurrection, 'And they that Hear shall live.' For all shall not live, at least with such life as ought alone to be called life because it alone is blessed. For some kind of life they must have in order to hear, and come forth from the graves in their rising bodies. And why all shall not live He teaches in the words that follow: 'They that have done good, to the resurrection of life' – these are they who shall live; 'but they that have done evil, to the resurrection of judgment' – these are they who shall not live, for they shall die in the second death. They have done evil because their life has been evil; and their life has been evil because it has not been renewed in the first or spiritual resurrection which now is, or because they have not persevered to the end in their renewed life. As, then, there are two regenerations, of which I have already made mention – the one according to faith, and which takes place in the present life by means of baptism; the other according to the flesh, and which shall be accomplished in its incorruption and immortality by means of the great and final judgment – so are there also two resurrections – the one the first and spiritual resurrection, which has place in this life, and preserves us from coming into the second death; the other the second, which does not occur now, but in the end of the world, and which is of the body, not of the soul, and which by the last judgment shall dismiss some into the second death, others into that life which has no death.

Source: Augustine of Hippo, City of God, *Book 20, trans. Marcus Dods, in Philip Schaff (ed.),* Nicene and Post-Nicene Fathers, *first series, vol. 2, Buffalo, NY: Christian Literature Publishing Co., 1887.*

9.3 Gregory of Nyssa, from *On the Making of Man*

Gregory argues that the resurrection promises a return to the perfect, pre-fall state. He suggests that evil is limited and cannot last eternally, but that good will prevail. Thus the image of God will be finally restored in human beings.

17.2 When the Sadducees once argued against the doctrine of the resurrection, and brought forward, to establish their own opinion, that woman of many marriages, who had been wife to seven brethren, and thereupon inquired whose wife she will be after the resurrection, our Lord answered their argument so as not only to instruct the Sadducees, but also to reveal to all that come after them the mystery of the resurrection-life: 'for in the resurrection,' He says, 'they neither marry, nor are given in marriage neither can they die any more, for they are equal to the angels, and are the children of God, being the children of the resurrection [Luke 20.35–36].' Now the resurrection promises us nothing else than the restoration of the fallen to their ancient state; for the grace we look for is a certain return to the first life, bringing back again to Paradise him who was cast out from it. If then the life of those restored is closely related to that of the angels, it is clear that the life before the transgression was a kind of angelic life, and hence also our return to the ancient condition of our life is compared to the angels. Yet while, as has been said, there is no marriage among them, the armies of the angels are in countless myriads; for so Daniel declared in his visions: so, in the same way, if there had not come upon us as the result of sin a change for the worse, and removal from equality with the angels, neither should we have needed marriage that we might multiply but whatever the mode of increase in the angelic nature is (unspeakable and inconceivable by human conjectures, except that it assuredly exists), it would have operated also in the case of men, who were 'made a little lower than the angels' [Ps. 8.6] to increase mankind to the measure determined by its Maker …

21.1. Wickedness, however, is not so strong as to prevail over the power of good; nor is the folly of our nature more powerful and more abiding than the wisdom of God: for it is impossible that that which is always mutable and variable should be more firm and more abiding than that which always remains the same and is firmly fixed in goodness: but it is absolutely certain that the Divine counsel possesses immutability, while the changeableness of our nature does not remain settled even in evil.

2. Now that which is always in motion, if its progress be to good, will never cease moving onwards to what lies before it, by reason of the infinity of the course to be traversed: for it will not find any limit of its object such that when it has apprehended it, it will at last cease its motion: but if its bias be in the opposite direction, when it has finished the course of wickedness and reached the extreme limit of evil, then that which is ever moving, finding no halting point for its impulse natural to itself when it has run through the lengths that can be run in wickedness, of necessity turns its motion towards good: for as evil does not extend to infinity, but is comprehended by necessary limits, it

would appear that good once more follows in succession upon the limit of evil; and thus, as we have said, the ever-moving character of our nature comes to run its course at the last once more back towards good, being taught the lesson of prudence by the memory of its former misfortunes, to the end that it may never again be in like case.

3. Our course, then, will once more lie in what is good, by reason of the fact that the nature of evil is bounded by necessary limits. For just as those skilled in astronomy tell us that the whole universe is full of light, and that darkness is made to cast its shadow by the interposition of the body formed by the earth; and that this darkness is shut off from the rays of the sun, in the shape of a cone, according to the figure of the sphere-shaped body, and behind it; while the sun, exceeding the earth by a size many times as great as its own, enfolding it round about on all sides with its rays, unites at the limit of the cone the concurrent streams of light; so that if (to suppose the case) any one had the power of passing beyond the measure to which the shadow extends, he would certainly find himself in light unbroken by darkness; even so I think that we ought to understand about ourselves, that on passing the limit of wickedness we shall again have our conversation in light, as the nature of good, when compared with the measure of wickedness, is incalculably superabundant.

4. Paradise therefore will be restored, that tree will be restored which is in truth the tree of life; there will be restored the grace of the image, and the dignity of rule. It does not seem to me that our hope is one for those things which are now subjected by God to man for the necessary uses of life, but one for another kingdom, of a description that belongs to unspeakable mysteries.

Source: Gregory of Nyssa, On the Making of Man, *trans. H. A. Wilson, in Philip Schaff and Henry Wace (eds),* Nicene and Post-Nicene Fathers, *second series, vol. 5, Buffalo, NY: Christian Literature Publishing Co., 1893.*

9.4 Thomas Aquinas, from *Summa Theologica* (1)

Aquinas here explores the question of whether humans have the capacity to understand God in his essence. The beatific vision is not primarily about seeing God, but rather concerns the capacity to comprehend the perfect being. Aquinas considers three ways in which humans could attain the vision of God and concludes that God provides us with the means to know him by giving the vision as well as the means to understand it.

Question 92. Whether the human intellect can attain to the vision of God in His essence?

Even as we hold by faith that the last end of man's life is to see God, so the philosophers maintained that man's ultimate happiness is to understand immaterial substances according to their being. Hence in reference to this question we find that philosophers and theologians encounter the same difficulty and the same difference of opinion. For some philosophers held that our passive intellect can never come to understand separate substances … In like manner certain theologians held that the human intellect can never attain to the vision of God in His essence. On either side they were moved by the distance which separates our intellect from the Divine essence and from separate substances. For since the intellect in act is somewhat one with the intelligible object in act, it would seem difficult to understand how the created intellect is made to be an uncreated essence … Now since the perfection of an intelligent being as such is the intelligible object, if in the most perfect operation of his intellect man does not attain to the vision of the Divine essence, but to something else, we shall be forced to conclude that something other than God is the object of man's happiness: and since the ultimate perfection of a thing consists in its being united to its principle, it follows that something other than God is the effective principle of man, which is absurd, according to us, and also according to the philosophers who maintain that our souls emanate from the separate substances, so that finally we may be able to understand these substances. Consequently, according to us, it must be asserted that our intellect will at length attain to the vision of the Divine essence, and according to the philosophers, that it will attain to the vision of separate substances.

… [S]ince in every knowledge some form is required whereby the object is known or seen, this form by which the intellect is perfected so as to see separate substances is neither a quiddity abstracted by the intellect from composite things, as the first opinion maintained, nor an impression left on our intellect by the separate substance, as the second opinion affirmed; but the separate substance itself united to our intellect as its form, so as to be both that which is understood, and that whereby it is understood. And whatever may be the case with other separate substances, we must nevertheless allow this to be our way of seeing God in His essence, because by whatever other form our intellect were informed, it could not be led thereby to the Divine essence. This, however, must not be understood as though the Divine essence were in reality the form of our intellect, or as though from its conjunction with our intellect

419

there resulted one being simply, as in natural things from the natural form and matter: but the meaning is that the proportion of the Divine essence to our intellect is as the proportion of form to matter. For whenever two things, one of which is the perfection of the other, are received into the same recipient, the proportion of one to the other, namely of the more perfect to the less perfect, is as the proportion of form to matter: thus light and color are received into a transparent object, light being to color as form to matter. When therefore intellectual light is received into the soul, together with the indwelling Divine essence, though they are not received in the same way, the Divine essence will be to the intellect as form to matter: and that this suffices for the intellect to be able to see the Divine essence by the Divine essence itself may be shown as follows.

As from the natural form (whereby a thing has being) and matter, there results one thing simply, so from the form whereby the intellect understands, and the intellect itself, there results one thing intelligibly. Now in natural things a self-subsistent thing cannot be the form of any matter, if that thing has matter as one of its parts, since it is impossible for matter to be the form of a thing. But if this self-subsistent thing be a mere form, nothing hinders it from being the form of some matter and becoming that whereby the composite itself is[1] as instanced in the soul. Now in the intellect we must take the intellect itself in potentiality as matter, and the intelligible species as form; so that the intellect actually understanding will be the composite as it were resulting from both. Hence if there be a self-subsistent thing, that has nothing in itself besides that which is intelligible, such a thing can by itself be the form whereby the intellect understands. Now a thing is intelligible in respect of its actuality and not of its potentiality: in proof of which an intelligible form needs to be abstracted from matter and from all the properties of matter. Therefore, since the Divine essence is pure act, it will be possible for it to be the form whereby the intellect understands: and this will be the beatific vision. Hence the Master says that the union of the body with the soul is an illustration of the blissful union of the spirit with God.

Source: Thomas Aquinas, The Summa Theologica Supplement, *trans. Fathers of the English Dominican Province, London: Burns, Oates & Washbourne, 1924–34.*

---

1 Literally, 'and becoming the "whereby-it-is" of the composite itself.'

9.5 Thomas Aquinas, from *Summa Theologica* (2)

Aquinas defends the notion of purgatory. He asserts that Scripture does not state anything clearly about purgatory, but that the revelations made to Fathers of the Church and to other holy people mean that this can be taught authoritatively by the Church.

Whether there is a Purgatory after this life?

From the conclusions we have drawn above it is sufficiently clear that there is a Purgatory after this life. For if the debt of punishment is not paid in full after the stain of sin has been washed away by contrition, nor again are venial sins always removed when mortal sins are remitted, and if justice demands that sin be set in order by due punishment, it follows that one who after contrition for his fault and after being absolved, dies before making due satisfaction, is punished after this life. Wherefore those who deny Purgatory speak against the justice of God: for which reason such a statement is erroneous and contrary to faith. Hence Gregory of Nyssa, after the words quoted above, adds: 'This we preach, holding to the teaching of truth, and this is our belief; this the universal Church holds, by praying for the dead that they may be loosed from sins.' This cannot be understood except as referring to Purgatory: and whosoever resists the authority of the Church, incurs the note of heresy ...

Nothing is clearly stated in Scripture about the situation of Purgatory, nor is it possible to offer convincing arguments on this question. It is probable, however, and more in keeping with the statements of holy men and the revelations made to many, that there is a twofold place of Purgatory. One, according to the common law; and thus the place of Purgatory is situated below and in proximity to hell, so that it is the same fire which torments the damned in hell and cleanses the just in Purgatory; although the damned being lower in merit, are to be consigned to a lower place. Another place of Purgatory is according to dispensation: and thus sometimes, as we read, some are punished in various places, either that the living may learn, or that the dead may be succoured, seeing that their punishment being made known to the living may be mitigated through the prayers of the Church.

Some say, however, that according to the common law the place of Purgatory is where man sins. This does not seem probable, since a man may be punished at the same time for sins committed in various places. And others say that according to the common law they are punished above us, because they are between us and God, as regards their state. But this is of no account, for they are not punished for being above us, but for that which is lowest in them, namely sin.

Source: Thomas Aquinas, Summa Theologica, *Appendix 2, Articles on Purgatory, trans. Fathers of the English Dominican Province, London: Burns, Oates & Washbourne, 1924–34.*

9.6 John Calvin, from the *Institutes of the Christian Religion*

Calvin considers the nature of heaven and suggests that we can only begin to grasp at the richness of life with God. He also warns that the imagery used in the Scriptures to describe hell is intended to communicate utter misery, which is primarily caused by being separated from God.

Chapter 25. Of the last resurrection

10. But since the prophecy that death shall be swallowed up in victory (Hosea 13:14), will then only be completed, let us always remember that the end of the resurrection is eternal happiness, of whose excellence scarcely the minutest part can be described by all that human tongues can say. For though we are truly told that the kingdom of God will be full of light, and gladness, and felicity, and glory, yet the things meant by these words remain most remote from sense, and as it were involved in enigma, until the day arrives on which he will manifest his glory to us face to face (l Cor. 15:54). 'Now' says John, 'are we the sons of God; and it does not yet appear what we shall be: but we know that, when he shall appear, we shall be like him; for we shall see him as he is' (1 John 3:2). Hence, as the prophets were unable to give a verbal description of that spiritual blessedness, they usually delineated it by corporeal objects. On the other hand, because the fervor of desire must be kindled in us by some taste of its sweetness, let us specially dwell upon this thought, If God contains in himself as an inexhaustible fountain all fulness of blessing, those who aspire to the supreme good and perfect happiness must not long for any thing beyond him. This we are taught in several passages, 'Fear not, Abraham; I am thy shield, and thy exceeding great reward' (Gen. 15:1). With this accords David's sentiment, 'The Lord is the portion of mine inheritance, and of my cup: thou maintainest my lot. The lines are fallen unto me in pleasant places' (Ps. 16:5, 6). Again, 'I shall be satisfied when I awake with thy likeness' (Ps. 17:15). Peter declares that the purpose for which believers are called is, that they may be 'partakers of the divine nature' (2 Pet. 1:4). How so? Because 'he shall come to be glorified in his saints and to be admired in all them that believe' (2 Thess. 1:10). If our Lord will share his glory, power, and righteousness, with the elect, nay, will give himself to be enjoyed by them; and what is better still, will, in a manner, become one with them, let us remember that every kind of happiness is herein included. But when we have made great progress in thus meditating, let us understand that if the conceptions of our minds be contrasted with the sublimity of the mystery, we are still halting at the very entrance. The more necessary is it for us to cultivate sobriety in this matter, lest unmindful of our feeble capacity we presume to take too lofty a flight, and be overwhelmed by the brightness of the celestial glory.

...

11. While all the godly with one consent will admit this, because it is sufficiently attested by the word of God, they will, on the other hand, avoid perplexing questions which they feel to be a hindrance in their way, and thus keep within the prescribed limits. In regard to myself, I not only individually refrain from a superfluous investigation of useless matters, but also think myself bound to take care that I do not encourage the levity of others by answering them. Men puffed up with vain science are often inquiring how great the difference will be between prophets and apostles, and again, between apostles and martyrs; by how many degrees virgins will surpass those who are married; in short, they leave not a corner of heaven untouched by their speculations. Next it occurs to them to inquire to what end the world is to be repaired, since the children of God will not be in want of any part of this great and incomparable abundance, but will be like the angels, whose abstinence from food is a symbol of eternal blessedness. I answer, that independent of use, there will be so much pleasantness in the very sight, so much delight in the very knowledge, that this happiness will far surpass all the means of enjoyment which are now afforded ...

12. Moreover, as language cannot describe the severity of the divine vengeance on the reprobate, their pains and torments are figured to us by corporeal things, such as darkness, wailing and gnashing of teeth, inextinguishable fire, the ever-gnawing worm (Matt. 8:12; 22:13; Mark 9:43; Isa. 66:24). It is certain that by such modes of expression the Holy Spirit designed to impress all our senses with dread, as when it is said, 'Tophet is ordained of old; yea, for the king it is prepared: he has made it deep and large; the pile thereof is fire and much wood; the breath of the Lord, like a stream of brimstone, does kindle it' (Isa. 30:33). As we thus require to be assisted to conceive the miserable doom of the reprobate, so the consideration on which we ought chiefly to dwell is the fearful consequence of being estranged from all fellowship with God, and not only so, but of feeling that his majesty is adverse to us, while we cannot possibly escape from it. For, first, his indignation is like a raging fire, by whose touch all things are devoured and annihilated. Next, all the creatures are the instruments of his judgment, so that those to whom the Lord will thus publicly manifest his anger will feel that heaven, and earth, and sea, all beings, animate and inanimate, are, as it were, inflamed with dire indignation against them, and armed for their destruction. Wherefore, the Apostle made no trivial declaration, when he said that unbelievers shall be 'punished with everlasting destruction from the presence of the Lord, and from the glory of his power' (2 Thess. 1:9). And whenever the prophets strike terror by means of corporeal figures, although in respect of our dull understanding there is no extravagance in their language, yet they give preludes of the future judgment in the sun and the moon, and the whole fabric of the world. Hence unhappy consciences find no rest, but are vexed and driven about by a dire whirlwind, feeling as if torn by an angry God, pierced through with deadly darts, terrified by his thunderbolts and crushed by the weight of his hand; so that it were easier to plunge into abysses and whirlpools than endure these terrors for a moment. How fearful, then, must it be to be thus beset throughout eternity! On this subject there is a memorable passage in the ninetieth Psalm: Although God by a mere look scatters all mortals, and brings them to nought, yet as his

worshippers are more timid in this world, he urges them the more, that he may stimulate then, while burdened with the cross to press onward until he himself shall be all in all.

Source: John Calvin, Institutes of the Christian Religion, *III.25, trans. Henry Beveridge (1559), Grand Rapids: Eerdmans, 1989.*

9.7 William Perkins

Perkins describes the state of the elect before and after the final judgment. Heaven is both life with God and perfect glory, and the elect will be free of all the sin of this life. He continues that there are those who are predestined for reprobation, according to God's will.

THE FOURTH DEGREE OF THE DECLARATION of God's love is glorification. Glorification is the perfect transforming of the saints into the image of the Son of God. The beginning of glorification is in death, but it is not accomplished and made perfect before the last day of judgment. The death of the elect is but a sleep in Christ whereby the body and soul is severed: the body that after corruption it may rise to greater glory, the soul that it being fully sanctified may immediately, after departure from the body, be transported into the kingdom of heaven ...

THE LAST DAY OF JUDGMENT SHALL BE on this manner. Immediately before the coming of Christ the powers of heaven shall be shaken. The sun and moon shall be darkened and the stars shall seem to fall from heaven at which might the elect then living shall rejoice, but the reprobate shall shake every joint of them. Then the heavens being all set on fire shall, with a noise like to that of chariot wheels, suddenly pass away and the elements with the earth and all therein shall be dissolved with fire. At the same time, when as all these things come to pass, the sound of the last trumpet shall be heard sounded by the archangel. And Christ shall come suddenly in the clouds with power and glory and a great train of angels.

Now at the sound of the trumpet the elect which were dead shall rise with those very bodies which were turned to dust and one part rent from another shall by the omnipotent power of God be restored; and the souls of them shall descend from heaven and be brought again into those bodies. As for them which then shall be alive, they shall be changed in the twinkling of an eye and this mutation shall be instead of death. At that time the bodies shall receive their full redemption and all the bodies of the elect shall be made like the glorious body of Christ Jesus; and therefore shall be spiritual, immortal, glorious and free from all infirmity. Last of all when they are all convened before the tribunal seat of Christ he will forthwith place the elect severed from the reprobate and taken up into the air at his right hand: and to them being written in the book of life will he pronounce this sentence, Come ye blessed of my Father, possess the kingdom prepared for you from the foundation of the world. Matt. 25.33.

THE LAST JUDGMENT BEING ONCE FINISHED, the elect shall enjoy immediately blessedness in the kingdom of heaven. Blessedness is that whereby God himself is all, in all his elect. And it is the reward of good works, not because good works can merit, but by reason of God's favour who thus accepteth works and that in respect of the merit of Christ's righteousness imputed to the elect.

Blessedness hath two parts: eternal life and perfect glory. Eternal life is that fellowship with God whereby God himself is, through the lamb Christ, life unto the elect. For in the kingdom of heaven the elect shall not need meat, drink, sleep, air, heat, cold, physick, apparel or the light of the sun and moon, but in place of all these shall they have in them God's Spirit, by which immediately they shall be quickened for ever.

Perfect glory is that wonderful excellency of the elect whereby they shall be in a far better estate than any heart can wish. This glory consisteth in three points: in that they shall still behold the face of God which is his glory and majesty; in that they shall be most like to Christ, namely just, holy, incorruptible, glorious, honourable, excellent, beautiful, strong, mighty and nimble; they shall inherit the kingdom of heaven, yea the new heavens and the new earth shall be their inheritance.

The fruit that cometh from both these parts of blessedness is of two sorts: eternal joy and the perfect service of God. The parts of God's service are praise and thanksgiving. The manner of performing this service is to worship God by himself immediately. In heaven there shall neither be temple, ceremony nor sacrament, but all these wants shall God supply together with the Lamb, that is Christ. This service shall be daily and without intermission.

THUS GOD in saving the elect doth clearly set forth his justice and mercy: his justice, in that he punished the sins of the elect in his Son's own person; his mercy, in that he pardoned their sin for the merits of his Son. All these things the Lord himself doth thus decree and in his good time will accomplish them to the glorious praise of his name.

Thus much shall suffice for the decree of election. Now follows the decree of reprobation. The decree of reprobation is that part of predestination whereby God according to the most free and just purpose of his will hath determined to reject certain men unto eternal destruction and misery, and that to the praise of his justice. In the scriptures, Cain and Abel, Ishmael and Isaac, Essau and Jacob are propounded unto us as types of mankind, partly elected and partly rejected.

Source: Ian Breward (ed.), The Work of William Perkins, *Sutton Courtenay: The Sutton Courtenay Press, 1970, pp. 246–50.*

9.8 John Wesley, from *Sermon on General Deliverance*

In his sermon, the General Deliverance, *Wesley takes as his text Romans 8.19–22. He argues that the future promises of God are not just for humanity, but for all of creation and for all species. Although Wesley asserts that all creatures will be perfected, he maintains that God has a particular concern for human beings.*

1. But will 'the creature,' will even the brute creation, always remain in this deplorable condition? God forbid that we should affirm this; yea, or even entertain such a thought! While 'the whole creation groaneth together' (whether men attend or not), their groans are not dispersed in idle air, but enter into the ears of Him that made them. While his creatures 'travail together in pain,' he knoweth all their pain, and is bringing them nearer and nearer to the birth, which shall be accomplished in its season. He seeth 'the earnest expectation' wherewith the whole animated creation 'waiteth for' that final 'manifestation of the sons of God;' in which 'they themselves also shall be delivered' (not by annihilation; annihilation is not deliverance) 'from the' present 'bondage of corruption, into' a measure of 'the glorious liberty of the children of God.'

2. Nothing can be more express: Away with vulgar prejudices, and let the plain word of God take place. They 'shall be delivered from the bondage of corruption, into glorious liberty' – even a measure, according as they are capable – of 'the liberty of the children of God.' A general view of this is given us in the twenty-first chapter of the Revelation. When He that 'sitteth on the great white throne' hath pronounced, 'Behold, I make all things new;' when the word is fulfilled, 'The tabernacle of God is with men, and they shall be his people, and God himself shall be with them and be their God' – then the following blessing shall take place (not only on the children of men; there is no such restriction in the text; but) on every creature according to its capacity: 'God shall wipe away all tears from their eyes. And there shall be no more death, neither sorrow, nor crying. Neither shall there be any more pain: For the former things are passed away.'

3. To descend to a few particulars: The whole brute creation will then, undoubtedly, be restored, not only to the vigour, strength, and swiftness which they had at their creation, but to a far higher degree of each than they ever enjoyed. They will be restored, not only to that measure of understanding which they had in paradise, but to a degree of it as much higher than that, as the understanding of an elephant is beyond that of a worm. And whatever affections they had in the garden of God, will be restored with vast increase; being exalted and refined in a manner which we ourselves are not now able to comprehend. The liberty they then had will be completely restored, and they will be free in all their motions. They will be delivered from all irregular appetites, from all unruly passions, from every disposition that is either evil in itself, or has any tendency to evil. No rage will be found in any creature, no fierceness, no cruelty, or thirst for blood. So far from it that 'the wolf shall dwell with the lamb, the leopard shall lie down with the kid; the calf and the young lion together; and a little child shall lead them. The cow and the bear

shall feed together; and the lion shall eat straw like the ox. They shall not hurt nor destroy in all my holy mountain' (Isaiah 11:6, &c).

4. Thus, in that day, all the vanity to which they are now helplessly subject will be abolished; they will suffer no more, either from within or without; the days of their groaning are ended. At the same time, there can be no reasonable doubt, but all the horridness of their appearance, and all the deformity of their aspect, will vanish away, and be exchanged for their primeval beauty. And with their beauty their happiness will return; to which there can then be no obstruction. As there will be nothing within, so there will be nothing without, to give them any uneasiness: No heat or cold, no storm or tempest, but one perennial spring. In the new earth, as well as in the new heavens, there will be nothing to give pain, but everything that the wisdom and goodness of God can create to give happiness. As a recompence for what they once suffered, while under the 'bondage of corruption,' when God has 'renewed the face of the earth,' and their corruptible body has put on incorruption, they shall enjoy happiness suited to their state, without alloy, without interruption, and without end.

5. But though I doubt not that the Father of All has a tender regard for even his lowest creatures, and that, in consequence of this, he will make them large amends for all they suffer while under their present bondage; yet I dare not affirm that he has an *equal regard* for them and for the children of men ...

God regards his meanest creatures much; but he regards man much more. He does not *equally* regard a hero and a sparrow; the best of men and the lowest of brutes. 'How *much more* does your heavenly Father care for you!' says He 'who is in the bosom of his Father.' Those who thus strain the point, are clearly confuted by his question, 'Are not ye *much better* than they?' Let it suffice, that God regards everything that he hath made, in its own order, and in proportion to that measure of his own image which he has stamped upon it.

6. May I be permitted to mention here a conjecture concerning the brute creation? What, if it should then please the all-wise, the all-gracious Creator to raise them higher in the scale of beings? What, if it should please him, when he makes us 'equal to angels,' to make them what we are now – creatures capable of God; capable of knowing and loving and enjoying the Author of their being? If it should be so, ought our eye to be evil because he is good? However this be, he will certainly do what will be most for his own glory.

7. If it be objected to all this (as very probably it will), 'But of what use will those creatures be in that future state? I answer this by another question, What use are they of now? If there be (as has commonly been supposed) eight thousand species of insects, who is able to inform us of what use seven thousand of them are? If there are four thousand species of fishes, who can tell us of what use are more than three thousand of them? If there are six hundred sorts of birds, who can tell of what use five hundred of those species are? If there be four hundred sorts of beasts, to what use do three hundred of them serve? Consider this; consider how little we know of even the present designs of God; and then you will not wonder that we know still less of what he designs to do in the new heavens and the new earth ...

Source: **Wesley's Sermons,** *from http://new.gbgm-umc.org/umhistory/wesley/sermons/60/*

9.9 Charles Haddon Spurgeon, from his sermon on 'Heaven and Hell'

The text for this sermon is Matthew 8.11–12. Spurgeon has first talked of heaven before going on to describe the path to hell and the fate that awaits those who are cast out of heaven.

Now list to me a little while – I will not detain you long – whilst I undertake the doleful task of telling you what is to become of these 'children of the kingdom.' Jesus Christ says they are to be 'cast into utter darkness, where there is weeping and gnashing of teeth.'

First, notice, they are to be *cast out*. They are not said to *go*; but, when they come to heaven's gates, they are to be *cast* out. As soon as hypocrites arrive at the gates of heaven, Justice will say, 'There he comes! there he comes! He spurned a father's prayers, and mocked a mother's tears. He has forced his way downward against all the advantages mercy has supplied. And now, there he comes. "Gabriel, take the man."' The angel, binding you hand and foot, holds you one single moment over the mouth of the chasm. He bids you look down – down – down. There is no bottom; and you hear coming up from the abyss, sullen moans, and hollow groans, and screams of tortured ghosts. You quiver, your bones melt like wax, and your marrow quakes within you. Where is now thy might? and where thy boasting and bragging? Ye shriek and cry, ye beg for mercy; but the angel, with one tremendous grasp, seizes you fast, and then hurls you down, with the cry, 'Away, away!' And down you go to the pit that is bottomless, and roll for ever downward – downward – downward – ne'er to find a resting-place for the soles of your feet. Ye shall be cast out.

And *where are you to be cast to?* Ye are to be cast 'into outer darkness;' ye are to be put in the place where there will be no hope. For, by 'light,' in Scripture, we understand 'hope;' and you are to be put 'into outer darkness,' where there is no light – no hope. Is there a man here who has no hope? I cannot suppose such a person. One of you, perhaps, says, 'I am thirty pounds in debt, and shall be sold up by-and-by; but I have a hope that I may get a loan, and so escape my difficulty.' Says another, 'My business is ruined, but things may take a turn yet – I have a hope.' Says another, 'I am in great distress, but I hope that God will provide for me.' Another says, 'I am fifty pounds in debt; I am sorry for it; but I will set these strong hands to work, and do my best to get out of it.' One of you thinks a friend is dying, but you have a hope that, perhaps, the fever may take a turn – that he may yet live. But, in hell, there is no hope. They have not even the hope of dying – the hope of being annihilated. They are for ever – for ever – for ever – lost! On every chain in hell, there is written 'for ever.' In the fires, there blaze out the words, 'for ever.' Up above their heads, they read 'for ever.' Their eyes are galled, and their hearts are pained with the thought that it is 'for ever.' Oh! if I could tell you to-night that hell would one day be burned out, and that those who were lost might be saved, there would be a jubilee in hell at the very thought of it. But it cannot be – it is '*for ever*' they are 'cast into utter darkness.'

But I want to get over this as quickly as I can; for who can bear to talk thus to his fellow-creatures? What is it that the lost are doing? They are 'weeping and gnashing their teeth.' Do you gnash your teeth now? You would not do it except you were in pain and agony. Well, in hell there is always gnashing of teeth. And do you know why? There is one gnashing his teeth at his companion, and mutters, 'I was led into hell by you; you led me astray, you taught me to drink the first time.' And the other gnashes his teeth and says, 'What if I did? You made me worse than I should have been in after times.' There is a child who looks at her mother, and says, 'Mother, you trained me up to vice.' And the mother gnashes her teeth again at the child, and says, 'I have no pity for you, for you excelled me in it, and led me into deeper sin.' Fathers gnash their teeth at their sons, and sons at their fathers. And, methinks, if there are any who will have to gnash their teeth more than others, it will be seducers, when they see those whom they have led from the paths of virtue, and hear them saying, 'Ah! we are glad you are in hell with us, you deserve it, for you led us here.' Have any of you, to-night, upon your consciences the fact that you have led others to the pit? O, may sovereign grace forgive you. 'We have gone astray like lost sheep,' said David. Now a lost sheep never goes astray alone, if it is one of a flock. I lately read of a sheep that leaped over the parapet of a bridge, and was followed by every one of the flock. So, if one man goes astray, he leads others with him. Some of you will have to account for others' sins when you get to hell, as well as your own. Oh, what 'weeping and gnashing of teeth' there will be in that pit!

Now shut the black book. Who wants to say any more about it? I have warned you solemnly. I have told you of the wrath to come. The evening darkens, and the sun is setting. Ah! and the evenings darken with some of you. I can see gray-headed men here. Are your gray hairs a crown of glory, or a fool's cap to you? Are you on the very verge of heaven, or are you tottering on the brink of your grave, and sinking down to perdition?

Source: Charles Spurgeon's Sermons, *from http://www.spurgeon.org/sermons/0039. htm*

9.10 Jonathan Edwards, from his sermon 'Heaven is a World of Love'

In this sermon Edwards states that heaven is the place where God dwells, and all is perfectly lovely. In heaven the saved are joined to the Church universal, and reunited with those who have previously died in the faith.

The apostle speaks, in the text, of a state of the church when it is perfect in heaven, and therefore a state in which the Holy Spirit shall be more perfectly and abundantly given to the church than it is now on earth. But the way in which it shall be given when it is so abundantly poured forth, will be in that great fruit of the Spirit, holy and divine love, in the hearts of all the blessed inhabitants of that world. So that the heavenly state of the church is a state that is distinguished from its earthly state, as it is that state which God has designed especially for such a communication of his Holy Spirit, and in which it shall be given perfectly, whereas, in the present state of the church, it is given with great imperfection. And it is also a state in which this holy love or charity shall be, as it were, the only gift or fruit of the Spirit, as being the most perfect and glorious of all, and which, being brought to perfection, renders all other gifts that God was wont to bestow on his church on earth, needless.

...

I. The CAUSE *and* FOUNTAIN *of love in heaven*   Here I remark that the God of love himself dwells in heaven. Heaven is the palace or presence-chamber of the high and holy One, whose name is love, and who is both the cause and source of all holy love. God, considered with respect to his essence, is everywhere – he fills both heaven and earth. But yet he is said, in some respects, to be more especially in some places than in others. He was said of old to dwell in the land of Israel, above all other lands; and in Jerusalem, above all other cities of that land; and in the temple, above all other buildings in the city; and in the holy of holies, above all other apartments of the temple; and on the mercy seat, over the ark of the covenant, above all other places in the holy of holies. But heaven is his dwelling-place above all other places in the universe; and all those places in which he was said to dwell of old, were but types of this. Heaven is a part of creation that God has built for this end, to be the place of his glorious presence, and it is his abode forever; and here will he dwell, and gloriously manifest himself to all eternity.

...

II. To the OBJECTS *of love that it contains*   And here I would observe three things: –
  1. There are none but lovely objects in heaven.   No odious, or unlovely, or polluted person or thing is to be seen there. There is nothing there that is wicked or unholy. 'There shall in no wise enter into it anything that defileth, neither whatsoever worketh abomination' (Rev. 21:27). And there is nothing that is deformed with any natural or moral deformity; but everything is

beauteous to behold, and amiable and excellent in itself. The God that dwells and gloriously manifests himself there, is infinitely lovely; gloriously lovely as a heavenly Father, as a divine Redeemer, and as a holy Sanctifier ...

2. They shall be perfectly lovely. There are many things in this world that in the general are lovely, but yet are not perfectly free from that which is the contrary. There are spots on the sun; and so there are many men that are most amiable and worthy to be loved, who yet are not without some things that are disagreeable and unlovely. Often there is in good men some defect of temper, or character, or conduct, that mars the excellence of what otherwise would seem most amiable; and even the very best of men, are, on earth, imperfect. But it is not so in heaven. There shall be no pollution, or deformity, or unamiable defect of any kind, seen in any person or thing; but everyone shall be perfectly pure, and perfectly lovely in heaven. That blessed world shall be perfectly bright, without any darkness; perfectly fair, without any spot; perfectly clear, without any cloud. No moral or natural defect shall ever enter there; and there nothing will be seen that is sinful or weak or foolish; nothing, the nature or aspect of which is coarse or displeasing, or that can offend the most refined taste or the most delicate eye. No string shall there vibrate out of tune, to cause any jar in the harmony of the music of heaven; and no note be such as to make discord in the anthems of saints and angels ...

3. Shall be all those objects that the saints have set their hearts upon, and which they have loved above all things while in this world. There they will find those things that appeared most lovely to them while they dwelt on earth; the things that met the approbation of their judgments, and captivated their affections, and drew away their souls from the most dear and pleasant of earthly objects. There they will find those things that were their delight here below, and on which they rejoiced to meditate, and with the sweet contemplation of which their minds were often entertained; and there, too, the things which they chose for their portion, and which were so dear to them that they were ready for the sake of them to undergo the severest sufferings, and to forsake even father, and mother, and kindred, and friends, and wife, and children, and life itself. All the truly great and good, all the pure and holy and excellent from this world, and it may be from every part of the universe, are constantly tending toward heaven. As the streams tend to the ocean, so all these are tending to the great ocean of infinite purity and bliss. The progress of time does but bear them on to its blessedness; and us, if we are holy, to be united to them there. Every gem which death rudely tears away from us here is a glorious jewel forever shining there; every Christian friend that goes before us from this world, is a ransomed spirit waiting to welcome us in heaven. There will be the infant of days that we have lost below, through grace to be found above; there the Christian father, and mother, and wife, and child, and friend, with whom we shall renew the holy fellowship of the saints, which was interrupted by death here, but shall be commenced again in the upper sanctuary, and then shall never end. There we shall have company with the patriarchs and fathers and saints of the Old and New Testaments, and those of whom the world was not worthy, with whom on earth we were only conversant by faith. And there, above all, we shall enjoy and dwell with God the Father, whom we have loved with all our hearts on earth; and with Jesus Christ, our beloved Saviour, who has always been to us the chief among ten thousands, and altogether lovely; and with the Holy Ghost, our Sanctifier, and Guide, and Comforter; and shall be filled with all the fullness of the Godhead forever!

Source: Jonathan Edwards Sermons, *from http://www.biblebb.com/files/edwards/charity16.htm*

9.11 Helmut Thielicke, from *The Evangelical Faith*

In this passage Thielicke discusses the return of Christ and the final judge-ment. He argues that when Christ comes into the world, it will be flooded with light and this itself will be a process of judgement as the darkness of the world is shown for what it is.

The signs of the end are not just personal (oppression by demonic forces, the approach of death, etc.). They are also cosmic symbols denoting world catas-trophe (Matthew 24:29ff.). Our references of the structures of the fallen cosmos, which we have interpreted as man's objectified secularity, have pointed us not only to the individual dimension of death and eternal life but also to the cosmic dimension of the end of the world and the coming of the kingdom of God.

Paul sees both dimensions together. Individually death means a change of form. We have to die; 'in the midst of life we are in death.' But for those who are united by faith with Christ's death on the cross, death is no longer the wages of sin (Romans 6:23). For through the Spirit they acquire a share in eternal life, no longer snatching at this life in order to be like God. Thus death ceases to be judgment, the closed barrier of finitude. The broader cosmic aspects are worked out in Romans 8:18–23. With man all nature is subject to the law of threat and anxiety and death. In solidarity with man it yearns for redemption. But the sorrow of creation does not disclose its secret in terms of natural laws, i.e., as fate or *moira*. Paul regards this suffering of nature as part of man's history with God in rebellion and grace. Animals do not fall (that would be real mythology). Man, the goal of creation and in some sense its representative, falls. His breach with God has a universal dimension. If it is not a dogmatic truth it is also no romantic anthropomorphizing to say that one has only to look one's dog in the eye to get an impression of its longing for redemption. When Goethe once came upon a puppy just being born he took it by the ear, noted with astonishment how it was straining toward the light, and suggested that this was what St. Paul meant when he spoke about the sighing of the creature.

The Spirit who helps our weakness as a pledge of future glory (8:23, 26), and gives us certainty regarding the future, enables us to face the background of a world of death and against all appearances still hope for an all-embracing redemption. The certainty that he gives is mediated by the love which is poured by him into our hearts (5:5). This love responds for its part to God's preceding love which has come to us in Christ's death for the wicked (5:6) and which remains faithful to us through the vicissitudes of history and nature right up to the final victory of the lordship of God …

We cannot affirm more than the fact of this second advent. As the coming of the new aeon of God's lordship it is outside our time. It transcends our history insofar as this is the way from the fall to judgment and is bounded by death. The forms and categories which we have to describe it are all shaped by our being in this world. The signs are the final encounter of this history-transcending factor with history and they are given only in the light of this transcending factor. The epistemological limits to what we can say are indicated indirectly by Paul when he tells us that our knowledge is now partial (*ek merous*) and that we only have the promise of a knowledge that matches our being known (1 Corinthians 13:12). What is able to cross the limits of what we can say is neither knowledge nor even faith, which will be lost in sight, but only love (1 Corinthians 13:8). This is the continuum which unites my here and now with the first and second comings of the Lord …

To speak theologically about the Parousia is fundamentally to do no more than interpret 'rejoicing in the Lord' (Philippians 4:4), and to find its basis in the Lord's nearness (4:5) both as his own nearness and the nearness of his coming …

Source: Helmut Thielicke, The Evangelical Faith, *vol. 3, trans. Geoffrey Bromiley, Edinburgh: T. & T. Clark, 1982, pp. 436–46.*

9.12 Karl Rahner, from *On the Theology of Death*

Here Rahner explores the phenomenon of death and the meaning of death for the Christian. Rahner discusses the way in which death is both fulfilment and end or emptying, and argues that Christians should be prepared to completely surrender themselves to death.

We may continue our investigation by asking: what precisely is it in the natural essence of death which makes it possible for it, through death as an act of man, to be changed into an event of salvation or of damnation, according to whether it is encountered either in faith or in godlessness? Our answer is this: it is the darkness, the hidden character of death. This reply, of course, needs some explanation. We shall have to recall a number of points to which reference has already been made in the first part of our discussion. Death appears, in unsophisticated experience to be the end of the whole man. Not, of course, in the sense that man simply and absolutely ceases to exist, or that the 'soul' ceases absolutely to exist and only that remains which is still open to empirical inspection, i.e., the corpse. This extreme interpretation of death would proceed on the supposition that what escapes the observation of our senses has no existence whatsoever; this supposition is without logical grounds and for many reasons (which we cannot discuss here) absolutely unacceptable in the present context. We hold that the spiritual, simple and personal principle in man, the soul, for ethical as well as for ontological reasons, can and must continue to exist. But death presents itself as an end, in our experience, in the sense that the whole of man somehow comes to the end of that finiteness which is characteristic of human life. This statement is valid for the soul too; at least to the degree in which, on the one hand, death appears as a phenomenon of the whole man, because it is experienced as the death of this particular man and not merely of his flesh. On the other hand, there is no reason to think that the soul, because it continues to exist after death, remains unaffected by this consummation, which occurs when our time of life runs out. ... Death is for man a dark fate, the thief in the night; it is an emptying, an ending. This simultaneity of fulfilment and emptiness, of actively achieved and passively suffered end, of full self-possession and complete dispossession of self, may, for the moment, be taken as a correct description of the phenomenon which we call death.

... No human experience will ever be able to reveal whether death is truly a pure perfection or a pure end of the man who died. Death is, indeed, hidden from the experience of man. Since this darkness of death is the result of the real-ontological, dialectical union of spirit and matter in the essence of man, we must say that this darkness belongs to the natural essence of death. This unity of opposites, in its mysteriousness impenetrable for mortals (though not for mortals who are dead, we would suggest), is the natural basis for the fact that the concrete death of man can be either salvation or damnation, punishment for sin or an act of faith.

By reason of this veil of darkness, death can be the punishment, the expression of sin; for this veiled perfection of man deprived of grace is opposed to his supernatural destiny, which still abides and which of itself tends always to an open perfection from within, which man empirically experiences and which includes his bodily nature. We suggested earlier that in some way, Adam would have died even in Paradise, in the sense that his earthly existence would have entered upon some final stage; we can now indicate with greater precision the difference between the consummation of the life of man in Paradise and the end of the human being who, in Adam, has fallen. Adam's death would not have been hidden in darkness. His end would have been the perfection and preservation of the personal reality effected in life, an end undisguisedly and tangibly experienced. The fact that the achievement of death done is enacted by man into the empty end of death suffered, and the resulting fact that death as a human act is covered with the veil of death as suffering, visibly manifests the absence of divine grace. Death, therefore, is the penalty of sin.

In this way, death becomes not only the penal consequence of sin, but also a culmination of sin itself, mortal sin in the most proper sense of the word. Since death is hidden in darkness, the concrete and final interpretation of this hidden situation can come to man only from God. On account of its darkness, man should and ought to understand the concrete existential situation of death, in so far as it is his own deed, as the culmination of that anticipatory attitude (all initial form of faith) in which man surrenders himself, in unconditional openness, to the incomprehensible God, without presuming to know of himself what that sovereign liberty of God may, in this dark and therefore incomprehensible death, decide concerning him. This in turn makes it possible to understand how death can be a mortal sin. For theological reasons we have already noted that death cannot be conceived merely as something passively suffered, a destruction coming upon us from without, but must also be conceived as an act of man, coming from within.

Obviously, it could not be an act of man, if it is conceived as an isolated point at the end of life. Death has to be understood as an act of consummation (a concept which an ontology of the end of a spiritual being can fully justify) which is achieved through the acts of the whole life in such a manner that death is axiologically present all through human life. Man is enacting his death, as his own consummation, through the deeds of his life. Thus, death is present in his deeds, that is, in each and every one of his free acts, the acts by which he freely disposes of his whole person. Consequently, the death present in the acts of life can be, explicitly or implicitly, mortal sin. In order to point out even briefly how man may make a mortal sin of the deeds of his life, we have only to indicate how he can, more or less explicitly, understand and enact his death as sin all through his life, and not merely at its end. We have no interest, obviously, in considering how each mortal sin, in some implicit and informal way, may also include a false and sinful understanding of death.

We have already suggested that death, because of its darkness, is faced rightly when it is entered upon by man as an act in which he surrenders himself fully and with unconditional openness to the disposal of the incomprehensible decision of God, because, in the darkness of death, man cannot dispose of himself freely and knowingly. Conversely, we might also say that mortal sin consists in the will to die autonomously, when death's opening towards God (which is contained in its darkness) is denied and the divine disposal of our supernatural destiny rejected, according to which death is both penalty for original sin and participation in the redeeming death of Christ. To be more precise: the sinful understanding of death in the deed or act of life could be related either directly and explicitly to the openness of human death, as though death were only a natural phenomenon, or to the two essential components of man, body and soul, the specific ontological dialectic of which reaches its highest and final tension in death.

Source: Karl Rahner, On the Theology of Death, *trans. C. H. Henkey, New York: Herder, 1961, pp. 46–54.*

9.13 Karl Barth, from *Dogmatics in Outline*

Barth here emphasizes that the resurrected person is not a different being, but perfected humanity. Resurrection completes and makes sense of this life, and is God's ultimate 'yes' to the goodness of humankind.

A Christian looks back, we said in the preceding opening statement. A Christian looks forward, we now say. This looking back and looking forward constitute the life of a Christian, the *vita humana Christiana*, the life of a man who has received the Holy Spirit, who may live in the congregation and is called to be in it a light of the world.

A man looks forward. We take a turn, as it were, of 180 degrees: behind us lies our sin and before us death, dying, the coffin, the grave, the end. The man who does not take it seriously that we are looking to that end, the man who does not realise what dying means, who is not terrified at it, who has perhaps not enough joy in life and so does not know the fear of the end, who has not yet understood that this life is a gift of God, who has no trace of envy at the longevity of the patriarchs, who were not only one hundred but three hundred and four hundred and more years old, the man who, in other words, does not grasp the beauty of this life, cannot grasp the significance of 'resurrection'. For this word is the answer to death's terror, the terror that this life some day comes to an end, and that this end is the horizon of our existence ... Human existence is an existence under this threat, marked by this end, by this contradiction continually raised against our existence: you can not live! You believe 'in Jesus Christ' and can only believe and not see. You stand before God and would like to enjoy yourself and may enjoy yourself, and yet must experience every day how your sin is new every morning. There is peace, and yet only the peace which can be confirmed amid struggle. Here we understand, and yet at the same time we understand so overwhelmingly little. There is life, and yet but life in the shadow of death. We are beside each other, and yet must one day separate from one another. Death sets its seal upon the whole; it is the wages of sin. The account is closed, the coffin and corruption are the last word. The contest is decided, and decided against us. Such is death.

And now the Christian man looks forward. What is the meaning of the Christian hope in this life? A life after death? An event apart from death? A tiny soul which, like a butterfly, flutters away above the grave and is still preserved somewhere, in order to live on immortally? That was how the heathen looked on the life after death. But that is not the Christian hope. 'I believe in the resurrection of the body.' Body in the Bible is quite simply man, man, moreover, under the sign of sin, man laid low. And to this man it is said, Thou shalt rise again. Resurrection means not the continuation of this life, but life's completion. To this man a 'Yes' is spoken which the shadow of death cannot touch. In resurrection our life is involved, we men as we are and are situated. *We* rise again, no one else takes our place. 'We shall be changed' (I Cor. 15); which does not mean that a quite different life begins, but that '*this* corruptible must put on incorruption, and this mortal put on immortality'. Then it will be manifest that 'death is swallowed up in victory'. So the Christian hope affects our whole life: this life of ours will be completed. That which is sown in dishonour and weakness will rise again in glory and power. The Christian hope does not lead us away from this life; it is rather the uncovering of the truth in which God sees our life. It is the conquest of death, but not a flight into the Beyond. The reality of this life is involved. Eschatology, rightly understood, is the most practical thing that can be thought. In the eschaton the light falls from above into our life. We await this light. 'We bid you hope', said Goethe. Perhaps even he knew of this light. The Christian message, at any rate, confidently and comfortingly proclaims hope in this light.

It is true that we cannot give ourselves, or persuade ourselves that we have, the hope that our life will be completed. It must be *believed*, in death's despite. The man who does not know what death is does not know either what resurrection is. It needs the witness of the Holy Spirit, the witness of the Word of God proclaimed and heard in Scripture, the witness of the risen Jesus Christ, in order to believe that there shall be light and that this light shall complete our uncompleted life. The Holy Spirit who speaks to us in Scripture tells us that we may live in this great hope.

The Lord's Supper ought to be more firmly regarded from the Easter standpoint, than is generally the case. It is not primarily a mourning or funeral meal, but the anticipation of the marriage feast of the Lamb. The Supper is a joyous meal: the eating of His, Jesus Christ's, flesh and the drinking of His blood is meat and drink unto life eternal in the midst of our life. We are guests at His table and so no longer separated from Himself. Thus in this sign the witness of His meal is united to the witness of the Holy Spirit. It tells us really, you shall not die but live, and proclaim the Lord's works! *You!* We are guests at the Lord's Table, which is not only an image; it is an event. 'Whosoever believeth in me, hath the life eternal.' Your death is put to death. You are in fact already dead. The terror you face you have already completely behind you. You may live as a guest at this table. You may go in the strength of this food forty days and forty nights. In this strength it is possible. Let this prevail, that you have drunk and eaten; let all that is deadly round about you be conquered. Do not nurse your sorrow tenderly; do not make a little garden of it with an overhanging weeping willow! 'We do but make the cross and pain the greater by our melancholy.' We are called to a quite different situation. 'If we died with Christ, we *believe* that we shall also live with Him' (Rom. 6.8). The man who believes that is already beginning here and now to live the complete life.

The Christian hope is the seed of eternal life. In Jesus Christ I am no longer at the point at which I can die; in Him our body is already in heaven (Question 49, *Heidelberg Catechism*). Since we may receive the testimony of the Lord's Supper, we already live here and now in anticipation of the eschaton, when God will be all in all.

Source: Karl Barth, Dogmatics in Outline, *trans. G. T. Thomson, London: SCM Press, 1949, pp. 153–5.*

9.14 Hans Urs Von Balthasar, from *Mysterium Paschale*

In this extract von Balthasar discusses Jesus' descent into hell and what this means for the scope of salvation. He suggests that there are two aspects to Holy Saturday, preaching or proclamation and liberation. Von Balthasar is concerned not to minimize the significance of this ministry of Christ, nor to maximize it beyond what Scripture allows.

As trinitarian event, the going to the dead is necessarily also an event of salvation. It is poor theology to limit this salvific happening in an a priori manner by affirming – in the context of a particular doctrine of predestination and the presumed identification of Hades (Gehenna) with Hell – that Christ was unable to bring any salvation to 'Hell properly so called', *infernus damnatorum*. Following many of the Fathers, the great Scholastics set up just such a prioristic barriers. Once agreed that there were four subterranean 'reception areas' – pre-Hell, Purgatory, the Hell of unbaptised infants and the true Hell of fire – theologians went on to ask just how far Christ had descended and to just what point his redemptive influence extended, whether by his personal presence, *praesentia*, or merely by a simple effect, *effectus*. The most frequent reply was that he showed himself to the damned in order to demonstrate his power even in Hell; that in the Hell of infants he had nothing to achieve; that in Purgatory an amnesty could be promulgated, its precise scope a matter of discussion. The Pre-Hell remained the proper field of play of the redemptive action. In the light of our remarks above, this whole construction must be laid to one side, since before Christ (and here the term 'before' must be understood not in a chronological sense but in an ontological), there can be neither Hell nor Purgatory – and as for a Hell of infants, of that we know nothing – but only that Hades (which at the most one might divide speculatively into an upper and a lower Hades, the inter-relationship of the two remaining obscure) whence Christ willed to deliver 'us' by his solidarity with those who were (physically and spiritually) dead.

But the desire to conclude from this that all human beings, before and after Christ, are henceforth saved, that Christ by his experience of Hell has emptied Hell, so that all fear of damnation is now without object, is a surrender to the opposite extreme. We shall have cause to speak of this again later, but even at this stage we have to say that precisely here the distinction between Hades and Hell acquires its theological significance. In rising from the dead, Christ leaves behind him Hades, that is, the state in which humanity is cut off from access to God. But, by virtue of his deepest trinitarian experience, he takes 'Hell' with him, as the expression of his power to dispose, as judge, the everlasting salvation or the everlasting loss of man.

...

Seen theologically, Purgatory cannot take its rise elsewhere than in the event of Holy Saturday. Even if, in First Corinthians 3, 12–15, Paul makes use of an Old Testament language and draws in the eschatological judging fire of the 'Day of the Lord' for the 'probation' of man, the criterion for that judgment is none other than the 'foundation', Jesus Christ. The eschatological fire can, no doubt, test the works raised on this foundation and in certain circumstances burn them up totally, but it saves the human being himself 'as through fire'. What is in question is not purification but putting to the test. The fire is the instrument of an eschatological judgment, but that judgment is not exercised by, simply, the devouring wrath of God. On the contrary, indeed, it is exercised by him who is solidary with us, Jesus Christ. The Pauline text, whose background is the fire of the Day of Yahweh, has nothing in common with the language of Matthew 25, 41 whose backcloth is the Jewish representation of Gehenna. Despite all the exegetical objections that Origen's account may arouse, he was theologically correct: in 'being with the dead', Christ brought the factor of mercy into what is imaged as the fire of the divine wrath.

...

Catholic dogma must, in any case, speak of a 'universal purpose of redemption' (ever against the restrictions of a doctrine of double predestination). A negative confirmation of the theological rectitude of this approach is furnished by those Scholastic speculations which, by postulating a pre-Christian 'Purgatory' in Hades, find themselves involved in insoluble contradictions ...

(b) The 'loosing of the bonds'

If one asks about the 'work' of Christ in Hades, or, better, since we have described that work as a purely passive 'vision' of sin in all its separateness, about the 'fruit' Christ brought forth there, we must, in the first place, guard against that theological busyness and religious impatience which insist on anticipating the moment of fruiting of the eternal redemption through the temporal passion – on dragging forward that moment from Easter to Holy Saturday.

To be sure, one can, as the Eastern Church customarily does, see the decisive image of the redemption in the *descensus*, that is, in the breaking down of Hell's gates and the liberation of the prisoners. Times innumerable the icon-painters depicted that scene, the true Easter image of the East. Here the entire work of the *Triduum Mortis* is perceived as a single movement which on Holy Saturday reaches its supreme dramatic intensity. Whereas the Western images of Easter always show the risen Christ alone, the East makes us see the soteriological and social aspect of the redemptive work. That is only possible by an anticipatory interpolation of the Easter event into the time of Holy Saturday, and by the transformation of a victory which was objective and passive into one that is subjective and active. The preaching of the first centuries, itself superseded to some degree by the Easter mystery plays of the Middle Ages, yielded more and more to this understandable need. That preaching, and those plays, preserved an important theological theme increasingly lost to view in systematic theology. But in preserving one theme they obscured another, which only recent liturgical directives have revalidated in excluding from Holy Saturday the alleluia Chant.

1 Peter 3.19 speaks in the active mood of *kçrussein*, 4, 6 in the passive mood of *euangelizesthai*, Acts 2, 23 of *luein*, the sufferings or bonds of death, with God

442

as subject. Accordingly, two themes compete for predominance: the theme of preaching or proclamation, and that of liberation or redemption.

The *proclamation*, in its sheer objectivity, and inasmuch as it is *evangelion* or good news, should be understood as an action which plants within eternal death a manifesto of eternal life no matter how that proclamation is made, or which persons are its heralds, or what the positive, or less positive dispositions of those whom the proclamation concerns. This removes at a stroke the problem, so pre-occupying for the Fathers, of how those already dead can be subsequently converted, and not only of the possibility of such a postmortem conversion but also of the number of those thus converting.

The theme of *liberation*, that is, of the salvation offered to the dead, as the content of this proclamation, must be understood no less objectively. Just as Jesus' condition in death is scarcely described in its subjective aspect, so here too the subjective effect of the proclamation on the 'spirits in prison' hardly enters into the reckoning. The dramatic portrait of the experience of triumph, of a joyful encounter between Jesus and the prisoners, and in particular between the new Adam and the old, is not prohibited as a form of pious contemplation, but it does go beyond what theology can affirm. It is here most particularly that the exigence for system-building must be checked. Otherwise it would move forward unhindered to the construction of a doctrine of apokatastasis.

On Holy Saturday the Church is invited rather to follow at a distance … It remains to ask how such an accompanying is theologically possible – granted that the Redeemer placed himself, by substitution, in the supreme solitude – and how, moreover, that accompanying can be characterised if not by way of a genuine, that is, a Christianly imposed, sharing in such solitude: being dead with the dead God.

Source: Hans Urs von Balthasar, Mysterium Paschale: the Mystery of Easter, *San Francisco: Ignatius Press, 2000, pp. 176–81.*

9.15 Alan Lewis, from 'All Things New'

Here Alan Lewis reflects on the meaning of mission. He establishes that mission properly belongs to God, and that the Church is invited to participate in it. The purpose of mission is ultimately the establishment of the new heaven and earth.

Because the Church serves and enacts the history of the trinitarian *missio Dei*, the scope of mission can be nothing less than cosmic. For the Father whose glory is that history's goal is no one other than the Maker of the cosmos. And the God who makes heaven and earth is incomplete, unfinished, until heaven and earth have been remade and thus completed. Things and persons exist, rather than nothing, because God chooses not to be alone, but to call forth worldly mirrors of uncreated glory, and creaturely analogues of the Creator's personhood – thus risking disappointment along with joy, repudiation as well as partnership. Creation thus expresses and reveals who God is: the inconceivable conjunction of lordly power and hungry, hazardous love.

Yet if creation is the act of God's own being, how can that being be complete, its hungers satisfied, its lordship uncontested, until the evil, sin and death which mar and thwart creation have been overcome? God will become at last the Maker, and the triune mission reach its goal, when creation and salvation coincide, and all the things that God has made have been restored, through the Alpha and Omega, who says 'I make all things new.' To sever the End from the Beginning, redemption from creation, or posit a scope of the one narrower than of the other, is thus at root a slander on the power and love of God. It denies that God completes what God begins; presumes that God loses what God loves; and thus attributes final failure to the Maker's very self.

Thus a second deception in missiology is that the Bible anthropocentrically narrates the salvation of the human race, or its chosen remnant, against the pretty, but inert, disposable backcloth of the natural order and the wider cosmos. That alleged background is, in truth, foreground; and its creatures principals upon the stage. *Our* story, central but not solitary, belongs within a history whereby *all things* are made by the Word of God, estranged by human sin, accompanied in pain and bondage by the groaning Spirit, reconciled by the peace of Christ. The drama of Adam's disobedience and the obedience of the Second Adam is enacted between the Garden of Eden and the Garden of the New Jerusalem; just as today humanity's fate is indistinguishable from 'the Fate of the Earth.' Thus does evangelism merge with ecology and ethics; and our 'vertical' relation to our Maker and Redeemer intersects with that 'horizontal' responsibility and mutual dependence which binds us with our fellow creatures in one common, global home.

Not that God's creative and redemptive love for the cosmos implies, as some sceptically fear and others romantically propose, a pantheistic confusion of nature's God with nature. Everything made by the hands of the Eternal Word and Creator Spirit is summoned to exhibit and extol the transcendent otherness of its Maker; just as divine sovereignty over nature, flesh and time is confirmed and clarified by God's presence, incarnate, crucified and risen, within the bodily matter of the universe. That ultimate affirmation of creature-hood also finally dedivinizes and deposes creation as its own redeemer. From these events springs the Church's missionary task to tell all the world the Good News that its Creator has become a creature; but also to expect 'every creature in heaven and earth, under the earth and in the sea,' humbly to render to its Creator and the incarnate, wounded Lamb 'blessing and honor and glory and might for ever.' *Trinitarian mission is not anthropocentric, but cosmic; yet not pantheistic, but incarnational.*

...

Thus contemporary experience conspires with Scripture to have us hear afresh the call to take Christ's name, in word and deed, to all the nations, beginning in Jerusalem; and to understand anew that the substance of our preaching is the promise of a New Jerusalem. There, all things are renewed and unified, in a community of forgiveness, justice, peace: a new order, in which the whole of heaven and earth participates – by the Spirit, confessing Christ, to the glory of the Father. The eschatological, global goal of mission has its origins in the Trinity itself. Through the Church – and undoubtedly beyond her – God is shaping creation as a whole into a community which shares in and resembles the fellowship and unity of the triune family.

Given this correspondence between God's eternal community and the coming community of God's creatures, missiology today justifiably questions the privatism of much past evangelism. Where human sociality, in the image of the Father, Son and Spirit, is the missionary vision, systems and structures as well as individuals will be brought under the transforming impact of God's grace. That necessitates political engagement; and above all, those acts of solidarity – however offensive to the forces of power, law and inequality – without which all talk of human togetherness and Christian fellowship is disingenuous. Hence the legitimate new criterion of 'orthopraxis' – provided that missionary activism does not succumb to anti-intellectualism. For doctrine secures the identity of the community of faith, enhancing our effectiveness as a dynamic prolepsis of the new community of heaven and earth. By theology, too, every penultimate political program of the Church is subjected to the ultimate, iconoclastic criticism of the cross of Jesus; and she articulates the *reason* for her hope. That radically differentiates her actions, despite their superficial similarity to those of other, humane but this-worldly, allies in the struggle to let the Father's heavenly will be done on earth.

There can, however, be no authentic analogy of divine community which is not as personal as it is communal. As the intra-trinitarian persons and relations are unique, so human community in God's image actually makes possible true individuality and personhood. Responsible Christian mission sacralizes neither collectivism nor bourgeois individualism, but seeks the liberation of each woman and man, interdependently with all humanity, for their own life-fulfilling knowledge of the love of God. Holistic evangelism tramples our phony fences between politics and piety, the body and the soul, the emotive and the economic – not to the detriment of any dimension of reality, but that the salvation of the whole person might be realized by the whole world. God's purposes – and God – will not be finished until all things that make us human, and all things that constitute the cosmos, have been made new, in tandem. *Global mission is not individualistic, but communal; yet not one-dimensional, but organic.*

Source: Alan Lewis, 'All Things New', Austin Seminary Bulletin 103:4 (October 1987), pp. 6–13.

9.16 Jürgen Moltmann, from *The Coming of God*

Moltmann suggests that a primary characteristic of life in Christ is joy. He argues that God gives not just 'grace upon grace', but also life upon life. The joy of Christ in this life is but a taste of the joy that will characterize resurrected life.

'From his fullness have we all received, grace upon grace' (John 1.16). The approach by way *of the fullness of God* (Eph. 3.19) which 'dwells bodily' in Christ leads us beyond the traditional ideas about the self-glorifying *will of God* and the self-realizing *nature of God* and makes the *interplay* of all blessing and praising, singing, dancing and rejoicing creatures in the community of God more comprehensible.

In order to grasp *the fullness of God*, we are at liberty to leave moral and ontological concepts behind, and to avail ourselves of aesthetic dimensions. The fullness of God is the rapturous fullness of the divine life; a life that communicates itself with inexhaustible creativity; an over brimming life that makes what is dead and withered live; a life from which everything that lives receives its vital energies and its zest for living; a source of life to which everything that has been made alive responds with deepest joy and ringing exultation. The fullness of God is radiant light, light reflected in the thousand brilliant colours of created things. The glory of God expresses itself, not in self-glorying majesty, but in the prodigal communication of God's own fullness of life. The glory of God is not to be found, either, in his laborious self-realization by way of his self-emptying, but follows upon that on the eternal day of resurrection.

The glory of God is the feast of eternal joy, and the Gospels therefore continually compare it with a wedding feast: 'Enter into the joyful feast of your master' (Matt. 25.21). Jesus's friends are wedding guests (Mark 2.19; Matt. 9.15; Luke 5.34), because they are people belonging to God's kingdom. Their final fulfillment is imagined in Rev. 19.7 as 'the marriage of the Lamb'. Even 'the heavenly Jerusalem' comes down from heaven to human beings 'like a bride adorned for her husband', according to Rev. 21.2. In Luke, the announcement of Christ's birth is proclaimed as 'news of a great joy' (Luke 2.10). According to John, Jesus's joy will remain in those who are his, so that their joy 'may be full' (John 15.11). For the coming of Christ is the arrival of God's kingdom, and the first human reaction to it is profound joy.

The resurrection of Christ means the overcoming of death's power and the appearance of imperishable, eternal life. The first human reaction to this is unrestrained Easter jubilation. Here the divine life opens and communicates itself. The Bible calls this *charis*. The divine life communicated is also eternal life, life in participation in the divine life. But it is not just life in 'the world beyond', 'life after death'; it is an awakening, a rebirth, already here and now, and the endowment of earthly life with new vital energies.

The *charis* communicates itself in countless *charismata*. These are not just 'gifts' of grace. They are new living energies as well. We are interpreting *charis* too narrowly if we only relate grace in a legalistic way to indicted sinners. *Charis* is life drawn from the fullness of God, and it shows itself in new livingness and exuberant joy. The reaction to *charis* is *chara*, joy. It is this joy that is called 'true faith'.

For human beings who desire to live and have to die, everything draws to a point in death. If death is the end, then all delight in living is as transitory as earthly life itself. But if life comes from the fullness of God, then this life is divine life, and manifests itself in us in the resurrection life. Consequently for Christian faith the resurrection of Christ was from the very beginning the open plenitude of God, and the joy that is called faith was Easter rejoicing.

> The day of resurrection, let us be light on this feast. And let us embrace one another. Let us speak to those who hate us. For the resurrection's sake we will forgive one another everything. And so let us cry: Christ is risen from the dead. (Orthodox Easter Liturgy)

In joy over the open fullness of God, out of which we receive not just 'grace upon grace' but also – as we can now say – life upon life, the life we live here and now is already transfigured and becomes a *festive* life, life in celebration. The joy brings music and imagination into this life, so that it is not just lived but is also shaped and given expression. Then life does not just go forth, it is *set* forth and moulded by God and human beings. Lived life itself becomes a song of praise. Even in pain and fear, community with the crucified Christ brings into life sparks of trust and candles of hope.

Do believers have this joy for themselves in a world hostile to them and to life? No, for them the transfiguration of life in Easter joy which they experience is no more than a small beginning of the transfiguration of the whole cosmos. The risen Christ does not come just to the dead, so as to raise them and communicate to them his eternal life; he draws all things into his future, so that they may become new and participate in the feast of God's eternal Joy: 'Through thy resurrection, O Lord, the universe is illumined ... the whole creation praises thee, day by day offering thee a hymn' (Orthodox Easter Liturgy). Out of the resurrection of Christ, joy throws open cosmic and eschatological perspectives that reach forward to the redemption of the whole cosmos. A redemption for what? In the feast of eternal joy all created beings and the whole community of God's creation are destined to sing their hymns and songs of praise. This should not be understood merely anthropomorphically: the hymns and praises of those who rejoice in the risen Christ are, as they themselves see it, no more than a feeble echo of the cosmic liturgy and the heavenly praise and the uttered joy in existence of all other living things.

The feast of eternal joy is prepared by the fullness of God and the rejoicing of all created being. If we could talk only about God's nature and his will, we should not do justice to his plenitude. Inappropriate though human analogy is bound to be, in thinking of the fullness of God we can best talk about the inexhaustibly rich *fantasy of God*, meaning by that his creative imagination. From that imagination life upon life proceeds in protean abundance. If creation is transfigured and glorified, as we have shown, then creation is not just the free decision of God's will; nor is it an outcome of his self-realization. It is like a great song or a splendid poem or a wonderful dance of his fantasy, for the communication of his divine plenitude. The laughter of the universe is God's delight. It is the universal Easter laughter. *Soli Deo Gloria*.

Source: Jürgen Moltmann, The Coming of God, *Minneapolis: Fortress Press and London:* SCM Press, 2004, pp. 336–9.

9.17   Wolfhart Pannenberg, from *Systematic Theology*

Pannenberg here argues that the divine love has entered into the created order and so God begins the process of transformation which will culminate with the perfection of all things and participation in the life of God.

The goal of the ways of God is not beyond creation. His acts in the reconciliation and eschatological consummation of the world are oriented to nothing other than the fulfilling of his purpose in creation. But why, then, did he not give creation already its definitive, eschatologically perfected form? In this question we see again the offense taken at God's permitting of evil.

From the days when the early church fathers dealt with this question, the answer of Christian theology has been that the permitting of sin and the resultant evils expresses the risk that is involved in the freedom with which God willed to endow his creatures, angels and humans. In my own presentation I have made this answer both more general and more precise by stating that permitting evil and its consequences is implied already in the independence of creatures in general. In this way I have included nonhuman nature in my discussion of the theme, just as fundamentally early Christian theology already did in its doctrine of angels by referring to a fall of angels (cf. Jude 6; 2 Pet. 2:4) before the human fall. Some degree of independence is an essential condition of the existence of the creature alongside the eternal being of God. But with independence it is only too easy for the 'impossible' transition to be made to autonomy in the creature's relation to its Creator, and all the easier the more the creature's independence takes the form of an active shaping of its own existence and of the related conditions. This is supremely true in the case of us humans and our ability to choose among different possibilities of willing and doing, an ability that many still call freedom although it is in fact only a totally inadequate if necessary condition of true freedom, the freedom of the children of God (2 Cor. 3:17). The ability to decide among possibilities of conduct is a high form of creaturely independence but also a very fragile form because the actual use of this ability can so easily lead to the loss of the independence for which God created us, namely, to our enslavement to the forces of sin and death.

By ordaining his creation for independence, God took a risk himself, the risk that the autonomy of his creatures would make him seem to be nonessential and even nonexistent. For the creature that emancipates itself from God, the fact of evil strengthens the appearance of God's nonexistence. The result is the ingratitude of creatures in their autonomy vis-à-vis God, their related unwillingness to accept the finitude of their own existence, and a good conscience in making a moral protest. Nevertheless, by his reconciling action God stands by his creation, and does so indeed in a way that respects his creatures' independence.

This independence does not end in the eschatological consummation. Indeed, by means of this event it abides in its true sense, as the actualization of the true freedom of the creature. But it is also still the condition of the mutuality of eschatological glorification in which creatures are not only glorified but also for their part glorify Jesus Christ and the Father. We can speak of this mutuality only because creatures have an existence with its own center and characterized by spontaneity in relation to God and their fellows. Hence the glorification that accrues to them cannot imply their absorption into the life of God. Instead, the spontaneity of the glorification of the Father who is manifested in his glory by the Son is the medium in which the glorification of creatures themselves takes place by the Spirit.

...

Articulated in various ways, the emergence of the eschatological future of the eternal God in the time of the creature is to be understood as the way in which the divine love declares itself. Even though itself eternal, the love of God brings forth time, works in time, and is thus present in time. As the future of God breaks already into the time of his creatures and is present to them in their limited time, God grants his creatures both existence and fellowship with himself. Thus the creation of each individual creature is itself already an expression of the divine love that grants existence to each creature, enabling it during the time of its existence to share in the vital power of the divine Spirit. God's reconciling action above all, however, is an expression of his love, causing the future of his kingdom to break into time already for those who open themselves to it in faith. The coming of the divine love into time culminates in the event of the incarnation. The fact that God is present with us in his Son to give us a share in the filial relation of Jesus to the Father, and thus to give us eternal life, means that regardless of our creatureliness we may participate in the fellowship with the eternal life of God. This carries with it for believers a guarantee of the future of salvation and an assurance of the love of God by the granting of the Holy Spirit as a lasting gift that can raise up their mortal bodies to eternal life in the future of God. Only the eschatological future of God will consummate this revelation of his love in the consummating of creation for participation in God's own eternal life. But by the gift of the Spirit believers are already certain of it. As those who are reconciled to God they thus live now in a state of peace with God (Rom. 5:1).

Only the eschatological consummation in which God will wipe away all tears (Isa. 25:8; Rev. 21:4) can remove all doubts concerning the revelation of the love of God in creation and salvation history even though the love of God has been at work already at each stage in the history of creation. Only in the light of the eschatological consummation is the verdict justified that in the first creation story the Creator pronounced at the end of the sixth day when he had created the first human pair: 'And God saw everything that he had made, and behold, it was very good' (Gen. 1:31). Only in the light of the eschatological consummation may this be said of our world as it is in all its confusion and pain. But those who may say it in spite of the suffering of the world honor and praise God as their Creator. The verdict 'very good' does not apply simply to the world of creation in its state at any given time. It is true, rather, of the whole course of history in which God is present with his creatures in incursions of love that will finally lead it through the hazards and sufferings of finitude to participation in his glory.

...

On the whole path from the beginning of creation by way of reconciliation to the eschatological future of salvation, the march of the divine economy of salvation is an expression of the incursion of the eternal future of God to the salvation of creatures and thus a manifestation of the divine love. Here is the eternal basis of God's coming forth from the immanence of the divine life as the economic Trinity and of the incorporation of creatures, mediated thereby, into the unity of the trinitarian life. The distinction and unity of the immanent and economic Trinity constitute the heartbeat of the divine love, and with a single such heartbeat this love encompasses the whole world of creatures.

Source: Wolfhart Pannenberg, Systematic Theology, *vol. 3, trans. Geoffrey W. Bromiley, Grand Rapids, MI: Eerdmans, 1997, pp. 642–6.*

9.18 John Zizioulas, from *Lectures on Christian Dogmatics*

The eschaton, Zizioulas argues, is the reality of the future, and the past. The Church offers glimpses of what life perfected in Christ will be like and life in the Spirit transcends the boundaries of past, present and future.

For the Orthodox, the historical reality of the Church relates to the Eucharist and so to that reality which comes to us from the eschaton. This eschatological reality reveals itself to us by means of sacraments and icons, which must be described in terms of an eschatological and iconological ontology. These sacraments and images are created as the Holy Spirit draws us and all our history into relationship with the end time, the reconciliation of all partial kingdoms in the true history of the kingdom of God. To ask whether the true Church is the *historical* or the *eschatological* Church is to fail to grasp that the eschaton is the reconciliation and integration of all history and therefore the truth of history. The eschaton is the summation and truth of all time and all kingdoms, and thus the eschaton is the truth of the world, of which the Church is the foretaste.

For this reason we must not isolate history from eschatology. The liturgy shows that the divine Eucharist is both a historical *and* an eschatological event. Remembrance does not mean recalling an event that is simply past, an event borne away from us by the stream of time. It requires a conceptual revolution to grasp that the liturgy is both an eschatological and historical event, and that it is a historical event *because* it is first the eschatological event in which all histories are called into being and gathered up into one.

We have said that the liturgy is an eschatological and historical event. However, how can it be both at once? In the Western intellectual tradition we remember what is past, not what is still future to us.

The Western tradition is constituted by its historical awareness, since it assumes that specific historical events are what is most fundamentally true, so all its scholarly efforts are directed to capturing or recovering the truth of historical events. This means for instance that when we ask about the authority of the councils, and want to identify where this authority begins and ends, we have to say that the authority of that council cannot be sourced merely in the event of that council, but also over the much longer event of the reception and acceptance of that council. Each conciliar decision is accepted in the fullness of the Church and so over time. Of course, it is not easy to accept such a degree of indeterminacy, for we want to identify an unchanging principle or institution or particular historical moment that we can date. This preoccupation with the givens of history is part of a larger yearning for security. Objective data takes the element of the unknown, and with it, the burden of responsibility away from us. It is important to seek the truth of events and to record them in the way that they occurred, but such scholarship is not only historical but also historicist, in that it claims such 'historical' knowledge precisely by divorcing events from their meanings.

The historical event is one apprehended by the mind and so constrained by the boundaries of the mind. When this is the case, what role is there for the Holy Spirit? We have a Christology at work here, because it is understood that we are in search of a series of past events, the cross, tomb, resurrection, ascension which fit into a timeframe, 'under Pontius Pilate', 'on the third day' and so on.

Yet we also have to come to terms with the thought that the liturgy also remembers what has not yet taken place. In the prayer 'We offer unto thee in all and for all' of the Liturgy attributed to St. John Chrysostom we read the words:

> Remembering, therefore, this commandment of salvation, and all those things which came to pass for our sakes: the cross, the tomb, the resurrection of the third day, the ascension into heaven, the sitting on the right hand, *the coming again a second time in glory*, Thine own, of thine own, we offer unto thee in all and for all.

This is the commandment of Jesus to his disciples to take and eat from his body and drink from his blood, in remembrance of him. However, it is perhaps not easy to see why we say that we are *remembering* his coming again in glory. How can we remember an event that has not yet taken place?

When we refer to remembering the future we part ways with the main Western intellectual tradition. The Church confesses that the Holy Spirit brings the future into history. Our kingdoms are founded on opposition to one another, each kingdom is in competition with every other. The peace of God, sustained by the rule of God, brings to an end this conflict between all partial kingdoms. The Holy Spirit invades the territory we hold against all others, and brings us into the rule and the peace of God, 'In these last days, I shall pour forth from My Spirit, on all flesh' (Acts 2.17). The Spirit brings all other rules and kingdoms, under the rule of Christ, bringing about the peace of Christ by which all things are reconciled and made peaceful. Christ brings the rule and peace of God into history.

Pentecost is the fulfilment of all times. Though many Christians assume that Pentecost and the Holy Spirit illuminate them personally, enabling them to grasp the events of history and so to grow in the knowledge of Christ, this is only a partial understanding. The Holy Spirit frees us of all the various confinements that hold us within our individual histories or the histories of our nation or social group. The Spirit draws us into the vastly larger dimensions given by the future, in which we are free to be fully present to one another, each of us to all others without limit. The life the Holy Spirit gives us is not divided, but all at once, so for the first time we may live knowing that all Christians, past, present and future are present to us, in a communion not delimited by space or time.

What we experience in the divine Eucharist is the end times making itself present to us now. The Eucharist is not a repetition or continuation of the past, or just one event amongst others, but it is the penetration of the future into time. The Eucharist is entirely live, and utterly new; there is no element of the past about it. The Eucharist is the incarnation live, the crucifixion live, the resurrection live, the ascension live, the Lord's coming again and the day of judgment, live. We cannot go to it casually or without repentance for it is the event in which all events are laid out and examined. 'Now is the judgment of the world' (John 12.31). This 'now' of the Fourth Gospel refers to the Eucharist, in which all these events represent themselves immediately to us, without any gaps of history between them.

The whole force of the Western intellectual tradition attempts to separate history and eschatology and fit Christian doctrine into its historicist and immanent mentality. Either the end times is a separate chapter that will take place 'afterwards', or it is the charismatic experience of a select few, set apart from the historical community. However, the eschaton means the end of all separate, disconnected times, the reconnection and reconciliation of our separate histories and the arrival of their future and fulfilment. All the continuity of our histories comes from outside them, from the end times, so there cannot be any final reckoning of our history apart from the eschaton which gives it its coherence and future.

The Eucharist is the communion of all things penetrating into our presently mutually antagonistic 'communions'. The fulfilled communion that is the Church is brought into being for us now by the entrance of the future reality of communion into our presently divided communities. Only a properly *pneumatological* Christology can give us the ecclesiology that understands the Church as the witness of the future.

Source: John Zizioulas, Lectures on Christian Dogmatics, *London and New York: T. & T. Clark, 2008, pp. 153–5.*

9.19 Kathryn Tanner, from *Jesus, Humanity and the Trinity*

Tanner explores the nature of death and distinguishes between biological and religious death. She argues that despite the reality of death, we live eternally with God through the life-giving power of God.

As parallel modifications in Christian accounts of creation suggest, what is required here is an account of a saving relationship with God that undercuts the religious importance of the question whether the world will end. Just as creation in its essential meaning does not refer to what happens in the beginning (in contradistinction to what happens after), so the central claim of eschatology must not refer to what happens at the end (in contradistinction to what happens before). Understood in that way the eschaton – consummation in the good – would have to do primarily with a new level of relationship with God, the final one surpassing what we are simply as creatures, beyond which there is no other – the relation with God discussed in previous chapters as life in the triune God, as that becomes possible for us through the Father's sending of the Son in Christ by the power of the Spirit. What is of fundamental religious interest for the question of salvation is the character of this relation to God and not what the world is like or what happens to it considered independently of that relation – say, at its end. One retains a religious interest in the future of the world *as it exists in this new relationship with God*, that is, one wants to know what consequences this relationship with God has for the world. But the world has this future whether the world, considered in itself, ends or not and whatever the process by which it does; the world will have this future, irrespective of such events, because it has this future in virtue of the character of its relationship with God whatever its state, whether or not the world ends, and whatever the process by which it does. The relationship holds whether the world continues to exist or ceases to exist.

To see the sense of these last remarks, it is important to see how life in God is a way of developing some typical biblical moves that already relativize or undercut the religious significance of the difference between biological life and death (or life as existence and death as cessation of existence).

First, there is the dominance particularly in the Old Testament of a wider (so-called metaphorical) use of 'life' and 'death', where life refers to fruitfulness and abundance, longevity, communal flourishing and individual wellbeing and death is a catch-all for such things as suffering, poverty, barrenness, oppression, social divisiveness and isolation. According to these more extended senses of life and death, one can be dead while alive; death enters into the course of life as the threat of such things as sickness, impoverishment, and lack of fulfillment. One can also enjoy a death that imitates life – in old age, surrounded by one's posterity. 'Your descendants will be many and your offspring like the grass of the earth. You shall come to your grave in ripe old age' (Job 5:25–26).

A second, similar sort of relativization of the difference between biological death and life is suggested by Old Testament passages in which 'life' and 'death' seem to refer to the *way* one lives or dies, in particular whether one lives (or dies) for God (and for others). One lives, in this sense, to the extent one dedicates one's life to the God who is the source of life in all its extended senses, to the extent that one keeps faith with a relationship with God by maintaining the form of life that relationship with God requires. All the goods of life – in our first, extended sense of the term 'life' – are blessings that stem ultimately from relationship with God. To die is to break with this life-giving, blessing-bestowing relationship with God and the covenant it forms; to live is just to place oneself willingly and joyfully within it. 'I have set before you life and death, blessings and curses. Choose life that you … may live, loving the Lord your God, obeying him, and holding fast to him; for that means life to you and length of days …' (Deuteronomy 30:19–20).One can and should hold fast to God whatever the dangers and vicissitudes of life; in this sense one enjoys a gift that cannot be lost, a blessing of life that survives every trial and tribulation, every threat, that is, from the forces of death. Whatever the adversity one can take comfort in the fact that 'Yahweh is my chosen portion and my cup' (for example, Psalm 16:5), 'my refuge' (Psalm 73:28); indeed, in such circumstances it becomes clear the way God's 'steadfast love is better than life' (Psalm 63:3).

But can the relations with God and neighbour that spell life be sustained across the fact of biological death? (Spiritualizing those relations, in the way the last biblical quotation suggests, can only go so far; it is therefore an ulti-mately unsuccessful way of relativizing the difference between life and death.) Does death not disrupt one's relationship to the life-giving powers of God? 'I shall lie in the earth; you will seek me, but I shall not be' (Job 7:21). 'For Sheol cannot thank you, death cannot praise you; those who go down to the Pit cannot hope for your faithfulness' (Isaiah 38:18). To what extent then does our second sense of life in relational terms genuinely relativize the difference between continued existence and its cessation?

For the Old Testament, the worry I am now raising primarily concerns the effect of biological death on an individual's relation to God. The death of indi-viduals may be final for them but not for the community, which continues to exist in relation to God. Thus, a single generation of the community might be cut off from God and suffer a grievous downturn, but presumably there might still be hopes for the next.

Despite a sense of the finality of death for the individual him/herself, worries about individual mortality can be quelled in the Old Testament by a more primary concern for the community and by a sense of the dead indi-vidual's continuing existence for it – through offspring or communal memory. So, the finality of his own individual death is softened in this way by Jacob on his deathbed: 'I am about to die, but God will be with you, and will bring you again to the land of your ancestors' (Genesis 48:21). One can participate beyond one's death in the ongoing life of the community through one's chil-dren, but even 'eunuchs … shall receive from me something better than sons and daughters: a memorial and a name in my house' (Isaiah 56:3–5, NEB).

This sort of response to the irrevocability of personal death is lost, for us, however; with scientific descriptions of the end-time, all human communities, along with the cosmos itself, seem to suffer as irrevocable a death as any individual person. The problem posed by personal death, in short, is now simply writ large for us. Are there biblical perspectives, particularly Old Testament ones in which the finality of personal death is assumed, that might be of help here in discussing a relation to God unaffected by death, perspectives on personal death that might be extended by us moderns to the whole of the cosmos marked for death?

Old Testament passages suggest, first of all, that the dead are not cut off from God because God is the Lord of both life and death. Death is a sphere within God's power, God's reach, and therefore (one presumes) the dead are not lost to God. 'The Lord gave, and the Lord has taken away; blessed be the name of the Lord' (Job 1:21). 'There is no god beside me; I kill and make alive; I wound and I heal' (Deuteronomy 32:39; also, for example, 1 Samuel 2:6–7). Therefore, 'where can I go from your spirit? Or where can I flee from your presence? If I ascend to heaven, you are there; if I make my bed in Sheol, you are there' (Psalm 139:7–8). In keeping with such ideas, maintaining relationship with the God who gives life would not seem to require the destruction of death (as a more apocalyptic outlook requires). Death does not have the power to separate one from God. Such a confidence, without the development of any explicit ideas about life after death, may underlie Psalms 16, 49 and 73. Thus, in a context where literal death seems to be at issue ['those who are far from you will perish; you put an end (to them)'], the psalmist exclaims, 'my flesh and my heart may fail, but God is the strength of my heart and my portion forever' (Psalm 73:26).

'Eternal life' (in some of its New Testament senses) develops this suggestion that not even death can separate us from the love of God and others. One with the Word, Jesus is not separated from God on the cross; exactly here (as everywhere else in Jesus' life), the light and life of God enter into darkness and death, to heal and save. In virtue of a continuing union with the Word that death cannot obstruct, the humanity of Christ, as its own powers of life perish on the cross, is able to draw upon the life-giving power of God so as to be resurrected and brought glorified to the Father. United with Christ, we too are inseparable from God: 'Neither death, nor life, nor angels, nor rulers, nor things present, nor things to come, nor powers, nor height, nor depth, nor anything else in creation, will be able to separate us from the love of God in Christ Jesus our Lord' (Romans 8:38). Because we are united with the life-giving humanity of Jesus by the power of the Spirit across the fact of our deaths, as our lives perish of themselves, lose their own powers of living, God gives to us God's own powers of life so as to maintain us. As in the case of Christ's crucifixion, where the divine powers that are always his are put to special use in a victory over death, this life of Christ is also ours now by grace, to be employed by God in a special way at our deaths. In virtue of our relationship to the life-giving powers of Christ's humanity, our lives are lived now, as after death, in and through God's own powers of life: 'I have been crucified with Christ; and it is no longer I who live but it is Christ who lives in me. And the life I now live in the flesh I live by faith in the Son of God, who loved me and gave himself for me' (Galatians 2:19–20). But these life-giving powers of Jesus' humanity do not overcome our deaths until we suffer them, at which time the only power of life we have is God's own.

Because it runs across the fact of death, life in Christ is eternal life. There is a life in the triune God that we possess now and after death, in Christ through the power of the Holy Spirit. Ante and post mortem do not mark any crucial difference with respect to it. Death makes no difference to that life in God in the sense that, despite our deaths, God maintains a relationship with us that continues to be the source of all life-giving benefit. Even when we are alive, we are therefore dead in so far as we are dead to Christ. Separation from Christ (and from one's fellows in Christ) is a kind of death despite the apparent gains that might accrue to one in virtue of an isolated, simply self-concerned existence. Eternal life, moreover, is one's portion or possession despite all the sufferings of life and death in a way that should comfort sufferers of every kind in tribulation. In all the senses of death, including the biological, we therefore live even though we die, we die to the Lord; so then, whether we live or whether we die, we die to the Lord; so then whether we live or whether we die, we are the Lord's (Romans 14:8).

Source: Kathryn Tanner, Jesus, Humanity and the Trinity, *Minneapolis: Fortress Press, 2001, pp. 103–8.*

9.20 Valerie Karras, from 'Eschatology'

In this extract, Karras argues that feminist theology has largely ignored the resources of Eastern Christianity. She seeks to demonstrate that some of the traditional approaches and problems of eschatology can be reframed if 'either–or' distinctions are replaced with 'both–and'.

As with other areas of theology, so, too, in eschatology I believe that feminist theology is still operating largely within the framework of Western theology. Feminist theologians have rightly critiqued the anthropocentric focus of much traditional Western eschatology. Their solution has been to shift the locus from humanity to creation, replacing the anthropocentric focus of patriarchal Christian theology with the cosmocentric focus of ecofeminism. In reality, however, this is not so much a shift of focus as a broadening of it, a recentring which is not really. Humanity is no longer central in and of itself, but it remains part of the focus as a part of creation. In other words, ecofeminist theology's cosmocentric focus has broadened traditional eschatology's telephoto lens from an extreme magnification focussing on humanity alone to a wider view of the cosmos in which humanity exists, but it has kept the lens focussed in the same direction – creation.

What I propose is that we not merely broaden the vision seen through our lens, but that we reverse the direction in which the lens is pointed: from the created to the Creator, from the cosmos to God. If, as feminist eschatology has rightly noted, our existence as humans can only be seen within the context of our participation in the bionetwork of creation, then both humanity in particular and the cosmos as a whole can only be seen in relation to that which has given them existence and sustains that existence. Ecofeminism's understanding of the cosmos as the body of God is an important attempt to articulate this relationship, but it has inverted the order, thereby making the cosmos – and, derivatively, humanity – normative in and of itself. Thus, the restoration of both the cosmos and humanity is seen primarily as a quantitative process rather than a qualitative one. There is little focus on the future because, if one does not understand the ultimate goal of existence as something transcendent, then that future existence will look similar to the present – it may be 'better', but it won't be substantially *different*.

...

This theology of the transfiguration of creation brings us to humanity's distinct role as mediator. But, in order to understand humanity's mediatorial role, we must first understand what it means to be a microcosm, to be human. Many feminist theologians reject the biblical creation story with its emphasis on the special status of humanity vis-à-vis the rest of creation. Instead, they promote a 'common creation story' characterised by humanity's total identity within the evolutionary fabric of creation, usually with no transcendent connection to the divine substantially different from that shared by the rest of the universe. But, we can accept evolutionary theory (the common creation story) as a description of the process of creation and of one aspect of anthropology (the physical and biological aspect) while also retaining the theological truths of the creation accounts in the first chapters of Genesis. In other words, again we must reject an either/or approach, this time with respect to anthropology and biblical interpretation.

...

This model of humanity as mediator provides us with an eschatological vision which is 'both/and' as opposed to 'either/or'. It is an unrealised (future-oriented, transcendent) eschatology that simultaneously has realised (present-oriented, ecofeminist, immanent) implications. It is this vision of humanity already realised as microcosm, together with humanity's not yet realised goal of mediator, which provides the rationale for an eschatology which recognises that the Kingdom of God is in our midst (Luke 17:21) while concurrently seeking it (Matthew 6:10) as something not yet come – now, and not yet.

There is a similarity among patriarchal Western theology, feminist theology, and Eastern Christian theology in the emphasis all place on a future utopian society – the 'Kingdom of God' – as the goal of human existence, a goal which is not yet achieved. Consequently, all three theological threads recognise that the social, political, economic, and cultural inequities of various human societies not only are not normative for humanity, but are an aberration from the condition of paradise and far removed from the Kingdom of heaven. This recognition is not a modern development; it is part and parcel of historical Christianity's understanding of the 'fallen' nature of corporate humanity. For instance, John Chrysostom (a monk-priest from Antioch who became archbishop of Constantinople in 397) in his 22nd Homily on Ephesians identified slavery as 'the fruit of covetousness, of degradation, of savagery'; in homilies on Genesis and 1 Corinthians, he asserted that the subordination of woman was a consequence of humanity's fall from grace. He clearly recognised human inequality as a divergence from the prelapsarian and eschatological norms.

But, while all three of these theological systems agree that the current condition of the human community falls far short of what it is meant to be, they differ as to whether it *can* reach its potential in the foreseeable future. That is, is the Kingdom of God achievable within the bounds of normal history? Can we construct a human society which is radically different from the way human societies are currently structured? This is the essence of the distinction between realised and unrealised eschatology: the former answers 'yes' to this question, the latter answers 'no'.

Historically, Christianity in both its Eastern and Western traditions has had an unrealised eschatology. Despite Chrysostom's recognition of the fallen nature of social inequalities, he did not call for the radical reform of either political or social structures. In fact, like many in both East and West, he considered such inequality normative for our current condition, necessary for the smooth functioning of a society filled with persons driven by ego and passions rather than love and self-emptying. Chrysostom was willing to allow for deviation from this norm where a personal spiritual situation called for it, but such deviation did not, for him, upset the validity of the norm.

Source: Valerie Karras, 'Eschatology', in Susan F. Parsons (ed.), The Cambridge Companion to Feminist Theology, *Cambridge: Cambridge University Press, 2002, pp. 248–55.*

461

9.21 Robert Jenson, from 'The Great Transformation'

Jenson argues that the End necessitates a final judgement. This is not primarily to determine the fates of individuals, but rather to restore righteousness and to put relationships right between enemies. This reconciliation, Jenson suggests, is itself the life of the eternal kingdom.

Since it is the Bible that proclaims a final judgement, our first task is to remind ourselves of what that book means by judgement. In Scripture, judgement is intervention to restore righteousness, that is, to set a community right. The notion is something like the following. In the community of Israel, or the church, or by extension a community viable for more than a moment, each person occupies a unique position over against all the others, constituted by a specific set of what we would now call rights and duties. Righteousness prevails when each person takes his or her such location as an opportunity of loving service to all the rest. To the extent that such love fails, the community is disordered and *un*righteousness prevails. Whether it is then a parent intervening in a quarrel between siblings, or a jury and judge determining the facts and the law, or the Lord intervening to judge all Israel, judgement is action to sort out a polity not living in love. So the prosperous landholder in Israel who does not use his prosperity to serve his impoverished neighbours, who, e.g., strips his fields so clean that there are no gleanings, commits injustice, and the town elders must reprove him in the gate and compel him to more communally responsible behaviour. And if the created magistrates do not function, eventually God intervenes to save the community from its own lack of love.

The *Last* Judgement is simply a judgement that encompasses the entire human community and after which another will not be needed. It will be the act of God in which all the accumulated injustice of history, of the total human community, is put right, and humanity is made one vast network of unique persons each taking his or her uniqueness as the opportunity of love for all the rest. So a child's disobedience will be set right between him and his parents, and the bombings of Coventry and Dresden between Germany and the Allies, and the eternal mutual oppression and violence of races and classes; and for that matter the hegemony involved in my presuming to write this essay, will all be put right.

Plainly, the last judgement just described is not the last judgement of much apocalyptic imagining, a sorting operation on individuals, to pick them out for heaven or hell. I do not mean to deny that individuals will be judged. The robber baron will be condemned for his exploitation of the helpless, and reparation made. The brutal parent will be rebuked and the harm done to the child repaired. And perhaps this will not be accomplished without excluding some from the blessed community altogether, so that indeed there comes to be a final community of love and another one of hatred, called hell. But that sorting is not the primary reality of what we may await. The primary reality of what we may await is the establishing of universal and perfect justice, which on the biblical understanding of justice is the same as the establishing of universal and perfect love.

This setting right should not be seen as a sort of preliminary, clearing the decks for the establishment of universal bliss. This setting right is itself the *content* of the eternal event of bliss. What happens as final salvation? Precisely *that we are set right* with each other, that I have the *joy of God's rebuke* for my sin against my brothers and sisters, and the joy of seeing the repair of my injuries to them, at my cost. The point is of fundamental importance, for it is just so that it is *me*, in *my* identity as the sinner I am, who lives the joy of the kingdom. The blessed eternity will be as it were the eternal expansion of one great *reconciling*.

Finally, on this line, the Last Judgement must be also *our* act of mutual forgiveness and reparation; we must be reconciled with one another. The proposition would be Pelagian, if a final mutual reconciliation were construed as an event prior to entry into the kingdom, and so as a sort of condition of entrance. But my proposal is that reconciliation, including this last aspect, is the life of the kingdom itself.

Source: Robert Jenson, 'The Great Transformation', in Carl Braaten and Robert Jenson (eds), The Last Things: Biblical and Theological Perspectives on Eschatology, *Grand Rapids, MI: Eerdmans, 2002, pp. 38–9.*

9.22 Rowan Williams, from *Tokens of Trust*

In this extract, Williams discusses the affirmation of belief in the 'resurrection of the body' in the Nicene Creed. He explains that although the nature of the afterlife is essentially a mystery, there are certain things which can be said. There will be some continuity between this life and the next; humans in heaven will continue to be embodied and relational beings. Heaven is not an escape from human bodies or nature, but a transformation of them.

The Church makes sense only when we see that it exists to get acclimatized to peace and praise, to bring us now into the atmosphere where what pervades and shapes everything is the life of God the Holy Trinity. So it's natural to move on to these declarations about our final destiny. But as we do, we should notice that we're not asked to declare a belief in 'eternal life' in general or in 'immortality'. In the Apostles' Creed this is most startling because we say we believe in 'the resurrection of the body' – or rather, in the original, 'the resurrection of the *flesh*'. If we have – as most of us do – a vague idea that religion commits us to believing in 'life after death', and that this involves a sort of shadowy reproduction of ourselves floating up towards the sky (remember all those cartoon images from childhood), this phrase gives a bit of a jolt. Do we actually want this particular lump of bone and fat and hair that we know so well to have an eternal future? And isn't there a hint of something, well, rather creepy about such language?

It is one of the hardest doctrines to state convincingly in the present climate. We are a fantastically materialistic society, but we often seem to have no innate respect for bodies, and to imagine that the body really is only the envelope for an identity created by the mind and will (it's one reason we get into such a mess thinking about human embryos – a bodily human organism but with no trace of anything we could call a mind or a will, so we can readily jump to the conclusion that it can't have ordinary human 'rights'). Christian faith says that since God has come to encounter us in this world of material bodies, *as* a material body, and since God continues to use material things and persons to communicate who and what he is, we can't suppose that life with him will ever simply sidestep our material life. The Bible speaks rather seldom of life with God in heaven; it is more inclined to talk about a renewal of creation, 'a new heaven and a new earth', as in the last book of the Bible. Life with God, it seems, is life in a *world* that has something in common with the world we now inhabit.

This is where it gets difficult. Our imaginations set to work and we produce pictures of the new world, the world we'd really like to live in; only they seem so often to produce only embarrassing clichés. Look at those pictures of the new heaven and new earth that you sometimes see in the glossy publications of some religious sects that claim to explain the real meaning of the Bible to you: the painful truth is that they can't help looking like holiday brochures of the naffest variety. The path to thinking about eternal life is strewn with cowpats and elephant traps; yet there it is, in Bible and Creed: 'the resurrection of the flesh', the new world. How do we do justice to what the tradition demands and still avoid the pitfalls?

Perhaps we can start from first principles. We are who we are because we live in a context that makes us who we are – a human context but also a non-human environment. We've seen already that our relation to both community and material context is intrinsic to the life of faith, not an afterthought or a luxury. Our holiness is bound up with other people and with the things of the world. Our relation with God is made visible (or not, of course) in how we conduct these everyday relationships. So if we believe in life with God that does not just evaporate at our physical death, it must still be life in community and context, life in a world where all our relationships with things and persons are fully anchored in the Trinitarian love of God and fully transparent to that love.

God knows – literally – what that might mean. But that seems to be the nature of the challenge and the promise of our faith. The gospel treats us seriously, in our wholeness; it promises a new world and it directs us to the central story of a bodily saviour whose material flesh and bones are not just left around in the world but raised and transfigured into something recognizably continuous with earthly life, yet dramatically different. The resurrection of Jesus and the hope of eternal life with God become the ground of a promise that, whatever exactly this means, God does not redeem us by making us stop being what we are – beings who live in community and context. If God holds on to us through death, he holds on to every aspect of us – not just to a specially protected, 'immortal' bit of us. Whatever life with God is, it is not something more abstract or more isolated than what we now know …

In our present life, the 'immortal diamond' [of Gerard Manley Hopkins' poem 'Nature's Bonfire'] is inseparably bound up with all the mixed and not very impressive stuff of human nature. And when resurrection arrives, it is not that all the rest falls away, but that the 'diamond' now takes in everything. It is not that the diamond is one bit of us that survives; the implication is that it is the precious possibility of relationship with God in the whole of our human nature.

And so the experiences of an anticipation of heaven that we have associated with 'seeing the Church' are important because they are quintessentially experiences of community and context. We may well be – well no, we just are – quite unable to give a description of heaven, but we can say, 'It cannot be less than this'. People are sometimes rather shocked if you say that Christianity does not believe in the immortality of the soul; but in fact, while the Bible and the tradition talks about 'immortal' life, they don't assume that this deathless existence is something reserved for a part of us only, as if there were a bit of us that didn't have a future and a bit that did, the solid lumpy bit and the hazy spiritual bit. We have a future with God as *persons*, no less. The life that is given us by God in our mortal and material relationships takes in all of that, and on the further side of death (which by definition we can't *imagine*) nothing is lost.

Our hope has nothing to do with some natural feature of our existence, a soul that has natural immortality. Although this came to be taken for granted in the early centuries of the Church and deeply affected much of what we are used to hearing on the subject, the hope described in the Bible is connected not to any aspect of our lives but to God's faithful commitment to the whole of what he has made. And, to be fair to earlier Christian generations, while they usually *did* assume the immortality of the soul, they never lost hold of the larger promise of resurrection. In the Middle Ages, you will find writers describing the frustration of the soul after death as it waits for the Last Judgement when it can be reunited to the body. We don't have to accept the rather convoluted theories they worked out in order to tidy this up; but we can recognize that they understood the hope of eternal life as hope for persons not ghosts.

Source: Rowan Williams, Tokens of Trust, *Norwich: Canterbury Press and Louisville: Westminster John Knox Press, 2007, pp. 139–43.*

Details of Authors and
Sources of Documents

1. Councils and Documents

Barmen Declaration (1934) The confessional document of the Confessing Church, which was a union of Lutheran and Reformed Christians in Germany united by their opposition to Hitler. It was later influential in the life of the East German Church and in South Africa. Written largely by Karl Barth (q.v.).

Chalcedon, Council of (451) The fourth ecumenical council, brought together to oppose various errant conceptions of how Jesus Christ could be both fully human and fully God. The Chalcedonian definition remains influential in christological discussion, but is now also controversial, with some writers suggesting it must be discarded as merely irrelevant to modern ways of thinking, and others insisting it remains a necessary and useful doctrinal standard.

Confession of Dositheus (1672; also known as the Synod of Jerusalem, or the Synod of Bethlehem) Dositheus (1641–1707) became the Orthodox Patriarch of Jerusalem in 1669, and called a synod to oppose moves to align Orthodoxy with the Reformed churches. The resulting confession is mostly written by him, and represents the closest approach of Orthodoxy to Tridentine Catholicism.

Constantinople, Council of (553; also called 'Second Council of Constantinople') Fifth ecumenical council called by Emperor Justinian to settle the Monophysite and Nestorian christological controversies stemming from Chalcedon. It ruled out any possible Nestorian interpretation of Chalcedon by condemning the *Three Chapters*, a group of writings viewed by Monophysites as hopelessly Nestorian, and upheld the authority of Chalcedon.

Constantinople, Council of (381) The second ecumenical council, which settled the Arian controversy in favour of Nicene (q.v.) orthodoxy. The so-called Nicene Creed is traditionally believed to have been written by this council, and remains the central doctrinal standard of the Christian churches in both East and West.

Didache (early second century; also called 'Teaching of the Twelve Apostles') From the period of the Apostolic Fathers, the *Didache* is a catechetical work, which purports to contain the apostles' teaching concerning Christian practices including baptism, fasting, communion and church organization.

Genevan Confession (1536) Traditionally ascribed to Calvin, now usually considered to have been written by William Farel. Whoever the author was, this is a representative of the confessions that proliferated around the time of the Reformation and afterwards, as new churches sought to define their continuity with the Christian tradition, and their differences from other groups.

Lumen Gentium (1964; also called 'The Dogmatic Constitution on the Church') A principal document of the Second Vatican Council (q.v.), it is noteworthy for centring ecclesiology in a trinitarian theology of communion, its more positive appraisal of non-Roman Catholic Christians, and holding out the possibility of salvation for unevangelized believers in God.

Mystici Corporis Christi (1943) Papal encyclical issued by Pope Pius XII on the Church as the Mystical Body of Christ. It stated that the Roman Catholic Church is not *identical to* but *subsists in* the Body of Christ, thus making theological space for non-Roman Catholic churches. It emphasizes that the Body of Christ includes the laity with the clergy and encourages the former's active participation in perfecting the Body of Christ.

Nicaea, Council of (325) The first ecumenical council, called by the recently converted Emperor Constantine to decide on the Arian controversy. The Council's decision eventually triumphed, but not until after several decades of struggle ended by the Council of Constantinople. The creed promulgated by the council, usually known as the 'Creed of Nicaea' is rarely used today, but is reaffirmed by later ecumenical councils such as Constantinople and Chalcedon.

Scots Confession (1560) The first confession of faith of the Reformed Church of Scotland drawn up in four days by John Knox and five other ministers. As a typical Calvinist document it emphasized justification by faith, election and the true Church identified not by lineal descent but by correct preaching of the Word, right administration of the sacraments, and discipline. It remained the confessional standard until being superseded by the Westminster Confession (q.v.).

Schleitheim Confession (1527) The earliest known Anabaptist confession adopted by a Swiss Brethren Conference overseen by Michael Sattler. Written in a context of persecution, it does not detail central Christian beliefs but highlights seven distinctive topics central for Anabaptists: baptism, the ban, communion, separation from the world, shepherds, non-violence, and the oath.

Thirty-Nine Articles (1563)   One of the key theological documents of the English Reformation and of the subsequent development of Anglican identity. Their history is complicated (although the first definitive text was produced in 1563, it owes much to Cranmer's Forty-Two Articles of 1553, and a final revision took place in 1571). They were intended to establish the Church of England as a Reformed church, occupying a middle position between Roman Catholicism and Anabaptism and other radical movements.

Trent, Council of (1545–63)   A council called by the Roman Catholic Church in response to the Reformation, which reaffirmed various Catholic teachings and practices as proper in the face of Reformed objections. It met in three stages over an 18-year period.

Vatican I (First Vatican Council; 1869–70)   A council of the Roman Catholic Church, which is famous mainly for defining the infallibility of the pope, when speaking *ex cathedra* and making official pronouncements on matters of faith and morals.

Vatican II (Second Vatican Council; 1962–65)   A council of the Roman Catholic Church, famous for its reforming of church practice in various areas (for example, the saying of Mass in languages other than Latin). Theologically, the Council issued two 'dogmatic constitutions', one on the nature of the Church (*Lumen Gentium*) and one on divine revelation (*Dei Verbum*). The former has widely been interpreted as being more affirming of other Christian denominations than had previously been the case in official church pronouncements.

Westminster Confession (1646)   A leading Reformed confession of faith written by predominantly Church of England theologians in response to a request from the English Parliament. Drawing on the European Reformed tradition and the ecumenical creeds, it is a systematic exposition of Calvinist orthodoxy consisting of 33 chapters that cover the breadth of Christian faith. It was adopted by the Church of Scotland in 1647 and has exercised significant influence in Presbyterian and other Reformed churches.

World Council of Churches (WCC; founded in 1948)   Ecumenical organization based in Geneva, Switzerland, it is 'a fellowship of Churches which accept Jesus Christ our Lord as God and Saviour'. It was established by the merging of the *Life and Work* and the *Faith and Order* ecumenical organizations, and in 1961 the International Missionary Council merged with the WCC to become its Division of World Mission and Evangelism. Representing most Protestant and Eastern Orthodox churches, the WCC is not a church, nor does it issue orders or directions to the churches. Rather it works for the unity and renewal of the Christian faith by seeking a common witness and Christian service.

2 Individual writers

Abelard, Peter (1079–1142) Philosopher and theologian, who famously developed a moral influence theory of the atonement. His main work is *Sic et Non* (*Yes and No*, 1120), in which he discusses the role of faith and reason in theology.

Anselm of Canterbury (c. 1033–1109) Born in Italy, he joined the abbey of Bec (in northern France), and became prior there. He later became Archbishop of Canterbury (England). Key writings include two arguments seeking to prove the existence of God, the *Monologion* and the *Proslogion*, and an important discussion of the atonement, *Cur Deus Homo*. An influential collection of prayers and meditations has also circulated under his name, although recent scholarship has questioned the authorship of some of these.

Apollinarius (c. 300–392) Bishop of Laodicea and opponent of Arianism. In his zeal to emphasize Christ's deity and the unity of Christ's one nature, he denied that Christ has a rational human soul thus undermining Christ's full humanity. Apollinarius and Apollinarianism were condemned as heretical at the Council of Constantinople (381, q.v.).

Aquinas, Thomas (c. 1225–74) Born in Italy, he became a Dominican friar and went to Paris to study, dividing the rest of his life between there and Italy. Regarded as the greatest medieval theologian, his work grew out of the need to reconcile the newly recovered philosophy of Aristotle with Christian doctrine. The *Summa contra Gentiles* and the *Summa Theologica* were his major writings, but he produced many others, and was an able commentator on Scripture, Aristotle and other writers.

Arius of Alexandria (c. 250–336) Theologian, arch-heretic, famous for saying 'there was a time when the Son was not', Arius denied the full divinity of Jesus and rather affirmed he was the most exalted of all creatures. He was opposed by Athanasius and condemned at the Councils of Nicaea (q.v.) and Constantinople (q.v.).

Athenagoras of Athens (second half of the second century) Philosopher and apologist, he used Neoplatonist concepts to interpret the Christian faith. He wrote *Plea Regarding Christians*, and *On the Resurrection of the Dead* is attributed to him.

Athanasius (c. 296–373) From Alexandria in Egypt, he accompanied the then patriarch to the Council of Nicaea. Soon afterwards he became patriarch himself. Much of his life was spent defending the Nicene doctrine that the Son, Jesus Christ, is of the same substance (*homoousios*) as the Father, that is, fully divine. The opposing position, denying the deity of Christ, was known as Arianism, and was very popular, forcing Athanasius to endure five exiles. His key writings are *Contra Gentes* ('Against the Pagans'), *Contra Arianos* ('Against the Arians'), and a *Life of St Antony*, which became a major text in the rise of monasticism. *Letters Concerning the Holy Spirit to Serapion* (*Ad Serapion*) is a late work extending the defence of the true deity of the Son to the Holy Spirit.

Augustine of Hippo (354–430)   Born in North Africa, his early life was spent in a quest for a satisfying philosophy, through which God led him to Christianity, a journey described powerfully in his spiritual autobiography, the *Confessions*. He became Bishop of Hippo (also in North Africa) and devoted his great intellect to the pressing theological controversies of the day, writing in defence of the goodness of creation against the Manichees, against the idea that human beings are free to save themselves by good works, as suggested by the Pelagians, and in defence of the reception of repentant sinners back into the Church against the Donatists. *On the Trinity* is a profound meditation on the triune nature of God that he worked on for decades before releasing it hastily in an unfinished form, because pirate copies were circulating. Arguably the most important theologian of the Western Church.

Aulén, Gustaf E. H. (1879–1978)   Swedish Lutheran theologian and bishop, he is best known for *Christus Victor* (1930), in which he argues that the classic model of the atonement is victory over death and hell, as taught by Irenaeus of Lyons (q.v.) and Martin Luther (q.v.).

Baillie, John (1886–1960)   Church of Scotland theologian, minister and ecumenist. A prolific author, he is best known for his devotional writings, especially *Diary of Private Prayer* (1936), *Invitation to Pilgrimage* (1942) and *A Diary of Readings* (1955). Among his most notable theological works are *Our Knowledge of God* (1939), his Bampton lectures published as *The Idea of Revelation in Recent Thought* (1956) and his posthumously published Gifford Lectures, *The Sense of the Presence of God* (1962).

Balthasar, Hans Urs von (1905–88)   Swiss Roman Catholic theologian. His major work, appearing in three multi-volume parts (*The Glory of the Lord*, the *Theo-Drama* and the *Theo-logic*), is a massive, erudite and complex attempt to discuss theology in terms of the three classical transcendentals: the beautiful, the good and the true.

Barth, Karl (1886–1968)   Swiss-German Reformed theologian. He studied under the great teachers of liberal Christianity in Germany, but was profoundly disillusioned when working as a pastor by the failure of that theology to speak to the needs of his people, and by his former teachers' support for militarism as the First World War began. He found in the Bible a 'strange new world', where God spoke a fundamental challenge to all human efforts and constructions from without. He taught for a time in Germany, before being dismissed for refusing to swear allegiance to Hitler.

471

He was the main author of the Barmen Declaration (q.v.), the doctrinal standard of the Confessing Church, set up to oppose National Socialism. Forced to return to Switzerland, he began writing the *Church Dogmatics*, a massive work that, although unfinished, is undoubtedly one of the major texts of the Protestant theological tradition. In it, Barth focused on God's revelation of himself in Jesus Christ and, in conversation with the Scriptures and with writers throughout the Christian tradition, sought to understand what that meant for every reality.

Basil of Caesarea ('*The Great*'; c. 330–79)   Bishop in what is now Turkey. One of the 'Cappadocian Fathers' (the others were Gregory of Nazianzus (q.v.) and Gregory of Nyssa), who developed the doctrine of the Trinity which lay behind the decisions taken at the Council of Constantinople (q.v.), and the Nicene Creed. His works include *On the Holy Spirit*, a defence of the claim that the Spirit is divine, and to be worshipped alongside the Father and Son.

Boff, Leonardo (b. 1938) and *Boff, Clodovis* (b. 1944)   Brazilian brothers, both significant liberation theologians. Leonardo became famous as a result of the Vatican's objections to his *Church, Charism and Power*, as a consequence of which he was silenced and later left the priesthood and the Franciscan order. Clodovis is Professor of Theology at São Paulo; his major work thus far is *Theology and Praxis* (1987).

Bonaventure (1221–74)   Franciscan scholastic theologian. His main works were commentaries on the *Sentences* of Peter Lombard (q.v.), *Itinerarium mentis ad Deum* and *Breviloquium*. A central theme of his theology is the ascent of the human soul towards God.

Bonhoeffer, Dietrich (1906–45)   German Lutheran minister and theologian and member of the Confessing Church. Among his best known works are *Letters and Papers from Prison* (ET published in 1953), *The Cost of Discipleship* (ET 1948), in which he combats 'cheap grace', and *Ethics* (ET 1955), which christocentrically recasts the Christian's relation to history, society and politics. He was executed by the Nazis in 1945.

Bosch, David Jacobus (1929–92)   South African missiologist, ecumenist, Dutch Reformed minister and opponent of Apartheid. His most famous work is *Transforming Mission* (1991), which is a classic text on missiology.

Bromiley, Geoffrey (1915–2009)   Professor of Church History and Historical Theology at Fuller Theological Seminary in California. He is best known for his translation work, especially Karl Barth's (q.v.) *Church Dogmatics*, the *Theological Dictionary of the New Testament*, edited by Gerhard Kittel, and other authors including Jacques Ellul, Helmut Thielicke, Wolfhart Pannenberg (q.v.) and Ernst Käsemann.

Bultmann, Rudolf (1884–1976)   German New Testament scholar, who spent much of his life as Professor in Marburg. He used existentialist philosophy to interpret the New Testament, and engaged in a process of 'demythologization', that is, reinterpreting miraculous elements in existentialist terms. His works include a very significant *Theology of the New Testament* (1948–51, ET 1970) and a commentary on John's Gospel (1941, ET 1971).

Cabasilas, Nicolas (*c.* 1320–90)   Byzantine lay theologian and liturgist. His *Commentary on the Divine Liturgy* and *Life in Christ* are classics of Eastern Orthodox sacramental theology.

Calvin, John (1509–64)   Born in France, he was converted to the Reformed cause and spent most of his adult life as pastor in Geneva. His writing centred on two foci: biblical commentaries and the *Institutes of the Christian Religion*, in which he collected thematic and controversial material arising from his commentating into an organized structure. The latter went through several editions, the final and definitive version being published in 1559.

Clement of Alexandria (*c.* 150–*c.* 215)   Early head of the famous *catechetica* school in Alexandria in Egypt (where Origen (q.v.) was later to teach), although he was forced to flee from there by persecution. His *Stromata* and other writings are attempts to relate Christianity to the Alexandrian culture of the day, which was heavily influenced by Greek philosophy.

Coakley, Sarah (b. 1951)   Anglican theologian, priest, philosopher and Professor at Cambridge University. She has published works on Patristics (*Re-Thinking Gregory of Nyssa*, 2002/03), feminist theology (*Powers and Submissions*, 2002), Christology (*Christ without Absolutes*, 1994), theology and science (*Pain and Its Transformations*, 2007), and practical theology (*Praying for England*, 2008).

Congar, Yves (1904–95)   French Dominican Cardinal who was one of the leading twentieth-century Roman Catholic theologians. Best known for his work in ecclesiology and pneumatology, Congar drew from biblical, patristic and medieval sources to revitalize the discipline. He was an ecumenist who exercised a major influence at the Second Vatican Council (1962–65). His major work is his three-volume *I Believe in the Holy Spirit* (1983).

Cyprian of Carthage (200–258)   Bishop of Carthage and martyr. His most famous work is *On the Unity of the Church*, in which he develops what has become traditional ecclesiology. It contains classic statements like 'There is no salvation outside the Church' and 'He cannot have God for his father who has not the church for his mother'.

Cyril of Jerusalem (*c.* 315–386)   Bishop of Jerusalem who lived in the midst of the political turmoil of the Arian controversy which led to periods of exile. Famous for his *Catechetical Lectures* which give important insights into the worship of the Palestinian church of the time.

Cyril of Alexandria (d. 444)   Patriarch of Alexandria most known for stressing the unity of Christ and opposing the Christology of Nestorius.

Dionysius, (Pseudo-) (*c.* 500)   A shadowy Syrian mystic whose works were originally thought to be by Paul's convert in Athens (Acts 17), and so to be possessed of apostolic authority. He combines Christianity with Neoplatonism in an influential synthesis. The *Mystical Theology* describes the ascent of the soul to God.

Edwards, Jonathan (1703–58)   American Puritan theologian, famous for his involvement in the Great Awakening (the American equivalent of what in Britain is known as the Evangelical Revival) in the eighteenth century. As a result of his experience of sudden conversions during the revival, he wrote several works analysing religious experience, of which *The Religious Affections* (1812) is the most famous. His wider theology was a profoundly creative attempt to hold together the Puritan synthesis in the face of new scientific and theological ideas.

Fiddes, Paul S. (b. 1947)   Leading British Baptist theologian who has written widely on topics as broad as *The Creative Suffering of God* (1988), *Past Event and Present Salvation* (1989), the Trinity (*The Trinity in Worship and Preaching*, 1991, and *Participating in God*, 2000), eschatology and literature (*The Promised End*, 2000), and Baptist ecclesiology (*Tracks and Traces*, 2003).

Forsyth, P. T. (1848–1921)   British Evangelical theologian, who sought to relate the gospel to the modern mind. Known for his work on the doctrine of salvation, a Christocentric soteriology lies at the heart of his theology. His main works include *The Person and Place of Jesus Christ* (1909), *The Cruciality of the Cross* (1910) and *The Soul of Prayer* (1916).

Francis of Assisi (*c.* 1182–1226)   Known for his commitment to the life of poverty, evangelical zeal, spirituality and personal charisma, he committed his life to follow the example of Jesus. He is the founder of the order of Franciscan friars.

Gregory of Nazianzus (*c.* 330–*c.* 389)   One of the 'Cappadocian Fathers' (the others were Basil of Caesarea (q.v.) and Gregory of Nyssa (q.v.)), who developed the doctrine of the Trinity which lay behind the decisions taken at the Council of Constantinople (q.v.) and the Nicene Creed. Gregory's *Theological Orations* were preached in Constantinople before the Council began, and represent a high point in theological preaching. At the Council itself, he appears to have been a leading figure.

Gregory of Nyssa (*c.* 335–394)   One of the 'Cappadocian Fathers' with his brother Basil of Caesarea (q.v.) and Gregory of Nazianzus (q.v.), he was a theologian and Bishop of Nyssa. He defended Nicene orthodoxy against

Arianism and Apollinarianism by working out Basil's distinction between *ousia* and *hypostasis* with regard to the doctrine of the Trinity. His classic theological work is *Catechetical Orations* which is a systematic treatment of Christian doctrine for catechumens.

Gunton, Colin E. (1941–2003)   British theologian, who taught systematic theology at King's College London for over thirty years. He was ordained in the United Reformed Church and was a prolific author in most areas of Christian doctrine including the doctrine of creation and the Trinity. Perhaps best known is *The One, The Three and The Many* (1993), a theological analysis and critique of modernity.

Gutiérrez, Gustavo (b. 1928)   Peruvian theologian, Dominican priest, and commonly regarded as the founder of liberation theology. Best known for *A Theology of Liberation* (1971), which resolutely combines theology with praxis, calls for redemptive solidarity with the poor and emphasizes the socio-economic and political aspects of Christian soteriology and discipleship.

Heron, Alasdair I. C.   Was Professor of Reformed Theology at the University of Erlangen in Germany. His best-known works are *A Century of Protestant Theology* (1980) and *The Holy Spirit* (1983).

Hildegard of Bingen (1098–1179)   German mystic of noble birth, she received visions from a young age. She described her visions in her main work *Scivias*. She was an abbess, composer, poet and author of theological, botanical and medicinal works and created her own alphabet.

Hilary of Poitiers (c. 315–67)   French theologian. He supported Athanasius (q.v.) in the Arian disputes and was banished to Phrygia, where he became familiar with Eastern theology, which influenced his writing. *On the Trinity* is his major work.

Hodge, Charles (1797–1878)   American theologian. He graduated at the College of New Jersey (now Princeton) in 1815, and in 1819 at the Princeton Theological Seminary, where he became the first Professor of Oriental and Biblical Literature in 1822. In 1840 he was transferred to the chair of exegetical and didactic theology, to which subjects that of polemic theology was added in 1854. His more important essays were republished under the titles *Essays and Reviews* (1857), *Princeton Theological Essays* and *Discussions in Church Polity* (1878).

Hooker, Richard (1554–1600)   Church of England theologian and leading opponent of the Puritans. He suggested the Church of England had failed to complete a fully biblical reformation. His main work is his eight-volume *Laws of Ecclesiastical Polity*, in which he argued for a middle way between Roman Catholicism and Puritanism.

Ignatius of Antioch (*c.* 35–*c.* 107)   Martyr bishop of Antioch. Little is known about his life. En route to his martyrdom in Rome he wrote a series of letters containing important information on the early Church. His letters, now part of the Apostolic Fathers, are an important example of primitive Christian theology, particularly ecclesiology.

Irenaeus of Lyons (*c.* 130–*c.* 200)   Born in Asia Minor, where he heard the teaching of Polycarp, who in turn had learnt from the apostle John. He became Bishop of Lyons (France), and wrote against the various deviations from the 'rule of faith' that he discovered in his major work, *Against Heresies*. His theology is marked by the doctrine of recapitulation, whereby Christ became a second head of the human race, undoing the failure of Adam, and by a strongly trinitarian account of divine action, particularly in creation.

Irving, Edward (1792–1834)   Scottish minister, preacher and theologian. He sought to reintroduce the charismatic dimension into Protestantism and taught on the Holy Spirit and eschatology. He was expelled from the Church of Scotland for his views on Jesus Christ assuming a sinful nature and was the forerunner to the Catholic Apostolic Church. His works include *For the Oracles of God* and *For Judgment to Come* (both 1823).

Jenson, Robert William (b. 1930)   American Lutheran theologian, heavily involved in defending orthodox trinitarian Christianity against all forms of modern accommodation. His two-volume *Systematic Theology* (2001) summarizes many of the themes of his earlier work and seems destined to become a major work of late-twentieth-century English-language theology.

John of Damascus (*c.* 675–*c.* 749)   Greek theologian, perhaps best known for his defence of the use of icons in the iconoclastic controversies. His *Exposition of the Orthodox Faith* is a remarkable piece of systematic theology which in many ways summarizes the Patristic Greek tradition, at times quoting more or less directly from an earlier writer at length.

Justin Martyr (*c.* 100–65)   Early Christian apologist and philosopher who converted to Christianity and was later martyred. In his *First Apology* and *Second Apology* he defended Christianity to the Roman Emperor and Senate, and in *Dialogue with Trypho* he sought to prove the truth of Christianity to an educated Jew named Trypho. He is important for his Christian interpretation of the Old Testament and his description of the sacraments of baptism and the Eucharist.

Kähler, Martin (1835–1912)   German Lutheran theologian who was Professor of Systematic Theology at the University of Halle. He is best known for his collection of essays entitled *The So-Called Historical Jesus and the Historic, Biblical Christ* (1892), which resisted the scholarly trend of separating the Jesus of history from the Christ of faith.

Karras, Valerie A. Teaches Church History at Perkins School of Theology at Southern Methodist University in Texas. She is a Patristic and Byzantine Christianity scholar whose main work is *Women in the Byzantine Liturgy* (2005).

Kasper, Walter (b. 1933) German Roman Catholic Cardinal and Tübingen theologian well known for his contributions to Christology, notably *Jesus the Christ* (1976) and *The God of Jesus Christ* (1986). Kasper is currently President of the Pontifical Council for Promoting Christian Unity, is prominent for his ecumenical work, and has written *A Handbook of Spiritual Ecumenism* (2007). He is also known for working towards reconciling Catholics and Jews.

Kierkegaard, Søren Aabye (1813–55) Danish philosopher/theologian who opposed Hegel's philosophy and reacted against the formal Christianity of his day to stress the need for a radical personal commitment to Christ. Many of his works were written under various pseudonyms, allowing him to work from within different intellectual positions. The *Philosophical Fragments* are ascribed to the pseudonym Johannes Climacus, who is perhaps best regarded as someone examining the logic of Christian faith from without.

LaCugna, Catherine Mowry (1952–2007) American Roman Catholic feminist theologian who, through *God for Us the Trinity and Christian Life* (1993), sought to make the doctrine of the Trinity relevant for Christian living. Building on the work of Karl Rahner (q.v.), LaCugna proposed a moratorium on language of the immanent Trinity and instead emphasized the importance of the economic Trinity.

Lewis, Alan E. (1944–94) Professor of Theology at Austin Presbyterian Theological Seminary, Texas. In his main work *Between Cross and Resurrection* (2003), Lewis develops a theology of Holy Saturday, and while writing he suffered from and finally succumbed to cancer.

Lombard, Peter (1095–1160) Medieval theologian and Bishop of Paris. A student of Peter Abelard (q.v.), Lombard's major work is his *Book of Sentences* (1158). It combines scholastic logic with numerous citations of Patristic and medieval writers and became the classic medieval theological textbook.

Luther, Martin (1483–1546) German theologian and one of the main Protestant Reformers. His theology might be considered to be built on three great slogans: through faith alone (*sola fide*), through grace alone (*sola gratia*), through Scripture alone (*sola Scriptura*). The first demands that human beings are not saved from their sins by any merits they accumulate in the sight of God, but only through faith in Christ. The second insists that there is no other mediator between God and the sinner but Christ, and so denies any mediatory role to the Church and its priesthood (or to the saints). The third demands that there is no other source of authority for Christian faith than the Bible, although Luther clearly respected the ancient Christian tradition as being faithful to Scripture.

McFadyen, Alistair I. (b. 1961)   British theologian at Leeds University, his main works are *The Call to Personhood* (1990) and *Bound to Sin* (2000).

McFague, Sallie (b. 1933)   American feminist theologian concerned with relating theology to contemporary issues. Describing the world as God's body, her works include studies on the relation between theology and metaphor (*Speaking in Parables*, 1975, and *Metaphorical Theology*, 1982) and theology and ecology (*Models of God*, 1987, *The Body of God*, 1993, and *A New Climate for Theology*, 2008).

Moltmann, Jürgen (b. 1926)   German Reformed theologian and Professor Emeritus of Theology at Tübingen University. Innovative theologian, who has written on most areas of Christian doctrine, but is best known for his *Theology of Hope* (1967), a key text in the rediscovery of eschatology, and· *The Crucified God* (1974), which develops Martin Luther's theology of the cross.

Nestorius (d. *c.* 451)   Bishop of Constantinople, he is known for denying that Mary is *theotokos* (mother of God). Cyril of Alexandria (q.v.) believed this denial undermined Christ's divinity and so opposed Nestorius, leading to his condemnation as a heretic at the Council of Ephesus in 431. His name is associated with the heresy Nestorianism, the heretical belief that Christ has two individual natures, the human and the divine, that are joined in conjunction rather than in hypostatic union.

Newbigin, Lesslie (1909–98)   British missionary and theologian. Newbigin served for 35 years as a missionary in India, in the process becoming one of the first bishops of the Church of South India and a leading figure in the World Council of Churches. On returning to Britain, he found, famously, that it had turned into a mission field, and he began writing and working to explore a missionary engagement with Western culture.

Niebuhr, Reinhold (1892–1971) American theologian, who became involved in the social gospel movement and was committed to a prophetic Christianity, which relates Christian revelation to political and social ethics. Professor of Applied Christianity at Union Theological Seminary in New York, his writings represent a critical reaction to liberal Protestantism. His best-known work is his two-volume *The Nature and Destiny of Man* (Gifford Lectures for 1939; two volumes 1941–43), which opposes Renaissance humanism with a biblical anthropology with its emphasis on creation, fall, atonement and Christ's second coming.

Origen (*c.* 185–*c.* 253)   Egyptian theologian and exegete. He was head of the catechetical school in Alexandria, but later moved to Caesarea and established a school there as a result of a dispute with his bishop. He was arguably the greatest biblical interpreter of the Patristic age, working on textual criticism as well as exegesis. *On First Principles* is a systematic account of the Christian faith, which is perhaps too influenced by aspects of the Greek philosophical tradition, but nonetheless intellectually outstanding. Many of his teachings were later condemned as heretical.

Owen, John (1616–83)   English theologian, who supported Cromwell during the Civil War and Protectorate and was for a time Vice-Chancellor of the University of Oxford. Increasingly recognized as a profound theologian, he is perhaps the outstanding mind of English Puritanism. His voluminous writings cover many areas.

Palamas, Gregory (1296–1359)   Orthodox theologian and Archbishop of Thessalonica. He taught that God cannot be known in his essence but can be known in his energies (in God's actions towards creation) through spiritual disciplines. His best-known works are *The Triads* and his two-volume *Homilies*.

Panchovski, Ivan (b. 1943)   Bulgarian theologian known for writing on pneumatology and theology and the natural sciences.

Pannenberg, Wolfhart (b. 1928)   German theologian who studied under (among others) Karl Barth (q.v.). He has attempted to take history more seriously than he believes Barth did, seeing God's revelation as mediated through history, and exploring Christology from a historical perspective. In recent years he has also been interested in the interaction between theology and other academic disciplines, not least the natural sciences. His three-volume *Systematic Theology* (1988–93; ET 1988–94) is a major work of late-twentieth-century theology.

Pelagius (d. *c.* 410)   British monk and theologian who travelled to Rome and was shocked both at the moral laxity and the widespread belief that humans are intrinsically evil. In contrast to this he argued that humans are free and good by nature, and since perfection is possible it is therefore obligatory. Famous for his theological debate with Augustine, his views are associated with a denial of original sin, affirming complete human freedom and salvation by works. Pelagius was declared a heretic but his views continue to exercise significant influence.

Perkins, William (1558–1602)   Church of England Puritan theologian and minister. He is known for developing the 'Golden Chain', which diagrammatically sets out the order of salvation according to Calvinist double predestination.

Rahner, Karl (1904–84)   German Roman Catholic theologian, influential at the Second Vatican Council (q.v.). Influenced by existentialist philosophy, he sought to explain theological meaning by appealing to transcendental experience that is common to all human beings. Much of his work is in shorter essays, many of which are collected in 23 volumes of *Theological Investigations* (1961–92). *Foundations of Christian Faith* (1978) is a summary of his thought.

Richard of St Victor (d. 1173)   Scottish monk and mystical theologian. He spent most of his time in the Augustinian abbey of Saint-Victor in Paris and his best-known works are *De Trinitate* (*On the Trinity*) and his mystical writings.

Ritschl, Albrecht (1822–89)   German Protestant theologian for whom justification was central to his theology. His main works are *Christian Doctrine of Justification and Reconciliation* (1870–74), *Instruction in the Christian Religion* (1875), *Theology and Metaphysics* (1881), and his three-volume *History of Pietism* (1880–86). He distinguished between 'fact' and 'value' judgements, consigning many central Christian beliefs, such as Christ's divinity, to the latter.

Robinson, H. Wheeler (1872–1945)   British Baptist theologian and Old Testament scholar. He was well known for his contributions to Old Testament Theology, soteriology and pneumatology, including the notion of 'corporate personality' in which descriptions of individuals in the Old Testament (like the Servant in Deutero-Isaiah) refer to Israel as a whole.

Ruether, Rosemary Radford (b. 1936)   American feminist theologian. *Sexism and God-Talk* (1993), perhaps her most significant book, is one of the major texts of feminist theology.

Russell, Letty M. (1930–2007)   Feminist theologian of Yale Divinity School, who pioneered feminist theology in theology, ethics and biblical studies. Her works include *The Future of Partnership* (1979), *Feminist Interpretation of the Bible* (1985), *Church in the Round* (1993), *Human Liberation in a Feminist Perspective* (1995) and *Dictionary of Feminist Theologies* (1996).

Saiving, Valerie   Feminist theologian who wrote the influential essay 'The Human Situation: A Feminine View' (1960). Arguing that characterizing sin as pride reflects male experience, she proposed a radical redefinition of sin that addresses female experience, with important consequences for soteriology.

Schleiermacher, Friedrich Daniel Ernst (1768–1834)   German theologian who sought to defend Reformed orthodoxy in the face of post-Kantian philosophy. His *On Religion: Speeches to its Cultured Despisers* (1799, 1806, 1831) was an attempt to find a place for religious experience, defined as a sense of absolute dependence, within the burgeoning Romanticism of his generation. *The Christian Faith* (1830–31) is a classic of Reformed theology, attempting to explore the whole of doctrine from this understanding of what religion is.

Schweitzer, Albert (1875–1965)   German theologian, medical missionary and musician. His best known work, *The Quest for the Historical Jesus* (1906), ended the 'quest' because he argued that the liberal Jesus was a fabrication and never in fact existed. He is known for emphasizing the apocalyptic character of Jesus' ministry and the importance of Jesus' proclamation of the kingdom of God.

Smail, Thomas A. (b. 1928)   Scottish Episcopalian priest and a leading theologian within the British charismatic movement. He emphasizes the trinitarian character of Christian living and calls for a firm theological basis for the charismatic renewal. His writings include *The Forgotten Father* (1980), *The Giving Gift* (1994), *Once For All* (1998) and *Like Father, Like Son* (2006).

Sobrino S.J., Jon (b. 1938)   Spanish Jesuit theologian working in El Salvador. Liberation theologian who seeks to reconcile orthodox theology with his work among the poor, emphasizing a 'theology from below'. His main works are *Christology at the Crossroads* (1978) and *The True Church and the Poor* (1984).

Sölle, Dorothee (1929–2003)   German theologian and political activist who was Professor of Theology at Union Theological Seminary, New York and Honorary Professor at the University of Hamburg. A leading exponent of liberation theology to the West, her major works include *Suffering* (1975), *Christ the Representative* (1967) and *Thinking about God* (1990).

Song, C. S. (b. 1929)   Taiwanese theologian whose writings discuss the interactions between Christian faith and contemporary social-political and cultural-religious situations, especially those of Asia. His works include *Christian Mission in Reconstruction* (1974), *Third Eye Theology* (1979) and his three-volume *The Cross in the Lotus Land* (1990–94).

Spurgeon, Charles Haddon (1834–92)   Influential English Baptist preacher. He pastored the congregation of the New Park Street Chapel in London, later the Metropolitan Tabernacle, for 38 years.

Storkey, Elaine (b. 1943)   British Evangelical feminist theologian, she has written numerous works including *What's Right with Feminism* (1985), *Contributions to Christian Feminism* (1995) and *Conversations on Christian Feminism* (with M. Hebblethwaite, 1999).

Stylianopoulos, Theodore   Professor of Orthodox Theology and New Testament at Holy Cross Greek Orthodox School of Theology, Massachusetts, USA.

Strauss, David F. (1808–74)   German theologian famous for his two-volume *Life of Jesus, Critically Examined* (1835–36). He refused to accept that the gospel miracles were either historical or simply fabrications and so he proposed the third category of 'myth' drawn from Hegelian philosophy.

Tanner, Kathryn (b. 1954)   Professor of Theology at the Chicago Divinity School. She writes on traditional theology (*Jesus, Humanity and the Trinity*, 2001), and theologically engages with politics (*The Politics of God*, 1992) and economics (*Economy of Grace*, 2005).

Tertullian, Quintus Septimius Florens (*c.* 160–*c.* 220)   African theologian. Most of his work was polemical, arguing against various heretical teachings. His argumentative style relies on all the rhetorical tricks of his legal training, and is often both entertaining and overwhelming. He saw the attempt to harmonize Christianity with the best pagan thought of the day, Greek philosophy, as the root of many of the errors that he opposed.

Theophilus of Antioch (d. *c.* 180)   Bishop of Antioch and early Christian apologist. His sole surviving work is *To Autolycus*, which defends Christianity and contrasts it with paganism.

Thielicke, Helmut (1908–85)   German Protestant Evangelical theologian and influential preacher best known for his three-volume *Theological Ethics* (1955ff.) and his three-volume systematic theology, *The Evangelical Faith* (1968–78).

Tillich, Paul (1886–1965)   German theologian who was forced to emigrate to America in 1933, and decisively influenced American theology. His 'method of correlation' is an attempt to bring together the present perceived needs of human beings and biblical and theological symbols. His three-volume *Systematic Theology* (1953–64) summarizes his thought.

Torrance, Thomas Forsyth (1913–2008)   Scottish theologian who studied under Barth (q.v.). He has been particularly influential with his discussions of the Trinity, his work on the relationships between theology and science, and his writings on theological method. *Theological Science* (1969), perhaps his best-known work, brings together the latter two themes, arguing that theology and natural science each have their own proper method and are each fully rational.

Vigilius (d. 555)   Pope from 537. His time as pope was full of political intrigue and pressure in the debate between Nestorian, Chalcedonian and Monophysite Christology. Caught between the pressure of the Emperor Justinian and popular Western conviction, he wavered and changed his mind but eventually defended the Council of Chalcedon.

Wesley, John (1703–91)   English Anglican priest, theologian, preacher and founder of Methodism. Prominent for being a leader of the eighteenth-century Evangelical revival and theologically Arminian, he emphasized justification by faith and Christian holiness. Best known of his works are his *Notes on the New Testament, Sermons, Journal* and *A Plain Account of Christian Perfection*.

Williams, Rowan (b. 1950)   Welsh Anglican theologian and Archbishop of Canterbury since 2003. Prolific author on philosophy, Patristic and modern theology, spirituality and religious aesthetics, his main works include *Resurrection* (1982), *Arius* (1987), *On Christian Theology* (2000), *Lost Icons* (2000), *Tokens of Trust* (2007) and *Wrestling with Angels* (2007).

Wilson-Kastner, Patricia A. (1944–98)   American minister and Professor of Homiletics. Her earlier works focused on feminist theology, chiefly *A Lost Tradition: Women Writers of the Early Church* (1981) and *Faith, Feminism, and the Christ* (1983). Her later works were mostly liturgical and include *Imagery for Preaching* (1989), *The Heart of the Matter* (1998) and *Praising God* (with Ruth Duck, 1998).

Wright, N. T. (b. 1948)   Church of England New Testament scholar and former Bishop of Durham. Currently research professor in St Andrews. His major works are the six-volume 'Christian Origins and the Question of God' series, the first three of which are *The New Testament and the People of God* (1992), *Jesus and the Victory of God* (1996), and *The Resurrection of the Son of God* (2003).

Yong, Amos   Ordained Pentecostal minister and Professor of Theology at Regent University who has published on Pentecostal theology, pneumatology, theology of religions, theology and disability and world Christianity. His main works include *Discerning the Spirit(s)* (2000), *Toward a Pneumatological Theology* (2002), *Beyond the Impasse: Toward a Pneumatological Theology of Religions* (2003) and *The Spirit Poured Out on All Flesh: Pentecostalism and the Possibility of Global Theology* (2005).

Zizioulas, John D. (b. 1931)   Metropolitan Bishop of Pergamon and Greek Orthodox theologian. Zizioulas has been a significant figure in the ecumenical movement, and has sought in his academic work to uncover and reappropriate the thought-world of the Greek Fathers. His major work so far is *Being as Communion* (1985).

3 Time chart

c. 544–484 BC	Heraclitus
c. 540–470 BC	Parmenides
427–347 BC	Plato
348–322 BC	Aristotle
c. 336–264 BC	Zeno (Cleanthes 331/30 – 233/2 or 231; Chrysippus 281/278 – 208-205)
c. 15 BC–*c.* 50 AD	Flavius Josephus
c. 35–*c.* 107 AD	Ignatius of Antioch
early second century	*Didache*
d. *c.* 160	Marcion
d. *c.* 165	Justin Martyr
d. *c.* 180	Irenaeus, Bishop of Lyons
c. 150–220	Tertullian of Carthage
d. *c.* 180	Theophilus of Antioch
second half of second century	Athenagoras of Athens
d. *c.* 215	Clement of Alexandria
204–270	Plotinus
d. *c.* 253	Origen of Alexandria
d. 258	Cyprian of Carthage
c. 250–336	Arius of Alexandria
c. 295–373	Athanasius of Alexandria
c. 300–392	Apollinarius
c. 315–368	Cyril of Jerusalem
315–367	Hilary of Poitiers
325	Council of Nicaea
c. 330–379	Basil of Caesarea
c. 330–389	Gregory of Nazianzus 'Cappadocian Father'
c. 335–394	Gregory of Nyssa 'Cappadocian Father'

c. 360–435	John Cassian
381	Council of Constantinople
c. 352–428	Theodore of Mopsuestia
354–430	Augustine of Hippo
c. 390–*c.* 463	Prosper of Aquitane
d. *c.* 410	Pelagius
d. *c.* 444	Cyril of Alexandria
d. before 450	Vincent of Lerins
d. *c.* 451	Nestorius
451	Council of Chalcedon
c. 480–524	Boethius
c. 500	Pseudo-Dionysius
c. 490–575	John Philoponos
553	Second Council of Constantinople
d. 555	Pope Vigilius
560–633	Isidore of Seville
580–662	Maximus the Confessor
c. 675–749	John of Damascus
ninth century	John Scotus Erigena
b. *c.* 1010	Pope Gregory VII (pope 1073–85)
c. 1033–1109	Anselm of Canterbury
1079–1142	Peter Abelard
c. 1095–1160	Peter Lombard
c. 1098–1179	Hildegard of Bingen
c. 1123–73	Richard of St Victor
1126–98	Averroes
1132–1202	Joachim of Fiore
c. 1170–1253	Robert Grosseteste
c. 1182–1226	Francis of Assisi

c. 1221–74	Bonaventure
c. 1225–74	Thomas Aquinas
1266–1308	John Duns Scotus
c. 1285–1347	William of Ockham
1296–1359	Gregory Palamas
c. 1320–90	Nicolas Cabasilas
c. 1330–84	John Wyclif
c. 1342–1420	Julian of Norwich
c. 1370–1415	Jan Hus
d. 1382	Nicholas Oresme
1401–64	Nicholas of Cusa
1420–95	Gabriel Biel
1463–94	Pico della Mirandola
1480–1528	Balthasar Hubmaier
1483–1546	Martin Luther
1509–64	John Calvin
1519–1605	Theodore Beza
1527	Schleitheim Confession
1536	Genevan Confession
1542–91	John of the Cross
1542–1621	Robert Bellarmine
1545–63	Council of Trent
1548–1617	Francisco Suárez
1548–1600	Giordano Bruno
1554–1600	Richard Hooker
1558–1602	William Perkins
1560	Scots Confession
1563	Thirty-Nine Articles
1564–1642	Galileo Galilei
1577–1635	Richard Sibbes

1583–1648	Edward Lord Herbert of Cherbury
1596–1650	René Descartes
1615–91	Richard Baxter
1600–79	Thomas Goodwin
1616–83	John Owen
1623–87	François Turretin
1623–62	Blaise Pascal
1632–77	Baruch Spinoza
1632–1704	John Locker
1642–1727	Isaac Newton
1646	Westminster Confession
1670–1722	John Toland
1672	Confession of Dositheus
1685–1753	George Berkeley
1692–1752	Joseph Butler
1694–1768	Herbert Samuel Reimarus
1703–58	Jonathan Edwards
1703–91	John Wesley
1711–76	David Hume
1729–81	G. E. Lessing
1724–1804	Immanuel Kant
1768–1834	F. D. E. Schleiermacher
1770–1831	G. W. F. Hegel
1772–1834	Samuel Taylor Coleridge
1792–1834	Edward Irving
1800–72	John McLeod Campbell
1800–82	John Nelson Darby
1801–90	J. H. Newman
1802–76	Horace Bushnell
1804–72	Ludwig Feuerbach

1805–80	J. C. Blumhardt
1808–74	David Friedrich Strauss
1809–92	Charles Darwin
1813–55	Søren Kierkegaard
1818–83	Karl Heinrich Marx
1822–89	Albrecht Ritschl
1829–95	R. W. Dale
1834–92	Charles Haddon Spurgeon
1835–1912	Martin Kähler
1844–1900	Friedrich Nietzsche
1846–1922	Wilhelm Herrmann
1848–1921	Peter Taylor Forsyth
1851–1921	B. B. Warfield
1851–1930	Adolf von Harnack
1865–1917	James Denney
1865–1923	Ernst Troeltsch
1869–1937	Rudolf Otto
1869–70	First Vatican Council
1872–1945	H. Wheeler Robinson
1875–1965	Albert Schweitzer
1879–1978	Gustaf Aulén
1884–1976	Rudolf Bultmann
1886–1968	Karl Barth
1886–1960	John Baillie
1886–1965	Paul Tillich
1889–1951	Ludwig Wittgenstein
1892–1971	Reinhold Niebuhr
1893–1979	Georges Florovsky
1902–66	Otto Weber
1903–58	Vladimir Lossky

1904–95	Yves Congar
1904–84	Karl Rahner
1905–88	Hans Urs von Balthasar
1906–45	Dietrich Bonhoeffer
1908–85	Helmut Thielicke
1909–98	J. E. Lesslie Newbigin
1912–80	Geoffrey W. Lampe
1912–2001	Gerhard Ebeling
1913–2008	T. F. Torrance
1915–2009	Geoffrey Bromiley
1919–2004	Langdon Gilkey
b. 1923	George Arthur Lindbeck
b. 1926	Jürgen Moltmann
b. 1928	Gustavo Gutiérrez
b. 1928	Wolfhart Pannenberg
b. 1928	Thomas A. Smail
1929–92	David Jacobus Bosch
1929–2003	Dorothee Sölle
b. 1929	C. S. Song
b. 1930	Robert William Jenson
1930–2007	Letty M. Russell
b. 1931	John D. Zizioulas
b. 1932	Alvin Plantinga
b. 1933	Walter Kasper
b. 1933	Sallie McFague
1934	Barmen Declaration
b. 1934	Eberhard Jüngel
b. 1934	Richard Swinburne
b. 1936	Rosemary Radford Ruether
b. 1938	Leonardo Boff

b. 1938	James Hal Cone
b. 1938	Jon Sobrino SJ
1941–2003	Colin E. Gunton
b. 1942	Denys A. Turner
1943	Mystici Corporis Christi
b. 1943	Elaine Storkey
1944–94	Alan E. Lewis
1944–98	Patricia A. Wilson-Kastner
b. 1947	Paul S. Fiddes
1948	Founding of the World Council of Churches
b. 1950	Rowan Williams
b. 1951	Sarah Coakley
1952–2007	Catherine Mowry LaCugna
b. 1954	Kathryn Tanner
b. 1955	Christoph Schwöbel
b. 1956	Alan J. Torrance
b. 1961	Alistair I. McFadyen
1962–65	Second Vatican Council

4 Glossary of technical terms

affections: roughly, 'emotions'; those ways in which a person is affected by a moving event or message.

anathema (Greek 'accursed thing'): a formal pronouncement of the Church repudiating certain doctrines and those who hold them. The effect is to remove the person anathematized from the fellowship of the Church. Traditionally used at the end of formal definitions of doctrines by councils to make explicit the positions that they intended to reject.

apostles, apostolic: while there is some discussion over the various uses of the title 'apostle' in the New Testament, in theology it tends to refer to those (including Paul) who received teaching directly from Jesus Christ, and were sent by him to teach others. Apostolic doctrine is thus true doctrine, and it is a mark of the Church that it is 'apostolic', that is, in continuity with the apostles and their teachings.

Arian, Arianism: heresy (q.v.) named after Arius, a presbyter from Alexandria, who was denounced at the Council of Nicaea (q.v.). Arianism flourished after the Council and was not finally overcome until the Council of Constantinople (q.v.). The essence of Arianism is the belief that the Son who was incarnate in Jesus Christ is somehow less properly divine than the Father. The great Arian slogan, 'there was [a time] when he was not', placed the origin of the Son in time, in contrast to the eternity of the Father. As with many early heresies, it is not entirely clear what Arius himself thought, but the error that bears his name remains a perennially attractive distortion of Christianity, as it avoids the 'scandal of particularity'.

atonement: the reconciling of the world to God through the work of Jesus Christ.

beatific (Latin *beatus*: 'blessed'): an adjective describing those things that pertain to the life of the blessed in heaven. The 'beatific vision' is the sight of God that is the chief joy and reward of the saints.

canon, canonical (Gk *kanon*: 'rule, measure'): (i) 'canon' is the general term given to an authoritative decree of a council, as in the 'Canons of the Council of Trent'; (ii) 'canon' also refers to the collection of authoritative books that make up the Scriptures, and 'canonical' describes a scriptural book.

catholic (Gk *kath houlou*: 'according to the whole'): originally, the term was used to describe the oneness and universality of the Christian Church. In the face of divisions and disputes, it became a test of orthodoxy: that which is generally believed by the whole of the Church must be true, and local novelties are false. Often now used as shorthand for 'Roman Catholic', that is pertaining to the Roman Catholic Church, as opposed to any other denomination.

charism, charisma, charismatic (Gk *charisma:* 'gift'): a charism, or a charisma, is a gift of the Holy Spirit given for service in the Church. Historically, it has been used to describe the particular gifts given at ordination, but in the late twentieth century a far wider meaning became current, which recalls the biblical teaching that the Spirit is at work in all members of the Church.

Church militant and triumphant: the Church is composed of all who confess the name of Christ, living and dead. The 'Church militant' is that part of the Church still engaged in 'warfare' or struggle; that is, those who are still alive. The 'Church triumphant' is that part of the Church that has triumphed and received God's reward; that is, those at rest in heaven.

covenant: God's commitment of himself to Israel and to all human beings, particularly involving the forming of divine–human relationships. ('They will be my people, and I will be their God.')

dialectic: in ancient and medieval usage, simply the art of logical disputation, of constructing an argument well. In modern usage, it refers more to the union of opposites in some manner, as in Hegel's metaphysical dialectics, where thesis and antithesis combine into a synthesis, or Marx's historical dialectic, where the clash of opposing social forces will inevitably finally result in the coming of communism.

dogma, doctrines (Gk *dogma*: 'teaching'): a dogma is an authoritative teaching of the Church (for example, the dogma of the incarnation), or of a particular church (for example, the dogma of the immaculate conception in the Roman Catholic Church). Dogmatics is the study of dogma, differing from 'theology' (if at all) by the particular attention paid to authoritative pronouncements.

ecumenical, ecumenism (Gk *oikoumene*: 'world'): relating to the whole world of God; so an 'ecumenical council' is one summoned from the whole Church whose pronouncements are binding on the whole Church. In recent years, 'ecumenism' has come to mean 'working for the unification of the Church', and ecumenical can also relate to this. There is another, related, recent usage where the union desired is not just of the Christian churches, but of all religions.

episcopate, episcopal (Gk *episcopos*: 'overseer, bishop'): 'relating to bishops'; the episcopate is the order of bishops.

expiation: compensation or atonement for wrongdoing.

filioque: (L. 'and the son'): refers to the clause in the Nicene Creed stating that the Holy Spirit 'proceeds from the Father *and the Son*'. The words 'and the Son' were not part of the original creed and have never been included by Eastern Orthodox churches. It was first added in the West around the tenth century and disagreement over the clause contributed to the schism between the Eastern and Western Churches.

generation: a term referring to the relationship of origin of the Son to the Father within the Trinity. Also 'eternal generation'.

Gnostic, Gnosticism (Gk *gnosis*: 'knowledge'): originally a collection of early quasi-Christian sects that all stressed the need to possess hidden knowledge which only they could reveal. Used more generally in theology of any system that demands elite knowledge, in place of the publicly declared gospel of what God has done in Christ.

gospel: The good news of what God has done in Jesus Christ, particularly the forgiveness of sins in his death and resurrection.

heresy, heretic: technical terms referring to teachings, and to those who hold them, which superficially appear to be theologically acceptable, but which have been judged by a church council to be seriously erroneous.

homoousios (Gk 'same substance'): refers to the indivisibility of the Father and the Son who, though distinct, are of one or the same substance. The term was first used in this context at the Council of Nicaea to further emphasize the rejection of the Arian view that the Son was of a different substance, or type of being, to the Father.

hypostasis, hypostases: this Greek term means something like the 'essential substance' or 'real essence' and was originally used in Christian theology to denote substance (*ousia*) or nature. However, from the fourth century it was more commonly used in distinction to substance, to describe nature, or specifically in terms of the Godhead, that is, distinct but not separate. Thus it is often used of the persons of the Trinity, as in the formula *mia ousia, treis hypostases* (one substance, three persons).

iconoclastic: the destruction or rejection of icons. Icons are depictions, usually of Christ or a saint, produced according to strict rules. In Orthodox theology icons are understood to be quasi-sacramental.

Imago Dei (L. 'image of God'): that which sets human beings apart from all other species (see Gen. 1.27–28). There is considerable debate in Christian theology as to what the image is and to what extent it was damaged or destroyed in the Fall.

incarnation: the event of God the Son becoming a human being, the Jewish man Jesus Christ.

justification, justify: to 'justify' is to declare or make righteous; justification is the declaring or making righteous of sinners by the life, death and resurrection of Jesus.

liberal, liberalism: describing a school of nineteenth- and twentieth-century theology which is positive about natural human abilities and sceptical about central Christian miracles (variously, the virgin birth, the resurrection, the incarnation).

liturgy, liturgical: refers to the ordered public worship of God; more specifically it refers to authorized texts for use in worship.

Logos (Gk 'Word'): God the Son, who became incarnate in Jesus Christ. (See John 1: 'In the beginning was the *Logos*, and the *Logos* was with God, and the *Logos* was God … and the *Logos* became flesh, and pitched his tent among us.')

Marcionites: followers of second-century Gnostic Marcion who believed that the God of the Hebrew Bible was a God of vengeance and wrath, and was not the same God of love who was revealed by Jesus Christ. Marcion consequently rejected the Hebrew Bible and much of what we now recognize as the New Testament, with the exception of an edited version of Luke's Gospel and ten of Paul's Letters.

ontic: the state of being or reality.

ontology, ontological: relating to the study of being or reality.

pagan: in theological usage, someone who is not a Christian believer.

paraclete: a Greek word that variously means consoler, advocate, comforter or one who intercedes. The word is used in the Johannine writings and was understood by the early Church to refer to the Holy Spirit.

Patristic: relating to the period of the Church Fathers, *c.* AD 100–700.

Pneumatomachians: this Greek word literally means 'spirit-fighters'. It refers to a theological position that emerged in the second half of the fourth century which denied the divinity of the Holy Spirit. The arguments echoed those about the nature of the Son earlier in the fourth century and Pneumatomachians denied that the Spirit was of the same substance as the Father and Son.

probole, probolai: the Greek word literally means 'throwing forward'. Theologically, it refers to the argument that Jesus' divinity is a result of his divine begetting.

prolation: a proclamation or utterance.

propitiation: the work of Jesus in providing satisfaction for sin, or appeasing the wrath of God.

providence: God's action in sustaining and directing the world he has created. Often used as a cirumlocution for 'God' – 'providence has decreed that …'.

quiddity: a Latin term meaning essence of an object, or the properties of a substance.

ruach: a Hebrew word that can mean wind, breath or spirit.

Sabellian: named after the third-century priest Sabellius, Sabellians argue that rather than being three persons, God is one person with three modes of being. So God does not exist as Father, Son and Holy Spirit, but rather can be perceived as Father, or Son, or Spirit. This belief is also referred to as modalism.

Socinian: one who denies the deity of Christ. Distinguished from Arian and Unitarian largely by historical context: Arianism describes the patristic heresy, Socinianism the European Reformation resurgence and the largely British and American enlightened form of the same belief.

Spinozism: a monistic philosophical system based on the thought of seventeenth-century Dutch philosopher Baruch Spinoza. Spinoza argued that all of reality is made up of a single substance.

Theosis: the final stage of the process of transformation in which humans become like God, or attain union with God. Cf. Athanasius' famous dictum 'God became a human being, so that human beings may become divine' (*On the Incarnation* 54:3, *PG* 25:192B). Mostly associated with Eastern Orthodox theology.

unction: this can refer to either the process of anointing, or the ointment which is used for anointing. Extreme Unction is one of the seven sacraments and refers to the practice of anointing the sick or dying.

Unitarian: unitarians believe that God is one and cannot be triune. Unitarian can refer to a theological position, or to membership of the Unitarian Church which grew out of mainstream Christianity in America and Britain in the nineteenth century.